ALSO BY HUGO VICKERS

The Unexpurgated Beaton: The Cecil Beaton Diaries as He Wrote Them (ed.) 2003

Alice, Princess Andrew of Greece 2000

The Kiss 1996

The Private World of the Duke and Duchess of Windsor 1995

Loving Garbo 1994

Royal Orders 1994

Vivien Leigh 1988

Cecil Beaton 1985

Debrett's Book of the Royal Wedding 1981

Gladys, Duchess of Marlborough 1979

We Want the Queen 1977

BEATON IN THE SIXTIES

Cecil Beaton—a self-portrait

BEATON IN THE SIXTIES

THE CECIL BEATON DIARIES AS HE WROTE THEM, 1965–1969

INTRODUCTION BY
HUGO VICKERS

ALFRED A. KNOPF NEW YORK 2004

This Is a Borzoi Book Published by Alfred A. Knopf

Published in the United States by Alfred A. Knopf, a division of Random House, Inc., New York.
Distributed by Random House, Inc., New York.

www.aaknopf.com

Originally published in Great Britain in slightly different form by Weidenfeld & Nicolson, London, 2003

Knopf, Borzoi Books, and the colophon are registered trademarks of Random House, Inc.

Library of Congress Cataloging-in-Publication Data

Beaton, Cecil Walter Hardy, Sir, 1904–1980.
Beaton in the sixties : the Cecil Beaton diaries as he wrote them, 1965–1969 /
introduction by Hugo Vickers.
p. cm.
Includes index.
ISBN 1-4000-4297-6
1. Beaton, Cecil Walter Hardy, Sir, 1904–1980—Diaries. 2. Photographers—England—Diaries.
I. Vickers, Hugo. II. Title.

TR140.B4.A3 2004
770'.92—dc22 2004048296

All photographs and drawings by Cecil Beaton, courtesy of Sotheby's Picture Library, London, and the collection of Hugo Vickers.

Manufactured in the United States of America

First American Edition

For Alice
with love
from her father

CONTENTS

ACKNOWLEDGEMENTS

This is the second volume of Cecil Beaton's diaries that I have edited, once again working from the notes I kept when engaged on his authorised biography in the 1980s. Some of these I typed myself, but I was much helped by Sue Morris to whom I dictated a great number, and also by Hermione Weguelin, who bravely tackled a large batch on her own. As ever, it was Cecil's handwriting that was the hardest part. When I mentioned this before, some reviewers were quick to suggest that the first volume might be full of mistranscriptions. I am sure there were some—indeed I know there were some—and all I can say is that had I not been working on Cecil Beaton's handwriting for the best part of a quarter of a century, there would have been a great many more.

In the production of the diaries, I would again like to thank my editor, Ion Trewin, who, rare among editors, again added more details to footnotes and identified elusive figures for me. Working with him is always a pleasure, and if someone had sat with us taping the asides that emerged in conversation as we went through the text, they might have a different slant on a number of the figures mentioned. Luckily we were not taped.

Gillon Aitken and Lesley Shaw have helped me as usual with my tricky dual role as editor and literary executor, and so too has Doreen Montgomery, Cecil's literary agent since the 1950s, never failing to tackle complicated issues on behalf of the estate.

I spent the usual day at St. John's College, Cambridge, and would like to thank Jonathan Harrison for putting up with something of a whirlwind invasion. I would also like to thank the enormously generous team at Sotheby's, who have provided photographs for this edition and extra ones for the hardback American edition, Lydia Cresswell-Jones, Grace Worthington, Juliet Hacking, and Sue Daly.

For help with identifying elusive figures, I am grateful once again to my friend, Richard Jay Hutto, who has responded with e-mail and faxes of obituaries of complicated American figures; Baron de Redé, Mr. Roderick Coupe, Mr. Jimmy Douglas, and M. Bernard Minoret in Paris; Mr. Samuel Adams Green; my New York editor, Shelley Wanger; the Countess of Avon; Mr. Philip Hoare; Mr. Hugh Montgomery-Massingberd; Mr. Michael Romain; Mrs. Sally Bedell Smith; Mr. Ilya Haritakis; Mr. George Vassiadis; Mr. E. G. E. Embiricos; Mr. Charles Kidd; Mr. David Warner; and Mr. Charles Duff.

Once again, Google.com proved an invaluable search engine for this work as for so many other things. Thanks to Ilsa Yardley for her help with the copy-editing, and to Victoria Webb, who coped with all the detailed proof corrections. Since the publication of the English edition, M. Etienne Grafe has kindly helped solve some further mysteries and proved an eagle-eyed proof-reader. So did Mr. Mitchell Owens.

I would like to again thank Philip Gosling and Elizabeth Sharland for putting me on board the *Seabourn Sun* and *Queen Elizabeth 2*, thus enabling me to make strides forward in the transcription and editing of this book, in exchange for some lectures on board.

But most of this work was done at home, so I must also thank Mouse, Arthur, Alice and Georgie for bearing with the long hours that I was confined to my desk, sometimes at unsociable times.

Hugo Vickers

July 2004

BEATON IN THE SIXTIES

INTRODUCTION

The first volume of Cecil Beaton's "unexpurgated diaries" covered the last decade of his life, 1970–80, whereas this book covers the period immediately preceding it, 1965–69. Those who read the first volume will have found a rather different Cecil Beaton from the man in his own published diaries, of which there were six volumes between 1961 and 1978. Cecil Beaton was the master retoucher and he presented the written portraits in much the way he presented their photographs, retouched until he had them exactly as he wanted them.

He disguised what he really thought and he omitted much. It would not have been in his interests to publish the full unexpurgated version in his lifetime and, indeed, at that time he would have incurred a considerable "reading" bill with his libel lawyer. But more than two decades have passed, a generation of his friends have likewise died and it seemed more interesting to know what he really thought than to read the earlier sanitised versions.

He once declared that he sometimes had great fun hating certain people. He must have written the sharper portraits with a kind of malicious relish. But had it proved that he was just against everyone, then there would have been no point in giving the diaries an airing. Beaton was that rare creature, a literate photographer. Not only did he have an all-seeing eye and the ability to capture a moment on celluloid, but his brain also worked like that. He had but to see something for a flash and it was fixed in his head. He would then go home and—to use modern terminology—"down-load" these images into his diary.

In the first volume, one of the most interesting passages was his description of the funeral of the Duke of Windsor in June 1972. I was present on that occasion, likewise acutely interested and aware of what was going on. His account is, however, much better than anything I could have written, since he was a master at setting the scene as if reviewing a play: he observed and noted all the key points and he was better informed than I would have been at that time, since he knew the participants in the unfolding drama. He also took the trouble to match his experiences with those of others present, and gave a more than fair overview of the characters of the Duke and Duchess of Windsor and that earlier drama (the Abdication) which had locked their lives together for ever.

If there is a concluding thought about the volume of diaries from 1970 to 1980, it is the slightly depressing one that it marked a time of sharp decline. With the benefit of hindsight, there are hideous indications of the approach of the crippling stroke in 1974; ill health and a degree of attendant depression mark many of the passages. Perhaps because Cecil saw himself as a man increasingly on the sidelines, there was added bitterness and waspishness.

This volume is somewhat less waspish than its predecessor, because Cecil was much more in the swim. His energy knows no bounds and he is busier racing from one celebrity to the next, from one artistic endeavour to its successor. The scope of his friendships was very wide, and he is unique in his generation for being at the centre of so many different, though always fascinating, worlds, including writers, painters, playwrights, actors, film stars, "squillionaires," royalty, the aristocracy of many lands and the owners of the finest houses, not to mention vineyards.

As the editor of both volumes, I have enjoyed this volume more, since it is livelier and more or less wholly bereft of self-pity. It has led me to some fascinating characters. In full, for the first time anywhere, is the horror of being on board a holiday yacht with Greta Garbo. There are the famous figures such as Picasso, Truman Capote, Barbra Streisand, Mick Jagger, Andy Warhol and "Coco" Chanel, with the crescendo in 1969, working with Katharine Hepburn. But for me, if I may be allowed a personal reflection, the pleasure has been in some of the lesser-known characters. These diaries have led me to the entertaining books by Alice-Leone Moats (notably a fascinating discourse on the stud Porfirio Rubirosa); to Philip van Rensselaer, escort of Barbara Hutton, and his memorable fall from grace; to the sad, twisted, yet not unsympathetic figure of theatre critic T. C. Worsley, who lived with the knowledge that he had prised his younger brother's fingers from his thighs, leaving him to drown, while he had survived—and there are a host more.

In *The Unexpurgated Beaton,* I gave a full digest of Cecil Beaton's career. Here it is only necessary to remind the reader that Cecil was a man of many parts—photographer, artist, writer, designer for screen and theatre, and arbiter of style. He was a man whom Jean Cocteau described as "Malice in Wonderland" and Cyril Connolly as "Rip-van-With-it." Kenneth Tynan noted that if he arrived at your party, he would give the impression that he had just come from a very much better one upstairs. Tynan also wrote of Cecil's failed play, "It was as if an avocado pear had been squeezed and discharged syrup." Cecil was an elegant man, as much photographed himself as photographing other people. Above all, he was that very rare creature, a "total self-creation."

The brief outline of his career was that his father was a timber merchant and his mother the daughter of a blacksmith. Cecil was born in 1904 and followed, in 1905, by a brother, Reggie, who sadly committed suicide when quite young, and two sisters, Nancy (1909–99) and Baba (1911–73).

His love of photography was engaged by spotting a photograph of Lily Elsie (the "Merry Widow") lying on his mother's bed. He was soon dressing his sisters up as early models.

He went to Heath Mount School in Hampstead, to St. Cyprian's, on the south coast, and to Harrow, where he prospered in the art school. He did little work at St. John's College, Cambridge, but relished the theatrical life of the university.

His breakthrough into a more glamorous world came thanks to meeting Stephen Tennant, who soon had him photographing the glamorous debutantes of the day. From that early beginning, all else followed. The photographs and the sitters became more sophisticated, he entered the world of the theatre, ballet and later opera, he designed memorable films such as *Gigi* and *My Fair Lady.*

He took the formal wedding photographs of the Duke and Duchess of Windsor in 1937, photographed Queen Elizabeth (later the Queen Mother) in 1939 and all the Queen's children as babies, as well as the Coronation in 1953.

During the war he was a Ministry of Information photographer, travelling all over Britain, and later the Near East and Far East. And so his career developed on all fronts. He even managed a tortured affair with Greta Garbo.

He produced many important books, including *The Glass of Fashion*, a survey of the people who had most influenced fashion in his lifetime.

In 1968, during the period covered by these diaries, his career was crowned with an important exhibition of his photographs at the National Portrait Gallery. Even then he did not give up, pressing on with his photography, painting, publishing more volumes of diaries and attempting to make a success of his play, *The Gainsborough Girls*.

Eventually, in 1974, he suffered a serious stroke from which he made a valiant but only partial recovery. He died at Broadchalke on 18 January 1980, four days after his 76th birthday.

This book, like its predecessor, was first published to mark Cecil Beaton's centenary in 2004 and affords the opportunity to read his private thoughts, to learn what the man behind the mask was thinking.

1965

As the New Year of 1965 began, Cecil was to be found living at Pelham Place in London and Broadchalke with his friend, Kin,[1] *met in San Francisco during Cecil's work on the Warner Brothers film of* My Fair Lady. *Cecil had persuaded Kin to give up his life in San Francisco and to come to London to study at the Courtauld Institute. Kin had arrived in the summer of 1964, so they had been ensconced together for some six months, by and large happily, though Cecil had to make certain changes to his life and should perhaps have made more.*

Hardly had the New Year opened than the news broke that Sir Winston Churchill,[2] *who had reached his 90th birthday on 30 November 1964, had suffered a cerebral thrombosis and was suffering circulatory weakness following a cold.*

His elderly doctor, Lord Moran,[3] *became a familiar sight on television news broadcasts and in the newspapers, emerging in his dark overcoat and Homburg hat from Churchill's home in Hyde Park Gate to deliver the latest bulletin. The country waited nervously for the great man to die. As his daughter, Mary Soames, put it, "We marched about the parks in the grey chill days, killing time, while time killed him."*[4]

Cecil was now back, working in England, and regularly took the train from Waterloo to Salisbury, escaping from the busy round of London life to the

[1] Kin (b. 1934), Californian teacher.

[2] Rt. Hon. Sir Winston Churchill, KG (1874–1965), wartime Prime Minister.

[3] Lord Moran (1882–1977), Churchill's doctor, who caused considerable controversy by publishing his diaries, an account of his patient from a medical point of view—*Winston Churchill—The Struggle for Survival* (1966).

[4] Mary Soames, *Clementine Churchill* (Doubleday, 2002), p. 537.

tranquillity of his garden at Broadchalke. Sitting in the train, he would look out for a small house near the railway line, with a sign in the window advertising "Brides." He would look at it wistfully and say, "There but for the grace of God go I!"

It was the height of chic for a bride to be photographed by Cecil and relatively rare. He took the official photographs at the wedding of Princess Margaret and Antony Armstrong-Jones[1] *in May 1960, and from time to time, for old friends, he would make an exception and become a bride photographer.*

Cecil loved Lord and Lady Lambton[2] *for their originality and eccentricity, and for their complete disdain for normal conventions. But he was also a little nervous, for he remembered that it was Tony Lambton's aunt Violet, the Countess of Ellesmere,*[3] *who had thrown his sister Nancy*[4] *who had been brought there in innocence by Stephen Tennant,*[5] *out of her ball in 1928, causing an enormous society row, known as the "Ellesmere Ball" scandal, which occupied columns of print in the society papers in the summer of 1928. Thus any connection with the Lambtons caused Cecil to remember his earlier social insecurity. This was wholly one-sided. The Lambtons found such attitudes hard to understand though they identified it in Cecil.*

Lucinda Lambton,[6] *then aged 21, Lord Lambton's eldest daughter, was marrying Henry Harrod, elder son of Sir Roy Harrod,*[7] *the economist and author of biographies of John Maynard Keynes, and* The Prof, *about F. A. Lindemann, and his wife, Wilhelmine ("Billa") Cresswell, who in old age became a friend of the Prince of Wales.*[8]

[1] HRH The Princess Margaret, Countess of Snowdon (1930–2002), and Antony Armstrong-Jones, later first Earl of Snowdon (b. 1930), photographer and designer, and something of a rival to Cecil. The Snowdons were divorced in 1978.

[2] Lord Lambton (b. 1922), later a government minister, who resigned in 1972 and went to live in Italy, and his wife Belinda ("Bindy") Blew-Jones (1921–2003).

[3] Lady Violet Lambton (1880–1977), married fourth Earl of Ellesmere. The famous ball took place at Ellesmere House on 9 July 1928. *See* Vickers, *Cecil Beaton* (2002), pp. 103–6.

[4] Nancy Beaton (1909–99), married 1933, Sir Hugh Smiley, Bt (1905–90).

[5] Hon. Stephen Tennant (1906–87), aesthete, poet and novelist manqué, later the reclusive squire of Wilsford Manor, near Amesbury. A self-confessed genius who, flatteringly, scattered the sobriquet on a number of his friends.

[6] Lady Lucinda Lambton (b. 1943), writer, photographer and broadcaster, now married to Sir Peregrine Worsthorne.

[7] Henry Harrod (b. 1939); Sir Roy Harrod (1900–78).

[8] HRH Prince Charles, Prince of Wales, KG (b. 1948).

The young Harrods had two children, Henry Barnaby, born in July that year, and Nathaniel, born in March 1967. The marriage was to last eight years, ending in divorce in 1973.

FENTON, NORTHUMBERLAND 20 JANUARY 1965

Came up on the night sleeper for Lucy's wedding.[1] Awful effort and every journey is a nail in coffin but am devoted to the family and felt I should make the effort. Also I knew, with so many eccentric personalities involved, it would be amusing. And it was.

A pre-nuptial gaiety in cold dark King's Cross Station with Lucian Freud and Ann [Fleming], Paddy Leigh Fermor and Joan, Ali F. [Forbes][2] etc. Arrival in north before daylight, cold, bleak moor scenery, Cheviot Hills, and our goal a turreted black and white Gothic house with light blazing in every window, and they had been blazing since five o'clock this morning when the chefs had started cooking for the wedding breakfast. Fires were also blazing in the hearth of every room and the corridors were a serried mass of blue hyacinths which, with the wood fires, scented the air. Tony appeared bleary-eyed in dressing gown, likewise Judy [Montagu], then Diana [Cooper][3] bare-footed with head tied in nightcap. Big joking at big breakfast.

Tony, whom I like in spite of his appalling caddishness, said that the bridegroom's mother was appearing at the wedding in a dress she'd bought for £20!—that the father had got drunk last night. (Later Billa and Roy explained they were so worried—L. L. had refused to speak to her fiancé on the telephone, shouted that the whole thing was a mistake, which the Harrods thought too, hence Roy took to the bottle, fell, hurt his eye and had to be guided to bed, screams from six children, extraordinary rustic chef decorations, a cross of grapes that someone said was part of Churchill's imminent

[1] The wedding took place on 16 January 1965.

[2] Lucian Freud (b. 1922), painter; Ann Fleming (1913–81), widow of Ian Fleming and former wife of second Viscount Rothermere (1898–1978); Sir Patrick Leigh Fermor (b. 1915), author, and his wife, Hon. Joan Eyres-Monsell (1912–2003), and Alastair Forbes (b. 1918), journalist, reviewer and uncle of Senator John Kerry—an explosive group to contain in one train carriage.

[3] Judy Montagu (1923–72), daughter of Rt. Hon. Edwin Montagu, married (1962) Milton Gendel; and Lady Diana Cooper (1892–1986), legendary beauty, actress, ambassadress and author.

Lucy Lambton and Henry Harrod at their wedding, January 1965

funeral decor, or as Paddy suggested, looked like part of a voodoo rite in Haiti. A peacock of fruit, a swan made of bananas and violets.

Bindy, still in plaster with broken leg,[1] shouting to people to leave her Clapham Junction bedroom, while she dressed the children's hair. Tony shouting to the bride in the bath, "Why in the world didn't you sign that document

[1] Lady Lambton suffered various serious accidents. Having recovered from a serious go-karting accident resulting in badly shattered legs, she later drove in front of a lorry on the A1.

as you were told? Now the whole thing is ruined and we'll have to pay death duties." Lucy, walking around in a bath towel, preparations at their height, great excitement under the generalship of Judy, a preview of the church at Wooler, garish decorations of daffodils, with sun coming through them gave wintry glow, Bindy dressed and looking large and ungainly in white velvet, frogging bows, white fur and Victorian hair and tiara.

Bridesmaids moss-green Anna Kareninas, Ned, Hussar, likewise with fur hat, Judy's minute child[1] dressed as a daffodil to strew flowers in bride's path as she came down it.

Lucy not wanting dugget, preferred to walk along the muddy path in the churchyard, made a delightful picture of bride with raven-haired highwayman bridegroom as half an hour later, after singing Child's hymns, snow and snow, "we plough the fields and scatter," processed against the sun, through the gravestones, with an excited village populace of gay-faced simpletons gawking and smiling. Military precision as the cars brought the cortège back to the black and white castle. For the Breakfast the board not only groaned but bellowed with the suckling pig, the geese, gammons of beef, hams, game pastries and eclairs (of which I had brought 300 with me on the night train). Mulled claret made of marvellous claret, the bride nervous, shrieking at her sisters with a frown on her face and brandishing a knife at the photographers who wanted the conventional picture of her cutting the cake.

How it all went so smoothly Tony did not know, for any moment there could be a clash of temperament. The bride asked Desmond Guinness[2] why he'd come to the wedding and shouted at nannies who proffered their behinds when the photographers tried to take pictures of the children.

Seeing Michael Wishart[3] she asked him what he thought of the wedding. "I thought you looked beautiful," he said. "I don't want to hear that sort of thing. What did you think of the wedding?" "Oh, it was beautiful, magical with the flowers and the Mozart *cantata*." "I don't want that sort of rubbish. I want to know what you'd write if you were describing it for the newspapers."

[1] Ned Lambton (b. 1961), now self-styled Lord Durham, heir to the Earldom of Durham, which was renounced by Lord Lambton in 1970; and Anna Gendel (b. 1963).

[2] Hon. Desmond Guinness (b. 1931), President of the Irish Georgian Society 1958–91.

[3] Michael Wishart (1928–96), artist and author of *High Diver* (1977), a dark account of his traumatic life. Cecil bought several of his paintings.

POST-MORTEM ON THE WEDDING

Jokes about the two families by each family. Judy to Roy: "You're not so much escorting the bride's mother as wielding a hunking cripple up and down the aisle." The bride has telephoned. She remembered every detail, the wedding did not go by in a haze. She only did not remember many of the people but saw some old servant 20 years dead. "How's Henry? He's not here," remembered Lucy.

He is calm of disposition, says "Other people would find Lucy difficult but she does not upset me." He writes a letter and finishes the crossword puzzle while she is railing about the marriage being an abortive idea: "I must give it up now." Roy naturally disturbed, Billa too. Not so Henry. Later Bindy is given by a child a batch of congratulatory telegrams too late for arrival before the couple departed. Jokes about Aunt Maddy and then the laughter stops. "My heart looks forward to seeing you with ecstasy and trepidation—Love Henry." We discover that this was sent earlier to "Miss Lambton" marked "Personal and confidential," and should have arrived early yesterday morning. People were a little embarrassed at this joke session going wrong, as indeed they should be.

Harrods very keen to see the newspapers and the photographs, and reading about the reports when eventually they arrive.

More than anything else Cecil loved to be at Reddish House, Broadchalke, quietly supervising changes and improvements to the house, the creation of a studio in which to paint, making changes in the garden, and inspecting the various successes and failures he found there. It was the nearest thing he could have to an Arcadian idyll. His diaries are full of stories about domestic dramas involving cooks who came and went, some markedly better than others. He was happiest when at Broadchalke with Kin, or when his secretary Eileen Hose came to stay, or friends such as Alan Tagg and Charles Colville.

At this time he was particularly interested in painting and even wondered if this might be a new late-life career.

All these weeks I have been painting, sometimes with a modicum of satisfaction though often with that appalling feeling of frustration one only knows when one's high hopes are dashed to despair.

All the while Kin was with me and all the while he was sympathetic to every mood. I had thought he might be a difficult character but this was not the case. He is always mindful of my ill humours, makes excuses for my bad behaviour, likes being alone with me, does not need neighbours, does not want company. We have reached a new intimacy, when we have jogged along quietly together from day to day with nothing to do but read, listen to music, watch television. It has been a further stretch of our life together and because it has not been a "highlight" it has been important as showing that we can relax together and be content in one another's company even through the most prosaic of times.

After a bad cook left, there came a new cook, Mrs. Paycock, and Cecil's spirits lifted.

Then came the glorious night when Mrs. Paycock appeared. She was given trout and steak to cook. Eileen,[1] Kin and I cheered the meal. It was as if our taste buds had been given back to us. Everything had its flavour once more. The sauces were delicious and at last each meal became a pleasure instead of a dreary necessity.

We are now doing everything in our power to make Mrs. Paycock (her husband is held behind the Iron Curtain) feel part of the family so that we can rely on her as a friend and an artist.

Kin's image must be changed. He is no longer the romantic fey creature I met in strange circumstances in San Francisco. He is a wholesome good person who is identified with my life, with my interests completely. A good, sterling character who makes allowances for my weakness but encourages me only along the path of righteousness. He is a good influence on me though I try consciously not to let him take complete charge of my tastes and inclinations. I have devoted less time to listening to him talk about his theories on painting and music than I would like. I would have liked to have spent less time on my own work, yet here is a rare opportunity to paint. But we talk as if we are to be

[1] Eileen Hose (1919–87), Cecil's secretary from 1953 until his death, by which time she also ran the household, and whom he once described as "my best friend."

together for some while yet. His course at the Courtauld goes on for two years and I am beginning to think that that meeting was one of the miracles that have happened in my life. For we really are very much together in understanding and in our mutual interests. The fact that we each have other interests of our own does not upset us in any way.

For a long year in 1963, Cecil had worked on the film of My Fair Lady *in Hollywood. Though this had given him many opportunities, he hated being ensnared in Hollywood for such a long time. Now the film opened to great acclaim across the world. Cecil, who had worked so hard and for so long, was finally able to enjoy it, the memories of feuding and in-fighting a thing of the past. Above all he had hated the director, George Cukor,[1] a mixture of personality clash, combined with Cukor having power over Cecil by his contract. There had been a blazing row one day when Cukor failed to look at some designs that Cecil wanted to show him.*

At last I believe the bogey of unhappiness created by my rift with Cukor has been expelled and that I can look back on the film making with a certain pleasure. The opening in Paris was certainly an event of pure pleasure, and of gala, and the praise that I received was important for it came from the people I revere.

Now the opening in London is about to start and I only trust that the death of that great man, W. C. [Churchill] will not ruin the celebrations, which we have looked forward to for so long. However, it is no use contemplating disappointment.

DAVID WARNER[2]

David Warner, half ape, half lanky hero, came to be photographed. He is incredibly shy, but thawed a little. When I asked him to come to supper that

[1] George Cukor (1899–1983), Hollywood director of the Spencer Tracy–Katharine Hepburn films, but best known for not directing *Gone with the Wind.*

[2] David Warner (b. 1941), North Country actor cast as Henry VI in the Royal Shakespeare Company's production of *The Wars of the Roses* at the age of 23. His film career included *Tom Jones* (1963).

night he giggled in his glass of whisky and said, "Oh no, I'm far too shy. You mustn't tempt me." He went off with his knapsack on his back, saying he would be back at 10:30. When he came into the crowded room, he walked up to Princess Margaret and said, "You're the only person I know in this room. Did you hear about my High Camp Lunch?" "No, where?" "At the Palace." Whereupon he and Princess Margaret were deep in conversation for the rest of the evening. He is a natural and in spite of his strange looks and the face covered with spots he has great charm (and, of course, a stroke or two of genius) and it is full marks to the Queen Mother's daughter that she recognises here is someone quite out of the ordinary.

REDDISH 23 JANUARY 1965

Happy to be back here after ten-day absence. It has been a restless period for me with the last round of *MFL* [*My Fair Lady*]. The days have been filled with interviews on the air and TV, and these make one tired but dissatisfied at not having done the job as well as one could. The critics for the film have been as I thought, not entirely satisfied, the direction without style, without a point of view, and no one has dared take risks—result a static photographed version of the stage play. Yet friends and the public adore it, thank heavens.

I gave a gala dinner [at home] for Audrey [Hepburn][1] and Jack Warner.[2] The latter brought his tart, who calls herself for no known or explicable reason—and she is very vague when asked for an explanation—"Lady Scarborough." Kistie Hesketh,[3] who came to dinner, happens to be the niece of Lady Scarbrough,[4] but this did not phase the tart who, on her best behaviour and appalled when Jack Warner became a bit too much at ease as he sat next to

[1] Audrey Hepburn (1929–93), played Eliza Doolittle in *My Fair Lady.* Cecil photographed her in all the extras' clothes for the Ascot scene.

[2] Jack L. Warner (1892–1978), president of Warner Bros., a man lacking in most of the social graces. Last of the four brothers.

[3] Christian McEwen (b. 1929), married second Lord Hesketh (1916–55).

[4] Katherine McEwen (1899–1979), married eleventh Earl of Scarbrough, KG (1896–1969), Lord Chamberlain.

Princess Margaret, whispered, but not too softly for Andrew Devonshire[1] to overhear and be enthralled, "Don't say shit in front of the Princess." Later Mrs. Cartwright [the cook] and the daily woman heard the tart say to Warner, "Let's get out of here" and Jack whispered, "Sssh!" Mrs. C. was shocked that such people as Warner and tart should have been invited into this company. It is amazing to me that Warner has not been able to learn a little about behaviour in the last 40 years of his successful career as a tycoon.

Audrey, on the other hand, behaved impeccably as ever, enthusiastic, interested in everything and everybody, outpouring, outgoing, generous, not sycophantic. I thought she looked scraggy and tired, others thought her unbelievably attractive and Princess Margaret and she had a quiet talk in which each said "I've always wanted to meet you." The gala was a real success and I was thrilled that Jonathan Miller, Ken Tynan[2] and David Warner should add their lustre to the golden scene. So many people enjoyed looking around and asking, "Who is that?" A most agreeable part of any party are the post-mortems. Princess Margaret is good at them. She described how Diana (Cooper) had apologised for not dropping her a curtsy, bat blind. "Oh, but I'm sure you did curtsy." "No, no, I was ramrod." Pss. Mt. also described how Rachel Roberts was a bit tight and, very noisily vociferous, said, "Don't know what I call you" but went on shouting. Rex [Harrison][3] interrupted, "You call her Ma'am." No response, so Rex and Pss. Mt. shouted, "You call her Ma'am, you call her Ma'am." (Incredibly Tony [Snowdon] did the most brilliant imitation I've ever heard of "Miki" Sekers!)[4]

Mary Herbert,[5] also good at vignettes, described David Warner glued to Pss. Mt. until she abruptly left him and he then, alone and friendless, lurched into the food with the rapaciousness of an escaped prisoner.

[1] Andrew, tenth Duke of Devonshire, KG (1920–2004), until lately a government minister.

[2] (Sir) Jonathan Miller (b. 1934), stage director; and Kenneth Tynan (1927–80), acerbic critic, who later wrote *O Calcutta!*

[3] Rachel Roberts (1927–80), Welsh actress, remembered for her portrayal of emotional pain and sexual ferocity in such films as *Saturday Night and Sunday Morning*. She was the fourth wife of (Sir) Rex Harrison (1908–90), actor who played Professor Higgins in *My Fair Lady*. They married in 1962 and divorced in 1971. She committed suicide with an overdose of barbiturates.

[4] Sir Nicholas Sekers (1910–72), managing director of West Cumberland Silk Mills, trustee of Glyndebourne Arts Trust and Chichester Festival Theatre.

[5] Lady Mary Hope (1903–95), married sixteenth Earl of Pembroke and Montgomery (1906–69). Lady-in-waiting to HRH Princess Marina, Duchess of Kent.

OPENING OF *MY FAIR LADY* 21 JANUARY 1965

I went off to the national opening of *MFL* in low spirits. It was Baba's[1] birthday and I was pleased to give her the treat of going in a £100 seat, but my family seldom come up to scratch and always appear apathetic about my work. The nieces had all been given seats for the press show, but not once did Baba say that they had even liked the picture. This shows a lack of imagination on her part, but oh, the troubles, sadnesses that are created by this and by an amateur lack of understanding of the effort put into almost any professional job of work. It is preposterous that a man of 60 should be upset at the lack of bouquets from persons of close blood but fair tastes, yet it dunches.

However, the evening was not a disaster. The much feared supper *à deux* was avoided by our joining the Devonshires[2] and their party in the Savoy Grill. This was great fun. But the opening was an anticlimax after Paris. The people, unknown Jews who could afford the £100 tickets. They looked ugly and dreary, and the climax to the horror was when we were all lined up to be received by Pss. Alexandra,[3] but instead had to bow and shake hands with my hated Lord Louis Mountbatten,[4] Jack Warner (with his CBE worn round his collar), Mrs. Cunningham Reid[5] and her son, and two other Reid relations. When eventually Princess Alexandra arrived, she was everything that she should have been, calm, collected, dignified and a great beauty.

Now it is time I forget the whole bloody business and I have come down to the snow-covered countryside to get on with my painting and to stay a while without the upsetting influences of press and publicity. I hope now to do a little reading and to have a little trickle going into the long emptied bucket.

[1] Barbara "Baba" Beaton (1912–73), Cecil's younger sister, married Alec Hambro (1910–43). She was born on 21 January.

[2] Tenth Duke of Devonshire, and his wife, Hon. Deborah Mitford (b. 1920).

[3] HRH Princess Alexandra, Hon. Lady Ogilvy, KG (b. 1936), always a particular favourite with Cecil.

[4] Admiral of the Fleet the Earl Mountbatten of Burma, KG (1900–79), president of the Society of Film and Television Arts. Assassinated by the IRA.

[5] Hon. Mary Ashley (1906–86), divorced wife of Captain Alec Cunningham-Reid (ca. 1896–1977), maverick MP. She was Edwina Mountbatten's sister, then known as Mary, Lady Delamere.

Cecil was happy to concentrate on his painting. This was his major preoccupation in the coming months, culminating in an exhibition at the Lefevre Gallery. His diaries throughout 1965 return frequently to his soul searchings as to the quality of his work and the possibility of exhibiting it. He loved nothing more than to rise early at Broadchalke and to work until his back ached and inspiration palled. He was deeply self-critical.

Presently he would convert the potting shed at Reddish House into a new studio, a short walk across the courtyard from his kitchen. In this studio, in later years, Eileen Hose, his secretary, worked. And it was where he kept his rows of manuscript diaries, and the portfolios containing his sketches, stage and film designs and other drawings.

PAINTING

There is no telling how a painting is going to come out. Unlike photography, when the results are more or less as foreseen, one can only hope and pray that with sustained effort through many vicissitudes the picture on the canvas may have a pleasant life of its own.

About two months ago I started to paint, from a small postage stamp photograph that I had kept for many months cut from a newspaper. The picture was a real success. My delight was the inspiration for many bigger and better portraits. Alas, they were not to be, nothing automatic. The initial success of John Russell,[1] the critic, who has one of the faces that I admire, like a clown white and pulpy, was followed by another of [Lew] Hoad,[2] the tennis player. Kin came into the studio at the right time, gave me encouragement, told me not to continue with this particular picture. But from then on uphill battles fought each week. Now I am here for a second trip of ten days' duration. I work until I ache in every limb from fatigue. I am too tired to read. There are no interruptions, no alibis, and yet the pictures are not as good as the two originals. I become very desperate and time rushes by.

Kin is an exceptional critic, can look on any sort of aesthetic manifes-

[1] John Russell (b. 1919), chief art critic of the *New York Times,* married to Rosamond Bernier, art historian.

[2] Lew Hoad (1934–94), Australian tennis player who won Wimbledon in 1956 and 1957.

tation and judge it on his own terms. He was very helpful about my week's work, and encouraging too. I didn't know whether I'd done something quite idiotic, pointless and affected. But no, he was amused, surprised and then started to tell me where I'd succeeded, where I'd failed. The failures stemmed from an overemphasis, a lack of elimination, not knowing where to stop, not realising the fundamentals. He tells me where to put the emphasis, what colour is warming with another, and gets me on a new track with high enthusiasm.

Sir Winston Churchill finally died peacefully at his home in Hyde Park Gate shortly after 8 a.m. on Sunday, 24 January. After the Lying-in-State at Westminster Hall, the State Funeral took place at St. Paul's Cathedral on Saturday, 30 January, attended by the Queen,[1] *the Royal Family, many foreign kings and queens and heads of state, including President de Gaulle*[2] *of France. There was a memorable BBC television commentary by Richard Dimbleby,*[3] *and the coffin was conveyed in the launch,* Havengore, *up the Thames to Festival Pier, and then from Waterloo Station by train to Bladon, in Oxfordshire to be buried near Blenheim Palace, where he had been born.*

CHURCHILL'S FUNERAL — 30 JANUARY 1965

The poor old celluloid doll lay peacefully in bed, his marmalade cat beside him, while his remaining energies seeped away. Then the marvellous old baby was no more, and with death came the full realisation of the grandeur of this man.

During the last years I believe he has taken considerable interest in the arrangements for his own funeral. At all times of day and night he would summon someone to talk about the cortège, but even he would have been surprised by the magnificence of his State Funeral and the depth of feeling his death has created throughout the world.

I have a cold in the head. This has reduced my vitality and resistance. The result was that while watching TV from 8:30 to 1:30 this Saturday morning

[1] HM Queen Elizabeth II (b. 1926).

[2] General Charles de Gaulle (1890–1970), President of France 1959–69.

[3] Richard Dimbleby (1913–65), broadcaster, author and newspaper director. This was one of his last commentaries. He died of cancer later in the year.

I must have shed lotions of tears. Never before have I watched TV for so long. Never before have I been so absorbed, so interested, so moved. The most unexpected things suddenly got one's most delicate spot, the face of Lady Churchill[1] asking for instructions as to procedure, with small jerky little steps, yet marvellously dignified, a face in a crowd, another sample of selflessness and pure feeling.

Eileen had written to describe how she had joined a queue for two and a half hours to see the catafalque in Westminster Hall and the great emotion that had come from the extraordinary silence.

Today there were bands and show, the navy, the army and the air force, and kings and queens and heads of state galore, and all the most important personages in the land. But it was the fundamental simplicity and gravity of the occasion, the passing of a great man, that had made so many people devote their time to his memory, people who had to put up with great cold and discomfort in England at the worst time of the year. One could see the clouds of cold coming from the Queen's mouth. One could see the spectators jumping up and down, flailing their arms to try to get some circulation going. One could not imagine the torture of the bandsmen manipulating with bare fingers the cold metal of their instruments.

Kin, sitting by my side, was less moved, but impressed. He said he thought only England could put on such a show that was perfect in all its details. He thought the service in St. Paul's a very masculine one in its taste, and the music, the lesson (on the Resurrection) and the bugle playing of the "Last Post" twisted one's guts.

The sounds of the procession, the marching boots, the horses' hooves, the distant military orders, the gun salutes, the flapping of a frightened bird's wings were all part of the spell.

In some ways I have never particularly liked Churchill. He could be gruff and coarse and rude, and very frightening. But now that one hears his speeches again, given such extra point by his own delivery (the sibilant actorish enunciation of Olivier[2] was quite degrading) made one conscious of his

[1] Clementine Hozier (1885–1977), married Sir Winston Churchill. Created Baroness Spencer-Churchill in her own right 1965.

[2] Laurence Olivier (1907–89), actor, his Richard III was considered definitive; first director of the National Theatre. He and Cecil quarrelled in the 1940s. Later Lord Olivier.

great mixture of energy, humanity and goodness, to say nothing of his humour, his wit, his eloquence. Perhaps the most moving of all the morning's viewing was to see shots of the crowds queuing towards Westminster Hall while Churchill's wartime speeches were relayed to us once more, and one realised that the little man in the coffin had a magnificence that will transcend time.

Don't know the reason but there is a devil lurking in me which longs to flaunt danger. The last time I saw Churchill at his home when his mental powers were in a poor state, he would look at me with big baby eyes and I would feel like winking at him. Why oh why? He would be quite capable of exploding: "Now, young man, what is that all about?" and one could imagine him taking off in magnificent terms about the folly of taking advantage of an old man who might appear gaga, but in fact was anything but . . . This devil must not be encouraged.

Juliet [Duff][1] returned from a long, tiring day after W. C.'s funeral. "No, I'm not a bit exhausted. I had such a wonderful seat in the Cathedral, just behind the Churchill family, that I'm elated."

Clarissa,[2] most moved by the scene by the Tower, with toy guns going off, and the pipers in their green and saffron kilts, and the party of bearers and the Earl Marshal[3] standing to attention as the group moved off. Said the cold in the carriage was appalling, that the last hot-water bottle proffered soon became cold, that Bert [Duke of Marlborough][4] coughed and sneezed and talked too much for the solemnity of the occasion, that she could not see anything or hear anything but the horses' hooves. Only on television at night could she see the soldiers, the processions and hear the bands, how Clemmie, 78, never wept and bore up beautifully, and how they all felt touched by the posses gathered at country stations and footballers standing to attention as the

[1] Lady Juliet Duff (1881–1965). See biographical note on p. 59–62.

[2] Clarissa Churchill (b. 1920), married, as his second wife, Rt. Hon. Sir Anthony Eden, KG, later first Earl of Avon (1897–1977).

[3] Bernard, sixteenth Duke of Norfolk, KG (1908–75), Earl Marshal from 1929. He organised the coronations of King George VI in 1937 and of the Queen in 1953. He was responsible for Churchill's funeral as it was a rare State Funeral.

[4] Tenth Duke of Marlborough (1897–1972), head of the Churchill family.

special cross-country trains raced by to reveal Churchills galore all eating and drinking Médoc.

The "private" burial very short but moving.

Telephoning to Betty Somerset[1] after the Churchill funeral, she said, "I can't throw it off—like falling in love."

She was deeply touched by Clemmie who "looked frightened, muttering, 'How kind you all are. Where do you want me to go next?' "

The Duke of Norfolk, "the Pig Duke"—had the face of the man on the moon, upside down, or we were looking at it the wrong way up.

A quiet weekend with Kin here for a short time, both of us feeling a little under the weather. We talk nonsense. Kin says we're bumbling about a bit. "Yes. It's all part of experience," but we have a funny little phase, I lying in bed, Kin sprawling at the foot of it. I relate a telephone call to my sister [Nancy Smiley] and how strange both sisters are at never mentioning my work to me. They have just seen *MFL* and neither had given me a dewdrop. It isn't as if I'm parched for them, but it seems to me such an unprofessional way of behaviour. Surely one is trained to make some reference to a person's work unless, of course, one positively hates it all and thinks it's beyond speech. Kin said he thought perhaps N. and B. were so accustomed to my work being admired that they felt they could not possibly add anything to the general acclaim. "Not a bit of it. They think I'm a complete wash-out. They can't conceive how it is that I've succeeded in any way. They know I'm a boob. They know I can't paint or write or do anything on my own. They think I'm hopeless, a baby. They never make allowances. When the porter put me on the wrong part of the train so that I could not get out at Alton, Nancy said, 'Oh, you're such a baby.' "

Cecil enjoyed a long phase in the country, painting most days, wearing an old mauve suit and 25-year-old tweed trousers with holes in the knees. Nevertheless, he worried that time was passing.

[1] Bettine Somerset (1900–73), wife of Captain Robert Somerset and mother of the eleventh Duke of Beaufort.

14 FEBRUARY 1965

It is two years since that night when at that strange locale, among the black leather toughs, one very beautiful fawnlike creature in olive green smiled the sweetest most tender of smiles at me.[1] After an appalling beginning, we could not understand each other's language, my offer of a drink, of an introduction to friends, all was refused, yet uncharacteristically I plodded on, and left in the Volkswagen; there came a miraculous decision when my new friend wheeled his car round abruptly, braked and said, "This is where I live. Come up."

How far we have travelled together since then! And I don't mean geographically! For we have been to many parts of the world together and for the last seven months Kin has remained here, thousands of miles from Stockton Street.

But our relationship has travelled through so many phases that we don't realise how much emotion has been used up to create the present happy state of affairs when we live together in complete trust of each other, trying hard to please the other, and have succeeded in making one another blissfully contented. The night I went to the Tool Box was the luckiest of my later life. It has made a momentous difference to my peace of mind, to my contentment, assurance and inner well-being. I am even proud that I can behave so well to another human being and feel completely unselfish in my attitude and demands.

As for the person I discovered in the haze and darkness, he could not be a more superior human being. After all these months together he seldom says anything unintelligent, unwise or not good. He is funny, full of laughter, unspoilt, enchantingly young and coltish, and ceaselessly beautiful. In every light, in movement or static pose, in sport or sleep, he is a continuous delight to the eye, and as adornment to my house and my life he is the most prized possession and of the greatest value to me. I can never be thankful enough for these two years, which incidentally seem part of the most recent events, [but] are in fact the latest events, are in fact the latest thing to happen to me. After two years, Kin is my Stop Press news.

[1] Cecil met Kin in a nightclub in San Francisco, called the Tool Box, in 1963.

DAVID WARNER

He talks non-stop on the telephone, then after one and a half hours of yapping, runs from his flat, so he is difficult to get hold of, yet if the miracle happens, he answers with a very businesslike "Flax[man] 4873." His accent North Country, his shyness overcome. He gave us tickets for *Eh?*, the Livings[1] play about an idiot boiler man. Not since the boyhood days of the Aldwych farces have I laughed so much. At two points the nonsense had reached such a pitch that I could not see what was happening on stage, so great was my laughter and so copious my tears.

David looked so fantastically comic in every situation, grave, gaunt, lilylike. His body of infinite grace, his absurdly long thin thighs in the most stove of trousers. His wild frame hunched, his canary silk hair never still, his face always so. A born actor, every reflection and reaction is unexpected, unbanal. There is nothing of ham in him. One could watch for ever. Most impressed by his versatility, this was zany of all parts after *Richard II.*[2]

He came to supper at home afterwards. His parents were amazed that he should want to go on the stage, and he was surprised at himself for as he looked at himself in the glass, he knew he could never get anything but strange character parts. Yet here he was—a star, at the top of his profession, with only one role at Stratford next season, that of *Hamlet.*[3] How did he feel about the part? He wasn't studying, it would happen. He always relied on his instinct. He was certainly doing exercises to increase his muscles and taking fencing lessons, but he wasn't the sort to have theories. He just got up and acted. Yet he could be very accurate in his analysis of what his work represented. They were all trying, at the Old Vic, to have the news commentator's sense of urgency. He

[1] Henry Livings (1929–98), playwright. *Eh?* played at the Aldwych from October to December 1964, also starring Donald Sinden and Brenda Bruce. Peter Hall directed it as a film, *Work Is a Four Letter Word* (1968).

[2] *Richard II* (1964). Warner's performance was described as "every inch a king, a poet-king prone to petulance—lolling on the throne at the tournament, lashing out with a whip at John of Gaunt, smashing the mirror with his fist, clanking his chains at Pomfret like Marley's Ghost" (Michael Romain, *Theatricals—the Scenic Art of Henry James and David Warner* [Merton College, Oxford, 2001], p. 13n).

[3] *Hamlet* (1965). Warner played Hamlet as a man "dwarfed by the towering figure of his father's ghost" (Romain, op. cit. p. 13).

David Warner, Shakespearian actor, London, 1965

admires and reveres great actors but does not go to see them, particularly not in films. Seems to have little curiosity about the stage as an art medium, and said so far his speciality had been in *Wet Kings*, and is said to be almost unfriendly in his remoteness to fellow players. Is simple, likes ordinary savoury food, likes money, doesn't have much of either, but now he's been given a film job[1] to fill in until *Hamlet*. This gives him money and his first trip to Paris.

He was sad his spots had not cleared up, and he said that to go off to Paris for the first time with a large boil on the end of your nose certainly undermined confidence. Don't know that I really get on well with him, but certainly he seems to have everything that makes for a good actor. He is intelligent, alive, energetic, has a face that can change into many different categories, can be gaunt, ugly, cretinous and also beautiful in a sensitive ivory-carving manner.

[1] *Morgan: A Suitable Case for Treatment*, directed by Peter Hall.

He left late at night, Peter Schenneil with dyed hair, tight black trousers and knapsack on back. For his first glimpse of Paris with all its hidden nuances of late-nineties naughtiness, in which no doubt he planned to take part. Too sad about all those spots, especially the one on the end of his nose.

Cecil invited Sir Frederick Ashton[1] *to stay at Broadchalke. The two men had worked together on several ballets and would have considered themselves friends, but not without a certain acerbic quality to their relations. Jealousy, suspicion of treachery in the professional sphere and the differences between one man working on his own and the other in a great national institution (Covent Garden) led to a certain mistrust. Years later Alastair Forbes met Cecil at Hackwood and said how nice it was to observe him and Freddie getting on so well. "I haven't* really *forgiven him," was Cecil's verdict.*

FREDDIE ASHTON

I see Freddie fairly intimately when working together on a ballet. We talk on the telephone. We are cosy with each other, but the fact that one has someone staying in the house, by putting them under an obligation and by giving one the responsibility of their safe-being, the visitor is more clearly defined. Fred showed up as a new character!

When first I saw him way back in the twenties, he gave an imitation of Queen Alexandra[2] at a bottle party at Todd's and Garland's.[3] The imitation was perfection, bringing up the entire aura of this parma violet-scented old royal harridan. I remember being envious of someone of my own age having such confidence as to perform in this brilliant intellectual world.

Throughout the years that followed Freddie always played the role of outsider looking in. His own analysis of himself was of scum and he was always trying to get even with the hierarchy. The fact that he was queer was never forgotten by him, or for that matter by anyone who watched him walk-

[1] Sir Frederick Ashton (1904–88), choreographer.
[2] HM Queen Alexandra (1844–1925), Danish princess and widow of Edward VII (1841–1910).
[3] Dorothy Todd (1883–1966), editor of *Vogue* in the 1920s, and Madge Garland (1898–1990), later Lady Ashton, a fashion guru and journalist. They were a lesbian duo for some years.

ing with such short, mincing little steps. But in spite of the faggoty walk, there was iron in those limbs and it is that hard structure that has come through today.

We are contemporaries and although I have lost my hair and my face has gone for six, I am still more or less recognisable as a relic of the person I was. Hardly Freddie. He has put on weight, developed an enormous lower chest. He has a hernia as a result of lifting Karsavina[1] as a willowy young man. Freddie's face has become very exaggerated, the lips more pursed, the nose beakier, the eyes waterier, the colour is almost purple but all this is overcome for he has developed the most miraculous self-confidence. This exudes authority. He now has the assurance of a tsar, and I must say that when walking slowly with fur cap and stick in the garden, this is just what he reminded me of. I suppose that a ballet master always has great authority, that by degrees he becomes accustomed to ruling with unswerving power over the little rats at the barre. But Fred is now a grand old man. He has acquired the authority of being able to talk and move slowly, to give a big knowing look, to know the value of a pause. Seeing him sit, like Buddha, and listen to the younger generation (Kin!) or to make his summations was like watching someone with 20 years added to his own 60.

Fred is a born mimic. It is more expressive for him to indulge in pantomime than in speech. He now imitates Alice Astor[2] picking cheap dresses out of a rack, or his choosing one card out of a pack with such knowledge that eventually his point is going to be made and his audience become convulsed with laughter that he is not afraid to take his time. I don't think I know of anyone who has become before my eyes, in my lifetime, a grand old man. It is achieved by knowing himself through and through and by never pretending to be anything he is not, by not wasting time in insincerities, by taking the opportunity each time he talks to someone, not of merely conversing but of finding out more of them, or of developing a relationship. Watching him look at a book that someone is showing him is to watch a pantomime of someone

[1] Tamara Karsavina (1885–1978), Russian ballerina, leading dancer of Diaghilev's Ballets Russes 1909–22, author of *Theatre Street* (1930).

[2] Alice Astor (1902–56), married Raimund von Hofmannsthal and later David Pleydell-Bouverie. She was a great supporter of Ashton ballets. She died in mysterious circumstances in New York.

showing deep interest, yet that interest is 100 per cent (when he is bored by something, he is ruthless enough to discard it without manners).

As the years pass by, he is much happier. His ambitions are fulfilled in his work, he no longer hankers avidly for money, or more success. He is less and less interested in "society," and more interested in growing his garden, planting trees and watching, he does a marvellous imitation of it, his cat in ecstasies in the catmint.

The weekend was a revelation as well as an entertainment for me as Kin roared with amazed laughter at Freddie's imitations of Margot, Lopokova and Baylis.[1] I felt sad that Fred's physical condition is so weak. He has trouble in digesting his food, and has a tiresome Christian Scientist maid[2] who prevails upon him to ignore medicines, but I felt pleased to see someone swimming so serenely into old age, and without racks and torments and without feeling that life had passed him by. He has become a most fulfilled and contented person.

Cecil's time at Broadchalke was enlivened from time to time by visits to Stephen Tennant at Wilsford Manor, and occasionally from him at Reddish. Now living in eccentric circumstances, a virtual recluse, he spent much of his time in bed. Wilsford was adorned with his paintings, shells and other objects that took his fancy. Every visit to Stephen was memorable, for one reason or another, and the proceedings were controlled by his whims and flights of fancy.

Stephen Tennant after six months of silence rang up from his neighbouring citadel to talk about Pavlova.[3] "Do you know her face was white and shiny, like the pip of an apple? And she stayed in the same hotel as I did in Paris, surrounded by about five Russians. She wore turbans, showed no hairline, and was the first woman I ever saw to wear dark blue on her eyelids." When was all this? "When I was 15." That must have been over 40 years ago, yet his conversation had such an immediacy that I felt that Pavlova was alive today.

[1] Dame Margot Fonteyn (1919–91), prima ballerina, born as Peggy Hookham, Lydia Lopokova (1892–1981), ballerina; and Lilian Baylis (1874–1937), theatrical manager who ran the Old Vic.

[2] Mrs. Lloyd, Ashton's first housekeeper, who came to him in the late 1940s. His friends noticed that he doted on her and worried that he might even marry her.

[3] Anna Pavlova (1881–1931), prima ballerina.

ALAN TAGG[1]

Alan used to be so timid that it was impossible to hear his whispers behind a curtain of fair hair. Now he has blossomed, and when given a sympathetic audience can be devastatingly funny for long leisurely spans of time.

He has been beguiling us with anecdotes of his recent visit to America and each story is told with such exactitude of dialogue, and is in itself so carefully chosen and individual that we get the very essence of his experiences.

A delightful aspect of Alan's humour is that once something has struck him as funny, it is always funny, and can be enjoyed over and over again with pristine relish. Suddenly he will explode with mirth and in explanation tell us that he has just remembered something he heard one woman say to another in a bus ten years ago. What was it? Do let us share the joke. "Well, one woman said, 'I washed it for her when she was eighteen, I washed it for her when she was twenty-one, I washed it for her when she was married, and I washed it for her after her first-born, but I'm never going to wash it for her again.' "

DAVID HOCKNEY[2]

As a child, I was, like most Edwardians, brought up never to waste a mouthful of food. If you can't finish your lunch, you'll have it cold for supper. "Waste not, want not" was drummed in and somehow my father always instilled into us a fear of the workhouse.

How very different the youth of today. David Hockney arrived (to be painted) on his way from Bristol. He turned up in his car, wearing the thinnest of synthetic or nylon windbreaks, over a T-shirt. "Noh, I'm not *corld.* Is it *corld* outside? I get into my *carre* and the heat's automatically on, and I get out at the *plaice* I arrive at. You may think this *cuppe* is a bit daft, but I bought *ert* at

[1] Alan Tagg (1928–2002), stage designer of over 80 West End productions from *The River Line* with Paul Scofield in 1952 to Peter Shaffer's *Lettice and Lovage* in 1987. He assisted Cecil with his work and was a frequent visitor to Broadchalke.

[2] David Hockney (b. 1937), artist, born in Bradford.

David Hockney in the winter garden at Reddish House, 1965

'*Arrods* because I wasn't lookin' *whaire* I was goin' and I knocked over all the hat stall, and I put the woman to so *mooch* trouble I thought *ah moost* buy *someunt*!"

Likewise nothing seems to surprise him. A boy from the most humble family in the Midlands, he arrived to learn to be a *paintah* in London without any misgivings. "It was most extraordinary at the College. After a bit they wouldn't give me any more *canvass,* we paints, because I hadn't got any *munnaigh,* so that's how I got interested in engraving. In the *engraivin'* dept, they let you have the *stoof* free, but even so they said I was *waaistin'* their copper plates because I did static isolated line drawings of figures, and they said I should use up all the copper by covering it with patterns. Before someone came and gave me a prize for that picture you bought, they never thought anything of my work. Now I paint twenty pictures a year and Kas[1] sold the lot and I teach.

[1] John Kasmin (b. 1934), London art dealer. Founded Kasmin Ltd. with Sheridan, Marquess of Dufferin and Ava, in 1961.

"I luv America, and I teach there quite a lot. They're not good at rendering. They can't paint a sphere, so I set the class to paint a door. They all got canvases the size of a door and painted as realistically as possible, and we had an exhibition of all the doors down a corridor. It looked *naice.* But I couldn't get *oop* in the morning. I was supposed to start at eight-*thairtee* but I'd *paaint* at night and then go out to the pools until they closed, and that'd be 2 o'clock, and perhaps it was 3 or 4 before I got to *baid,* so I couldn't get up at 8 o'clock, so I'd go in at 10:30 and stay till I but *nohwon* seemed to *caire.*"

It staggers me how an unprepossessing, even eccentric, freak like this can be so at home in the world. When I first went to America I was too scared to ask a policeman which was downtown. Not David. He arrives in Los Angeles without knowing a soul. He gets arrested at 3 in the morning for jaywalking but he makes friends with lots of healthy people and goes off in a truck with one to get his driving licence. "Where's your car?" "I haven't got one, but this is my friend's *trook.*" He drives it around with the instructor who thinks him mad, but gives him a permit although he has failed on four points. Hockney then buys a car and starts to drive it on the St. Berna[r]dino Freeway. He can't get off, and drives on and on until he comes four hours later to Las Vegas. Here he remains an hour, then comes all the way back. It gives you confidence to be driving for ten hours on end.

I looked at him in amazement. No wonder his face seemed so bland. He seems to have no hurries, no problems, no fears or anxieties. "I just draw static figures. *Noh,* I *dorn't* have an easel. I just prop my canvases on a chair. The only trouble was my paints took so long to dry, I had to be working on four pictures at once, but now I have Crilla paint and that's *mooch* easier. No, I'm in *noh* hurry to get back to London. I'm not doing any painting for another month or two."

I'm afraid he left me feeling very sorry for myself, particularly vis-à-vis my paintings in which I don't know where I am even aiming at, let alone achieving what I want.

In April, Cecil paid a second visit to Prince Felix Youssoupov, the Russian prince, who had lived in exile in Paris for many years. Felix Youssoupov, born in 1887, had a dashing history behind him not only as a prince from one of Russia's oldest and richest families, who lived in St. Petersburg with a beautiful wife, but more so as the murderer of Rasputin.[1]

The Youssoupov Palace was enormous and known for its grand soirées, having its own exquisite theatre. The Prince had bachelor rooms to the left of the main entrance.

On the night of 29–30 December 1916, at the time of the Russian Army defeats, he and Prince Dmitri[2] *lured the "Mad Monk" Rasputin to the palace, with the intention of disposing of him as a wicked influence over the Tsarina Alexandra,*[3] *which he had acquired due to his seeming ability to contain the suffering of her haemophiliac son, the Tsarevich.*

Youssoupov was forced to dramatic lengths in order to murder Rasputin. A meeting with Princess Irina Youssoupov,[4] *his wife and the niece of the Tsar, was presented as bait. The Princess was actually in the Crimea at the time, and in order to convince the Monk that she was entertaining upstairs and would soon come down, the gramophone record of "Yankee Doodle Dandy" was played over and over to give the impression of a party.*

Youssoupov attempted to poison Rasputin with cakes filled with cyanide of potassium, he then shot him, but Rasputin staggered on, so they shot him again. Finally they trussed him up and lowered him into the Neva. When found, he was pronounced dead from drowning.

Youssoupov and his accomplices were banished from St. Petersburg. He was made to live at Rakitnoe in the province of Kursk. Thus he escaped the fate of many of his relations. Some years later, he won substantial damages from MGM when they portrayed the murder on screen. He settled in relative penury in Paris, where he remained officially married to his wife, though openly homosexual. He acquired a friend in the form of a shabby monk, who was so smelly that it made

[1] Gregory Rasputin (1871–1916), the "Mad Monk," son of a peasant, who became the Tsarina's confessor in 1907, succeeding in keeping the ailing Tsarevich alive by hypnosis. An orgiastic maniac with evil influence.

[2] Grand Duke Dmitri (1891–1942), only son of the Grand Duke Paul and Princess Alexandra of the Hellenes, and first cousin of the Tsar.

[3] Tsarina Alexandra (1872–1918), daughter of Grand Duke Ludwig IV of Hesse, and of Princess Alice, daughter of Queen Victoria.

[4] Princess Irina (1895–1970), only sister of Prince Dmitri, a woman of exceptional beauty, who married Prince Felix Youssoupov in 1914.

entertaining Youssoupov impossible. Lady Diana Cooper, tolerant of many Bohemians, drew the line at inviting them to dine at the British Embassy due to the monk's less than appealing aura. Youssoupov lived on in Paris until his death in 1967 and here Cecil found him in April 1965.

PARIS—SECOND VISIT TO PRINCE FELIX YOUSSOUPOV APRIL 1965

"*Chien méchant*" the black iron door warns the visitor, though the dog responds to the ring of the bell by a furious yapping while the Prince sometimes does not hear the first summons, and one waits anxiously lest some arrangement has gone wrong and he is unavailable. But today he appeared on the second ring, and the "*chien méchant*" was too old a pug to be really much of a menace. The Prince, too, has failed a bit in the last two years. His eyesight is poor and his face was badly shaved, with white whiskers covered with powder, and the eyes were no longer *maquilléed.* However, on this visit, conversation and intercourse seemed to flow much more easily, though nothing much else in the atmosphere had changed since I was last here. (In fact, today there was a smell of fish cooking) and I was right in my supposition that a coveted book on Pavlova that I had formerly seen on a table in his bedroom would still be in place. It was and luckily the Prince asked if I would like to borrow it. To all intents and purposes it is mine, so my mission was successful.

But successful in other ways too. It was a lively meeting this time. The Prince said that Paris was for every taste but no one became a friend here. He had lived here since 1949 and had not made one friend. People were only interested in money and power. The rich were incredibly rich and so were the poor. He said the only women he ever loved were his wife and Pavlova, that he could not understand why Paul Getty[1] was so keen on him, and even spent money telephoning across the Channel, for Getty was no homosexual. But maybe he liked the things he said to him, e.g. "You will never be happy if you go on like this," that Getty had sent the biggest box of caviar he had ever seen. "It was very amusing." Perhaps people knew he had a certain intuition about them and that's why he got on terms so easily.

[1] Paul Getty (1892–1976), oil millionaire, normally remembered for his exceptional parsimony. Owner of Sutton Place, near Guildford.

The Duchess of Windsor,[1] after he had played the guitar at a dinner at her house, asked, "What do you think of me, Felix?" "I don't think you'd like it if I told you. But you have no sex, not female or male, but you have a Wallis sex, and without you the Duke could not live. You are his oxygen tent." I left the house on a scene of pandemonium. A young Frenchman asked why the Prince wore a table napkin in his breast pocket. The Prince looked down and exploded with laughter. Only royalty can laugh as he laughed. He went to the cupboard to search for a handkerchief. Among a litter of crumpled rubbish he brought out table napkins, short pants, anything but a handkerchief. As he did, so he roared and roared, with tears pouring down his face. It was a nice way to leave him.

Alan Jay Lerner[2] had longed to follow the success of My Fair Lady *with a musical on the stage, based on the life of the legendary couturière, "Coco" Chanel.[3] He wanted Cecil to design the costumes. The musical did eventually take place, causing Cecil considerable grief, in the autumn of 1969.*

CHANEL APRIL 1965

Brisson[4] charged me to see Chanel re the possibility of the musical that Alan Lerner is said to want to do. (It will probably never come to anything.) But the fact that Chanel is still alive and in full sail is quite wonderful and one should not take for granted that old people can live for ever.

This visit to the rue Cambon was like many another. The mirrored palaces below were now heavily populated. The apartment upstairs more than ever filled with glitter of gold lacquer, ormolu and crystal. The menagerie of animals from Persia has grown. Chanel in oatmeal with facings of crimson and navy blue, looked thinner, but otherwise of an extraordinary girlishness. She

[1] Wallis Warfield Simpson (1896–1986), married HRH The Duke of Windsor, KG (1894–1972), who abdicated the throne to marry her.

[2] Alan Jay Lerner (1918–86), lyricist of the pair Lerner and Loewe. He wrote the words for *My Fair Lady, Gigi* and *Camelot.*

[3] Gabrielle "Coco" Chanel (1883–1971), dress designer, and founder of the house of Chanel, who liberated women's fashions in the twentieth century.

[4] Frederick Brisson (1915–84), stage producer, married to Rosalind Russell. He had been trying to get the musical into production since 1954.

was talking her head off to her staff as she waited to take me out to lunch at her *petite auberge* (the Ritz) opposite. She has no cook in her apartment *ooh la la.* Things were getting more and more difficult. She didn't like the look of the way things were going with the government. She didn't know if she would do another collection, and there were no craftsmen, no one took trouble, the food was no good in Paris any more because it takes "time" to prepare sauces. Arm in arm, we walked to the Ritz, where she ordered lunch only as a Frenchwoman can. The asparagus must be *tiède,* not frozen, the taste went, and there was much talk about the steak being *à point,* and not *sanglant.* Then, having got rid of the menu, she devoted herself to me, or was it to me that she talked? Or was she just talking for talking's sake? She did not really show much sign of judging whether I was present or not. It did not matter if my mind wandered, because the flow went on so much longer than one could ever give attention to. Only a pity a tape recorder was not hidden, for much must have been useful. Her generalisations were apropos fashion (anti-Courrèges)[1] the theatre with the bad manners of modern authors who were so interested in one's making pi-pi, and abstract painting, anti much but so prolific that one does not take her complaints as valid. They are a game played on a certain level. The rat-tat-tat continued. Our heads became lower on the table and closer. Her eyes like pansies, with dark heavy lashes, her skin very clean and her aura delightfully perfumed, with hands that are like a peasant's. She kept fluttering a pair of gloves and I noticed that only the hands had become old.

Much that she said was incomprehensible, and although many would have been bored to distraction with the onslaught, it was enough for me to breathe in her physical presence, for taking everything into consideration, she is utterly individual, completely French and such a rare phenomenon that there will be no one to take her place. She is certainly one of the greats.

Cecil then travelled to Notre-Dame de Vie, the villa on a terraced hillside near Mougins, in the South of France to photograph Picasso. By this time Picasso had achieved that rare distinction of fame and fortune within his lifetime. The Tate Gallery had mounted a comprehensive exhibition of his work in 1960, which was seen by 450,000 people. Even Russia was persuaded to send several works from the

[1] André Courrèges (b. 1923), couturier, opened his fashion house in 1961.

Hermitage. In 1964 the Bavarian government had paid the then exorbitant sum of £90,000 for a single portrait, creating the world record for the largest sum for a work by a living artist. Early in 1965, the Tate paid £60,000 for Les Trois Danseuses, *in a hail of controversy.*

Picasso, born in 1881, was 83 at the time of Cecil's visit, and living with his second wife, Jacqueline Roque, his model, whom he had married in 1961. He had lately been involved in considerable and unsuccessful litigation to try to prevent his former mistress, Françoise Gilot,[1] *from publishing her memoirs not only in magazine serialisations but also in book form.* The Times *described this book as "probably the most intimate and in some ways the most unpleasant biographical work about Picasso."*[2] *John Richardson,*[3] *Picasso's biographer, came to see some merit in the work for its insights into Picasso's character, but at the time the artist was enraged by such descriptions as "He took his hands away. Not suddenly, but carefully, as though my breasts were two peaches whose form and colour had attracted him; he had picked them up, satisfied himself that they were ripe but then realized that it wasn't yet time for lunch."*[4]

The old artist was to live on until April 1973, dying at the age of 91.

28 APRIL 1965

It is strange that at an age of over 60, I should be able to work myself into such a nervous condition at the idea of photographing Picasso. I was certainly extremely on edge. I remember when I first photographed him in the early thirties, at that time I could speak very little French. In the meantime every professional photographer in the world and thousands of amateurs too have had a field day with him, and I remember Liberman[5] saying it was tiresome that once one had photographed him he never had enough and begged, "Come back tomorrow."

[1] Françoise Gilot (b. 1921), Picasso's mistress between 1943 and 1953. She was the mother of Paloma Picasso. The book, called *Life with Picasso,* co-written by the American art critic Carlton Lake, was published in France and the United States in 1964, and in Britain in 1965.

[2] *The Times,* 9 April 1973.

[3] John Richardson (b. 1924), art historian, whose first volume on Picasso won the Whitbread Prize in 1991.

[4] *Life with Picasso* (1965), p. 26.

[5] Alexander Liberman (1912–99), managing director of *Vogue.*

This was not possible for me when three years ago I attempted to see him. He was rattled, worried. Douglas Cooper[1] passed Madame P.[2] on our way to Cannes, and although we had been refused, she was surprised we did not stop and come up to the house.

This time I planned, as before, to stay with Douglas Cooper at his marvellously romantic Château de Castille[3] and come under my own steam to Mougins. I sent a telegram as from le Petit Beaton from London, to warn him of my arrival. This was well received, and *politesse* was in the air. When I telephoned and asked Madame P. if she would pose, she was shy. "I am not beautiful, just *une bonne petite bourgeoise.* Can you come now?" "No, I'm arriving only tonight in Cannes." "4 o'clock tomorrow? Ravi." But I was somewhat sleepless my last night at the Castille and I was restless for the early-morning taxi to arrive and take me to the train. Was this the right part of the train? Would it arrive on time? I had worked myself up into such a state of anticipation by the time I arrived at the Grand Hotel, Cannes, that I had a bad headache and only a few minutes to enjoy the effects of two aspirins before going off to Mougins and Notre-Dame de Vie.

The taxi driver was not sure of the way so we asked a group standing in a cottage door. "*Le Grand Peintre, eh bien,* 250 metres on the right and up, up the hill." I realised what a tremendous amount of canvases must have been sold to pay for this long winding drive that curled to the top of the mountain. Suddenly, a closed gate, with a bell. The driver rang. No answer. I would not be surprised if they did not answer. It would be like the end of *Washington Square.* But suddenly, a voice asked who was there? "Mr. Beaton?" "Cecil Beaton. Yes." "Then wait."

The door eventually opened and suddenly we arrived at a courtyard filled with flowing wisteria to be welcomed by Madame P. at the door. She is very squat and short-necked. She wore a blue silk coat and white trousers, hair immaculate. She was very polite. "Pablo says it is 20 years since he last saw you." A great welcome from Picasso. "Oh, I am pleased that you are here. We must

[1] Douglas Cooper (1911–84), see biographical note, p. 48.

[2] Madame Picasso (Jacqueline Roque) (1927–86). A model of Picasso's, she eventually married him in 1961. She mourned him grievously and shot herself dead on 15 October 1986.

[3] Douglas Cooper's villa, the Château de Castille in Provence.

Pablo Picasso at Mougins, 1965

embrace." I kissed him on two soft clean-shaven cheeks. Also present were M. and Mme. Gomez[1] (she who specialises in Balthus)[2] and the room was a kaleidoscope of brilliant objects and colours against a sunny white background.

[1] André Gomez and his wife Henriette, from whose collection *Le Grand Paysage* by Balthus was sold for $760,000 in 1997.

[2] Balthus (1908–2001), painter.

Picasso, sad to relate, has grown older, and it has taken the form of shrivelling him. He was never slim but he had a strength that has now diminished. There is something sad about his eyes, which have lost something of their brilliance. And whereas before they were black, they now seem a paler brown. In fact, he was altogether a symphony of brown, beige, mushroom. His skin was pale cigar-leaf and his hands, pointed fingers, rather heavy, were a darker shade. The teeth like old ivory and the whites of the eyes parchment. He wore a biscuit-coloured woollen pullover and patterned velvet trousers of cinnamon and snuff. There was a gash of green paint on one arm, a sleeve was worn to tatters, a hole also in the black stockings, neat white leather shoes.

Lots of fun about the passage of the years. Yes, he remembered my photographing him like Whistler's mother, and featuring the toys on his mantelpiece. No regrets about the dead or the past. We must go on even if it was madness. The number of paintings he did! Sometimes eight in one day. We must see everything in one day. We left the sitting room for another white simple drawing room with such a mass of letters, pottery, drawings, stacks of canvases, that it was impossible to take in more than an occasional detail. Passed the dark dining room covered with parcels, pictures, books, sculpture, the walls lined with pictures stacked back to wall, to the hall, packed with packing cases and canvas (pale, honey-colour effect) against white walls.

Down to the basement (formerly the hall in the Guinnesses'[1] time) now just a cemetery of statuary, some lifelike, some abstract, constructions of wire, steel, painted tin. P. wondered about turning on extra lights for photographs, enjoying being taken bored, amused, flattered. He had a semi-queasy expression on his face. But I found it difficult in my excitement to photograph him as he had evolved a technique of being photographed by others and fell into his habitual poses. Square on to the camera with wildly staring eyes. This was nevertheless a field day and I only wish I could have had a more pliable sitter, who would take on other shapes with his sculpture. The amount of work was utterly staggering, but there is more. "Come, you must see everything."

Mme. P. was marvellously self-effacing and managed to be out of the camera line all the time. And when I tried to take her she seemed generally

[1] The villa had belonged to Benjamin Guinness (1868–1947), father of Loel Guinness, Meraud Guevara and Tanis Phillips.

unhappy and shy. We then circled a wide staircase to come upstairs to one huge painting room after another, each filled with pictures, some in execution, others stacked face to the wall. Everywhere huge daubed colours of the shapes we have become accustomed to. But to me the latest work seems to have lost exactitude. The line is not good, the brush stroke so coarse and rubbed. A lot of curious painting with every sort of trick employed. Perhaps he dipped the paint into a cork and pressed that into the canvas. A smell of Ripolin and everywhere stacks of tins of paint. I noticed no brushes. The sun poured through the shutters which due to today's great wind slashed backwards and forwards. Perhaps one went into four different rooms filled with new paintings, then on to a huge glassed-in terrace with a superb view of distant purple mountains. Here a mass of blue Ripolin canvases of monstrous women, all somewhat indecent according to Victorian standards. I clicked and clicked, hoping for the best. In my excitement and emotiveness I had moved a piece of sculpture that I thought was made of card and found it of iron. Points dug into my thumb and the blood poured. Nothing to do but suck and forget. Some of the time the sun came through on to the floor to enable me to take good patterned compositions, but much of the work was pretty humdrum stuff and God knows whether I have got the exposures right.

Back in the first sitting room we sat around the circular table and talked. But I went on taking pictures betimes and it was not as if he minded. Madame would make some very good heads.

The scene represented the attraction of conversation, for the party was tremendously amused and happy just to sit and talk without the necessity of drinking. After I had taken as many pictures as I felt I could in this particular light, I got out my sketchbook and started to make notes. But I find that after the excitement of taking photographs my energies are too dissipated for drawing and I did pretty badly, and I kept turning the pages and Picasso rushed from his chair. "Why don't you do what Degas did and have pages of paper that is transparent so you can turn over and trace the good bits and correct the bad?" He was tremendously enthusiastic about this idea and his eyes popped. It was another facet of his extraordinary display of vitality.

Once he demonstrated to Mr. Gomez the advantages of the modern (Knoll) swivel chair he sat in. He almost twirled himself into space. All his actions are quick ones. His arms raised in a fork. His body is too nervous and strong to be graceful generally. When he turns his head his body turns too. He jumps from place to place like a boy skipping. He talked of his working at night. It was then so quiet and no one to disturb. Sometimes it was 3 o'clock before he stopped, so he liked to get up late in the morning. He didn't need much sleep but liked to rest and read. When someone complained that they hadn't been able to sleep P. had said, "So much the better for you. Sleep is a waste." He is strong. He is accustomed to moving sculpture. He did an imitation of his mother in her rocking chair. Her feet could never touch the ground. He asked Mme. Gomez why she was here. "Specially to see you." That reminds me of Alice Toklas[1] who arrived one day and said she had come specially to see him. "Now you have seen me now you can go." Alice was not amused. But Picasso is fond of Alice and helps her in her financial crisis now that she has been bled by Gertrude's revolting relations who have snooped on the apartment, taken everything from it and then turned her out. How beastly can relations be?

Although he moved a lot, he sometimes stared very intently at me, and his stare still has the power to intimidate. He laughed at me holding four sharpened pencils in my hand and said, "After that you're going to paint me?" Suddenly he said he thought I was a painter. I had the eyes of a painter like Chardin or Fragonard, but not of a photographer. Most photographers had the eyes of their lenses. Photographs were too mechanical, drawings more alive more—I can't remember the word—and colour photography added nothing to black and white.

Madame Gomez went into the next room to talk business with P. and Madame P. said that, while on the subject of intimidation, she still found Pablo someone that she could never take for granted. She had been married for 11 years and each day she was more impressed by his honesty and naturalness. He was so great that she felt always it was a privilege to be with him and take care of him. This shows how much she loves him. Her eyes linger on him. She dashes forward in distress if the wind blowing a small canvas on to another has smudged. She wraps his jumper across his chest when he comes out into the cold. She brings him a large glass of milk.

[1] Alice B. Toklas (1877–1967), heavily moustached friend of the American writer Gertrude Stein (1874–1947). Author of the celebrated cookbook.

Cecil with Picasso at Mougins, 1965

Jacqueline admitted she would like to go to Paris, that they seldom went out here, not even to the bullfights any more. But Pablo only liked to work and here was his native world, on the mountain top. He had already made three new studios and he wants now to fill a fourth. This at 84 is not bad. She is obviously happy to look after this man and has no ulterior motives, is utterly non-venal, and unlike the Gilot, whose book was now discussed.

Picasso said that he was a great admirer of Princess Margaret (with her long face), but please not to tell people otherwise someone will write a book about it. If he told me that sometimes at night when he is working late, rather than walk to the lavatory, he pees out of the window, he does not want me to put that in a book. It was awful to have someone in the house with you for ten years and know that they were putting everything in a book. Would they ever have a Customs control. "Are you writing a book? If not swear not."

The fact that his two children have been turned against him is a very great upset. He is deeply disturbed by the whole thing.

The art dealers asked if he admired any new painters. "*Ah, oui. Pignon*[1] *et Balthus.*" He said he is publishing some lithographs of Shakespeare and someone had written that before he had made his drawing, she didn't know Shakespeare had sex appeal. Whisky brought. A convivial scene sitting in this cluttered room, the centre of which was taken by a bowl of deep pink roses from the garden. Really romantic they are, said Madame P. who had made the delightful little posies of daisies, tulips and small bright almost wild flowers put around the room in odd pots. After a while my head became quite stiff on the shoulders and I was completely exhausted. Time to go. The picture-dealing Madame had almost to be turned out of the house. "I have to paint," said the Maître. It is marvellous that he has such fun at his time of life. He believes in all his jokes. And some of them are good. But seeing the place littered with literally thousands of pictures today one saw a great number of pictures that do not deserve to be seen and probably will never be exhibited. Some were wild blobs and smudges of a ruthlessness that was really very unpalatable. Sad that someone who can draw with the exactitude of Ingres and the freedom of a Japanese master now does thick smudges that have no apparent drawing. But no doubt I am wrong again. I was nonetheless somewhat suffocated by so many, too many neo-classical heads and tortured buttocks and graffitiesque twats. There were too many photographs of Picasso around, but no, I must end on a note of charity. For he was kindness itself to me and I know he is so great that any deficiencies in his latest work are probably merely my lack of appreciation of them.

Eventually the two Picassos came out to the wisteria-covered courtyard to bid us goodbye. The light was fading. The grey stone was fading like opals. The wolfhound was like a grey pearl. Picasso's teeth looked very dark ivory as he smiled. "So good to see you looking so well," I said and he ran to touch the wood and the wisteria. He does not like age and the process of getting old. "Come back again in twenty years, but come back sooner as well." Eyes melting with amusement and kindness as we all waved and waved, and then circled down the mountainside.

[1] Edouard Pignon (1905–93), artist who shared an atelier with Picasso at Vallauris 1951–2.

PICASSO (CONTINUED)

Stands legs apart, hands deep in pockets. He clips his own white hairs. (At the back of his hand the pores are open and dark, giving a dotted effect.)

At one moment he took two little square paintings off the wall. They were of Rousseau's mother and father. He was very pleased that they were unframed and had on them the hooks with which Rousseau fondly hung them on his own walls.

Cecil had been staying with Douglas Cooper at his magnificent home, the Château de Castille, in Provence. Cooper was an art dealer, who amassed the world's most important collection of Cubist paintings. His business ethics were not always of the highest. He was an adviser to Wildenstein, and the world expert on Gauguin. John Richardson, who spent some years as his companion, left a devastating account of him in his memoir, The Sorcerer's Apprentice *(1999).*

DOUGLAS COOPER

Douglas Cooper is not a person that I could be fond of. I used to loathe him with poison. He has improved and I have become less critical, and I do admire his cleverness. He seldom says a futile thing. He is fantastically well documented, never forgets a detail and is very good company, daring to be more unpleasant than most people think wise. Also, he has got a really superb flair and taste, not only in pictures but in his house.

To find such a place as the Château de Castille in the first place, and then to overcome all the difficulties from French incoherency, and transforming the ruin into a living entity was something that few would be prepared to do. It is now comfortable and unbelievably beautiful, and the latest addition of a Picasso terrace is a trial of skill, taste and tenacity. He has spent a fortune on pictures that are now worth twenty times what he gave for them. He has spent inordinately on other works of art and the water supply is now adequate. But the bedrooms are utilitarian to the point of being monastic and this is as it should be. No money squandered on pelmets, it goes on things that are worthwhile like the collection of de Staels in my bedroom.

I love this part of the world and it was good to be there again when the lilac, white and dark purple iris and the tree peonies were out. Marie[1] (though threatened with the sack for drunkenness) cooked as deliciously as only a Frenchwoman can. The Graham Sutherlands[2] were in the offing, so conversation was spiked and peppery. (Graham describing how David Sylvester[3] went on eulogising a bottle of Algerian wine that G. had put and served in a decanter, Kathy describing Jane Clark's drunkenness, repeating what nasty things had been said about Douglas.)

A group came in for Sunday night supper including an intelligent Belgian cinema producer, Raoul Lévy,[4] the Hugo's[5] etc. It was all very entertaining, until Douglas was stricken ill with fever of 104, went red in the face and sweated, and I was left alone in the house to await the train to take me to Cannes.

It was terrible suddenly to feel trapped. The rain came down in gusts and the landscape seemed very flat. Douglas would have no pity. He lay feeling rotten with his high temperature, but he knew there was nothing to worry about. The doctor had given him piqûres. He would recover in two to three days. Meanwhile he now lay in bed, would have turtle soup and salad and oranges for dinner. I watched him. His self-sufficiency quite amazing. He kindly looked up a place in the Michelin where Eileen could spend a holiday. He turned the pages violently in ugly, clumsy hands. He wore glasses but could not see. He was like a blind mole. The lettuce and salad dressing ran down his cheek and chin. He moved in paralytic jerks. "No, I'm all right, I don't need anything," he said, and I feel he meant it. He doesn't need love or friendship or companionship. He and Marie are sufficient in this stronghold of modern art, beauty and canniness. Douglas has almost arrived at the point where his ambition has left him. All that remains is his intelligence and that seems to satisfy him. Fighting French authorities, getting the better of lawyers, rivals and ene-

[1] Marie Desvignes, Cooper's tyrannical housekeeper. She was eventually dismissed.

[2] Graham Sutherland (1903–80), portrait painter, and his wife, Kathy (1905–91). John Richardson did little for his posthumous reputation. See *The Sorcerer's Apprentice.*

[3] David Sylvester (1925–2001), art critic.

[4] Raoul Lévy, Belgian film director.

[5] Jean Hugo (1895–1984), painter and great-grandson of Victor Hugo, and his second wife, Lauretta Hope-Nicholson, with whom he had seven children.

mies, he is a lone wolf and somehow one is not even sorry for him, and he certainly does not ask for sympathy, not even praise. "No, I don't need anything."

GROWING OLD (ONCE MORE)

29 MAY 1965

Was lying on my bed with hair awry, having spent the afternoon sleeping and writing, when Mrs. Paycock (whom I consider so infirm that she must be cosseted) came in to ask me at what time I was leaving for the weekend at Wilton. Oh, I said, soon after tea and I wished I hadn't to go. It's so damn cold out and I'm not sure that Wilton will be as warm as it is here. "Oh, but I should think Lord Pembroke[1] would have a well-heated house. He's old, isn't he?—like you are." (This blow follows close on my seeing the photograph of myself in the London *Vogue.*)

Don't know if it is a question of age or whether it is just human nature that makes me more conscious of my moods. I have touched every piece of wood in the Forest of Arden, been very lucky and happy in recent years. No great cataclysm has sent me reeling and so much has been agreeable that only minor irritations have crossed my way. These generally created by my having, through over-fatigue, reacted too violently to petty setbacks. But last week my mood took such control that a situation arose that created an atmosphere that I haven't yet known and which has continued for nearly two weeks. My relationship with Eileen has been so congenial and sympathetic that not during all these 12 years since she has been with me has there been anything wrong between us. Very occasionally I might speak a bit abruptly to her if I were finding a situation stubborn. But never anything but the greatest admiration and affection for her. Until this lovely sunny Saturday when we, Eileen, Kin and I, drove to Swindon to visit Ann Fleming in her new house. It was a long way to go for lunch and we motored on further to see the Morris house at Kelmscott, then called at Clarissa Eden's [Avon's] house en route for home.

By now I was very tired and irritable, and it was a mistake for me to

[1] Sidney, sixteenth Earl of Pembroke and Montgomery (1906–69). Cecil had known him since the 1920s when he attended his 21st birthday ball at Wilton and was thrown into the Nadder by some young "hearties."

suggest that Eileen drive the car home. There is something about her driving (always so personal a thing) that I find irritating to a minor degree. Eileen had kindly looked out our route on the map and mistakenly suggested that it would be a shorter and more direct route to go via Amesbury. As it happens, this is an ugly road with lots of traffic, and it is Clarissa's way to come over the Plain. On the way home Eileen suddenly took a wrong turning and having bottled up my irritation [I] became utterly furious when I realised that she was going home by the same longer ugly route. I slapped my hand on my knee, shouted "We will not go home that way" and became inarticulate with fury.

Eileen was told to give up the wheel and lay in the back of the car knocked out with shock. I drove at 80 miles and was home in a very short while. Eileen ran to her room, and although Kin did his best to make dinner talk bright and agreeable, Eileen's eyes were mostly on her plate, and the whole of the next day she was still resentful and knocked off her pedestal in spite of repeated apologies.

This shock was to her the last of many setbacks. She I overtire. She has had her holiday suddenly postponed (by Hal)[1] and life is not joyful for her. Her zest has been missing. It was a very great shock to me. I love Eileen and only want to make her happy. And this not from selfish reasons, although if she were to lose her sympathy and enthusiasm for me it would be a cataclysm of such dire magnitude that I could not imagine anything more awful.

But the "row" has created an atmosphere that in my somewhat debilitated condition has been like an illness. I have felt everything changed, as if I had jaundice, and my low spirits have even made the marvellous atmosphere of Reddish seem like dross. The burgeoning of spring has gone for nought and even Kin's kindness has not alleviated the pain.

By degrees the details of everyday existence absorb one, but that this unreasonable explosion should have happened has ruined something. As [J. M.] Barrie[2] said of a baby, "It is never quite the same once you have caused it to cry." Perhaps the lesson is that at my age I must not allow myself to

[1] Hal Burton (1908–87), who collaborated with Cecil on many theatrical projects, in particular advising him on the many re-writes of *The Gainsborough Girls,* Cecil's own play. A friend of Eileen's.

[2] Sir James Barrie (1860–1937), author of *Peter Pan.*

become so overtired and on edge that if the mood is not good, and with age the mood plays a larger part, then nothing is worthwhile.

Cecil was in for an unpleasant shock, shortly after this incident.

BROADCHALKE JUNE 1965

It's been a disappointing summer. This sounds like a weather report, but this year somehow the portents were good. We had an early burst of hot sun, then continuing rain. We thought that next week, after the farmers had got their mills filled, we could look forward to high summer. Week after week went by cold, wet, windy. The result an epidemic of flu colds. Kin caught a snorter from the place where he has his hair done. The germs passed to Eileen who was run down, depressed, who got it badly in the chest, then to me.

I felt rotten on the Monday morning when, still in bed, Kin returned from taking guests to Salisbury station and, seeing that all was quiet, pulled a chair up to my bedside, and asked, "Can we have a little talk. Let's talk about England." "Don't sit on the chair, sit on the foot of the bed." He sprawled across my feet.

"It's been a year since you arrived," I said.

"A year tomorrow, yes, and I feel I haven't made any progress here, I make no contribution and I can't go on playing a role where I just sit back and count for nothing. I listen to the talk and I don't participate, and no one wants me to. They're really all very friendly and kind but they don't connect. You're the only person that I've come here for and you're the only person that I like. I make very few friends in America, but here not one. I don't understand the people. They're so busy being clever with themselves. And they've got a lot to be pleased with, that they don't give a damn about you.

"England bugs me. People say this country is beautiful. It's not. And the climate and the rain are so depressing. You can't go for a walk without coming across a bungalow. It's too small. When I shut my eyes I see the hills around San Francisco and the light. It isn't just being homesick; it's missing what I need. I don't like the East coast of America. I'd rather live in England than the East, but something happened when I discovered San Francisco."

Of course I protested, "People do like you here. You could not be more admired and loved. No one has taken against you. You have fitted in so well." But the slow realisation came (as a complete shock) that Kin was going to leave me. I had not for one moment expected this. He had seemed perfectly contented here, pleased to go out with me whenever anything was planned, equally glad if there was nothing on the agenda and I was busy working so that he would go to his "little room."

I had wondered, a few weeks back, why he had decided going on a holiday to Greece with his friend Ed, and when I had asked why he had laughed. "Oh, lots of reasons." "Financial?" "Partly." He is too honourable to have had the holiday at my expense, then to come back and break the news of his decision. "It's not good for me to be dependent on you. You make everything so agreeable. You have been so kind. I feel like a shit but I can't give up my life. I want to teach and if I were to stay here ten years I'd be too old. There have been so many advantages which I know I'll miss when I go back, but I've got to live my own life. I have written to Cal University to ask for a teaching job, and to my family, and to Ed and Gene."

I realised there was nothing to say in protest, no use in trying to prevail upon him to alter his mind, no use trying to make it more difficult for him. There was nothing to do but try to hold back my feelings. This was impossible. I saw myself suddenly so lonely. After this wonderfully happy year here and the excitement of the year in California, everything had dropped out of my world. I saw my life suddenly so unfulfilled with all the inadequate, makeshift friends, the activities and affairs that mean nothing.

I saw all the things that I would be missing, Kin's playing Schubert or Bach as early-morning music, his schoolboy gangling, loping into the room, nose-wrinkled smile, his untidiness and the liveliness and high quality of the books in his room, our discussing all our pleasures and enthusiasms, sharing every situation, analysing every friend and event, the good companionship on motor tours.

I wept so much that breathing became difficult. My whole frame shook in an orgasm of misery. "There's nothing to look forward to now!" Kin, a cry from the heart said, "Oh, Kek!" "I feel amputated, bereft." I could only moan, "Oh, dear" and weep more. For Kin it must have been very unpleasant.

Eventually, after an hour's hysteria (it is strange how in any crisis in my life there is quiet in the outside world—the telephone strangely enough did not ring all morning), I felt that we were only working ourselves into an even greater frenzy, so staggered towards the bathroom. My walk was limp, I turned on the bath tap and stood, one hand flat to a cheek, crying and staring into space. Kin came in. We embraced. "It's so sad that we like one another so much and live in such different worlds." For the rest of the day I felt like an invalid, weak and limp.

I tried not to talk too much about events when later that evening we drove to London. I dreaded the night. When I woke up in the middle of the night, I quickly asked myself what was wrong—had there been a death in the house? I remembered and, with my raw new sorrow, found it difficult to turn over and go to sleep. When next morning Kin came into my room and saw the misery on my face he too collapsed and we remained sobbing in one another's arms.

Three or four weeks later

I have grown accustomed to this very sad decision, understandable, but misguided too, and have become reconciled to the fact that all the little extraneous excitements and frivolities will take the place of something that has been really serious and worthwhile, and which I am not likely again to be able to find. But for me it is only a loss, that there are no redeeming factors to tide me over the misery and the complete and utter break. For that is what it surely must be, living so far apart we are never likely to become so close to one another as now, and life moves on so quickly and so emptily.

Years later Kin said that Cecil had hoped for two years with him. He was surprised how much Cecil's influence remained with him, and his abiding memory was of his integrity.

Cecil could perhaps have integrated him more fully into his life. In London Kin lived in a small room at the top of the house. At Reddish, too, he was given far from the best room. Cecil's friends were indeed divided in their opinions of Kin, some enjoying his company, others finding him intellectually pretentious and regretting his absence of small talk. It was an unlikely coupling and probably always doomed to failure. Truman Capote believed that Kin's departure broke Cecil's heart.

VISITS TO PARIS

JUNE 1965

I like to keep my finger on the pulse of Paris, but I'm beginning to wonder if the pulse isn't failing. Certainly it now costs so much money to make the discovery that it is hardly worth the outlay.

Taxis are so scarce at the times one needs them that in order to get from exhibition to museum, from shop to social gathering, it is impossible to arrive on time. A hired car, as I discovered, costs the earth, and even those people whom I think of as not being particularly rich, spend a fortune on trivialities. (Lilia Ralli's[1] hair cost £75 last week, three dressings, washings, sets and extra pieces for hire.) The suits I was foolish enough to buy from Cardin cost twice as much as Savile Row and the Guy de Rothschild[2] party at Ferrières where the hideous 1890 palace was hung with cobwebs cost £3,500! However, there are moments when in spite of all the chatter, the nonsense, the feckless frivolity, one still senses the fact that Paris is more alive to the vagaries of fashion than anywhere else. Cardin[3] described a woman (whom I had not even noticed) at the Fair Lady Ball, dressed in mushroom-colour and topaz. He suddenly became inspired. He evoked not only the period of 1913 but the years preceding. She was not dressed in Poiret 1910, with swirling skirt caught here and here (his voice became like Sarah's) but she wore a looser line, her poses were rounded, softer, her complexion was pale powdery mauve made up as at that time, not for overhead lights but candles at eye level. She was made up with *papier poudré* and she sat sideways on her chair with arm extended to her parasol. This impersonation was worth a visit, as was Yves Saint Laurent's[4] "Bar." This is a piece of furniture made by a young sculptor to hide the cocktail bottles, shakers and ice container, a thing of steel beauty, a thing of inspiration and the beginning of a whole new line of furniture.

[1] Lilia Pringo (d. 1977), Greek, born in Athens, married Jean Ralli. She was an intimate friend of Princess Marina and Princess Olga. She was a girlfriend of Cecil's in 1937 and remained a lifelong friend. Later she worked for Christian Dior.

[2] Baron Guy de Rothschild (b. 1909), head of the famous banking family, married to Marie-Hélène van Zuylen (1927–96). Marie-Hélène was one of Paris's most famous party givers.

[3] Pierre Cardin (b. 1922), avant-garde couturier, who opened his fashion house in 1950. Previously he worked for Schiaparelli and was head of Dior's *tailleur* atelier from 1947.

[4] Yves Saint-Laurent (b. 1936), reclusive couturier and head designer at Christian Dior, who opened his fashion house in 1962. Famed for putting ladies of fashion into trousers.

But these instances are rarer than before. The modern paintings are of little interest, the clothes as superb as ever, but even the rich cannot buy the embroidered dresses that cost £1,000 each. Nobody talks politics. The premier goes out to dinner parties and even Malraux[1] is at every lighted candle. There is a story of his entertaining de Gaulle at a gala at the theatre which summarises de Gaulle's vanity. In the interval the two men retired to the men's room to pee. As they were standing side by side Malraux, somewhat desperately, made conversation: *"Quand même c'est une belle pièce."* To which de Gaulle replied, *"Regardez ailleurs."*

10 JULY 1965

It's been the social fortnight of the year. Pretty silly and not very entertaining on the whole, but a certain amount is necessary for my career, and other things like obligations and weaknesses crop up that make inroads on one's time and energy. The Chatsworth ball[2] was quite a failure, and the Ferrières "do," although unforgettable as a sight, was too exhausting, taking altogether about 12 hours of one's time. But the *My Fair Lady* soirée[3] at the Cascade in the Bois redressed the balance. This was so amusing that although I danced all night I awoke next morning feeling 20 years younger.

The festivities in London. Two days running I had lunch parties for Lilia Ralli on a visit and after they were over Kin and I stood on the doorstep at Pelham waving off Ali Forbes. He put the car in gear and drove off without turning to acknowledge our cheers. "So much for that lunch party," said Kin. "That was long forgotten. That took place two and a half minutes ago."

But last night's outing was different and rather remarkable. We were

[1] André Malraux (1901–76), writer.

[2] The Chatsworth ball given by the Duke and Duchess of Devonshire in honour of the coming of age of their son, the Marquess of Hartington.

[3] Hélène Rochas, widow of Marcel Rochas, and head of the Rochas perfume empire, gave a ball at the Grande Cascade du Bois de Boulogne inspired by *My Fair Lady* on 22 June. Some of the team from Chez Castel, the nightclub, came as costermongers, having eaten onions. The Duke and Duchess of Windsor were there. Cecil admired Hélène Rochas's beauty, especially at the 1971 Proust ball.

bidden by Solly Zuckerman[1] to assemble at 7:20 in the Elephant House at the Zoo. It was to be a dinner to inaugurate Tony Snowdon's Aviary. Princess Margaret had told me with excitement, "Mummy's coming." But not only were the Snowdons late, but Mummy too, so that we stood around a long while with drinks or canapés in our hands, watching these huge primeval animals being washed or playfully entertained by their keeper. Under the new arc lights of Casson's[2] house, the animals appear at their most remarkable, huge, slow-moving, strangely textured, extraordinary and unaccountable. The juxtaposition of these great primitive animals with the ultra-sophistication of this evening's guests made about as great a contrast as one could find. When Royalty arrived, the tour continued. Spellbound, we all watched in wonder the marvellous interweaving of the giraffes, playfully licking the manes on each other's necks, gyrating their dappled bodies in such unaccustomed ways. The Queen Mother,[3] fatter, dumpier and more Scotch than ever, looked up with infinite wonder at these great rhinoceroses, emus and zebras.

When we went to the Aviary—an extraordinary mind has conceived such a curious mélange of struts and cantileverages—the scene was almost as strange with the Queen Mother, her head encased in a peasant scarf, Princess Margaret done up like Empress Josephine walking over hard ground and being spotted by tourists on a barge trip of the Regent canals, and waving back as at old friends.

When the evening was over at midnight, Princess Margaret and Tony asked me if I'd like to come back to their house to prospect for backgrounds for a photographic sitting. We drove to Kensington P. in Tony's new grand car, an Aston Martin (worth over £4,000) with dashboard as complicated as that of an aeroplane. We roared through the London streets and as we got out on arrival, he tore the coat of his dinner jacket. P.M. very solicitous, he quietly angry. The house done up almost entirely by Tony, and a great success. Jacksons supplying Kentish mouldings and cornices and niches, Michael Duff[4] supplying slate slabs for floor. Elsewhere Tony has carpentered doors, book-

[1] Lord Zuckerman (1904–93), hon. secretary, Zoological Society of London 1955–77, president from 1977.

[2] Sir Hugh Casson (1910–99), architect and artist, later President of the Royal Academy.

[3] HM Queen Elizabeth The Queen Mother (1900–2002).

[4] Sir Michael Duff, Bt (1907–80), Lord Snowdon's godfather. He lived at Vaynol, in Wales.

cases, has made furniture out of packing cases and veneered doors. His own room is a workshop-study of incredible efficiency. He has inherited his Uncle Oliver [Messel]'s[1] love of detail. As a perfectionist only his talent is of today. In the modern idiom T. is of a much more technical nature (all the drawers are handleless and are apt to contain tape recorders, relays for gramophone etc.).

Apart from the hall, the drawing room is the most conventional room with its family photographs and pale colours, but the pictures are modern and the bedroom and bathroom and kitchen are all of the very latest styles in comfort, utility and labour-saving. Oliver's use of remodelled old junk most successful here with lots of Gothic put around the Gothic bathroom where the *chaise percée* is of fruitwood and the towel rack is octagonal and in reach of the bath. Remnants of the Ascot railings white ironwork used for a terrace in the garden etc. "We haven't got very much money, you see."

A search for photograph settings. Princess Margaret held a torch lamp while T. and I looked at the garden. (There is a patch of long grass under the trees that should come in very useful for groups with the children.) Then came back to talk about the distribution of the pictures in the US, which they visit in the autumn. Tony, on my side, fighting against the negation of the press rules. We all inveighed against Richard Colville.[2] Tony said he's a swine. He would never speak to him again for the way he talked of Jeremy Fry.[3] He said that the Queen did not need publicity and handled the press with that mistaken frustrating attitude of mind. Tony said if the pictures are generally released the British papers will publish them but not *Vogue, Harper's, Life* or any of the big magazines. Could we not settle that this could be used for *McCall's,* that for *Saturday Evening Post,* Princess Margaret, inhaling cigarette smoke through a long holder, suddenly became worried. She looked gaunt, older and more beautiful. "But you're bulldozing me into something that Lilibet [the Queen] may not like. I must ask Lilibet about it." Tony adamant: "We've moved on. This isn't twenty years ago. You've got to be realistic. It's ridiculous for Cecil to

[1] Oliver Messel (1904–78), interior decorator and ballet set designer.

[2] Commander Sir Richard Colville (1907–75), Press Secretary to King George VI 1947–52, and to the Queen 1952–68. Known for his fierce attitude to the press.

[3] Jeremy Fry, designer who lived at Widcombe Manor, near Bath. He would have been Armstrong-Jones's best man but was deemed unsuitable at the last moment.

give all to Blau.[1] It's a waste. Besides, Blau takes such an appalling cut. No, you let me manage it." An argument of ferocity ensued.

Earlier in the evening I had watched with intent Tony show his independence. The Queen Mother had been asked to sign the Visitors' Book to the Members' Room at the Zoo. Two ballpoints were produced, one red, one blue. Great discussion as to which the QM would use. Red decided upon, signature accomplished, writing so thin. "I can't even write with those things." Further discussion about Princess Margaret, she decides, too, on red. Then Tony. He must use a ballpoint too. "No, I've got my own pen." "It'll be different." "No, no, no!" The QM watches him write his name in thick juicy ink and in fury throws her arm through the air.

Tony, lying back without his coat, argued more and more. Suddenly in a rage rushed out of the house and got into his car. "Tony, Tony." Princess Margaret goes after him. "Where are you going? Are you going to take Cecil home?" "Come and get in here, Cecil." We drive down Kensington Green at enormous speed. "This is a lot of shit," says T. "If we let Colville have anything to do with it, it'll be another complete cock-up." "I'll fix it. You let me do the arrangements. If I may, I'll send some of the pictures of Margaret which she doesn't like. If you put a strong light directly on her face she'll close up her eyes just out of tiresomeness and in certain lights her face looks fat and pulpy like Lord Harewood.[2] Perhaps now I've gone too far." And as a framed photograph I'd taken away of the QM (to be further retouched) fell off my lap, I said, "And the Queen Mother's gone for six." We had clocked up 3 o'clock in the morning.

SIMON AND JULIET

Lady Juliet Duff and her companion Simon Fleet were integral features of Cecil's Wiltshire life. They lived at Bulbridge House, Wilton, and entertained a mixture of society and theatrical figures.

Juliet was born as Lady Juliet Lowther on 9 April 1881. She was the only daughter of the fourth Earl of Lonsdale and his wife, Lady Gwladys Herbert, a sis-

[1] Tom Blau (1913–84), who ran Camera Press.

[2] George, seventh Earl of Harewood (b. 1923), Princess Margaret's first cousin.

ter of the thirteenth and fourteenth Earls of Pembroke. Juliet was therefore a first cousin once removed of the sixteenth Earl of Pembroke, who was living at Wilton in the 1960s.

Had she been a boy, Juliet would have succeeded to the Earldom and to immense riches. Her father was a slightly pathetic figure, somewhat despised by his younger brother, Hugh, who envied him his wealth since he tended to be seriously in debt. Her mother, Gwladys, was tall and beautiful, and somewhat flighty.

When Juliet was not yet one, her father succumbed to a cold, and suddenly took a turn for the worse, dying, embarrassingly, at a small house he had taken in Bryanston Street to entertain actresses. His body had to be smuggled back to the family home in Carlton House Terrace. (His wife being in Monte Carlo.)

The title and the fortune passed to Hugh, who became known as the "Yellow Earl," the magnificently extravagant, and eventually bankrupt, fifth Earl of Lonsdale, KG, champion of boxing, and well known on the turf.

In 1885 Juliet's mother went on to marry Lord de Grey, who succeeded as second Marquess of Ripon in 1909.

As Lady de Grey in the 1890s, she had established opera seasons for the de Reskés, and Oscar Wilde dedicated his play, A Woman of No Importance, to her. E. F. Benson wrote of her, "At heart she was a Bohemian, while socially a great lady on a pinnacle . . . higher than any other . . . She wanted a definite 'stunt' to occupy her . . . When the Russian ballet appeared in England her interest in the affairs of Covent Garden swiftly revived."

By this time, the Marchioness had become a close friend of Queen Alexandra. Both she and Juliet were keen promoters of Diaghilev. They raised funds for him and were earnestly supportive. The Marchioness died in 1917.

Juliet had married, in 1903, Sir Robin Duff, second baronet, and had two children, Sir Michael Duff and Veronica Tennant. Her husband was killed in action in 1914 and she later married (in 1919) a man called Major Keith Trevor, whom she divorced in 1926, resuming the style of Lady Juliet Duff. She lived partly at 3 Belgrave Square and also at Bulbridge, a Pembroke house.

There was hardly a figure in the world of society, literature, the arts, ballet, theatre and cinema that she did not know, provided they were sufficiently prominent. She was muse to Maurice Baring and Hilaire Belloc. The Oliviers and even the American actress Ruth Gordon were entertained by her. She was also the source of many stories that amused the neighbours. She took the Lucky Strike *heiress, Doris Duke, to see the Double Cube Room at Wilton. Pointing out the tapestries, she told her that they were a gift from Henry VIII to the Herberts. "I'm not interested in textiles," replied the American.*

Walking round her garden at Bulbridge, Somerset Maugham congratulated her on her "Queen Hortense" roses. "Don't be a silly old bugger," she remonstrated. "They are Queen Olga of Württemberg." Another time he looked out of the windows and commented, "The c-c-cows are lying down. That means it's g-g-going to rain." "Not in Wiltshire, it doesn't," replied Juliet.

Her companion, Simon Fleet, was born as Simon Carnes in 1910, but changed his name to Fleet in the 1940s. He was originally discovered by Lady Diana Cooper in 1931, when he toured in the cast of The Miracle *with her. They ate Mars bars together in the interval of productions. Later Juliet adopted him as her "jagger" or "walker" (as he would now be called), and they lived together for over 40 years. Simon was the producer of* Heil Cinderella, *a wartime pantomime to raise money to buy cigarettes, games and comforts for the Armed Forces.*

Simon was a friend of the ballet designer Sophie Fedorovitch,[1] *who bequeathed to him her little house in Bury Walk, Chelsea, known as the "Gothic Box," where to this day a plaque records her occupancy. In 1955 Simon edited a private book about her entitled* Sophie Fedorovitch, Tributes and Attributes, *with contributions from Frederick Ashton, Cyril Beaumont, Dame Ninette de Valois, Oliver Messel, Cecil and others. In a curious, but not un-typical, Fleet operation, this was accompanied by a 20-page booklet, entitled* Sophie Fedorovitch, A biographical sketch, *with the note: "This biographical sketch was written as an introduction to the book,* Sophie Fedorovitch, Tributes and Attributes, *but it did not reach the printer in time."*

Though under Juliet's wing, Simon remained very much his own man and his London life was perhaps more adventurous than that led at Bulbridge. He was a particular friend of Queen Victoria's grandson, Lord Carisbrooke, who paid a regular visit to him at the Gothic Box, and also of Jacques Fath. He was not averse to alcohol and there was an unfortunate incident, at a party given by Cecil at the Café Royal after the opening of the London version of My Fair Lady, *when*

[1] Sophie Fedorovitch (1893–1953), Russian-British stage designer and one of Ashton's closest collaborators.

Simon, briefly free of Juliet's scrutiny, became thoroughly drunk, rubbed his face against that of Princess Grace Radziwill, ran his fingers through Lady Lambton's hair, made a pass at Daisy Fellowes and slipped his hand up Pamela Churchill's skirt.

Later in the evening, Cecil was alerted at the Milroy that Simon had been seen being frogmarched into a Black Maria and conducted to Savile Row police station. The Earl of Dudley,[1] *in a far from alcohol-free condition, rang the police station and assured them that though he did not know Fleet personally, he was "a decent enough sort of fellow" and secured from them the promise that he would be allowed to go home when he finally sobered up.*

Diana [Cooper] was the first to discover the charm and rare qualities of the companionship of Simon when the two were touring in *The Miracle.*[2] Later Juliet, after a bad start, realised she had found her life friend and thenceforth never let him go. For nearly forty years, now, they have been inseparable. Simon has enjoyed the many comforts and amenities of the life Juliet was able to offer him but the fact that he could meet Somerset Maugham and the Duke of Kent[3] and be enfolded in the life of the Pembroke family was bought at the cost of his having to give up his freedom and great ambition to succeed in some capacity in the theatre.

Someone who knew Simon at school said that without doubt he was the most ambitious boy of the three hundred. He may have changed—people do—he may have settled for being "no great shakes," and yet when one sees him off guard he looks desperately melancholy. Yet as a person his semi-gigoloesque life has not softened him. He has always kept a door open to "life," to the unexpected, to the rough as against the smooth.

In his few moments off duty he has done quite a lot of work, has learnt to be quite an authority on antiques, and shows in conversation that he has imbibed much knowledge from the books (seldom the recently published ones) that he has read. As a companion he is second to none. Unselfishly, he will down tools and, at a moment's notice, make a fiesta of a search with Diana

[1] Eric, third Earl of Dudley (1894–1969).

[2] *The Miracle,* play produced by Max Reinhardt in the United States in 1923.

[3] W. Somerset Maugham (1874–1965), author and playwright and HRH The Prince George, Duke of Kent, KG (1902–42), fourth son of King George V.

for a dog. Every motor expedition to and from Bulbridge at the "weekers" results in a discovery of a new route, an unknown antique shop or a curious character at a coffee shop, a garage. He can tell with amazing spontaneity and with pantomimic acrobatics how he was followed for miles in the country by an irate motorist who was a member of the Preservation of the Countryside and had spotted him throwing out from his car a discarded pork pie that he had not wished to attract the cats in his dustbin of the Gothic Box, where he lives. This summer we have sat around on chairs blissfully amused by Simon. He has been at his best.

Juliet has been at her worst.

For many, many years, Juliet has been a great figure in my life. She even had an influence on me. Her taste, inherited from her mother [Lady Ripon], has always impressed me. She has always been "game" for funny stories, the joke on her, and she has had a certain elegance and sense of eccentricity that is appealing. But I have never really liked her, nor she me. At first, she was very undecided as to whether she would "take me up" or not. At the time of my first appearance in London, she was a great figure with Diaghilev, sitting in his box at the first night of the new ballet season.

It was to a large supper party in her Belgrave Square house that she first invited me. The 50 guests were already seated at a long table in the marble swan decorated dining room. They were drinking pink champagne, a drink always served by her mother. Most of the men guests were in dinner jackets. I, arriving late, had to walk the length of the room to greet my hostess. I was in a tailcoat, having come on from some other beano that warranted such apparel.

Emerald Cunard,[1] on seeing me, created a little rumpus of displeasure, for only a few days before had she put a poker through my recently published *Book of Beauty*,[2] declaring that I was a "low fellow." Juliet was now in a quandary. As hostess she must be polite to her invitée, but although she never liked Emerald, she did not wish to incur her displeasure. With one gracious smile I was bidden to sit out of earshot and sight of Emerald and from that day

[1] Emerald Cunard (1872–1948), born Maud Burke, married Sir Bache Cunard. One of the great hostesses of her age and mother of the wild novelist Nancy Cunard (1896–1965).

[2] Cecil published his *Book of Beauty* in 1930, a mixture of photographs by him of the beauties of the day, sketches of those who eluded his camera and prose portraits written by him but touched up by the Wiltshire novelist Edith Olivier (1872–1948).

on Juliet has been a constant source of amusement. I don't think she has ever genuinely grown to like me. She knows that I am kinder than she is, and that I do more good things for people, but she resents my hostility to certain enemies who, although they are not really her friends, she is apt to uphold. Certainly in the last few years our irritation with each other has increased. As a friend she never does a kindness, as a neighbour she is competitive.

As the years pass, Juliet's once enormous income has diminished, and she has had to retrench, but likewise her innate meanness has taken a severe hold and, like her son and mother, she is incapable of putting her hand in her pocket if there is anyone around to foot the bill.

Recently this passion for parsimony has become so exaggerated that I do not know how Simon can manage to remain civil. A cocktail party is arranged by Juliet in Simon's London house. It is a success and several young people remain enjoying themselves with no particular reason to leave. Simon asks Juliet if they couldn't be invited to an impromptu supper. "No, get rid of them and we'll go to a little restaurant in the King's Road." An Italian proprietor asks, "A bottle of Chianti?" "No, water." "What to eat?" "Spaghetti." "And then?" "Nothing." At 9:15 the bill is presented and Juliet, out on the street, says, "Well, we got away with that for 12s. 6d." The fact that the evening was ruined did not enter her mind.

The slate mines have been doing badly in Wales and the income that Juliet received all these years, tax free, does not do for her what it did. So, she must sell a Fabergé ornament or a Boilly painting from the very vast collection of valuable works of art and furniture that she still possesses. But her economies increase. Under the pretension that her butler, Andrews, is overworked, and that Mrs. Andrews's feet give her hell, she seldom invites friends for the weekend where at least six guest rooms remain empty. If neighbours are invited over for drinks, there is little encouragement for them "to help themselves." Whenever possible, she will arrange to take herself and Simon off to have meals elsewhere.

Dicky Buckle,[1] now at Clarissa's Rose Bower in the village, has suited

[1] Richard Buckle (1916–2002), ballet critic of the *Sunday Times*, author of biographies of *Nijinsky* (1976) and *Diaghilev* (1979). He had rented Lady Avon's cottage at Bowerchalke. Later he settled at Gutch Common, near Semley, and was part of Cecil's group of Wiltshire neighbours.

her mood marvellously for, although servantless, he has been made to cook for her party whenever she has made an exception and asked people for Christmas or a Bank Holiday. Even Dicky rebelled when Juliet telephoned to say she was sorry she couldn't ask him to lunch on Saturday as Clarissa [Avon] was invited and that would make them eight, but could they all come to dinner with Dicky. A myriad stories there have been of Juliet's meanness.

But lately we have become alarmed. For Juliet's health is very poor. She has fallen several times and although Gottfried[1] has reduced her blood pressure from the danger point, she does not look as if she is long for this world. We are not aghast at the prospect of her death, but we are all most exercised that out of stupidity and meanness Juliet will leave Simon very badly off, in fact, with nothing at all.

It has recently been brought to bear, with the death of that old multi-plus-millionairess, Helena Rubinstein,[2] how the old ghouls die without more than a thought to their dependents, best friends and companions. For years, Patrick O'Higgins[3] has taken care of that *insortable* woman, bringing her to every party, spending his nights with her in Paris and London when he longed to see his friends. That he did so much for her didn't come in the realms of business relationship. Yet when she dies she leaves him as much as a servant would get, a tip of $5,000. Many other such instances have made us all gang together to try to do something about Juliet not following suit. Diana has been racking her brain as to the best way of approaching the subject and only I was foolish enough to stick my neck out. Of course, I got pole-axed and Juliet hated me just a little more for my uncalled-for interference. But as the subject was then on the *tapis,* Simon himself often would talk about his future. "Oh, you'll be able to look after yourself," said Juliet. "It would look so badly in the newspaper if the heading read, 'Earl's daughter leaves all to lover.' " Simon exploded, "You're too old to be news value."

When Simon insisted on mentioning the subject of his receiving some of the furniture, Juliet would put her fingers in her ears and say she did

[1] Dr. A. R. Gottfried, Viennese-born doctor with many fashionable clients. He continued in practice at 75 Wimpole Street until 1979.

[2] Helena Rubinstein (1871–1965), founder of a vast cosmetics empire.

[3] Patrick O'Higgins (1922–80), who worked for Helena Rubinstein and wrote a book about his experiences, *Madame* (1971).

not wish to hear anything unpleasant. Simon admits that it would be very easy for him to get everything she possesses (there is little money, but valuable possessions) by going on "strike," by disappearing even for a fortnight. Without him to fetch and carry, she would be lost. She even begged Simon not to go to a ball at the Ormsby-Gores,[1] saying, "You'll drink too much and then if you're found under the influence in possession of your car, you'll get sent to prison and I'll be immobile."

Juliet could not bear to be without her prop, and would soon come to her senses and to terms. But Simon says he cannot become a blackmailer, and admits that rather Juliet is blackmailing him, and Andrews too, by keeping them, knowing that they would not leave her, and yet never "raising their salary." Andrews, all these years, has been paid £5 a week, half the wage of her gardener.

Meanwhile Juliet is 86, and Simon nearing 60. Diana would love to have him become her "jagger" and would certainly see that in the last analysis Simon would not be left stranded. But as the situation stands, it is difficult for Diana to see Simon. She can only telephone to him midweek when he is in London. (Even I find it impossible to talk to Simon in the country for if by a fluke he should come on the line, it is wrested from him by Juliet, who fails to inspire me so the conversation dies quickly) and Simon remains loyal to his eccentric friend, as he calls her. But his loyalty is stretched tight. Simon seldom complains but sometimes he confesses he would like to scream yellow, pull off his wig.

Simon motored off to fetch Buckle from his cottage, leaving Juliet's son, Michael,[2] with Caroline[3] and their adopted son, in charge. Immediately I broached the subject. "What is Juliet going to leave Simon?" I asked Michael. "I'm afraid she's not got much to leave—no money." "But furniture?"

"Well, the Jacob suite will come to Vaynol, naturally, and I'll give Simon some furniture."

[1] Jane and Victoria Ormsby-Gore, elder daughters of fifth Lord Harlech.

[2] Cecil's footnote: "Michael dislikes his mother and always has. He now says she is living too long."

[3] Lady Caroline Paget (1913–76), daughter of sixth Marquess of Anglesey. Married Michael Duff in 1949. The adopted son, Charles, was born the same year.

"But I don't mean furniture. He's got enough for the Gothic Box, but something that will bring him in cash."

Caroline interspersed, "From what I hear, Michael gets the downstairs furniture and Veronica [the sister][1] the upstairs, and there's going to be a lot of *va et vient* up and down those stairs when Juliet dies."

"And does Simon, after all these years, get nothing?"

"What about the linen?" asks the adopted son.

Michael, very cross, says, "That of course comes to Vaynol."

Then, doggedly, I continue, "But you mean Simon after all these years will get nothing?"

"Oh, of course I'll give him something," says Michael, who is just as vague and as intentionally mean as his mother. Meanwhile Juliet, to save Andrews trouble, asks Simon to put logs on the fire, give the guests the minimum of drinks, turn off the radio and drive her to have her hair done in London.

I have told Simon that I will not continue to labour the subject, that it's now up to him to help himself, but nothing will come of it. It is sad to see that these selfish people get away without ever rewarding the devotion of the few who have made their life so much less difficult, and it will do Simon no good that after the event I vent my spleen on Juliet as I now do on Helena Rubinstein.

GARDEN REPORT, REDDISH

JULY 1965

This summer can be written off as far as the garden is concerned. Never have we had less days of sun. After a false optimistic alarm when for four days in early spring we sweated and ate lunch out of doors, there has been nothing to encourage growth in the plots. Moreover, when anything was brave enough to blossom, either rain dashed the petals or wind broke the stalks and after spending so much money in high spirits on the candidiums the lily disease took hold so fast that not only the stalks but the buds were blighted. This depressing for me and for Smallpeice who toils non-stop.

[1] Veronica Duff (1904–67), married Group Captain John Tennant. He was killed in action 1941.

Cecil and his gardener, Jack Smallpeice, in the garden at Reddish House, Broadchalke, 1965

In every free moment Cecil continued to paint.

The discoveries in painting continue through the long hours. Apart from the technical problems of keeping a consistency of paint or brush strokes, of doing only what the medium can tolerate, other ineffable problems arise as to where emphasis should be, what colours do to one another, how to achieve calm or brilliance etc. But at the moment my greatest problem, and one that I have really only solved in the [John] Russell picture, is how to simplify right down to essentials.

This cannot be done by eradicating with paint, wash or rag, but has to be conceived first in the mind as the only length to which it is possible to take the picture. I don't know how to arrive at this, but maybe with time I will be firmer in my determination to discard the un-essentials. At the moment I am trying hard to learn that the less one puts into the canvas the more successful the result is likely to be, and yet this does not always work.

The summer passed by and it was time for the holidays. It was also time for the long-dreaded departure of Kin.

Always a sadness at leaving England for the summer holidays. It means that when one returns the summer in the country will be over. I was less sad to leave this year as it has been such a beastly climate showing no signs of recovery and it would have been awful to remain moping at the departure of Kin.

As it was, he and I both left early on the same morning. His early call and exit down the stairs was as if to the execution. I watched him go from the front door, I in my pyjamas. He had two heavy bags to carry. He gripped his lips very tight and looked very serious. It was as bad a moment, I like to think, for him, as it was for me. The taxi turned into the crescent. His outstretched hand was stiff and taut. I went back to bed, for an hour, not to sleep, but to moan at my loss, and to feel desperately sad.

The long journey to Athens was something to keep my mind occupied with new impressions.

Cecil had been invited on board Baroness Cécile de Rothschild's[1] *yacht,* Siëta, *for a cruise around the Greek islands with a boat party that included his old friend Greta Garbo, with whom he had enjoyed a rather tortured love affair in 1947–8, which had limped on and off for some years. Also on board were Count Friedrich von Ledebur,*[2] *an enormously tall Austrian, whose diverse career had included working in Hollywood and being married to the poet Iris Tree, and Princesse Jeanne-Marie de Broglie,*[3] *later Christie's representative in France.*

I arrived at Vougliameni, the appointed bay where the yachts were harboured. Greta was the first I saw, sitting with her back to the quay, she had tied her hair back into a small pigtail with a rubber band. The effect was pleasing, neat and Chinese but the hair has become grey. The surprised profile turned to reveal a big smile. It was almost the same, and yet no, the two intervening years since

[1] Cécile de Rothschild (1913–95), unmarried daughter of Baron Robert de Rothschild, sister of Diane, Alain, Elie and Edmond.

[2] Count Friedrich von Ledebur (1900–86), Austrian aristocrat and film actor.

[3] Jeanne-Marie de Maillé de La Tour Landry, divorced wife of Prince Guy de Broglie. She had a son and a daughter.

we've last met have created havoc. I was appalled how destroyed her skin has become, covered with wrinkles, double chin, but worse the upper lip has jagged lower and the skin has perished into little lines, and there is a furriness that is disastrous. But no sign of defeat on Greta's part. She was up to her old tricks. "My, my, my! Why can it be Beattie? My Beat!"

Under the influence of Kin I took the opportunity to talk to her and told her of Kin's exit this morning after one year and how much I would miss him. "One whole year! My, my!" And this was the only talk we had during the entire trip. There could have been so much to discuss. Perhaps it was only natural that she didn't want to talk of Schlee's death,[1] but there are so many things that we could have shared. At first I was riled and irritated by the "Is," "that sos," and "never minds," "don't ask questions," "not going to tell yous" etc. I couldn't imagine that there was not to be one moment of truth, but no. She was behaving like a mad child most of the time and that is all she wanted. So I soon learnt to talk gibberish like a monkey and she seemed perfectly content.

Cécile was serious, heavily Rothschildean and slightly preoccupied lest her guests, Frederick Ledebur and Princesse de Broglie, would not turn up. But they did and soon were settling down to our shipboard life. At first I was so knocked out by the air and the sun that I slept most of the day as well as the night. Soon one day passed into another without any apparent differentiation. All effort poured away from me. I realised how incredibly I had wasted all summer idling and how depleted a condition I was in. As a result I could not summon up any energy to write consecutive diary, but made the following notes:

Cécile is very happy to have Greta on board for she is besotted. She snickers at everything Greta does, even if it is a slap directed against herself. She says, "It's G's childish side that should be encouraged. People have always tried to take from her, not give to her." But Cécile has now become Mercedes de Acosta[2] and she gets exactly the same treatment. Cécile makes just the same

[1] Georges Schlee (1896–1964), Russian émigré, who married Valentina Sanina (1894–1989), in her day a wonderful dress designer. Schlee had eventually more or less dropped his wife in favour of Garbo but continued to live in the same building with Valentina on the 14th floor, and Garbo on the 9th. He travelled everywhere with Garbo and was described by Kenneth Tynan as "a sort of Kafkaesque guard, employed to escort her to her next inscrutable rendezvous."

[2] Mercedes de Acosta (1896–1968), poet, playwright and author, but remembered as one of the most dramatic and celebrated lesbians of her generation. She made the proven claim "I can get any woman from any man," and was known to have had affairs with Garbo, Marlene Dietrich, Eva Le Gallienne, Ona Munson and many other ladies.

Greta Garbo, temperamental boat guest

mistakes. She has not learnt not to ask questions or to avoid discussing anything of Greta's past. Of course, it is difficult not to want her to talk of her art, but it has to be stage-managed so carefully.

Cécile and Greta have recently been for two weeks in Sardinia where Greta slept well and behaved beautifully, even socialising with a great group of strangers, but the *Siëta* being a small boat, echoes all the sounds of the night and Greta was unable to sleep in her cabin. Moreover, she had a stomach upset and my Enteroviaform came to her rescue only just in time, for if Greta had not recovered there was talk of Cécile having to take her home. Greta was terribly unkind to Cécile—I was shocked—and Greta at night came to her cabin door and said, "I've got a temperature, isn't that frightening! You see I should never travel!"

Cécile's devotion continued unabated in spite of Greta's complaints: "Why don't we have salad all dumped together with the other dishes?" "It's too much food." "Why can't we have dark bread?" Cécile enquires after Greta's health.

"Don't ask no questions" is the reply. Cécile, stricken, was worried enough after the temperature scene to ask next morning, "How do you feel?"

"Won't tell you."

"Then I'm glad you're better."

"How'd you know I'm better?"

"I'm jumping to conclusions."

"Don't jump." Greta has the last word.

Cécile brings the top of a garment to Greta's cabin. Here is the top of your bathing suit. "I know it is, but how do I know now where I'll find the other part?"

"My shoes, they-re *feelthy.* I wash 'em."

"Why not put them in fresh water?"

"No. First in the *veem,* then in my cabina."

"But let me wash them. It amuses me to do it, but after lunch, because lunch is ready."

"*Naaow.*"

"Lunch is ready."

"What, you mean lunch is ready now?"

"Well, we said we'd have lunch at 1 or 1:15."

"Why don't you give me a straight answer? What is the time now?"

"One o'clock."

"Then I wash them now straight away."

G. has incredible unswerving strength of character, never is swayed, never explains, never hates, but dislikes. Ruthlessly cuts out rather than compromising (re Mercedes).

In Skopelos an unshaven old native came up to know if he could help us. He could speak no known-to-us language but we understood him to ask our nationality. I said "Here we have *Suedoise.*" G., furious, said, "Now you cut that out."

I then went on to introduce in pantomime the Austrian, French, English. After thirty years she is still wary of the public pursuing her. She talks nonsense to me, passing a café, gesturing and turning her head. "What are you saying?" I ask.

"Just up to my old tricks."

Later she criticised me for drawing attention by making Frederick pose. I was angry and said I didn't mind drawing attention to myself. Her sense of humour is very alive. She remembers things that have amused her years before, my asking the Queen Mother to fold her hands on her lap and being too fat to do so, and the Queen of Persia[1] asking "Will it be in colour?" "No." Also remembers silly stories, bald man going into drug store, "Are you sure this hair restorer will succeed?" "Yes." "Then give me two bottles and a comb and brush." The pansy who was told by the director to walk down the stairs in a more manly fashion. "You don't expect me to play a character part for $7 a day?"

Some of the stories she told on this trip are those that I have quoted her as telling me twenty years ago, e.g. Chaplin[2] and the paralytic.

But this is all very childish and she has not developed in the last twenty years. She has no interest in topics to do with either of the last world wars or films, plays, books. She talks in snippets about food, but interrupts others' talk and the flow of conversation. She refused to talk about her family, friends or career.

She has a slight flair for modern painting (likes Jawlensky[3]) but never remembers names and is full of regrets. "Oh, if only I knew how he made that chocolate soufflé." (She couldn't make it!) "Why can't I? If only I wasn't such a different human being." "I started to read it (lobster), but shucks! I gave it up. I suppose I'll have to try and dig it up somewhere."

By being so solitary all these years she has never learnt to speak grammatical English. The result is that in her beautiful, touching voice she used the idioms of the Hollywood electricians. Sometimes it is almost impossible to understand her, and since I am the only one on board to "kid" her at all have asked, "Would you please translate that last sentence into Swedish."

Cécile, while we were anchoring in a marvellous green bay surrounded by forested hills, remarked how wonderful it was to be woken by the

[1] Princess Fawziah of Egypt (b. 1921), sister of King Farouk. She married (1939) Muhammad Reza Pahlevi, Shah of Persia (1919–80), divorced 1947. Cecil photographed them in Tehran in June 1942.

[2] Charles Chaplin (1899–1977), film actor and director. Knighted 1975.

[3] Alexei von Jawlensky (1864–1941), Russian-German Expressionist painter. Garbo owned several of his works and these were sold at the Sotheby's sale in New York following her death.

tinkle of sheep bells and the calls of the shepherd. Greta appeared. "I couldn't sleep. Did you hear that bloody shepherd? Fancy being woken by a shepherd!"

In this cruel harsh sunlight on board one sees every crinkle and crevice in the most cruel way. I have, hawklike, watched her in all lights, without mascara even. This is a severe test and she does not like to be seen without this armour and only ever appears this natural if she is sunning early before the rest of us, or if she has gone to bed and returns to complain about the noise.

She is fully conscious of her lost beauty and, while oiling her wizened arm, says, "I once saw an old man . . . oh, it's disgusting." But here I go again, criticising nature. Yet at other times, and under stark conditions, she can still be extraordinarily beautiful. The angle of nose jutting unhesitatingly from the profile is unaltered. The nose is cut with a high deep bridge and the eyes are deeply set, so that there is always a cavernous shadow above the lid. With age the cheekbones have become more modulated and firm, and the teeth though they have lost their dazzling whiteness (no doubt partly due to the non-stop smoking) are still in being and bold, and by slanting inwards complement the perkiness of the nose (incidentally used to catch in a wonderful way the reflection of the studio lights).

In the apricot-coloured light of evening she still looks absolutely marvellous and she could be cleverly photographed to appear as beautiful as ever in films. But it is not just her beauty that is dazzling, it is the air of mysteriousness and other intangible qualities that make her so appealing, particularly when talking with sympathy and wonder to children or reacting herself to some situation with all the wonder and surprise of childhood itself.

DATELESS IN SCIATHOS

AUGUST 1965

It is 8 in the morning. The others have gone on shore to buy honey cakes while the ship is refuelled. Greta put her head out of the cabin and said, "Wait for me," so I suppose the others waited, for Cécile would never go without Greta. Stubbornly I have stayed put in my cabin to finish my volume of Proust and now I have left the yellowing trees in the avenue des Acacias and taken up my pen to try to capture the atmosphere.

On the surface and because we all are civilised human beings the atmosphere is light and "sportif," emotions under control, but I find that I am not the only one to sense the vibrations of rancour, jealousy and criticism that exist beneath the surface. Last night after our dinner in the *quai* when the others had left our disappointing taverna for coffee in a café, Jeanne-Marie de Broglie and myself sat eating baklava at a cake shop and we for the first time discussed our fellow travellers.

No more unselfish, sweet-tempered person exists than Jeanne-Marie. Looking like an Ingres model of 18, it is incredible to think that she is a mother of grown children with quite a career as an art dealer; so sweet and open is she, that it is surprising to find that she does form her impressions, not always favourable, of those she loves; less in a spirit of complaint than of analysis she discussed our hostess, with whom she shares a cabin. Therefore there is no question of ever reading more than a page of a book without being interrupted, for Cécile's restlessness has become so neurasthenic that she cannot be alone, for one moment, nor can she stick to any subject for long, except on the subject of Greta, by whom she is obsessed. With Greta she is a kid hypnotised by a situation. She is willing to become Greta's slave, she only wishes to be badly treated by Greta, and she will snigger with glee. But it is not a good way for her to spend these years, now that she is feeling more than ever the lack of a man in her life.

Today she told me of how fate had ordained that she should come to Paris on a certain day earlier than she intended, to find Greta and Schlee at the Crillon before leaving the next day for New York. They dined together. Greta left with her companion at 11:30, she to walk a little, whereupon he had a heart attack, went to a bistro, asked the proprietor to telephone Greta, became worse and on the way to the hospital died. Greta meanwhile receives a call from an unknown man whom she cannot understand because he speaks French. She tells him to call Cécile, who is given the news, and from now on Cécile fills the role of Schlee in Greta's life, Schlee and Mercedes combined, for I cannot think that Greta treated Schlee as badly as she does Cécile.

Cécile brings to Greta's cabin the top of her bathing dress: "I found this for you. It is the top of your bathing dress."

"I know it is but now where shall I find the other part?"

Greta walks along the shore in a petulant mood. Cécile follows ten yards after her. Only when a pile of rocks brings her progress to a halt does Greta turn to welcome Cécile.

Jeanne-Marie remarked that she had been fascinated to watch "the Queen," that in a bathing cap she still looked beautiful with the well-known line of her forehead and neck, that she could be continuously funny and her clowning was wonderful. But she is always so critical. "Did you notice when Cécile asked if she wanted eggs and bacon she said, 'You're not to order them or they'll get cold or I'll have to come when I'm not ready. I'll come when I'm ready and order them then and then they'll be hot'?" At dinner she remarks, "How beautiful this fruit looks, but it's all rotten, not ripe, hard, uneatable."

Even Frederick Ledebur, great gentleman that he is, so wise and understanding and forgiving, has remarked when Greta's being so critical of everything. But no one is as critical as I am. Not because I have any resentment or prejudice, but just because having loved her so much it is a nightmare for me to see to what inevitable paths her negativeness and selfishness have brought her.

Yesterday was not Greta's worst day, she felt quite well, but it was a pique day. While I wrote diary next to her on deck she was restless and bored. When we bathed she rested on shore, when we were about to leave she bathed. At lunch she moved plates, fumbled with cigarette apparati, always needing something, and remarked in childish or critical terms on the food, "Could I have a half-lemon? I can't get anything from these slices. This is goodie. Shall I try some coffee?"

Otherwise she was out of the conversation and I was determined that the meal should not go by without any topics to be discussed and so worked hard in spite of interruptions from both Cécile and Greta. We talked of movies, of today—Greta silent. She did not even know that Jeanne Moreau had made a film of *Mata Hari.*[1] She had never heard of Antonioni, Fellini, Richardson[2] or the like.

She remained stubbornly silent while the pros and cons of Dietrich were discussed. She took no part in an explanation of Expressionist painting.

[1] *Mata Hari* (1965) with Jeanne Moreau (b. 1928), French actress of stage and screen, best known at this stage in her career for *Jules et Jim.*

[2] Michelangelo Antonioni (b. 1912), Federico Fellini (b. 1920) and Tony Richardson (1928–91), influential directors.

When Jeanne-Marie asked the date of Augustus, Greta said, "I know nuttin'." One sees that those endless days and evenings doing nothing have resulted in negation. She has never let any new impression or influence come into her head for more than a moment in the last twenty years. The funny stories of Chaplin she tells me are those she told me when first I met her. She bothers not to learn the names of even the people she has perforce yet to see. I doubt very much if she has even learnt Jeanne-Marie's name and refers to her as "this lady."

In the morning on arrival at Sciathos Cécile suggested taking a picture of Greta and me. "No, I don't want to be photographed." Greta seemed jealous of my friendship with Jeanne-Marie so I tried to be sweet and took her in front of the others to walk up the white street of this charming village. Conversation was sadly forced and not one bit interesting. Greta had spotted some American tourists who had spotted her and this was of more amusement to her than seeing a new place in a strange land.

The evening sunlight fading to make the colours hum more and more melodiously was a pleasure to us all. Greta did not seem to notice the magical effects, of which she in pink with pink and white striped trousers became a part and in this light she became as beautiful as her legend. But it is a legend that does no longer exist in reality. If she had been a real character she would have left the legend, developed a new life, new interests and knowledge. As it is, after thirty years she has not changed except outwardly, and even the manner and personality has dated.

Poor old Marlene Dietrich,[1] with her dye and facelift and new career as a singer, with all her nonsense, is a live and vital person, cooking for her grandchildren and being on the go. That is much preferable to this other non-giving, non-living phantom of the past.

From there the Siëta *sailed to the island of Trickeri, where the boat party enjoyed bathing.*

[1] Marlene Dietrich (1902–92), celebrated German film actress and diseuse, a deal more generous than Garbo, upon whom, to some extent, she modelled herself in her early career. She was still travelling the world with her repertory of songs, her tight tube evening dresses and capacious mink coat. She ended her life a genuine recluse in her apartment in Paris, unlike Garbo, who was known as "a recluse about town."

TRICKERI—ON THE MAINLAND

Yesterday was a halcyon day in all respects. We arrived at a small olive-planted island that appeared to be deserted, and bathed close to the shore in pellucid waters, for the captain warned us of the danger of sharks. It was difficult to imagine anything as violent as a shark in these calm waters but Frederick, having demonstrated at breakfast how to baffle a wasp (by twirling one's thumb in quick circles) then gave us the drill if one met a shark—splash the surface of the water with your flat hands and put your face beneath the water and make a loud noise causing bubbles to rise. If the shark is then not terrified, dive at it. In no event turn your back on it and swim away.

Greta, still somewhat piano and petulant, meanwhile had landed on the shore and while we bathed, went for a smart walk among the olive trees. Within a few minutes she was seen at a great distance keeping up a great speed in her tall straw hat, but having abandoned the top to her bathing suit. A while later she returned radiant, her eyes blazing, teeth shining in a great grin. "You have no idea how beautiful it is! It's holy!" She described the uninhabited island of rows of olive trees, stretching for ever to the horizon. For the rest of the day her mood was marvellous. She was reborn, she became radiant and her spirits soared. Indeed, the island proved to be a wonder. By walking over a steep precipice, leaving our grey-blue seas behind, we came to the grey-treed summit to find a brilliant blue ocean lying before us, and in every direction one looked, there was a new variety of beauty to beguile the eyes. We walked and swam and were happy, and by the time we returned to the big boat, it was for a 3:15 lunch of moussaka and other Greek or Turkish delights. The siesta was a long and calm one of satisfied sleep. Then our evening expedition.

This augured well from the start when an old Greek woman welcomed us ashore wearing marvellously disintegrated clothes, green and yellow head shawl, burgundy and grey pleated skirts and aprons. She held a twig of olives and posed like Dorelia John.[1]

We walked through the groves to come upon a small harbour and village of extreme charm, with whitewashed buildings, an eighteenth-century

[1] Dorelia McNeill (1881–1969), wife of the artist Augustus John.

church and two vast cypress trees, old women like statues, mules, a goose, a pale rose tree, and everywhere the marvellous opalescent light of sundown. Thence to the top of a hill, and to a large cloistered building and church. It appears there was never a monastery here, that it was built as a keep against invaders, but the whole complex of buildings had infinite charm and, at this hour particularly, a serenity that struck us like a spell.

The exterior of the church possessed a cycladic head and eighteenth-century carvings of animals, and its interior a beautiful sweep of balustrades following stairs and balconies that swept along the tall domed ceilings, icons, dying roses tucked into the Madonna's silver collar.

By degrees we made friends with villagers and old women bowed from their cloistered arches with the dignity of Proust duchesses. Then we discovered that part of the cloisters were now transformed by a German into a pension. We saw, with delight, the bedrooms, so simple yet all that the soul requires, and the dining room, in peasant style, appeared so appetising. The light became even more beautiful, our mood more halcyon and, fond of everyone, we lingered before walking home through the olives, determined to come back to this place with a loved one, or with a load of work. A village girl came up to know if Greta was who she was. No one offered the information, G. hiding her "smiling" face. Then, as we retreated into the darkness she went back and told the girl that she indeed was who she was. The girl was delighted. Greta showed in many ways that she can be kind and good and adorable. At dinner she was in the highest spirits and told funny stories and said that if she were ruling the world, she would outlaw all violence (including boxing).

She talked with enthusiasm and experience about where you can get good cooking. Food is one of her only subjects, but she was best of all as an imitator, a clown. There is a Greek sailor on board who has the most extraordinary hollow voice. She has this perfected. She talked about the Kabuki actors and said that although at first she found the noises they made an offence to the human race, on a second visit she was fascinated. And she was able to reproduce exactly these noises. She described a female impersonator in the troupe who she said had the most "sexy" look of any woman she had ever seen. Regarding someone with slowly lowering eyelids, a shock was sent down your spine.

I was happy to have this different impression of her, and to discover that she can look, in certain moods and in evening light, just as delightful as ever one could imagine her to be.

Next day, after a bathe, we left this ravishing island, waving as the sails flapped in the wind to the little posse of people waving back to us from the monastery garden, all longing to return to this fabulous place in the spring when the whole island is carpeted with flowers.

The rest of the day given over to rough seas. We arrived at a bay on the mainland quite ruined by man. It was a shock to return to the ugliness of bourgeois taste. The others went ashore to buy chickens from three hags at a farm while I drew Jeanne-Marie badly. We discussed later, when the others went to bed, our hostess, how she never listens, is so brusque with Frederick, how she cannot remain still for a moment and from the moment of waking smokes cigarettes non-stop. Jeanne-Marie asked why Greta had wept at dinner. Was it because she had interrupted Greta's complaints that there was no chicken leg in the dish, by saying that they never served chicken legs on this boat? No, I think Greta was out of the French conversation. The second whisky had gone to her head, and maybe she thought a little of Georges Schlee. Anyhow, she is apt to cry on occasion. I remember motoring with her to Reddish when suddenly she wept and I was so upset. She said it was nothing, that sometimes the mood overtook her.

Jeanne-Marie asked if Greta was ever interested in my work—never asks any questions, never looks at it, shows no interest in what I am doing.

This is what happened at breakfast on deck this morning. Greta arrived last, looking rather raddled as if she had had a sleepless night (but we know better than to ask how she slept). After a little child's play she asked if the coffee was strong and hot. (Yesterday there had been a commotion when she said, "I can't be *that* wrong. It must be Instant Coffee!" "No, it's Maxwell House." "It can't be. Like the people of Missouri I want to see. Show me the tin." An enormous new tin of Maxwell coffee was brought. No apology, just, "Well, it must be rather stale and has lost its strength.")

Cécile, in-taking cigarettes, then asked me if I had designed *Dame aux Camélias* with Nureyev.[1] "Yes." "It was beautiful, so good that I wrote you,

[1] Cecil designed *Marguerite and Armand* in 1963.

Greta, to go and see it." Greta nodded. "Did you go?" Greta nodded. "Did you like it?" Greta nodded. After a moment I began to get irritated, closed like a clam and soon left the breakfast table. But I'm sure Greta hadn't, as the expression she uses has it, "the foggiest idea" why I was in any way put out. It is, of course, stupid to expect her to make any comment on one's work, but it shows an incredible lack of imagination not to realise that people *do* like to have the results of their efforts noticed, but not one word even, though I know she has seen it, of *My Fair Lady.*

Later I realised this reticence was caused more by Cécile's inquisitiveness than lack of generosity towards me. Luckily my mood soon changed and the day was agreeable.

Perhaps it is about time that the cruise should come to an end.

ADDRESS UNKNOWN TO ME

Arrival before lunch at another almost unpopulated island, free from the winds that have been so violent recently that ships have been wrecked and lives lost in the Cyclades. Lucky to have taken this northern course and avoided (with only one exception) the tempestuous seas.

Today's island was grandiose in outline and scale, dotted with olives and partitioned with stones; the landscape itself made a tremendous impression on the others, but only later when we inspected it on foot was I so impressed by the Braque-like colours of acorn-coloured earth, yellow-dried thistle, ever-changing olives and silver slabs of rock mottled with white and black markings. The going was very difficult. In fact, we had recourse to a native Greek who had lived in Australia and who could speak English, to save us from climbing over this appalling stone desert. This man tending his sheep and goats (there are natural salt wells) on mules that with delicate hoofs spring from rock to rock. Even the Greek admitted there were too many stones and the island was too dry, but it was his home and what else can you do?

Greta today in good spirits, obviously feeling well. We do not ask her how she has slept but we talk in whispers the moment she retires to her cabin, the crew are told to stop their cacophonies, the visits to the loo at night are as

Cécile de Rothschild and Garbo

perilous as if one were a cat burglar going for a safe. We have developed the shipboard rhythm so that now one has no idea of what time of the day it is, let alone what day of the week.

I still sleep ten hours a night and an hour in the afternoon. I am beginning to lose flesh round the centre and under the chin, although I enjoy an eggs and bacon breakfast and two plate-covered meals. Reading a bit, drawing Jeanne-Marie and trying to photograph Greta, who today did a brilliant take-off of a Comédie Française love drama with Jeanne-Marie. Her words of French are used to miraculous effect and she was inspired, a brilliant glowing performance that made one regret more than ever that G. has given up for nothing else her fruitful career. Certain French phrases or words—*coffre-fort, épatant* are favourites—strike her ear and she uses them to alarming effect, and she made us roar with laughter as she leant forward to plump, honest and true little Jeanne-Marie saying *"ma souffrance me mange."* The crew, too, are fascinated by her clowning and the captain goes off into paroxysms of mirth at her imitations of his radio talks to Athens: "Sexy Sieta, Saita, Santa, Sexy Sànta." She is the star with star quality wherever we go, and it is remarkable that at 60 she still combines the qualities of beauty and clowning and naturalness to such a degree. It makes one realise that all these last 20 years she could have been used to such effect, thereby justifying her existence.

FOLLOWING DAY—STOPPING AT ANOTHER BAY ON THE MAINLAND NEAR PETALÍ

Again G. was in fine fervour, laughing and clowning and being very attractive in her childishness. I have long given up any idea of having any conversation with her. Nothing important in her life or mine to be discussed. Childlike and often delightful badinage is all that one will get and, given this supposition, it is good light entertainment. Perhaps because, as a result of the last ten days, I now find it impossible to use my brain (except to listen to Frederick or to converse with Jeanne-Marie). At breakfast today these two were involved in a yelling match, F. furious with J.-M. for reducing the landscape to Cézanne level. "Why can't you enjoy life? The reality instead of bringing it to the level of a bloody picture!" "I'm not, merely using terms of reference. The architecture of these hills and olive groves is as delineated as in a Cézanne."

To Cécile the landscape was redolent of mythology. To me this is not the case although, if ever, it should be now for I am reading the *Odyssey*, though in an appalling translation. For myself I find I must often concentrate hard, fix my eyes on the scene before me, consciously to enjoy it. Natural landscape is not one of the things that gives me most pleasure, except on occasions, and these are mostly at my favourite hour of dusk.

Today G. and I walked along the white sands, past a pitiful little camp of four lesbians and the local shack restaurant to the heights of a cypress-clad buff-coloured mountain, looking over two ultramarine bays, then returned to lie on hot rocks in the sun. A bathe in fresh cool water and lunch took us to

4 o'clock. By the time the siesta was over, we had arrived at civilisation in the form of a white bourgeois 1900 house with turquoise shutters, a municipal pier–like entrance and gardens. We had arrived at Petalí. Suddenly we realised how much we would now miss, how strange and remote and far from civilisation the days at Trickeri had been.

Suddenly we were back in a world of drinks and gossip and banalities. The Embiricos[1] are kind and have welcomed us warmly. We enjoyed their civilised paths to the sea for a sweet pea sunset bathe; Greta, like a native woman carrying a bundle of clothes on her head, was a funny and beautiful sight. Then back to café society, with new people to learn, including the pretty daughter of the house and her cinema director fiancé, and Brigitte Bardot's sister,[2] a sad phenomenon, like the star but lacking everything. Greta, eyes to heaven with boredom and regret, and the clock ticked on so that we all went to bed later than we have since we embarked.

PETALÍ

The bells of sheep coming down from the mountains to drink. The creaking in the corridor of someone going to the loo. The clink of the latch in the pumping of the water, a member of the crew coughing, water lapping against the side of the ship, a distant whir of a motor boat, deckhands treading heavily above. A door slams, a dynamo starts to make electricity with a great whirring. The captain goes off to fish with a great rumble of spluttering engines, more coughing from the crew, and much conversation, more pumping of loos, then with a mighty roar the engines of the boat are put in motion, every rhythm is taken up in turn. At first the sounds are of the tapping of a hundred frenzied typists, then later the rhythms change to a shuttle service of wooden pens

[1] André Embiricos (1895–?), Greek shipping magnate and one-time beau of Mona Bismarck, and his American wife, Beatrice. His daughter, Cornelia, about to marry a Schroeder, is now deceased.

[2] Marie-Jeanne Bardot (b. 1938), known as "Mijanou," married (1962) Patrick Bauchau, a Belgian film director and actor. She hated being known as "Bardot's sister," was lured to Hollywood with promises of contracts, but dressed as Bardot. She returned to Paris and ran a soft-furnishing business.

clanking each other with hollow sounds, steam rollers arrive in their dozens. Then abruptly the noise stops for a great mechanical wheeze as the medieval clanking of the anchor being raised makes the boat shudder anew. With a terrible grinding the anchor falls again, the motors are turned off, ropes are being strained and whine like tortured dogs. There is no chance of sleep now for two mates are busy scraping the sides of the ship with emery paper.

As it was late before we returned to the ship last night Greta is giving gyp to Cécile who apologises abjectly. (She is the best-humoured person, never says a swear word and, upset to find a hole burnt into her shirt, said calmly, "That's a pity.") Greta, with crustacean contorted face, is ruining the effect by continuing the ticking off too long. "It's cruel. It's cruel to human beings." It was not a good day for anyone. Even Jeanne-Marie was showing signs of the undercurrents. She wished to escape with Reynold's book on Cézanne, but she was not left in peace. Only Frederick managed to shut himself away from the bad vibrations and, determined to evade the Embiricos clan, he accompanied Greta and myself on a long trek through the island.

The heat of the sun made it a strenuous expedition through the scrub and stone, and the pace at which he forages is quite astonishing, and no doubt if we had not been following his velocity would have been doubled. As it was, we walked to a secret bay where we bathed in the nude. By now Greta's good spirits had returned, for she is a "Virgo," the child of nature, and becomes positively happy in the sun, sea and loneliness of the landscape. She lay in the sun for a long while, hating to have to return to the others.

Lunch took us back to the hideous bourgeois Embiricos house where talk was of mundanities (how Queen Frederica[1] would not be prised out of this house after she had taken possession, and behaving with typical Prussian lack of sensitivity), but the presence of the young leavened the whole atmosphere.

Eventually back for a siesta but alas not as long as that enjoyed by the Embiricos family (the beautiful little bride-to-be being woken at 7:30 p.m.). We made an expedition to another island and walked high among the olive orchards, and visited a toothless semi-blind crone who, it appears, is the bastard of the first King George of Greece.[2] Her stone house struck Jeanne-Marie

[1] HM Queen Frederica of Greece (1917–81), wife of King Paul, KG (1901–64).
[2] HM King George I of Greece, KG (1845–1913). He was born Prince Wilhelm of Denmark.

and myself as being utterly ravishing, and gave us feelings of longing to own it. Frederick's godlike strides took us too far. I rebelled. Exhausted, we bathed in a cove with stinking grass. F., furious, said, "Nobody ever listens to me. We should have gone elsewhere. Never bathe where fresh water cannot get to you."

The first of the packing. Tomorrow we spend the night in the Embiricos boat while the *Siëta* returns to Athens. Then the evening spent with the Embiricos crowd, where the young people danced in an astonishing way (I thought the Bardot sister quite mad), but Cornelia enchanting even when un-bridal-like she joined the conversation about what to do to ensure marital bliss, what perversions to avoid. The younger generation are certainly not *pudique* and husband-to-be said he had been very amused by a book on onanism.

The bride showed us her wedding dress in its white box and tissue paper, a work of art in muslin from Castillo. Greta had given her all at lunchtime when she kept the room in gales of laughter with a description of how her breasts had sagged, yet how she could never strap on one of those awful binding contraptions, and tonight was tired. Yet tired and aged as she was, particularly in contrast to the 20-year-olds, she has still enormous beauty and spirit, and her attitude to the young is not self-conscious and envious but one of natural curiosity and admiration.

Back to our boat for the last night's sleep.

Greta, Frederick and I, intent on our goat climb of the mountains, were seduced into going to a cove where we thought the great crowd would not intrude. No sooner had we arrived, stripped naked and stepped into the sea, than a distant boat roared towards us. It was a funny scene, Greta trying to get to shore in time on her behind. I, bare-arsed, walked out. Frederick was marooned with his white patch of skin and huge, hanging balls, an embarrassment to him and all who would study the unusual sight.

Our last lunch on board was not as agreeable as it would have been if Greta had suited her mood to the occasion. She continued to criticise, to give the hostess hell, and the hostess sniggers with happiness, thrilled to be saving the lost soul, but merely being used as a convenience by Greta.

Cécile was now preoccupied with the complications of paying for the trip, the food, the oil, tipping the captain £40, and sending telegrams for her chauffeur and maid to meet Greta and her in Lausanne. It takes a lot of organisation to do a cruise like this and an appalling amount of money.

The wealth of Cécile is fabulous, but like all rich people she wants to be loved as if she were poor. She is terribly selfish, and her money has ruined her. Nonetheless she is one of the nicest rich women that I have come across.

Another visit to the old crone on the island, to see inside her house. The old woman wept, was inconsolable, showed us her room with pictures and mirrors all covered, and strips of black on the bed, on the tables and chairs. Beatrice Embiricos, married for 20 years to a Greek and spending at least two to three months a year here, has not learnt to speak one word of the language and was therefore incapable of saying one word of consolation to the widow, who needed help, who was in such a stab of grief that the sight upset Greta so much that she herself wept.

Followed a photograph sitting of the young bride in her exquisite costume standing before the village church in which she will be married. The evening sun did its best and the girl looked like a Byzantine figure while the "group" watched and helped and made suggestions.

An evening of gaiety, somewhat desperate. I was physically worn out, and although I had loved the trip and it was just what was needed, yet I felt that enough time had been spent on it. Greta's lack of conversation and her wilfulness could be a bore, and I felt that to delay would be to see the film run a second time. But up till the last, Greta had given one moments of such unexpected beauty that one realised without a doubt why she was so much more remarkable and beautiful than anyone else who had been in films. Her gestures are sometimes unbelievably moving, as when going late into the sea one night the water was cold as she walked from the shore, and she clasped her hands as if in prayer. This evening she appeared at the window of her cabin, her hair hanging and her bath towel hanging to show part of her breasts, and the eyes were quite fantastically deep-set and tragic. This appearance, in fact, was to declaim on the unfairness of her siesta being ruined by flies, but she was like a great beauty of tragedy. Whatever she does is touched with a sort of genius, a "star" quality that gives indications of immortality. She is on the highest plane, never vulgar, always incredibly sensitive and subtle, and with a hint of sadness and spirituality that is always with her, on any occasion, however banal, so that when meeting a crowd of strangers, just by remarking on the food of the day or the child, she can beguile them with her mysteriousness.

Only once on this whole trip did I notice one moment when this magic escaped her (sometimes she looks terrible, haggard, ghastly, but still it is the wreck of the great figure of mythology). Once, however, this magic left her for a moment. We were swimming and as I came towards her I did something that surprised her and made her laugh, that made her into an ordinary, well-preserved ex-beauty. I looked at the teeth, long and slightly discoloured, and realised what she would have been like if she had been an ordinary woman and not, in spite of all her faults, a phenomenon of the utmost rarity.

At sundown we were all brought from our faithful friends on the *Siëta* to the Embiricos boat [*El Petal*]. Cries of joy at the sight of so many large cabins, so many bathrooms, so many loos, even a bidet. We were perhaps not as tactful as we should have been in keeping our praises toned down in front of Cécile. Suddenly the *Siëta* seemed very sporting, but small and squalid. I had two hot baths. Dinner at Embiricos' (after a cocktail visit to see Perry's hideous house) where gaiety was perhaps forced at first but the young people's happiness was infectious and eventually we were all doing the Shake or at any rate attempting the most difficult and unseemly motions. Greta now full of regrets that we were leaving, and the Embiricos begged us to remain on the boat, Cécile even willing to cancel all her plans. But I could not listen to the too well-known nonsense of "Oh, how I wish we hadn't done this, but could do that." I left Greta's regrets to sleep.

Early departure of Frederick. I saw through my porthole while peeing, his kind good eyes full of gratitude and friendship as he waved. Breakfast on deck, Greta disliking the biscotte instead of bread, looked her worst. Should she bathe with the others? If she did, then they'd take her coffee away. When in the sea she noticed Cécile using the towel Greta had brought from her cabin. "That's my towel and you're making it all wet!" This from the person who has been living off Cécile, who is her last desperate port in a storm. When I asked Greta to take off her spectacles for a snapshot, she refused. Her mouth turned down at the corners. I wished I hadn't taken the picture. It is everything I dislike about her.

The waving goodbye was not very happy either. She looked drab, and I was sad for her, sad for myself, yet grateful that I had not got myself straddled by such an impossibly difficult human being. Cécile, reading her mail, looked like an old businessman. I felt sad for her going off with Greta on a tour of punishment. Jeanne-Marie and I got into a boat with our luggage and thence in a waiting car for a dangerous drive towards Athens, that most hideous of modern cities.

Cecil left the claustrophobic atmosphere of Cécile de Rothschild's yacht, with the petulant Garbo making demands on hostess and guests alike, and set off to stay with Count and Countess Brandolini at their palazzo in Venice. This visit brought a number of old ghosts back to life to haunt him, and a number of new society dramas to amuse him. Brando Brandolini, his host, was married to Christiana Agnelli, who was the granddaughter of Princess Jane di San Faustino, who held sway over Venetian society at the time of Cecil's first visit in 1926 and was invariably clad in white nun's robes.

VENICE AUGUST 1965

When I arrived in Venice surprisingly early to be greeted with such a heart-warming welcome by all at the Palazzo Brandolini, I realised that every effort to get here had been worthwhile. The smiling, amused faces, the atmosphere of comfort and luxury and friendliness was worth travelling many continents to discover. In the best possible spirits, and health, I settled down to enjoy the benefits of a hospitable household that with expertise has avoided all the more squalid forms of reality, while keeping *au courant* on all that makes life interesting and agreeable.

Before long a new world had opened. Brando[1] was a wonderful guide to Guardi. Without him I would never have discovered so vividly the difference between the best and the lesser. Without him to point out the felicitous I would never have noticed the understanding, the sense of scale, the measure, the minute knowledge of stress and emphasis that were given by the cunning placing of shadows, groups of people (all with such individuality, even those at the back of a crowd, all with their counterpoint of flow of movement, flowing cloaks to emphasise one sweep). The Watteau trains of the women to balance

[1] Count Brando Brandolini (b. 1918).

Count and Countess Brandolini in the Palazzo Brandolini in Venice, summer 1965

another trend, and the discipline and subtlety of his colours are masterly beyond belief. This was a revelation. This alone worth the journey from Milan by car, for without Brando to be guide on a wet Saturday morning I would never have had the tuition that was inspiring, that could only come from someone as developed in his sensibilities and as *rusé* in the art of living the aristocratic life as Brando.

The exhibition was a revelation. For the first time I realised the superiority of Guardi to Canaletto, Bellotto and that time, and to think that the poor man was never acknowledged in his lifetime and had to take his paintings into the piazza to hope for a sale.

It was interesting to see how acute this group of friends are in assessing the quality of people. By a remark or a smile, they know when someone shows themselves to be common, or coarse or pretentious. Their bright eyes never miss a point.

Philip Van Rensselaer[1] provided comic relief with his frankness about being a gigolo to Barbara Hutton,[2] how he became disgusted by his greed, and had to leave though he got large cheques from her of $40,000 worth of stocks. "But I couldn't go on. It was too tiring. I had to take sleeping pills, and have champagne and eggs, and I hated waking up at the end of the day, and others like"—mentioning other pretty boys and their boyfriends—"all made so much more than I did. Now I'm broke, or at any rate can't afford to live in New York or Paris, so I think I'll take a flat in Tangiers."

Philip, who has received terrible reviews for his new book,[3] tells us that he is going out to talk to Lina Rothschild[4] in order to put her in his new book. Anyone telling him anything goes into this *pot-pourri.* "May I go and see those two old ladies in black tomorrow? I'd like to hear what they say and put them in my book." Philip tells us Barbara Hutton hates being married, but adores honeymoons.

[1] Philip Van Rensselaer (b. 1928), self-confessed sybarite, who descended from the famous Governor Van Rensselaer, the Dutchman, who owned 700,000 acres along the Hudson River in New York. Though impecunious, he was good-looking and entertaining and had gone to Venice in July 1957 with a friend, Norma Clark, had been invited to a ball by the Brandolinis. There he had met Barbara Hutton, soon becoming her travelling companion. When she tired of him, he asked for compensation of $1 million. Meanwhile, he was taken up by the Brandolinis and stayed with them for several summers. Eventually, things went wrong and in his memoirs, *Rich Was Better* (1990), he tells the story of how, feeling slighted, he stole some precious objects from them. He also wrote a book about Barbara Hutton, entitled *Million Dollar Baby* (1979). He once declared, "I'm drawn to the squalid glitter and blackmailing creatures of the international set where everything goes and anything is possible."

[2] Barbara Hutton (1913–79), famous as a "poor little rich girl." She was a Woolworth's heiress and married many times, her husbands including Cary Grant, Kurt von Reventlow and Porfirio Rubirosa, the noted Dominican playboy.

[3] *The House with the Golden Door* (1965), a light novel based on Barbara Hutton and the rich who gathered in Venice each summer.

[4] Lina (Georgina) Blanc, who married (1958) Edmond de Rothschild (b. 1926), son of Maurice de Rothschild.

Brando, whose analyses of people are brought to the finest art, is delighted with the visit of Diana [Cooper]. She arrives for lunch on foot, early, having walked all over Venice and having found a typical hat for herself in the Merceria, a coarse straw with a shaving brush sticking out at the back. She has called at Harry's Bar en route and eaten some chicken rissoles. These have caused the old-fashionedly violent lipstick to run down at the corners of her mouth. This is rectified before the host arrives from the Lido. She moves in a gauche, gaunt way. Brando is delighted. "She still has the direct look of beauty and she's a real aristocrat, not a bit of refinement about her. She has the peasant quality of the real thing."

19 AUGUST 1965

It is good to have memories, but I do not feel very stimulated for the present if I compare it with the past. The early days here were my beginnings. My first visit, on borrowed money, was my first real glimpse of the "abroad" and of Italy. The impression made on me by St. Mark's, and its gold and its colonnade, was indelible, and little glimpses of the life led by the grand, elegant world will always remain with me.

There is a fat and horrid woman of journalistic brashness in America. Her name is Alice-Leone Moats,[1] but she will always remain for me the exquisite little cherry-faced girl with sleeked-back golden hair that I saw with an armful of tuberoses being driven past in a gondola. The cool completeness of this independent little creature was something that was to be coveted. Who could aspire to achieve this glorious picture of romantic privilege? The American girl had all the atmosphere of Henry James.

. . .

[1] Alice-Leone Moats (1911–89), intrepid traveller and journalist on the international scene, who visited Russia before World War Two. Author of a number of books, including *No Nice Girl Swears* (1930), *Lupescu* (1955), *The Million Dollar Studs* (1977) (in which, among others, she tells the story of the rigid stud Porfirio Rubirosa) and various autobiographical works. She was a columnist with *Collier's*. Her books were entertaining, and more frank than was usual in those days. In *The Million Dollar Studs*, she told the story of how Rubirosa was spotted in the men's room. "It looks like Yul Brynner in a black turtle-neck sweater," declared Jerome Zerbe, the witness (p. 203).

Venice. One arrives every time with surprise and delight. One seldom leaves with regret.

Cecil returned to England and settled at Reddish, where Eileen came to stay, and Alan Tagg joined them, in order to "buffer the loneliness caused by Kin's absence."

RETURN TO ENGLAND—REDDISH

The Indian summer, which one had relied upon to compensate somewhat for a totally grey and wet June and July, disappoints. In spite of cold winds and rain gusts, I continued to wear my tropical clothes and rope-soled shoes as I enjoy the late garden flowers, those that remind one of summer holidays, asters, stocks, Japanese anemones.

Alan told me of how, in my absence, he and Eileen were staying here and lunched with Dicky Buckle on the latter's birthday. A great effort had been made: banquettes and flower-decorated tables put out on the lawn of the minute cottage for at least 12 guests. Juliet was one of them and, as is now customary, was being rather difficult, wanting a rug as she was feeling chilly, refusing food, then, too late, changing her mind. Dicky nonetheless was most attentive and intent on amusing her. His eyes sparkled as he told her of the wonderful early-morning surprise. "I have Erich Alport[1] staying with me (he is without interest to Juliet—a crashing bore) and while I was downstairs preparing his breakfast, Alan and Eileen crept into the cottage—I'd opened the front door to let the sun in—and placed on the dining-room table the most marvellous bouquet you have ever seen, all from Cecil's garden, but so beautifully arranged with care and originality, mallows and carnations, and sweet peas, all the most wonderful variations of pale colours, and then underneath it, also beautifully arranged, some fruit and village sweets, bull's-eyes, candied violets . . ."

The description was abruptly halted by Juliet lighting a cigarette and asking, "And what did you give Erich for breakfast?"

[1] Erich Alport, Jewish refugee and long-time friend of Buckle's, who frequently travelled with him. Buckle described him as an "obstinate spoilt child," who "was prepared to endure hardship in the cause of research" (Buckle, *In the Wake of Diaghilev* [Collins, 1981], p. 203).

STEPHEN TENNANT

Alan [Tagg] and I visited the haunting and haunted Wilsford in the spirit of adventure, for one never knows with Stephen if an invitation is to be countermanded at the last moment, or whether on arrival his mood prevents him from making himself available. He had today indulged in some artifice about friends not coming down from London so he could give us all his attention. As usual the house was cold, untidy, undusted and today it was strangely dark. Stephen made a late entrance down the stairs looking so ghastly that I cringed at the idea of having to greet him with a kiss. "How are you?" "Oh, I'm exhausted with happiness."

He laughed and gave Alan all his attention, or rather only an occasional line of dialogue was delivered in my direction as Stephen sat, feet crossed, in the hall and gave forth on his own terms. "Let's talk about Shakespeare. I always think Shakespeare was full of theatre, so theatrical, and of course the poetry! He has Juliet say such beautiful lines: 'The mask of night is upon my face.' Isn't that lovely? I always think that if I had been born in Shakespeare's time, I would have loved to play all his heroines. You see, it wasn't till very late that it was considered respectable for women to go on the stage. Now, Alan, which order do you think it would have been best to play in. Juliet first, then Desdemona and Rosalind. I'm so glad you like *As You Like It* and then the Queen in *Macbeth,* Lady Macbeth, no the Queen in *Hamlet,* Gertrude, yes, yes. Oh, how lovely it would have been! Now do have some tea."

Old Ford, the coachman, brought in a tray of kitchen crockery and some stale bought cakes and the talk turned to Billie Burke and Flo Ziegfeld.[1]

They were married for years, but Billie Burke nearly went mad that he never had anything to say at breakfast. "Speak rubbish, just use words! So long as you say something!"

Then the topic switched to Pavlova. Suddenly Stephen was in his stride. He evoked the dancer in a most remarkable way, and he cannot have been more than 16 when he saw her. Would it be 40 years ago? He said that her

[1] Billie Burke (1885–1970), actress, and Florenz Ziegfeld (1869–1932), director of the Ziegfeld Follies.

taste was poor. She was not an intellectual, but that magic sprang from her mere presence on the stage. She was bewitching and something emanated which made audiences incapable of ever forgetting her. Her movements were of a swooning nature. She could be so light that you felt she was attached to strings, that many of her dances did not bring out much effort on her part, that the swan was evolved in an hour and contained a very few steps. Her choice of music was tinny and too pretty-pretty, but her curtain calls were the greatest part of the entertainment, for she played with the audience. She enjoyed the fun of appearing at odd, unexpected parts of the stage, and was amused by her own antics.

Off the stage she was not like an artist. She was hearty and full of laughter. Together they would go to see Pearl White[1] movies, and she would never talk of her work. She wished to be utterly "private" and chose an uncelebrated hotel in Paris. She looked like a little Indian god with skin drawn tightly over the bones, hair scraped back and wore navy-blue on the lids of her deep-set eyes. She was never well dressed, wore coats and skirts and turbans. Seldom has an artist had such continuing fame. Wherever she went the houses were packed, seats impossible to procure. There was nobody like her now. But then where were the great personalities? Where the great playwrights? "Oh, come off it, Stephen! What about Pinter? Osborne's[2] pretty good too." But one realised that Stephen has just put a time limit on himself. He has closed his eyes to anything that has happened in the last 25 years.

We were hearing fascinating little details about things that everyone else had forgotten. But Stephen had not continued to be interested from the moment the last war started. He never looks at a paper or magazine. No new book arrives in his house. Little wonder that he has, apart from his eccentricity, become such a period piece. Even his vocabulary is dated, although his use of words is his one remaining talent (the drawing is now dissipated). Stephen produced an old *Horizon* for Alan to admire, something Stephen had written about me 20 years ago. He produced a piece of paper on which he had written something about me this morning. But the electric light was not strong enough, nor the daylight, and the reading ended in gales of laughter. He pre-

[1] Pearl White (1889–1938), American leading lady in silent serials. Author of *Just Me* (1919).

[2] Harold Pinter (b. 1930) and John Osborne (1929–94), noted playwrights of their generation.

sented Alan with some posters of Mexico done 25 years ago, and a caricature of Delysia[1] for me done 35 years ago.

The exertion had caused Stephen to break out in a sweat. In desperation he combed back his greasy, messy, straggly curls; with straight clean-cut hair, he suddenly showed that he still has a birthright of distinction.

As we threatened to leave, Stephen's blandishments became more desperate. "Come and look at the water lilies, and the perch. Have another cup of (cold) tea." But he appeared crushed when I said we had to go on somewhere else. "Oh, you've got another visit." "Just tennis. I'm going to play tennis with the Longmans,"[2] to which Stephen triumphantly asked, "Oh, wouldn't it be better just to watch?"

Alan, safely in the car, buried his head in his hands with laughter and tears. "But you know he got out of our visit more than we did. He wouldn't answer any of our questions. We couldn't control the talk. He wouldn't give. He just stage-managed proceedings to his liking. He never learnt anything about us. He's the most selfish person there's ever been, and he's tough. He's ruthless. It's no good feeling sorry for him. He's not sorry for himself. He keeps those Fords under ruthless control. He's leading just the sort of existence he wants to. Don't let's fool ourselves that he needs sympathy from us."

Cecil then spent an evening with the American dancer and choreographer, George Balanchine.[3]

BALANCHINE 10 SEPTEMBER 1965

What a very different opinion Balanchine holds on Pavlova. Although of the same generation as Stephen, he told me he thought she was awful. "She had such bad taste and chose such dreadful music. She liked Hungarian composers and dainty tippety-tip dances. Ta-ta-ta-ta-ta-ta-ta, dumb, dumb, dumb, dumb.

[1] Alice Delysia (1889–1974), musical comedy star.

[2] Mark Longman (1916–72), publisher, and his wife Lady Elizabeth Lambart (b. 1924). They lived at Bishopstone House, near Salisbury.

[3] George Balanchine (1904–83), choreographer.

Turn! And her feet were so ugly. Such large, lumpy shoes. They looked as though they'd been pounded by iron, and were so solid, but still so big. And her dresses! She'd dress up as a marquise with a beauty spot, and do the gavotte. It was awful, but the audiences loved it. They didn't know any better in those days. They loved the dying swan, just for one reason. It's awfully boring and there are only two movements in it, and the hands go flap, flap, but the audience know she is going to die and so they're all waiting for it to happen. But she wasn't an artist. She didn't get along with Diaghilev because she was so selfish. Yes, I knew her. She wasn't interesting. She didn't inspire me. She asked me to do something for her. She was very businesslike, but our arrangement never came to anything."

It was Balanchine night for me last night. I broke my long sojourn in the country to go up to London to see the American ballet which, after two unsuccessful seasons here, has suddenly met with a total triumph. There was no advance booking whatsoever, but the praise of the critics at once filled the opera house and the applause was that of an excited and knowing audience. For me, and obviously for the majority of those present, these ballets have renewed my interest in the art. I had seen one swan too many. I could not bear to see Margot going mad as a wronged village maiden, or Nureyev[1] in dowdy tights and excruciating wig posturing as a prince. It didn't interest me if someone did 69 fouettés.

Suddenly Paul Taylor[2] came along with his small troupe and did abstract dances. This was exciting. Then Balanchine shows us the stage full of his pupils grown to the mature age of 18, and by putting them to make new shapes and patterns, by using the suppleness of their bodies in a completely unclassical way, one was suddenly entranced and stimulated. His "episodes" to music by Webern[3] reproduces the strangeness that one used to feel on going to the theatre. This was the unexpected and the surprising. We did not watch to see how well the dancers did the known steps, but one was spellbound by the freshness of invention, the shock of unexpected attitudes. Likewise the "movements" of Stravinsky has given one a pep pill. One is sitting forward instead of

[1] Dame Margot Fonteyn and Rudolph Nureyev.

[2] Paul Taylor (b. 1934), American dancer and choreographer.

[3] Anton von Webern (1883–1945), Austrian composer.

lolling back, one is intent, and amused too. This is a combination of lunacy and beauty. Sometimes indecency comes in too, but with subtlety and refinement, or decadence. The Japanese ballet, *Bugaku,*[1] with the beautiful empty setting, white with scarlet and emerald-green rostrum, and the clean laundered transparent white costumes of Karinska[2] put one into a mood to enjoy strange happenings. We were not disappointed. The rituals were danced with utter seriousness but in themselves were extremely curious, even bordering on the comic. But one knew the dancers to be dedicated artists and one had too much respect and admiration to laugh at their incredibly unlikely posturings. The bride, to the accompaniment of the swooning of a hundred cats, was being adorned for the wedding ceremonial. The men too were preparing the groom for the occasion. The lovers mate in an incredibly lascivious dance, if dance it can be called, for if so you won't forget that nonsense of Pavlova in the gavotte. Here the heel is the important part of the foot and if the toes are pointed it is so rare an occurrence as to be a lovely shock. The dance of bride and groom continues in a smooth dream of the 198 positions of love. There is something utterly pure and honest about this love play. The heart does not beat in the female breast, though perhaps it plays second role to the sexual organ in the man. The woman goes through her vile indecencies with the most pristine and youthful innocence. She is a butterfly, a snake, an insect, a flower making love, and because she is the newcomer, Mimi Paul,[3] we are in at the birth of a star. The long-neck coolness, the calm surprise, the gazelle-like cleanliness of her poses, her arms, her hands, her legs, her feet, produce an effect that is quite unknown. How can a girl of 18 know instinctively about style? She is a goddess, an empress, a harlot, a debutante, a flower. She is God's latest, greatest gift to Balanchine.

After the congratulations backstage (and a vain search for the elusive Mimi, who had already gone home and had left her dressing room, not on the floor with the principal dancers, but with the assisting dancers), we then went to the supper party given by the violinist, Nathan Milstein,[4] who is one of George B.'s greatest friends.

[1] *Bugaku,* arranged by Balanchine in 1963.

[2] Madame Karinska (1886–1983), Russian born costume maker, who won an Oscar for her work on the costumes of *Joan of Arc* (1948). Much favoured by Cecil.

[3] Mimi Paul (b. 1942), American dancer from Tennessee.

[4] Nathan Milstein (1903–92), violinist born in Odessa.

Milstein, hearty, sympathetic and humorous, jockeyed one on to eat and drink. We were all merry and I was particularly pleased to find myself next to George (on his other side he held hands with his love, Suzanne Farrell,[1] like a poetical granddaughter of Pauline Rothschild,[2] with her head bent so low on one side that she appeared like a bird with its head tucked under one wing).

I have worked with George (*Swan Lake* of course) but have never felt anything but his coldness and my own inadequacy. Tonight he was at ease and I too. We talked of the genius of Karinska, of my thrill at discovering what beauties she has created with my designs for *Traviata.* George said, "There is no one like her. When she is gone, it will be finished, and the same with me and with you too. We will not survive another 20 years, but then something quite different will happen. It will never be the same."

He told me that nowadays he had to be very careful about the projects he undertook to do. "You see, I can only teach people by showing them myself how it must be done, and it is terribly tiring. I can't do all this jumping and dancing much longer, and so I must not take on something that will take me four months to prepare unless it is really worth it, and it's not worth it in opera. I like singers to stand still, but it is much harder to get them to do it than to make dancers dance.

"If I do *Apollon*[3] in London, then you must send the boy to me. It will be cheaper and I can't afford the time to come to the Savoy and drum it into him. I must have a boy who is content to do everything I tell him. He mustn't have any other ambition. Nureyev came to see me shortly after he fled from Russia, but he wanted to dance on circuit and make extra money. He wanted to be the star. He didn't want to be part of a ballet. He is too selfish and a dancer cannot afford to be selfish. You will soon spot a selfish dancer. Nureyev will end up badly, you'll see. He'll be like Pavlova."

[1] Suzanne Farrell (b. 1945), American dancer from Cincinnati, who became the star dancer of the New York City Ballet.

[2] Pauline de Rothschild (1908–76), born Pauline Potter, married Baron Philippe de Rothschild (1902–88), owner of the Mouton vineyards.

[3] *Apollon Musagète,* haunting ballet by Balanchine with music by Stravinsky, which Cecil wanted to be played at his funeral.

When he told Dicky that he loved to laugh at critics, and he loved Dicky's jokes, he said, "Please make jokes about us on Sunday." Dicky, flushed with wine and the occasion, said that he had been so impressed by something written by Andrew Porter[1] in the *Financial Times* that he told him he was so much better than he was, and wouldn't he like his job? Dicky is certainly honest in so many unexpected and daring ways, and was very beguiling and delightful tonight, but why is it that one does not like him completely?

George has impeccable manners. He has the frankness and honesty that can make him behave with naturalness under every circumstance. ("We have to be photographed with officials," he said apropos Evangeline Bruce[2] coming backstage.) Although he was certainly hungry and ate anything that was offered him, he would never grab for a bread roll himself or ask for another slice of cheese. He has a white vellum complexion, his hair is lank (perhaps dyed), his cuffs are those of a seigneur. It is a good way of getting old, for he never kids himself about old age, his work or the opinion that others have of him. He is certainly one of the best there are today.

FOOTNOTE

Footnote, which should not be a note on which to end a genuine paean. The success of the season, the adulation of the critics, has resulted in appalling jealousy and outrage at Covent Garden. Freddie [Ashton] knows this has been a mortal stab. "I too can make them do contortions *and* pornography . . . I'm very pleased they've had such a success, genuinely pleased, but it's been out of all proportion."

It is quite obvious that the influence of this visit will soon be felt, and profoundly so, in this opera house, and if we have less cygnets and swan princesses, then more often am I likely to make the effort to go.

[1] Andrew Porter (b. 1928), music critic of *Manchester Guardian, Financial Times, New Yorker* and *Observer.*

[2] Evangeline Bell (1914–95), wife of David Bruce, American Ambassador to Britain. She wrote *Napoleon and Josephine.*

Cecil spent three weeks at Reddish House, with few visitors, working quietly on various projects. It was a time when the garden was full of scents and "the damp leafy smell that presages the beginning of the autumn." His sister Nancy came to visit him, reminding him of his mother.

Cecil was in Monte Carlo when he heard of the death of Lady Juliet Duff on 23 September 1965.

MONTE CARLO—JULIET 25 SEPTEMBER 1965

Juliet has conked.

There was no doubt about it. She'll be missed by a lot of her friends, and by me especially. Recently I have been at Broadchalke alone when she was away and the fact that she was not available to invite to dinner or to go over to Bulbridge was very marked. I began to feel the first possibilities of loneliness.

Sometimes during the evening I was too tired to get on with writing or even reading seriously and was delighted when Juliet returned full of news of trips to Brighton and Devonshire. After a lull it was pleasing to have the supreme Faggots' Moll to dinner on Sunday with Simon, Chrissie Gibbs[1] and Dicky Buckle. Often Juliet does her best to wreck an evening in my house. She is restless and determined to cut the evening as short as possible. She interrupts the flow of conversation, is extremely competitive and can be altogether so exasperating, but one has had to make allowances that this is a woman of 84. The revelation is astonishing, for she does not react like an old woman, and she [is] always surrounded by young men, the younger the better.

This Sunday, however, she was at her best, rather piano, but content to sit back and listen to the talk, which was very racy. Occasionally she made a contribution about Diaghilev or someone she considered came in the category of eccentric, under discussion. Simon, rather tipsy, was in his most delightful vein and at the end of the evening (11:30 struck up), he ran his hand down Juliet's arm and said, "You looked so pretty in your rose-coloured dress."

Next morning Chrissie Gibbs was posing in my new studio when, at the end of the morning, Juliet and the boys suddenly appeared to take him away.

[1] Christopher Gibbs (b. 1938), wild child of the 1960s turned Establishment figure and doyen of the London art scene. Antique dealer.

Juliet looked tremendously surprised to see the studio. Her habitual expression, with eyebrows raised, was laughably exaggerated. She liked the studio, her voice breathless with surprise, passed a remark about the nose of Chrissie being too *bombé* and then departed. "When are you going up to London?" The usual question, she: "Tomorrow." But on the morrow she became dizzy in the bath, lost consciousness, regained it enough to ring the bell. Andrews pulled her out of the bath and the local doctor, an old-fashioned idiot, told her to rest. Next day she keeled over getting out of bed. Andrews to the rescue. She lay resting, had a brain haemorrhage at 11, lost consciousness and died at 7:30.

She had said to Simon earlier, "I don't want to give the doctors a lot of trouble. I've had a very happy long life, and I'm quite contented to go. I just don't want to be paralysed or be a nuisance." She confessed she had never had a day's illness, and this is almost true, and she certainly had the most painless and easy death. It happened so quickly that though for a long time I had known she was "for it" I was shocked and poor Simon stunned. He blubbed, then took some stiff drinks and discovered the nobility of death. "She looks so wonderful lying there, just like her mother, her face less broad, and with a sweet smile. It was a sweet death."

Although in many ways I disliked Juliet and found her appallingly selfish, superficial and unreal, yet she has played a large part in my life.

Her name, so beautiful and strange, was a part of one's own personal vocabulary. She was always there. She, tall and gangling, silly as she was, was a perpetual joke, but a distinguished joke, never sordid. And of course her obituaries are everything that she would have wished and are a part of social history (even if of another day).

Her scrapbooks, Queen Mary Christmas cards and junk mixed with Fabergé. The servants all rallying at her death, devoted and sad, Lily sponging the blood that spurted from the mouth and combing the hair.

Cecil had been invited to Monte Carlo by Princess Grace[1] *to design a poster for the forthcoming centenary of the principality in 1966. She invited him because she thought of him as the epitome of the Edwardian era.*

[1] HSH Princess Grace of Monaco (1929–82), married (1956) HSH Prince Rainier (b. 1923), the reigning Prince. She was formerly the film star Grace Kelly and died as the result of her car losing control on the Corniche.

MONTE CARLO

25 SEPTEMBER 1965

There is every reason to believe that I was conceived here. My parents spent their honeymoon at the Hôtel Hermitage and nine months later I was born. One of my earliest memories is of a photograph of my proud and smiling parents standing in an exotic garden with the spikes of the black feathers in my mother's hat complementing the cacti and palms of the background. (My mother's dress was of rose velvet and a morsel of it remains in the attic at Reddish.)

I came here suddenly on the invitation of Princess Grace to discuss doing a poster for the centenary celebrations. Monte Carlo was built by Garnier,[1] in 1866. I suppose it is a sign of old age that I hated the idea of not returning to Broadchalke after three days in London, especially as the sun was shining for the first time, but it is a tyranny if the morning glories prevent me from moving and in any case the late roses were over.

For a while it was amusing, even exciting, to be once more in this fantastic rococo nirvana. No doubt my delight was aided by the fact that I was here expense free, with all luxuries thrown in, as a guest of the principality. Now I could stay at the Hôtel de Paris, which had always been beyond our means when my poor mother, during her last winters, came here trying to sop up a little winter sun.

It is a hotel which I had looked upon with covetousness when in my early years, and I had forgotten how amusing is its patisserie decor of huge cream-coloured ladies linking garlands amid the arches of electric lights. Occasionally I had been invited to meals in the Louis XIV room, and the service and food were unlike anything that one would find elsewhere today. Going out on to the balcony of my room, the illuminated port below with the silhouette of the castle above presented a pretty picture. I explored the place, adored the bad taste of the casino with its medallions and incrustations, and from the liver-coloured marble hall (with its painted ceilings) I was deeply stirred by the view back through the entrance hall with the illuminated garden like a green and gold and red backdrop beyond. The parterres have been planted with arums, salvia, orange marigolds and cockscombs, and the effect

[1] Jean-Louis-Charles Garnier built the casino at Monte Carlo between 1879 and 1885.

with the avenue of receding palm trees and the velvety dried grass was (if one accepts the fact that it is awful, really in Edwardian bad taste) as pretty as can be imagined in its originality.

Haunted by memories, I walked around, by the Promenade where there used to be the horrible . . . pigeons, and where I once saw Lillie Langtry with her still violet eyes. Ghosts of the past were flitting by, Otéro, Gaby Deslys, Vesta Tilley[1] (even Juliet kept haunting me afresh), but there was new interest here now that Rainier had married Grace Patricia Kelly. (The fact that she was a film star is played down.) It is amusing to hear how the Court is kept up with style, and how as royal as any queen the pretty Princess has become.

The welcome that I received was impressive, a Mercedes to bring me from the airport, gladioli and whisky and an invitation to lunch with Their Serene Highnesses, in my room. The Palace with the sentry boxes, the tourist crowds and medieval archway, was impressive. Into a painted courtyard with twirling marble staircases and carriages and coaches emblazoned and bedecked, standing at the ready. Many ADCs, sentries and attendants.

We were shown along a terrace by the gardens, where an enormous curving and swirling azure-blue swimming pool has lately been built. Here the Princess doing the honours, with scraped-back yellow hair and a face that has coarsened in the 12 years since I last saw her. But she is still pretty and still *photogénique* in the extreme. At first my critical eye was cruel. The complexion was roughened by the sun and the jaw a bit squarer, and her manner was metallic. She spoke French with not a trace of American accent. She was a bit too gracious maybe, but she had to do the honours and make the introductions. Why criticise her for being too expert?

The fellow guests were not of a high order, unknown Monegasques and hangers-on and appendages, Sam Spiegel, Jacqueline Delubac, the Plesches, Rory Cameron.[2] The children very American, with their newly bearded father,

[1] Lillie Langtry (1852–1929), actress, known as the "Jersey lily," Caroline Otéro (1868–1965), "La Belle Otéro," courtesan; Gaby Deslys (1881–1920), singer and dancer; and Vesta Tilley (stage name of Lady de Frece, 1864–1952), male impersonator.

[2] Sam Spiegel (1901–86), Hollywood producer; Jacqueline Delubac (1907–97), film actress and the third of five wives of the playwright and actor Sacha Guitry; she bequeathed her Picassos, Degas and Manets to the Musée des Beaux-Arts in Lyon; Dr. Arpad Plesch (1889–1974), millionaire with interests in Haiti, and his wife "Etti" Wurmbrandt (1914–2003), two-time winner of the Derby as an owner; and Roderick (Rory) Cameron (1914–85), owner of La Fiorentina on Cap Ferrat.

Princess Grace of Monaco and her daughter, Stéphanie, Monte Carlo, September 1965

were swimming. The Princess clapped. "Time to come out." The Prince appeared in a dark-grey alpaca shirt, has let his figure go to pot and has a new row of upper teeth, hair getting white. He bowed to his guests, strangely enough with hand in pocket, but is pleasant, quite witty and intelligent. Much better than his press.

Lunch was enormous, prosciutto and pear, turbot, steak, cheese, ice cream, fruit. No wonder Princess Grace says she is 12lb overweight. Today's lunch knocked me for a loop. Talk about the *Centenaire*, the vileness of Onassis[1] wanting to destroy the casino, and all the architecture in favour of modernisations. Talk of new activities in science labs and the new Monte Carlo. One could not fault Princess Grace, and one realised what a great stroke of fortune it was that these two should have met and so soon fallen for one another, for she is first rate at the job and beautiful, efficient, hard-working, energetic and full of new ideas. And it is a great position to be the

[1] Aristotle Onassis (1906–75), Greek shipowner, who had interests in the Société des Bains de Mer at that time. He was the lover of the prima donna Maria Callas whom he left to marry Jacqueline Kennedy, widow of President John F. Kennedy, in 1968.

head of this rich piece of territory, and land values are going up all the time. It is a Croesus possession, becoming richer all the while. Little wonder the Mercedes.

Later that evening I went again into the casino and by now the freshness had worn off and I realised the shoddiness, the deadness. This was a living cemetery. It is impossible to recall the early days, to pretend that the Edwardian elegance can return. The old are dead, no more are there Russian grand dukes. No more *grandes cocottes,* no women of fashion.

The rooms were half empty and those occupying them were beatnik teenagers in sandals and blue jeans, and peasants and roughnecks, cheap American tourists, a few old crones with green painted faces, red-dyed hair, old men with wall eyes, women with goitres and so thin that they are like a silhouette. One woman had a perpetual twitch, another so humped that she had to hold on to chairs or rails when leaving her seat to change money. Some empty rooms have slot machines, some serve sandwiches.

Everywhere I looked there was some sign of how the mighty have fallen. Perhaps the glory of Monte Carlo can be replicated for one night, but it is dead, dead, dead, and I can't get away quick enough; in fact, am leaving right away.

Cecil enjoyed four days in Paris before returning to hear more about the death of Juliet.

Of course, her death has provided many another funny story and to assuage the guilt of laughter we say how much Juliet would have been amused to hear how Mary Herbert had come over to Bulbridge to advise about the funeral ("you must insert that it is private, family only, otherwise members of the Royal Family will send down representatives") and how she suggested going out to discuss it in the garden. "But why outside?" asked Simon. "*Pas devant les domestiques!*" It seems that the sight of Michael and Veronica scattering Juliet's ashes in the orchard was tragi-comic with Michael saying, "Darling Mummy's in a polythene bag."

But everyone has behaved better than could be expected. Michael, who can be so greedy, had only one moment of aberration when in addition to the Jacob furniture willed to him, he said "And I want that and that and that," until Mickey Renshaw,[1] the trustee, remonstrated that he must respect his mother's will.

Simon has been left the contents of the house but it may easily turn out that he has very little left after duty is paid and Sidney Herbert and the Vaynol estate have all put in their greedy claims. Simon has proved himself utterly unselfish, unvenal, and saintlike. Diana has behaved typically: "I can't feel sad. It was such a good end, and she'd had enough." And Michael has written that he admired her, she was a great character, and if he hadn't been her son he'd have been more of a friend.

FRIDAY, 18 OCTOBER 1965

This is the day I should have supped with the Queen of Spain.[2]

I couldn't resist putting this enclosure in my diary, although in fact the invitation had not given me a shimmer of excitement and it was very easy to refuse the Ambassador's[3] request to go with a small party to see a Coward revival[4] and on to supper.

My painting of much greater importance and my whole ten days in the country has been a joy. To feel that one day can pass into another without having to stir stumps, without the effort of conditioning one to a change of scene, this gives one a holiday glow. Not that I haven't felt stale in my house. It is hard for me to regulate my work, and if in good condition will continue long after the war of attrition should be declared over. It is foolish to work against the clock, but even now, it's difficult to arrange one's schedule so that it is not necessary to hurry.

The sudden excursion to London was beneficial. I went to the K. P. [Kensington Palace] party, given to all the painters and sculptors by the Snow-

[1] Mickey Renshaw (1908–78), bachelor, who lived partly in Cyprus.

[2] HM Queen Victoria Eugénie of Spain (1887–1969), Battenberg granddaughter of Queen Victoria. A bomb was hurled at her carriage after her wedding to King Alfonso. Later she lived in exile in Lausanne, making regular forays to London, where she stayed at Claridge's.

[3] Marqués de Santa Cruz (1902–88), Spanish Ambassador to London 1958–72.

[4] Noël Coward's *Present Laughter,* which had been playing at the Queen's Theatre since April, starring Nigel Patrick, Richard Briers, Avice Langdon, Phyllis Calvert and Maxine Audley.

dons, and enjoyed myself so much that when after a day's interval from the studio I returned there, it was with fresh strength and impatience to get started again. Now, incredible as it seems, I have painted more than enough pictures for an exhibition. It was very exciting suddenly to realise that the years at the Slade and Royal College, and the time in the country, have borne fruit, however sour it may taste in the mouths of the critics. It gives me more satisfaction than anything I have done for many years, for I feel this is something that I can rely on in my declining years.

NEW YORK

Slight eyebrow raise at different code of manners. Taxi drivers seldom speak at all, or if so it is to slap you down. "Can't you see the 'Off Duty' sign on the top of the cab? If you'd look, there'd be no need to get excited."

Cross-town traffic jams worse than before. My difficulties of getting behind the Garment Trade Trucks on my way to Metropolitan Opera give me the prevailing ulcer. The strain of always being late. The tension ends in a headache, a strain to get through to the end of the day.

The agreeable welcome party at Vreelands'[1] (a dinner for the young) an exhausting (as usual) jaunt to the country, Cowles, Philip Johnson, that ass Astor (Brooke)[2] telling of how her aged mother is now calmer and quieter having been fed a mood drug. Before, she had thrown an umbrella at her daughter, now she was read to by two beautiful young men (*Midnight Cowboy,*[3] an erotic tale is the American favourite). Brooke, spoilt by riches, has now become pretentious, with her keeping up with the Wrightsmans.[4] She is bewildered at the Wildenstein loan exhibition of Impressionists. "Isn't this *something*?" "Yes, very pretty," I answer crossly. Then, short-sightedly, she looks at the catalogue and, pointing at the Gauguins, Cézannes, Monets and Bonnards, exclaims,

[1] Reed Vreeland (1899–1966) and his wife Diana (1903–89).

[2] Fleur Cowles; Philip Johnson (1906–2000), architect; and Brooke Astor (b. 1902), widow of Vincent Astor.

[3] *Midnight Cowboy,* later made into a film (1969) directed by John Schlesinger, and starring Jon Voight and Dustin Hoffman.

[4] Charles B. Wrightsman (1895–1986), oil millionaire, and his wife, Jayne Larkin (b. 1918).

"There's the Morton Schwartz! There's the Freylinghausen, there's the Lilyammilch, there's the Cutting Curtis. Do you prefer the Schiff Ogden or the Glübleselz?"[1]

How the rich are impressed with one another! It is not the poor who are keeping up with the Joneses, but the Paleys with the Whitneys,[2] and how the rich like to be given presents. Getting something for nothing delights them—whereas the poor are resentful of receiving kindness.

Dates made for Met, promotion talks on radio for my book, and occasional photographic sittings made each day a morass of anxiety. Will I get a cab? Looms a trip to Washington. During the one day I make a two-hour tour of the National Gallery, so am already tired before pictures are taken of Mrs. Bliss, Longworth, Graham.[3] Total collapse and sorrow for myself on return.

The triumph of Truman is salt in one's wound. The man of the moment is greedy for all aspects of his success, and never has there been a greater success. He says only words masterpiece and genius will suffice, and must be repeated every moment. I am on edge, deeply tired, and not one night's sleep will suffice. However, I have only myself to blame. But the prospect of Broadchalke looms attractively.

NEW YORK 10 NOVEMBER 1965

5 o'clock. The fitting of our "Violetta"[4] in her Karinska costumes was over. Everyone pleased. Discussions of no consequence could doubtless continue for half an hour or so, but, as usual, the watch hands were in advance, and I beat it back to the hotel for a final winding-up with Mrs. Smith, the pretty false-eyelashed blonde secretary who had been doing odd bits for me during my short stay here, now about to end. Mrs. Smith was indeed waiting in the

[1] Presumably these refer to the millionaire owners of the works of art, hence the emphasis. Cecil seems to have the names slightly muddled, possibly out of disdain.

[2] William S. Paley (1901–86), Chairman of CBS, and his wife Barbara "Babe" Cushing (1915–78), and Babe's sister, Betsey (1908–98), wife of John Hay Whitney.

[3] Mildred Barnes (1879–1969), wife of Robert Woods Bliss (d. 1962), collector living at Barton Oaks, Washington; Alice Longworth (1884–1980), daughter of President Theodore Roosevelt; and Katharine (Kay) Graham (1917–2001), owner of the *Washington Post.*

[4] Violetta was sung by Anna Moffo (b. 1932).

Alice Longworth, daughter of President Theodore Roosevelt, Washington, 1965

crowded hotel lobby. We ascended to the 30th floor and coped with a few telephone calls, chores, bills and oddments. I was keen to get rid of her by 5:30 when two naughty boys were due, one with a present of a beautiful, but somewhat pornographic drawing, a goodbye present. The day's work over, night had descended. The leavetaking of Mrs. Smith started when the lights dimmed. Am I going blind, or were the lights flickering weaker and weaker? Suddenly they went out. We looked out of the windows. Even outside was dark too. No lights in any windows. This very odd for New York! We could not believe our eyes. As far as we could see, across to Brooklyn, the only lights were those reflected from the lamps of the cars densely packed as they moved along the streets. By degrees, the traffic became more and more tightly jammed, for we noticed that even the traffic lights had gone out. Total blackout as far as the eyes could see. And for how many minutes would this continue?

We joked about the shock that the movie audiences would have as suddenly they were plunged in unexpected gloom. A ballerina in the middle of her pirouettes would find herself lost in Stygian darkness. Gradually we realised that not only was light cut but electric power also. How awful to think that subways were suddenly at this, the great rush hour, brought to a standstill and people would be caught stranded God knows how many stories high in elevators. Oh, God. Below we heard the roar of sirens, ambulances with jangling bells and fire engines with scarlet flashing bulbs. People in the streets like black ants hurrying, trying in vain to cross the road, motor cars incapable of crossing town. We would telephone to find out what had happened. The operator told us that no lines were available, that the power cut was complete and extended the entire length of the Eastern seaboard as far as Canada.

Pretty little Mrs. Smith suggested we play sardines. I was in no laughing mood. The whole situation seemed fraught with portentous possibilities. Was this sabotage, someone demonstrating against the government's policy towards Vietnam? If so, how long would it take to make the point? We waited, 20 minutes, half an hour, 45 minutes, still no light except that reflected from the diamond crocodile trying to pass down Park Avenue and the red glow of the ever denser traffic trying to get out of town. By now a few candles appeared at isolated windows.

The slow revelation came that not only were many people likely to be trapped in elevators and subways, but others were marooned away from friends or family, the frigidaire would start thawing and the food in the deep freeze would start to melt. Radio and television were out of commission, only those with transistors could hear what was happening. After an hour and a half, Bob LaVine[1] and Franco M. banged on the door. They were breathless but in high spirits, having walked up the 30 flights of iron stairs to my room.

Bob has never been funnier. He was inspired. He made fun of the situation. There was pandemonium downstairs in the lobby and an old woman was shouting, "I've got to get to Palm Beach," though, as Bob said, what she would find there at this time of the year would be negligible. Have we any candles? Couldn't Mrs. Smith make some? Hadn't we looked in the frigidaire? Had we any matches? A Texan on the staircase had gone to the 16th floor and handed on his book of matches, but by now that was finished.

We all drank whisky in the dark. Bob told funny stories funnily. Then he became tired. Franco took the helm. Mrs. S. was quiet, I was hopeless,

[1] Robert LaVine (d. 1981), costume designer, who also worked with Diana Vreeland. His boyfriend was Bob Prairie (d. 1989).

dunched, exhausted, depressed and somewhat in awe. Unbelievable that such a thing could happen in New York where everything depended on electricity. The overworked telephone operator said that the trouble had started with a power failure in Niagara Falls, that Philadelphia and Boston were dark. They hope to get the switches turned on in two hours. Mrs. Smith wondered whether she could go home alone. We waited. Crowds still jostling below.

The boys decided to go down the staircase with Mrs. Smith. A woman in the next suite came out in terror. She lent them a candle for the descent. Impotent, marooned, I returned to my room, sank on to my bed and mercifully slept. But it was not a peaceful sleep. I kept wondering what at worst could happen. I had missed my TV appearance tonight to an audience of 50 million. I had missed dinner. I had missed telephoning to Kin to say goodbye.

I slept and dreamt a lot of unpleasant dreams. Periodically I woke enough to lift the telephone receiver and ask if the communications were not mended. No, no news. It was 2 o'clock—3—4. Still no light and no one ringing me. At 5:30 was wakened by the lights going on again. Could I now call San Francisco? My call woke Kin. He had heard the news on the radio. It must be like the war, or like the *Book of Joshua*. We had a matter-of-fact talk. I felt desperately tired. Yawning, I turned and tossed but slept little. Would my aeroplane leave on time? Surely no aircraft could land in a blacked-out aerodrome. BOAC telephoned to say the flight was delayed by four hours. I slept. I woke to find the elevators still at a standstill. No breakfast. Margaret Case[1] rang to tell of her experience. It had been like the war. They had all met up in the hall of their apartment building. People who lived there and they never saw before had become friends, providing whisky. Old Colonel So-and-So had pondered that here we were sending people to the moon and yet couldn't regulate the amenities of ordinary civilian life. If one switch had done this what could a Russian bomb do? There was no water in their apartment building. Diana Vreeland sent the maid with two bottles of Portland water.

Stories of bonhomie in the war conditions. Everyone friendly, women with fur coats and chauffeurs giving lifts to everyone, Negress drivers giving preference to cripples, others benefiting by the crisis, overcharging for

[1] Margaret Case (1891–1971), worked for Condé Nast. Eventually she committed suicide.

matches and candles. Handbags being snatched in the dark. The operator told me, "Yes, they've got the people out of the lifts, I'm thanking God that I was not trapped. It would have given me a heart attack." Telephone communication again. Would I be wanted for TV tonight? If so, perhaps I would stay, but by degrees I realised that I was in no mood to stay. I was more unnerved than I realised. My bags packed. How would I get them downstairs? Someone said that the bellboys were running up and downstairs with luggage of people checking out.

The woman next door, who had given the candle last night, telephoned. I didn't know her but she and her family knew me as they were all in show business. She had a heart condition and it was bad for her to be frightened and she was frightened if she realised she was alone on the floor. If I was going down by the stairs, would I let her accompany me? The bags put out. She appeared, an old marmalade beehived woman wih short skirt and her fur coat wrapped in a bundle in a dustsheet. She'd kick it downstairs to prevent herself from carrying it. We started. I kicked the bundle. There is nothing more squalid than the backstairs of a New York hotel with its bags of garbage on each floor. I kicked the bundle down to the 21st floor, the old woman stopping to sit on the iron steps for a whiff of smelling salts. Her legs felt queasy with the unaccustomed exercise. We got to the 16th floor. "Is it 12 o'clock?" "Five past." I feared I might lose my plane. "You hurry on. Here's a waiter. He'll look after me." Marmalade mum told him of her heart condition.

Downstairs, pandemonium. Margaret Case in the middle, ordering me coffee. "He hasn't eaten since lunchtime yesterday." (My head ached with hunger.) But I was more concerned with the non-arrival of my luggage. A taxi shortage, so Margaret ordered a limousine. Two bellmen in sweaty exhaustion at last appeared with my heavy luggage. They had had to walk up 30 flights and then drag the bags down the same number of floors. "I wouldn't do that to a dog," I said in gratitude, over-tipping them and rushing out of the hotel, giving only a cursory goodbye greeting to Margaret.

Of course, the aeroplane was further delayed and I need not have panicked, but in my nervous condition I was never more relieved than when the plane took off for the six-hour flight and I felt that after I had eaten I could at last relax and think over and perhaps even laugh at some of the experiences of this terrifying nightmare when, as the *Evening Standard* said, "New York died."

Walls were hacked away to free people in lifts. "Any pregnant women in there?" someone shouted. "Give us a chance," came the reply. "We haven't even got to know one another yet."

Would the hospitals have their own electrical supply for brain operations, for people in oxygen tents?

Cecil went down to the country to resume his painting. He completed his poster for Monte Carlo and sent that off. Then, to his great shock, on 21 November Mrs. Paycock, his cook, whose fare he so enjoyed, announced that she would "like to have a change." His painting morning was ruined and he began to feel depressed. The approach of Christmas did not help his mood and he felt lonely without Kin.

His next mission was to photograph some Proustian characters in Paris, an invitation that came to him when he was in New York. He wrote his account on returning from Paris, where he had had an early call at the hotel, suffering from a bad stomach, and then, on the last lap of his journey, the train ride from Waterloo to Salisbury, he had been turned out of the first class compartment for not having the correct first class ticket.

Cecil wondered why he accepted every offer that came along. But this one held particular appeal as he was reading the two-volume biography of Marcel Proust by George Painter.[1]

TRIP TO PARIS

27 NOVEMBER 1965

It was an upheaval to go, and a strain to fit in other appointments, the chiropractor, the shopping and old friends, but the photography brought me in touch with people that I would otherwise never have known. The centring of the lights on one personality suddenly made them important. Otherwise I would have paid no attention to these people. But in their own way they were fascinating.

Living in one bedsitter with a minute bathroom behind the front door was the elegant, long-fingered Jacques Porel. At seventy he still has the

[1] George Painter (b. 1914), published *Marcel Proust—A Biography* in two volumes (1959 and 1965).

Jacques Porel, son of Réjane

allure of the twenties, though no physical resemblance or I would say temperamental similarity with his mother, Réjane.[1] Jacques was suffering from his colon and sorry for himself, but he remains full of verve and vigour, and he retold many of the anecdotes about himself that appear in the Painter books. Céleste,[2] the old housekeeper, was the next on our quest. She is now guardian of Ravel's house in Montfort-l'Amaury. And blotted her copybook by not being at home when punctually we arrived.

We discovered her to be a woman of a certain taste, with her lifetime's love devoted to Proust and his memory. Tears came back of her thick glasses as she talked of his *nacré* complexion, charm, kindness, never exasperated, never a martyr to his work. Terrified he would not finish his work before his death.

No greater contrast to this dead long-ago decorated house (twenties) could be found than that belonging to the last of our series, Princess Marthe

[1] Jacques Porel (d. ca 1985), author, father of the actress Jacqueline Porel and of Mark Porel, who appeared as Richard Hornig in Visconti's film *Ludwig* (1972). He was the son of Réjane (1857–1920), actress and manager.

[2] Céleste Albaret (1891–1984), Proust's housekeeper, author of *Monsieur Proust* (1976).

Princess Marthe Bibesco at her apartment on the Île-St-Louis

Bibesco.[1] If in ordinary life I had been invited to see her I would most likely not have had time to accept, and how much I would have missed! For the old lady, however tiresome and pretentious she may be, is a great character and her voice is calm and has much gracious to say. This is the old-world manner, and it is neither ridiculous nor obsolete when used with her tact and taste. She appeared in her writing clothes, a horror of white satin, crumpled and a bit stained, with a black hood over her head to camouflage the dewlaps. The face that was painted so beautifully by Boldini[2] is now a mess of porridge with eyes, mouth and chin slipped. She has little money left, yet the apartment has such style that I was fascinated. At the windows are rows of glass bottles with each a sprig of camel, dromedary, or mandarin fern. On a table in front of her Drian, 12 eighteenth-century perfume bottles each with white-wire carnation facing in the direction of Notre-Dame. The colours of the apartment worked, her

[1] Princess Marthe Bibesco (1888–1973), eccentric Romanian aristocrat and author.

[2] Giovanni Boldini (1845–1931), belle époque painter, who painted many beautiful women of the period.

parrot perched on a marbled Cupid on the white fireplace, a tapestry pale rose and biscuit, the velour coverings faded but powdered pepper.

The old lady, embarrassed and apologetic about her age, lived in the grand manner and told that Céleste had once refused her entrée into P.'s bedroom on account of her perfume being likely to give the invalid a further attack of asthma. Quotes of poems and letters of Proust's but always the feeling that she was more important than he was. "I was terrified of him. When he asked me to dance at a ball I fled. I was fifteen and wanted to have a good time, not be stuck with this terrifying man in the long black coat."

Cecil then visited Georges Mathieu,[1] *a painter, who was enjoying a certain success at this time. Not in the first rank of painters, Mathieu's work was nevertheless widely bought and exhibited. Some found him pretentious and he cannot be described as well-known to the general public today.*

The last sitter before taking the plane home was not on the Proustian track, but nevertheless was another example of how the process of photographing introduces one to stranger and unexpected people. [He] was the moustachioed painter Mathieu. In many ways he is like a modern-day Stephen Tennant, his house an unbelievable medieval fantasy, abstract art, good and bad mixed.

The door was opened surprisingly by this bowing factotum. "I am h-h-h-honoured by your presence," he said. I was struck by the hands, the decor of the hall. Opposite in the well of the staircase a frigidaire decorated with his calligraphic scrawls, an early throne, medieval flags, busts of emperors, their faces turned to the wall. But this is nothing—"Come upstairs." What one saw was outrageous. Scarlets, purples, mauves were the colours of the huge painting by him, of a huge table covered with velvet backed by books, and an unbelievable collection of objects, bottles, champagne bottles, busts of Voltaire (face to wall), ostrich feather penholders and a gilt throne (Italian) used by Sacha Guitry[2] in a French film. Everything mixed up, good and bad,

[1] Georges Mathieu (b. 1921), painter.

[2] Sacha Guitry (1885–1957), prolific French author and actor, who retained a precocious attitude throughout his life, insisting on acting in the plays he produced, over 90 of which were staged. His five wives included Yvonne Printemps and Jacqueline Delubac.

Georges Mathieu, eccentric painter

real Gothic furniture, mixed with cinema set plasterboard and fake early-Gothic paintings done by him with collages for five frames. Upstairs a mauve and carved wood Gothic bedroom looking out on to a neo-Gothic church (we went on roof), his own bed on three-sided square with coloured wine goblets and decanters with a still life of sweetcorn and feathers sprouting from the centre.

Unbelievable mess of paintings and tiny objects, coaches, trains, carriages, made in plastic. No snobbery, no style, no restraint. A vast terrible portrait of himself painted by an aunt reminded one of the portrait of Ludwig of Bavaria and his taste was somewhat similar. But by degrees one realised that there was really no madness here. An extraordinary sense of reality. "I don't like to put on fancy clothes just for a photograph." (I had suggested his putting on a purple velvet Louis XIV coat thrown over a chair.) "Take me as I am in life, but in Dalí[1] tricks." "Why do you frown in pictures?" "Because I look better." It took me some time to get over his pictorial onslaught.

[1] Salvador Dalí (1904–89), Surrealist artist.

This phenomenon minced about with pointed fingers and pineapple-cone hairdo. It was impossible to think that this man can be taken seriously. (His current exhibition at the Charpentier is selling out and he is represented in 40 museums.) He said that he started painting (a colour postcard of Selfridges illuminated for Christmas with buses and advertisements) in 1942. Suddenly read that Bach's music did not illustrate anything, why should painting? So he started his abstract (Tachisme) and now paints a picture in ten minutes. A great feeling of health and vigour emanates from this extraordinary fly-like creature. He seems happy and content in spite of being such an intellectual (rarely happens) although in response to my query said, "I'm content with myself but not with the rest of the world." I became almost envious that here was someone who has found his niche in life so completely, and is accepted seriously in spite of all his rather disturbing affectations.

Malraux pays him tribute. He gives demonstrations of his painting technique and is acclaimed throughout the world, and is, of course, in some ways completely mad. But it is he who laughs on the way to the bank, and after an engaging, absorbing hour in his company, I decided I liked him very much.

For myself I found the paintings very "flighty," not solid enough. But they have a success for the moment and he lives in the full realisation of his limited talent while Stephen's frustrations drive him to an unhealthy sort of madness.

1966

Cecil began the New Year in a poor state of health, suffering from shingles. He had been overtaxed by his three-week visit to New York and further worn down by his trip to Paris. He had completed enough paintings for an exhibition and had hoped to relax. December had proved a month of enforced "leisure" in which he had felt ill and unable to sleep.

He decided that all this presaged the onslaught of old age and that he should be more careful. He planned a visit to the Trees[1] *in Barbados after his exhibition was opened.*

Meanwhile Cecil contemplated the changes at Wilton, and attended the wedding of the heir to the title and the estate, Lord Herbert, to Claire Pelly, on 20 January 1966.

ANOTHER NEIGHBOURHOOD MILESTONE — JANUARY 1966

The generations tear by like comets, since I have come to live in Wiltshire—is it 40 years ago?—and the big house at Wilton has always had a major emphasis. The scene has changed considerably. The Edwardians[2] hung on long, bravely, with stiff upper lips, then petered out, and the younger generation,[3] already middle-aged, moved in from the Chantry House opposite the Park doors. (Unfortunately they brought little in the way of fresh blood to the

[1] Ronald Tree (1897–1976), Anglophile American, who had lived at Ditchley Park, and his second wife Marietta Peabody (1917–91).

[2] Fifteenth Earl of Pembroke and Montgomery (1880–1960), and his autocratic wife, Lady Beatrice Paget (1883–1973), daughter of sixth Marquess of Anglesey.

[3] Sixteenth Earl of Pembroke, and his wife, Lady Mary Hope, daughter of the first Marquess of Linlithgow.

house, continuing to entertain only the most staid and boring additions of the former prototypes. But they did bring their children, and the boy Henry[1] has grown to be a gangling youth with the possibilities of being a character, a personality, an individual. The boy Henry showed his independence by becoming engaged to a beatnik-looking girl who was at first greatly disapproved of. However, nothing that Henry did could ever be wrong, so Miss Claire Pelly[2] was welcomed into the upper echelons (though the Dowager remarked to her that this was the first time since 1379 that a Pembroke had married a commoner). Bea in fact was a Paget and there's nothing very illustrious about that!

Two days before the wedding a party was given for the young couple by Sheridan Dufferin,[3] which showed the changes that have taken place in the new world. Not one person was in evening dress, not a sign of a gala flower, no buffet with little cakes; beats, open necks, blue jeans, sweaters, shoulder-length hair for men and women, Shrimpton[4] the model, in football boots. One wonders what will happen to Wilton when this generation succeeds. Will they, at last, bring their David Hockneys and Pop Art to the Single Cube?

The wedding was more staid, though there was a Dickensian-dressed show-off group, Chrissie Gibbs, Mark Palmer,[5] the Ormsby-Gores looking as if they had been rummaging in the Wilton dress-up chest. There was the *mal occhio,* mad, frightening and horrible Mrs. Desmond Guinness[6] with old artificial flowers in her bird's nest hair and like some mad female impersonator creating alarming ambience wherever she wandered, but there were mainly the usual body of Pembroke friends, the autocratic society and its appendages, and its parasites, and it was these that gave a sense of continuity to an otherwise boring function.

It was the coldest, greyest, iciest, ugliest day of a bad patch of a bad winter, and yet in spite of late and unheated trains, the old standbys from Wilton had turned up, Mrs. Campbell, the widow of the vicar, in Edith

[1] Henry, Lord Herbert (1939–2003), later seventeenth Earl of Pembroke and Montgomery.

[2] Claire Pelly (b. 1943), now Mrs. Tertius Murray-Threipland.

[3] Sheridan, fifth Marquess of Dufferin and Ava (1938–88), art dealer and partner of John Kasmin.

[4] Jean Shrimpton (b. 1942), popular model and girlfriend of David Bailey.

[5] Sir Mark Palmer, Bt (b. 1941), described by the artist Michael Wishart as leader of the "Peacock Revolution."

[6] Mariga Guinness (1932–89), born Princess von Urach, wife of Hon. Desmond Guinness (b. 1931), co-founders of the Irish Georgian Society. Divorced 1981.

Olivier's time, and her now elderly daughter, Edith herself represented by her nieces, there were the old retainers, nearly a hundred of them, up by charabanc, purple nose Ray the butler, Andrews, very plump and Lily, Juliet's housemaid in her mistress's cut-down fur coat.

The Knightsbridge church chosen is one of the ugliest in London and although the bride, in wooden Victorian hairdo and beautiful cream paper dress, looked her best, and the pages and bridesmaids, copied from a Van Dyck portrait in the Double Cube, wore cream and coffee and cigar, dowdy unexpected, wonderful (the beauty of the Kent cherub,[1] golden-haired, open-eyed, at the pitch of perfection is a miracle of nature, but one that cannot last). Nonetheless it was not a beautiful wedding or occasion. The highlights were: the ivory face of the Dowager, "Auntie Beeswax," now grown like a monument, a Gothic statue, with, as Mary P[embroke] later said, a yellowing cowpat on her head, David [Herbert], pouterchested, the instigator of the romance, Patricia,[2] his sister, for the boshshot of her hat, a terrible gold pumpkin (she had spent the morning lying back having her hair done, her face done and her hat put on!) said to me the one moment that I will remember, of the bridal couple, ensconced in their car, driving from the church very slowly on the ice, and in a shower of paper rose petals waving to the friends.

Henry, at the height of his youthful beauty and elegance, waved with wide large gestures, leaning forward and smiling. One could gauge even through the window the expression of happiness, tenderness, the frank goodness in his eyes, the gaiety of his smile, the distinction of his body as he leant forward. This was his apotheosis. Never again will anything equal the poetry of this moment in his happiness. Poor Juliet was missed. Her house is being dismantled, alterations underfoot, the guests' bedroom being converted into nurseries and rooms for nannies. Another generation on its way.

How fascinating the detail! Michael Duff has an adventure in the barber's shop at the Carlton Tower. "Do you know of a masseur in the hotel?" "Yes, me." "No,

[1] George, Earl of St. Andrews (b. 1962), elder son of HRH The Duke of Kent. Lord Herbert was a godson of Prince George, Duke of Kent, and his mother a lady-in-waiting to Princess Marina.

[2] Hon. David Herbert (1908–95), feline bachelor, living in Tangiers, and his sister, Patricia, Dowager Viscountess Hambleden (1904–94), Lady of the Bedchamber to the Queen Mother, children of the fifteenth Earl.

I don't mean massage on the head. I mean body massage." "Yes, me. I'll ring you to say when I can come up to your room." 4 o'clock. Michael guessed there might be more in the air when at 4 o'clock the visitor arrived and, seeing twin beds, asked, "Are you sharing this room with anyone else?" Michael replied, "No" and the visitor said, "Good."

Simon [Fleet] too is capable of graphic descriptions. His account of a visit to Liberty's to change a sweater is hilarious. The very staid shop assistant told him he'd better try on the sweater. "But no." "Oh yes, you'd better." They walked down long corridors to a curtained partition where the shop assistant became no longer staid. When Simon had recovered his equanimity the shop assistant said "Nothing doing here," but put name and address in the package containing the sweater. Back in the showroom again became a model of conformity.

Simon laughs about David Herbert's "Paget" quality of seeing all his geese as swans. Simon recently conducted David to Wig Creations for a toupee. After wearing [it for] a year in Tangier, David brings it back for a clean-up. David said, "Do you know, when they saw it, they considered it the best kept wig from the tropics that they'd ever seen!"

Cecil's shingles turned into sciatica, according to his doctor, Dr. Gottfried. And the weather remained glacial.

Cecil exhibited 28 portraits at the Lefevre Gallery, in Bruton Street, between 27 January and 26 February 1966. Works on show included portraits of the actors Alec Guinness[1] *and David Warner, the art critic John Russell, and Picasso. Cecil did not name the sitters, who were variously described as "tennis player," "poet," "explorer" etc. The exhibition also included a New York hustler, some Mexican masks, wrestlers, torsos and a nude.*

29 JANUARY 1966

Oh dear! I'm a bit baffled, but I suppose my "shingled" health has much to do with my feeling incapable of much feeling. I can't really enjoy anything. I can

[1] Sir Alec Guinness (1914–2000), actor known for his ability to change into many guises, as in the film *Kind Hearts and Coronets.*

register visually, I can listen, take in a certain amount, but in many respects I am an invalid and I suppose that's why this important week has left me with less emotion than I would have hoped for. At any rate, so far, there have been no disastrous setbacks, though the serious critics have yet to write their pieces, if indeed they will condescend to do so at all.

This important week has been the one in which I have shown for the first time my oil painting to be appraised by the public. It is something I have long wanted to do and it represents, after the training in later years at the Slade, the result of a year's work in the studio here. During this year, there were days of elation when I really thought I had managed to do something worthwhile, and that I was on a new and interesting track. Of course, there were many failures, but if the "successes" were really successes, then something had been achieved. Now we must see if the successes did amount to anything in the open market. On Monday I came up by an earlier train than intended in order to view the hanging, and to price the pictures (£100 to about £700). It was a great surprise to find my old friends in a new guise, in glittering gold frames against a brilliant white background. They looked very bright, like Japanese paper flowers, and I was not ashamed of them. The gallery people themselves not at all specific or articulate about them, were friendly, enthusiastic, but slightly condescending, perhaps because they are accustomed to selling Bonnards and Boudins for thousands instead of hundreds.

Other reactions I awaited, impatiently, and it is extraordinary how difficult for a painter it is to find anyone to commit himself in a judgement. Everything said is as oblique as in a Pinter play. The press view was fairly pleasant. The questions asked were quite friendly, but the interrogators were more "whos" than "art," so nothing too tricky was broached. Then the opening, more professionally arranged than by any other gallery; they are accustomed to having a party for each show and it is superbly done with lots of various categories, buyers, "dressers," painters, and the effect is good. First on the list to appear was Pam Berry,[1] followed by Evangeline Bruce, a cachet already given, and then the anonymous crowd appeared in which there were a few familiar

[1] Lady Pamela Berry (1914–82), Lady Hartwell. Daughter of the first Earl of Birkenhead. Political hostess, whose husband Michael, Lord Hartnell, was the proprietor and editor in chief of the *Daily* and *Sunday Telegraph*.

faces. Friends would come up: "I've not seen the pictures yet. I'm going to do the rounds and tell you what I think." And then they beat it to the door like a shot rabbit. I would have liked to have heard what Tynan and Connolly thought. Garrett Drogheda[1] was impressed and Hockney said he liked Queen Victoria and that I had painted her as Van Gogh would have painted her. Patrick Procktor[2] also liked her and the funnier canvases. (Is this a clue that I should keep my tongue in my cheek?) I dare say there was a great deal of lurking jealousy. Francis Rose[3] found it difficult to tell me what he thought. He wanted to tell me that the "fuss" in the papers had been out of all proportion and why didn't he succeed. All he said for the moment was, "Well, Cecil, your exhibition shows that you have made a very great endeavour."

As for sales, so far they are not too good, six or eight pictures gone for £2,000. Perhaps it is good, but I must remember that I always knew these were very unsaleable subjects, that sales were not what was intended. One is going to be unhappy if one switches one's sights, suddenly wants success other than what one intended. But by and large, the reception to the pictures is in spite of my innate pessimism, very depleted physical condition, as I had hoped, they have startled a number of people and they have baffled all the friends who never look at modern pictures. They have, so far, not created any violent hitches on the part of the Francis Bacons[4] (perhaps because they have not been enough lauded in the right circles). But for better or for worse Miki Sekers said what I wanted to hear, that he applauded my moving with the times and facing up to the fact, and no longer a young boy indulging in prettiness, that it was the opposite of Oliver Messel, who never moved. Jakie Astor[5] said he admired my guts, my courage. So I suppose if one or two people one respects are impressed then that is all one can hope for, that and the fact that appalling cold douches have not descended (as of yet) and which would make it very hard for me to summon up enough courage to go back to the studio with the intention

[1] Kenneth Tynan, critic, and Cyril Connolly (1903–74), critic, who had been at St. Cyprian's with Cecil, and eleventh Earl of Drogheda, KG (1910–89).

[2] Patrick Procktor (1936–2003), artist.

[3] Sir Francis Rose, Bt (1909–79), wayward artist, who latched on to Cecil in his later years and was continually in some form of scrape, financial or otherwise.

[4] Francis Bacon (1909–92), artist.

[5] Hon. Sir John Astor (1918–2000), son of Viscount Astor and Nancy, Viscountess Astor.

of starting another show. It is perhaps going to be more difficult, now that I have not the most inspiring advice and strength of view of Kin, whom I consulted with throughout many vicissitudes, but perhaps he has sent me on my way, and I must have strength to go it alone.

As Cecil's departure for Barbados approached, he felt that for the first time he had had enough of his country house, not to mention his lingering illness and the long winter. He was still in pain from his shingles.

He flew to Barbados.

WEDNESDAY

It is now a week ago that I left England in that vast torpedo and arrived without any voice and looking so ill and tired that I scared my friends, at that wonderful stage setting designed by Ronnie Tree within a few yards of the sea. Coming around the garden entrance by night, one was suddenly given the most extraordinary stage picture of a vastly tall white coral house with soaring portico and a group sitting at a long stone table lit by candlelight. The surrounding trees were looped with garlands of other trees and parasite orchids grew in the bowls of the grey trunks. Only white and green plants were part of the decor. This gave one a rare frisson, one's remaining energy was summoned, I tried to croak, and soon staggered to bed and to a profound sleep.

Sadly, the week has been preoccupied with my health. I had mistakenly thought that once I arrived in the tropics, attacks of pain would leave me. I slept almost continually, the hot humid air induced sleep all afternoon after a nine-hour night. But I had developed an inner cold. I felt bronchial, still extraordinarily tired, and my pain continued in the right foot. I did nothing but rest and a little gentle sightseeing of the island. The club also designed by Ronnie, the house Oliver [Messel] is building himself, and of course every aspect of Ronnie's great creation, Heron Bay.

But after three days I had to draw stumps, house full for the weekend, I was to move on to Clarissa and Anthony[1] in their newly acquired plantation house. The change was welcome, a short time is enough for the gossip of the

[1] The Earl and Countess of Avon, who had a winter home on Barbados for many years.

The Earl and Countess of Avon at their home in Barbados, January 1966

"platinum strip," of hearing of the latest rows between the Munsters and their guests. The self-conscious chatter palls and at one moment the beach looked like London with the crippled Belsen body of Nell Ilchester and her stick, malproportioned Bert Marlborough[1] with his stick and the monstrosities passing to and from the Colony Club.

The Eden visit therefore came as a great relief and contrast. For these two exceptional people lead a life of almost complete simplicity. The house is almost bare of furniture, painted white with rush matting throughout, the gate-legged tables and chair are of mahogany, there are no attempts at decorations, white muslim curtains, and here in the garden Clarissa looks after the tropical plants while Anthony reads political biographies on the veranda. Or

[1] This was a closely linked set, Margaret (Peggy) Ward (1905–82), married to Count Paul Munster (d. 1968), her sister, Helen (1907–70), widow of the seventh Earl of Ilchester, and Bert, tenth Duke of Marlborough (1897–1972). Bert's son, the eleventh Duke, was first married to Susan Hornby, niece of Peggy Munster and Nell Ilchester.

she is busy with the coloured servants, being a perfectionist about the meals, which consist of local products, native fruits and fish (dolphins, flying fish, pawpaw, gower soup etc.). Neither of them is hurried, both seem completely contented with their quiet life, and it is very charming to see Clarissa, settled happily merely to look after her husband, and for relaxation to read eighteenth-century biographies (Crabbe, the son of the life of his father the poet). Because they have a visitor, three guests are invited for Sunday lunch, a great effort is made.

Then Clarissa drives me through the rows of sugar canes to see other plantation houses, Drax Hall, Clifton Hall, Malvern and Easy Hall. (I am so taken with the charm of this that for two days I envisage living there myself, but even in the moment of euphoria I realise the utter impracticability, and also the fact that I could not afford the vast sums that are asked for even the smallest property here. We witnessed a charming Ronald Firbank scene with coloured people assembled for the passing-out ceremony for a certain sect of fathers at Codrington.

We visited the delightful tombs in the St. John's church where Clarissa said she would like to be buried. Then early to bed, and late to wake, exquisite linen sheets, down pillows and a breakfast with toast and always a new pot of Oxford marmalade. In the vast bathroom always new cakes of soap, exquisite towels and hot water. It may be simple but it is exquisite. And now, after three days of recuperation, I am returning down to the coast feeling very much better than before, even if easily tired by talk or merely standing on my painful foot.

Cecil was pleased to be taken to visit Agnes Ernst Meyer, who was staying in the area with a house party of influential friends. He does not explain who she was. Agnes Ernst (1887–1970) had been a reporter and social activist in her younger days. She worked for the New York Sun *and was sent to interview the photographer Alfred Steichen in 1908. They became great friends.*

Agnes married Eugene Meyer, a Wall Street banker, who became Governor of the Federal Reserve, organiser of the Reconstruction Finance Corporation and the first president of the World Bank. He and Agnes were co-owners of the Washington Post, *and were the parents of the celebrated Kay Graham.*

They had a large and important collection of art.

MRS. EUGENE MEYER—BARBADOS FEBRUARY 1966

Ronnie took the Linlithgows[1] and myself to have a drink with a neighbour, something that happens regularly on this cocktail strip. But I was looking forward to this particular visit as it was to be to the house that the Heinzes[2] own, which was the scene of an appalling fight with Oliver Messel. But more interesting was the fact that the present occupant was an aged widow of whom I had [heard] great things. Nor was I disappointed. We were introduced to a group in a patio-like room (where the wind blew a bit too freshly). The Chief Justice of the USA, Earl Warren and his mossy little wife, Mr. and Mrs. Drew Pearson[3] etc. Then lying full length on a chaise longue, wearing an apricot and gold viridian negligee, a large white-haired, fat, doll-faced lady with thick spectacles and a deep voice, who immediately established herself as a great character.

From the moment of catching sight of her, I knew myself to be drawn to her, and I was fortunate that she asked me to draw up a chair beside her. For three-quarters of an hour I was entranced by the wise and jolly old lady who, in spite of a recent cataract operation and few visible teeth, gave me the impression of being at the height of her powers.

We talked of Steichen.[4] I told her that his pictures never "dated," unlike the work of other photographers, that I had been vastly influenced by him, but that he had never had any use for me, that he had disliked me from the beginning. I told my new friend that unlike Steichen who started life as a painter, I hoped to end as one. She then said, "There was a time in my life when I had to make the decision to have my portrait done. I did not like Sargent and although I was a great friend of Brancusi, I went to Desprain.[5] He called me to

[1] Charles, third Marquess of Linlithgow (1912–87), and his second wife, Judith Baring.

[2] H. J. ("Jack") Heinz II (1908–87), chairman of the international food company, H. J. Heinz, famed for its "57 varieties," and his second wife, Drue Maher, a considerable benefactress of literature and the arts, whom he married in 1953.

[3] Earl Warren (1891–1974), Chief Justice of the United States Supreme Court 1953–69, and his wife, the former Mrs. Nina Meyers, and Drew Pearson (1897–1969), columnist and radio commentator, who wrote a daily column called "The Washington Merry-Go-Round" from 1932, and his second wife, Luvie Moore.

[4] Edward Jean Steichen (1879–1973), painter turned photographer.

[5] John Singer Sargent (1856–1925), portrait and landscape painter; Constantin Brancusi (1876–1957), Romanian abstract sculptor; and Marius de Zayas (1880–1961), art critic and gallery owner.

see him. He told me to take off my hat and asked, 'Do you always wear your hair flat like that with a band of ribbon on it?' 'Yes.' 'Then I'll do your portrait. Your head has an affinity with the Greek.' He made his masterpiece of me. But imagine Brancusi's feelings. However, it stimulated him to do his best work. It was quite abstract and nothing like me, but he said it was my portrait, a huge, vast, magnificent piece of black marble."

Mrs. Meyer's humanity came through every sentence she composed, sometimes haltingly, but never not believed in. She talked of her friendship with Rodin.[1] He always made passes at his women friends and when Mrs. Meyer rebuffed him gently, saying she wanted none of that, Rodin seemed so relieved, and he would take her to the Louvre and teach her all he knew about works of art. Rodin's life was very turbulent, Rilke[2] madly in love with him, but Rilke too was always in a turmoil.

Rodin had wanted her to pose in the nude, riding a charger and waving a spear as the head of the Amazons. But she couldn't do a thing like that. She was far too modest. "I wish you *had* done that! Don't you regret that you didn't?" "I never regret anything that I know I could not do," she said.

This all happened in 1908, and what a wonderful time that was when the Russian Ballet, with Nijinsky[3] and Pavlova, came to Paris. Once she was lunching alone at a restaurant and a Goddess of Grace walked through the room. "My God, who is that?" she asked the head waiter. "That's Pavlova." Never have I seen anyone move like that! And Chaliapin,[4] at the height of his powers, was singing *Boris Godunov* in clothes of incredible magnificence lent by the Tsar. One night they were entering a restaurant for supper, and they noticed a group of Saltimbanques sitting around a fire eating their evening meal, and looking like Picassos of the Blue Period. "You must excuse me a little, while I join them," said Chaliapin. "You see I used to be just like them, one of them." I said I thought that romantic, touching. She said, "It shows what heart he had." She talked of the early years when she collected pictures. "I bought Cézannes because I liked them. I would have bought Van Gogh but my

[1] Auguste Rodin (1840–1916), sculptor.

[2] Rainer Maria Rilke (1875–1926), sensitive poet and author.

[3] Vaslav Nijinsky (1888–1950), Diaghilev's principal dancer.

[4] Feodor Chaliapin (1873–1938), Russian operatic bass singer of exceptional power who made his London debut in *Boris Godunov* in 1913.

husband didn't like them, never admired Gauguin, too tropical. It's never any good to buy anything for an investment. What I bought for $2,000 is now worth a million dollars today, and I can't afford to leave them to my children, so they have to go to the National Gallery." But today she didn't know of any young new painter whom she liked. Perhaps it was difficult for young artists today. In the eighteenth century you saw that a chair, a table, a window had the imprint of its time. Now there was no stability, dealers approached them with fantastic offers, then soon dropped them dead. They needed guidance, or at any rate an understanding of what present thought was about. That was why she was putting her house at Mt. Kisco to the use of a collection of physicists, scientists, writers, poets and politicians who could exchange ideas.

One weekend Robert Oppenheimer[1] was staying with her, and she asked him what he thought she should do with this great unwieldy house. "Just what you are doing." Having I believe, been responsible with her late husband for running several Washington newspapers and magazines, she is a natural executive.

"Do have some of that excellent Danish cheese." She told me that for the councils at Mt. Kisco she would have a marvellous chef and three magnificent meals a day. She called the coloured boy to give her another Scotch and soda, and she chain-smoked cigarettes. She obviously has a relish for enjoyment, and her life of hard work and excitement has left her with the complexion of a young woman. Although her interests are so much wider than mine, it was easy to understand her enjoyment of subjects that are quite closed to me, for so great is her mind that she is able to simplify everything to the essentials that one can comprehend. If she says of someone else that he is "great" you know that she speaks of an equal. She marvelled at the sincerity of the TV interview with Oppenheimer. He was not afraid of silent pauses, of talking slowly. All the world could watch that man thinking.

Apropos Anthony Eden, she used to be a friend, but was politically so opposed to him since Suez that she did not want to meet him for she knew it would be impossible to avoid a discussion. That would be sad.

[1] J. Robert Oppenheimer (1904–67), director and Professor of Physics, Institute for Advanced Study, Princeton, New Jersey 1947–66. He directed the development of the first atomic weapons during the Second World War, but got into trouble over the policy on hydrogen bombs. He was an advisor on the question of using atomic bombs on Japan.

Only for the sake of politesse did I yield my chair to another guest, and was very happy when Mrs. Meyer said, "I shall tell Steichen, when he comes to stay with me next week, that I have met you and that you're a very nice person." When a few moments later, Ronnie summoned us with his car to return to dinner, the banality and crassness of the Linlithgow conversation came as such a shock that I could hardly be civil. In fact, Mrs. Meyer had put the cocktail strip into perspective, and in our house only the young Simon Parker Bowles[1] seemed to understand at all when I tried to explain about the force of personality of this great old woman.

THE "PLATINUM STRIP"

The rich D. of Marlborough, Linlithgow, Rothschilds[2] sponge on Ronnie Tree's hospitality while they rent, at vast sums, their own homes in the sun.

Victor R.: "Why should I live in my own house when I can live free at Ronnie's?"

The P. Munsters, so snobbish, that for the privilege of having a duke to stay (the decrepit Bert) they are willing to move out of their own bedroom.

On the beach the meeting of the lame and the halt, like Lourdes, Nell Ilchester, a Belsen figure, and Bert, with their sticks.

PRODUCTION NOTE FOR A PLAY

Clarissa, patiently waiting for her telephone call, stretches as far as wire will hold, towards her bag, placed on floor. Her head is upside down in bag, with receiver at her ear. When she is asked, "Please, who shall I say is calling?" "Lady Avon. A-V-O-N. Yes, I'll hold."

The uniform belief, the certainty, the knowledge by their owners of the importance in a name. Not for one moment does Bert forget he is a duke.

[1] Simon Parker Bowles (b. 1941), now the owner of Green's Restaurant in St. James's.

[2] Victor, third Lord Rothschild (1910–90), zoologist and head of counter-espionage at M15 during the Second World War, first head of the Think Tank. His biography, *Elusive Rothschild*, was written by Kenneth Rose (2003).

In a manner which he knows is "offhand" yet pregnant with importance, the Marquess confides into the telephone, it is "Charlie Linlithgow—Linlithgow speaking."

No one here seems to realise that this group of survivors from another age is now quite aged, and they are, in reality, the old contemptibles, and they have to rely on one another, for few younger people could afford such long air journeys and such high stakes at gin and bridge.

The convalescence at Barbados has helped me more than I could realise. I arrived without a voice, frightened my friends by my appearance and for days on end I did little but sleep, and whenever I awoke to look in the bathroom glass, the reflection scared me. An old, tired, ugly man looked back at me, with red eyes and desperately drawn, as if on his last legs. Never before have I looked so old, so beastly, and the beastliness of proportion. My nose looked enormous, my eyes small and red.

After Barbados, Cecil joined Fulco di Verdura and Tom Parr for a holiday in Grenada. Verdura was recovering from an accident, having two years previously broken both his legs and more. He and Tom Parr hired a boat to explore the Little Grenadine Islands. There were problems with the crew and the weather was so rough that, soon after joining them, Cecil was "not only sick, but terrified." This storm over, St. Vincent provided them with a day and a half of pleasure, and as they reached calmer waters, Cecil revelled in blue skies that reminded him of Poussin, changed to Monet and then turned into abstract de Koonings, and even Turners.

They arrived on dry land and stayed at the Calabash Hotel, where they witnessed the traditional Carnival. This Cecil enjoyed, but his blistered lip and sunburn soon gave him "a jaundiced view of life."

Presently he returned to Palm Beach, on his way home.

The return to the luxury of Palm Beach has been a great solace and the days of doing nothing but sleep and swim and eat and gossip *must* have been beneficial, and my hosts could not have been more kind and understanding, allowing me to remain of an afternoon for five or six hours on end in my palatial bedroom.

And then he went to Philadelphia, and New York, which afforded him a few moments of amusement.

My amusement at Sam Green[1] (of the half-beard) inviting me to the party of the angry lesbian sculptor Kyorssa [sic].[2] "There won't be many people, not too crowded, as she's not all that popular."

The Wrightsmans, Laskers,[3] making fun of their efforts to help the deserving. How to a group of millionaires the chairman of the committee said, "Now that we have raised all this money we must go out and try to find some paralysed children"—or again—"We must thank these little orphans, for without them this great effort would never have been made."

Mercedes de Acosta was one of Cecil's oldest friends. Between them they had battled for many years with the cruel whims of Garbo with whom they had both been obsessed for many years. Now she was dying.

Mercedes de Acosta is dying by slow degrees. On the telephone she mumbled that three times she thought she was dying but just out of cantankerousness she had fought to live. But she cannot last long. I told Greta that she must, at least, send a p.c. Greta, upset, said, "Why must you bring up such a subject. I've got enough to cope with. I'm in trouble enough! I can't tell you what it is (I discovered a relation is ill in hospital, she motors each day to see him) but it's enough! I don't want any more troubles!" I have said before so did not repeat that I thought she would have terrible conscience when Mercedes did die.

When I complained to a friend of Garbo's behaviour, she said, "Well she has always made her own rules. They are not other people's rules, but she sticks to them." And this is true.

[1] Samuel Adams Green (b. 1940). This is the first mention of Sam in Cecil's diaries. See biographical note in *The Unexpurgated Beaton*, pp. 52–3.

[2] Chryssa (b. 1933), Greek artist, born Athens, who moved to the USA, 1954. She created the giant work, *The Gates to Times Square*, which stood in that square and are now in Buffalo.

[3] Mary Woodard Reinhardt (1900–94), New York industrial designer, who married in 1940 Albert Davis Lasker (1879–1952), already deceased by this time. Albert Lasker was a Texan and the founder of the modern advertising movement. His motto was, "Advertising is salesmanship in print." They were immensely rich and created the Albert and Mary Lasker Foundation.

No good trying to reform her, or change her. The only way is to be sweet to her. As usual, the visit was abortive, she was never free, she was not in a good condition. Her cough continued. She would have liked to "come round" but not just yet. She has had enough of Cécile de R., so sees nobody. Her formal apartment, in which she receives nobody, is more ridiculous than ever. Sad, but one cannot go on grieving. There are too many alternatives.

Amid the New York chatter it was so delightful to hear Sachie Sitwell's[1] talk, so witty, he described his passion as a young army officer for the ballet. Each evening he came up from Aldershot to see Karsavina, Nijinsky, and often he would hang around Diaghilev, who would find Sachie in a great state of agitation looking at his watch and saying, "I must get back to Aldershot by the midnight train." "Aldershot? Aldershot? *Qui c'est cette Aldershot? Elle est ta maîtresse?*" (What a wonderful name for a *grande cocotte*!)

A theme that begins to appear in these diaries is Cecil's disenchantment with Truman Capote. This was partly due to jealousy over his enormous success with the publication of In Cold Blood *and, as an extension of that, his annoyance that Truman was taking himself too seriously.*

TRUMAN

Success has changed him. He looks like a tycoon, thickset, well-dressed, no longer the little gnome of *Other Voices.*[2] (He says, "Bunny? Bunny? Why does Johnnie Ryan call me Bunny? I'm an asp!")

Truman has just moved into a new "luxury apartment." I do not like it. It is the new world, no one in sight, every hyper-gadget, a great view, but no personality. T.'s apartment has been decorated by a decorator. I miss his touch. This is expensive without looking more than ordinary. To have such a success as he has (*Cold Blood*)[3] is like having a major operation. Mercifully much of

[1] Sir Sacheverell Sitwell, Bt (1897–1988), poet and writer, the youngest of the three Sitwells.

[2] Truman Capote (1924–84) had a sudden infant prodigy success with his first novel, *Other Voices, Other Rooms* (1948), based in no small measure on the languorously posed portrait of the young author on the back of the jacket.

[2] *In Cold Blood,* Capote's "true account of a multiple murder and its consequences," the story of a wealthy Kansas farmer and his family who were brutally murdered and the two men who were hanged for it, was published in January 1966. It enjoyed instant success.

my jealousy and rancour was dispersed with a nice dinner we had together when we exchanged confidences. When talking of a trip to Mexico with Peter [Watson] I said, "That was so long ago, that was the beginning of my life." He knew why I said that. "You mean that was the first time you'd shared your life with someone." He talked of his twenty years with Jack [Dunphy],[1] how their habits have changed. They are greater, calmer friends, but not more remote. Truman goes off in his Jaguar, perhaps for two hours, or two days, but motors along the speedway for two weeks, stopping at motels, dead tired, takes four whiskies and sleeping pills to the bathtub, almost falls asleep in it, then on next morning. This is the only way he feels calm.

Switzerland makes him restless and he feels ill and has been a lot in hospitals. I secretly feel T. is in a bad state and may not last long. He has become a real neurotic case, best at talking about writing in which the quality of persuasiveness is the most important. Discipline, construction, is unimportant, but most of all is to create a mood to convince your readers of what you are writing.

APRIL 1966

The novelist Evelyn Waugh (1903–66) died in the lavatory of his Somerset home, Combe Florey, on Easter Sunday, 10 April 1966. Cecil and he had been at Heath Mount School in Hampstead, and on the first day of his first term, Cecil had been subjected to the indignity of Waugh menacing him and sticking pins into him. There was a lasting froideur *between them for the rest of their days.*

BROADCHALKE 11 APRIL 1966

So Evelyn Waugh is in his coffin. Died of snobbery. He did not wish to be a man of letters. It did not satisfy him to be counted the master of English prose. He wanted to be a duke and that he could never be, hence a life of disappointment and sham. For he would never give up. He would play the aristocrat. He

[1] Jack Dunphy (1915–92), Truman Capote's lifelong companion. A novelist and the author of *Dear Genius* (1987), an account of his life with Capote. They met in 1948.

would drink brandy and port, and keep a full cellar. He was not a gourmet, like Cyril [Connolly], but insisted on good living and cigars as being typical of the aristocratic way of life. He became pompous at twenty, and developed his pomposity to the point of having a huge stomach and an ear trumpet at forty-five.

Now that he is dead I cannot hate him, cannot really feel he was wicked, in spite of his cruelty, his bullying, his caddishness. But he was possessed, from time to time, and when having appeared rather charming and appreciative and even funny (though my hackles rose in his presence) he could suddenly shock by being overcome by a devil and doing completely devilish things. His snobbery, his cruelty, his bullying, was at its worst at White's. Here he impersonated an aristocrat in its most loathsome forms, bullied newcomers or non-members, and was altogether intolerable. But a few loyal friends saw through the pretence and were fond of him.

We had a row, never made a truce, and although I forgave him long past for being the first to bully me at my day school (the publishers cut out the bit about his baring his black pitted teeth in a further effect of frightening me).[1] He was my contemporary, born within a few miles of one another (I in Hampstead, he in Golders Green) and he has recurred in my life at intervals so that his death does come as a shock, in the empty phrase "Gives one to wonder," a phrase that prevents one being more specific about the meaning of death, its lack of meaning. It does not give me a twinge of regret or remorse. I am pleased not to see him again, but I am given a shock to realise how unnecessary it is to have died so comparatively young. Or is it not so young to die at 62? He had no real illness, just became aged through volition. He liked playing an elderly part. Talent in abundance and brilliance, a clear, quick brain, and sensitivity, even, of a sort, so much of a sham, so that the sham took over, and a sham elderly man has gone unnecessarily to his grave ten or fifteen years earlier than would have been usual. Oh, shades of Dr. Grenfell and the Heath Mount days.[2]

. . .

[1] Happily this was reinstated in the present editor's biography of Cecil, pp. 13–14, along with Waugh's version: "Our persecution went no further than sticking pins into him and we were soundly beaten for so doing."

[2] J. S. Granville Grenfell (1964–1929), headmaster of Heath Mount School.

PS Have been unfair. It seems Evelyn dies through sleeplessness. The drugs he took to send him to sleep at night became stronger and stronger, and to feel well when he was awake during the day, his drinks became stronger and stronger, with the result that his heart gave out. Returning from church yesterday, Easter Sunday, he had an attack and his unhappy life was over.

This from E. M. Forster, *The Longest Journey:*[1] "Between Rickie and Gerald there lay a shadow that darkens life more often than we suppose. The bully and his victim never quite forget their first relations. They meet in clubs and country houses, and clap one another on the back; but in both the memory is green of a more strenuous day when they were boys together."

Somerset Maugham said that he knew four months after his death he would never be heard of again. What a shock it would be for him to discover that his lifetime secret homosexuality would be the subject of articles, books and plays. His nephew Robin has "cashed in," as have Beverley Nichols, Godfrey Winn, and now Noël Coward with a sincere and rather ham-fisted play he has written about the romance with Gerald Haxton so that even Mother *Times* has given the names.[2] In fact, the romance with this drunken "nothing" has blossomed into a sort of bugger's *Tristan und Isolde.*

Cecil then went to photograph George Painter, who had lately produced the second volume of his biography of Marcel Proust (volume 1 in 1959, volume 2 in 1965). Cecil was fascinated by Proust, read both volumes and was intrigued to meet the author. Painter was assistant-keeper of fifteenth-century books at the British Museum, a post he occupied from 1954 to 1974. Cecil went to see him on 14 April 1966.

GEORGE PAINTER

A real angel of a man. At first his appearance is a shock with his shock-head of greying Indian-black hair, his roughly shaven skin, his warts, his unbrushed

[1] *The Longest Journey,* published in 1907, by E. M. Forster (1895–1970).

[2] Robin, second Viscount Maugham (1916–81), wrote *Somerset and All the Maughams* (Heinemann, 1966); Beverley Nichols (1898–1983) wrote *A Case of Human Bondage* (1966); Godfrey Winn (1908–71), wrote *The Infirm Glory* (1966–7) and Noël Coward (1899–1973) starred in his play, *A Song at Twilight,* which opened at the Queen's Theatre on 14 April 1966 with Irene Worth and Lilli Palmer also in the cast. Gerald Haxton (1896–1944) was Maugham's secretary and lover.

George Painter, Proust's biographer

shapeless suit, dusty shoes and runtish body. But after two seconds one is a victim of his charm, which emanates from his goodness and his sincerity. It comes as a shock to meet people who are completely pure and innocent, who have no truck with the world and therefore none of its dross rubs off on them. You know he is pure sterling and you at once throw away all reservations, all judgement and abandon yourself to the unique pleasure of the company of someone who lives in a world apart from buses, taxis, snobbery, stop press, but in a world of written words, a world of great minds and sensitive thoughts.

Welcoming me and pardoning my lateness, he quoted Charles Lamb. He told me he was beginning to write about Chateaubriand, but that he could not free himself of Proust. "It is impossible after eighteen years to get rid of him. He still absorbs me completely. He has devoured me. I am a wreck as a result of him. I am so tired that I am nothing. I cannot throw him off, yet I cannot write any more about him. I am drained to the last drop, and when I wrote about his death, I was unable to sleep for nights. I was ill. I identify myself with him so completely."

And how extraordinary to think of this rather farouche, simple young man immersing himself all these years in Proust and his world! He is so homespun and rough, so pure yeast rather than truffle. He is obviously bone poor, has no interest in money, commutes to the country where I am certain he eats very poorly, looked after by his dear wife. But he does not invite sympathy. He would never think of himself as anything but fulfilled and happy. Yet from an outsider's point of view one longs to give him a present of something he could not afford himself.

One wants to make him into something different and therein one makes a mistake, for he has made his life the way he wants it, and it is obvious that all his confreres at the British Museum have enormous respect and affection for him. I was in the usual quandary when taking photographs of knowing how to divide my attention between concentrating on the camera and listening to my subject. So much that Painter was saying was lost. Yet he was alive and my camera was able to record his enthusiasm. However, when the photography was over, we leant against the bookshelves in the badly partitioned-off room he has in the Museum, and talked about Angus Wilson who loves teaching at the University of East Anglia.[1] "But then he loves the young—I hate them!" I asked him about his thrown-away remark in volume 2 about Lantelme[2] being a lesbian. Was that possible? He explained, "Misia Sert told me that Lantelme came to see her and said, 'You want [George] Edwardes back, don't you? Well, you can have your husband on two conditions. I want all your jewellery, and when you've given it up to me, then you'll have to sleep with me.' "

He talked of the effort of writing his book. If there are good passages in it they have been composed as a result of hours, days, weeks of work. "Nothing has come easily. I have put everything into it and I'm a shell. I'm hoping later on to go, for the first time, with my dear wife, to Italy but at the moment I'm too tired to move."

Yet his eyes sparkle with the innocence and brilliance that you only find in pure, unharried, childlike people. There is no pressure, no hurry or

[1] (Sir) Angus Wilson (1913–92), novelist, was Professor of English Literature at the University of East Anglia 1966–78.

[2] Geneviève Lantelme (1887–1911), prostitute turned actress, painted by Boldini. In *The Glass of Fashion* (1954), Cecil described her at the theatre as "with the huge mouth of a carp, her hair a mass of frizz . . . slouched so low over the rim of the box that her pearls fell in cascades to the light brackets below" (p. 58). She drowned in the Rhine in mysterious circumstances.

flurry. In his moth and cinnamon–coloured world of the [British] Museum, he is remote from all the limitless tiresome little eventualities that crowd other people's lives, and which exhaust and deplete them. His exhaustion has been brought on entirely by intellectual effort. Now that he has made his effort and before he gets involved in the next, it is time to pamper and nourish him, but one knows that he would stand for only a very little of that treatment, that he is above thinking in terms of comfort, let alone luxury.

In April Cecil visited North Africa, staying in Tunis with Leo and Edwina d'Erlanger, then visiting Tripoli as a guest of Anna Maria Cicogna. Then, in May, Lady Diana Cooper came for the weekend, motored down by Simon Fleet, who spent much of this year driving her about. The visit inspired Cecil to write, "The trail she leaves behind her makes one realise the follies of trying to do her a kindness." Then it was Whitsun and Cecil looked back over the previous week.

WHITSUN, REDDISH 29 MAY 1966

Even if someone who is working on a project with me is staying in the house, I am not able to work with the same concentration as if I am here alone. Last weekend José [Pradera][1] spent all his days working out a solution to putting the three sets of *Lady Windermere's Fan* on a revolve.[2] By the end of the weekend we had managed to provide (in rough) models for the three acts. This a very quick job (even though I suffered at the constant alterations to the ballroom) but by the time José left, I felt the time was ripe for me to settle down to a real effort. But by now time was short. The three gouache "perspectives" took all the morning before my departure, leaving me only a very rushed while in which to rush out of the studio between rainstorms, to cut lilacs and peonies and put them around the house in celebration of the following day's visit of 40 blue-haired American tourists (enthusiasts of the Bath Museum) before catching, by a whisker, the train to London.

[1] José Pradera, theatre designer.

[2] Cecil had agreed to undertake sets and costumes for a new production of *Lady Windermere's Fan,* unwisely attempting to repeat his 1945 stage triumph. It played at the Phoenix Theatre from 13 October 1966 until April 1967, with Wilfrid Hyde White, Ronald Lewis, Coral Browne, Isabel Jeans and Juliet Mills in the cast.

This was a crowded visit, most of the time spent visiting doctor, osteopath and exercise woman (Gaffran)[1] in an attempt to rid myself of the lingering remains of shingles. But in between there were other engagements (a lunch by Weidenfeld for, it is said, his future mother-in-law. He is tapping the Whitney millions).[2] A lunch for Francis Rose and, unbelievably, his fiancée,[3] (not bad, a nurse by nature, an old-fashioned showgirl of the thirties, who will cosset him), and a visit, very disturbing, to St. George's Hospital to see Maud Nelson,[4] now having recovered from desperate illness enough to make plans for her future existence. To find myself with the old and sick, the ugly, the sad, was most distressing, and makes one realise one's good fortune.

Then at night there were three pleasant engagements, the two new short Coward plays,[5] with Ann Fleming, which we found unpardonably below standard. Then two embassy dinners. The Italians honouring E. M. Forster with a gold medal for his having, in early days, written about Italy in a favourable light. The Guidottis[6] are both extremely civilised, highly cultivated beings. He knows literature in many languages and is able to say Russian is no good in any other language, or Shakespeare possible, except German. They had gathered together a most delightful assembly of literary friends, Sebastian Sprott, the first undergraduate I knew to wear a scarlet tie, William Plomer, Joe Ackerley, Cecil Day-Lewis, Kenneth and Jane Clark (she a little worse for wear) and the Henry Moores.[7]

Soon the door opened and two neighbours from Broadchalke were announced: the William Goldings,[8] she sailing in, self-conscious but defiant in

[1] Charlotte Gaffran, masseuse based in Notting Hill Gate.

[2] George Weidenfeld (b. 1919), Cecil's publisher, later a life peer. He was on the point of marrying Sandra Payson Meyer. They were divorced in 1976.

[3] Beryl Norris, widow of Squadron-Leader Basil Montefiore Davis. They were married in 1967.

[4] Maud Nelson (d. 1969), Cecil's secretary for many years. See biographical note, pp. 377–78.

[5] On 25 April, *Shadows of the Evening* and *Come into the Garden, Maud* opened at the Queen's Theatre, completing Noël Coward's new sequence of plays as part of the National Theatre's West End season.

[6] Gastone Guidotti, Italian Ambassador in London 1964–8.

[7] Sebastian Sprott (1897–1971), a fellow undergraduate at Cambridge; William Plomer (1903–73), writer, later president of the Poetry Society; Joe Ackerley (1896–1967), writer and literary editor, author of *My Father and Myself* (1968); Cecil Day-Lewis (1904–72), author and later Poet Laureate; Henry Moore (1898–1986) and his wife, Irene Radetzky.

[8] William Golding (1911–93), author of *Lord of the Flies* (1954), and his wife, Ann Brookfield. They lived at Ebble Thatch, Bowerchalke.

a long trailing spangled gossamer [gown] with long gloves and beehive hairdo, he looking as if in hired clothes from Whiteleys. The last to make a theatrical entrance with a cane was pie-eyed, pissed, Christabel Aberconway.[1] The two Cecils sat together and he struck many a harmonious chord. On my left a Culme-Seymour sister of Drogo Montagu,[2] a difficult, dangerous character, but interesting if one refused to be bullied by her.

Huge decorated salmon were "chefed" by an Italian boy who misguidedly came to see us about getting a job as a cook, and when told we wanted a houseman begged not to let on that he'd come to see me, otherwise he'd be sacked. Rows of small spring flowers, badly arranged, stretched to the Ambassador (I felt sorry for him sitting between the two drunken ladies, their hair awry) to the Ambassadress with the adorable little old hero of the occasion, who held out in the most pointed, small girl's hand the recently acquired golden coin. "How can I wear it? Must it be pierced, and hung on a chain or ribbon?" he asked. "Your hand is the perfect setting for it," I remarked wishing to give a true compliment. "But I want to eat!" The coin was dropped on the floor, a scuffle. Morgan will never grow up. His arrival in London this morning was typical. It was arranged that he should arrive from Cambridge by a certain train, arriving at Waterloo, where in state he would be met by the Ambassador. It was a great day, great occasion. But Morgan, accompanied by Joe Ackerley, got into the wrong train at Cambridge and they found themselves in a slow one arriving at St. Pancras (?), Morgan decided it was not helpful to get rattled, but those sorts of decisions are not easy to abide by.

The dinner party continued as the waiters brought forth the routine gala foods and wines. Mrs. Golding had eaten most of the meal in her gloves, but now had relaxed enough to take them off. Christabel drunkenly was grabbing at the floral decor munching her teeth like a cow the cud. The women left and I had an innings next to Morgan with Henry Moore, pink-faced and healthy, holding the fort. He is a remarkable natural phenomenon, completely

[1] Christabel Macnaghten (1890–1970), author of *The Story of Mr. Korah,* married (1910) second Lord Aberconway. A friend of Rex Whistler. His brother Laurence wrote of her "she combined in wealthy middle age a mirror-polished poise with the steel-hard shrewdness of the sleuth."

[2] Lady Faith Montagu (1911–83), married secondly (1948), Sir Michael Culme-Seymour, Bt, of Rockingham Castle.

unspoilt by his enormous success. He is one of England's greatest exports, together with whisky. He last year made £300,000. Out of this he is allowed to keep £7,000, and his wife and daughter have to pay tax on any gift of sculpture that he may make them. Henry remarked on how rewarding it must be that Morgan had become so recognised. Gently Morgan answered, "Yes, it is good after so long to know that one's early efforts have given pleasure and one [is] still alive."

Henry complimented him on having made one remark that like very few others had always influenced him. He had always felt the truth of the remark: if the choice were for me to fight for my country or my friend, I would choose my friend. This has never been said before. "No, never so crudely," answered Morgan. Henry then asked what other remarks had influenced him. Morgan shut his eyes as if to go to sleep and quoted Michelangelo. Henry agreed with Michelangelo when he said that a piece of sculpture was good if you could roll it down a hill without it being broken. He himself was tremendously influenced by Voltaire's "You must cultivate your garden" and also by a book on Goethe he had lately read. He talked of the stress of his work. He became restless if he took more than a ten-day holiday. "But surely there is no dateline for a sculpture?" I asked in my ignorance. "You have to keep at it. Otherwise other people will be held up in the process, and it's a slow job. While I was tap tapping in my garden two country people the other side of the hedge stopped to watch. Suddenly one said 'Tap tap and nothing happens' and walked on."

Henry asked compassionately of Morgan's boyfriend Bob.[1] "He is a wonderful person, a good man, to be a probationer like that he must be a good man!" "Yes," replied Morgan. "It was a wonderful thing when I met him. He was just an ordinary policeman. I met him at the boat race (I think he said) and it was the best piece of luck. It sometimes happens. Has it happened to you?" I told of my meeting in the San Francisco night bar with Kin how desperate my overtures were, how each remark was even more stupid than the last, and how badly received they were by Kin. "But those halting beginnings led to so much else. It's wonderfully lucky when those things happen, and they

[1] Bob Buckingham, a police constable. The relationship survived Buckingham's marriage in 1932, and Forster died at their home in Coventry.

are less likely to happen later in life. You are very lucky. It's wonderful when those things happen."

Henry Moore had to leave early. "We have an hour and a half's drive back home." But the expedition had been worthwhile for it was a rare occasion for him, as indeed it was for all of us.

The following night at the Spanish embassy was an entirely different affair, elevated above the grand society Princess Margaret level by the playing of the grand old man Segovia[1] with his little sugar-mice fingers nimbly twitching over the steel strands of his guitar. I sat next to Lady Zia Wernher, who yesterday won the Derby.[2] She seems vague about the money involved, but has to pay £20,000 out of the £75,000 that she has won. The horse will be valuable for breeding purposes until he is twenty. Having made an effect with her I then shocked her by telling her that Lord Sefton[3] bored the pants off me and that I thought the young men of today with long hair were quite splendid.

It was with a longing for work and relaxation in the country that Eileen and I took first class tickets to Salisbury for what we both hope more than for anything, for sunshine and warmth.

SUNDAY, 29 MAY 1966

We have been more than lucky thus far. The sun is brilliant, the trees miraculous and the garden at last blooming with lilies of the valley, Nelly Moser, *Gloire de Dijon* and the last of the lilacs.

Cecil enjoyed "the glorious golden spell of sun," continued with his painting and was even able to snooze in the afternoon before resuming work at night.

[1] Andrés Segovia (1893–1987), Spanish concert guitarist, brought up in Granada, who came to England as a young man.

[2] Lady Zia Wernher (1892–1977), daughter of Grand Duke Michael of Russia, married to Sir Harold Wernher, Bt (1893–1973) of Luton Hoo. She won the 1966 Derby with her horse, Charlottown, ridden by "Scobie" Breasley. She was the leading owner in 1966, winning £78,075.

[3] The seventh Earl of Sefton (1898–1972), a racing peer and part of the Duke of Windsor's set who remained a friend after the Abdication.

5 JUNE 1966

I wish that I possessed the ability to make my way with the ordinary run of humanity in the way that Eileen does. I haven't the knack and must perforce listen to reports second-hand. Her stories of the backstage in the servants' world are positively dramatic.

Of their lies and dishonesties to one another, I am appalled, but more often am I amused by their wroughty humour. Our "butler" [Ray Gurton] at present in London has come from a spell with Peter Sellers and his wife.[1] He was paid £25 a week but never had a moment off as even when in one of his many cars Sellers would telephone to Ray: "Go up to nanny and tell her she's sacked. She's a cow." At three in the morning: "We're on our way home. We're passing through Berkeley Square now. See that hot soup is ready for us in seven minutes."

He has become accustomed to the violent rows, the hysteria and the bad manners, and he finds our household somewhat dull in comparison. Nevertheless there are moments. But he tells Eileen of the Sellerses and the Snowdons, and he does not think much of either party. Once Sellers was having lighting for some sculpture installed in the garden and asked Tony's advice which he was giving when Princess Margaret, sucking at a long cigarette holder, sidled up and asked, "Don't you think it would be better if," to which Tony answered her by telling her to piss off.

THEATRE DESIGN

Each time I'm asked to do the decor for a play or a ballet I am again under the misapprehension that the job can be done in a short space of time. I am admittedly one of the quickest, make up my mind and stick to it, unlike Oliver [Messel], who dithers for ever (and succeeds in developing an astonishing sense of detail). Even so I forget how much time has been spent not only in argument, conference and fittings, to say nothing of rehearsals, lighting etc., but the

[1] Peter Sellers (1925–80), film star of many guises and erstwhile Goon, had married, in 1964, the Swedish film actress Britt Ekland. They were divorced in 1969.

actual putting down of one's ideas on paper, and fitting them to become part of a composite whole is a wearisome and worrying process. I am less impatient than I used to be (I was extremely difficult in my pent-up enthusiasm when I started on this career and must have been a tiresome collaborator, for I would allow of no compromise). Even so I am on edge until the designs are on paper.

The present *Lady Windermere's Fan* has taken quite a lot of time already, and the director [Anthony Quayle][1] has not yet returned from filming in Italy to look at the drawings. But José has spent two long weekends here, put in a great deal of time in London, and I have been for six weeks thumbing through old magazines and making notes. I am hoping that by the end of the day I will have finished the three "furnished" perspectives and that then other aspects of the job will come along intermittently to allow for other activities.

THEATRE

JULY 1966

When John Perry[2] rang to know if I'd like to design a new *Lady Windermere,* I thought what fun. That'll mean doing a few new sketches. When as before I had cheated and made the costumes more Edwardian than Victorian (a fact taken up by James Agate)[3] this time I would stress the archaic, even Knossos, look of the Victorians. A jolly time would be had by all.

John seemed surprised at my acceptance, as well he might, when work started and the snags one by one cropped up. Casting is always disappointing. Even the biggest theatre names cannot get what they want. Substitutes are disappointing. Then the substitute starts being difficult. I'd hoped Vivien Leigh[4] would be Mrs. Erlynne, but her substitute, Coral Browne,[5] was soon on the telephone in tears. She had been shown her costume designs by Berman. She

[1] (Sir) Anthony Quayle (1913–89), actor and director.

[2] John Perry (1906–95), former boyfriend of John Gielgud, he managed H. M. Tennent for "Binkie" Beaumont, also his boyfriend.

[3] James Agate (1877–1947), theatre critic.

[4] Vivien Leigh (1913–67), actress and film star, by then divorced from Laurence Olivier. Cecil rather disliked her on account of a long ago row with the Oliviers.

[5] Coral Browne (1913–91), Australian actress remembered for many raunchy asides. Cecil had had an affair with her in 1941–2. She said of him, "He was a very passionate, very ardent man and quite unlike the way people normally think of him."

couldn't wear red satin. She'd look like a fire hydrant with her high diaphragm and necklessness. She was a common lady with a fat face and had to be dressed very carefully.

A meeting was called at my house. Compliments. Coral looked very well, after all these years. No trouble. The director Anthony Quayle sided with Coral. "She'd dress quietly to go to the Darlingtons. She wanted to catch Lord Augustus. She'd play it safe." "Nonsense. She'd wear her best and newest Paris frock and make all the English look like the Derry & Toms frumps that they are. She'd have authority, for she knew she was more alluring than anyone else Lord Augustus would see, and in France ladies (viz. Proust) *did* wear Mephistophelean dresses, and Proust wrote pages about the Duchess of Guermantes's scarlet slippers."

I would have been deeply upset if I'd had to abandon the scarlet, but managed to win this point, though I had to concede all ideas of Knossos and make the dress not of hard satin but of net. Next day I must ask Isabel Jeans to see her designs, as she was very worried at the idea of having *poudré* hair. After all, everything must be done for her as it was a thankless part. She had to get the story going. All her Act I was explanation; in fact, she was "Mrs. Plot"!

Alan Tagg was here from Chichester where he is the designer of this season's four plays. He said that if one wrote down detail by detail all the ignominies one suffered, one would never feel inclined to embark upon another production. There was the arrogance of the boss, John Clements[1] who, not quite a gentleman, is so determined to be one, and his authority must not be challenged. Rather than give in to the director who wished to be present at George Devine's[2] memorial matinée, the cast was corralled at Chichester at 9:30 in the morning. For two hours Clements kept them doing nothing. When two urns he has brought from his garden were considered unsuitable, he was determined to keep them on stage on pedestals, and only at the first performance, and without a word, were they not on view. At the dress parade Clements opined that a pale Goya dress needed a red rose on the waist. "Oh no," said Alan, fighting hard for his convictions. "Yes, a red rose. Next please!"

[1] Sir John Clements (1910–88), actor, manager and producer, who was director of Chichester Festival Theatre 1966–73.

[2] George Devine (1910–66), actor and first artistic director of the Royal Court Theatre, where John Osborne's *Look Back in Anger* was first presented in 1956. He died on 20 January 1966.

When these details are added up they make for an experience that is as painful as childbirth, but like slates of pain, one forgets them in retrospect and blithely embarks upon a new project.

THEATRE

Coral, when told that Barbara Jefford was to play Lady Macbeth to Wolfit's Macbeth said, "Poor bitch! She'll find he makes her letter scene into a postcard." And Wolfit appeared himself in the sleep-walking scene.[1]

COWARD

I went to lunch with Noël in his rented flat. "The Master's downstairs." Noël, sitting like a Buddha, put on a delightful show and I was glad to find him so completely satisfied with his great success. The critics have been kinder than at any other time in his career and the audiences are packed and have put on evening dress for him. He is oblivious of any shortcomings and it would be a wonderful exit for him. However, he will go on. We discussed his recent illnesses. He is violently anti Swiss doctors and described in gory details the ignominies and agonies he suffered. Then on to old age. I asked him what he thought the compensations were. "My bed. I've grown to love my bed so much. I can hardly leave it for a moment. To get into bed in the afternoon with a bad book is the greatest joy. And I love it so much I don't want anyone else to come near it."

A long session at the wig makers with the cast of *Lady W.* bringing with them their own egos in order of importance. First the star, C. B., then Isabel Jeans. Fantastic as it is, Iso is now over 70.[2] On stage she can look 40, but today she

[1] Barbara Jefford (b. 1930), actress with the Old Vic Company 1956–62, and Sir Donald Wolfit (1902–68), actor-manager, on whom Ronald Harwood based his play *The Dresser.*

[2] Isabel Jeans (1891–1985), actress. She had starred in the 1945 production of *Lady Windermere's Fan.* Cecil dressed her extravagantly as Aunt Alicia in the film *Gigi,* and she was desperate to be Mrs. Higgins in the film of *My Fair Lady.* Cecil also wanted her for this part but it went instead to Gladys Cooper. She was then 75.

was more than her off-stage age, blind as a bat, frowning, face screwed up into a pomander, thick legs, unsteady, hunched back, she unwrapped her head from the chiffon turban, revealing hair white and half old dyed gravy.

Now what was all this about making her wear a grey wig? The Duchess of Berwick was the mother of a very young debutante. She was witty and bright. She had to get the play going. She couldn't do that in a grey wig. She had to *feel* right and witty. A tall dowager's wig was affixed. She did not like it at all. She screwed up her small features into a knot of dissatisfaction. Six onlookers stood around, sympathetic, sad and embarrassed. Gently, Stanley Hall produced a strand of nut-brown hair. The little old lady suddenly became Isabel Jeans again. It is true the dowager's wig disguised her. "You see, this is more the colour of my own hair." We marvelled at such swift deception. Soon we all acquiesced. A faded brown was chosen. Suddenly the contorted little nut of a face was wreathed in smiles. The little old actress left the building with all the graces of an actress of the past. We were relieved. Next please. This lady is playing Mrs. Cowper Cowper. How about auburn? The text says "hair straw-coloured."

CHANEL

JULY 1966

It is quite incredible that she is today over 80. Her skin is drawn in tight wrinkles over the bone of her face, but her hands, her figure, are those of a middle-aged woman and her walk, her vitality and general animal grace are those of a teenager. When she says she is tired she lies back on the sofa with hunched shoulders, stiff like a wooden doll, but only for a moment does she remain recumbent.

Cecil had the chance to talk to, or at any rate to listen to, the great couturière.

She has learnt some very simple lessons and her aphorisms are repeated very often, but have the basic truth of the French photographer. She is like a modern Pascal or Rochefoucauld, talking of life being over when you can no longer cry, for without tears you cannot love.

Of luxury she said, "There are some things you can define only by the opposites. The opposite of luxury is not poverty because in the houses of the poor you can smell a good *pot au feu.* The opposite is not simplicity for there is beauty in the corn-stall and barn, often great simplicity in luxury, but there is nothing in vulgarity, its complete opposite."

During the last three days in Paris it was only to be expected that much time was spent talking about her. One realised that she is the stuff of which legends are made, and she is a wonderful subject for the musical in construction (whether or not she will sign up and give her OK to go ahead is a problem that Brisson must tackle, and one in which I do not wish to be involved).

During these two days, she gave a very remarkable display, reminiscing about her gypsy Auvergne-Provence childhood, at being so shocked by sex, at always demanding the best out of life. She talked of Balsan[1] and all he had taught her, and of the dresses that she started to make being before their time. She inveighed against her old friends, about *Vogue,* Vreeland, Liberman and Charles-Roux.[2] She can be devastating as only the French know how, but it is a tiresome display of spleen, unworthy of her greatness, and it is no use to argue, otherwise the row is never forgotten. Thus she is often embarrassing company and one wonders why she has not, among all the things she has learnt, come to realise that this is unattractive and against her own well-being.

Each time I left her presence it was in a condition of total exhaustion, Alan [Lerner], so nervous that he had to have a bath and change his shirt. My head ached. As I left her in her workroom with the swaying metallic bands running in and out of a thousand seams until five hours later she might have put another four dresses on the road to completion.

FOOTNOTE ON CHANEL

Her large-boned, eloquently articulated hands are so accustomed to plying material that even when she is talking at lunch she is pleating the table napkin

[1] Etienne Balsan (1880–1953), younger brother of Jacques Balsan, who married Consuelo Vanderbilt, Duchess of Marlborough. He was killed in a motor accident. Chanel began a love affair with him when she was 21.

[2] Edmonde Charles-Roux, editor of French *Vogue,* who wrote two books on Chanel, *Chanel* (1975) and *Le Temps Chanel* (1979).

and turning it round, squaring the edges, the fingers trembling with energy and sensitivity.

PARIS

Arriving from my holiday, tired and late at night at the Vendôme side of the Ritz Hotel, a large group of people were leaving after dinner. I was amazed to see one of them, a boy of about fourteen, pale pink faced, blond, bald, crew-cut, in blue serge suit, transfixed, stuck stiff like a crucified image with head up straight and enormous black egg-shape wide-open mouth. He remained thus with incredibly wide gape for several seconds. Thus did his schoolboy spirits show his surprise at seeing the vast, illuminated Vendôme Column. His behaviour was not noticed by any of his group but it made a lasting impression of delight on me.

Rich South American banker, also Finance Minister of his country,[1] entertains at restaurant on cruise. The bill is brought to him. He blinks at it, gives it to his wife to pay. "Didn't you know he can't add up? I always have to attend to the bills."

PARIS

Two taut days of photographing the new fashions on Fiona Thyssen[2] for *Weekly Telegraph* [*Weekend Telegraph*] undid all the good of the holiday. It was 3 before we were back in bed after a series of pictures taken in different locales (Winston's, Crillon and Maxim's). Nerves were frayed and we had to start again next day at Roger Vivier's.[3] Here his drunken friend remained in the

[1] Walter Moreira Salles (1912–2001), Brazilian banker, Ambassador in Washington in the 1950s and Finance Minister in Brazil 1961–2. His second wife, Elizhina, pleaded poverty when they were divorced, put on a jump suit and jumped out of a window to her death.

[2] Fiona Campbell-Walter (b. 1932), top model, married (1956), the art collector Baron Heinrich Thyssen-Bornemisza (1921–2002). Divorced 1965.

[3] Roger Vivier (b. 1913), shoe designer who promoted the stiletto heel and the platform shoe and designed the Queen's shoes for the coronation.

host's absence, and added to the tension by bawling out Fiona, Cherry Twiss[1] and all who were drinking Coca-Cola and eating croque monsieur in his bedroom. Stomach upheaved, either out of nervousness or a chill, but the return to London was anticlimactic to start with and built to a week of such frustration that it has taken me a day and a half of complete quiet in the country to regain equilibrium.

In London messages were always repeated wrong, results disappointed, crisis followed crisis. Out of *Lady W.* bothers with upholstery, furniture coverings etc., a plaintive call from *Family and Fortune*,[2] scenery somehow doesn't quite look right, what could be done? Schneider has not listened to me, and made all the women's dresses too skimpy. Must send to Paris for extra material. People *don't* listen. Scenery badly painted. I explained at early sessions I wanted the original maquettes to be followed. No trace of the personal touch and the builders only giving the painters three days to complete the Darlington set. A phone call from Twiss to say *Telegraph* are not using four of our sittings. A telegram from Alfred [Lunt] in New York. No furniture for Act I designed—conditions at Met "hectic beyond belief."[3]

Vogue photography for their fiftieth aniversary, Nicko Londonderry[4] wearing incredible jewellery given by some grand duke to a former Lady L. "Will you come in to see the colour tests tomorrow?" Yes, but they put the whole lot through at once. Editor Beatrix Miller[5] is disappointed with the results. Eileen telephoned all over England for Nottingham lace curtains. They are now obsolete, but I insist. Rush to country for *Modess Because* sittings because they pay me better than anything else. But Balmain's has made such a balls-up of one of the dresses that even I, who am adept at making silk purses out of sow's ears, will not touch this one. At last the models and editors and assistants leave the house, and I fling myself on my bed, hoping to remain here for some considerable time.

[1] Cherry Twiss, model.

[2] Cecil designed Julian Mitchell's play *A Family and a Fortune*, based on a novel by Ivy Compton-Burnett.

[3] Cecil had been designing a production of *La Traviata* at the Metropolitan Opera House in New York, under the direction of Alfred Lunt (1893–1977).

[4] Nicolette Harrison (d. 1993), married (1958) ninth Marquess of Londonderry. She appeared to produce a male heir who proved to have been sired by the singer Georgie Fame. Divorced 1971, she committed suicide.

[5] Beatrix Miller, editor of London *Vogue*.

. . .

Only funny thing in Anita Loos's disappointing autobiography.[1] A quote from one of the Mizners, going around with such-and-such was like taking a trip down the sewers in a glass-bottomed boat. Even so the publishers bogged it by omitting the preposition "a."

Don't quite know why I've never liked Ned Rorem.[2] Maybe his pastry feminine features in a masculine body with its deep voice, something under a stone about him physically, smelly, cheesy, snotty. He's quiet and menacing but not interesting. I was very prejudiced against his *Diaries*,[3] and the countless photographs of him brought back my dislike of him, but on reading the book am amazed to find how frank a portrait it is of himself, to what extent he has the powers of analysis and the real talent to write something fresh and startling.

DEATH

Of course, the thought of one's own death rises to the surface more often as one gets older. Instead of looking at the "engagements" or "births" in the newspaper one looks at the "deaths" and as time passes the score becomes astonishingly high of those one knows who [have] gone on. The last month has been particularly rich in mortalities. Diana Vreeland's adored Reed[4] has given up the ghost, eaten to bones by cancer. Frank O'Hara,[5] a young American poet of great distinction who, for a while, acted as my secretary, died as a result of a beach taxi swerving violently into him when the driver was blinded by oncom-

[1] *A Girl Like I* (Viking, New York, 1966), by the diminutive author Anita Loos (1888–1981), famed for her novel *Gentlemen Prefer Blondes*. The autobiography is far from disappointing.

[2] Ned Rorem (b. 1923), composer and obsessive publisher of his own diaries.

[3] *The Paris Diary of Ned Rorem* (George Braziller, New York, 1966). Besides a lot of soul searching and revelations about his love life, and the love that Marie-Laure de Noailles had for him, the book contains one very black joke. In 1953, the atomic spy Julius Rosenberg was electrocuted with his wife. A cruel joke soon circulated in Paris. Before going to the chair, Mr. Rosenberg asked a number of questions about the mechanism. "The guard answers, '*Ne vous en faites pas, mon ami—on va vous mettre au courant*' " (Rorem, op. cit., p. 124).

[4] Reed Vreeland died in New York Hospital on 3 August 1966, aged 67.

[5] Frank O'Hara (1926–66), poet. He died on 25 July, having been hit by a beach buggy.

ing lights. Monty Clift,[1] no great friend, but a brilliant actor and a reformed drunk, rang me to know if I'd go to see a Swedish film, and two weeks later was dead in bed. These are comparatively young people. It was only to be expected that old Reginald Kennedy-Cox, a neighbour, should succumb, and I suppose that living ghost, "Jolly" Jack Minster, had by now reached a respectable age. So too "Topsy" Lucas, but oh dear, it hurt me to read of her demise.[2] She was so youthful in spirit. In my Cambridge days she meant a lot. She was the beginning of the opening of a door on to the intellectual world.

Nonetheless it came as a great shock to me when, in a television interview, Muggeridge[3] said to me, "We'll both soon be dead!" My reaction was to say, "Well, you may be, but I won't." And yet why do I think I shall survive till I'm over 80? My mother's family have all been great survivors. And my father and his brothers lived long, and I suppose I have the feeling that I will have to survive longer than I wish. This may be proved today, or tomorrow or next time I take an aeroplane. But I am secretly preparing to have to face all the ardours of old age, the being passed by, the disappointment, disillusionments and bitterness. The ignoring of one's work, the despising by the young of one's attempts at humour. Although I don't look forward to this, I can see that it is going to be difficult, at any particular stage (unless, of course, scandal or tragedy in a big way strikes), to say, "This is enough."

Meanwhile mirrors become ever less friendly, self-photographs a disaster, and even the body strikes its own blows, stomach upset more easily, backbone asserting itself and brain less capable of concentration (I find even these entries become more futile). But one is buoyed up by the memory of what one was and I feel as I used to be, even if I do not behave or look as I feel. There is comfort in the illusion.

[1] Montgomery Clift (1920–66), introspective, romantic actor on stage and screen. He had descended into the world of drink and drugs. He died on 23 July.

[2] Sir Reginald Kennedy-Cox (1881–1966), founder of the Docklands Settlements and playwright, who lived in the Close, Salisbury, and died on 27 July; Jack Minster (1900–66), theatrical producer, who attempted to stage Cecil's play *The Gainsborough Girls* under a new title, *Landscape with Figures,* and died on 1 August; and E. B. C. ("Topsy") Jones (1892–1966), novelist, first wife of F. L. Lucas (1894–1967), Fellow of King's College, Cambridge; she was part of Cecil's early life at Cambridge, a considerable influence on undergraduates, and later a reviewer. She died on 30 June.

[3] Malcolm Muggeridge (1903–90), journalist, editor, author and television guru.

. . .

Is it the fashion to decry oneself, to make oneself out even more stupid than one is? To repeat one's mortifications to others, even to brag about them. It is a trick that I excel in.

Talking to Kin on the telephone from Reddish to San Francisco, he paid me a compliment. "You've strength and energy! It's as if you had three balls."

That I should have agreed to do the Ivy Compton-Burnett play[1] was in the nature of a madness, for although the play is one of distinction and gives me a chance to do something different, nevertheless although a small production, it has created as many problems as the bigger. To be fitted in also was a meeting in Paris for the Chanel musical [*Coco*], another visit to Paris for the photographing of the fashions for the *Weekly Telegraph*, yet another visit to see clothes for *Modess* (this a money-maker if all goes well) and visits to New York for the long-postponed production of *Traviata*. Little wonder, then, that I now find myself limp and depleted, unable to settle down to read, to have to leave my Vol. III[2] untouched for five months, and the studio likewise ignored.

What lesson to learn? That when offers arrive to decorate a musical of *Trelawny* etc., that the designing of costumes is only the beginning of a long haul of unpleasantness, delays, disappointments, bad craftsmanship, boredom of watching and waiting until one's nervous system cannot find the necessary strength to endure the final pinpricks.

Just as I am about to leave the theatre at Brighton after the successful first night of *Lady W.*, Anthony Quayle, a most fair and sensitive director, asks if I would change the leading lady's last act hat as it disturbs her wig so much putting it on and off. That is too much. If she had disliked it, if the management revolted against it, but it was a witty, unexpected object (taken from Gustave Moreau's sketch for *Salomé*) and if the wigs were in bad shape, the management should afford a hairdresser to stand by for every performance on the road.

[1] *A Family and a Fortune.*

[2] Cecil was working on volume 3 of his diaries, the controversial one, since it contained the story of his love affair with Greta Garbo. It was eventually published as *The Happy Years* in 1972, causing a furore in the press. Cecil half regretted publishing it and many took a dim view of him for doing so.

Returning home to London, a letter awaits me from cry-baby Alfred Lunt. "Wherever you are I wish you were here. We're having worries. The trunks to be used as chairs and table are too low and too narrow. The bed is in the wrong position." Then from Oxford an SOS, to alter the set for *A Family and a Fortune.* The company find it too open. Their voices get lost, the litter in the corners is insignificant. Could this not represent the ghosts of the past, ancestors memorabilia? (A good idea this.)

A list of new properties is made out that covers two sheets of paper and one secretly knows that these improvements will not lengthen the run of the play, which can really only expect a very limited audience even in London. (It has been limping around the provinces to very poor attendance.) One must be grateful that *Lady W.* has a prosperous future, but in future one must realise how the acceptance of an offer is likely to lead to tiring and nerving travels, to many weekends spent away from one's home and garden, and the creation of a restless staccato state of mind that prevents one from settling down to the life that well-ordered people of my age should lead.

ISABEL JEANS

Isabel Jeans, an old warhorse of the theatre, still feels at 70 the excitement of the fire horses when the bell goes. Fitting her mauve evening dress at Berman's, she turns with blazing eyes. "Have you heard they're already sold out at Brighton?"

KIN

It is over a year now since that early morning when, with grim-set jaw, he got into a taxi and left for his beloved California. It was lucky that a few hours later I myself was leaving for a holiday in Greece. But the wrench of parting from someone who had become so close, who in fact was my bulwark against the world, has remained as painful as I knew it would be. Particularly when I am in the country do I long for his sympathy and companionship. With him I feel a complete unit in the world. At night the absence of him from the little room next to mine is very acute.

. . .

It needed careful juggling to fit in all the dates for this late summer's activities. On Tuesday, after the Bank Holiday, Simon [Fleet] and I set off by car from Broadchalke to Brighton on the last lap of chores to photograph *Lady Windermere.* It was a lovely sylvan drive through woods and downs, and our spirits were high and I felt less than the usual panic at the responsibility ahead. For four hours I photographed, every scene of the play, every character taken to the "dock" where I found an ideal daylight studio, and at the end of the evening performance I felt that the last details had been cleverly attended to.

Coral B's new felt hat had been successfully launched and a list of further things to do left with the stage manager and wardrobe mistress, when Anthony Quayle, the director, bombards me at the Pass Door. "When can we have a proper painting session, so that Act III can come up to the level of the other two acts? Oxford? Manchester?" I see now that on my return from New York, there will be quite a lot more to do. I make my escape in Simon's car, tired out and headachy.

Then in London I must think in terms of New York, and the great project at last to take place on the Metropolitan stage. Binkie Beaumont[1] then rings me: "We have made a great mistake. The cast is excellent, with one exception. We will have to get rid of Anthony Ainley[2] as Windermere, and the photographs in which he appears must not appear and others will have to be taken in Oxford of his replacement." Will it never end?

For two or three months the schedule has been appalling, not a day to waste, not a day to be found to go down to Brighton to see Francis Rose's exhibition (an omitted chore which has created great bitterness in the artist's sensitive make-up). Then at last all working up to the departure for New York and to start on the last lap of the *Traviata.*

But on arrival there is no word from the Met. They are panicking with the turntable breakdown. No one read the instructions so 500 chorus, camels, horses, sheep, goats and Leontyne Price[3] got on to the German machinery and instead of whirling in a circle, heard a crunch as the giant table groaned and

[1] Hugh ("Binkie") Beaumont (1908–73), theatrical impresario, whose company, H. M. Tennent, dominated the London theatre world for two decades.

[2] Anthony Ainley (b. 1937), son of Henry Ainley. He later starred as Dr. Who.

[3] Leontyne Price (b. 1927), soprano, American prima donna.

sank into itself. I did not wish to get involved as the frustrations, delays and disappointments of the others came to my ears soon enough.

Meanwhile my life was given its true colours by the presence of Kin. For thirteen months we have not seen one another. There were moments when I wondered whether we would ever be as happy as during that year in England. Then he appeared. He looked as young and as American as when I first knew him, not the long romantic hair of London. He proved as intelligent and quick as I remembered, made sense of my halting muzzy sentences, got through to the core of every subject, and for four days we enjoyed each other's company to the exclusion of all others in the town.

HAVE RETURNED 3 OCTOBER 1966

The three weeks in New York were bypassed as if in an incubator or deep freeze. I lived in a hotel room that had no individuality, ate food that was without character, answered the telephone ceaselessly, went through the endless list of people I must telephone, even managed to write a few notes, but nothing positive stirred my intellect. No new thought went through my brain. I doubt if I learnt anything.

This, of course, precludes the first five days which were not given to New York for they were occupied happily and entirely by Kin. He had come from Washington where he was staying with his parents to be in New York with me. It was our reunion after thirteen months.

The rest of my New York visit was spent preserving my strength and trying, under the most difficult conditions, to get through the finishing stages of the production of *Traviata* on which I have been working for over two years.

Aubrey Ensor,[1] schoolmaster at Heath Mount, writes to Eileen, "I hope all goes well with Cecil. It usually does!"

Little does he realise!

[1] Aubrey Ensor, Heath Mount schoolmaster, who danced round the classroom singing the popular theatrical hits of the day and possessed 36,000 postcards of actresses.

In 1962 Cecil had photographed the great courtesan Cléo de Mérode (1881–1966) in Paris. She had been very particular about what she allowed to be published, and he was aware that she would not hesitate to sue him. So he lodged some untouched photographs of her with Camera Press for posthumous publication. He was fascinated by her Belle Epoque past, and also intrigued to find her up to date with modern music, and a "fan" of the energetic pianist, John Ogdon (1937–89).

CLÉO DE MÉRODE 18 OCTOBER 1966

Cléo de Mérode died yesterday, aged 91. At the turn of the century she was voted the most beautiful woman in the world. Till the last time I saw her she had the quality of beauty. She had sold her king's jewels, and possessions, was extremely hard up, and covered her half-dyed hair in an old woollen cap that was frayed at the nape. She pottered about, hunchbacked, in carpet slippers and a dressing gown over her dress. But she was still interested in life, listened to the radio with curiosity and had no bitterness, no regret for the past. She really is (and not La Belle Otéro) the last of the *grandes cocottes* of the Belle Epoque and I am sorry that I won't be able to telephone to her on my next visit to Paris. I enjoyed listening to her deep, gruff voice, and I enjoyed taking flowers to her. She represented to me the make-believe glory of the past.

Well, Lady Winderbag's version II is safely delivered. It's been a long accouchement. The trip round the provinces prolonged the agony, for new problems were being raised all along the line. The replacement of Lord W. by another actor produced pandemonium in the cast and everyone became unsure of themselves. For my part it was like getting blood out of stones to get everything finished that one knew two months ago must be done. Always one hears "Can we leave this to London?" and one knows that by London the management will have closed down on further expenditure. Again this happened. It would have been easy to go off to the races, but I have to fight for the last drop. At last we corralled the scene painters to put the necessary work into the oriental filigree of Darlington's room. At last José added fringe to curtains with Copydex, the Louis Seize table was disguised, the poppies and marguerites placed in the ballroom, and after a terrible row about the wigs, everything was to my liking.

Then the horrible time when one greedily looks for the reviews. One is always disappointed. One thinks mistakenly that this revival will be of interest. But the theatrical event of the week is the Brook production of the Vietnam play.[1] Then the critics are divided, one saying exactly the opposite of the other. Some have said my clothes are vulgar and without taste. On the whole they have been full of praise and two in particular have written such eulogies as I have never had before.

But now I hope to calm down and stay a little in the country, looking after my health and building up resistance. The last six months have been very highly pressurised. There hasn't been enough time for anything. But now the horizon looks clear for at least a month or two so I am trying to regain a lost sense of freedom, to look in different directions, to find new people and to regain a lost sense of fun.

29 OCTOBER 1966

I was very curious to see the anti–Vietnam War *US*, which Peter Brook put on on the same night as the opening of *Windermere* and naturally stole all the newspaper space. For not only was this not a revival of a revival of a revival etc., but a most "shattering"—to use Brook's word—assault on the complacency of an audience. Prejudice against the hated Brook apart, I found the evening thoroughly objectionable. It was not a question, as I had imagined, of being horrified, shocked, stunned, rather of being irritated, unnerved by the unnecessary noise (everyone had to shout through a microphone) and ashamed of the puerile attempts of the author at satire, the actors at acting and the composer as musician.

The evening was over for me by the first interval. By this time two hours of banshee, end-of-term rowdiness had lowered one's resistance.

However, the evening illustrated the fact to me that never from one moment to another is one safe. The unexpected, in all its forms, is always lurking. It can strike at any moment.

It struck next door to me. On the stage some English actors were imitating American war correspondents relaying the US progress in Vietnam.

[1] Peter Brook's production, *US*, opened at the Aldwych in London at the same time as *Lady Windermere's Fan.*

Suddenly my friend Simon Fleet, whom I had taken as guest to the theatre, shouted in a loud, slow, well-articulated voice, "Why don't you Americans occupy Gibraltar so that we British can keep it for ever and ever?" The whole theatre shocked, stunned. Proceedings stopped, laughter, desultory applause, the atmosphere electric, before the correspondents said, "Can't answer that Sir. We're only the actors."

Suddenly one was the focus of a drama. Journalists applaud, excitement, foreboding. The only person who seemed unmindful of the fuss was Simon. I am staggered at his lack of self-consciousness, yet find it very alarming. Anything can happen any minute, older nerves are frayed by stress and drink or sadness (all three for Simon since Juliet's death), the possibility of surprise can be quite serious.

REDDISH

Eileen and I came down for longed-for weekend of quiet reading and relaxation. Eileen has fought off the germs that have laid low every other member of the household. But country air and peace would give her added strength. I am at the end of a six-month spate and after a year's interval want to start work on diary Vol. III.

Meanwhile our peaceful country activities are encroached upon by messages from Kensington Palace. In view of the leakage of the new baby's picture,[1] could we hurry our proofs through? Could they be sent round by messenger within the hour?

DIARIES END OF OCTOBER 1966

Have been reading with enormous pleasure Harold Nicolson's diaries edited by his son Nigel.[2] I can really hardly fault the book although I have been on the

[1] Cecil had photographed Princess Alexandra's infant daughter, Marina Ogilvy, who was born on 31 July 1966.

[2] Nigel Nicolson published the first of three volumes of *Harold Nicolson: Diary and Letters* in October 1966. The first volume covered the years 1930–9.

lookout to do so on every page, for I have never liked Harold Nicolson, have always mistrusted him, considered him a phoney. I don't know whether I've resented his "getting away" with *so* much, being a fairly successful politician, at any rate respected by Churchill, Eden and group, a worthy critic, a figure in contemporary literature, a personality in the glittering world, a father, a loving husband, a gardener, and all the time a man with a most greedy lust for young men.

Perhaps it is more the greed than the lust that irritates me. Perhaps it is just that I dislike his obvious lusting. Although furtive of eye, no one shows his feelings more nakedly than Harold. He digs into a second helping of suet pudding, his double chins pucker, as he looks at a hefty schoolboy bicycling by. Harold's fly buttons pop through the air like rockets. Physically he is repellent to me, the pig features in a fat bladder, the awful remains of schoolboyishness, the pink cheeks, the crinkly hair, the offensive pipe. I have had angry arguments with James P.-H. [Pope-Hennessy][1] about him. I have tried to like him. I have asked him to dine. It didn't work. Yet here is a book full of very frank self-revelations. He comes out of it with enormous charm, a man of great perceptiveness, fairness and sincerity, altogether admirable.

So good is it that I have thought several times during the past few days of trying to write these notes each day in the way that Harold has for so many years. What happened this week?

Back from the country in time to take the Ogilvys[2] to Lady Winderbags. Difficult to find the right people for such an evening. It is no good my trying to impress them with grand people, so perhaps the theatre. Whom do I know that is young enough? Leslie Caron[3] is intelligent, a leader in swinging London and a star; Georgina Ward,[4] struggling actress, that gives her the right status, and she is engaged to Ali Forbes and he is ideal for every gathering.

The evening is easy, thank God, and Princess Alexandra has just the right touch with everyone. Coming out of the stage door, a crowd has collected. She asks, "Did you enjoy the show? This is the man who did the sets!" Supper, ham mousse, beef olives, cheesecake with cherries. Ray did well, Cor-

[1] James Pope-Hennessy (1916–74), author.

[2] HRH Princess Alexandra (b. 1936), and her husband, the Hon. Angus Ogilvy (b. 1928).

[3] Leslie Caron (b. 1931), French actress, who had starred in the film *Gigi* (1958).

[4] Hon. Georgina Ward (b. 1941), actress, married to Ali Forbes between 1966 and 1971.

nelius back in the fold to serve dinner and Mrs. Cartwright who later demonstrated to Georgina how to fold the napkins to look like water lilies.

The following night was empty, so I rang Tom Parr at the eleventh hour to know if he'd like to go to a movie. While cruising in the Caribbean he said he liked being called up at the last minute. He had got something to do. In fact, he was having 40 people to dinner and to hear a quartet. The arrangements must have taken him weeks. He kindly invited me, I accepted. The evening was special. Few make such an effort. In Nancy Lancaster's tall vaulted room[1] the string quartet played Mozart, Haydn and Brahms, in a room in which Haydn had himself played. Only music lovers were invited, Rhoda Birley,[2] Diana [Cooper], Londonderrys.[3] It was a surprise delight.

By the Thursday night total exhaustion. After a visit from a Greek hairdresser I was incapable of making further effort. Eileen, Ray and I were all exhausted by the week's activities, which had included the start of a new book, sorting out photographs for *The Best of Beaton*;[4] giving instructions about the treatment of the cat's abscess in the country; buying a Blue Period Picasso etching, an investment, in exchange for the money long owing me at Redfern; calling Kin in San Francisco to see if he was free for Christmas (no, with his family); having a showdown with Geoff,[5] my assistant, about lack of assistance; Dr. Gottfried (ears still blocked, foot still shingled), Dr. Svenson, to stretch the spine; the start of Christmas shopping (Elizabeth David's[6] shop for the first time). In one hour I spent £72, Eileen on my return said, "Good."

No, I don't think I'm a Harold Nicolson. In fact, I'm going through a very disorganised patch with these notes, realise that for a very long time past they have been no good whatsoever, and since I've learnt nothing new, am in a poor way altogether. With my physical appearance gone, there is nothing left

[1] Nancy Lancaster (1897–1994), who ran Colefax & Fowler for many years. Their headquarters were in Avery Row, near Claridge's Hotel.

[2] Rhoda Pike (1900–80), married (1921) Sir Oswald Birley (1880–1952), portrait painter. She lived at Charleston Manor, Sussex.

[3] Alastair, ninth Marquess of Londonderry (b. 1937), and his wife Nicolette Harrison.

[4] *The Best of Beaton* (1968), a visual celebration of decades of Cecil's photographic work, with an introduction by Truman Capote.

[5] Geoffrey Sawyer.

[6] Elizabeth David (1913–92), cookery expert.

for me to employ but my talents and they seem to be employed in a very unsuccessful way. Oy veh![1]

REDDISH NOVEMBER 1966

Two days in London this week mostly taken up with caring for my back. Svenson, the chiropractor, tells me it is very stiff and will cause trouble later on. I have put something out of place (when doing exercises under the tuition of Charlotte Gaffran), the ensuing pain and immobility has made me feel very old and depressed. (Yes, it's nearly gas oven time!) The doctor and dentist also played an important part. (I generally enjoy the relaxation of a visit to the dentist but this time he drilled on a nerve in the "small" of a tooth.) Looking at old negatives for *Best of Beaton,* a visit from a stranger was mildly interesting, and dinner with Ivan Moffat[2] and his wife was stimulating as usual, but a Weidenfeld gala for Maurice Bowra[3] was a flop. No plays, no real thrill and was pleased to escape.

THE GILBERT MILLERS[4]

I don't know if it might be possible to write a symposium of all the laughs that there have been at the expense of Gilbert and Kitty during the last forty years. They are a continual source of gossip, of rows, apologies and outrageous behaviour of all sorts. Perhaps a play could be made.

Kitty, rich, worldly to the point of madness, insatiable, full of energy, never tired, never secure. Gilbert, a cad, a beast, with certain disarming qualities of charm, brashness.

Perhaps I will write down a few of their foolishnesses.

[1] This popular Jewish phrase was often used by Greta Garbo to cover a miscellany of reactions.

[2] Ivan Moffat (1918–2002), screenwriter.

[3] Sir Maurice Bowra (1898–1971), celebrated Oxford don. He published *Memories* at this time. Cecil once told Kenneth Tynan that he thought in all Weidenfeld galas for 100, there was a dinner party of six desperately trying to get out.

[4] Gilbert Miller (1884–1969), theatrical impresario, and his wife, Kitty Bache (1900–79), daughter of the American banker Jules Bache.

The latest to keep the telephone wires buzzing is of their arrival to stay with Merle Oberon[1] in her new house in Acapulco. It seems Acapulco is in the news and the Millers could not resist being there this winter and they invited themselves to the "film star's" whom they hardly knew. They arrived at midnight and were shocked that Merle was already asleep, that no servants had waited up to unpack for them.

Complaints right and left. Gilbert drops food on his shirt-front at each meal, brought only two evening shirts. Kitty gives these to the maid to be laundered. Kitty is summoned to Merle's "opium bed." Merle (I'm bored with cinema star behaviour) says, "I'm sorry we haven't a laundress here. The staff cannot do the guests' washing. If you are uncomfortable, my husband could help you with tickets to get back to New York. They're impossible to get for ten days." But by 6 o'clock next morning the Millers are on their way to New York, furious, for they have given their servants a month's holiday, although Merle had only invited them for a week. On leaving Merle discovers they have taken with them all her clothes hangers.

Kitty, hideous beyond recall, once said at the end of an Atlantic crossing, to Natasha [Wilson],[2] "Oh it's a disaster. I couldn't sleep a wink last night, and Gilbert will expect to see me coming down the gangplank this morning looking like Hedy Lamarr."[3]

While on subject of the silly set:

Elsa Maxwell[4] discovered Paul Getty, the richest man in the world. She did not know him, but decided to honour him by giving a party for all the swells in his honour. She took the whole of Maxim's, filled it with red roses and invited 200 people. Getty, on her right. Gradually, towards the end of the evening, the penny dropped and Getty realised he might have to be landed with the bill. He slid out to the men's room and then home. When the bill came, four

[1] Merle Oberon (1911–79), film actress, born Estelle Merle O'Brien Thompson; played Cathy in *Wuthering Heights* opposite Laurence Olivier.

[2] Princess Natasha Paley (1905–81), married Jack Wilson, theatrical impresario, in New York.

[3] Hedy Lamarr (1914–2000), Austrian film star of the 1920s and 1930s, who went to Hollywood in 1937, after the sensation of appearing nude in the 1933 film *Extase*.

[4] Elsa Maxwell (1883–1963), inveterate party giver and columnist.

or five pals clubbed together for thousands of dollars. From then on Maxwell wrote that Getty was the meanest and the most boring man in the world.

The [Loel] Guinness house so draughty. It's a storm vent. You could test a plane in it.

The impoverished millionaires in reduced quarters. "So you're going to have lunch in their servants' quarters. Perhaps you'd like to have lunch tomorrow in my servants' rooms."

Minnie Fosburgh,[1] absurdly sentimental, listens to Fulco [di Verdura] with tears in her eyes. He is describing how he was bringing bathing shorts for his holiday. He had some from Rome and London, but those that he got in an ordinary shop in Madison Avenue were every bit as good. "When it comes to making bathing shorts America is as good as anyone, if not better!" Min leans forward and clutches his arm saying in deep-felt emotion, "Thank you."

Maurice Bowra told me the following:

Sibyl Colefax[2] staying at Stinchcombe (Stench) with Evelyn Waugh, is broken in on while lying in the bath (no locks even on loo doors), shouts cheerfully, "I won't be two twos!"

Cecil contemplated a visit to New York, partly to attend Truman Capote's lavish "Black and White Ball" ostensibly to honour Kay Graham, but more to celebrate the new-found riches, derived from In Cold Blood. *The ball was held at the Plaza Hotel on 28 November 1966, and those not favoured with an invitation left New York. The ball was inspired by the black and white scene designed by Cecil for* My Fair Lady.

REDDISH 20 NOVEMBER 1966

I will be going (DV) to Truman's £10,000 party. About this I have mixed feelings. I would feel that I had missed quite an event if I didn't go, but I know I

[1] Minnie Cushing (1906–78), wife of the homosexual painter James Whitney Fosburgh (1910–77).

[2] Sibyl Halsey (1874–1950), widow of Sir Arthur Colefax, a hostess of the 1920s and 1930s.

will be angry. It seems to me such a terrible waste of money to spend so much in one evening. After six hours he will have nothing to see for his cheque except a lot of press clippings. The foolishness of spending so much time organising the party is something for a younger man, or a worthless woman to indulge in, if they have social ambitions.

What is Truman trying to prove? At any rate it is a masterstroke of publicity though of the wrong sort. Cocteau fought to keep himself away from the costume balls of de Beaumont.[1] As much as he would have liked it, he knew that his image was being made too frivolous if he was photographed in *Vogue.* So he kept away. Now things are different. Truman had delivered himself of a very good book. Nothing can take away the fact that as a popular writer, of the greatest sales, he has "arrived." That this is a book of importance is also undeniable. The party will be a very brilliant occasion with all café society present, but while the two bands are blaring and the champagne drunk, who will remember the two murderers but for whose garrulous co-operation, as Jonathan Miller remarked, the book could not have been written. It is going to be very hard for me to hide my feelings.

When I told others that I had to bestir myself once again and take myself across the Atlantic, my plaintive voice was met with cries of envy. "How lucky you are to get away from this long winter."

"Yes, but if only I could have stayed on until after Christmas. Now is the time to remain in the country."

Cecil arrived at the St. Regis, which he had left two months before, for a three-week visit.

In December Cecil visited New Mexico to photograph the artist Georgia O'Keeffe (1887–1986). She first went to New Mexico in 1929, and had lived at the small shepherding village of Abiqui, on the banks of the Chama river, not far from Santa Fe, since 1931. Cecil had always wanted to see this part of the world.

The artist was hard to find, since she rose at 5 a.m. and went to bed at 9:30. Cecil made five telephone calls before he got through to her. The telephone

[1] Count Etienne de Beaumont (1883–1956), who gave legendary fancy dress balls, for which Cocteau sometimes wrote the opening speeches.

was answered by "an interested cooing deep voice sounded full of enthusiasm, yet veiled."

"You'd better have your lunch here as you won't be able to get it anywhere else." (Not so gracious.)

"Is there anything I can bring?"

"Well, we've a bit of smoky cheese, but perhaps you could bring whatever you like in the way of cheese. You get it from the Westminster (?) market. Yes, 50 miles is a long way to motor for cheese."

The voice sounded as if it belonged to a Grant Wood character, but it was not at all articulate and described the mountains as "colourful."

Cecil set off with his assistant, Charles Biasiny, and in due course they arrived on the outskirts of a dirty-looking Indian village "of mushroom-coloured adobe."

Large gates of strong wire faced us. With unprepossessing tin signs, we were warned "Keep out," "Beware of dog," "Dangerous dog." Two large chow puppies, Bobo and Chia, appeared only mildly interested, but no human being was in sight. This was obviously Miss O'Keeffe's home for here was the skeleton-skull of an ass, or a horse, or a stag, her "signature tune." At last, and with a twinkle of welcome in her eyes, the old lady herself appeared to open sesame.

With one hand I proffered the bag of groceries and with the other the bunch of carnations. She looked incredulously. "Flowers?"

"Why yes. Do you hate them?"

"No, not at all. But you must have had such difficulty in finding them. We have so few here. We never have any in this house."

Since twenty years have passed since last I saw Georgia O'K., it was not surprising to find her hair had become grey, that she was now elderly rather than middle-aged, but the atmosphere she created was the same, with her rugged bony face, her smooth hair and her neat, well-ordered clothes. Today she looked extremely dressy in a lesbian suit of charcoal grey with tucked-in fine linen shirt.

Charles later said to her that he was sure she was wearing a Spanish suit. O'K., shocked, replied in her deep drawl, "Why no! It's the product of my New York tailor!

"Once the dogs get accustomed to you, they won't bother you. They're very well trained, though once one of them did bite a neighbour, and she sued, and my insurance company had to pay up. It was an awful nuisance because I had to write so many letters before I could get any other insurance company to take me on."

Once inside the rough wooden front door, all was well. This really was the house that was all that it was cracked up to be. Walls hung with bones, skulls, antlers, rope and stacked with wooden logs, stones. On the ground pebbles and stepping stones of flag. Inside a large adobe room with adobe floor ("I discovered it's so easy to clean with a hoover!"), with sparse modern furniture, huge sofas, an early Rothko (in fact O'Keeffe, but in pale blues, greens, whites), half in a corner, Japanese flags with a blob of scarlet for cushions and the only colour. Bookshelves filled with oriental art books, health diets and gramophone records of Bach and Vivaldi. Pebbles of all smooth sizes at the windows. "Every time I go out I bring back rocks." Hi-fi, utter simplicity, utter luxury.

The adobe dining room all mushroom-coloured had polished table of infinitely beautifully grain texture, "the most important ingredient is New York soot" and the bleached wooden chairs were each covered with a goat skin. "It's good to have the warmth at your back."

Another darker little room was the summer dining room ("it's so cool it's where we store the apples") and the almonds and onions were displayed in long baskets on shelves. The room smelt fragrant, so too the pantry, which was lined with neatly arranged bottles of herbs, with dried foods and from the ceiling dozens of beautiful Mexican baskets were hanging. "In the summer they are filled with fruit, but in winter we try to keep them out of the way."

What could be more luxurious than this house? Complete in every way with the great attraction of simplicity in all things. Nothing ugly encroached. Even the tins in the kitchen were beautiful, so too the vases and bowls and pots.

A large studio with long "picture window" on to the panorama of mountains was warm, clean, polished, efficient, white and off-white, every neat gadget displayed as part of a still life. The latest *Life* and *Time* magazines struck an incongruous note. A row of empty white canvases already in silver frames hung in a line on the walls. She seemed in no hurry to start painting. She seemed in no hurry at all. She walked about with droopy, eagle-hooded

Georgia O'Keeffe at her home in New Mexico, December 1966

eyes, a sardonic expression on her mouth, a marvellous subject for photography. It is impossible to take a bad photograph of her.

The talk was not of painting, even her painting, and I believe she likes discussing other painters or theories of art, but of the country and the mountains which she loved so that she has a whole range to admire and gaze at from her almost entirely glassed-in bedroom. "Come and see the new road they have built. It makes a pretty curve from up here." With slightly screwed-up eyes she pointed her fine nose at the distant range and due to the cold brought out a handkerchief to dry a tear from her eye. "If you want to use a toilet, I'll unlock that yellow door."

Fearing the sort of "Men's Room" I visited at the local garage, I was amazed to discover a large bathroom, with large bathtub, washing basin, toilet, all finely furnished with good rugs, rows of coloured glass bottles, new cakes of the most expensive soap. At 12:30 we started to eat our lunch, Miss O'Keeffe lit a pile of faggots in the hearth, carved the steak, passed the brown bread crust, opened a bottle of red wine, brought out the salad and the great array of cheeses (I ate the smoky remains). Everything tasted as it should, of itself. Obviously G. O'K. is in all things a perfectionist.

I started to tell her how surprised I was to find her being carefully looked after here when I had concocted a speech telling her it was not safe to live entirely alone. "Suppose you fell from your horse." But she interrupted me: "It's not true. It's never true what they say, except that I do try hard not to be interrupted. I'm so far here that when people come to see me, they feel it is a big adventure and as it's taken them so long to get here they feel they must stay and before you know it a whole day is gone. And I don't want to see many people, only those I know well, and to know people well you have to see a lot of them. I'm not really interested in human nature. When I was living with Stieglitz,[1] I saw enough of it to realise I didn't like it, and I don't want to be bored any more. I've been bored long enough and I don't want to make conversation. Stieglitz never talked, so I had to take the initiative."

I asked about Steichen. "Yes, he was Stieglitz's pupil but like a lot of other young men he wasn't grateful to the master, and he behaved—well I don't suppose I should go into that now, it's not necessary—but Stieglitz put a lot of interesting people in his way to photograph—sure, and Rodin and Duse.[2] No, Steichen wasn't really a very pleasant character." But all that was part of New York life and she was glad that was over. Here she was able to walk, look at the mountains, sleep and enjoy nature.

It was wonderful not to have to talk to people, she'd talked to too many friends of Stieglitz. Yes, there were neighbours, the nearest was 25 miles

[1] Georgia O'Keeffe first met Alfred Stieglitz (1864–1946), the photographer, in 1916. She became his second wife in 1924 and they remained together until his death.

[2] Eleonora Duse (1859–1924), Italian actress.

away but she didn't see him any more since his marriage. He had been a delightful, articulate companion, but he brought his new wife to dine and she had made the mistake of confiding all her troubles and from that moment on the two were *persona non grata.* I felt G. O'K. could be pretty ruthless, she is obviously a great character and selfishness enters into her being. Reading between the lines, both Charles and I felt that she had actively hated Stieglitz. I had the impression that she had little time to read and I was surprised when she did not understand the word "anachronism." "If you don't explain what that means I'll have to get out the dictionary when you've gone."

She was as busy as six people here, looking after the house even when she was not painting. Lately she had not been well and not yet strong enough to start painting. "It's no use if you're not feeling [up to] it. It's only a waste of good materials and of time too." She showed us some of her paintings and to me they were frightful. I disliked very much cavernous slices of chocolate colour representing the Grand Canyon, and her clouds from an aeroplane were very sentimental. In fact, she has attained an important position in the history of American painting (for being the precursor of Rothko) but her influence has been nil. She herself an exception—unique.

The fact that she is now acclaimed and renowned gives her obvious satisfaction. The fact that the paintings are sold to museums for large sums is one of the reasons she is able to lead such an equable life though she is, of course, at the opposite end of the pole from her sister, Mrs. Anita Young, who must be one of the richest widows in the US, in spite of the fact that her husband, fearing that his fortune was being impaired, shot his face off in the Renaissance-style Palm Beach house.[1] When I mentioned her sister it was with certain misgivings, as rumour has it that the sisters dislike one another. On the contrary G. O'K. wanted to hear about the vast house, as big as a hotel, and as solid as the Escurial, with which the Renaissance palace is being replaced.

Having seen the house, I described how the sister had built a hill on which to place the building and that there were extravagances such as

[1] Anita O'Keeffe (1891–1985), married Robert Young, a Texas businessman who made a fortune on the railroads, and bought a house in Palm Beach called Fairholme. They became friends with the Duke and Duchess of Windsor in America after the Second World War. Robert Young shot himself in the billiard room at Fairholme in 1958.

cathedral-like windows for the servants' wing and a bathing pool that was being suspended, in order that any leakage could be mended from beneath. "Yes, I believe my sister had trouble with her other swimming pool. She is very practical. I must go and see the house, and get her to pay for a lot of my pictures she has on the walls."

After lunch we motored about 15 miles to the Ghost Ranch House in which G. O'K. lives during the summer. "It's all I like. I'd like to give up the other house. It takes so much looking after. Imagine having two men to rake that gravel, but I can't get anyone to come out and look after me at this other place, it's too far away."

Camouflaged among the scrub, at the foot of a high ridge of mountains lay the small flat red adobe-shaped bungalow where the nature lover feels ever more in touch with the elements. Not content with her bedroom of plate glass situated with a full view of the mountains, the old "salt" sometimes lugs her bed on to the roof and sleeps under the stars. She is equally busy here, walking, blinking at the mountains and the stones. Only now her riding days are over.

Here again the same "decor" of animal skulls ("there's a bone yard near that I visit quite a lot") the same simple orderliness. Boards hung up with an arrangement of pincers, tweezers, secateurs, thread, all the things that she might need for stretching her canvases. Bottles full of new paintbrushes, Mexican muslin to prevent strangers from peering in at the windows (how on earth she is not robbed, let alone murdered, I do not know).

For twenty years she has been here looking at every stone, watching the changing sky and becoming part of a country so barren that it takes 40 acres of pasturage to feed one cow, and where water is so scarce that unless animals are in the farms the occupants must allow the water to be passed on to those who need it more. It is all very rugged and primitive, and it is this quality that appeals to this woman of rare refinement.

As she trundles among the stones in her low-heeled shoes, wearing a man's cape and hat, her arms have a bold sweep, her hands are like plates, with the fingers never far apart. She looks at you with an honest regard. She is sunburnt and wrinkled but not stained or blotched. In fact she is one of the few who gain rather than are impaired by age.

Cecil visited Kin in San Francisco, and then returned to Britain in time for Christmas. A preoccupation was the sudden death of Simon Fleet on 11 December. During the year since Juliet Duff had died, Simon had been much in the company of Diana Cooper. But he drank too much, and it was probably in a state of alcohol that he fell downstairs at his little home in Chelsea, the Gothic Box, and died.

REDDISH 24 DECEMBER 1966

This is what I have been looking forward to for a long time. A spell in the country by myself with no particular chores to do, and no midweek date in London. In fact, the reality is not quite as halcyon as I had planned it for the unexpected and sudden death of Simon distresses me a great deal, and I find myself being reminded of his presence (his name the last to be written in the Visitors' Book, the leather-bound address book he gave me and the advice now being taken about grassing over the long gravel walk across the lawn).

Simon was to have spent the holidays with me here quietly and he would have been, as ever, a most companionable asset. I am not, in fact, feeling lonely, but am ruminating about the unexpectedness of events and how none of us ever knows when the axe is going to fall. Simon seemed recently to have come into his own as a character, and was never more entertaining or full of interesting and unexpected information. He had become a London personality and it is only now, a week after he fell down his staircase and fractured his skull, that by putting little pieces of gossip together one realises that perhaps, without Juliet as anchor to his life, he was unable to cope and had in fact become desperate in many ways.

He did not eat regular meals, he drank in excessive bouts, perhaps he entertained subconsciously a death wish. Escorting a friend along the street, he said, "Do come back for a moment to the Gothic Box (where he lived, a house his for always) and isn't it sad that I have to leave it?" On other occasions he said he did not care if the result of the examination he was to have turned out to be cancer. After the infinite sadness that Simon was too young, feckless and frivolous to die, one is slightly consoled by the fact that he has possibly been spared a dreadful *dégringolade.* But who knows?

Anyhow, I am here, at Reddish, alone, with a half-dozen new books I want to read and the shelves full of all those I have had no time to enjoy while engrossed with all the nonsenses that have been so completely absorbing for almost the whole of my grown-up life.

At dinner Edna O'Brien[1] has only just arrived and she is talking of masturbation. Loelia Westminster[2] is convulsed as Arthur Marshall talks of woman's time. The "hostess" says, "Now lots of mothers are worried because their 13-year-old sons show no interest in girls and are going in for masturbation." "Have no worry!" is her advice.

Three nights ago a little group of intimates came to dinner, Caroline and David Somerset, Anne and Michael Tree, Judy [Montagu] and [Milton] Gendel.[3]

Mrs. Cartwright, the help, had such a good time listening that she refused to leave the dining room as the story was related of how Bertie Landsberg's wife came to Michael to ask him if, since they all decided he was the ideal person, he wouldn't oblige them by going to Switzerland to inject his spermatozoa into a test tube so that their daughter could have a child. Michael was flattered, but could not be left alone with the girl out of embarrassment and said he couldn't possibly go to Switzerland as he couldn't do anything into a test tube!

Caroline took up the line: "Call me when you're ready. I'll leave you to yourself for a bit." David said, "I couldn't do it alone. I'd be impotent like the Duke of Westminster" (who, it seems, was rogering a woman knowing her husband was in the next room and could never do it again). "If the hospital nurse helped, that would be better. I find uniforms rather exciting."

Caroline: "I'm very jealous that Michael should have been chosen and not you, David."

David S.: "If I have to go to bed with another woman I'll scream!"

Talk, then, of the first time. Were you a virgin? Did it hurt? Caroline: "Not a bit, it must have been all that bicycling that prepared me!"

"Oh, we don't believe that old pummel chestnut!"

. . .

[1] Edna O'Brien (b. 1936), novelist, best known at this time for *The Country Girls*.

[2] Loelia, Duchess of Westminster (1902–93).

[3] David and Caroline Somerset (later Duke and Duchess of Beaufort), Michael Tree and his wife, Lady Anne Cavendish, and Judy Montagu and her husband, Milton Gendel.

Anne talks of the current boom in burglaries. "They always defecate after doing the job. It's the sign of the professional. Well, it must be rather a windy job going through people's drawers, and they are so relieved when it's over they just go ohhh! all over the floor!"

"I do wish doctors wouldn't be so coy, can't bear them to talk about 'placie.' They should just 'ask' have your bowels moved today? When my mother [the Duchess of Devonshire][1] went to her doctor and told him she'd got a stomach upset, he asked, 'Is it soup or porridge?' and she never went back."

By December 1966 Kenneth Clark had completed a documentary about the royal palaces, which was a joint venture by the BBC and ITA. He had been asked to do this as he had served as Surveyor of the King's Pictures. It proved something of a disaster. Looking back on it, Clark thought he should have been boundlessly enthusiastic and that he should have avoided the "bump of criticism" that he found it hard to conceal. In fact, he thought the script should have been written by Sir Arthur Bryant and read by Richard Burton.

He conceded that he should have spent longer on it, and regretted that it had been filmed at a time when the Queen and the Duke of Edinburgh were away, so they had not been consulted. He admitted that he failed to capture the right tone.

There came the dreadful day when he had to show it to the Royal Family. "When they finally saw a rough cut it was without sound, and I had to speak the text from my script while the royal corgies bit my ankles. It was a total failure. The Queen and the Duke of Edinburgh disliked it so much that they would, I believe, have liked to veto the whole film. She was persuaded not to do so by Kim Cobbold, the Lord Chamberlain."[2]

Cecil reported on the horror of this showing.

K. Clark told me that he has taken nearly a year to do the TV film on the Queen's palaces. It was interesting, with for once, a running commentary by someone with a first-class brain and an extraordinary knowledge of all forms of art manifestations. He brought a greatness to the subject. He did not give us any

[1] Lady Mary Cecil (1895–1988) married tenth Duke of Devonshire, KG, Mistress of the Robes to the Queen 1953–66.

[2] This account is drawn from Kenneth Clark, *The Other Half* (John Murray, 1977), pp. 209–10.

of the *Woman's Own* gush about the glorious little lady of the throne. He talked of kings and queens as real people in history. He criticised from a very lofty plane some of the works of art in the palaces and, although giving great credit where it was due, was probably a little condescending about the position of Zoffany and the specialists in "conversation pieces" in the world of art masterpieces. But the whole effort was successful, lively and of real interest. And this is in itself difficult for the Palace, on guard against any digression from the banal.

When the film was first submitted to Court officials, he was told to delete the word "sycophants," when describing those surrounding Henry VIII. When the Royal Family were to be shown the film, K. Clark and his chief assistants were present, hoping to receive final acclaim for something of which they were proud.

When, after the showing, the lights went up, the Queen rose to her feet with a face of iron. K. Clark approached, hand outstretched, waiting for congratulations, to be met with an irate, "Did you *have* to be so sarcastic?"

K. Clark replied, "Well, Ma'am, if you didn't like the film, you must admit the photography was good. May I present the photographer?"

But HM swept out, followed by embarrassed courtiers. Prince Philip[1] lingered long enough to ask K., "How do you *know* the people guzzled at the palace banquets?"

"Because half the population was undernourished. Few had good meals. This was an occasion for a tuck-in."

The only one to show an interest was Prince Charles, a nice, sensitive boy, who would be interested in works of art if his father were not determined to knock "all that sort of rubbish out of him."

Soon afterwards David Attenborough invited Clark to do the highly successful series of 15 television films called Civilisation.

REDDISH CHRISTMAS EVE 1966

It is Christmas. My sisters are feeling guilty that I have been left alone. (Simon, dead one week, was supposed to have been a companion.) But I am not sorry

[1] HRH Prince Philip, Duke of Edinburgh (b. 1921).

for myself. I enjoy the rare pleasure of being alone. In fact, it is a necessity for me to have occasional spells when I can redress the damage of overcrowding my mind. In general so many things happen so quickly upon one another that they are soon forgotten, leaving no residue of experience.

26 DECEMBER 1966

No complaints about social life being dull in the country when one has neighbours like the Heads. Whenever one goes over to the house that was in Alys Essex's day so suburban and ordinary and is now so full of style and taste, one is galvanised by the intense interests of the characters who bring such zest to every day. Antony is vastly intelligent and has an appreciation for the things that most members of White's consider beyond the pale. Dot is one of the great characters, becoming ever more eccentric and always "true."

On Christmas Eve, Cecil joined the Head family for the evening, and talk presently alighted on Jackie Kennedy attempting to prevent the author William Manchester from quoting her on a variety of matters including her dislike of the "boorish Johnsons."[1]

"Have you come across that man?" Antony asked. My only contribution was Mrs. J. at the opening of the new Met Opera in New York. At the first interval, anyone connected with the opera productions were bidden to take part in a radio programme describing the scene for the great American public. The evening was one of intense emotion for me (frustration and irritation that Bing[2] had made it impossible for us to rehearse, jealousy and admiration that Zeffirelli[3] had managed to demand of Bing all that we would have wished) and

[1] Lyndon Baines Johnson (1908–73), President of the United States of America 1963–9, and his wife Lady Bird (b. 1912).

[2] Sir Rudolf Bing (1902–97), general manager of the Metropolitan Opera, New York, 1950–72. By 1987 he had fallen victim to Alzheimer's disease, was reported missing for several weeks and eventually found in a Caribbean honeymoon cottage with a new Lady Bing. Many legal dramas ensued. By 1990 he was confined to the Hebrew Home for the Aged in the Riverdale section of the Bronx. Author of *A Knight at the Opera* (1981).

[3] Franco Zeffirelli (b. 1923), Italian director of opera, film and theatre.

suddenly all feeling was spent and I was amused to see the ritual of the microphone. The lady in charge of the programme had invented a mute technique whereby she ordered her charges. Finger language was enforced by a rougher treatment whereby men were pulled into place by their coat ends, and women round their waists. It was quite rough-house for most.

I was surprised to find Mrs. Johnson, with a slab of extra hair on the top of her head, as if a cowpat had fallen on her crown, and a harsh grimace of a smile that only occasionally was turned off, was treated with no greater care; in fact, she came in for particular attention from the lady impresario, who seemed to take a delight in spinning her around as if a top. When I told Lewis Douglas[1] of my surprise that so auspicious a personality should be given such cavalier treatment—in fact, handled as if she were a sack of potatoes—[he] said, "Well, confidentially, I think that's just what she is!"

Anyhow, Mrs. Johnson herself did not seem to mind the rough handling and continued to stretch her lips (and nostrils) in the widest of smiles while in silence we all waited for the radio advertising to run its course so that the opera opening could then hold the attention. The impresario, eyes-a-goggle, with first finger to her lips, was seeking silence, while doubtless the announcer recommended some new motor type, breakfast cereal or deodorant. At last the commercials gave way to culture. A beaming figure of the world of music told the whole continent that here in the new 50 billion quadrillion opera house was a most distinguished gathering, first and foremost, the First Lady. "Now, Mrs. Johnson, will you tell us your impressions of this evening?"

Mrs. J., finally punched, buffeted, pivoted, pushed and elbowed by the impresario, re-stretched her lips and nostrils and gasped for air, gushed for emotion. Her eyes popped, she looked around wildly for the oxygen bag. Then into the mike she confessed, in a raucous Southern accent, "Oh! It's like faireeland! Oh, it's so glam-er-uss, it's, oh, I don't know, when I saw all those chandahleehrs, I thought they looked just like stars!" By now Mrs. Johnson had found her own supply of oxygen and, non-stop into the microphone, she told the great American public just how impressed she was at being present at such a wonderful occasion.

[1] Lewis Douglas (1894–1974), banker, American Ambassador to London 1947–50. His daughter, Sharman, was a close friend of Princess Margaret.

No one around seemed at all impressed by her presence, and my last glimpse of her was when the impresario got an underarm hook on her and twisted her round to join the milling crowds. Only then for a moment, as if a muscle had been cut, did the grimacial smile fall into a grim line that showed the determination of the woman behind the façade.

26 DECEMBER 1966

It is extraordinary how in the ordinary day's conversation the most important events are seldom mentioned. We read in the papers of some "general" happening of vast importance to us all, yet it is only the "personal" that is mentioned at church. This week, one of the most important milestones in English law has been reached, and hardly any of my friends, even those most closely involved, have mentioned the fact that at last, the recommendations of the Wolfenden Report regarding the behaviour of homosexuals[1] have been accepted. We are now almost at the point where two adults of the same sex who consent to have sexual relations with one another are no longer breaking the law. No more important event has happened since the declaration of peace. Yet few people seem to have looked back to remember with what anguish their natural inclinations made them law breakers.

Of recent years the tolerance towards the subject has made a nonsense of many of the prejudices from which I myself suffered acutely as a young man. Even I can only vaguely realise that it was only comparatively late in life that I would go into a room full of people without a feeling of guilt. To go into a roomful of men, or to a lavatory in the Savoy, needed quite an effort. With success in my work, this situation has become easier, but when one realises what damage, what tragedy has been brought on by this lack of sympathy for a very delicate and difficult subject, this should be a great time of celebration.

If Queen Victoria had possessed more understanding than we could expect of her (not sure of my facts here), the world would have been without

[1] The Wolfenden Report, instigated by Lord Wolfenden (1906–85). In 1954 Lord Wolfenden chaired the Committee on Prostitution and Homosexuals, campaigning vigorously for the implementation of the report, which was published in 1957. It led to a change in the law relating to homosexual activities between consenting males over the age of 21.

so much suffering. Fear of blackmail, fear of prison, fear of loss of all worldly hope in their professions could have been avoided by thousands. Politicians would not have suffered the sudden axing of their career from the moment of "scandal." The mind boggles at the differences that could have been brought to humanity, but the thought occurs that if the law had been different, it is quite possible that we would have had at least a half-dozen more *Importance of Being Earnests*.

For myself I am grateful. Selfishly I wish that this marvellous step forward could have been taken at an earlier age. It is not that I would have wished to avail myself of further licence, but to feel that one was not a felon and an outcast would have helped enormously during the difficult young years.

BOXING DAY AT THE BIG HOUSE

Mary [Pembroke] gives the impression to all who know her only by sight of being extremely strait-laced and conventional beyond bearing. Up to a point this is true, and her lack of imagination in certain ways, not to do with human feelings, is exasperating. Nonetheless I am fond of her, for she has the qualities that make a genuine friend. Once she has decided that you are her friend, she will give you her complete trust. In front of her friends she can relax, when she relaxes it is to the extent that strangers would not imagine it possible to be the same person that they know.

At Christmas time her Hope family relations come to the Big House for the jollifications. The old dressing-up box is ransacked for charades, but occasionally Mary will think up a special turn. There was to be one this year. It was seriously discussed.

Not too much sherry, not too much booze at dinner (food filthy, clear soup surely from a tin, tasteless slices of turkey in a white sauce, flavourless profiteroles. How is it that no matter *who* the cook may be, certain people's food always tastes good or bad?). Not too much jollity. Perhaps that wore thin at last night's charades. But, at the designated hour, Mary, handsome, conventionally dressed and coiffed, retreated to prepare for her turn. Desultory conversation, a lot of false alarms. Then the record player was turned on by Diana [Herbert]. A young Hope came in dressed as a king, and suddenly, wild-eyed, but still Mary, although disguised as Salome, a huge woman with yellow locks, thick, blackened eyebrows. It was a complete surprise, and as such it was fascinating. The younger generation may know about rock and pop, and LSD and consenting adults, but this was something true of the ruling classes of a hundred years ago.

I came away ashamed of myself for being unamused. After all, it isn't every day that Mary lets her hair down, and after all, Mary is a countess.

IRIS TREE[1]

She is being given painful rays in an attempt to defeat the cancer that has been growing inside her. The treatment makes her terribly tired and she moves slowly, nonetheless her great spirit surmounts all disabilities. She may, one moment, be sitting hunched in a chair, as if not even in the room in which we are all talking, then suddenly she comes to life with verve and brilliance, with wit, with fun, with impersonation. "If I were rich, I would buy a lot of very interesting people to have around me. I would buy all of you. I'd say I'll bid £50!—£100, £250, £300, £500." She is master of overtiming, of going on too long. "In our early days when we were photographed, the photographer dived under the black velvet and said, 'Now you must keep still while I count. Now, ready, steady, go. One, two, three, four, five, six, seven, eight, nine, ten, eleven, twelve, thirteen, twenty-one, twenty-two.' "

Diana is propping up the heavy hanging heads of some hyacinths in a bowl. "I can't think why they fall. I propped this one up only this afternoon." "It's higher since then," says Iris.

She is here for the weekend and happily her visit coincided with the final service for the much missed Simon, when his ashes were scattered in the orchard at Bulbridge beneath the plaque inscribed in the wall: "Juliet lived here."

Simon [Fleet] has gone out in such a blaze of glory. No one has had a more beautiful memorial service. Dicky Buckle, after the care with which he

[1] Iris Tree (1897–1968), poet, variously married to Curtis Moffat and Friedrich von Ledebur. She performed in *The Miracle* with Diana Cooper, the production where they met the young Simon Fleet.

Iris Tree, poet, 1965

stage-managed the funeral, brought his great gifts of organisation to the planning of a service unlike anyone else's. A beautiful little city church, St. Mary's Abchurch by Wren, with dark panelling, Gibbons carving, domed ceiling, was the venue. The flowers were simple, obelisks of eucalyptus leaves studded with carnations, John Betjeman recited a poem by Eliot, Dicky delivered himself of the best oration of a friend I have ever heard, and a row of trumpeters from the Blues added enormously to the Shakespearean effect quoted by Dicky with their clanking spurs and boots as they moved in line to their seats and finally blew a fanfare that sent shivers through all the veins of one's body.

Then the urn containing Simon's ashes was brought to Bulbridge. Andrews, an acolyte, preceded Gerald,[1] priest, brother, through the garden so full of memories of Simon, to the orchard. The faithful friends, including Diana C[ooper], Michael and Caroline Duff, Christopher Gibbs, Rosemary and Joan Olivier,[2] David Herbert, Sidney and Mary [Pembroke], Henry and Claire [Herbert]. Then, after a moment, Iris, feet planted well apart, arms stiff

[1] Rev. Gerald Carnes, former Acting Bishop of Haiti, then Vicar of Hampton Wick.

[2] Rosemary Olivier (1903–2002), and her sister Joan Collen (1901–*dec*).

to the side, declaimed a composition from Isaiah which she had learnt. Her voice rang true and bold, not a hesitation, a triumph after her illness, her face became incandescent.

The funeral oration was interrupted by signs of life continuing, schoolchildren passing by the other side of the wall, builders at work on Bulbridge roof, a jet aeroplane crossing the sky. But these only made our small ceremony the more poignant. Gerald read a prayer, and we slowly walked back, through the orchard and garden, sad that never again would we meet Simon or Juliet here, but glad that Simon, who had never succeeded in anything but "living," had died triumphantly, leaving behind a host of friends whose lives had been enriched by his selflessness, his goodness and sense of fun.

Iris, in her cerulean-blue cowboy's hat, now very serious, sad and ill, came back here to continue her struggle for survival. As we watch her, we are desperately sad, for Iris [is] like Simon, in that she has had no public acclaim for her remarkable talents. The best friend of Diana, who owes so much of her personality and character to her, she is one of the great people I have ever known.

Iris, standing back of Diana, who is helping herself to curry at the hatch: "Excuse me saying so, Diana, but it must be the rice first!"

1967

The exhibition of primitives that used to belong to Abdy,[1] sold and resold at Christie's.

"It was the only cemetery where I needed a handkerchief."

22 JANUARY 1967

I have almost got beyond being shocked by the speed with which time passes and we all become old. Yesterday was Baba's (the youngest [sister]'s) birthday. Someone had found a snapshot of N. and B. taken when children at Sheringham, left as a book-marker in a library book. Dated 1913. The owner had made a mistake as Baba, appearing as six or seven in the photograph, was born in 1912. That makes her 55. The fact that I am 63 now begs the question—time is now rushing by and out. Nothing can prevent it rushing by without one's realising it, except some momentous happening, and that is not necessarily welcome. Meanwhile one's work is all, and that takes longer as the years go by. Perhaps one knows a bit more about the job in hand, and is more of a perfectionist. But how lucky one is to have this soporific! This last week I have been concentrating on Vol. III. Each morning, first thing, before exhaustion sets in, I turn to the new start with enormous pleasure. What would one do to fill the days if there wasn't this work? I long for leisure, to enjoy exhibitions and plays and to see people quietly, but one finds disappointment is very often just

[1] Sir Robert Abdy, Bt (1896–1976), the collector.

around the corner. Meanwhile one is set in one's mould, but the turnings are always different and they keep one going. Can one ask for more?

After six months of *pourparlers,* a lorry drove up with a lot of moss-coloured stones. These the beginnings of our new plans for the garden, to do away with beds, to have lavender, rosemary and rose bushes instead of bedded-out things.

Everything arrives at once. Bricks, paving and the trees for little Japan, the prunus and flowering fruits that are to dot the hill opposite my bedroom. We are planning for posterity. We are creating an act of faith and one wishes that this had been done before. The only thing that prevents me making the major alterations is money. I never know what my financial situation is. Eileen is in charge. I rely on her to warn me when we have spent too much. I'd like very much to do alterations to the guest rooms, to have each its own bath, to clean and simplify. But Eileen says we must not do this for another two or three years. How she knows this I do not know. But here's hoping there will be no cataclysm. One can be poor when young, but never later on in life.

RE ZENA DARE'S[1] 82ND [80TH] BIRTHDAY

"Don't let's talk about old people looking young, but about young people looking old. It's so much more interesting."

Cecil then visited Paris and called on Chanel.

PARIS

Chanel is going mad in a rather interesting way. She is a remarkable person, a great character, a woman of extraordinary taste. She is a swine. She behaves monstrously to people who have worked for her for years, she has few friends

[1] Zena Dare (1887–1975), British actress who played Mrs. Higgins in the London production of *My Fair Lady* for a record-breaking number of years. She was a heroine of Cecil's formative years.

left, for those she had have either been appallingly treated, or are willing to continue merely to be audience to her incredible self-indulgences.

The last collection—said to be her final, but since it is a success she is already saying she will make another—has tired her. Her body is as strong and lithe, her mind as alert, but she now has no sense whatsoever of time or of other people. The machine rattles on while the clock ticks.

After seeing her collection, I had to listen for two hours while she talked about the Duke of Westminster and the grandeur of her life with him.[1] She, it seems, was the only person among a crowd of sycophants who stood up to him, showed her independence by stamping on the jewels he offered her or threatening to leave forthwith.

Not one word of how she would like me to work with her on the forthcoming musical, though when, with intolerable headache caused by the heat and the exhaustion, I made my excuses, she launched off on an attack on the present fashions, yet how we must make her clothes in the production of the future and not of the past (no attention paid to plot, no feeling towards reality).

Following day, I am invited to lunch to discuss the forthcoming production. We wait, we converse. It is 2:15 when she appears. One word of apology and she is off again, the one man band. She seems rather surprised when after the meat course at quarter to three I have to leave. But it would not have been a long session in any case as Chanel was off to Trouville to offer her role in the film to Elizabeth Taylor.[2] It is humiliating to have to put up with such nonsense. No payment is worth this. As it is, I am not yet under contract, nor do I wish to be until I see the final script. I'm afraid this next project is going to be a disaster unless things go very different from the way they are now.

The advertisements announce "Last week of Beaton's beautiful bravura." The revival of *Lady Windermere's Fan* has not been a success. It has not paid off its original costs. Some of us blame the theatre, the Phoenix is badly situated, gets no one in off the street. I blame Juliet Mills[3] for being without grace or glam-

[1] Chanel lived with Bendor, second Duke of Westminster (1879–1953) during the late 1920s.

[2] (Dame) Elizabeth Taylor (b. 1932), film actress, then married to Richard Burton. Cecil particularly disliked her. See *The Unexpurgated Beaton*, pp. 260–61.

[3] Juliet Mills (b. 1941), daughter of Sir John Mills and sister of Hayley Mills.

our. Binkie says, "We made a mistake in letting Mrs. Erlynne wear scarlet when she was trying to ingratiate herself to English society." Anyhow, whatever the reasons, it has failed to click, while the rival *Rivals,*[1] thought poorly of and badly reviewed, is filling the Haymarket, but worst blow of all, the appallingly vulgar production with beat-up film actresses of *Ideal Husband*[2] has been a great hit and has coined in millions for all concerned.

Before leaving Paris, Cecil visited the Tutankhamen exhibition, at the Petit Palais, some years before the famous 1972 London opening. Large crowds prevented him getting in, but one evening, driving to dinner with Lilia Ralli, they spotted no queues and were able to see it.

In March Cecil paid a visit to Morocco, where he was confronted with the Rolling Stones, then at the height of their controversial rise to stardom.

MOROCCO

I have abused myself:

I have even abused my house in the country. Instead of making it into a place where I can have an idyllic life of relaxation, away from the stress of my London activities, it has become a factory, a laboratory, a workshop. Too often have I allowed myself to come away to bed in such a state of exhaustion that it has been difficult to lose consciousness without the aid of a sleeping draught.

I know that work is the most important thing left to us, but I have become a maniac. Not a moment is lost. That extra stint is put in, the added paragraph or painted readjustment, before making the business call to London. Only rarely, when the TV has little to recommend it, do I allow myself a free evening at leisure.

I feel stiff and terribly old by the time with aching eyes, neck and back, I rouse myself with difficulty out of the sofa. It is remarkable what an output is

[1] *The Rivals* played at the Haymarket from October 1966 until September 1967, with Sir Ralph Richardson, Daniel Massey, Geoffrey Toone, Keith Baxter, Margaret Rutherford, Moray Watson and Marilyn Taylerson. It was directed by Richard Todd.

[2] *An Ideal Husband* had been revived at the Strand Theatre and ran for two years.

achieved. But is it worth it? The strain has gone on too long, and now I have had to come away to do nothing, to lie in the sun and swim in the pool, and find myself close to myself. It is not easy. It is not entirely pleasant. I face up to the horrible realities. My body is misformed, my head a mess, my brain a morass, my powers of concentration on anything new have eroded. These long moments of truth are very depressing.

Ira Belline (d. 1971), the daughter of a Russian Tsarist admiral and a niece of Stravinsky, had fled Russia with her family at the time of the Revolution, and worked in restaurants, as a seamstress and for the Diaghilev Ballets as a designer. She became one of the leading costume designers in Paris in the 1930s. After the Second World War, she settled in Morocco. She opened a flower shop, and later an antique shop. Etienne de Beaumont bequeathed her a furnished house for her lifetime, which proved too expensive, and finally Barbara Hutton bought her a house in the Palmeraie, just outside Marrakesh.

IRA BELLINE, MARRAKESH MARCH 1967

This is my paradise. If I were asked to live in Paris in great luxury in a big house I would never dream of exchanging it for this.

It is a house of no importance or personality, but it has thick white walls, and 72 olive trees grow around it. She and her brother own the farm. They sell tomatoes and carrots. They have two native boys to help, and the wife of one of them comes to work in the house. Otherwise, nothing. Ira is poor now that her job with Barbara Hutton[1] is over, and B. has not given her the promised pension (she cannot take away the house as it is bought in Ira's name). But Ira won't hear a word against B. or anyone else for that matter.

To begin with I thought her in a bad way, her hands tremble. She cannot remember a name. She seems to have little enthusiasm apart from her countless dogs, her turtles, which inhabit an almost empty swimming pool. "They love the dirt of it," she said. But by degrees I realised that without ambitions of any sort, without actually being in want, she is quite happy. In fact,

[1] Barbara Hutton had recently bought a palatial house in the Kasbah, Tangiers, which for some years Ira ran as housekeeper-companion.

with this little property to look after, she does not need friends. She does not seem to need books, certainly not natural possessions. She is perhaps one of the few happy people I know.

She talked of her first job at Chanel, as a refugee from Russia. The *vendeuses* and the mannequins were all prostitutes. Ira was shocked at their language and before had never heard the word *merde.* They would arrive back from lunch dead drunk, and lie on their dresses, until Chanel would rush at them and kick them down the mirrored stairs.

Chanel never had heart, wanted to marry Capel,[1] was *éblouie* by Dmitri,[2] and made Russian dresses under his influence. At one party ten out of twelve women wore her black Chantilly lace dress. Her colours, never bright, were beige, navy-blue and white, and *Bois de Rose.*

AN EVENING WITH THE "STONES" MARCH 1967

It was a temptation for me to get off the plane at Tangiers and join Robert Fraser[3] who was to spend a weekend with a group that would include Mick Jagger.[4] I thought at last an opportunity to photograph one of the most elusive people, whom I admire and am fascinated by, not determined whether he is beautiful or hideous.

But my exodus from the photographic excitements at home was dictated by my run-down state of health, so on I went to Marrakesh, where I knew nobody (except Ira Belline) and for four days was quite by myself. I overslept

[1] Captain Arthur ("Boy") Capel (d. 1920). He was the father of Cecil's friend June Osborn (now Lady Hutchinson of Lullington).

[2] Grand Duke Dmitri of Russia (1891–1942). Half brother of Natasha Wilson, he was an accomplice of Felix Youssoupov in the murder of Rasputin.

[3] Robert Fraser (1937–86), man of the moment art dealer, whose star was briefly high in the 1960s. "He went to prison for the Rolling Stones," declared Diana Vreeland. He was one of the first figures in the art world to die of AIDS. Harriet Vyner wrote his biography, *Groovy Bob.*

[4] (Sir) Mick Jagger (b. 1943), lead singer with the Rolling Stones. He was then involved with Marianne Faithfull, and had left England to escape the furore involved with being "busted" at Keith Richards' home near Chichester.

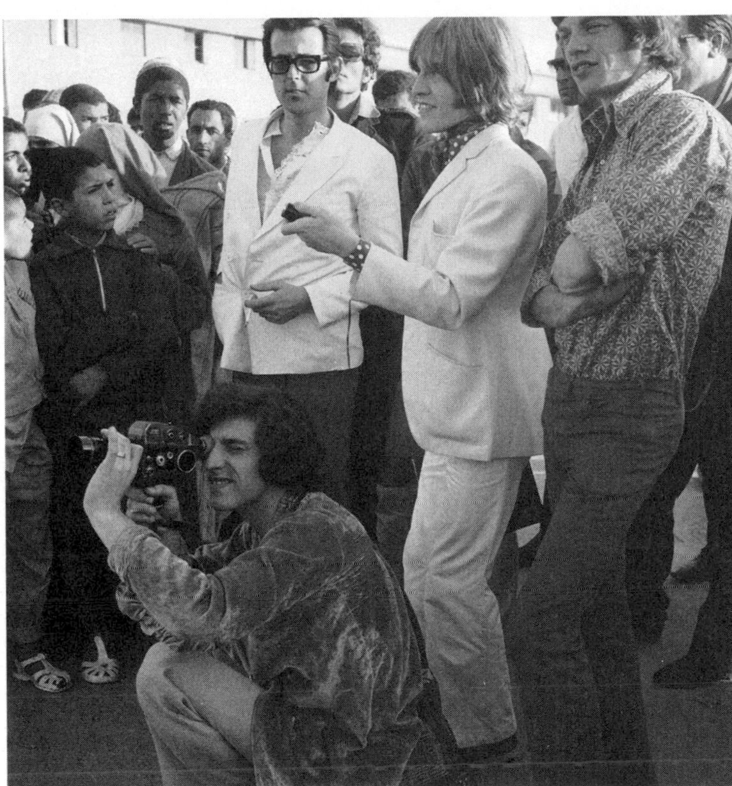

Gallery owner Robert Fraser, Brian Jones, and Mick Jagger in Morocco

and became introspective, extremely displeased with myself and hating all that I saw of myself in the nude. On the Tuesday evening I came down to dinner very late, and to my surprise, sitting in the hall, discovered Mick Jagger and a sleepy-looking band of gypsies. "Where is my friend the art dealer?" I asked. Robert F., wearing a huge black felt hat and a bright emerald brocade coat, was coughing by the swimming pool. He had swallowed something the wrong way. He recovered and invited me to join the others for a drink and then, by degrees, for an evening out.

It was a strange group, three "Stones," Brian Jones and his girlfriend, beatnik-dressed Anita Pallenberg,[1] dirty white face, dirty blackened eyes, dirty canary-yellow wisps of hair, barbaric jewellery. The drummer, Keith (?)[2] of the Stones, an eighteenth-century suit, black long velvet coat and the tightest pants,

[1] Brian Jones (1942–69), Rolling Stone, and his then girlfriend, Anita Pallenberg (b. ca. 1945), film actress.

[2] Keith Richards (b. 1943), guitarist with the Rolling Stones, still part of the group in 2004.

and a group of hangers-on, chauffeurs, an American man with Renaissance-type hair, a "Moroccan" expert (also American) from Tangiers etc. I was intent not to give the impression that I was only interested in Mick, but it happened that we sat next to one another, as he drank a Vodka Collins, and smoked with pointed fingers held high. His skin is chicken breast white, and of a fine quality. He has enormous inborn elegance. He talked of the native music, how the American had played him records of a Turk from near here, which music included the use of pipes that were the same as those that were heard in Hungary and were also the same that were used in Scotland. He liked Indian music. He would like to go to Kashmir, Afghanistan, would like to get away. England had become a police state, with police and journalists prying into your lives. Recently 20 policemen had invaded the house of the drummer in the country to search it for dope (no charges have been made). The papers had written completely false accounts. He was going to sue the *News of the World*. He'd done nothing to deprave the youth of the country. He liked to get away from the autograph hunters. Here people weren't curious or badly mannered. I noticed he used quite old words, he liked people who were permissive. By degrees the shy aloofness of the hopped-up gang broke down. We got into two cars (the Bentley I was in had driven from Brian Jones's house in Swiss Cottage to here, and the driver was a bit tired and soon got very drunk. The car was filled with Pop Art cushions, scarlet fur rugs, sex magazines).

Immediately the most tremendous volume of pop music was relayed at the back of my neck. Mick and Brian responded rhythmically, and the girlfriend screamed in whispers that she had just played a murderess in a film that was to be shown at the Cannes Festival.

We went to a Moroccan restaurant, tiles, glasses, banquettes, women dancers. Mick preferred to be away from the other tourists. He is very gentle, with perfect manners. He commented the usual style of decoration gave little opportunity for understanding to the artist. He indicated that I should follow his example and eat the chicken in my fingers. It was so tender and good. He has much appreciation and his small albino-fringed eyes notice everything. "How different and more real this place is to Tangiers, the women more rustic, heavy, lumpy, but their music very Spanish and their dancing too." He has an analytical slant and compares what he is now seeing with earlier impressions and with other countries.

Mick Jagger in Marrakesh, 1967

We talked of mutual acquaintances. David Bailey had been too busy being married[1] to take any good photographs during the past year. His film was not erotic, he wished it had been, it was merely black and white, and obviously avant-garde. He liked the new ballet, *Paradise Lost,* but [was] bored by Stravinsky's *Les Noces.* (Tchaikovsky he called the composer, but he showed he hates US chorales as much as I do, and is limited in his field of music to that which he had studied since he was 11 years old, and which he is never tired of absorbing.)

"What marvellous authority she has," listening to a coloured singer. "She follows through." He sent his arms flying about him. I was fascinated with the thin concave lines of his body, legs, arms. Mouth almost too large, but he is beautiful and ugly, feminine and masculine, a "sport," a rare phenomenon. I was not disappointed, and as the evening wore on, found him easier to talk

[1] David Bailey (b. 1938), enduring photographer, who married that year, as his second wife, Catherine Deneuve (b. 1943), the French film actress. They were later divorced.

with. He was sorry we'd not been able to converse when we met at that fancy dress party (Christie's). How could he remember? He asked, "Have you ever taken LSD?"—"Oh, I should." It would mean so much to me. I'd never forget the colours. For a painter it was a great experience. Instead of one's brain working on four cylinders, it would be 4,000. You saw everything glow. The colours of his red velvet trousers, the black shiny satin, the maroon scarf. You saw yourself beautiful and ugly, and saw other people as if for the first time. "Oh, you should take it in the country, surrounded by all the green, all those flowers. You'd have no bad effects. It's only people who hate themselves who suffer."

He had great assurance about himself, and I have too. "No, believe me, if you enjoyed the bhang in India, this is a thousand times better, so much stronger." He'd let me have a pill: "Oh, good stuff. Oh no, they can't stamp it out. It's like the atom bomb. Once it's been discovered, it can never be forgotten, and it's too easy to make LSD."

He didn't take it often, but when he was in a congenial setting, and with people he liked. Otherwise it didn't work so pleasantly. Maybe he took it about once a month. We walked through the decorated midnight souks. He admired the Giacometti-like drawings, loved the old town, was sad at the sleeping bundles of humanity. Brian Jones said he had not seen such poverty since Singapore. Mick was full of appreciation for the good things we saw, the archways, the mysterious alleyways.

THE SKY SPANGLED WITH STARS

Again we bundled in the cars. Again the gramophone records, turned on at volume. By now the Moroccan chauffeur in front was quite drunk and driving on the wrong side of the road. When we shouted in warning, Brian said, "There's no traffic!" I was quite alarmed as to whether we would get home safely. We all trooped up to our bedrooms on this floor. Gramophone records turned on, but by now it was 3 o'clock and my bedtime.

They seem to have no magnetic call from their beds. They are happy to hang about. "Where do we go now? To a nightclub?"—"It's closed"—"Well, let's go somewhere and have a drink." Never a yawn and the group had been up since five o'clock this morning, for they motored throughout the day through the desert from Tangiers with the record players blaring. It is a very different way of living from mine, particularly from that of the last four days. It did me good to be jerked out of myself. Mick listened to pop records for a couple of hours and was then so tired that he went to sleep without taking off his clothes. Only at 8, when he woke, did he undress and get into bed and sleep for another couple of hours.

At 11 o'clock he appeared at the swimming pool. I could not believe this was the same person walking towards us, and yet I knew it was an aspect of him. The sun, very strong, was reflected from the white ground and made his face a white, podgy, shapeless mess, eyes very small, nose very pink and spreading, hair sandy dark. He wore Chanel *Bois de Rose.* His figure, his hands and arms were incredibly feminine. He looked like a self-conscious suburban young lady.

All morning he looked awful. The reflected light is very bad for him and he isn't good at the beginning of a day. The others were willing only to talk in spasms. No one could make up their minds what to do or when.

A lot of good humour. I took Mick through the trees to an open space to photograph him in the midday sun, thus giving his face the shadows it needs. He was a Tarzan of Piero di Cosimo. Lips of a fantastic roundness, body white and almost hairless. He is sexy, yet completely sexless. He could nearly be a eunuch. As a model he is a natural.

Ira Belline came to lunch. Mick left the others to join us. In a sweet, natural, subtle way, he showed we were friends. Ira was charmed, gave him compliments, said how imaginatively he and his friends were dressed. He reminded her of Nijinsky upon whose lap she sat as a child. Mick talked of the struggles to success. It had seemed slow, those four years, and now it had come, he didn't want anything more than a good car. He didn't want possessions. He would like a house somewhere with 30 acres. He wanted to work less. They'd worked so hard. He'd arranged for his money to be paid over the next 30 years. He didn't want vast sums, but he had recently had fantastic offers to make films. One was intriguing. He'd be a Mexican with dark skin and curly hair, but he wouldn't appear as a pop singer.

The group lying around the swimming pool, eating a lot. Then we went sightseeing in the town, to the market square, and the souks, and to see the new young Getty[1] house (very sensible beautiful 1830 Moroccan house with just the right garden). While watching the native dancers, Mick was convulsed by the rhythm, every fibre of his body responding to the intricacies. Likewise Brian who, with microphone, was recording the music. Then in a quiet moment he blared it forth. Each of these "Stones" is utterly dedicated to the music they love; they are never tired of learning, of listening, of enjoying (they are furious at the phrase "background music").

Unfortunately they seemed to have got into bad hash habits. Brian, at one point, dozed off. "Are you asleep?"—"I just tripped off." Before dinner, a long spell in Robert Fraser's room when cookies were eaten and pipes were smoked. This meant that they did not arrive in the restaurant by 10 o'clock. The chef had left. Awful row. Embarrassing scenes. Mick came down at 10:15 p.m., to be told there was nothing but cold food. (The sideboard looked very appetising to me.) Oh, he was furious. He couldn't stomach that stuff. It turned him off. He told the maître d'hôtel he was "very silly"! He was quite angry, and chef d'hôtel too. I must say a scruffier-looking gang could never be imagined. The photographer, Michael Cooper,[2] Keith, with green velvet blouse open to his navel, in a red coat with tarnished silver fringes round the sleeve, absolutely gone. Robert, wild and unshaven. I tried to calm the scene, Mick told of an occasion when they had such a row that the food was thrown about, and of course it got into the papers.

I was determined, having waited so long, to eat my dinner. I chewed my way through *rouget*, and cold turkey. The others, meanwhile, having found a sort of restaurant that would be open until 2 o'clock, were content to sit without any idea of hunger or impatience. Brian went into a drugged sleep.

Mick intended to leave alone tomorrow (he finds travelling unpleasant, fills up on pills and becomes incredibly offhand). He said he'd like to see me in London and was pleased we'd been able to meet each other here.

There are moments when little is said but a few grunts, tough banalities, but much is sensed. I feel he is his real self. I watched him walk through the series of glass front doors of the hotel and look back for the driver, his hand

[1] (Sir) Paul Getty (1923–2003), then married to Talitha Pol who died in 1971. A long history of disasters and illnesses was before him, until he emerged under the guidance of Christopher Gibbs as one of the great benefactors of Britain's cultural life.

[2] Michael Cooper (1941–73), photographer.

on one side, the picture of grace, and something very touching, tender and appealing about him.

I wonder what the future can bring to someone so incredibly successful at such an early stage? Will the hash wreck his life, or will it go up in the smoke of the atom bomb with all the rest of us?

PS They never seem important, never in a hurry. Their beds can wait, their meals too. They do not mind if the drink ordered arrives or not. The hash settles everything. Their wardrobe is extensive. Mick showed me the rows of brightly shining brocade coats. Everything is shoddy, poorly made. The seams burst. Keith himself had sewn his trousers, lavender, dull rose with a band of badly stitched leather dividing the two colours. Brian at the pool appears in white pants with a huge black square applied on to the back. It is very smart in spite of the fact that the seams are giving way, but with such marvellously flat, tight, compact figures as they have, with no buttocks or stomach, almost everything looks well with them.

Not one book in their rooms. A lot of crumbs from the hash cookies, or the kif pipes. The most obvious defect of drug taking is to make the addict oblivious to the diet and general slothfulness that he conveys. The photographer, Michael Cooper, is really dirty, with his shirt open and trousers to below the navel. Unshaven, he spends a lot of time scratching his long hair. No group make more of a mess at the table. The aftermath of their breakfast with eggs, jam, honey everywhere, is quite exceptional. They give a new meaning to the word untidiness.

We must reconsider our ideas on drugs. It seems these boys live off them, yet they seem extremely healthy and strong. We will see.[1]

The party, minus Mick, loses all its glamour. Brian Jones seemed in a more communicative condition and smiled a lot. His voice is quite affected, unlike the rawness of the others, and he makes attempts at politeness. He even apologised for falling asleep at table last night. "It was very bad-mannered," he drawled with a bit of a lisp. I asked him about their work. They'd started off playing blues, by degrees developed their present style, altering their instru-

[1] Brian Jones did not survive, but the others, notably Mick Jagger, are still going strong in 2004.

ments, and now they spend much more time than before experimenting, playing back tapes, and now, for example, the sitar holds a more prominent role. They continue the tapes, more alterations, play back another tape. Elvis Presley, now a back liner, was very important in the history of modern music, and Ray Charles.[1] Ray, who still went on doing what he believed in and it was good, unlike the tuxedo Las Vegas gang, in their tweeds (Sinatra and Crosby).[2] Keith and Mick generally write their own words and music. They thought the best of "pop" came from the US.

At about 3 o'clock they were joined by the others, who had been house hunting. "I'd like to buy a house"—"I'd like to have a good car"—"Put a call through to London, will you?" and again there was another row with the waiters. The chauffeur, Tom, returned from Casablanca and was furious to be told there was no more hot food. The kitchen empty. Likewise the photographer—where had he been to be so late? Just waiting. He of all people to complain. Little wonder that the elderly waiter became furious. "You're a lot of pigs. You should go to the market square, the Medina, and eat your food there. That's where you belong! I am not going to serve any of you again."

Robert F. rushed out to complain to the manager. Gosh, they are a messy group. No good getting annoyed. One can only wonder as to their future. If their talent isn't undermined by drugs etc. They are successful rebels, all power, but no sympathy and none asked.

SPRING 1967

After his encounter with the Rolling Stones, Cecil travelled over the Atlas Mountains from Marrakesh to Tangiers with David Herbert, a trip of several days. Besides the beauty of the scenery, it was a chance to catch up on the breed of gossip in which Herbert excelled and which Cecil relished.

[1] Elvis Presley (1935–77), Ray Charles (1930–2004).

[2] Frank Sinatra (1915–98), singer, said to have Mafia connections, forever retiring and yet returning to the fray, and Bing Crosby (1901–77), best remembered for his perennial favourite "White Christmas" and his collaboration with Bob Hope (1903–2003), in the "Road" films.

SANS NEZ, SANS RACE

David's a great one for remembering funny stories in complete detail. The phraseology remains exact after 35 years. Viz. Mrs. Pat Campbell[1] complimenting Norma Shearer's[2] husband on his wife's "pretty little eyes *and all.*" It is the last two words that make the laugh.

And he certainly has a gift for friendship and during his life has known very intimately a great number of interesting people. When he was 18, he used to spend evening after evening with Mrs. Pat in London and, when she was staying in New York, she would call him and ask him, "Are you doing anything tonight?" and if he was busy and suggested a meeting for dinner tomorrow, she would say, "I don't know that I could wait that long."

One afternoon they went together to a hat shop. "At my age I can't buy a hat. It must be a 'good' hat." David had no money to buy her one, but the proprietor of the hat shop became so enamoured of Mrs. Pat that she said she did great justice to her hats. "They've never looked so well on anyone else."

"Oh, how kind of you to say so. I'm so blown up and hideous nowadays, and I used to have eyes like pools."

Eventually Mrs. Pat left the shop with three free hats and, at the door, turned to the proprietor and asked, "Would my autograph be of any help?"

I tried to influence David to write down his character studies, as they could have a certain interest, and any profit he might make from a book would be untaxed and of great help to house and garden in Tangiers.[3]

From his sister Patricia [Hambleden], he has a number of jokes about the Royal Family. Once in India, the Queen [Mother] was making a speech to the parched natives, who had been suffering from an exceptionally serious drought. In her peroration she said, "And I hope very soon that the rains will

[1] Mrs. Patrick Campbell (1865–1940), actress.

[2] Norma Shearer (1900–83), film actress. She was married to Irving Thalberg (1899–1936), executive producer at MGM, and the man responsible for such films as *The Barretts of Wimpole Street* and for hiring the Marx Brothers.

[3] David Herbert took Cecil's advice and produced a very readable book of memoirs; *Second Son* (1972). He delivered himself of a further volume, entitled *Engaging Eccentrics* (1990), of which one reviewer wrote, "The author finds it hard to keep himself off centre stage for more than a few paragraphs at a time."

come to irrigate your lands, and that you will all be restored and refreshed." Whereupon, with a tremendous crack of thunder, the heavens opened and there was a downpour from heaven. Soaked, they made their way to the car, and as they drove through the cheering populace, the Queen Mother, smiling and waving to the people, said to Patricia, "And if I'm ever sacked from my job at home, I can always come here and practise as a witch doctor."[1]

Jokes about special loos being constructed in Africa. One for the Queen with a crown on it and one for Patricia. On the second visit to these little huts in the centre of the forest the QM said, "This time I'm going to use yours—just to see how inferior it is to mine!"

Dancing with David at a ball at the Palace, one of Ambrose's cronies suddenly appeared singing from a balcony, "She's so right and so wrong!"

Princess Marina, arriving by helicopter to do some stunt, said, "I'm so excited at the idea of all these lovely Welsh choirs that we're about to hear." Whereupon the Mayoress snapped, "We're in Shropshire."

But, of course, the book would not have to be a string of comic stories, but a real description of the characters of the people he'd known so well.

Cecil spent a few more days in Marrakesh.

The American "choirs" singing "Love Is a Many Splendoured Thing" and "Five Coins in the Fountain" and the like nauseated me to such an extent that I did not think I could remain in the Assardi Hotel for more than a day. But, by degrees, I realised it had its benefits. The pool was heated and I spent much time exercising in it, and the straightening out of my back and shoulders was one of the prime reasons for my holiday.

The food was good and its dining room less depressing than the Mammounia. It was almost a week after that I departed to join David at Mammounia and from there started on a short trip.

Cecil and David drove over the Atlas Mountains to the Gazelle d'Or, near Taroudannt, which struck Cecil as "a phoney tarted-up luxury nightclub." They were happier at the "cheaper Sala'am with really frosty Moroccan decor," though

[1] When Herbert told the present editor the story in 1980, the location had changed to Rhodesia, which is more likely. In fact, the incident occurred in Kenya in 1959.

Cecil was pleased to be invited to photograph the Gazelle d'Or by the management. They went on to Agadir, and Mogador. Cecil took photographs. He noted:

I, with great excitement, clicked until dark. How lucky I am to have this interest of the camera. Although David says he is never bored, there is nothing to keep him from the drinks tray.

Strange interludes along the not quite deserted promenades after dinner, a dark stomping landscape with prowling youths in the moonlight.

On the fourth day, at Essaouira, the pair discussed David's forthcoming book.

Talk of David's book to be called, I suggest, "The Younger Son."[1] Talk of Wilton in 1914 war, of the young men dying in their dozens, of his seeing nothing but khaki and nurses in white.

At dinner, a younger lobster, David said that he never stopped giving thanks for the luck in his life. His father had been so understanding. "You always fall so in love with such unsuitable people and I love you for it." And his uncle, Sidney Herbert[2] (who had left him so much), asked, "And do you go in for these strange practices with your lovers?" David answered, "No, it's too painful." Uncle replied, "Yes, I found it so too!"

[On] David's father: "Your mother always wanted you to get some job, but you never wanted it. You said you knew how to be happy doing nothing, and you have succeeded. You've made a perfect life for yourself, made a lot of people happy, and it's just worked out the way you said it would."

Presently they arrived at Tangiers.

The three days in David's house were interesting. It is a long time since I have been surrounded by people with the aristocratic attitude underlying everything. Although David loves his fellow human beings, and is almost too Christlike with ugly urchins, beggars and waiters, he is very conscious of

[1] It was called *Second Son.*

[2] This was probably either Herbert's cousin, Sir Sidney Herbert (1890–1939), or Hon. Sir George Herbert (1886–1942), younger brother of fifteenth Earl of Pembroke. The money was left by Sidney to "Geordie" and then to David.

whom he considers above the others. These aren't the intellectuals, the artists. Taking me to a shop to buy presents, he said, "The best people have bought these bags, Lady Diana Cooper and Lady Kitty Farrell."[1]

He laughs about the Queen Mother's lady-in-waiting (his sister) and Mistress of the Robes (her friend, the Duchess of Abercorn)[2] crossing the street in Essaouira in bath towels to bathe in the sea. A marble statue falls into the goldfish pond: "And it's my great-aunt," yet it has been refreshing to recollect some of the atmosphere of something that is completely past.

Although he [David] reads no newspapers, he is completely *au courant* with the world of people, who is divorced, or cheating or dying. His mother's influence, both good and bad, is tremendously strong.

He has been good about not inflicting me on boring neighbours or consuls. We have pottered in the garden and slept, and one day has imperceptibly slid into another, and I have had long periods of wakefulness before being called in which to think about Kin's lack of writing, about my Vol. III and its consequences, my prospects of happiness as age and ill health increase.

I have not come to any conclusions (except that at the present moment I would say I don't want to live to be anywhere near as old as most members of my mother's family), that I should take a leaf out of David's book and remain where I want to be and let people come to me, rather than them having me always on the run. I feel I have read little, made no discoveries, but have taken time off to do nothing and that this is something I thought I could never do. It has worked, and with luck the benefits may last a week or two after my return.

VAYNOL

Michael shares with his mother and his cousin, David [Herbert], a fantastic memory.

The following stories have always amused me, but I never remember them, so here to jog the memory.

[1] Lady Katherine Farrell (b. 1922), twin sister of seventh Marquess of Anglesey. She was Lady Diana Cooper's niece.

[2] Lady Kathleen Crichton (1905–90), married (1928) fourth Duke of Abercorn. She was Mistress of the Robes to the Queen Mother (1964–90).

EMERALD CUNARD

Emerald, escorted by Chips[1] to the first big wedding after the war, Duke of Northumberland marrying Duke of Buccleuch's girl.[2] Queen Mary[3] etc. present, all the great names of British aristocracy. Chips: "This is wonderful! This is beautiful. You see all the people here. Well, we've preserved them all. That's what we've been fighting for."

Emerald (mock innocent): "Why? Are they all Poles?"

Emerald, introducing lunch guests to Lord Duveen:[4] "And this is little Poppy. She's very intelligent. She says all the pictures in the National Gallery are fakes, and Poppy knows, you know."

Re Lady Armstrong-Jones: introduces: "My beautiful daughter, Gwyneth."[5]

"Blodwin, how many times have I told you not to wipe out Sir Armstrong's tooth glass with the chamber cloth?"

Irate talk at club about a peer.

"The chap should be shot." Expatriates: "A disgrace." Suddenly *The Times* is lowered. An angry old man explodes, "Lord—. I'm sick of hearing about him. If a peer of the realm cannot be allowed to bugger a boy scout, I don't know what the world's coming to!"

Re Lilian Braithwaite,[6] showing off brooch given to her by Ivor Novello:[7] "Can you see it?"

Michael remembers the physical characteristics of beings who have gone before.

[1] "Chips"—Sir Henry Channon, MP (1897–1958), remembered as one of the significant political and social diarists of his time.

[2] Hugh, tenth duke of Northumberland, KG (1914–88), married (1946) Lady Elizabeth Percy (b. 1922), daughter of eighth Duke of Buccleuch.

[3] HM Queen Mary (1867–1953), widow of King George V.

[4] Lord Duveen (1869–1939), art dealer, who worked with the aid of Bernard Berenson.

[5] Margaret Roberts (d. 1943), wife of Sir Robert Armstrong-Jones (1857–1943), and her daughter, Gwendoline (1905–85) who married Hon. Sir Denys Buckley. Margaret was the grandmother of Lord Snowdon.

[6] Dame Lilian Braithwaite (1873–1948), stage actress.

[7] Ivor Novello (1893–1951), actor in spectacular musical romances.

Lady Colefax, while talking to H. G. and B. B.,[1] would be rearranging all the objects on the dining table in front of her.

Lady Granard[2] sends silver boxes etc. flying the length of the table.

Lady Crewe[3] continually dusting her mouth with a sideways pendulum swing of a chiffon handkerchief.

Hiding behind a pillar at her own party at Crewe House, she says, "If I were you, Michael, I wouldn't venture in there. It's a terrible party. With any chance I won't have to face them, and take my advice, stay away."

Michael also relished the fact that Lady Crewe would never, out of shyness, or self-satisfaction, demean herself to wait with the other patients in a Harley Street waiting room. Arriving on time at her dentist, she would send in the chauffeur to enquire if the dentist was running a little late, or was ready for his next appointment. If it was a question of waiting, the car would drive her round the square until eventually she could be shown straight into the dentist's chair.

Michael's fund of unnecessary knowledge is reached when he asks, "Did you know that, out of kindness, Simon [Fleet], every Thursday afternoon, used to bugger Drino Carisbrooke?"[4] One afternoon, when the performance was over and Drino was standing naked on the bed, he noticed a crown above, on the curtain. "That's a Schleswig-Holstein crown, what's it doing there?"

"I don't know. I just bought it."

"Well, you're not entitled to have it. It belongs to the Schleswig-Holstein family."

. . .

[1] Sibyl Colefax, hostess, H. G. Wells (1866–1946) and Bernard Berenson (1865–1959), art historian, living at Villa I Tatti, north of Florence.

[2] Beatrice Mills (d. 1972), daughter of Ogden Mills of New York, she married eighth Earl of Granard (1874–1948). As an owner, she won the 1964 One Thousand Guineas with *Pourparler.*

[3] Lady Margaret ("Peggy") Primrose (1881–1967), married first Marquess of Crewe, KG (1858–1945). She was the daughter of fifth Earl of Rosebery, KG.

[4] Alexander, first Marquess of Carisbrooke (1886–1960), son of Princess Beatrice and thus a grandson of Queen Victoria. He married (1917) Lady Irene Denison (1890–1956). He lived at Kensington Palace.

Lopokova[1] once shared a sleeping apartment on a train from Spain to Paris with Mata Hari. Lopokova was on the top bunk. "We were very polite. She was obviously made for man's delight, very big and round, with a precise, clear wheeling of the body." But she was not allowed into France, and although stopped at the frontier, Lopokova did not know that she was a spy.

HAROLD NICOLSON

Have been reading N.'s Vol. II[2] with as much pleasure as his first pre-war diaries. Again I wonder why it has been that, in spite of being told again and again by his friends, James P.-H. [Pope-Hennessy] and others what a fine fellow he is, I've never liked the man.

Again he proves himself to be such an honest good character, sensitive to others, far-searching about himself, unvulgar, noble-minded, and with an eye to the comic. Often he is able, in the written word, to make me blub; in fact, I finished this book in a blub of tears. But when scrutinising the photographs I again see that I am as put off by his physical appearance as I was in life. How unfair this is, especially as he is the first to denigrate himself in all respects. But the Cupid doll mouth, the paradoxical moustache, the corpulence of hands and stomach all give me a *frissant* [sic] and there is no getting over the fact that I could never become a friend of his. Sad because he could have been a help and guide and an influence for the better.

Cecil had one surviving aunt, Cada Chattock, the youngest sister of his mother. She was not as potent an influence on him as his other aunt, Jessie Suarez, but nevertheless he retained a residual loyalty and affection for her. As with many families, the myth and the reality were different, and though he kept in touch with Aunt Cada regularly, he also felt guilty that he did not do more.

[1] Lydia Lopokova (1892–1981), ballerina. Married Maynard Keynes (1883–1946), first Lord Keynes, economist.

[2] *Harold Nicolson: Diaries and Letters 1939–45*, edited by Nigel Nicolson (1967).

AUNT CADA, REDDISH

6 MAY 1967

I don't do enough for Aunt Cada, who is 87, blind and lonely. I telephone her whenever I can, but that is not enough. So when she telephoned to suggest coming for the weekend, arrangements had to be remade, and when she appeared, white stick, smart hat and fashionable suit and all, I noticed that the five years' interval between seeing her had become apparent. Her face has lost its aquiline shape. Her dead eyes have not any light in them. Her hair has become just an old lady's white hair. She seemed more infirm, and sadly spilt some of her tea on to her suit.

Yet no sooner settled and rested from the tiring journey than she took on terrific impetus and never stopped talking. Her angel guardian and daughter, Tecia,[1] sat interested by her side, but contradicting and interrupting quite unnecessarily. As the evening wore on, drinks time and dinner time approached and passed, Aunt Cada never paused for breath. If I started to tell a tale, I had to shout not to be interrupted. I would soon become exasperated. Little wonder that Tecia was irritable, on edge, nervy. At dinner, T. would say, "No, you're not to eat more strawberries. You'll be ill. No more wine. No, you're wrong. The story wasn't that." After dinner T. contradicted and shouted in opposition to such an extent that I suggested, "It's your mother's story. Let her tell it. It doesn't matter if she gets it wrong." But I was becoming so on edge that I suggested Tecia should go out to the kitchen to yak a while with the voracious Mrs. Culverhouse. This worked well, in that Tecia was out of the room for almost an hour while Aunt Cada held forth with me.

Since she is blind, I need not hide my restlessness and looked round the room to see what should be done in the way of alteration, setting to rights, improvement. I soon became pulp in the face of this non-stop avalanche.

Stories of Aunt Jessie being the first woman to go over the Andes.

Then suddenly Cada wished to go upstairs and the evening was over. Tecia returned from the kitchen. She looked starry-eyed. "Oh, you've no idea of the strain. I don't know how I can last out much longer. The old lady's indefatigable, strong as an ox, and my nerves [are] cracking. I've been to the doctor.

[1] Tecia Fearnley-Whittingstall (1907–92), Cada's elder daughter.

I'm all blown up. Look at my ankles and feet. They won't get into my shoes, and yet when I *do* go away for a holiday, I deflate again and become quite thin. It's all nerves. You used to be exasperated with your mother in her last years. Well, I've had 15 years of this.

"Those three beautiful sisters were indestructible, all spoilt, all all-conquering, all having their own way, to the extent of fighting with one another, all living to the ripest of old age."

I felt too weak to talk, just axed with sadness, horror, and when I retreated to my room, gratitude overcame me that my troubles have thus far been so small in comparison with those of others, who bear them with such extraordinary fortitude.

Even after sporadic glimpses of my Aunt Cada during the short visit, I found myself utterly exasperated. I cannot imagine how Tecia must feel. At dinner I was quite rude. Non-stop conversation from the poor, blind old lady.

REDDISH MONDAY, 11 JUNE 1967

It is 8 o'clock and there is time to hear the news. I am looking out of the window at the green scene when I hear that war has been started in the Middle East.[1] Israel and Egypt were saying the other was the first to be the aggressor.

The awful sinking dread singes through from the groin to one's solar plexus. At once one thinks, not of the suffering, the pain, the killings in the far land, but one selfishly thinks of home, of oneself. If the war spreads one will soon be involved. Even if only remotely, by the rationing of fuel. Oh Lord! That we should once more have to undergo such privations. It seems such a little time ago that we had to conserve our allowances, perhaps scrounge an extra can of petrol? And the continual dread. The encroaching anxiety.

But miraculously the Israelis, against all odds, brought about in three days a complete reversal of the Middle East picture. By fighting a brilliant campaign, Dayan[2] has overthrown the Egyptians and Jordanians, Nasser[3] is humiliated and the particularly anguishing picture we have lived with all these years

[1] War broke out on Tuesday, 5 June.

[2] Moshe Dayan (1915–81), Minister of Defence in the Israeli Cabinet.

[3] Gamal Abdel Nasser (1918–70), President of Egypt 1956–8, and United Arab Republic 1958–70.

has changed, and no one can be more delighted than our neighbour up the valley, Anthony Eden,[1] who miraculously, in spite of a plastic duct and continuous fevers, has lived long enough to feel he has been vindicated and his bogey destroyed.

On 12 June 1967 Lord Avon celebrated his 70th birthday after years of indifferent health.

It was quite an extraordinary atmosphere of event, joy, achievement that pervaded the pretty Georgian home at Alvediston that Clarissa and Anthony have recently bought. It was Anthony's 70th birthday celebration, and no one could have had a more wonderful birthday present than the events of the last week, which have meant that, in principle, Anthony's much criticised policy on Suez and his distrust of Nasser were correct. Clarissa, generally so cold and reserved, admitted this evening that she was "stewed." She could not have been more enchanting in her gaiety and, in an aside of happiness, said "I never thought Anthony would live long enough to see himself proved right. It has been the most wonderful time with the bulletins and friends ringing to give the latest news."

Anthony, sunburnt and wearing a maroon-coloured velvet dinner suit, seemed to be the picture of health and radiance. He was surrounded by his loyal *confrères* and a few members of his family. Bobbety Salisbury[2] had made a speech that was eulogistic, but neither embarrassing nor sentimental. Oliver Lyttelton,[3] whose desire to amuse has increased with the years to the extent that he is a real bore, made one funny joke. "The evening's been a great success. Only one setback. Nutting's[4] chucked." Lord Scarbrough,[5] having motored from Yorkshire, was pissed to the world, but would try to talk. Lambton[6] motored from London. A surprising group, young Lord Brooke,

[1] Anthony Eden, Earl of Avon, KG, who had just moved to the Manor House, Alvediston. He had been Prime Minister during the Suez Crisis of 1956.

[2] Robert, fifth Marquess of Salisbury, KG (1893–1972), doyen of the Conservative Party.

[3] Oliver Lyttelton, first Viscount Chandos, later KG (1893–1972), former Conservative Cabinet minister.

[4] Sir Anthony Nutting (1920–99), who had resigned so memorably over Suez.

[5] Roger, eleventh Earl of Scarbrough, KG.

[6] Viscount Lambton was one of Eden's great friends and admirers.

Nicholas, other young Edens, Ronnie Tree, Antony Head, and the Hoffs[1] (whom I brought). The house very pretty with a goodish collection of pictures cleverly invested by A., and then good quality wedding presents. Nicholas handed round tulip-shaped glasses of Elizabethan (II) vodka! This was real dynamite and tasted like aquavit, and took one's breath away as it went down one's chest. Bottles of champagne popped, and the gathering was fraught, but private, very English, understated and poignant. My mind went back to the morning at Reddish when Clarissa came into my bedroom, sat down on the brown and buff tapestry chair and asked, "Do you think I should marry Anthony Eden?"

KARINSKA

Recently Karinska was struck down with a gammy leg. In fact, she had broken her hip. When her nephew brought her a bouquet, Karinska, with typical Russian gloom, said, "Oh no. I don't want to lie and watch them die!"

In June, Cecil went to Royal Ascot, an event he should have enjoyed since he had made it such a feature of My Fair Lady *with his elegant and funny costumes for the "Ascot Gavotte" scene, both on stage and in the recent film.*

But now he felt old and tired, sometimes overworked, at other times restless. He fought this, but dreaded "the look of empty boredom" that older people's faces often showed. His visit to Ascot brought home to him how far he had moved on from what he called "childish pleasures."

MY LAST ASCOT

JUNE 1967

As a snobbish boy, I was always dunched when my mother's request for tickets to the Royal Enclosure at Ascot were turned down. Nothing would have given me more pleasure than to parade with my family in a condition which proved

[1] Lord Brooke (1934–96), later eighth Earl of Warwick; Lord Avon's great-nephew, Nicholas, Viscount Eden (1930–85); Lord Avon's son and heir by his first marriage, Ronald Tree; Viscount Head; Raimund von Hofmannsthal (1906–74) and his second wife, Lady Elizabeth Paget (1916–80).

conclusively that, as the *Tatler* would say, one was "In Society." But the slap in the face came back again and again from Lord Churchill[1] on behalf of the Queen.[2]

Eventually "society" went for six. Now practically anyone who can pay the few guineas necessary is welcomed, and with the opening of the floodgates that brought in Jack Hylton,[3] Binkie Beaumont and any starlet available, I was given the OK. But it was too late. By the time I was there, the grand ladies in their *Fair Lady* dresses had all died. Fashion and exclusivity had gone. It was no good trying to give artificial respiration to a dead donkey. The Ascot weeks that I spent in the pleasant company of Mrs. Nancy Lancaster were really rather an effort. The horses were pretty, the jockeys' colours very unexpected, but I know nothing of racing, don't know the technique of when a jockey rides well, so little wonder that I am bored, and very tired.

However, now the rules have changed. You need not buy an RE [Royal Enclosure] ticket for a whole week. For one day it might be fun. I went under the best auspices, with Jakie Astor and Chiquita,[4] whom I love. He is a member of the Jockey Club, can make things easy. Delightful lunch at their flat, easy car journey, till the queues started half an hour from the course. Jakie was witty and more intelligent than I could possibly have been. He is a bright boy, charming. Chiquita was quiet and sympathetic, as a companion ideal.

Then all sorts of forgotten snobberies rose to the surface, awful distractions, awful unimportant things assumed importance. Very depressing to witness these things again. Arrival on the course perfectly timed. The Royal Procession was coming towards us. Some people with a banner were running in front of the oncoming horses. "Stop the murder at Vietnam," the police were slow on the mark, but no embarrassment to the Royal Family, who, unexpectedly, were wearing, instead of the usual pastel, colours of great vividness. The Queen in violet, the Queen Mother in puce, a mushroom puff of puce tulle on her head. Jaipur[5] in a marvellous turban of ochre and scarlet, and this change of colour is one of the things that have happened.

[1] First Viscount Churchill (1864–1934), Lord Chamberlain 1902.

[2] Presumably Cecil meant King George V.

[3] Jack Hylton (1892–1965), former bandleader who became theatrical impresario, also a racehorse owner and breeder.

[4] Hon. (Sir) John Astor (1918–2000), and his wife, Ana Inez "Chiquita" Carcano (d. 1992), daughter of the Argentinean Ambassador to Britain.

[5] The Maharaja of Jaipur (1911–70), a keen polo player, often at Smith's Lawn, Windsor.

Pop Art has infiltrated itself even to the Royal Enclosure. Seeing this tribune of women in the serried ranks was quite a pretty surprise, for everywhere there were large touches of brilliant magenta, orange, eye irritant viridian. Edwardian Ascot must have been entirely pastel-coloured. Here was a change that one enjoyed. But not the others. The quality of the material was so poor. The plastic and the nylon look so crummy in the outdoors. The retina irritant imitation leather shoes and handbags are part of the Roxy Floor Show. The crocheted shift, the miniskirts and little girl fashions are not right for here.

But then I am not right for here. Loelia [Duchess of Westminster][1] gave me a look of surprise: "What are you doing here?" It was no wonder that I didn't enjoy myself, that I pretended to be interested in the sights, in the awful phenomenon. It was not boring to be irritated, as I was, by the smugness of some of the members of the Royal Family and their retinue. It was not boring to go into the Holy of Holies, the Jockey Club restaurant for a short drink of iced coffee and to hear Lady Sefton[2] call her husband a bugger. It was not boring to lose £1 each way on Mrs. Engelhard's horse,[3] and the sight of the French Ambassadress[4] in Mizza Bricard's *art nouveau* picture hat adorned with water lilies was the one fashion note that gave me a slight tremor. But I was in a great state lest we should *not* leave before the last race (and thus avoid the worst of the traffic).

I returned home crushed with fatigue, but worse, worried and depressed that my powers of enjoyment had entirely gone from this form of entertainment. Perhaps the fault lies more in my choice. For me, at my time of life, to go off to such a function was perhaps asking for trouble. It is not suitable. It is something that does not interest me any more. At 63, I must find

[1] Loelia Ponsonby (1902–93), third wife of second Duke of Westminster, later Lady Lindsay of Dowhill. This she would have said in a voice that was a mixture of amused welcome but with a sharp hint that Cecil had moved out of his orbit and had no right to be there. Part of her own curious insecurity.

[2] Josephine ("Foxy") Gwynne (1903–80), wife of seventh Earl of Sefton, a stalwart of the hunting world and an inner member of the raffish circle of the Duke and Duchess of Windsor.

[3] In 1967 Charles Engelhard (1917–71), the inspiration for Ian Fleming's *Goldfinger* in the James Bond books, won the St. Leger with Ribocco. He was famed in racing circles as the owner of Nijinsky, who won so many classic races in 1970. He won £55,502 as a winning owner in 1967. His wife, Jane Brian (1917–2004), was a well-known art collector and philanthropist.

[4] Martine Hallade, wife of Baron Geoffroy de Courcel (1912–92), French ambassador to London (1962–72).

things to take the place of the things that interested me in my adolescence. Otherwise I am in for a disappointing time, and a wretched old age.

THE THEATRE

The theatre is another form of enforced entertainment that I am finding hard to enjoy. Early on in life it was enough for me to watch the curtain rise on an illuminated set and to peer at the make-up on the performers' faces. Now this is hardly enough. The well-known situations, the clichés and the acceptance of ordinary standards of behaviour that we see in the usual commercial play does not give me anything but excruciating uneasiness.

I have become expert at deciding to quit the theatre at the first interval. But after the trouble, time and expense of getting to the theatre by "curtain up," this is not a satisfactory way of spending the evening.

Occasionally, however, an evening in the theatre stands out as giving me utter contentment. This was the case recently when, at Hampstead, Roy Dotrice[1] gave an extraordinary imitation of old age in a one-part play about John Aubrey of Broadchalke. This entertainment, derived from Aubrey's diaries, showed the old professor on waking, and going through the domestic chores and thinking about life and general matters as he did them on the last day of his life.

Dotrice's understanding of and love and sympathy for old age was one of the best pieces of histrionic art I have ever seen. It was completely in the framework of today's taste and was part of an evening of exquisite pleasure.

The strange play, *Rosencrantz and Guildenstern Are Dead,*[2] also gave me a rare lift for it embodied in a different, oblique, way, the lure of the theatre. The romanticism, even mysticism of the players, the backstage, the changing of scene and the innate poetry. But this sort of occasion is rare. Even Shake-

[1] Roy Dotrice (b. 1925), actor. He played in Patrick Garland's adaptation of John Aubrey's *Brief Lives,* which later played at Golden Theatre, New York, in 1967, and at the Criterion, London in 1969, taking the world record for the longest-running solo performance, over 400 performances.

[2] *Rosencrantz and Guildenstern Are Dead* opened at the Old Vic on 11 April and played until July, with Edward Petherbridge and John Stride.

speare is treated with such gross disrespect (by Zeffirelli and others), that one only comes away from the play angry at the wrong emphasis. The lesson to be learnt is that one must choose with greater care. The reason that sister Nancy thinks she is giving me a treat by inviting me to see *The Beaux' Stratagem* at Chichester is not enough to warrant my putting aside work for a whole day and being exhausted, angry and frustrated as a result of the long expedition, the only really enjoyable part being the drive through the lanes of many trees at their last white blossoming on the way to the ugly Festival Theatre.

One must choose and decide with greater care, then the possibilities of disaster can be to a greater extent avoided, but even so the element of the unexpected is lurking so that one can never safeguard oneself. Even in safe-guarding there is danger, for one is apt to close too many doors. That is also a part of old age. One must keep the doors open, but only those that one feels have a good chance of opening up life-enhancing vistas.

Cecil liked to be in touch with the young and relished all that the talented youth of the 1960s were exploring, partly since his group had done much the same in the 1920s. He was therefore particularly interested in Christopher Gibbs. And Gibbs has testified to the kindness of Cecil to "us youngsters."

CHRISSIE GIBBS JUNE 1967

Chrissie Gibbs, delightful, intelligent, extremely well informed, has become one of the leading "dopists" in a certain young set in London. It is amazing that he had not been run in by the police, who have been after him for the last two years. Like all who take dope, and he is said to confine his activities to marijuana, he is elusive, evasive, and difficult to approach on the subject.

When he asked me to have dinner quietly with him, I thought the evening would be interesting in the revelations that he would give me in reply to my interrogation.

The evening was different. I returned to Pelham extremely late, having been out all day, in a state of near collapse. Even a strong drink would not be the means whereby I could go through the evening forthwith. Was dinner really at 8? Yes, a message had come through from Mr. Gibbs's secretary earlier in the day. "Dinner at 8 at Mr. Gibbs's house." I rang to ask if it would matter

Marianne Faithfull and Christopher Gibbs, 1967

my being a little late? No reply. Ten minutes later I rang again. Would it matter being late? "Not at all. Take it easy."

I took a bath. I felt a great devil lying luxuriously in hot water while the day's exhaustion flowed out of every pore, and then in a fresh shirt and suit taking a taxi to Cheyne Walk 40 minutes late.

On arrival I found Jane Ormsby-Gore, with her baby Saffron[1] lying in a sleeping basket, smoking marijuana cigarettes. She was calm and sad about the tragic accident that had killed her mother four days before. She spoke sympathetically about the misery that her father still must face, each time some

[1] Hon. Jane Ormsby-Gore (b. 1942), married (1966) Michael Rainey, then a trendy tailor, and their son, Saffron Rainey (b. 1967). Her mother, Lady Harlech, had been killed in a car crash.

Mick Jagger and Anita Pallenberg on the set of *Performance*, 1968

new aspect of his loss occurs (the snapshots that he took on that last Sunday's tea party will one day be returned from the printers).

Michael Cooper, the photographer, joined her in smoking (I had a puff or two) and in condolence, while Chrissie bustled about his dark-panelled rooms doing nothing in particular and certainly never settling down to talk.

Half an hour later Michael Wishart, freshly out of a nervous-nursing home, came to call for Jane. She snatched up the basket and they disappeared. "Mick's coming to dinner," said Chrissie, "bringing Marianne Faithfull,[1] but I can't think where they are." At 10:15 they appeared. Mick, in a gold brocade coat with tight coffee-coloured trousers, was vellum-white of face, grey of hair and

[1] Marianne Faithfull (b. 1947), pop singer.

Mick Jagger on the set of *Performance*, 1968

so huge of mouth that it was quite indecent. He shrugged a bit, made no pretence of manners and settled down to look at a picture book. Marianne, with white suety face, the usual drowned blonde hair and smudged eyes, and a large tear of her dress under the arm, fluttered and made "groovy" conversation. She took an occasional and casual deep puff although she said she and Mick had been back to his "pad" to get high after the awful evening at the Court Theatre where (unprofessionally) they had left after the first of two of the Joe Orton plays.[1] Also present, by now, was Prince Stanislas Wasserpee Wipper Püdler Wittensteinpesse or some such name,[2] which surprised us when it was brought into prominence as being that of the friend arrested with Brian Jones for being in possession of [drugs].

I remember seeing Prince Stanislas two years ago at a freak Dufferin party when he walked around, a huge, white and black Hamlet, wearing, in spite of the heat, a heavy black cape. He looked extremely self-conscious and po-faced, was said to be a promising pop singer. The promise has come to nothing. Tonight he was still dressed as Hamlet, with stripes of sequins on his blouse and his shoes painted psychedelically in silver, magenta and gold. He showed a large white décolletage, had a vast Adam's apple, huge white hands with fingers covered with rings. Byzantine black pageboy hair, white face with potato nose, he was quite revolting-looking. Throughout the long evening he spoke not at all.

In spite of the impediment in his speech, the most articulate member of the group was Robert Fraser who, since he was arrested with the Rolling Stones, has, I believe, been dis-intoxicated from his nervous habits, but hard dope has taken its toll on his appearance. He has the usual pallor, the five o'clock shadow, the tie badly in need of a pull up, the greasy hair.

All dopists have a habit of never bringing to a conclusion any given topic of conversation. A few isolated remarks go off into thin air and one feels coarse-grained if one continues along the same line. This does not make for stimulating discussion.

I made cursory attempts at conversation with Chrissie, but his heart wasn't in his replies. At 11:30 we went off in taxis to the Baghdad House Restau-

[1] Joe Orton (1933–67) had just rewritten *The Ruffian on the Stair* and *Erpingham Camp* for the stage double bill *Crimes of Passion* at the Royal Court Theatre.

[2] Count Stanislas Klossowski de Rola, son of the artist Balthus.

rant in Fulham Road. Here in the club-like atmosphere of the basement we found others of the gang, Mark Palmer,[1] more rodent-like than ever with his greasy blond hair over his nose; Michael Wishart, looking as if he needed to go back to the nursing home; the youngest Tennant girl[2] dressed like an aged twenties figure with dark glasses, LSD frizzed hair, a miniskirt over thick purple woollen stockings and rows and rows of clairvoyant beads.

Also present Jane O.-G., her husband, Michael Rainey, badly shaved, with shoulder-length hair, asleep, "out," with his head on a shoulder, and near by the flashing lights and roar of jukebox, the baby Saffron in the shopping basket.

I remarked that the baby was being brought up in a strangely foetid atmosphere. Chrissie jumped to his friend Jane's defence. "She's being very careful about how she brings the child up. She's read all the books, has theories of her own. It's going to be a vegetarian and is really beautifully looked after." At this moment the baby started to wail. The sleeping beauty of a father awoke, strove in his tight hipster pants to pick up the baby and while the Jute [juke] gave us Indian zither music, the baby screamed and the father showing off to full advantage his beautiful lean hips, patted the baby on the bottom, swirled round, jigged up and down, did all the nursemaid tricks. Jane looked on vaguely.

I tried to talk to Mick but he shrugged, twitched his eyes, contorted his mouth and screwed up his face. He was hungry. He wanted "fewd." Little plates of mush were brought. He put a cake of pap into the huge mouth. I was, by now, in a trance of fatigue. Robert Fraser extolled the virtues of Andy Warhol's[3] *Chelsea Girls* film. Wouldn't I like to come and see it? He had it at home (it runs for four hours). I wondered if I should be a devil and make a night of it, put a sign "Do not disturb," forget about Miss Gaffran for exercises

[1] Sir Mark Palmer.

[2] Hon. Catherine Tennant (b. 1947). She later married Mark Palmer. Their daughter, Iris, became a well-known model.

[3] Andy Warhol (1928–87), painter, film maker, diarist and inveterate party-goer, who shocked the world with his depictions of Campbell's soup tins. *Chelsea Girls* (1966) was a sequence of interwoven life stories, the first underground film to catch the imagination of the general public. It was variously hailed as "the *Iliad* of the Underground" and as a "grotesque menagerie of lost souls whimpering in a psychedelic moonscape."

at 8, about the first appointment at 10, the following at 11, 12 and 1. But no, I hadn't the strength. I said, "If you'll excuse me" and it was 1 o'clock when I left to walk home up the deserted Fulham Road, leaving the night to them to turn into something or nothing.

Cecil suffered a burglary at Reddish House, with all the attendant feelings of invasion and upset that accompany such things. "A fashion sitting employing the little phenomenon Twiggy[1] had been arranged for my day." When it was over, Cecil went down to the country to inspect the damage. It could have been worse. The bedroom gave him the worst shock:

All drawers opened and ransacked, and over the bed flow all Kin's letters, snapshots of us taken in California, Garbo's snapshots, messages, all the memorabilia hidden in the locked iron coffer which, denuded of its secret hoard of cash and surrounded by garden implements and a poker, lay bashed open upside down on the floor. This sight was upsetting. It made me realise that one has absolutely no privacy, that everything can be bared to the world. The contents of this box were innocuous enough, but what if they had not been? In any case I did not want these things to be seen, and now everything was on view for police and servants alike.

In contrast to pop groups and the younger generation, Cecil was still as excited to meet a survivor from the past. He went over to Wilton to meet one of three surviving granddaughters of Queen Victoria, Princess Alice, Countess of Athlone. The Princess, born in 1883, was the only daughter of the haemophiliac Duke of Albany. In 1904 she married Prince Alexander of Teck (later Earl of Athlone, KG), who was Queen Mary's brother. At this time she was a sprightly figure, who travelled to Jamaica each year by banana boat. She lived at Kensington Palace, and frequently travelled by bus. She wrote her memoirs, For My Grandchildren, *in 1966 and lived until she was nearly 98, dying in January 1981.*

[1] Twiggy (b. 1949), wafer-thin model (real name Lesley Hornby), who proved unusually enduring—an actress notably in Ken Russell's film of *The Boy Friend.*

PRINCESS ALICE, LADY ATHLONE

I'd never met this little woman before but lately, when going through all the early bound magazines from Sweden, had seen pictures of her at her wedding and in her early life. I was struck by the tiny-ness of her waist, and the *potelé* little bosom and rounded hips that were pushed out from the corset. Now the Princess, playing croquet under the cedars of Lebanon at Wilton, was distinguished as an 80-year-old lady.[1] The remains of beauty are still there, though the waist has gone, together with her porcelain complexion, and the teeth are now false, anonymous.

But unlike most Royalty, and perhaps she has the advantage of being very "minor," she has a directness that is healthy and her shyness is well under control.

The Pembrokes continue in their tradition of the Edwardian house party and had assembled 12 for this weekend, which was now, on Sunday evening, at a low ebb (half of the guests having departed), and it was in quite a relaxed atmosphere that, the croquet over, we were relaxing (after a long hot weekend that had made the flowers look a bit blown) in the library having a drink before dinner.

The Princess talked on her Topic A, which was of Queen Victoria.[2]

The following points interested me.

The children were all very much in awe of this auspicious little figure. It was always being drummed into them that they must behave in front of her so that when she appeared they quaked.

But she was easy and good-humoured, laughed a lot and had two long bird-claw-like teeth in front that appeared whenever she was amused. (Princess Victoria,[3] known as "The Snipe," inherited them.)

The Queen had no figure, an avalanche of basalt black, and wore little white lawn collars and cuffs that were immaculate. I think the word for the neckpiece was "tucker." The tucker was not worn high round the neck in the

[1] In fact she was then 84.

[2] HM Queen Victoria (1819–1901).

[3] HRH The Princess Victoria (1868–1935), second daughter of King Edward VII and Queen Alexandra. She was a spinster, who frequently "sneaked" on the royal princes to George V.

fashion of the time (others wore whale-boned collars) but was quite décolleté (and therefore dowdy). The Queen was very clean and always smelt refreshingly of rose water.

The Queen did not possess a style or dress sense, yet when she went to Paris, the Empress[1] was considered a grande dame, while the Queen was real "*Reine.*"

She was often making a hat, plaiting straw together and the Princess was furious at having to wear this hat, which she considered hideous, and the Queen would be angry when the children played with her spinning wheel.

At Windsor, Balmoral and Osborne, there was always too much food, the sideboards heavy with cold and hot meats and fowls. Always two soups, clear and thick, fish, eggs, choice of meats and capons, and so much for the servants to take away, such a waste.

Mrs. Gladstone said, "Willie[2] always likes sleeping between the Queen's sheets."

A jolly little woman, having a lot of fun out of life up to the end.

In September, Cecil and Lord Pembroke made an expedition to Sweden together. The rest of the time Cecil preferred to be in the country, but was inevitably drawn back to London.

LONDON WEEK

On Tuesday, the glorious long spell of sunshine continuing, I delayed my return as late as possible. My first date was a dinner with Ann Fleming. I could not remember what it was in aid of, but I felt it would not matter if I arrived 20 minutes after 8. But I was not counting on the loathsome Mrs. Barbara Castle[3] (of the expensive "hairdos") and her new electric trains. The service all along the line was disorganised and we arrived, after halting at every station, an hour late. Ann's dinner was a typical gathering, Jewish, Liberals, politicians, foreign

[1] HIM Empress Eugénie of France (1826–1920), wife of Emperor Napoleon III.

[2] Rt. Hon. William Ewart Gladstone (1809–98), Prime Minister 1868–74, 1880–5, 1886 and 1892–4, and his wife, Catherine Glynne (d. 1900).

[3] Rt. Hon. Barbara Castle (1911–2002), then Minister of Transport in the Labour administration. Later a life peer.

officers, dowdy-looking ladies, excellent food, good talk. I sat next to Ian Gilmour[1] who surprised me by being pro-Nasser and Arab, while Solly Zuckerman and Max Rayne[2] wanted to jump on him. I drank champagne, talked afterwards of the new generation in the person of Penny Cuthbertson (Baby Jungman's daughter)[3] whose independence and courage I admire. But in spite of the entertainment I must get home, for the morrow would be crowded and I must get into training, and I knew a letter was awaiting me from Kin.

Letters about the burglary to answer, questionnaires for insurance, photographs for my book, and NPG exhibition, and the usual rush to be ready for an interview and to go to join a mysterious group (Bath, Queensberry, Bishop of London, O. Lancaster, J. Miller, Roy Harrod, F. Ayer etc.)[4] for *Queen* magazine, taken by a very go-getting, tough Lord Lichfield,[5] who had been out so late at Annabel's in the company of "The Pill," Miss Lynda Bird Johnson,[6] that he had had no time to shave.

Nice summertime interlude for lunch with Bindy Lambton and lots of her children, Rose,[7] 14, in a state of acute self-consciousness, her white-painted face gouged by two huge Dutch doll painted eyes; the little Ned [Lambton], five years old now, and less beautiful but still a character and my favourite, Isabella,[8] adorable, and unlike the others in that she has a quality of gentleness. Bindy, vast and crippled by her accident, like Lileth. After alfresco lunch everyone leaps into heated swimming pool.

[1] Sir Ian Gilmour (b. 1926), later a Cabinet minister and now Lord Gilmour of Craigmillar.

[2] Sir Max Rayne (1918–2003), later Lord Rayne, Chairman of London Merchant Securities.

[3] Penelope Cuthbertson, daughter of Teresa Cuthbertson (b. 1907) who was one of the Jungman sisters. Penny married (1985) Hon. Desmond Guinness.

[4] Sixth Marquess of Bath (1905–92); twelfth Marquess of Queensberry (b. 1929); Rt. Revd. Robert Stopford (1901–76), 114th Bishop of London (1961–73); (Sir) Osbert Lancaster (1908–86), cartoonist; (Sir) Jonathan Miller, director; Sir Roy Harrod, the economist; and Sir Freddie Ayer (1910–89), philosopher, who were all photographed together. The group was meant to show "you can judge a man by the company he keeps."

[5] Patrick, fifth Earl of Lichfield (b. 1939), photographer and man about town. A great-nephew of the Queen Mother.

[6] Lynda Bird Johnson (b. 1944). She was staying in London as a result of which David Bruce, the American ambassador, and his wife Evangeline had been obliged to "chuck" a weekend with Cecil, soon after his burglary. At the time he described Lynda as "that horrid daughter of that horrid President of the United States." She married (1967) Major Charles Robb, U.S. Marine Corps.

[7] Lady Rose Lambton (b. 1952), married Oliver Musker, another sixties wild child, who at one time nearly married Marianne Faithfull.

[8] Lady Isabella Lambton (b. 1958).

I go round the town with an assistant to photograph a yard of discarded cars, but the effect was not what it had been, and things one sees from a taxi window are no longer the same when one returns a week later. The Park afforded not very unusual and interesting pictures, and I came back feeling that no contributions had been made to my book.

The younger generation in the form of Stella Astor, Christopher Sykes and Martha Laycock[1] graced my house, and were snapshoted with a distorting lens. A beautiful man from Big Sur came in and made me wonder if beauty were enough.

The heat became oppressive—the Italian Ambassadress's[2] fight to open a window in her drawing room after two dozen of us had sat at a long table for a formal dinner in which there were gaps of silence due to certain people turning in the wrong direction (this always happens at this embassy and once the Ambassadress sent a note down to her daughter not to talk to Mr. B., as she was causing a hiatus). Gasping for breath, I returned.

Twiggy to be photographed. She is an easy little marvel of photography, can't look wrong, followed in the heat by Lord Reay,[3] a strange, enigmatic extension of an eighteenth-century portrait. The Dufferins likewise come in for a "sitting" that is very informal and they talk of dope, many of their friends not having been able to arrive at their party as such strong "cookies" had been passed round after dinner. Then the peers go off to vote for the amendment of the laws on homosexuality.[4] A great event in history that this should have been achieved. What a difference if Lord Queensberry's ancestor had had his great-grandson's sense of enlightenment. O. W. could have given us half a dozen more *Importance*s and early life for so many of us made less difficult.[5]

Nothing to do for the evening so I took off to the country again and, arriving at 9 o'clock in Broadchalke, I sat on the terrace looking at the garden, the trees, the sky fading, the birds flying across the open space, or flapping

[1] Stella Astor (b. 1949), daughter of Hon. (Sir) John Astor; Christopher Sykes (b. 1948), photographer and author, son of Sir Richard Sykes, Bt; and Martha Laycock (b. 1949), daughter of Sir Robert Laycock, married David Mlinaric.

[2] Madame Guidotti.

[3] Hugh, fourteenth Lord Reay (b. 1937).

[4] Following the Wolfenden Report.

[5] John, ninth Marquess of Queensberry (1844–1900), father of Lord Alfred Douglas (1870–1945), who accused Oscar Wilde (1856–1900), the Irish playwright, of perversion in 1895, as a result of which Wilde was imprisoned in Reading Gaol.

their wings in the Fragonard hills. Utter quiet. The stillness was almost haunting, not a leaf in the tallest tree was moving, complete quiet. A slight rumble of distant thunder? No, a far-away aeroplane. Turned round and went away and left behind complete and eerie silence.

In August Cecil rented Reddish House to two Americans. He went to stay with the Trees at Mereworth after a visit to the National Portrait Gallery to discuss his forthcoming retrospective exhibition with the young director, Roy Strong,[1] *"such a nice odd character, a real addition to my acquaintance, owl-eyed, funny, calm, and so unimpressed with his success at half my own age."*

Cecil visited Sissinghurst, where Harold Nicolson was living a widower.

TO SISSINGHURST AUGUST 1967

Even three [five] years after V. S.-West's[2] death the garden is still her triumph. What would there be to see in August? A purple, lavender, mauve border, an orange yellow garden, a white, grey, pale-greenish garden, each a triumph of horticultural knowledge and imagination.

The populace crowd over the private dream come true and there, sitting cross-legged in the sun, is the remains of Harold N. After his stroke he is really just a clockwork dummy. He smiles, his eyes are bright, but he is clothed in the anonymous vestments of old age, scraggy white moustache, bald white hair, pendulous stomach. But his brain does not work any more, just vague automatic answers in reply to something he doesn't understand.

"Your purple border is wonderful. Congratulations," I said.

"I haven't been out much lately. I haven't seen it," he replied, and to other questions he gave a good-humoured low benevolent growl.

It is sad that he does not have the satisfaction of realising the great success of his diaries, but he seems contented in his animal state of relaxation and inactivity, which could presumably continue for another fifteen years.[3]

[1] (Sir) Roy Strong (b. 1935), director of the National Portrait Gallery 1967–73, then director of the Victoria and Albert Museum 1974–87. He brought the NPG to life, not least with the Beaton exhibition in 1968.

[2] Vita Sackville-West died on 2 June 1962.

[3] Harold Nicolson only lived until the following year, dying on 1 May 1968.

Cecil also visited Firle, the estate of Lord Gage,[1] *where Duncan Grant,*[2] *the painter, was living.*

"Duncan says"—"Duncan did this"—"Duncan was there"—"Duncan's arriving." This all my Cambridge days. Duncan was an unknown god to me. When, years later, I eventually met him, the glamour had gone. He had become aged and passé. The Bloomsbury manner and quiet, breathless voice remained, and the charm, but none of the qualities that made others breathless was there. We went to see him today.

His house is a museum. He has lived in it for 45 years. It is unchanged since the day he and the Omega Workshop decorated it.

It was like seeing the set for a French play in a provincial theatre, fascinating.

In this house he lived with Vanessa and Clive Bell. Although known principally as a homosexual, he had a child by Vanessa, now said to be the most untidy, ugly woman alive.[3] Here for 45 years he has painted and decorated, and continued to live his essentially Bloomsbury sort of life. It is now a completely "lost" period so it was interesting to see these rooms today in the company of such bright contemporaries as Anne and Michael Tree, who were aghast at the self-painted wallpaper, like something in a mad whorehouse, the painted chimney pieces, with every inch of moulding and panelling trellised or dotted, crossed or marbled to frame Pomona with her bulging cornucopias of paint and all the "standby" figures of this school. Nothing was left to its own resources. Even the radiator was decorated with tile top and braided frieze, from which cords of brown and grey fringe hung to the ground. The dining table was a thing of beauty, a subject for Vuillard, large, circular, and painted in concentric circles in various tones of pink and shrimp. It has acquired a delightful patina with the years, and today in the centre stood an off-white cracked pot containing three of the darkest full-blown red roses, one mauve and a white rose. It was an invitation to bring out the palette and brushes.

[1] George, sixth Viscount Gage (1895–1982).

[2] Duncan Grant (1885–1978), Bloomsbury painter.

[3] Angelica Bell (b. 1918), officially the daughter of Clive Bell (1881–1964), writer, and his wife, Vanessa Stephen (1879–1961), sister of Virginia Woolf (1882–1941). She married the Bloomsbury writer David Garnett (1892–1981).

Not so the studio. This really was in too great a state of disrepair and disorder. The decorations were peeling or fading in mildew. Pomona was about to crash from her oval canvas and one felt that the stacked canvases had not been gone through for many years. But Duncan presided with the authority of someone who was still someone. He is on terms with any stranger. He is not apologetic about anything.

Present were two Woolfs who are publishing a recently discovered seventeenth-century cookbook to be illustrated by Duncan. It all seemed very unnecessary and tiresome, and no money can come to anyone for it. But the talk was civilised for there was great respect for the past and for the fact that here was something that could show how others had led as civilised lives as they.

Talk about neighbours, Connolly hating to be the tenant of Gage, but hating to have to leave his house, Gage always liking to keep his tenants on the move, of Lydia Lopokova, now seldom seeing anyone and welcoming no one before teatime as she is apt to be about the garden in the nude. Talk about the garden, which grows on its own without intervention, but what to do about the bulrushes in that pond? He so liked to see a reflected patch of sky but the bulrushes had completely taken over, and he didn't know how to get them cleared away, about getting someone to mend the road, or attend to the lights in the studio, or painting out the peeling bathrooms, or even finding time to shave himself or have his hair dyed black.

But the drinks were liberal, and one's eye was cosseted by flowers carefully chosen and arranged, and one knew that the host was completely contented with the way he continued to live in a world that had almost entirely forgotten him.

LONDON WEEK

Tuesday—Felix[1] and a Japanese film. Later *The Man in the Glass Cage* about Eichmann,[2] pretentious and last act surprise but a theatrical event with Pinter

[1] Felix Harbord (d. 1981), interior decorator.

[2] In fact, *The Man in the Glass Booth*, a play by Robert Shaw about Adolf Eichmann (1906–62), German Gestapo Chief, who escaped after the war, but was found in Buenos Aires and executed. It opened at St. Martin's Theatre on 27 July 1967.

ambiguity in atmosphere. But Pleasence's[1] remarkable performance ruined by a *deus ex machina,* the long-forgotten Sonia Dresdel,[2] coming out of the audience and focusing all attention for the rest of the play on herself.

Friday to Sandwich, an intended nostalgic return to the scenes of early holidays, where rather poor we enjoyed a rented cottage life away from the crowds and feeling that the grand elite of Sandwich Bay, if not near at hand, gave the whole place a tremendous cachet. But my return as one of the elite of the Bay (staying in the huge Astor[3] house) was short-lived, as Michael [Tree], spoilt and erratic as he is, decided that the four of us must return on Saturday to Mereworth where the bed I had vacated last Monday had hardly become cold.

However, I did see that Sandwich isn't what it was when the Prince of Wales lived in an oak-beamed monstrosity, with Mrs. Dudley-Ward and daughters nearby in a coastguard's cottage.[4] The big "Bay" houses are now turned into flats (no servants to be got) and the large hotel is faring badly.

The return to Mereworth in a rainstorm with charabancs and motors of all sorts filled with perambulators and boats etc., filled with holidaymakers on their way to Ramsgate and Margate in clouds of water, was indeed a sad sight. But the sun made Sunday a memorable day. Looking out early, the world was golden with bright blue shadows, a Monet landscape of vast trees. It was altogether a wonderful patch of weather and the gardens full of all that I love with black shadows under the trees.

The spell continued as next day I drove to Stratford for Scofield's *Macbeth* (sadly unmoving due to current mania for Brechtian non-emoting).[5] On next early morning to Paris to take photographs of Rex Harrison in a Feydeau film, something that I really considered as a job that was only undertaken because it is the way that I earn my living.

[1] Donald Pleasence (1919–95), actor who also played villains in many films.

[2] Sonia Dresdel (1909–76), British stage actress invariably cast in masterful roles.

[3] The Astors had a house called Rest Harrow at Sandwich.

[4] The Prince of Wales's affair with Freda Dudley-Ward (1894–1983) was known in society, though not generally known. The daughters were Angela (later Lady Laycock), and Penelope (later the wife of Sir Carol Reed, the film director).

[5] Paul Scofield (b. 1922), actor; his *Macbeth,* directed by Peter Hall, later transferred to London, to mixed notices.

PARIS, HÔTEL CRILLON

I don't know why the rich, when deathly and old (and above all American) depress and disgust me more than any other human beings.

I had a solitary dinner recovering from the exhaustion of the last two days of film studio delays and hot air, in the luxury of the Crillon grill. The dinner, *foie gras* and kidneys, was excellent, but the whole atmosphere of needless luxury struck me as being so useless and ridiculous and revolting that I came to bed feeling I had escaped from the jaws of hell.

The sparsely sprinkled dining room was inhabited only with Americans. Not one of them appeared to justify their existence. None possessed a kind look in their eyes, or a vestige of sympathy, warmth or gaiety. They all looked like something preserved in an embalming liquid in a bottle. No knowledge of allusions, no wit, sensitivity, just taking for granted that others should work to the bone for them. Little wonder the French have shown their antipathy and disdain.

Opposite were naïve women from the South hanging on the words of every stranger like a wasp on an equiliser, readily amused, nodding at anything, easily frightened, one saying repeatedly "What worries me . . ." These were the best in the room, one old scarecrow in black lace, dyed hair in topcrust, would have no wine, no mineral water, no aperitif, would start with consommé chaud—she explained to the waiter "that means hot consommé."

A group of nine Americans in a circle in the hall. A wild-eyed woman is doing the honours. "Now let me present. This is Mrs. Taylor. This is Mr. Taylor. This is Mr. Taylor. This is Mr. Taylor. This is Mrs. Taylor. This is Mr. Taylor. Mrs. Taylor. Mr. Taylor." Smirks, beams, pursed lips, gimlet eyes.

The group move to the restaurant. They are waited upon by waiters trained like acrobats, highly skilled at manoeuvring on the high wire with plates and forks and salad bowls with the exquisite dressings they have made.

By far the worst was the elderly couple sitting next to me, the man rich, very old, with no reservations left towards his nagging loathsome white slug wife. In a drone she went on without ever looking at her husband, "Oh, get me a ring, something outstanding. I need a new——. Look what I need. This melon is very low in calories. Anything can happen here. This is getting to be a bit like home."

"What is?" Silence.

"I'll read you Annette's letter: 'I didn't have to ask him for money. He just gave it me. If you want me to do any shopping for you let me know in good time.' Am I to write to her and say I don't like the way she writes? I should have a letter from Melissa in the morning. Where's the bill? That's not so cheap; 30–80 per cent plus 13. Here's 40 cents. Am I rich!"

When the two staggered out, the white slug-rat was wearing creased pea-green trousers. What loathing crossed my face.

FLEA IN HER EAR, PARIS — AUGUST 1967

I know from experience how difficult Rex Harrison can be. He was all goodness and light arranging that he would be pleased to be photographed by me as Poche[1] tomorrow. He would be ready, made up at 12 o'clock. Rather than take a few pictures there and then, I agreed to the delay though I know Rex likes to delay as much as possible, until he is in a bad mood.

I arrived at the Boulogne Studios punctually, Rex's Rolls-Royce not there. I waited half an hour in exasperation, then got the studio to send me round to the Bagatelle. In the sun-flecked gardens I forgot my irritation, and [it] was amusing to see a painter in front of the green scene of trees, lake and grass painting a stylised all scarlet picture.

On returning to the studio Rex's car was parked outside. I waited. Eventually I went up to beard him. No word of apology could ever pass his lips. He said, "How did you enjoy seeing the Bois?"

The photography went well. I beat my own record for the number of pictures taken, literally hundreds, and I felt, with few exceptions, they all had a certain freshness of appraisal. What interested me most was that I found I was playing the part of a director and giving Rex all sorts of instructions about qui-

[1] Rex Harrison starred in the dual role of Chandebise (the lawyer) and Poche (the hotel porter) in the joint U.S.–French production of a Feydeau farce, *A Flea in Her Ear* (1968), which also starred Rachel Roberts. He made the film in a last-ditch attempt to save his marriage to Rachel.

etening down the eyes, a softer look, not exaggerating the character, and I found myself inventing all sorts of business which I'm sure will find its way into his performance on the screen, Poche picking his nose, de-waxing with a finger his ear, standing stiff against a wall to "make himself scarce" in the brothel, yawning fit to kill.

Rex was tremendously enthusiastic, his vast "ego" flattered to the fullest, and I must admit that he gave, as usual, a perfectionist's performance. He minds, he takes infinite trouble. This characterisation is all important to him. He minds nothing of riots in Hong Kong, the war in Vietnam, the Arab–Israeli and Czech situations. He turns myopically to the script once more.

Having done a great stint in the morning, we lunched together (denigrating Sir Laurence [Olivier]). Then Poche turned to Chandebise and the inventions continued until utter exhaustion was long forgotten. I felt young and energetic and happy, my 40-year-old assistant Jean being worn out long before me.

Rex would have gone on posing until the moment when he would suddenly say, "I can't be expected to do any more work," but the ugly moment never came. He complained to the Publicity person that I gave him a real workout, but even though they were tired smiles, we all smiled at the end of the long day.

ON THE SET

It is clever of the producer to make this Feydeau farce in a French studio. Here all the artisans are really dedicated artists, they understand their job and appreciate what they are asked to do in the way of reconstructing the art nouveau period. Everyone is concerned, and Jacques Charon,[1] the director is an artist. He works with joy. Everyone seems to be happy. It is so much easier when everyone has respect for each other's talents. How different was the atmosphere on the set of *Fair Lady.* Cukor[2] was a dictator of Nazi proportions

[1] Jacques Charon (1920–75), French actor, who had originally directed the play at the Comédie-Française.

[2] George Cukor had had Cecil under contract for several months in 1963, while he directed *My Fair Lady.*

with his henchmen thugs ruling over the whole unit with terror and menace. To be on the set was to be in the lobby of the gas chamber.

Of course, Cukor was in terror of [Jack] Warner who, having spent so many millions on the picture, started to panic and run for home, with the result that the pressure to finish was the chief concern of all responsible. But it was typical of Hollywood to go on making the mistakes for which [it] has been criticised and almost driven out of business during the last 20 years. But nothing will change Warner. He will blindly continue to make the same old mistakes, and somehow manage to die with an extra million in the bank.

Cecil continued to observe the guests and staff of the Crillon before leaving Paris.

SUMMER 1967

For several summers, Cecil accepted an invitation from some rich friends to stay with them, or go on a cruise on their private yacht. Such hosts were Charles and Jayne Wrightsman, rich collectors then living in New York City (see biographical note, The Unexpurgated Beaton, *pp. 95–7).*

On this particular trip, Radiant II *sailed to Yugoslavia, taking in Pula, Trogir, Split, Dubrovnik, Korĉula and Kotor, before reaching Corfu. As usual, Cecil studied his fellow travellers and his hosts.*

THE CRUISE—DON'TS FOR CHARLES

JULY 1967

Never be late. Philip Johnson,[1] who enjoys being ragged himself, is a master of Charles's cynicism and frankness: ("Why don't you two go to the Blue Grotto tonight? It's a marvellous place for married people who aren't getting along too well") says, "If you're ten minutes early, you're still late for Charles."

"Never have a cold, or Charles will catch it and name the cold after you."

[1] Philip Johnson (b. 1906), Cleveland-born architect in the modern aesthetic movement, considered as one of the great architectural minds of the twentieth century. In the 1960s he designed the Kline Science Center, at Yale University (1962), the New York State Theater at Lincoln Center, New York, and the New York State Pavilion at the World's Fair (1964). His best-known book was *Philip Johnson: The Architect in His Own Words.*

"Never drag the wicker furniture on deck."
"Never use sun oil."
"Dive at an angle to the ship, but parallel."
"Don't walk decks with wet feet."

GENERAL TALK

On Met Museum's directors' meeting, Jackie and Bobby Kennedy, Clare and Henry Luce,[1] her LSD addiction, his millions and her fighting for more than she had been left, $30 million, the President, Vietnam, pot, the sea, sailing, other vessels, the wake of a ship, the shoals of flying porpoises, the editorials in *Washington Post* and *Newsweek.*

TOM HOVING[2]

Tom Hoving, seeing fragment of a head with hand over its mouth: "I've lost my passport."

Extrovert. "Don't step back or you'll tread on old Venetian dog, that's raw sewage," imagination (impersonation of guidebook), healthy, diving off deck, big breakfast, tremendous physical vitality, gestures, gesticulating, twist of head on thick trunk neck, hair that waves as soon as sea water dries in sun on head, long, strong fingers, heavy long legs, alert insect eyes, grinning smile that reveals small badly coloured teeth. A phenomenon, mind as alert as body, a well-rounded man.

Next day suddenly all is changed in a flash. One eye pops wider, his hair curls, he holds forth too indiscriminately. He has no regard for others, he slaps down his wife. One realises that he is oblivious of his physical attractions

[1] Jackie Kennedy (1929–94), Senator Robert Kennedy (1925–68), Clare Booth Luce (1903–87) and her husband, Henry Luce (1898–1967).

[2] Tom Hoving (b. 1931), director of the Metropolitan Museum of Art in New York 1966–77. In his book, *Making the Mummies Dance* (New York, 1993), Hoving left his own description of Cecil on this cruise: "Cecil Beaton was a living encyclopedia of social small talk, titillating anecdotes, and major-league gossip—all in flowery good taste. Cecil never stopped flitting around or chattering. His eyes never quite focused on you, so busy was his search for someone of greater importance" (*op. cit.*, p. 114).

because they are not there. One wonders how one could have been so subservient and willing to heed to his assault.

Presently the yacht arrived at Corfu.

CORFU

Cypresses and old olive of extraordinary height, and trunks pitted with holes like Gaudí architecture. Poverty, perfume of hot grass at evening. Empress Elisabeth's[1] hideous Achilleon Palace, the palace full of japonaiserie, Temple of archaic beauty of Perseus and the Dragon with serpents, the most beautiful of all we have seen.

CORFU, THE ROYAL FAMILY VISIT TUESDAY

Arrival by motor boat of Queen Frederica[2] and daughter Sophie.[3] The Mumhun reminds me of Clare Luce, a German equivalent. Then, due to the accent and voice, of that old trouper, Marlene Dietrich. All my prejudices are out. Is the smile too ready-made? What is she after now? What is this act all about? Meanwhile the daughter speaks in the same voice as Princess Marina ("charmming!"), but is easier, with a sympathetic chuckle, spotty non-chin, bulging low cheeks but pretty eyes and easy conversationalist.

The King,[4] very boyish, puppy fat, silken hair, sexy, hirsute eyebrows, button mushroom nostrils, with drooping lids, and baby teeth, arrives from Athens, grateful to be asked to take off his coat in the air-conditioned drawing

[1] Empress Elisabeth of Austria (1837–98) visited the Achilleon Villa (built 1889–91) in spring and late summer until her death. Later the Kaiser owned it for a time.

[2] HM Queen Frederica of the Hellenes (1917–81), daughter of HRH The Duke of Brunswick, and granddaughter of the Kaiser. Married (1938) HM King Paul of the Hellenes, who had died three years before, in 1964. Known as an energetic Queen of Greece, whose dabbling in politics was eventually the undoing of her son, King Constantine. Later she spent some time in India involved with a guru.

[3] HRH Princess Sophie (b. 1938), daughter of King Paul and Queen Frederica. Married (1962) HRH Prince Juan Carlos of Spain (b. 1938). Now Queen of Spain.

[4] HM King Constantine II of the Hellenes (b. 1940). King in Greece between 1964 and his flight in 1967. Married (1964) HRH Princess Anne-Marie of Denmark (b. 1946). An Olympic oarsman.

Queen Anne-Marie of Greece

room "lounge." His Queen [Anne-Marie], pretty complexioned, but too young to show any character, and dressed in a most uneventful way. An ugly unmarried sister, Irene,[1] is the most serious and a good pianist.

Evelyn Waugh wrote that the presence of Royalty was like heavy thunder in the air. These people much less heavy than their equivalents in England. I have Queen F. on my left, giggling, Sophie on right. The Mum is deaf, but I have her better ear. She talks of her vegetarianism, started because she had seen so much suffering and did not wish to inflict more on animals, fish or anything that loved its mother. I laughed. "What about whitebait?" She was sur-

[1] HRH Princess Irene of Greece (b. 1942). She studied the piano with Gina Bachauer. When the family went into exile, she followed her mother to India. She now lives in Madrid.

Queen Frederica of Greece

prised at my laughter, but has the sense to laugh at herself. "I did not like my mother,"[1] she added.

Re LSD and drugs, this was like taking a glimpse of heaven but paying with shoddy money. Should be done by isolation (immolation?) and fasting.

Re her politics. She was called fascist, yet had worked on our side against the Germans during the war. The British papers had been monstrous but the people had wanted fair play. She related being set upon while walking outside Claridge's, how with Princess Sophie, she had been shaken, then the police had intervened with her attackers. She asked the daughter to report on progress as she walked on in a dignified way. "Two are on the ground" and now, "They are closing in on us." She walked faster, and only when in the mews at the back of the Italian embassy did she run and ring a door-bell (and thereby give Marti Stevens[2] the story of her life).

[1] She certainly did not. The Duchess of Brunswick was not invited to Sophie's wedding, and a fearful row ensued when some journalists were imprisoned following an interview conducted with the old Duchess in 1962, when she complained of being neglected by her daughter. This was deemed to be treason in Athens.

[2] Marti Stevens, cabaret singer, actress (*All Night Long*, 1961), and close friend of Marlene Dietrich. Daughter of Nicholas Schenck (1880–1969), who created the Loews Entertainment group.

"Good, right!"—Queen slang.

Then she heard the King telling the story to the three rapt ladies of the revolution.[1] He had been seeing a Rock Hudson[2] film and hating it, so that he decided to see another. By remaining so long, he probably saved himself from being hijacked in the road to his country home. In the middle of the night he was telephoned by his secretary to say there was a revolution. "Who are they?"—"Don't know." He spoke in whispers as he telephoned his mother. Guns put to the door. "We are here to protect you." Army officers, some of whom he did not know, were the instigators. The King furious and likely to "shout" if the rebels did not allow him a constitution with his own appointed PM.

Everyone who is not popular considered a Communist.

Meanwhile no bloodshed. Everything cleverly organised like clockwork, and now that the whole excitement had died down, they begin to realise that changes *had* to be made, that the regime could have been Communist and the family put behind the Iron Curtain, and the army now beginning to find it hard to cope with all difficulties, and more amenable to the King's suggestions.

This seems to be odd considering the youthfulness and lack of experience of the King. Yet he is a figurehead and very popular, his wife is so pretty and young, and a son and heir just born.[3]

This more or less the King's story. But the day was spent by the guests on board trying to piece word for word everything he had said, filling in the gaps and questioning much that remained baffling. Having gone so far as to say he could not possibly believe the family did not know what was in the wind, that each member of the family was here to tell their fabricated story.

From the fragments I heard this seems impossible and I cannot believe that such a young boy is capable of taking on such a difficult role in public affairs. Judging from his appearance, he seems utterly genuine, simple and straightforward. Little of his mother's blockbusting ambition seems to have come through.

[1] There had been the "Colonels' Coup" in Athens on 21 April 1967, during which the military seized power in the name of the King. The King and his family were confined to the Palace for some days.

[2] Rock Hudson (1925–85), enormous American film star, known for particularly mannish roles, who nevertheless succumbed to AIDS to universal shock.

[3] King Constantine and Queen Anne-Marie had a daughter, Alexia, born on 10 July 1965, and their first son, Crown Prince Paul, was born on 20 May 1967.

Anyhow arguments continued, piecemeal, and so many tiresome interruptions or beside the point questions were raised that I thought it best to come straight to bed, before I showed signs of exasperation with any of my close inmates.

Queen F. asked Charles, "How much does this yacht cost you?" Answer not given. One of the children asked Jayne the same question. She genuinely didn't know.

Talking of the vast sum he has to pay on the insurance of his furniture and works of art, Charles said, "The collection Jayne and I started to make 20 years ago is now worth 17 million." The valet flies back to NY with Charles's luggage. There is $260 excess to pay.

The taxi driver at Corfu asked $100 for their two jaunts of sightseeing.

JAYNE

"The Hovings didn't reply to our invitation for two weeks." I could write their dialogue: "I hate the rich. I'm not going to spend time with that crowd. It's bad enough having to go to a social dinner party to encourage a lot of people to give to the museum, but to be locked up with that bunch!"

SHIPBOARD LIFE

Most of us realise we are under careful scrutiny and try to show ourselves in the best light. Hoving, who was dazzling at the outset, has become a friend, non-stop "show off," ruthless to his pathetic wife, a go-getter mixed up in the world of art and high-powered business, a troublesome combination. How can he have such enthusiasm for a medieval reliquary and concentrate only on those who are to help him in his career?

After a week, certain of us loathe his incessant interruptions, his whistling, his raucous badinage, his greed, his self-interest. Deeda [Blair][1] even confesses she hates the way he swims.

[1] Deeda Blair and her husband, Ambassador William McCormick Blair, were on board.

After a large vodka cocktail, I make great efforts to break down his wife's barrage of uncommunicativeness. I ask her what is her husband's Achilles heel. Apart from suggesting that he is incapable of wandering and wondering alone like she can and does. She does not know where it can be. "We must try to find it, and you must dig into it mercilessly when you've found it."

Next day she says I'm a feminist and marvellous. I am surprised and rather appalled to think how easily I can make an effect with her. If I am in danger of becoming conceited, then I only have to realise the utter lack of any ripple I have made on the husband's consciousness. I just don't exist.

Cecil then caught sight of himself in the glass opposite his bunk, which provoked one of many similar horrified self-examinations: "I am horrified. Aloud I exclaim, 'Oh, that's terrible!' The deep lines at nose to mouth are like black tracks. The mouth is a slit, the head on top baldly bullet-like, and the wild hair sticking cockatoo fashion out above the ears is that of King Lear."

He wondered how others tolerated him and considered the similar fate of friends.

Randolph Churchill, looking old, grey, like a haggard hawk, has been on the brink of death for three years. The other night he told me that he was now happier than he had ever been. He was at last doing something that satisfied his life, his book on his father,[1] the best thing he had ever done, his contribution to the world, and the fact that he was no longer restless was balm to him. I really believe he was being sincere, but it is hard to understand how he can feel this way. His eyes look so abysmally sad.

My hostess on this boat—would she be veering towards her 50th birthday?—has said that the last ten years had been her happiest.

I have known great happiness with Kin. (Perhaps the long silence from him was one of the main reasons of unrest this summer) and of a sort that has not happened before in my life. For that I am grateful, and with luck that may continue, but otherwise the peaks have not been so high even if the depths have not been as low as they used to seem.

[1] Randolph Churchill (1911–68) wrote the first two volumes of the official biography of Sir Winston Churchill. The remaining volumes were the work of Sir Martin Gilbert.

The cruise took the passengers to Capri, Ischia, Santa Margherita, Portofino, Villefranche and Saint-Tropez.

Cecil had some thoughts about what he found in the South of France, including "the dégringolade *of Alan Searle,*[1] *lost in fat and high living since M.'s death."*

THE SOUTH OF FRANCE

The S. of France bringing memories of my early adult days. Villefranche, where at the Welcome Hotel such strange things happened, when Bébé, Boris, Cocteau,[2] Francis Rose etc. all were bursting with youthful mischief. Monte Carlo, where probably I was conceived, since my parents spent their honeymoon at the Metropole Hotel.

Cap Ferrat, my first winter trip abroad when I stayed at Primavera[3] with Stephen [Tennant] and thought the summit had been reached.

St. Juan, where I felt more miserable than ever before, waking with a hangover to find Peter [Watson] not in the bed next to me. He had taken advantage of my drunkenness to go off with Oliver [Messel].[4] Cap d'Antibes, at the Eden Roc, the Bright Young Things were photographed and I thought I would like nothing more than to be part of such a life. St. Tropez, which we visited on Daisy Fellowes's yacht, *Sister Anne,* before the place became famous, and we wandered in the little park and bought exquisite paper hats from a woman who then became renowned for her taste.

But all so changed. Monte Carlo a mass of skyscrapers and commercialisation. It seems Rainier only wants to make a Brighton out of it. The roads an inferno of petrol fumes and worse. Modern cardboard boxes dotting the hillside. Hideous, vulgar, lacking in all charm, a place to be avoided.

. . .

[1] Alan Searle (1903–85), secretary and boyfriend of W. Somerset Maugham. He inherited much from Maugham, not without incurring the displeasure of Maugham's family.

[2] Christian (Bébé) Bérard (1902–49), artist; Boris Kochno (1903–90), his friend and the former secretary to Diaghilev; and Jean Cocteau (1889–1963), artist, writer, playwright and film director.

[3] Lady Grey had guests staying in March 1927. Here Cecil met HRH Princess Louise, Duchess of Argyll, daughter of Queen Victoria, who presently became his first royal sitter.

[4] This was a fraught affair. See Hugo Vickers, *Cecil Beaton: The Authorised Biography* (1985–2002), *passim.*

There are few restaurants where the food is still superb. But the prices are unbelievable. The Wrightsmans allow their guests to take the party to a good restaurant whenever we spend a night ashore. We dined at the Château de Madrid with Kay Graham. Luckily it does not hurt her to fork out since she is rich, rich, rich. With her, cocktails, wine and champagne were drunk with the dinner of fluffy egg over artichoke, poulet à l'estragon, and Grand Marnier soufflé.

My turn came the next evening. Two magnums of white wine with lobster pastry, loup de mer and ice cream. By this time we were reduced to seven. My bill came to nearly £60. One of the company said that when he returns from paying this, he'll be wearing a miniskirt. The allowance for the English abroad is £50.

Of course, I do not resent contributing to a wonderful, luxurious holiday, but I resent contributing to de Gaulle's economy and the General seems this week, in Quebec in particular, to have gone off his pinhead.

Cecil was glad to return to the familiar territory of Broadchalke, albeit not for long, since Reddish was presently to be let to two Americans for August. He revelled in the delights of his garden in summer.

I come down to the country by the earliest train possible. The landscape is everything that I love, with dry grasses in the hedges, corn golden counterpanes on the hills and all cottage gardens ablaze. We have waited so long for this effulgence that it is silly to go away when the growth of green is so rich.

I am sitting on my terrace. The cracks in the flagstones have given forth a tremendous display of thyme and night-scented Virginia stock, the grey plants have sprouted, the new roses have grown, the lavender is sprawling. I sit beaming with pleasure at the green scene before me. Is it because it is my own that I love it so much? It seems to me now far more beautiful than any of the things I've seen abroad. It is lush and yet restrained, the colours wonderfully controlled. The glorious sunshine we have enjoyed for so many weeks on end has not dried the lawns for there have been occasional rain storms, and now all at once in bloom are the favourites that I've loved from childhood holidays. The pale yellow hollyhocks, the Japanese anemones and the phlox, so peppery pungent. The trees are green and darkest black. There are poppies and marguerites in the long grass, and convolvulus trailing like rambler roses.

The curtains in front of me were pulled to reveal a bright summer morning. The sun casting shadows across the lawn, picking out the high points of the distant trees, the newly planted orchard, and the garlands of new dawn roses still flowering without cease, the green and pale-pink shown in great contrast against the cerulean-blue of the cloudless sky.

I was too delighted to be able to tear myself indoors. The morning went by doing all sorts of things that prevented work. I could not have been more happy.

DIANA VREELAND SEPTEMBER 1967

Diana Vreeland, on arrival in England: "This is a marvellous country. Everyone finishes their sentences and looks you straight in the eye."

Went to the Old Vic to see Olivier in *The Dance of Death.*[1] It is his best part. His stylised hammy acting suits the turn-of-the-century play and his innate coarseness is used to good effect. Edgar is bumptious and common. Olivier enjoys showing these aspects of a person that in many ways could be identified with the real Olivier himself. I am prejudiced. I don't like Olivier as a person, but everything I dislike about his personality became part of Edgar, and the range and variety of his voice were indeed remarkable, and he used a real actor's restraint and tact, and only when taking a curtain call could one detect a supercilious patronage of the star among lesser fry.

ALAN TAGG

Alan Tagg has a marvellous ear for words. He remembers exactly why a remark made 20 years ago was amusing and on repeating it goes into gales of laughter.

We were talking of John Gielgud,[2] who has directed a "little family

[1] Laurence Olivier was playing the spiteful Captain Edgar in Strindberg's *The Dance of Death,* which also starred Robert Stephens and Geraldine McEwan. It opened at the Old Vic on 21 February. He portrayed a man deserving of both hatred and compassion, and some critics claim it as one of his finer late-life roles.

[2] (Sir) John Gielgud (1904–2000), actor, with a particularly memorable voice, and director.

comedy" for which Alan has done the decor. John, always tactless, has developed the art of saying exactly what is on his mind to the most farcical extent. In his deep, throaty, almost military staccato he keeps up a flow of speaking his mind without ever any understanding of the reaction it may have on others. At the beginning of the rehearsal he says, "You're beginning to be very good. I'm *very* pleased with you all, except, of course, Beryl (Beverley?). You've got it all wrong, no good at all. Beryl (Beverley?) explodes into noisy tears. John, stricken with embarrassment and, avoiding a row at all costs, is not seen for dust.

One poor girl does not notice that a piece of scenery has been placed in her way, falls over it with a painful thud. "Oh, Dilys, *do* please be graceful!" instructs John. He decries himself, surprised when [Tony] Richardson and younger directors pay him a compliment. "They seem to like my work! Of course I'd like to do something with a modern author. But they send me things I don't understand. This new Joe Orton play[1] for example. All the cast say the most awful things to one another and a policeman dresses up in drag, and then a huge plaster statue is brought in of Sir Winston Churchill, which they all proceed to smash. Then they all try to put it together again but they can't find the cock. The cock has disappeared. Where's the cock? Great scene looking for the cock. Then at last they find it and are glad that they then don't have to stick in that silly cigar. Don't understand a word of it. Wouldn't touch it, and they offered it to Ralph[2] and he wouldn't touch it either."

Re young actors: "Their skin is in such a bad condition. David Hemmings[3] and the like, all covered in spots and boils, but they don't seem to mind, and they have a great success with girls. In my youth one would have had no success with girls, or boys. I remember I had acne all down my back, covered, and I wouldn't have stripped off for all the world."

Vivien Leigh, stage and screen actress, had won Oscars for her parts in Gone with the Wind *and* A Streetcar Named Desire. *In the 1940s she and Laurence Olivier had incurred Cecil's displeasure over arguments in connection with* The School

[1] *What the Butler Saw,* eventually produced in London, with Ralph Richardson, in March 1969.

[2] (Sir) Ralph Richardson (1902–83), actor then playing Lord Emsworth in BBC's adaptation of P. G. Wodehouse's Blandings novels.

[3] David Hemmings, actor, then married to Gemista Ouvry.

for Scandal, *for which Cecil had done the costumes. She had suffered from manic depression for some years and her marriage to Olivier had collapsed. The Oliviers were divorced in 1960, and Vivien had then lived in contentment with the actor John Merivale. She had died on 8 July that year.*

John relates, on returning from Vivien Leigh's memorial service, a terrible blunder. Poor Larry found himself sitting next to Jill Esmond.[1]

A loathsome angle on this situation is told at Maggie Smith's[2] brother's home that night where Olivier, with Miss Plowright[3] present, says, "I was sitting next to a fat old woman who kept looking at me. She would keep turning her head in my direction, and blow me, I discovered it was my first wife."

There are some things that must not be repeated. How awful that Olivier should relate of all people, to Kenneth Tynan, about the ghastly picture of Vivien's death . . .

Betty Somerset has strange intuitions. She can spot a witch a mile off. She is intimate with the elements, with the mind and the sea, and she describes the importance of sounds. "I'm most haunted by trains, those old-fashioned trains that we have no more, when they used to go up a hill in Scotland, and in America. I've never been there, but from films I know the haunting hooting of the trains. It's like the cry of a curlew. It stops the blood."

(I remember being so haunted, mostly miserably, by the train sounds when travelling with Peter [Watson] across America, so long ago.)

Betty is convinced that Ava W.[4] is a witch ("I knew it the first time I saw her forty years ago") and thinks it possible she is responsible for the fact that her white sparrow, an intimate in her garden for five years, was never seen again after Ava's last visit.

[1] Jill Esmond (1905–90), actress and film star, who was Olivier's first wife. She later shared her life with a lady friend.

[2] (Dame) Maggie Smith (b. 1934), actress.

[3] (Dame) Joan Plowright (b. 1929), actress, whom Olivier married in 1962.

[4] Ava Wigram (1896–1974), widow of Sir John Anderson, later first Viscount Waverley (1882–1958), Lord President of the Council and Chancellor of the Exchequer.

DEBO DEVONSHIRE[1]

Debo Devonshire, a natural. She has taken to the job of being a duchess (one unsuited to her and her husband that of a duke, and which at first was difficult beyond comprehension) with all the poise and humility that you only find in the best in England. "It's such hard work running the place which is like a hotel and a museum." She copes with far more than her husband who is only intermittently on the job, not so Debo. It is to her that the agent telephones. "We have shot 450 grouse today. What do we do with them?" Meetings galore, speeches, diversified interests, but above all the great sense of ready heady humour. Immediately phrases are coined. Jokes abound, and her eyes and those of her devotees sparkle with happiness: "15 vestal virgins heading for the coast"—"Procol Harum the genius."

Cecil then went to New York for his winter visit.

NEW YORK

18 NOVEMBER 1967

Each visit used to be a milestone. Although I haven't been here for a year, the aeroplane journey, arrival and first impressions seemed more routine.

Staggering the change that one week can bring, and the amount of variety. London, Broadchalke and the problems that now seem quite remote.

I have my apartment here to decorate, photographic appointments, discussions, with Weissberger[2] about possible stage jobs, or decorating the *Queen Mary* on Long Beach. There is a rush to relax, to see old friends, Serge [Obolensky], Vava [Aldeburg], Truman [Capote], Lincoln [Kirstein],[3] and newer ones too.

Now Truman has given me, as a Christmas present, a genius doctor for the skin, who burns off one's blemishes.

[1] Hon. Deborah Mitford (b. 1920), married Lord Andrew Cavendish (1920–2004), who became eleventh Duke of Devonshire in 1950 because his elder brother, the Marquess of Hartington, was killed in the war.

[2] Arnold Weissberger (1906–81), Cecil's agent in New York.

[3] Lincoln Kirstein (1907–96), choreographer, who founded the New York City Ballet.

DINNER WITH TRUMAN NOVEMBER 1967

Much better impression than of yore. Less interested in society and personalities. Keen on a young group of TV directors, producers. A businessman, he says he thinks of everything, but there was one thing Lazar[1] thought of that he hadn't thought of, getting the film company to pay 50 cents on every hardcover of *Cold Blood* has resulted in an extra $2½ million for Truman. The film company didn't spot the clause.

T. has infinite self-belief. He is the cleverest, the smartest, the operator, but he is the artist, with a perfected technique, so that he now can give all his efforts to the imaginative effort of creation. He is a legend. He can thumb his nose at everybody, doesn't give a fuck, is coming right out in *Playboy* with his credo, against the Jewish mafia, the critics, Ken Tynan, [President] Johnson, the lot. He knows he can succeed, others farm and *suck*, he creates from a blank page while the others are dependent. He is less dependent on people, only likes being alive.

Has had a shock when the doctor told him he had seriously damaged his nervous system, that it could never be 100 per cent right, that the arteries had hardened. He now drinks only wine, has smoked, as from yesterday, his last cigarette.

With millions in the bank, he has an extraordinary sense of security. He chooses, he is inundated with requests, but is tough about turning them down. He is so intelligent in life that I feel envy of his capacity for finding new people, new interests, new forms of work. Nothing remains static with him. He even looks very different from the person I saw last year, cleaner-cut, more sophisticated. The little Southern elf has gone.

His closest love is for Charlotte, the dog. He is taking the house in Palm Springs because here the dog suffers less from asthma and (with tears falling down his cheeks) he hopes to give Charlie a very happy last year of his life.

Cecil found much of his New York existence "a growing menace" of pressure and deadlines. He struggled to earn dollars, which he found hard to come by following

[1] Irving Paul Lazar (1907–93), famously bespectacled theatrical and film agent, known as "Swifty" Lazar. He gave a celebrated Oscar® night party each year.

the recent devaluation of the pound, but he welcomed an invitation to travel with Charles Engelhard and his wife, Jane.

It does not matter if the Cadillac is ten minutes late, for the aeroplane waits on one's wishes, and throughout the day there are people waiting on one's wishes. No question of there not being a chauffeur to greet the delayed plane's arrival. There are two. But even though these are arrangements brilliantly carried out, that at every point along the line there are attendants to smooth the path, it takes a certain amount of serenity to cope with such high-powered activity. This Jane has. I doubt if she is ever really rattled. She has a man's mind, feminine intuition and a superbly adjusted technique to living with the multiest of millionaires. She has even made it easy for me to relax, and although the day was one of fantastic contrasts, the early bell and desperate attempts to get lawyer Weissberger and other calls before leaving, the snow scene to the airport, the terrifying speed of the little jet, the Washington Capitol surrounded by snow, blossom, trees, the snow scene of the Library [of Congress] steps, and suburban wooden houses, and the arrival after snow in the tropics of Florida, and the revelation of the Engelhard plantation, with its guests and servants galore, this was all very much for one day.

However, the reveille has taken place the following morning. The sun is out, we are to go on a boat trip fishing. It is all too easy and extremely good for the nerves. The tension is down and I realise what an unnecessary strain much of the last week has been.

NICE COMPLIMENT FROM MARIANNE MOORE[1]

"You're a great example to us all. You're so modest. You exact the most of yourself." Since her inconvenient birthday, she was recently 80, she has had a kaleidoscope of a life.

After a while she hopes to be thawed out. New York has recently had many disgraces and robberies and so forth.

[1] Marianne Moore (1887–1972), American poet.

DIANA VREELAND, HER FANTASY

Some may see Charles Engelhard, the gold, platinum, uranium tycoon, as a tough, obese business genius with fairly unattractive manners and a terrible physical onslaught. To Diana he is "le Roi Soleil." "Put a wig on him, then take the nose, he already has the stick, and watch his walk! With one foot forward! Why, he's from all the pictures!"

"Those were terrible pictures we published. They were taken by an intellectual. It won't happen again. If we have an intellectual working for *Vogue,* he's running the elevator!"

D. V. on Jane Engelhard: "She has a sense of splendour. Everything is played very close to the chest. Of course, she's Catholic, but doesn't show it. I believe everyone is religious, but when it's discussion, they just look away."

TRUMAN CAPOTE

We dined together at the Lafayette. T. much thinner than he was a year ago and different. More suave, the lines all drawn tighter. His tremendous success has "told" in many ways. He speaks with ultimate authority, he is a millionaire and it has done something to his attitude of mind. He minds less about what people think. He is extremely courageous. It was a friendly, intimate evening, and we discussed work and technique while personalities were mercifully forgotten. Thank God no mention of his horrible party last year.

Of more interest was an interview he has given to *Playboy* for $20,000. It took him five weeks to polish and to have the last word. But in it he sounds off against all his pet hates. He gives his views on politics, other US writers, Ken Tynan and the Jewish mafia! There will be fury to begin with, but he feels everyone will come crawling to him. He's most interested in the Hardy group, a set of young people who are putting his short stories on television, and redoing *The House of Flowers.*[1] He is interested in a new genius, a face doctor, a skin

[1] A musical version of Truman's short story, with a score by Harold Arlen, which closed after 165 performances. The original story was based on a visit by Capote to Haiti in 1948.

specialist, who is redoing his face for a TV appearance. (Truman will give me a course of treatments for my blemishes as a Christmas present.)

He has been suffering from "nerve frictions" or some such, and has been told by his doctor that irrevocable damage has been done to his nervous system by smoking, that the arteries had started to harden and that he would never smoke another cigarette. His hands trembled so that he could not write or light a cigarette when he first woke up in the morning. He had had to have five calming pills today. Now the hands are quite firm as he held them out full length, but by the end of the evening he had drunk a bottle of white wine (it was easy for me to note this since, as a result of severe headaches produced by half a glass of wine (!) I have had to go "on the wagon").

Truman talked of his ever increasing desire to be alone. In the country he saw nobody, except Jack [Dunphy] and even to go across to Jack's neighbouring house for dinner was quite an effort. He would often prefer to be alone and go to bed with a book.

His millions talk with an authority that was not objectionable this evening, but can be so on occasions. They have put Truman into a different category of person, and although I feel I have lost him as a close friend, am glad that my former unfavourable impressions of him were balanced in his favour tonight.

A week's interval. Would he read what I had written about my photographs for our joint publication? Yes, and later he would meet me at the Fosburghs[1] for a drink, and would return the mss. He thought it all right. He had made some alterations.

Greedily I looked later to see these alterations, knowing they would be improvements, but they did not exist. Truman no doubt thought at the time of telling me that he had altered my mss. But it worries me that what he thinks is the truth is often so far from the actual fact. He has written that he himself considers lying the least important of the sins, but I am even more worried when I wonder if his sense of the truth is not influenced by the pills that he takes.

At the same time as the call about the Fosburgh meeting, he telephoned to tell me that he'd seen Peter Glenville,[2] who had been very spiky and

[1] James Whitney Fosburgh and his wife "Minnie" Cushing.

[2] Peter Glenville (1913–96), stage and film director, whose film *The Comedians* came out in 1967.

sarcastic about me. He had laughed when recalling how Tony Snowdon had shown him his rough-cut TV film about geriatrics,[1] and how badly I had come out of it. Very bad it was for me. They'd done horrid things to me without my knowing it, had sent me up, had kept the camera rolling long after I'd thought the shot was over, had shown me "behind the scenes." Yes, Peter had laughed about it. Now I must at once see that the film was stopped, and quickly, before it was too late, before CBS bought it.

This distressed me a good deal (my distress augmented by a chill in the stomach no doubt brought about by going from the Engelhards' overheated swimming pool in Florida to the ice-cold of my air-conditioned bedroom). In my weak, overtired state (the last three days had been of great strain) I suddenly felt fed up. New York was the toughest of cities. Life here was a jungle affair, so tough to succeed, so easy to be toppled over, enemies lurking jealously everywhere.

Truman at the Fosburghs put on, at first, a Sinatra–Lazar act, was full of "in" gossip about the reason for the Guests being in debt, how "that creep" Mrs. Engelhard prevented some tart from stealing her husband, and I became a little upset. Then we talked about the South and he regaled us with stories of the opposition he met with in his determination to meet those various people in Death Row. Was it in Alabama that the warden of the prison had refused to let these "Do-Gooders" see the inmates of his pretty "tightly run" prison?

"I don't give a fuck if you've got permission from the Governor, you're not coming in here."

"Well, will you allow me to telephone the Governor?"

While Truman waited for the Governor to come to the phone, he watched the prisoners exercising in the yard. Suddenly a guard was set upon as he watched one of the prisoners turn and turn again a knife in the man's stomach. The guard fell dead in agony, bells, alarms, everyone rushing in circles, the murderer chased round the wall of the yard, then as he is cornered under the

[1] Lord Snowdon had made a TV film about old age, called *Don't Count the Candles*. It included interviews with some well-known old people, including Sir Alexander and Lady Patricia Ramsay (a granddaughter of Queen Victoria), and also scenes in old people's homes. Cecil had been encountered in the King's Road, claimed to have mistaken the nature of the film and agreed to appear in it. The film was shown on television on 4 April 1968 and Cecil's friends generally wrote to congratulate him on his performance.

window where Truman is watching, another guard staggers pop-eyed and dies of a heart attack.

Can this be true? If so, how is it that T. does not talk of such things rather than worthless gossip? But *is* it true?

His imagination is never at rest and it is fed with the food of everyday-life incidents. He says he will see the most "boring" people in order to root out stories. He does infinite research, so that he has a complete documentary, about the people who are coming into his stories. Recently he has made a new friend who is a neighbour at Littlehampton. He has taken this friend on his TV prison reform trips and has become intrigued that she has a lover.

"If you don't tell me who it is, I will find out and then, when I do, I'll let everyone know."

In the South, while staying in a motel, he hears his friend telephoning at night. On leaving, T. came down early to pay his friend's bill. He saw the telephone calls enumerated and said to the cashier that he must have the telephone numbers that were called. The cashier obliged. T. rang the number, found out the number belonged to some drearily married doctor and so reported the news everywhere.

He has a great talent for pumping people, and much of the information he gleans is of grist to his information, but the line between fact and fiction is very blurred.

As he leaves me, he impresses, "Now ring up your lawyer in the morning and see that film is stopped."

Next day I tell Diane V. that I have done just this (Arnold [Weissberger] suggesting that before threatening proceedings I write Tony a friendly letter asking to see the documentary). Diane then tells me how Truman has spent the evening at her house with Lee R. [Radziwill].

Truman had appeared on her doorstep as if from another world, in a daze. Throughout the evening he had repeated himself. He was in "a wild condition."

"Now we've all got to stop this. We must see the film. We must stop this happening to Cecil, whom we all love. But first we must see the film, because we mustn't let Cecil suffer unnecessarily." (He hadn't seen the film when he told me and I did suffer.)

The evening had been rather scary for Diane was convinced that Truman was under the influence of drugs. Did I know what he took? Did I take anything with him? Did I think he was getting Lee into mischief?

Truman goes to Alabama before Peter Glenville can telephone to deny absolutely that he has given anything but a favourable account of my treatment by the film directors. (To Arnold Peter gave a "rave notice.") I am now convinced that Peter is not lying. What is the point of Truman creating such a fabrication? It is one that will be difficult for him to extricate himself from.

I return to find Tony on the telephone. He is furious with Peter's unprofessional behaviour in regaling a lunch party about something he had seen privately. Derek Hart,[1] his co-producer, is in tears. Truman has really stirred up a hornet's nest and for what reason? Perhaps we have not heard the last of this story, but I wonder how Truman can continue to use his imagination in such dangerous ways. Has he reached the point where he can still keep to the facts—or has his imagination (aided by pills and other stimuli) now free rein to make of reality whatever he wishes?

I think that Diane's incentive to send for me to New York was to illustrate a feature on the Engelhards. She knew Jane to be a difficult but worthwhile subject, and perhaps I'd be the best at the job. It came as a shock to her, on arrival in New York, that after an expensive gala at Brooke Astor's new apartment (she has done all the wrong old hat things) that I said on going home with her that I thought Mrs. E. looked exactly like the female impersonator, Danny La Rue.[2] Little wonder that Diane telephoned to us in the middle of our session in Florida to know if all was under control.

Although this was to be the main session, others were fitted in. Mrs. Laurance Rockefeller.[3] No one could be less vulgar, or further removed from the life of NY City as most of us know it. Isolated in her millionaire's apartment, she leads a worthy but incredibly monotonous existence. "My husband broke the arm of this chair last night. We were playing cards as we usually do . . ."

[1] Derek Hart (1925–86), radio, television and documentary film producer, founding member and co-presenter of BBC *Tonight*. Earlier an actor, including Bob Dale in *Mrs. Dale's Diary* (1949–51).

[2] Danny La Rue (b. 1928), long enduring female impersonator, popular in high vaudeville.

[3] Mary French (1911–97), married (1934) Laurance Rockefeller, Chairman of the YWCA's World Service Council. They lived at 834 Fifth Avenue, New York.

The apartment contains a Monet and many extremely valuable pictures among the other trash. There are coloured snapshots of the family in frames, too many large comfortable chairs and sofas. Taste is something never aimed at. I feel an impostor coming here and secretly judging the ugliness of the juxtaposition, the low ceilings perforated with cinema lights, the ugly frames atrociously arranged, the lack of luxury. But I respect this timid quiet lady. I admire her haunted eyes, her wistful regard, her tentative smile. I know she is worthy and worthwhile, but after a bit I long to flee.

Another sitter, Mr. Ripley,[1] the director of the Smithsonian Institute [sic], has Johnny Walker[2] of the National Gallery by the jugular vein. Yet you would never know this soft, smiling, rather weak-seeming man with the quiet voice could be such a demagogue. A long way to go to photograph him, and how lucky that I took my camera and two rolls as Charles,[3] my assistant, was fogbound, and arrived eventually when all was over and forgotten.

Another enthusiast, or perhaps one could even say "crank," for such, superficially, is Dr. Steichen Calderone,[4] the daughter of the old photographic monster, and now an elderly grey-haired dowager who appears Mitford-esque with her deep-set turquoise-blue eyes, her beak nose, delightful teeth and disarming smile. She and her doctor husband, when their children left home, decided to present the meaning of sex to a larger audience.

"These things must be brought into the open, not made something furtive of which we are ashamed. Sex is not an act. It is a sense of being. One human being, made up of so many different characteristics, meets another with corresponding tastes and they love one another. That is important. The other thing is merely pelvic rationalisation. It's nothing, whereas sex whatever its focus is something we have got to understand. I don't prevail. I don't tell people that it is good or bad for them to masturbate. If you want to masturbate, do so. It's not for me to tell you not to, and I don't proclaim about the

[1] Dillon Ripley (1913–2001), ornithologist, and secretary of the Smithsonian Institution in Washington from 1964 to 1984.

[2] John Walker (1906–94), director of the National Gallery of Art, Washington. Author of *Self-Portrait with Donors* (1974).

[3] Charles Biasiny-Rivera, now director of En-Foco.

[4] Dr. Steichen Calderone (1904–98), President of the Sex Information and Education of the United States, which she founded in 1954, and daughter of Edward Steichen (1879–1973), photographer.

virtues or vices. It's all the same to me if your tendencies are heterosexual or homosexual, so long as they are true. Go to it."

When I asked her to smile for her picture, she said, smilingly, "Nowadays we don't say 'Cheese' to the photographer, we say 'Sex'!"

CHAX FORD[1]

A friend and a figure from the Tchelitchew past came back into my life after a long interval. The beautiful poetic boy of 30 years ago still is young in appearance and still charming and disarming. He does not seem upset that his promise has turned to nothing more than making home-made movies in Greece.

His enthusiasm is undiminished. I must go to meet a marvellous photographer, Jack Smith, who makes underground movies, whose *Flaming Creatures*[2] was banned and burnt by the police. There was one copy left and it was marvellous. Would I go to see it? I would, on Sunday evening. "But Chax, I'm so tired, could I lie down for a half-hour and come to fetch you at 7 instead of 6:30?"

I was grateful for the reprieve. Together we rattled downtown in the Subway, ten blocks lower than the Village, to an uninhabited part of the town, huge Italianate empty palace, business offices, black and peeling, hardly a soul on foot.

Chax gave a lurch against a scabrous door. It gave. We were at the foot of a curving staircase that was in an advanced state of disintegration. A water pipe had burst and, without anyone's knowing it, had flooded the staircase for days on end. The rot had long set in and the stench was utterly appalling. We

[1] Charles-Henri Ford (1908–2002), writer, who shocked many with his banned book, *The Young and Evil* (1933), which contained a page of the word "love," and is thus best read by those with minds wide open. Philip Hoare described it as "an overtly homosexual tale set in New York, with no discernible narrative or plot!" He was the boyfriend of the painter Pavel Tchelitchew (1898–1957). His sister Ruth Ford (b. 1920) was a well-known actress, who lived in the Dakota Apartments in New York.

[2] Jack Smith (1932–89), rival film-maker to Andy Warhol. Like Warhol, he made long films which took endurance to watch. He sought aesthetic delirium. He became paranoid after the banning of *Flaming Creatures* (1963) in 1964. He died of AIDS.

climbed high from the stink and came to an absurd studio-attic. "Jack! Jack!" No reply.

Eventually a wild fox of a fellow with a long white nose, a sandy beard and heavy boots appeared. His handshake was clammy. He croaked instead of speaking. He was gone but one heard the splashing of water and clatter of plates. Half an hour later a tray of coffee in tumblers appeared. A few people sat around making conversation, a Greek, an editor, a friend of Jack's in an equal state of dope, a marijuana pipe was handed around non-stop. Charles and I did not partake (the idea of putting the wet stem into my mouth did not attract me). When would we see the film? Croaks from Jack. After an hour Chax said Jack had always wanted to cut one scene out of the film and he was doing that just now.

What could I do? If I were to rise in a huff and leave, I'd be lost. Nowhere near here is a taxi to be found. Chax said Jack would be in a state of shock. After two hours of desultory waiting in this very cold Addams cartoon attic, Jack's hob-nailed boots were heard again. Now he was threading the spools on to the circular can.

At last the lights were put on. The film rolled and flip, it broke; 10, 20, 30 times this happened. I doubt if I've ever been more pent-up and angry. No laughing matter. We craned our chairs towards a small white square of screen high in the roof. At last the film started. The most mad and amateur nonsense of men dressed as women greeting one another, fluttering fans or making up their lips. Repetition was one way of making an effect. After a bit the effect was of complete exasperation. This was utter craziness. How could anything so appallingly bad ever be shown in public?

Yet there was about the whole a certain 1890 beauty. The earliest photographs reminded me of those screen pictures, the dowdiness, the lack of self-consciousness, the appalling perverse integrity or the camp attitude. It was supposed to be funny. It was grotesque in a rather beautiful way. There were obscenities mixed with angels, nuns, whirling dervishes of camp. The film was impossible, mad, bad, but withal beautiful. There were moments that were unforgettable. What more could one ask of an evening?

We ended up on 42nd Street, dining in the automat, and browsing in the pornographic bookshops where it seems nothing is now barred.

An evening in contrast to too many, an evening at the Salvation, a

Marat-Sade dance pit, with moving lights, played on a piano typewriter by a girl expert. Here one could watch for three hours on end without a moment of repetition.

The Electric Circus, a huge Gustave Doré psychedelic cavern, with colours and forms moving according to the rhythm of the music, very impressive in its integrity, and the people so strange to watch for a short while. I bought a bowl of miserable goldfish.

MARGOT FONTEYN

Eileen has a great deal more patience than I have. She has many uses for it, being victim on the telephone of the vagaries of the rich and spoilt people who speak more bluntly to her than when on comparatively good behaviour to me.

But even Eileen got exasperated with Margot Fonteyn. Months ago Diane Vreeland called us that she wanted a pictorial feature showing the greatness of the dancer as a "woman." The article accompanying the pictures was commissioned from Marguerite Duras.[1]

But Margot kept postponing the engagement. She is, admittedly, tremendously busy. She knows her days of retirement are not far off, and she is intent on making as many appearances and gaining as much money as she now possibly can. She flies to all parts of the world for an appearance with any sort of partner, and she now needs a day's sleep to recover from the exhaustion of the performance.

It is a bore to be photographed. She is entitled to say she does not wish to give us that time and I would understand. But the prevarications were endless. Margot would be in Paris between the 3rd and the 19th if I'd come over, but she couldn't pose on the 4th, 5th, 6th, 7th, 8th, 11th etc. etc. Then she was going to Sweden, then Texas. Then she didn't know where she would be. Then she couldn't be got in touch with for the secretary of Fred Ashton had given her up as hopeless. Eventually try her mother. Try her chauffeur. I sent an exas-

[1] Marguerite Duras (1914–96), French writer of impenetrable prose, who finally wrote an easily read book, *L'Amant*, published in 1984 and filmed as *The Lover*, which won the Prix Goncourt.

perated telegram to Diane who got Lee R. to take up the cudgels. It's the only time I've asked someone to do my work for me.

Vogue paid the fare and sent a car for Margot to come to NY from Dallas. She rang to know if she could be photographed in the house of Trumble Barton[1] where she was staying. No. If even one leg of a piece of furniture appeared in the background the pictures would be unpublishable in *Vogue*.

Margot arrived at my hotel quite punctually, very staccato and giggly. She said she was sorry I'd got the impression she didn't particularly want to be photographed by me. Rather than anyone she wanted me etc. and it was better that she come to NY than that I go to Texas. (Certainly I would have refused to go to Texas to photograph the girl from next door.)

Margot at over 50 still possesses the line and movement of youth. Her legs are long and straight and go into ballet positions, which look odd when she wears a very "way out" Saint-Laurent evening dress. Her spirit shines through. She is like a blade of young grass, but she is still the genteel, middle-class little English girl grown scraggy and lean. This is something audiences are not conscious of. They see only the artist in her, and this is as it should be. The artist is the important and all-rare phenomenon. It is the reason for her becoming a legend, and that is what she will be for future generations. To us who have known her so well, it is hard to disassociate ourselves from what we have seen in early stages, developing, via Constant Lambert[2] and others, into the *ballerina assoluta* who with time will have nothing on Pavlova, for such is the case of Mrs. Hookham's little girl.

Kin came to spend Christmas with Cecil, looking taller and better than Cecil had remembered. The pair got on so well that Cecil concluded, "I was transfixed. I felt that I would never want to work again, and there was no possibility of my doing so, when such a stimulating and delightful companion was around. I pray more than I have for a long time, prayers of thanks and gratitude for the happiness that had come into my life."

As the year ended, Cecil recalled his dealings with Garbo while in New York.

[1] Trumble Barton, known as "Tug," friend of John McHugh. Margot Fonteyn paid tribute to his kindness over many years in her memoirs.

[2] Constant Lambert (1905–51), composer and father of Kit Lambert, of The Who.

GRETA

I tried hard, on arrival in New York, not to get overtired and harassed. I must preserve myself for tough times ahead and so for this reason I did not get involved at once with too many people. I had no time. The time was not yet ready to telephone to Greta. She would answer, "Well, well, well, what a surprise! What do you know? Why Beat!" Then, when it would come to a question of making a date with her, "Well, I'm not feeling too chipper. I've not been out for goodness knows how long, so I'll have to let you know."

Instead I telephoned to Cécile who has come to New York to see Greta. Cécile had seen her for only four hours out of a week, and was a bit fed up. But Greta wanted me to call her. Truman, the little spy, had seen Greta in the street (had said Greta looked like one of those old women who used to trudge through the mud delivering Western Union cables) and informed her of my arrival. G. was surprised.

I went to have a drink (non-alcoholic, as I've been on the wagon the entire time in NY) at Cécile's. Greta was still there, having been out Christmas shopping all afternoon, and waiting for my arrival. Her cheeks were flushed and shiny pink. She had on a thick pixie hat, and her shoes were old and nobbled. They made her feet look poor and aged.

G. looked quite beautiful because she looked completely natural. Her skin was glowing and her eyes filled with so many expressions. Marlene Dietrich, on the stage, can still look marvellously young in an artificial way, but she is a monster. Greta is a real-live human being.

Greta listened to our talk of NY with surprise. The Electric Circus. What's that? and psychedelic decors, what could they be? and *Salvation*, and *Hair.*[1] Oh, what were all these things we were talking about? She never goes out, doesn't know a thing about life in New York. (If she were engaged in reading the great works or in studying *something* this would be great.) But the fact is that Greta now has little to talk about. "Oh, I wish I could."

[1] *Hair,* the sensational rock musical, in which full frontal nudity was seen for the first time on the London stage since the Lord Chamberlain surrendered his charge of censorship. It provoked jokes in magazines such as one actor leaving saying "I failed the medical" and that it was the only production where "the director was worried about the size of the part" etc.

We would all go out, four of us, to see the town on Friday.

I telephoned to ask Greta to lunch with me alone. I thought I ought to speak to her about the diaries and to confess that we were living on "borrowed time." But she had reneged on our night out plan and since she did not call me back as a result of messages left by her maid, she thought I must be going to badger her to reconsider her decision to come out on the town.

But no, I would never do that. I know too well how hopeless it would be and if she *should* accede would blame me for all that went wrong with the evening. So cars were cancelled and I left New York without having seen her alone, and I'm sorry to confess without any regrets whatsoever for not having done so.

How sad!

1968

Cecil began the New Year preoccupied with building works at Reddish House, adding a landing "library" and bathrooms to the guest rooms. The work unearthed some more serious problems, and he soon discovered that the landing had been on the point of collapse, and that the cisterns were about to burst. The cisterns also proved to be full of the decomposing bodies of rats, bats and birds, which the household had been drinking for years without realising it.

Cecil soon set off for America again, on his way to Palm Beach, and in due course to Australia for the first time. In New York he met the photographer David Bailey.

An evening with David Bailey was a revelation. At 30 he has made a fortune as a photographer with eight different companies in Switzerland and Liechtenstein. He allows himself to make only £10,000 a year in England and pays his accountant, who invents these wheezes, $90 a month. He is on the ball in a way that it is intelligent for an artist to be. I would like to be able to learn a few of his tricks. It would not mean that I become less of an artist, but more sensible about an important part of my life, and less worried when Mr. Blick[1] says that it will cost £250 to renovate the garage roof.

If I stay long in New York the activities gang up on me with such speed that again I forget the importance of taking time off to attend to the manipulation of my money, the lesson being that as soon as one senses one is

[1] Brian Blick, Cecil's builder at Broadchalke.

in a rut, either of illness or stagnation, or of overwork, it is good to pull stumps and move on to get a different perspective.

Now I have come away for a break. Nothing specific to do, but an attempt to cover new ground, and I plan to take time off, and even to go, most unexpectedly in view of my never having wished to go there, as far as Australia. Perhaps I am getting desperate.

In Palm Beach, staying with the Wrightsmans, Cecil attended an exhibition of "a scratch lot of sketches" at the Vigouroux Gallery, which proved "an excellent way of making money," and led to two commissions for portraits. A blonde woman asked him where he was going next. "Australia! Australia! That isn't a bit you!" Mrs. Vigouroux[1] *told him, "Your show's a smash hit. Do you enjoy being housed? It's the first opportunity we've had of housing one of our artists."*

CAPOTE JANUARY 1968

I feel I have lost Truman. Of course we all change, some develop, and success puts us in a different stratum. Truman has certainly changed. He is still nice to old animals and old people. He has a knack of making them feel he is their long-lost confessor (the fact he seldom follows through has not caught up with him yet). But his success has become so overwhelming that he is wasting little time on anything but the promotion of it. Perhaps this is wise, for he certainly can never have such success again. He might as well milk it, and this he is doing to the extent of personal appearances for his film all over the world and every end is tied up neatly. He knows the "returns" each week, not only of the books, but of the cinema attendances.

He makes the usual excuses, the weather, the after-Christmas lull, the uncertainty of the dollar. There is nothing he overlooks. His profits are Croesus-like. He spends fantastic amounts on doing long-distance telephone calls. He is living it up at a very high rate. All this is fine, but I cannot but feel sad and resent the undoubted fact that he has become condescending to old

[1] Mrs. Vigouroux, wife of George Vigouroux, at whose gallery in Palm Beach Cecil was exhibiting some paintings.

buddies, to newcomers, to all and sundry. He slaps an end to a telephone call by "Well, I'll call you tomorrow, eh?" He does not have his old curiosity about friends. He does not encourage me to elaborate on any story. I know he is pre-occupied or only wanting to interrupt. He has begun to believe his own press agent, and when drunk his bragging is vastly unattractive.

"I'm the greatest," he says, but not in imitation of Cassius Clay.[1] He is unique. His intelligence is remarkable. In his behaviour less wise. He does not seem to be building towards happiness. He speaks so disparagingly of possible rivals. He, the *numero uno,* is even unmagnanimous about Tennessee Williams,[2] Elia Kazan[3] whose heyday is long past and who can take no skin off his nose. He will resent more and more the young and the promising, and since publicity seems so important a yardstick now (he knows that I must resent his being the Elsa Maxwell[4] of his day and did not mention his forthcoming ball, which can only be a poor reflection of the first). It seems as if this phase should quickly be superseded by something likely to make him less notable in old age.

I stayed for three days with him in Palm Springs (the over-decorated house like an Oliver Smith setting[5] for an American drawing-room comedy) and by degrees found myself less and less able to communicate. Thomas Hardy made a marvellous substitute. When it was time for me to leave it was without any regrets. The telephone would continue to ring non-stop. He would spring to the attentions necessary. He would read the *Los Angeles Examiner* from cover to cover (perhaps on the track of a new subject). He would roar with laughter to himself at some Kansas women's account of being in a shoot-in. (His laughter is delicious—one of the rarest things about him.) But I felt the spirit of I. Lazar was round the corner and I didn't enjoy the world of Hollywood agents, thugs and dictators. I didn't like my friend to spend his time speaking computer language. I found myself thinking more and more about the people in Broadchalke.

[1] Cassius Clay (b. 1942), boxer, later known as Muhammad Ali.

[2] Tennessee Williams (1911–83), American playwright from the South and a particular *bête noire* of Truman's.

[3] Elia Kazan (1909–1995), theatrical director, who directed Thornton Wilder's *Skin of Our Teeth.*

[4] Cecil's remark was not a compliment.

[5] Oliver Smith (1918–94), stage designer, who was responsible for the sets of the stage version of *My Fair Lady.*

In January Cecil visited Kin in San Francisco. He then set off on his trip to Australia, travelling via Tahiti, Bora-Bora, where, despite the beauty of the place, Cecil felt "trapped," and other tropical spots on the way.

Cecil then arrived in Australia.

"Mr. Beaton? Will you come this way please?" For medical inspection. Embarrassing to be picked out for such unexpected and sudden attention, but I loved it.[1] "This way." Through the back of the economy class, through first, through officers, to Customs. An army of white-shirted, black-trousered and -toed inspection officers, "A Group Captain from Lord Casey[2] to meet you."

"The Queen's photographer's luggage."

I took to all this like a duck to water. The waiting Rolls motored its way, much stared at, as there are few "grand"-looking cars on the road. Conversation with apple-cheeked ADC with a strong accent. (My ears as well as eyes on sticks), pretty ironwork balconies on ramshackle early houses, the bridge, the new opera house, the white low-lying Admiralty House,[3] 1845?, with boats up and down the water at the flower border edges. The Old England pomp, the sentry, the arrival, another ADC at attention, and there to greet me the Caseys, bow, bow, exchange of politeness, smiles, jokes, the grandchildren, and an English setting, a Monet scene through the windows, bright and ugly gold-ness, but modern skyscrapers forming a backcloth, very impersonal, white, grey, dark-green, a huge bridge, a large English country house atmosphere, the beginning of Australia.

It's impossible to get to grips with reality. The town is there in its physical sense, but it seems there is no life in the streets (it is Australia Day weekend, a holiday, so that everyone goes away for a holiday). It is impossible to tell what sort of people live in the little houses, the coloured balconied shacks, the new villas, the apartment houses, or sleazy hotels, for we see everything from the igloo of artifice of the G. G.'s pedestal. The tradition of Empire being upheld in its glory is still evident here.

[1] Cecil told Diana Cooper that when he arrived in Australia, he was asked if he was "a bugger."

[2] Richard, first Lord Casey, KG (1890–1976) and his wife Maie (1891–1983). He was Governor-General of Australia 1965–9.

[3] Admiralty House, the official residence of the Governor-General.

Lord and Lady Casey at Pelham Place, 1967. Cecil stayed as their guest at Admiralty House, Sydney, in 1968. Lord Casey was Governor-General of Australia.

The life at A. H. is so formal, so comfortable and conventional that it is impossible to break through to today. Maybe I would have been utterly lost if I'd come here as unprepared as I am, and had not this auspicious background to my new venture. But after one and a half days here I find it very difficult to know what is happening outside this rarefied atmosphere. Competent secretaries enquire what help they can offer. They mean to carry through and they do. One's physical needs are cared for.

We meet punctually at mealtimes, ADCs prompt one, tell one where to sit (your back will not be facing the window). We make spasmodic conversation but it is never consecutive and is often interrupted, no subject is therefore fully discussed. This makes for great frustration.

Having slept for ten hours at night it is asked, "Would you care to rest this afternoon?" No, a plot has been brewing among the newly arrived guests. "We would like to venture forth on our own to see the city, the suburbs, even go to a bathing beach." A limousine is ordered, a brilliantly technically able she-secretary directs the chauffeur, fills us in with the information. "This is the Library, the Wall Street area, King's Cross, the Soho bit, this is the Chelsea or British part of the town, Kensington."

But today, Australia Day, every part is abandoned, as if for a plague. It is only when we get to Bondi that the beach life is amusing to watch, so much activity, surfing, competitors of all aquatic kinds, inspectors rushing out to sea, to preserve people from currents, sharks, or being battered on the rocks, young men training to be life savers giving one another the kiss of life, every colour and costume, a Pop Art kaleidoscope of young people, nothing sordid, everyone well disposed to each other, young (where are the old?) quite good-looking in an anonymous way, but no beauties, as you would see in Italy, surprisingly a lot of Negroes and Chinese.

The limousine continues its tour, this the Gold Club stretching for miles, here the park with the crowds listening to the soap box preachers. We long to get down and mingle and listen, but time is too short. We are due back to meet the grandchildren at 5 o'clock. We are frustrated. Over there is the zoo, the opera, the bridge, the new circular skyscraper, the pearly dome, then the boats for the regatta, the tankers, the boat that brought soldiers back from Vietnam.

It is all very remote. We would have liked to get to grips with nature in the raw, but back to the depersonalised drawing room, the attendant aides, the *petits soins.*

The guests escaped again and Cecil admired the opera house: "many shell backed. It makes all other opera houses look like coppers or kiosks. Situated on this commanding promontory to dominate the city in a manner worthy of the place that art and sculpture is given in all future plans. It is an act of faith on a scale worthy of Australia's fast increasing greatness."

Cecil continued his tour to Canberra on the hottest day of the year (104 degrees), still in the company of the Caseys.

The journey here was a revelation, no worry about whether we would miss the aeroplane, or be detained at Customs. No lining up or waiting. The entire staff moves with Their Excellencies (some, including the chef, going on in advance). We are lined up in the hall, the men in lounge suits, hats, the women likewise in hats and gloves, the flagged Rolls in position. "Will you go in the second car, please." No dallying. Four outriders in white crash helmets on motor bicycles start the cavalcade (other traffic jolted out of line if necessary), lined up saluting officers outside the aircraft.

Cecil enjoyed the amenities and the style of life in Canberra, though he thought much of it overdone and outdated. He appreciated that the Caseys had "curtailed a great deal of the pomp and ceremony, and do their best to see through the fog of formality."

All the while I could not help thinking how my friend Ava Waverley would have relished every moment of the grandeur of being curtsied to, having the people sign Their Excellencies' Visitors' Book. She very nearly did make it, but missed the greatest Cinderella story of our day by only a few pips.[1]

Cecil visited an estanza and inspected sheep-shearing activities, and was reunited with his friend Natasha Johnston, whose husband, Sir Charles, was then High Commissioner.[2]

Dined on her terrace with Natasha (who has broken her leg). She suffered in the heat and kept mopping herself. She is very Asiatic, and said her father-in-law at her wedding told Princess Marina, "This is the first time we've had a foreigner in the family," to which Marina replied, "And about time too."

Natasha's mother's brothers and sisters were all murdered in the Russian Revolution,[3] and she cannot yet read books on the Revolution without sleepless nights.

[1] Presumably Lord Waverley (1882–1958) nearly became Governor-General.

[2] Sir Charles Johnston (1912–86), High Commissioner, Australia 1965–71, and his wife, Princess Natasha Bagration (1914–84).

[3] Prince John, Prince Constantin and Prince Igor died with Grand Duchess Elisabeth at Alapaievsk in July 1918. Prince Oleg was killed in action in 1914.

During his visit, Cecil sketched Lady Casey and photographed Lady Johnston, and he made a drawing of Mo, Sir Charles Johnston's major domo, about whom Sir Charles had written a book.[1]

Going to do a drawing of the Johnstons' Mo. "That's jolly good of you."

No good turn goes unpunished.

Mo, the Arab from Cairo, has been Charles's servant for more than 25 years. Some while back I promised I'd do a drawing of him. Now he is on his last legs, about to retire, and this would be my last opportunity.

I'd spent a lot of the day trying to draw Maie, a *difficult* subject. Mo would be easy. He was. From the first stroke of the pencil I knew I was in for a good piece of work. I enjoyed the confidence of working on something that needed no kindness, no flattery. Mo did not move. Neither did he speak. In one hour the drawing was a triumph. Mo thought it marvellous.

"Take it in to the others, Mo, and see what they think of it."

While packing up my paraphernalia I waited to hear the cries of delight. Not at all. Charles said, "Yes, yes." Natasha: "He's put in all your chins, three of them." And no more. Nin Ryan[2] said, "But I think it's very good." Natasha, with broken leg, went up to her room without a word. (The concentration of getting up the stairs is quite strenuous, I admit.) I felt utterly dunched. The only satisfaction, a great one, being that I knew it was a very good drawing.

I did not much enjoy the evening that followed, a dinner with a number of important people, a minister, ambassadors etc. Fond embraces. I would take the drawing back to the Caseys for approval. But my joy at making the gesture had been sadly dampened.[3]

[1] Mohammed "Mo" Aboudi (c. 1901–76), found his way into Virginia Cowles's *The Phantom Major*, and Sir Fitzroy Maclean's *Eastern Approaches.* Having been a "sufragi" to Sir Miles Lampson in Cairo, he worked for the three Stirling brothers, and then attached himself to Sir Charles Johnston, remaining with him for 26 years. After leaving Australia in 1971, he returned to Egypt and worked for Hugh Leach, a bachelor First Secretary in Cairo. Sir Charles wrote his story in *Mo and Other Originals* (1971).

[2] Margaret "Nin" Khan (1901–95), widow of John Barry Ryan, was visiting Australia from New York.

[3] Nevertheless the Johnstons cherished the sketch, and it hung in their London flat until Sir Charles's death.

"The Seekers," the Australian pop group,[1] *came to tea with the Caseys, and presently Cecil went on to Melbourne, staying at Government House, a copy of Queen Victoria's Osborne. Cecil was much impressed by their culture centre and National Gallery. He lunched at the American Club "with two fashionable molls and a nice architect. Luckily our meal was in a private room, but going through the downstairs room one saw all the Melbourne equivalents of the lecture circuit ladies, very* embonpoint *with Queen Mother flowered hats and spectacles."*

He photographed Joanna Baillieu,[2] *"a nice exotic-looking girl, wearing much too much eye make-up and too much base, with adorable, fresh, unspoilt ever-young mother, as nice as to be found anywhere."*

He met Lady Potter, "a local Vivien Leigh,"[3] *and then returned to Sydney, where he stayed with James Fairfax,*[4] *in his house on the promontory of Darling Point.*

As in all rich houses a good collection of modern Australian painters. The local arts are most loyally supported. Calm, serenity. I feel extremely relaxed, more than for several years, I think it has a lot to do with Australia itself. That is why others here smile at each other when they have minor car mishaps. Their nerves are cushioned by the climate etc.

Saw local sights, the local H. Hokinson ladies at the Club, the circular Baillieu house, the nice Sheila Scotter,[5] the local Diana Vreeland, then the local newspaper tycoon, Packer,[6] gave a dinner. Talk of Lord Kemsley,[7] today's obituary giving deceased unwarranted praise (when he sold his newspapers to

[1] The Seekers, pop group formed in 1962, known for "The Carnival Is Over," "Georgy Girl" and "World of Our Own."

[2] Joanna Baillieu (b. 1946), daughter of John Baillieu and his wife, Elizabeth Darling.

[3] Susan, wife of Sir Ian Potter (1902–94), businessman and philanthropist, the first Australian share-broker to be knighted.

[4] James Fairfax (b. 1933), son of the newspaper tycoon Sir Warwick Fairfax. Director of John Fairfax Ltd. Sydney 1957–87. Author of *My Regards to Broadway* (1991). He lived at 5 Lindsay Avenue, Darling Point.

[5] Sheila Scotter, first editor-in-chief of *Vogue Australia,* and founder of *Vogue Living.*

[6] Sir Frank Packer (1906–74), chairman of Consolidated Press Holdings from 1954, and of Australian Consolidated Press from 1936. Married (1964) as his second wife June Porges. Father of Kerry Packer.

[7] James, first Viscount Kemsley (1883–1968), chairman of Kemsley Newspapers. He actually sold the business to Roy Thomson (1894–1976), later Lord Thomson of Fleet, for £5 million. He died in Monte Carlo on 6 February.

Thomson he did not warn his long-term staff but gave one of his old supporters an envelope. Thinking it to be a cheque, he opened it with trembling hands. It contained a photostat copy of the cheque for £90,000 which Thomson had given him for the sale). Lady Packer, very French and cuddlesome with a strange habit of grinning with nose screwed up and one eye tight closed.

Cecil bought three Brett Whiteley[1] *drawings, "erotic, almost pornographic, but very beautiful draughtsmanship, a miraculous line."*

An evening with "the boys" (several of us being quite elderly) at an inferno of noise, the Purple Onion, where a drag revue was amiable and everyone wonderfully friendly. Dancing wildly until 2 o'clock was a contrast to the 9:30 bedtime at Government House.

As he left Australia, Cecil looked back on his time there:

A country and people which bring out the best in one's nature. No anxiety, no nervous exhaustion, no worry in fact, certainty about the rosy future.

Obversely nothing very exciting, or galvanising. After a bit the cocoon lulls one into laziness.

The lack of snobbery, the complete lack of self-consciousness, so that people are without protective colouring, and show themselves openly to be what they are.

Cecil returned to San Francisco once more to find Kin awaiting him at the airport.

There in a dark-blue suit was my nicest friend awaiting me the other side of the glass door from the Customs office.

Forgotten were the Caseys and the ADCs and all the grandeur of Government House. Forgotten too the various people I'd met for the first time. The beach house outside Sydney[2] seemed very far away and remote. In a few

[1] Brett Whiteley (1939–92), Australian expressionist artist and the youngest artist ever to be collected by the Tate Gallery, London.

[2] James Fairfax took him to his beach house, not long before he left Australia.

minutes I was back in a grey slightly foggy scene, speeding along the highway with so much enthusiasm for my companion. So much to talk about, all that had happened in the last three weeks. At last the luggage opened and all its contents thrown about the nice familiar room, a bath and then a visit to the new house where Kin had been working so hard during his two-week vacation. Many alterations to the garden but the progress inside was scarcely visible. It will be a year before it is at least partly habitable.

So much to discuss: the Bora-Bora loveliness, the extraordinary arrival in grandeur after the bullying on the air trip, the impressions of the new country and the people I'd seen, the comparisons between the grand and the "camp" life related to such an understanding, sympathetic audience. We lay full length talking by the hour. Then Kin got up to put a pot roast into the oven. It was a late dinner that we enjoyed and still so much to discuss. On the morrow I would go to hear Kin hold one of his classes, talking on English literature.

This was a revelation. Mighty impressed I was. I could not understand how all the students did not fall in love with the teacher. He was so enthusiastic, so good and kind, welcoming everything they had to say in their analysis of an early Greek epitaph, then a jingle by Ogden Nash[1] followed by a Shakespeare sonnet. He dashed from one end to the other of a large screen blackboard chalking down notations with a speed faster than sight. An Olympic athlete of the mind at work. When a girl haltingly suggested that the meaning of punctuation was to give added irony, the teacher said, "How nice." He smiled and developed the theory. Three hours passed in a flash. I felt very privileged to be the one to go off to lunch (fish in an old-fashioned restaurant) with the prize performer.

The next two days were of an extreme happiness. It was as if we were discovering new and nicer things about each other, as if we had never known one another intimately for the past three (?) years. We shopped, bought daffodils, ate at Trader Vic's where we drank a large Mai Tai. "Rum seems to be good for us both." We recollected our first divulging our reactions to meeting one another after our first drinks at a Chinese bar. We talked about Kin's future, his love of teaching, but please not to waste his valuable time on giving too careful an examination to the student papers. The lectures teach him a lot, he is

[1] Ogden Nash (1902–71), poet.

inspired, he learns from their intelligent reactions, and his sense of analysis is given fractures when going through the papers of the more intelligent students.

I confided that during my trip I had seen Beverley Nichols[1] on a round-the-world trip trying to escape from the odour of his bad book on [Somerset] Maugham and how it had given me second thoughts about publishing my diary about Greta. Kin agreed that perhaps I should delay. It was something that could wait. If my conscience pricked me I should not put an increasing burden on myself.

We walked among the hippie drop-outs of Haight Ashbury. We went to the film of *Cold Blood.* Kin was moved by it as a study of death in relation to life. I saw it as an unsuccessful piece of drama. I was not involved, too conscious of bad direction, the lack of lyricism, the hackneyed performances.

We came back to the apartment as if it were less a return than a beginning. I prayed secretly in gratitude for such happiness. "Yes, experience does make it better." I left, not regretful that perhaps much time would pass before our next meeting, but happy and confident that our friendship is the most important thing that has happened to me.

Cecil then flew to New York on his way back home to Britain.

NEW YORK 19 FEBRUARY 1968

Jackie Kennedy's little girl's voice on the telephone asked a favour. "It may bore you most terribly but would you like to come with me to the Balanchine ballet on Sunday? He's dancing *Don Quixote* himself." I behaved rather badly on adjusting plans but Bob LaVine "understood" and so we went. First tea and caviar at the apartment. I found the children enormously improved. John[2] house-trained and quite bright whereas before he was wild and mad, Caroline[3] going to be quite a pretty girl, though when I told her so, she had not the experience of accepting a compliment. Jackie shows signs of the awful experiences

[1] Beverley Nichols, overly popular novelist, whose precocious fame did not endure after his death.

[2] John-John Kennedy (1960–99), the little boy seen on world TV saluting his father's coffin at the state funeral in Washington in 1963. America was shocked when he, his wife and her sister were killed when the plane he was piloting dived into the sea.

[3] Caroline Kennedy (b. 1957).

of the last four (is it?) years. Her white skin has shadows and creases as if underneath the surface something had broken out of a place, and when she smiles, there is a crease that spreads from between her brows down to her nose. Very odd. On a more superficial level, her cheeks have become quite inflated, bulging towards the chin, and late, at supper, I noticed that one eye turns in when she stares at you. Happily none of this shows in photographs and she is still the most photogenic person in the world, infinitely more so than her infinitely more beautiful sister [Lee Radziwill].

But she is on all counts a remarkable person, and this beyond the "build-up" that necessarily surrounds this tragic young woman. She has an enormous appreciation and subtle understanding of humanity, and wisdom beyond her years, and a naturalness that allows her to be funny and outspoken. She has innate distinction and this shows in every unexpected situation, when faced by some insensitive intruder, or tactless questioner. The fact that she has been idolised for so long has given her a sheen but not removed her from reality.

The ballet was a long drawn-out narrative affair of little distinction. Balanchine himself quite ineffective as the leading bore. Many of the scenic effects were in elaborate bad taste, monsters, giants, horses heads of papier mâché, were grotesque and ugly and above all silly. Sometimes the stage was suffused with steam, smoke. When a couple of revolver shots went off, Jackie nearly jumped out of her chair, and over the rail in the dress circle. I felt sorry for her in such a state of nerves.

Only some of the individual dances were inspired choreography and the presence of Suzanne Farrell gave the evening its transcendent beauty. At the end of Act II, Quixote comes in and goes off on a white horse, followed by Panza on a donkey. Animals are always a hazard on the stage, but these behaved well; in fact, the horse looked drugged, until suddenly just at the end of the act, as it stood centre stage, it decided to let loose a mountain of mustard-coloured droppings. The audience roared with laughter and the horse walked off. The curtains rose to the cast taking their bow behind this perfectly placed mountain.

When the composer, Nabokov,[1] came up to talk to Jackie, his opening gambit was touchingly modest: "Tonight the horse stole the show."

[1] Nicolas Nabokov (1903–78), Russian composer, brother of Vladimir Nabokov, author of *Lolita*.

Suzanne Farrell, Balanchine's star ballerina, New York, 1968

. . .

Lee Radziwill goes to a fortune teller in Paris. (Maybe she wants to hear she is to become a film star) and is told that her husband will find a glorious new mistress. On her return she tells the glad tiding to all the family. The children and Stas [Radziwill, Lee's husband] are full of coming events. Suddenly, Lee exasperatedly laments, "Oh Stas, the sooner that mistress of yours arrives the better it will be for all of us. I'm sick of her already."

Even the prospect of photographing the loathsome Eliz. Taylor[1] was enough to upset the week. Irrelevant calls, in person and on telephone from publicity

[1] Cecil had a long-standing antipathy towards Elizabeth Taylor, the film star.

staff and director. The more I heard about the project (she would bring 18 people) the more upset I became (she's everything I dislike). So I asked for a fee of 5,000 dollars. Although we need the money, the relief was overwhelming when we heard Universal would not pay such a price. Instead, it was pleasant to photograph the eccentric Australian, Barry Humphries,[1] for an under-the-counter £50.

Cecil entertained the Queen Mother to lunch at 8 Pelham Place twice, the first time in November 1962 and then again in April 1968.

THE QUEEN MOTHER TO LUNCH

Last time I was honoured in this way Edith Sitwell[2] was the *pièce de résistance.* Truman arrived an hour early and together with Eileen we watched from a top window as a huge ambulance drove up to the house, as a group of stalwart men moved to bring the poet out into the daylight. A pair of very long medieval shoes appeared, then a muffled figure and finally a huge golden melon of a hat. Edith was wheeled into place and given two strong martinis. I now remember little of the lunch except that the QM was very impressed by the food (the late departed Cornelius did a wonderful curry-seasoned pastry dish and we ended with summer pudding), thought Edith so warm, funny and human, and Truman, who told about the financial losses of Betsey Whitney's football team,[3] very intelligent. (Truman subsequently lied by telling US friends that he'd been such a success that the QM had told the Queen she must meet him and forthwith he was summoned to the Palace!)

This time the mood struck me as much calmer. A detective had arrived the day before to find the house and to see the police put up "No Parking" boards, but no boards arrived. When Eileen telephoned the police, they said they *had* no boards and no one paid any attention to them in any case. But they would send a "bobby" along. He arrived and struck up friendships with

[1] Barry Humphries (b. 1934). He created his alter ego, Dame Edna Everage, in the 1950s and watched her grow into an international superstar.

[2] Dame Edith Sitwell (1887–1964), author and poet.

[3] Betsey Cushing (1908–98), married to John Hay Whitney (1904–82), American Ambassador to Britain. Betsey was later one of Capote's victims in *Answered Prayers*.

the household, who were by now extremely excited. Miss Feeney,[1] elderly, virginal and deaf, was full of nervous giggles, Miss Bell, the retoucher, who never looks up from the job in hand, was already agog at the window.

The other guests arrived, Roy Strong in a psychedelic tie; Kistie Hesketh, hatless, dressed like a child's idea of a primrose by Courrèges; Leo d'Erlanger,[2] superbly mundane in a black coat and pinstripe; Jakie Astor, wearing a hat which he subsequently forgot, Irene Worth;[3] just right in non-colours and Diana Cooper, casual, the same as ever, with her habitual basket occupied by Doggie, the chihuahua.

The Queen Mother's huge limousine arrived as near as possible to the house and out stepped the smiling, delightful, familiar figure, dressed in brilliant puce and magenta, the colour dazzling if the material not of the first quality. But no complaints, everything is perfect. "The last time, poor Edith." The delightful hesitancy, wistful eyes. "Oh how nice and warm your house is. I'm cold from sitting to Mr. Ward.[4] Sitting produces its own coldness, doesn't it?"

Introductions. Roy and I sat at the QM's feet. I suddenly found myself nervous and stumbling over my words, Roy calm-headed. The topic, the lack of painted portraiture today. Would Graham Sutherland[5] be good to paint the Queen? "Why not you?" the QM asked me.

Lunch seemed to be long in being announced, and when at last we sat for the egg with the explosion on top, Ray, out of nerves, had cooked it too long. It was hard. I apologised. "I'm afraid the egg is cooked too much. It's hard."

"Oh, I like it like that."

I noticed the Queen took a fork to the egg, and later said "I always choose the wrong implements!"

Controversial subjects such as Lord Snowdon and his film were avoided, Prince Charles eulogised, and perhaps just a suspicion of criticism for

[1] Sheila Feeney, who helped Eileen with secretarial work.

[2] Leo d'Erlanger (1898–1978), banker.

[3] Irene Worth (1916–2002), actress, much liked by Cecil, who, in her own words, worked hard to make her famous.

[4] John Ward (b. 1917), portrait painter and Royal Academician.

[5] Graham Sutherland (1903–80), painter. He undertook portraits of Churchill (destroyed), Somerset Maugham, Helena Rubinstein and the Queen Mother, but never the Queen.

his father sending him to a tough school. "Now he doesn't need to be toughened any more."[1] The QM applauded the reappearance of the old *Tatler* and I described the attack on its existence by the *Observer.* "What's this I hear?" cried Jakie,[2] and conversation became general. Lots of big laughs were heard by the group in the office, Eileen, Miss Bell and deaf, virginal Miss Feeney, Eileen going to and from the post, passed the hall door and saw two glimpses, one of the Queen Mother a bite of food in her mouth, and second, with arm raised high, quaffing a large glass of Rothschild red wine.

Leo used the English language in a flowery manner that is seldom used by Englishmen but which is utterly delightful. The QM, on hearing a particularly well-phrased compliment, said, "Oh I must remember that." Then Diana, Doggie nestling in a shiver at her bosom, with vodka and wine under her belt, did a virtuosa piece on spending the weekend with "The Horse," Harold Macmillan,[3] and how Ava Waverley had been *décommandée,* how Ava had said, "Diana, aren't you going to buy anything new for the occasion?" The tale was so well told that the QM laughed from the gut. The fact that Macmillan was continually referred to as "The Horse" (reason unknown) added to her enjoyment. The little fat face crinkled except for two apples in the centre of the cheeks. These remained as round and perfect as always.

Diana's was the star turn, her imitation of Ava forthright, the greatest success.

The Queen's car had arrived. It must be ignored. Half an hour later the Queen asked Jakie the time. "Oh, I must go!"

"I want to thank you very much for being always such a support and good friend to me," I managed to spurt out as the Queen stood in the street, while a few onlookers gawked. The car drove away. Smiles, bows, waves.

The party was soon over for the other guests were late too. "But it *had* been a whizz, hadn't it?" said Diana.

Upstairs in the office, and down in the basement, were now giggles and hoots of laughter, a release of pent-up energy. Tension over. The bobby

[1] Prince Charles had been sent to Gordonstoun, a notoriously rigorous school in Scotland, which he hated.

[2] The Astors owned the *Observer.*

[3] Rt. Hon. Harold Macmillan (1894–1986), Prime Minister from 1957 to 1963. He was known in Diana Cooper's circle as "The Horse."

came to talk on the front doorstep. The salacious Ray told me that the policeman had told Mrs. Cartwright, "Something smelt jolly good. What was it they were having for lunch?" Mrs. Cartwright, overexcited, replied "Roast Dick." When Ray repeated this dirty laugh to Miss Feeney, she yelled with pent-up virginal laughter, and asked, "Whose Dick?"

EARLY SPRING

15 APRIL 1968

Clarissa [Avon] came to lunch yesterday, said she thought she'd hang on to Rose Bower Cottage as, although she adored her new house, everything was so expensive. "Oh, I don't know," I said. "I do," replied Clarissa ominously. Perhaps I am living in a fool's paradise. I haven't really made any big money for a big time and avid tax requests come in all the time. The success of the Palm Beach exhibition was encouraging, so now whenever possible I go to the studio to do a few sketches that might be of interest to these curious, still-rich people.

But the main line of my painting is hazardous. Very few successes lately and I don't know in which direction to go. It is difficult, especially as now I have the glorious opportunity of staying down here in the country for nearly two weeks on end.

This rare pleasure is this time somewhat mitigated by the effects of Lord Snowdon's first TV film, for I have perforce been thinking a great deal about old age and loneliness.

I was walking down King's Road, Chelsea the day before my July holiday trying to buy clothes for the cruise. Suddenly my name called out and an open car filled with tousled young men drove up to the kerb. Tony, Derek Hart and American technicians were making a film and wanted to photograph me. Naturally I thought the film was about King's Road types and said, "No, those are the people you should photograph" and pointed to the Procol Harum pop group[1] who, dressed in Genghis Khan moustaches, beards and burnooses, were about to step into a taxi. Tony looked apelike, then snapped back, "No, it's you we want; we've been trying to get in touch with you."

[1] Procol Harum, whose hits included "Whiter Shade of Pale."

"But I'm leaving for my holiday at dawn and working with Mark Peploe[1] on a book this afternoon."

"It'll just take twenty minutes. Couldn't we come to your house after lunch?"

"Couldn't you just do it here and now?"

"No, at your house."

"Well what's it all about?"

"It's"—giggle—hesitation—"it's about London."

"But I'm not swinging London."

"But it's about senior citizens."

"What's that mean?"

Giggle, giggle, Tony and Derek Hart behaved as if they'd just found themselves. "Well, come round to Pelham after lunch but as soon as Mark Peploe arrives I'll have to work with him."

After lunch the gang arrived, set up a movie camera in the front garden and Derek asked indefinite questions. I talked in circles. Tony said, "Try to be amusing. In life you're the most entertaining person I know. Try to get that likeness into your answers."

"But I don't really understand what this is all about. The wind's blowing so I can hardly hear you. Let's go indoors a moment and discuss things. Just what is this film about?"

Giggle, giggle, hesitation. "It's about experience. Do you feel the same now about things as you did at the beginning of your career?"

"Who else have you photographed?"

"Compton Mackenzie."[2]

"What did he talk about?"

"Oh, about his work."

When it dawned upon me that the film was about growing old and the ways to combat it, I warmed to the subject, having written notes for a play to be called *Time Table,* I talked about the various signs whereby one fell from one shelf of age on to another. Unfortunately, Mark Peploe never showed. He

[1] Mark Peploe, editor.

[2] Sir Compton Mackenzie (1883–1972), Scottish author. He was then aged 85.

was viewing the rushes of his South American films and completely forgot my appointment. Thus I was at the mercy of the gigglers. We drank whiskies and sodas. Who else could I suggest? Marlene D.? Would she do it?

Imagine my surprise when five months later Truman came to tell me in New York that he'd been to a Paley lunch and heard I was "shown up," seen in a most unflattering light in a film about gerontophilia. Telegrams, letters and telephone calls. "I assure you you're the best thing in the film. Everyone says so."

I asked various friends who'd seen the film. Truman was exaggerating, Alex Liberman said, "You are frank and charming, but I doubt the wisdom of your having done it."

Delays, procrastinations from Tony and Derek. They hadn't got a copy to show me. Only the night before it was to be shown in London (after the NY showing) was I invited to go to a private viewing. I was appalled to find myself at 64 as taking a large part in a film that had to do with senility, old people's institutions, old people being injected with youth hormones and glands, or being massaged, shaken, fitted for wigs. The fact that I looked extremely young and attractive helped, but the fact that under false pretences I'd been put into this particular setting made me extremely angry.

If I had known what the plan really was about, I could have refused to appear or if I had wished to be featured then I could have answered a little less glibly, and perhaps even said one or two things about the dignity or nobility of old age, an aspect that was almost completely lacking in this clever, snide and typically Snowdon-esque film.

As a result of the film a great deal of emphasis has been put on my age, not only in America (*Time* says I have trouble with my dentures) but here among friends and strangers. Worse—the effect is with me. It has made me feel venerable. I do not like this and the fact that Tony has managed to invade the privacy of my mind is something I resent. Now, when I am in the studio painting, I am apt to think about the past and the question of the future, and feel this is not of the occasion. I would like to have been prompted to these thoughts by other means than a con-trick. It gave me little satisfaction to telephone Tony and tell him I thought Derek and he had "pulled a fast one" on me, for I know Tony was only pleased to think he might have found himself in a lot of trouble, but had just managed to get away with it.

The poet Iris Tree died on 13 April 1968.

IRIS TREE 15 APRIL 1968

The life has ebbed out of Iris. For some time, now, she and her friends knew she was a goner. The old, dreaded cancer. She wanted to die in her favourite pine-studded stretch of France near Bordeaux, and her friends were afraid that she would have a seizure and be less well supplied with painkilling drugs by the French hospital staff than by kinder and more generous English doctors. However, she returned to die by slow but mercifully painless degrees in the house of her son Ivan [Moffat]. Her ashes are to be taken to be strewn under the pine trees.

And so one of the most rare and wonderful human beings has gone from us. Iris is someone whom, as a boy, I admired and wondered at from afar. How glorious that a young golden goddess should be able to show such independence, such originality and, to use an old-fashioned word, such Bohemianism. With her corn silk hair sheared in stiff pageboy fringe and bell, with her artistic clothes, golden tissues, leather, flowered jackets, she looked so unlike anyone else at that time. She posed for Augustus John portraits, sat to Epstein,[1] wrote poems, appeared as the nun in *The Miracle,* in a series of marvellous photographs taken by her husband, Curtis Moffat.

Then she married [Friedrich] Ledebur and went through an Austrian phase, bringing humility and added warmth and humanity to the group of artists living on the lake at Kammer, then together with Frederick, she led a life on horseback in California. She studied and taught at the Chekhov school at Carmel. She was always experimenting with existence. She did so many things that are now accepted as part of the new hippie scene for the first time.

Whenever she appeared, it was a delightful surprise, for she brought with her an unexpected candour and freshness. Nothing was ever formulated. She moulded everything anew. There were no set ways, no rules. This led to a marvellous freedom.

When she was living in an abandoned wooden tower, part of the playground part of the pier of Malibu Beach, she decided to give a party. Her guests

[1] Sir Jacob Epstein (1880–1959), sculptor.

mounted in circles to the top of the tower to sit on the wooden floor and eat four long fresh loaves of bread and to drink beer, while the talk was brilliant and Iris's dissertations and impersonations kept everyone entertained till dawn.

Arriving one day in Mercedes [de Acosta]'s sunny garden in California, Iris, who had been camping in the mountains for some weeks, asked if she might have a bath. She then proceeded to walk into the bath fully dressed, submerged herself entirely, soaped her hair, her clothes, her cotton skirt, her leather belt, her canvas shoes, then rinsing herself out, lay on the lawn to dry out. She emerged fresh as a child.

Her sense of wonder, her appreciation and love never lost the spontaneity of childhood.

Iris was a noble creature. Free of convention, of snobbery, fuller than anyone I know of understanding and lacking in censure of the badness of others, she had her real friends. They were not only her intimates, but the people she talked to as she sat by herself at a restaurant table or at a bar. She was on easy terms with all strata except those people who were pretentious and false.

Without a word she would turn away from them in self-protection, knowing that even to discuss them would sully her impeccable immaculate natural distinction. She was like a Geiger counter for spotting parsity of spirit in others. She never failed.

In many ways she was a precursor of Garbo, and Diana [Cooper]'s personality is founded on Iris's influence.

SATURDAY MORNING, 4 MAY 1968

Can't escape early enough from London, now that spring is here and so much growth to watch each day in the garden. Returned to an empty Pelham Place on a gloomy Sunday evening, relieved to be able to give in to the really bad cold I'd caught at Kistie's stately home.[1] Ray was out, the rubbish from the wastepaper basket put to one side, but not taken downstairs, no flowers, no mail or papers. The rooms cold. With a fur rug wrapped round my legs, I wrote a long

[1] Lady Hesketh lived at Easton Neston in Northamptonshire.

Gervase Griffiths and Patrick Procktor, Reddish House, April 1968

letter to Kin. He has not written to me for two months and I mind. I wrote a newsy, bright letter but added that I hoped he wouldn't continue his silence as it made me very sad. This long letter produced, as if by instruct, a letter from Kin next morning, nothing intimate to show that we were at all close to one another, just a description of what he is doing to his first house, and enclosing a map he'd made of the rooms and the furniture.

Dinner with Patrick Procktor made me realise how all the people I'd been with at Kistie's, though interesting and agreeable, were not really the ones I wanted to spend my time with. I am completely in my element with Patrick. We discuss every manner of subject and he always seems pithy, fresh and stimulating. His friend Gervase[1] had cooked the chicken and the pear pudding, his Tunisian travelling companion named Ozzie was present, and was like a Victo-

[1] Gervase Griffiths, an Oxford undergraduate, whom Patrick Procktor met in 1968 and with whom he was romantically involved for two years. Cecil photographed him in the nude.

rian life companion, like someone you'd pay to give cosiness to family life, a spinster, completely and utterly feminine. Ozzie, in spite of his "with it" manner, had the qualities of a Jane Austen character, while looking exactly like the portrait of Emily Brontë. Ozzie, tired after a quick trip to Denmark, smoked two hash cigarettes, then was sick and passed out on the day bed in the studio. I loved being in the company of Pat and G. (gosh, it's love in bloom) and stayed late drinking rum.

If only I could have given in, as Dr. G. [Gottfried] told me to do, and had not felt obliged to go with Dicky [Buckle] to the Danish Ballet. If only I had coddled myself, I would have been less ill for the following week. Agony getting through the long hot evening. Intervals galore, a fight to the bar, and then bells summoning one to another ballet, and a good gawk at the Royal Family with the King and Queen of Denmark[1] in the royal box. (The Queen dignified, very dowdy and not really animated enough, the Queen Mother surprisingly faded, Princess Margaret with an outrageous, enormous Roman matron head-do, much too important for such a squat little figure. Princess Anne,[2] her hair rather pretty and well dressed, and her eyes quite heavily painted. Luckily I did not see the common little Lord Snowdon, who was wearing his hair in a dyed quiff, but enjoyed at second hand the snobbish enjoyment of the evening, as exemplified by the sycophantic smiles of Lady Fermoy, Princess Georg of Denmark[3] etc.)

The most distinguished figure in the baby-blue frilled box was Lady Churchill,[4] a little baffled but nonetheless comporting herself with amazing dignity. A white-haired woman of over 80, with a new habit of not being able to keep her mouth (quiet) licking her lips all the while, yet who, with age, has become more noble and fine than ever before.

Next morning cold much worse as result of outing. Luckily could stay in (sorting photographs) until lunch with Roy Strong in his Victorian flat looking over the Catholic cathedral.

[1] HM King Frederik IX (1899–1972) and HM Queen Ingrid (1910–2000), born a princess of Sweden. They were in Britain for an Anglo-Danish Trade Week.

[2] HRH The Princess Anne (b. 1950), now HRH The Princess Royal.

[3] Ruth, Lady Fermoy (1908–93), lady-in-waiting to the Queen Mother, and Anne Bowes-Lyon (1917–80), wife of HRH Prince George of Denmark (1920–86), who served at the Danish embassy in London. She was a niece of the Queen Mother and mother of the Earl of Lichfield.

 [4] Baroness Spencer-Churchill, widow of Sir Winston.

He said he thought one never quite knew a person until one had seen where they live. His taste proved to be extremely restrained, intellectual and sombre, as one would have expected. Dark-brown and apricot walls with Old Master drawings, engravings, and Elizabethan theatrical designs in the dining room. The windows looking out on to the Roman Catholic cathedral, which he says the younger generation admire, while "oldsters" like myself are apt to find it an abomination.

The morning had been spent going through files of my old photographs and throwing prints around ruthlessly. Is this worth bothering about? No. But Roy and his henchmen at the National Portrait Gallery had discovered in some forgotten picture possibilities for posters, and had treated them with a deference and care that had touched me deeply. It was quite strange to see a mock-up for a poster of myself for the NPG, almost as if one were already dead.

Cecil had a weekend guest in the form of Whitney Warren (1898–1986), a social friend whom Cecil saw in San Francisco. Warren was the son of the architect Whitney Warren, who built Grand Central Station. As a result, he was able to live the life of a well-heeled bachelor, indulging his interests, which included art and gossip.

That most light-weight of all persons, Whitney Warren has been for a short visit. I ask him because he entertains me in San Francisco, and because of Kin I am hopefully able to think I shall return again and again. But really Whitney is the worst possible news.

Selfish to an appalling degree, snobbish, insensitive, he thinks only of himself all day and night. "Now, Eileen, will you go out of the room and bring me in a pencil and paper as I want to write down a list of seeds you'd like from California. Delphiniums, polyanthus, begonias? You don't like begonias?"

By this largesse he thinks he can patronise us. "I *like* what you are doing to the house. That makes sense to me."

He brings all conversation back to himself and his experiences. "This was the road I travelled last week on my way to Cornwall. Now listen"—as we are walking, he will stop in his tracks (I walk on), and he employs the child's trick of refusing to allow the conversation to be taken from him by elongating the "aaaaa" or "errrr." Likewise, he will not leave a place when asked, employs delaying tactics if he is enjoying himself, or is impressed. He is always fractious that a new appointment has been made for him. He has bought a Fantin-Latour, and don't we have to hear about it? He gave, three years ago, a Whistler to the White House. We are still hearing about that. He listens to nobody. He is a really worthless fool, an ass, that I'm ashamed of. I can't wait to get rid of him and have now decided that this is the last time he ever comes to Broadchalke.

Cecil held an exhibition of his theatre designs at Wright Hepburn Gallery.

Whitney Warren's departure on Monday morning gave me only a few hours to relax and recuperate, and these were spent doing a few last-minute "designs" for the show. The private viewers were not important in any field of activity. I knew very few, but they were the clients of the Wright Hepburn Gallery, which has built up a great interest in ballet and stage design. They managed to sell 18 of my exhibits after three hours of party talk. I returned home somewhat elated and, realising the interest in designs for "celebrity" costumes (Olivier and Margot and Nureyev went like hot cakes), I came home and, after a cold supper alone, finished seven more designs by 1 o'clock in the morning.

Next day a press show, very tiring because one has to be on one's guard all the time, followed by another private view. This time very few people, very few red tickets and I became not only exhausted but depressed. I suppose I should be realistic and know that this exhibition was successful in the unpretentious way that it set out to be, but nonetheless I was sad and dunched that it was not considered more of a success.

As if I had not held a glass in my hand for long enough, and made conversation with enough people, the Wednesday had to be a continuation of just such a procedure for this was the day on which my sisters and I had planned an obligation cocktail party at home. A crowd of 70 filled the room at Pelham. They were unexciting. They were, with very few exceptions, not my friends. They were the sort of people I have no longer any interest in, though to Nancy they are still respectable, important, even impressive. With a background of frenzied activity with the photographic files, in preparation for the National Portrait Gallery exhibit, with a TV appearance, there was little time to talk to Eileen. Many things now have to be put off for next week. Meanwhile, at any rate, a batch of negatives had been sent off to be printed, so it came as an appalling shock to me when, having slept or just rested, as I watched the springtime trees, still in pointillist dots of pale green, rushed by the train window, and as we packed into the car at Salisbury, Ray told me a neighbour had telephoned to say that Michael Bundy was planning to destroy his old dilapidated barn opposite and to build a modern concrete and aluminium erection for all his tractors. This would completely ruin my view and the entire village scene as seen from my hill. I felt utterly sick.

Cecil proceeded to take preventative action.

JAMES POPE-HENNESSY

It was a shock to hear it. The revelation to James must have been appalling. He has lately taken a youngish-looking young man (a wrinkled poor white skin like an undernourished Russian, but with curly grey-blond hair) to live with him. "It's so wonderful. I now have someone to look after me, to prevent me drinking, who's a wonderful chef. Do come to dinner."

I could not make out what sort of a person this was, interested in dog racing, football, very straight, yet seemingly devoted to James, for whom he had left his new wife and large home just recently. "When we met it was a *coup de foudre.*"

The [John] Cholmondeleys[1] were at dinner, a magnificent meal, and the two lovers seemed utterly contented, though I was baffled. Now it seems the young man was merely conning James. All the while in cahoots with his wife, and all the time running up enormous bills at the shops where James had an account. The last two weeks have cost James £500 in bills and no doubt he will discover worse losses in due course. All this apart from the loss to his pride, to his self-esteem, to his self-confidence. A really upsetting experience, and one that is quite new to me. I must try to hear all about it.

Cecil spent the weekend arranging his books in the recently completed library on the landing. He then heard of the death of Mercedes de Acosta, whom he had

[1] Lord John Cholmondeley (1920–86) and his wife, Maria-Cristina Solari.

known since the 1920s. She had played an integral role in his relationship with Garbo. She was a lesbian who once made the proud and substantiated claim, "I can get any woman from any man." Of her Alice B. Toklas declared, "You can't dispose of Mercedes lightly—she has had the two most important women in US—Greta Garbo and Marlene Dietrich." Mercedes died at her home, 315 East 68th Street, New York on 9 May.[1]

MERCEDES DE ACOSTA

So the tragic Mercedes has succumbed at last. Perhaps it is nearly ten years ago that she was stricken, and while near to death vowed that she would not give in. Her characteristic stubbornness has seen her through many years of pain, illness and sadness. I am only sorry that the pain, and the expense, and the fortitude have had to continue for so long.

I cannot be sorry at her death. I am only sorry that she should have been so unfulfilled as a character.

In her youth she showed zest and originality. She was one of the most rebellious and brazen of lesbians. She married, a nice man and bad painter (Abram Poole),[2] but refused to be known as Mrs. She was always M. de A. (never "Miss"). She managed not only to make a beeline for all the women who interested her, but by some fluke, or some genius gift of her own, became intimate friends. She, I'm not sure of the facts, informed Maud Adams[3] that her house was on fire, she became part of her life subsequently, as she did of Isadora Duncan, Marie Doro, Duse, Nazimova,[4] oh, countless women.

She had excellent, severe Spanish taste in her furnishing and in her interiors using only black and white, and was never willing to accept the vulgarity of so many American standards. She was strikingly un-American in her black tricorne and buckled shoes, highwayman's coat and jet-black-dyed hair.

[1] For the full saga of Mercedes de Acosta, *see* Hugo Vickers, *Loving Garbo* (1994).

[2] Abram Poole (1882–1961). Some of his portraits are in national collections.

[3] Maud Adams (1872–1953), actress, famed as Peter Pan in America.

[4] Isadora Duncan (1878–1927), dancer who was strangled by her scarf and the car wheel, who wrote Mercedes graphic poetry; Marie Doro (1882–1956), a Charles Frohman star; Eleonora Duse (1858–1924), Italian actress; and Alla Nazimova (1879–1945), Russian actress who performed in many Ibsen and Chekhov plays.

She was always about to write a play for Eva Le Gallienne,[1] or deliver herself of a novel or a thesis on Indian photography, but her sole publication, an autobiography,[2] was a big disappointment. She became rather idiotic, petty and petulant. Looking for grievances, she found them.

She managed to make it difficult for friends, impossible for her lovers. She became ill, she became poor, but she never became old. She had a gallantry that could be recognised in her sprightly step. When I telephoned to enquire if I could come to her in her bed of illness, she said, "It would give you too much of a shock. You see the pain has been so great behind the eye that it has entirely turned my hair white."

The one person who could have made her last years less lonely and bitter was Greta. If only she had sent Mercedes a bunch of flowers, it would have made all the difference. As it was, Greta felt that Mercedes, her long and once loved friend, brought her bad luck, that as a result of Mercedes recommending a quack doctor, Greta had almost become crippled (no signs!). It was this, more than the indiscretion of Mercedes writing about Greta,[3] that brought the friendship to a close.

Several times I tried to cajole G. to relent, to send a message to the pining, still adoring Mercedes. "I have enough trouble without that!" I had the idea of sending flowers to Mercedes and pretending they came from G. Would that I had done that. It would never have been discovered. As it is, after suffering the horrors of New York hospital treatment at the hands of rude nurses and doctors alike, all Mercedes's money has gone. She became threadbare. She pined to leave the vulgarity of Hollywood and New York to visit Europe once more. But she had not the wherewithal, or the money. Now, without a kind word from the woman she loved more than any of the many women in her life, Mercedes has gone to a lonely grave. I am relieved that her long drawn-out unhappiness has at last come to an end.

[1] Eva Le Gallienne (1899–1991), actress with whom Mercedes was in love in the early 1920s. She acted in Mercedes's play, *Jehanne d'Arc.*

[2] *Here Lies the Heart* (1960). Mercedes also published a number of novels, plays and volumes of poetry.

[3] Mercedes left one of the most vivid and insightful descriptions of Garbo's mercurial personality in her book *Here Lies the Heart* (1960), a book which many have criticized, and yet which is a classic of its kind.

TUESDAY, 14 MAY 1968

Am riveted by Cynthia Asquith's diaries. Of course, it is the period that appeals to me, but they give a really true inside glimpse of what high life and aristocratic life was like, and I enjoy her vanity. Many women criticise this. "Does she never forget a pass?" But one must not necessarily like all authors. I did like her. I find her aloof but sympathetic, and there was something a little mad about her pleasure in her physical beauty, which, incidentally, I could not see. She was like a cat that had finished the cream and she was continually licking her thin, upward-curving lips. There was something a bit gauche about her, which made her vulnerable and appealing, and she had that white pig look that I found fascinating. Anyhow I am under the influence of her diary, so, herewith:

After Sunday supper (hot livery soup, cold lamb, meringues and marrons, cheese and pears), drove Eileen and Charles [Colville] and Alan to get the last train to London after a particularly pleasant and relaxed weekend. Weather had been swinish lately, too much rain, mud everywhere, and no sun. But although the Sat. and Sun. were unsettled, there were a great many "high intervals" and these were taken full advantage of by the others who went for long walks, or took the car to sightsee, to shop, or to visit remote downlands (where on Sunday morning they came across a school of gliders, who spoke fascinatingly of their sport).

Unfortunately, I had not fully recovered from the really bad cold, caught at Easton Neston, when by some incredible bad luck I seemed to have caught another. Throat full of knives, nose swollen, eyes bunged, thought it wisest to remain indoors. However, feeling rather out of it all, and mistakenly imagining that "fresh air" would do me good, I went on a wonderfully pleasant expedition on the Sunday evening, through a Pre-Raphaelite glade, up a long hill which was completely remote and deserted except for foxes, badgers and frightened birds. Our delight at the beauty of the springtime hedges reaching its height when we came across banks of wild violets. They were the deepest purple and enormous. The country loot of cowslips, young beech leaves, bluebells, and even roses from the greenhouse filled the flower room, and in the panic to get the train one large bunch was left behind. I returned to a completely deserted house, the burglar alarm my company. By the fireside I looked through early negatives of myself at Harrow and Cambridge (what a horror I was!) in an unsuccessful attempt to find one particular picture for the forthcoming Nat. P. show. Altogether frustrated.

The Tempest was being given on TV, but my set was on the blink and I could not even get a clear sound. I felt it was my fault, as I have a jinx on these things. But the next day Brian Blick, still at work on the "landing library," could do nothing with it. Moreover, I could not discover why, when I put on the burglar alarm to test, that in spite of all doors being closed, the ground floor alarm buzzed at me angrily. (Later, I discovered the cellar door was open.) Feeling old and ill and depressed, I came to bed and sneezed, and dreamt about awful situation in which the Duchess of Windsor was present while I was being humiliated wearing a toupee that would not behave itself.

MONDAY, 15 MAY 1968

A great relief. I decided that I had been ill long enough and must take my cold seriously. No use fighting. I'd not go over to the studio. I'd remain the whole day in bed. Telephoned to put off Clarissa A. (who seemed in a bad temper) for tea and settled down to cosset myself with hot lemon and trays. Started to write diary Vol. IV, something I enjoyed as a change. I haven't worked at this sort of thing for a long while. I filled in bits about Greta's first visit to me in London, and also about Bertie Abdy and Henry Moore.[1] Eileen, telephoning from London, said that a minimum of mail awaited her. Mercedes [de Acosta] was dead, *Vogue* wanted me to photograph "Andrews"[2] for his article, the Wrightsmans had invited me to Greece in July, the carpets and *torchères* part of a group sent up to Sotheby's from here, had fetched £400, a help towards the landing library. Many letters of thanks for the "family" cocktail party etc.

In the writing mood, I could not stop until lunch made a welcome distraction, then more effort, until sleep overcame me. But the welcome noise of men working on the landing prevented me from dozing for more than half an hour. More diary, then slogging away at dreary letters, then more rearrang-

[1] Sir Robert Abdy, Bt, and Henry Moore, the sculptor.
[2] Andrews had been Lady Juliet Duff's butler.

ing of books. To find the right place for all that I have here will take for ever. I go about like Atlas, carrying great ton volumes from one shelf to another.

Then, when the cold was at its heaviest, I would have a long hot scented bath. I relaxed. It was a rare pleasure. Then dressing in time for *Panorama.* (TV sound better, but picture utterly distorted, so my enemy, E. Shinwell[1] looked like a wildly gyrating polyps as he tried to defend the leadership of the loathed Harold Wilson.)[2] Went through magazines for clippings, then threw them out, then with burning eyes, up to bed again. Mrs. Smallpeice meanwhile having made the room neat and spruce, with fresh bed, and I enjoyed the new placing and eliminating of furniture (changes throughout the house).

I started to read Cynthia Asquith and became so engrossed that an intended early night developed into a late one. I was deeply moved by Letty (Elcho)[3] being told of her husband's death in the 1914 war. She seemed, surrounded with her children, like a great Greek tragic heroine. I felt I was present in her bedroom. In fact, Cynthia brings back the unknown with such reality that I am transported back to the times when I was at my most impressionable.

1 JUNE 1968

At last hot blue misty sunshine. Just the wonderful summer days we have dreamt of. It is impossible to work indoors. I take the day off, go out into the garden before having a bath, plant hostas and primulas, and start weeding. Before I know it lunch is ready. The body aches, one can hardly, as Patrick White[4] says, alter oneself from being a half-closed knife. After a short sleep, more gardening. Then at last the delayed bath, but not too much time allowed

[1] Rt. Hon. Emmanuel Shinwell (1884–1986), later Lord Shinwell, post-war Labour minister.

[2] Harold Wilson had been Prime Minister since 1966. He remained so until 1970, returning between 1974 and 1976.

[3] Lady Violet "Letty" Manners (1888–1971), daughter of eighth Duke of Rutland. Married (1911) Hugo, Lord Elcho, heir to the eleventh Earl of Wemyss. He was killed in the First World War in 1916. She was the sister of Lady Diana Cooper and the mother of Martin Charteris. Later Lady Violet Benson.

[4] Patrick White (1912–90), Australian novelist and Nobel prize winner, whom Cecil met on his recent trip.

to soak, for dinner is at the Big House with Ma'am Darling [Princess Marina] and woe betide if you are late.

All the news, from every front, is bad. The Vietnam peace talks get nowhere. Wilson proves himself the most hated Prime Minister since Lord North and the Conservatives say they will not be able to clean up the economic mess, and it is said that the more unpopular Wilson becomes, the lower the opposition Edward Heath[1] sinks in public opinion. Air disasters, submarine disasters, African massacres and tortures, then comes the revolution in France. At first it is funny to think that de Gaulle should be so humiliated. Then one wonders who will fill his place when the rioting students and trade unions have won their battle. The Sunday papers write it is not a question of when but how de Gaulle will go. Then suddenly, by refusing to go, he stays and the revolution fizzles out. It has been pointless and it has done nobody any good.

There are many sick anti-French jokes as everyone is on strike and the corpse of *grandmère* is being eaten by the swarms of rats.

Cecil then had to go down to Broadchalke to deal with the rural council, as his neighbour, Michael Bundy, was threatening to replace his thatched barn with a concrete and aluminium shed.

REDDISH JUNE 1968

Leaving by the early train for a day's work in London, Mrs. Stokes, the daily, tells that she has heard on the radio that Bobby Kennedy has been shot.[2] The news is here in this small village only a few minutes after the event, and in fact before the great American public has yet heard of it. On hearing the news, Stas Radziwill telephoned Jackie Kennedy. It was four o'clock in the morning in New York, and she saw the light twinkling on the telephone by her bed. "Isn't it wonderful?" she says to Stas. "He's won. He's got California!"

"But how is he?" asks Stas.

[1] Rt. Hon. Edward Heath (b. 1916), Leader of the Conservative Party from 1965. Prime Minister 1970–4.

[2] Senator Robert Kennedy, who appeared to be heading towards the Presidency.

"Oh, he's fine, he's won."

"But how is he?"

"What do you mean?"

"Why, he's been shot!"

A bullet lodged firmly in his brain. Throughout the day the bulletins made us pray that he would die and not remain paralysed for the rest of his life. Stas flew to New York, but Lee, appalled at the idea of having to go through the agony of calming her sister's hysteria yet again, decided to await events. I dined with her. She had been looking at television horror all day (the photographs are incredibly dramatic) and looked beautiful, but distraught.

With the Wrightsmans, the evening was spent talking of Bobby and watching the latest news. When the Wrightsmans left (Charles having put his foot in it a few times vis-à-vis who would be the new President, and would David Harlech[1] marry Jackie), Lee asked me to remain while she tried to calm down before going to bed. In her dry, rather strangely hoarse deep voice, with gawky, amateur theatrical gestures of her hands, she held forth.

"You don't know what it's like being with Jackie. She's really more than half round the bend! She can't sleep at night, she can't stop thinking about herself and never feeling anything but sorry for herself! 'I'm so unprotected,' she says. But she is surrounded by friends, helpers, FBI. She certainly has no financial problems, but she is bored. She takes no interest in anything for more than two minutes. She rushes around paying visits but won't settle down anywhere or to anything. She can't love anyone. She wouldn't throw herself out enough. Of course she won't marry that fool David although he goes on about it all the time, but she may quit and start a new life. Meanwhile the new horror will bring the old one alive again and I'm going to have to go through hell trying to calm her. She gets so that she hits me across the face, and apropos of nothing.

"The last time I was in New York she asked me what she could send Margot Fonteyn, who was staying in my apartment, as a little present. She had

[1] Lord Harlech, a former British Ambassador to the United States, who had been widowed the year before, was considered likely to marry the President's widow. Instead, later that year, she married Aristotle Onassis, the Greek shipping millionaire.

turned off the telephone when I called so I left a message suggesting a case of champagne. I was woken by a screaming telephone. 'What's this about a case of champagne? Who do you think I am? A Croesus?' "

Then a diatribe against Lee being Tracy Lord (character Lee played in the Chicago Philip Barry play *Philadelphia Story,*[1] thus showing disapproval of this venture) and surrounded by a rotten lot of people without any sense of reality.

Lee makes the same gestures with her hands. "She's so jealous of me, but I don't know if it's because I have Stas and two children, and I've gone my own way and become independent. But she goads me to the extent that I yell back at her and say, 'Thank heavens, at last I've broken away from my parents and from you and everything of that former life."

"Jack used to play around and I knew exactly what he was up to and would tell him so. And he'd have absolutely no guilty conscience and said, 'I love her deeply and have done everything for her. I've no feeling of letting her down because I've put her foremost in everything.' But Jackie was hopeless even with him. She'd say, 'Look at my desk! I can't get through all those letters!' and he'd gently say, 'Send the whole lot down to me. I'll look after them.' She's lazy too. She never did anything at the White House that she didn't want to and always went away on Friday evenings for a long weekend. She was interested in converting the White House to her taste but even that was only for a short time!"

"But how can we help her? Could you find a strong man to bully her, to make her listen to him? Could we find someone to influence her into taking her painting more seriously?"

"No, she is not really interested. The cultural centre bores her. Everything bores her and as the years pass the situation only becomes more difficult."

My voice had gone and my headache was splitting when at last Lee drove me back to my house.

[1] Lee played Tracy Lord in this revival (which had enjoyed success as the film *High Society* with Grace Kelly in 1955). Lee was dressed by Yves Saint-Laurent and the production opened at the Ivanhoe Theater in Chicago on 20 June 1967. It attracted undue press and critical attention, most of it unfavourable.

BROADCHALKE

"You judge yourself too harshly. You're too hard on yourself." So said the nice 23-year-old German nude model for the weekend, who sat for me for half a face sketch. It is true my pictures do not delight me and I'm very apologetic about them. Perhaps I have, as Churchill said about Attlee,[1] "much to be modest about."

Randolph Churchill died.[2] Not a surprise, he has been a physical wreck for years. I suppose the brandy did it. It certainly sent him into paroxysms. I remember a night when I stupidly said, "Since we're old home week friends here, going to have a nice evening." Randolph then rushed in the room like an angry bull, black round the eyes and sweating. He at once became obstreperous, insulting Laura Dudley Charteris,[3] then at dinner he attacked Ian Fleming[4] for being a coward and staying at home during the war. He stood to his feet and shouted. I have never seen such a ghastly sight, as grey-faced, sweating, he looked at me on interrupting as if I were a viper. The evening ended in disaster, and I saw R. less for a while.

He had many other bad faults. He was rude to inferiors, arrogant, class-conscious, snobbish. But I liked him. He was game, courageous and enjoyed a good joke more than most. Could be very funny and tender. He supported me early, loved Tilly, Mona.[5] We went through a New York phase. He was very much part of the Diana/Duff [Cooper] scene. Then a blank. He appealed to me to see him more often. He knew he was a failure, and this made him vulnerable and charming, and on his last visit to New York he came to my room and talked with a great deal of feeling about old friends. He would be furious, and perhaps it's typical of his bad luck, that he expired on the same day as Bobby Kennedy and that in the newspapers he rates second billing.

. . .

[1] Rt. Hon. Clement Attlee (1883–1967), Labour Prime Minister 1945–51.

[2] Randolph Churchill died on 6 June.

[3] Laura Charteris (1915–90), married to Viscount Long, the third Earl of Dudley, Michael Canfield, and finally the tenth Duke of Marlborough. Randolph had been in love with her over many years.

[4] Ian Fleming (1906–64), creator of "James Bond." He was married to Laura's sister, Ann.

[5] Tilly Losch (1903–75), married to Edward James and the sixth Earl of Carnarvon, and Mona Harrison Williams (by then Countess Bismarck).

I don't really enjoy having people to stay. It is my fault for not relaxing and realising that all I need to do is to leave them to their own resources. But even if I do go to the studio to get on with a hand or a neck I feel that I must keep in touch, and even go so far as to make them feel they should keep in touch with neighbours. Sometimes the social dates don't fit. Dot [Head] is doing A levels, Sidney [Pembroke] is going to hospital about his leg, the D. Cecils are at Oxford, the Longmans[1] recovering from serious illnesses etc.

This weekend Julian Jebb[2] is an ideal guest, appreciate, cosy. Judy [Montagu] is absorbed by the hour in old *Tatlers* (getting information for her book about her mother and Asquith),[3] but Diana C. is a dynamo. I feel I have to keep her busy, either in talk or mobile activity of some sort. How silly of me. I have spent an enormous sum on providing bed and bathroom for each guest, and yet I am really most at ease and happy when I am completely alone.

Now, however, I have got the house full, I must try to make the best of it, take a guest away one by one, for private talk. Otherwise it is nothing but chat, try to get to know each one better.

Meanwhile the sun is out, so are the clematis and the first roses, and the garden is really just as it has been in our dreams for the last nine months of cold, hideous emptiness.

So much happens each day that the weekend papers might belong to another era, and letters from America arrive by air as if de Gaulle were quitting and Bobby Kennedy going to be their new President, instead of which the General is firmly ensconced and people are killed on the railway line as the crowds surge forward to see Bobby's coffin on its way to join J.F.K. in Arlington Cemetery.

I suppose because servants are scarce and one does so much oneself (I do comparatively nothing, can only boil an egg) that it becomes a ceaseless toil having people to stay. Of course Diana, Judy and Julian Jebb are all strong meat, ter-

[1] Mark Longman (1916–72), publisher, and his wife, Lady Elizabeth Lambart (b. 1924).

[2] Julian Jebb (1934–84), television interviewer and maker of arts programmes. His story is told in *A Dedicated Fan*, edited by Tristram and Georgia Powell (1993). He committed suicide.

[3] Her mother, Venetia Stanley, had an affair with H. H. Asquith, when he was Prime Minister in the First World War.

rific characters and never quiet for a moment. Diana not easy. Breakfast? Nothing? But this means she raids other people's breakfasts, or goes down at dawn for a feast from the ice box. No, Diana is a difficult guest. She has her meannesses, her economy. One of these eccentricities takes the form of never supplying her own cigarettes. She is always looking for a fag, or a light or an ashtray. And she has to be watched, lest she helps herself too liberally at the drink tray and gets sloshed, as she did on Saturday night. This is a tragedy, for a great person becomes a responsibility and a difficult problem. (Her brain remains so clear that one cannot slough her off, but her timing is out, she drools on and her speech is slurred.)

CYRIL CONNOLLY

JUNE 1968

Cyril Connolly has become so benign and benevolent. There is still a tang in his voice as he elaborates on the man who cannot understand people who have other people's family crested silver on their table or others' ancestors on their walls. Oh yaaas—"And who have to look from their windows to other people's property." But when one remembers how spiky and terrifying he used to be it is extraordinary to see how docile and tamed he is now. And he has become pretty, a pale pink celluloid baby, blush-rose cheeks and not fat, not obesely disproportioned.

We dined at the neighbouring Hobsons.[1] Cyril described his new house in Eastbourne. He and his Deirdre loved going every morning to the Italian shop to sit, among senior citizens, while they drink delicious coffee and cream, and ate cakes while reading the newspapers. It sounded like a trip to Italy. "But I suppose it is the lure of 'Flip' (the headmistress of St. Cyprian's School) that brought you back to Eastbourne?" "Oh yes, that coconut cake in the mornings, when one was in favour and taken on her shopping expedition into town. That's at the root of it all. How much do you remember of St. Cyprian's?" he asked. "Unfortunately very little. I can't even remember Orwell."[2]

[1] Anthony and Tanya Hobson lived at Whitsbury in Dorset.

[2] George Orwell (1903–50), the writer, was at St. Cyprian's School at the same time as Cyril and Cecil. He wrote an essay on his time there called "Such, Such Were the Joys."

"But," asked Cyril, "if we had started a love affair do you think it would have lasted?"

"Oh, a lifetime of course," I replied. Cyril exploded with laughter. When we all departed Cyril came up and said, "Goodnight, Darling!"

When the Marx Brothers were introduced to Mrs. Rittenhouse, one of them said, "We've heard so much about you, Mrs. Rittenhouse, we're getting sick of it." That's really what I felt about Mrs. Eleny (?) Strutt,[1] of whom [Beatrice] Lady Pembroke and old cronies have talked since my days at Ashcombe. One glimpse of her in her wheelchair (she is now at 85, immobile in body) made me realise what I had missed. A tremendous, wise, witty woman of experience, she exudes zest and enthusiasm for life, her great enthusiasm perhaps being her garden. We made an expedition to see it, and to see her whizzing about at great speed under the low-hung branches was a big experience. The sudden swift velocity gave great point to everything she said, and her Dutch accent too heightened her efforts. I thought her in appearance very like my mother, and also like Ena, the Queen of Spain[2] (who were said to resemble one another) and this touched me a lot.

Altogether it was such a treat to see such experience at work that it made me see that there are benefits to old age. Her timing, her authority, her naturalness and "not caring" could never be acquired by a younger person. She seemed quite at ease and calm in her gardening interests. "When that hedge is high, we are going to plant the field." (The hedge not yet planted. What optimism.) Seconded by Thompson, a wonderful factotum in charge of her old motor conveyance and her garden, with an old admiral in tow as part-time husband, she is perfectly satisfied with her lot in life. If she had been younger, she would have married the Duke of Wellington,[3] but as it is she's perfectly happy just to have him around as a convenience.

[1] Baroness Irene de Brienen (1884–1974), married first (1904), Captain Hon. Cyril Ward (1876–1930). Thus she was the mother of Countess (Peggy) Munster; Helen, Countess of Ilchester; and Nicolette Hornby. She married second (1934), Vice-Admiral Hon. Arthur Strutt (1878–1973). They lived at Hodges, Shipton Moyne, near Tetbury, Gloucestershire.

[2] HM Queen Victoria Eugenie of Spain (1887–1969), a granddaughter of Queen Victoria.

[3] Gerald, seventh Duke of Wellington, KG (1885–1972), aesthete and architect, married to the poet Dorothy Wellesley (d. 1956).

She talked of manure, soft silky sandy fertilisers, not sticky messes; she goes to the fundamentals of gardening, and though the results are not on a par with Alvilde Lees-Milne's,[1] the effect is remarkable. It just shows you that you can build a garden and a wood in any old flat field. Yes, if you have this remarkable person's zest.

J. Brody, who has commissioned me to design the club to be called Raffles, has given permission for a Bob LaVine, who is acting as my assistant, to call me whenever business warrants from New York. It is one of the most delightful aspects of the undertaking, for Bob is a bright, amusing and good friend. Apart from the exigencies of the club details—many thousands of details have been contended with—he gives me gossip of New York. He laughs, though I am horrified. When he tells me that Brody, after a morning's work from 9 o'clock, suggests at 1:30 that Bob may be hungry, "Then I'll give you a slip so that you can go down to the basement and eat at the waiters' table." How can one? But among the items on our last table was the information that four of my pictures, which had been sold by the Wright Hepburn Gallery, had been returned because their new owners had heard I was anti-Jewish, that I had written, "Kill the Jews!" This recurrent threat has continued with me for over 30 years now, and it isn't as if I had been anti-Jewish at any point in my life. Amazing how one mistake (using the word Kike—"love from Kike") can have such repercussions! It is a horrible thing to realise that there are still people vindictive enough to want to wish me harm. It is a great relief that these people have not, in this instance, done any very great damage, but it could be serious, and it is disturbing to know of one's unseen, unknown enemies, who have time on their hands and such bitterness in their hearts.

Taking Princess Marina to see *Hadrian the Seventh.*[2] In the first scene Rolfe upsets an inkpot and his landlady chastens him for his clumsiness. Princess Marina leans forward and asks me in her gruff voice, "Did that happen last time you saw the play?"

[1] Alvilde Bridges (1909–94), married to third Viscount Chaplin, and later to the author and diarist James Lees-Milne (1908–97). A distinguished gardener.

[2] *Hadrian the Seventh,* a play by Peter Luke based on Baron Corvo's novel, opened at the Mermaid Theatre on 18 April, with Alec McCowen and others.

On 1 July Cecil left for another holiday with the Wrightsmans, finding himself in the same cabin in Radiant II *as the previous year. They sailed to Dubrovnik, Corfu and Olympia.*

Then Cecil went to Venice.

The holiday, after three days in Venice, is about to be over (DV). Such a creature of habit am I that not for long am I able to keep away from work. This would be something to take into consideration if one were contemplating voluntary retirement. I have little appetite for long sessions of sitting about waiting in hotel lobbies or airport terminals. I'm not so sure I even like watching the reveille of others. Perhaps leisure is something that one has to acquire the use of. Certainly Brando [Brandolini] treats it like a virtuoso. The hours of the morning can pass in discussions of the varying pleasures of Morocco, the fight to preserve Venice from big business and the Communists, the new and "destroyed" appearance of Grace Radziwill[1] or the old mad films of Marlene Dietrich. All this with such zest that at times he leaps high in his bed.

Unfortunately, much as I enjoy his company, I am not relaxed enough to remain lying on the end of the bed and the next telephone call gives me the opportunity to plan a foolish morning buying rubbish to take home as presents from abroad.

THE AUNT'S STORY

This winter in Australia Maie Casey gave a cocktail party for us to meet the cream of Sydney, lots of painters who I didn't know of were to be there, and Dame Pattie [Menzies],[2] and Patrick White, the best novelist etc. It seemed to me a dreary party. Maybe I just had bad luck and got trapped by tiresome old women, so when I was taken up to a couple and Patrick White's name was mumbled, I imagined that this was just another dreary couple. Neither did

[1] Grace Kolin, first married to Prince Stanislas Radziwill and by then married to third Earl of Dudley.

[2] Dame Pattie Menzies (1899–1995), widow of Sir Robert Menzies (1894–1978), Prime Minister of Australia.

either do anything to encourage further acquaintance. I thought P. W. an ugly, sly, disappointing old fuddy-duddy. I was wrong. I was wrong in supposing there was a Mrs. White, I was wrong in supposing him to be a fuddy-duddy.

Only much later, too late, did I discover my mistake when the delightful Jimmy Stern[1] told me how much I would enjoy these novels. He sent me a couple, to be followed by *The Aunt's Story* with instructions to read this first.

In a way it ruined my summer's reading. To begin with the book afforded me enormous pleasure. It was a sort of revelation, but I found it hard to read in large doses. Then I would have the opportunity to read a great deal and my pleasure was expressed in a letter (or was it a telephone conversation to Jimmy's wife). I found this such a contradiction to everything I had imagined would come out of Australia. It was strange, morbid, weird, witty, funny and highly imaginative. But it was the extraordinary sensitivity and degree of perception that gave me such a delightful surprise.

By degrees *The Aunt's Story* hung fire. I found the South of France hotel too like Firbank (how annoyed P. W. would be). I got stuck. The book menaced me from the end of my bed. I took it on the cruise holiday, still found the Russians and strange people who went up in flames in the South of France pension difficult to wade through. But at last the Aunt leaves for Australia. The book ends on passages of such utter beauty that it has left a great impression and if I were to have time, or I were to be a serious writer, I would study all the works of this unprepossessing but I am told quite entertaining and charming character who incidentally is due soon to visit Jimmy in Wiltshire. Perhaps an opportunity to make up for a lost opportunity, although I doubt it.

AUGUST 1968

Cecil took a strong professional interest in other photographers, which found fruit in a work that he undertook with Gail Buckland, called The Magic Image *(1975). Thus, from time to time, he enjoyed encounters with others in his trade. Madame Yevonde (1893–1973) was a society portrait photographer, who was accorded a*

[1] James Stern (1904–93), novelist and critic. His legacy created the Stern Silver Pen Prize for Non-Fiction.

posthumous exhibition at the National Portrait Gallery in 1990. She once did a collection called Birds and Predators. *Lallie Charles (1869–1919) and Rita Martin (1875–1958) were sisters and rivals, popular in the early years of the twentieth century.*

YEVONDE AND LALLIE CHARLES

One learns a lot by seeing things done the wrong way. I went to the retrospective exhibition of photographs of the old thirties society photographer, Yevonde, because I saw in the paper that her pictures went back as far as Gaby Deslys, and it would fascinate me to see how this lady of pale artificially lighted photographs would produce results from someone who had only been photographed by classical daylight. She hadn't, for these photographs were taken in the sepia manner of the time, in lighting and pose, conventionally 1914 fashionable, and made before this photographer had "found" herself.

The exhibition was a terrible mess, every sort of print tacked up, and pictures very dated in style and content. It nonetheless was a help to me when choosing pictures for my exhibition. Had they the outdated look that was merely dreary?

But I came away from this antiquated haunt feeling a sympathy for its denizen, Yevonde obviously wondering at being 75, not able to give up, yet feeling that things weren't as good as they used to be.

Later someone told me that she had started her photographic career as a "pupil" of Lallie Charles, the society photographer of pre–World War One. I was so intrigued that when Yevonde wrote asking me to sit, I accepted.

The session was extraordinary in that the method of photographing was completely unlike anything of today. A huge brontosaurus on a heavy tripod, black velvet, slides and a second's exposure. It amused me and delighted me too, for Yevonde was obviously such a nice woman. When Ruby failed to put the plate at the back in time, Yevonde merely laughed (unlike Baron[1] who used to curse his assistants). She was nervous, shy at photographing another photographer, and quite bright and full of perception.

[1] Baron (1906–56), photographer, born as Baron de V. Nahum and something of a rival to Cecil, particularly since he enjoyed the patronage and friendship of Prince Philip. Antony Armstrong-Jones was one of his pupils. Baron's early death under the surgeon's knife cleared the way.

But the session was especially delightful because she told me quite a bit about the world I had glimpsed as a boy through the pages of the magazines.

Lallie Charles and Rita Martin were the two most successful portrait photographers of their day. Rita, concentrating more on the stage than society, was a serious rival, and now the two sisters were not on speaking terms.

Lallie Charles had a large retinue, travelled in a special coach on the train, put on the dog, kept her sitters waiting and was very temperamental.

A beautiful woman with long corn-coloured hair which she wore in a long bun at the back kept in place by two tortoise-shell crescents. When her sitter was particularly important, the Gaekwar [of Baroda] or some other Indian potentate, she would somehow contrive that the hair would fall from the crescents in a long cascade down the back of her long black charmeuse dress from Handley Seymour,[1] which ended in a long train. With this dress she wore a long hanging row of pearls.

Yevonde came as a highly paying apprentice and when I asked if she learnt much from the experience, she said, "Yes, manners. It taught me how to get along with people and my mother remarked how much my manners had improved." Yevonde loved the life of the studio and would be sent out into Baker Street to buy the flowers for the sitters to fondle. She helped with the arrangements in front of the lattice window. Lallie Charles's prints were done in daylight on IVP [or CVR] paper and the fact that people wrote complaining that they faded was what crashed her. The poor lady, after such work and success, went broke, died of cancer.

And I was late for my appointment with martinet Dr. Gottfried.

Loelia [Duchess of] Westminster told me that every night of her life, before cleaning her teeth and bed, she wrote a few notes of diary. If she could make anything interesting of our dinner at the Beits'[2] she is a literary genius. Never

[1] Madame Handley Seymour, who dressed the Queen Mother when she was Duchess of York and indeed made her wedding dress. She clearly longed to move her custom to Norman Hartnell (1901–79), but out of loyalty got Handley Seymour to do the dress for her coronation, while Norman Hartnell did those of the maids of honour. Then she felt able to switch her allegiance.

[2] Sir Alfred Beit, baronet (1903–94), South African collector, who lived at Russborough in Ireland, and was tied up by Dr. Rose Dugdale in 1974, and his wife, Clementine Freeman-Mitford (b. 1915).

has a more boring evening been endured by ten elderly people. Arriving late, I mentioned that pompous swine Lord Dudley, whereupon Alfred said, "Oh, Lord, he and Grace[1] are coming tonight." Worse to follow. Peter Quennell was bringing his new wife.[2] That's not all, the Thorneycrofts[3] were the final *bonnes bouches*. I could think of nothing interesting to ask anyone throughout the wasteful evening. The twenty eggs, the chicken and tarragon, and raspberries had been cooked in vain. The bills for decor might as well not have been incurred. Poor Alfred, he is so kind and nice, Clem too, but ouch! the emptiness. How much rather would I have stayed at home with my thoughts, however gloomy they may be.

Telephone from the Apple corp. to know if I'd be interested in photographing the Beatles.[4] Yes. Two men came to lunch, very intelligent, but very strange. I, speechless, waiting to ask questions. The Beatles wanted me to go round in a van with them and photograph them at various stops. Fine, but not this Sunday. Why? Well, couldn't you bring the American Ambassador [David Bruce[5]] too? A great deal of the hysteria surrounding the Beatles infiltrated itself into my quiet homestead and Ray told me that one of the men was heavily drugged, hence his slurred speech, his fat cheeks, flappy wrists. On arrival he had asked to go to a lavatory where he had injected himself, leaving behind him part of an ampoule. He then drank quite a bit of sherry and wine. But I suppose living at such high pressure, the Beatles couldn't keep going for long and have to calm themselves somehow. But it does seem to bring bad results so quickly and the huffy young man was so much too young to go.

Have been amazed at the likeness between Rolfe-Corvo and Francis Rose and also Charles James.[6]

[1] Eric, third Earl of Dudley, had married Grace Radziwill in 1961.

[2] (Sir) Peter Quennell (1905–93), author, and his last wife, Marilyn, formerly Lady Peek.

[3] Peter Thorneycroft (1909–94), Conservative Cabinet minister, and his Italian wife, Countess Carla Roberti.

[4] The Beatles (John Lennon, Paul McCartney, George Harrison and Ringo Starr) were then at the height of their fame, but verging on the eccentric, influenced by this time by Indian philosophers. The group finally dissolved in 1970.

[5] David K. E. Bruce (1898–1977), U.S. Ambassador to Britain 1961–9.

[6] Charles James (1906–78), brilliant but erratic dress designer.

"There was little or no warmth or affectionateness in him. Probably this was why he was so selfish and self-centred. No generosity. His humour, such as it was, was of a thin and rather sardonic kind.

"A sort of sub-species. He must have been very tough and elastic, or he would have been utterly crushed and destroyed by the opposition and enmity he met with and did so much to incite. Was there an element of greatness in him to account for this? Or was it perhaps something more analogous to that appalling saying of Parolla, 'If my heart were great 'twould burst at this.' "

The inevitable long-life battle against odds, hard luck etc.

IN A RICTUS OF RAGE

Patrick Procktor took tickets for *My Giddy Aunt,* a play featuring the very special Irene Handl.[1] She is one of the funniest women of today, but appears in the most appalling plays of which the latest seems to be the worst.

The evening was amusing only in laughing at the play itself and the appalling attempt at humour as demonstrated by the author and cast alike.

I have been so little to the theatre of late years that I did not believe such bad performances could have survived from my youth. Here were actors, some quite young, who were performing in a way that I felt sure went out forty years ago.

The evening was hilarious for Patrick who laughed so much that two women got up and changed their seats (theatre half-full). But most hilarious of all ingredients was the pianist who performed in a pink spotlight in the intervals. The programme read "At the piano Hero de Rance."[2] Hero was an aged Edwardian overblown rose type, the sort that was trained in musical comedy, cheery enough to split the atom, a huge jaw, flashing eyes, heavily made up in the old peaches and cherries and cream tradition, false hair, a strip

[1] Irene Handl (1901–87), actress, who played in the West End comedy *My Giddy Aunt;* also a successful novelist.

[2] Hero de Rance, theatrical pianist, without whose piano playing in the intermission of films and plays, no performance was quite complete. Likewise her name was a reassuring feature in the lists of those attending theatrical memorial services.

of enamel. She thumbed out old [Ivor] Novello tunes, smiled at the gallery, caught Patrick's eye and became flirtatious. That such things can continue in the West End of London is quite staggering, yet perhaps a little reassuring, for maybe there are younger people who still have a taste for the things that went out in my youth.

It was the genius of Roy Strong to suggest that Cecil should be the first photographer to have his work shown as a collection in a special retrospective exhibition at the National Portrait Gallery. Cecil was also the first living artist to have his work thus shown, and it was the first time that the occasional non–British subject appeared in the show. The exhibition was an extraordinary success and did much for Cecil's reputation, as well as effectively converting the National Portrait Gallery from being a morgue of old portraits into a lively museum, visited by a wide variety of the general public.

FORTY YEARS ON EXHIBITION

It has been a great strain organising the show for we have had to originate a scheme, and naturally there were many pitfalls. Work had to be redone a number of times and it seemed as if we were making no progress. Over and over the screens of Gertrude Lawrence[1] and Marlene Dietrich had to be made over. Negatives were mislaid or lost for ever. It was unnerving work and Eileen, generally so enthusiastic, said, "Are we ever going to enjoy this? So far it has not been pleasant at all."

I became very nervous. Time became so short before I'd be leaving again for America, and Dicky Buckle is not one to hide the fact when he is in a bad mood. However, he does not resent an argument and sometimes his spirits were so high that he sang or recited Shakespeare.

When I got testy with Eileen she said, "If we don't keep calm about this we'll be at each other's throats before we're through." On top of this activity, there were other strains. No time for Eileen to organise the inviting of people to a party for Liberman,[2] so I had to do this at odd moments early morning

[1] Gertrude Lawrence (1898–1952), stage star, who played in Noël Coward's *Private Lives* and many other productions.

[2] Alexander Liberman (1912–99), managing director of *Vogue.*

or at night, during a deserted London August. Little wonder Liberman said he thought I looked tired and was worried about my health. (Certainly the benefits of my holiday cruise are long since forgotten.) On top of this a grinding anxiety about finances. For a long time now I have been doing the things I like to do and these are not the things that bring in money. Meanwhile the money has had to go out at a great rate, on the alterations at Reddish, besides the continual drain from so large a staff. Altogether it has been a difficult period (the stars say better is in sight) and the strain has made its mark.

I left for New York without the necessary build-up of rest and relaxation for the onslaught to come and, on arrival in NY, the time sequences upset my equilibrium and my stomach. For days on end I had diarrhoea—rare for me in the US—and headaches, and I did not feel able to enjoy extracurricular activities. However, by the time Kin arrived five days later I had partly recovered, and enough to enjoy his most sympathetic presence. He made me realise how lonely I had been without him and how much of just that stimulus he provides. He made me realise my qualms about his taking our friendship for granted were unfounded. He made me realise that so much of my daily activity is uninteresting and only worthwhile if directly concerned with money and earning my living.

I realised that with his being so simple in his demands, so economical in his way of life, extravagant only in big ways (like buying the house next to the one he already owns) he is so much less vulgar than most of my friends and, by being always on the alert and ready to learn, his brain is always being exercised and prevents one from becoming utterly lazy. I realised what a good influence on me he is and how much he has changed me for the better.

He has put on weight. I am rather appalled, for the perfection is off the peach, and I fear that with his ulcer he may not be able to take off the extra weight and that in middle age (he is 35 next year) he will be a very large man indeed.

Last weekend in New York the city was deserted. By Sunday it became a plague city, no one on the sidewalks. I did not enjoy being there. I was lonely. I longed for Kin, but that couldn't be arranged. I filled in with other dates—D. Vreeland. We had a *horrid* lunch after she arrived half an hour late, Bob L.V. a session at his house when I had to leave on account of headache. It was all rather sad, but a necessary part of earning my living and I am lucky to have been away from home as little as I have this last year.

In a panic at the thought of remaining over the weekend in my NY hotel rooms (Kin away with his family) I made attempts to stay with friends. Bob LaV. was too busy to go to Fire Island, Truman working all the time on a TV was not going to Southampton. The Ryans[1] invited me to Newport where there is a dance. The negative point of Newport seems to be that it is impossible to get out. The train journey to Providence was interminable and harassing. Two big taxi rides and I arrived for dinner at ten o'clock. The Ryans equally late. Then very soon the pain started again. How would I get back?

The fog did not look like lifting for flying. Was it the weather or was it my increasing restlessness that made me feel so trapped? With the years I find myself bored with my surroundings (particularly if they are not my own) and longing to escape. This hit me very hard this weekend after a long day of making conversation with people with whom I have very little in common. We went to Bailey's Beach Club and here found an entirely different world from the rest. Everyone here so pleased and self-contained, assured, well-meaning, well-met. Some were shrewd enough to have become rich, others had riches thrust upon them, all were at ease, relaxed, out to amuse themselves as much as possible. I found the atmosphere nightmarish. When I first came to this country the attitudes were not as permissive as now. I was an outsider wanting to get inside. Now that I have got made, I can't wait to get out and back to the worlds where I belong. Old hatchet faces of the past loomed up from the haze of forgotten nonsenses, of months of wasted time. Now that I am, in their estimation, a celebrity the hard old faces welcomed me. The climax of this socialising came in the evening. We went to a dinner of 40 (with modern pictures paradoxically placed in a bourgeois house, beautiful). The noise in the dining room was such that conversation became impossible. I sat next to a crashing bore from Carolina. Food was revolting. Four or five hours of a ball faced me at 11:30.

Will I never learn? Why did I allow myself to make the mistake of

[1] John Barry Ryan III and his wife, Dorinda Dixon (D. D. Ryan). They had a cottage on Nin Ryan's property, Moorland Farm, Newport, Rhode Island.

going somewhere from which as soon as I'd had enough I could not escape? The decorations were expensive and well-organised. The party was on a huge scale, not too hot, an ideal set-up. But the boredom! Since I don't drink it was impossible for me to achieve the necessary degree of enforced euphoria. Others and older people seemed to be enjoying it, old women dancing ecstatically, old rich people laughing, showing signs of mountain-moving vitality, the decibels of their voices cracked the eardrums.

On the morning of Tuesday, 27 August, Princess Marina died at Kensington Palace from an inoperable tumour of the brain. Only a few knew that she was ill and she herself was unaware of the seriousness of her condition. She had gone out for lunch at the weekend, but tripped on the Monday evening and sank into a coma from which she did not wake up.

Cecil had been a friend of Prince George and Princess Marina since the early 1930s and took many excellent photographs of both of them. In widowhood, she became one of Cecil's special friends and they frequently went to the theatre together.

NEW YORK AUGUST 1968

The *Sunday Times* representative in NY called me to say that Frank Giles[1] in London had asked if I'd write an appreciation of Princess Marina. I had heard nothing of a serious illness. Her leg, always weak since paralysis in childhood, had conked out and she had been convulsed with laughter when she sank helpless to the floor in a marquee. But this must mean that she was dead. "Please find out."

An hour later the telex told me she had had an inoperable tumour on the brain, and had died painlessly and quietly. I was deeply shocked. Dreadfully sad. A blow that came very near. She was so very actual, and definite, and I had seen quite a lot of her of late. I'd telephoned just before leaving for NY to commiserate on the leg, and we had just been to see *Hadrian VII* and she told me how interested she was in the life of Corvo that I'd recommended.

[1] Frank Giles (b. 1919), editor of the *Sunday Times*, who resigned in 1983 after the paper had given credence to the so-called Hitler diaries.

HRH Princess Marina, Duchess of Kent

Kin was staying with me and I was busy with him and imbibing all that he had to tell me after a long interval, but even so for the next two days memories of Princess Marina kept coming back to me with such vividness that they were like interruptions to our conversation. "Excuse me but I do remember so vividly her talking about her interest in my romance with Greta. She thought it so surprising that I should feel this way." She thought more about one and one's problems than seemed apparent. She had a formal manner but a conspiratorial gift for intimacy, and in later years I really felt she was a true friend.

But how to write an appreciation that would be de rigueur and yet intimate enough to be interesting?[1]

I was leaving on the morrow, so I would spend the air journey making

[1] Cecil's tribute was published in the *Sunday Times* on 1 September 1968. Princess Alexandra wrote to Cecil to tell him how much she had liked his article; "as it was humorous and unpompous and she would have enjoyed it!"

notes. And this is just what I did. The Atlantic crossing took only six hours and went by very quickly while I wrote and rewrote what seemed to me very uninspired impressions. However, each further draft seemed to take me a bit nearer to liveliness and I arrived at London airport with something that could be bashed out on the typewriter for further polishing. But all the time I was writing I felt extremely sad, not so much for Princess Marina, for her death was sudden and painless and she did not know she was seriously ill. Moreover, her life was an empty one and she had little more to live for. But for people of my age the loss is great for she was so much part of an era, and she added so much to the early days. She was always so vividly around, even until now, so that with her going she leaves a very great gap.

Dined with James P.-H. and two of his friends at an Italian restaurant near to his house. He willingly wrote his name on the bill but when I passed £5 as a contribution, he could not resist keeping the note. "I can more than use this," he said quite unmindful of the fact that he would one day have to pay the restaurant bill. James's lack of financial understanding is too idiotic, and he goes on from bad to worse. Am afraid he will end very badly.[1]

REDDISH

It is very quiet here on my return. Ray, the servant, is away on holiday and most of the neighbours have left and I have no immediate work to do (although much that has to be done eventually before November and the exhibition) so I am thrown upon myself and my surroundings. Partly as a result of my "trip" I am quite pleased with myself, and as a result of my visit to New York and my being with Kin, I feel in a mood to be by myself and to keep utterly quiet, and although summer is fast dying, I am finding my house and my garden very sympathetic and comfortable, and everything is a great joy to me after the last two weeks in New York.

[1] Pope-Hennessy was done to death in 1974 by a man who thought he had the advance for a book on Noël Coward in his London flat.

JOHN GIELGUD'S RUTHLESSNESS—ANOTHER EXAMPLE

He is talking to Athene Seyler. "All the old actresses are a most terrible bore. Sybil, Edith, Gwen, Fay, Athene—not you, Athene."[1]

On a visit to Paris, Cecil encountered another photographer, this time the elusive and distinguished Henri Cartier-Bresson (b. 1908).

PARIS—CARTIER-BRESSON SEPTEMBER 1968

By the end of my first day in Paris I found myself feeling very relaxed for the first time in many weeks. There has been much pressure on me ever since I returned from the ten days' holiday in July, so much to do with the exhibition (and under frustrating difficulties), so much travelling (now even the journey to and from Salisbury can be a hazard with floods or strikes or the British Railways' growing inferiority, while one now may have to circle Kennedy Airport after an eight-hour journey for another six hours). However, although the day in Paris had been a rushed one, with photograph sittings at Courrèges and Ungaro, I had managed to sandwich in a visit to the Vuillard exhibition and do some necessary shopping. The change of environment robbed me of all feelings of responsibility and I rejoiced in the feeling that my skin was no longer constricting my body, that I felt at ease physically and mentally.

In this grand Rothschild house[2] there was a switchboard operator and a secretary apart from all the servants to help and make one comfortable. The old ladies' maid said, "We have spoons in this house, why do you stir your stomach powder with the end of a toothbrush?" But even the local telephonist could not cope with the difficulties of tracking down Cartier-Bresson.

I had wanted him for my show and had sent a telegram from London. He had telephoned when I was out. He had left no number. I begged the tele-

[1] Boring to explain a joke, but the actresses referred to were Athene Seyler (1889–1990), Dame Sybil Thorndike (1882–1976), Dame Edith Evans (1888–1976), Dame Gwen Ffrangcon-Davies (1891–1992) and Fay Compton (1894–1978).

[2] Cecil was staying with Elie and Liliane de Rothschild.

phonist to get his number when next he called. He would not leave it. For two days we missed each other. Magnum, his firm, could not tell me where he lived. A maid said he was out. He would not wait when we called and the telephonist said I was busy talking. Eventually he rang once more. He explained that he had simplified his life. He had sold his private aeroplane, had sold his car, had got rid of his telephone, at least he did not take incoming calls. But he added, "I do answer letters."

I asked him if he would come and be photographed for my show. No, but he would like to come and talk to me and photograph me. We had not met for 20 years. He would rectify that immediately and come round in a taxi. I realised that I could take a picture of him as he walked unknowingly across the grand courtyard. I prepared the camera (later discovering that I had given too much exposure) and soon a white-haired man with martial gait strode across the paving stones. Click click, once, twice, three times, four times. A moment later he was being shown up the side staircase to my room. He had aged, yes, but still had the eyes and general feeling of a very baby-like boy. (I quickly noticed he still had the unfortunate halitosis *in excelsis*.)

We sat each side of a desk drinking tea. "Well, won't you let me take even a back view of you looking out of the window?" I asked. "It's very important to include you among the photographers in my show since you are the one I admire the most." "There are three categories of people who should never be photographed—prostitutes, private detectives and photographers—and I take this very seriously. It's important that I am anonymous doing the sort of work I do. Once in Kansas I was photographing in a crowd and a young man said, 'There's the poor man's Cartier-Bresson.' You see I've thought a lot about what I do, spying on people, and I don't like anyone to do it to me. But I want to photograph you. There. There's a photograph!"

He leapt to his camera. But I was stubborn. "You see I want to bargain with you. It's my only card. If you photograph me, you must let me photograph you. It's only fair. If I let you take me, I've no chance to pull the strings." "Ah, there's another photograph." I told him how much I hated the way I looked in my old age and if I looked so awful it was only natural that I should photograph appallingly. Again he saw a photograph. Three in all he had in his mind. I held tight. He talked of his photography. He learnt everything he knew about the subject from André Lhote, the bad painter, and from Jean Renoir,[1] who was his spiritual father. (I told him that the evenings spent with the Renoirs were the most real of any I'd spent during that awful year in Hollywood.)

He gave me examples of his dedication to his art. He was about to negotiate with a publisher to do a book which would take him a year. He worked for *Holiday* magazine, touring America for five months and they used five photographs. He did not mind. He is never hurried, never ambitious, never out for money, but then he happens to be rich on his own. However he does see, and talk, like an artist. He is a bit pretentious.

The meeting drew to an end, a stalemate. He hoped I would let him photograph me when he came to London. Friendly smiles. He left. Then I was left alone wondering if I would, under the circumstances, dare to use the pictures I had snooped of him. After all, his whole life was spent snooping. But still. When I mentioned my qualms to Liliane R. she laughed. "Of *course* you must use them."

I'll always remember the pictures I took of Courrèges, the dressmaker, because they did not come out. The circumstances were felicitous. The bright autumn sun came through the shutters on to a white and mirrored room. This monkey-like sitter created a very interesting focal point in an interesting geometric pattern. A dozen variations on this theme, one better than the other. Courrèges himself, after a frigid start, showed signs of enthusiasm. He laughed. I did not like him. He is a fanatic for work, OK. He doesn't speak English, he doesn't know about me, no compliments exchanged. I find him like an ex–pro tennis player turned instructor. You can feel his dry skin and smell his dry sweat as he holds your hand, your racquet and tells you how to do a backhander. He is an athlete in this white world of fashion, but the white is not quite as white as it should be. His *vendeuses* or the girls standing around, answering telephones or reading a novel with brown paper wrapped over it, are not as pristine as they should be in their crocheted or knitted white *maillots.* One has a white leather skirt over her hips and it rides up when she sits

[1] André Lhote (1885–1962) and Jean Renoir (1894–1979), film director and son of Auguste Renoir, the painter.

and is definitely grubby. In one or two places the *maillots* have caught on a nail and been pulled out of place, or the wool is frayed. Their leather and shoes are bruised. The girls wear their hair in comic pigtails and are like schoolgirls, but the hair needs redyeing for the roots are beginning to show blue. Courrèges's gym shoes are quite dirty. This is amusing to see.

But of course this will not show in these dazzling white photographs. I took one reel of 35 on the 33 mm camera and got out quickly so that the master could continue with the designing. He complimented me on being so quick.

Next morning I called at the studio to be told that the film was "*vièrge.*" The film had not rolled through the camera. If Courrèges had been as pleasant as Ungaro[1] I would have telephoned for a retake. But I knew he would refuse and I had a few less good pictures on the Rolleiflex which would suffice. But I know I will always remember the geometric composition which did not come out.

PARIS—HOYNINGEN-HUENE[2]

Madame Dilé and Simone[3] at the *Vogue* studio had some very sad news to impart. They had just heard that Hoyningen-Huene had died of a heart attack in Hollywood, and thus went for them part of their past. George was a great figure in the studio in the early thirties and his photographs built tremendous excitement around them. Influenced originally by Steichen, he used that old bastard's rich lighting schemes to make far more elaborate pictures in which the props consisted of Greek columns, plaster horse heads and giant-size heads. He photographed models in draperies lying on the floor to look like flying figures in a frieze; he superimposed models among vast vases of flowers. He photographed personalities with daring and dash, and gave real glamour to a series of Hollywood movie stars.

Each time I went to Paris my visit pivoted around him. He took me to exciting places, he introduced me to Cocteau, he made me share his latest

[1] Emmanuel Ungaro (b. 1933), couturier, who opened his fashion house in 1965.

[2] Baron George Hoyningen-Huene (1900–68), photographer, with whom Horst lived for some years.

[3] Madame Dilé was a stalwart of *Vogue* for many years. Likewise, Simone.

enthusiasms. He bought an Arab house in Tunisia and it was when I accompanied him on a trip to the desert that he taught me to take photographs out of the studio, and to use the world around me for my own photographic ends.

He was fun to be with, hilarious, outrageous, unconventional. He could be wistful too and easily shocked, and something kept him back from daring. He tired of fashion, concentrated on architectural photographs and produced some dazzling books on Greece and Spain.

Then he became infected by some misbegotten theory that artistically and culturally Europe was dead. He made the mistake of settling in Hollywood. Here he taught young students his theory of photography, and embarked upon a complete pictorial documentation of film studios, photographing all the technicians at their work. After years the book was incomplete and never published. He then used his great talents as a bottle-washer for lesser talents, and he made quite a name for himself as a colour consultant for films with little artistic merit. The salary was good but the spirit seemed to have been knocked out of him and he was employed by a ruthless director to do such ignominious tasks as decorating a dressing room for a temperamental star while on location in India.

Of recent years he became more and more of a recluse, living in a book-lined, sculpture-filled house that exemplified his originality of taste. But it is sad that he never dared to take the plunge as a film director for which his talents, ahead of his time, would today be much appreciated.

There now follows the first of several entries, in which Cecil speculates about the illness of his friend and neighbour, Lord Pembroke. At first the gravity of the matter was not admitted. In those days, cancer was only mentioned if it were proven. Cecil obviously hoped for the best for as long as he could.

WILTON

A pall of gloom hangs over the "big house." Nothing is said, but the atmosphere that we used to expect is no longer there. We all know there is something wrong, but how wrong? The last person to know is Sidney himself, for it is he who is the cause of our worry. He has been in pain for six months now; in fact, longer, for he had already been suffering for a long while before he went to

London to see a doctor. He was taken to hospital and given treatments. When he returned we were told that the doctor had discovered a patch on the lung, that the fluid had gone to his knees and settled to give him great agony in the leg. He had been given cobalt treatment.

The gossips all said, "Surely that only means one thing!" The Hopes[1] are tight-lipped and in this case quite right to be silent. But now Sidney is no better, still living on painkillers, and neither Mary nor the children explain the situation. The house seems doomed as we jump to the conclusion that Sidney possibly will die by slow and painful degrees.

It is a shock for he seems so young, or he seemed so young before this, and he has inherited what he is so good at preserving, for such a short space of time. If he should die Henry, at the moment heirless,[2] would be the most reluctant possessor of so many responsibilities. Henry had hoped to "live," to become part of contemporary life before Wilton swallowed him up. But if one's fears are correct the change will bring sadness to everyone concerned. Meanwhile Sidney battles bravely but it is awful to see him suffering such agonising twinges as he moves his leg on the sofa.

CRICKET

I really only like the company of artists, of people who create things. I'm amused with all sorts of other people [for] a variety of reasons. They can be funny, decorative, or in some way impressive. But to come into the aura of artists is to breathe extra oxygen. The artist may be from any denomination of life, may not be at all interested in the visual arts, but they understand. So it was not surprising that I suddenly found myself in full sympathy with the Julian Breams[3] when Dicky [Buckle] took me down from his cottage on Gutch Common to see the guitarist about arranging the music for "our" exhibition.

At first I was put off by the house, very conventional, a long rather ugly rectory-type villa with formal flower borders. Inside the rooms lacked any real

[1] Lord and Lady Glendevon. Lord Glendevon was Lord Pembroke's brother-in-law.

[2] Lord Herbert had married Claire Pelly in January 1966. They had one daughter at that point, Lady Sophia Herbert (b. December 1966).

[3] Julian Bream (b. 1933), guitarist. He married Margaret Williamson, then in 1980 he married Isobel Sanchez.

Julian Bream, whose music accompanied Beaton's National Portrait Gallery exhibition in October 1968

taste or charm and Bream, balding, running to fat, squat and a bit complacent, seemed to be a very alien hearty type. His "wife" Margaret (they are not, in fact, married—technical reasons) an artist's wife type, gypsy-like. But by degrees Bream, with North Country accent, started to tell about himself and I was fascinated. He liked to walk, when on his tours, otherwise he'd see nothing throughout the world but hotel rooms and concert platforms. On his way back from Devon he stopped in Shaftesbury and walked towards Gillingham, discovered Gutch Common and decided he would like to live there. Now he enjoys his life recording in the Wardour Chapel, growing melons and tobacco plants. He works, mainly in the US, only in winter. Why work when you should be enjoying the rewards earlier work has already brought you? Margaret dispensed white wine, Sancerre, with an expert's appreciation. Bream played records of the guitarist Django Reinhardt,[1]—and the evening was utterly delightful.

Last night, in an effort to pin down Bream to giving us the music for the show, Dicky went back to the house after dinner. This time there was so much to discuss that it was difficult even to get on to the subject of our pro-

[1] Django Reinhardt (1910–53), Belgian jazz guitarist and founder, with Stephane Grappelli (jazz violinist), of the Quintet of the Hot Club in France in 1934.

gramme. Julian, as he has now become to me, was telling about his local cricket activities and how absolutely fascinating, absorbing, marvellous they were.

I told him how my early childhood had been made miserable by the fact that I showed no interest in the obnoxious game.

I give a great deal of thought nowadays to my old age. I notice so many inevitable changes taking place so that the usual will happen. My interests are more in the garden, in quieter things of the mind, much less interest in people and even a disdain for what is known as society. This used to be important to me. Now I am deadly censorious, can't be benign about these idiotic women who spend so much money on tastelessly adorning their hideous bodies, the men so desperately climbing the ladder of snobbery. I can't pretend or console myself with the knowledge that I learn anything new, or that my intellectual powers work on any but the most sluggish basis. But fortunately I still have my work to do and, when in doubt, go to the studio. Even if no pressing painting or sitter is available, there are filling-in jobs, or I take to this diary, and there is a great backlog of old diaries to read. But what if I should, as I now think, be unfortunate enough to live to a very great age? I will have exhausted my backlog, exhausted myself? Sometimes I think of starting again. Where? In Italy? In Provence? But wherever one is, one is always oneself.

In certain ways I try to improve, not to become entirely self-centred. I try to ward off my innate selfishness, perhaps mainly because I know that selfishness makes such miseries of us all. I don't have much talent for thinking in the abstract. Perhaps that is just as well. But the future can never really be *all* that exciting. Since I don't enjoy the excitements as much as before, perhaps I should realise that the best thing would be to settle down quietly, and perhaps in my mind's eye, that is what I am already trying to do.

18 SEPTEMBER 1968

As if I haven't taken *enough* photographs during my lifetime. The exhibition, covering forty years of work, represents only a flea bite of all that there is, yet the show must be brought up to date. Very important I show that I'm not just a bit of past rococo and the "Today" section must be the highlight.

There are a few disappointments in tracking down significant people. Lord Russell[1] said he spent too much time being photographed, and the model, Verushka[2] was always on the wing, but in spite of all the activity, I felt I must try to get a new picture of the Queen, and after advice from Patrick Plunket,[3] got a favourable reply from Martin Charteris,[4] who rang from Balmoral to say the Queen was not averse to my taking some new pictures of her. Later the phrase changed to "would be pleased" and it was added that I should take some pictures specially for new stamps to be issued in the Channel Islands.

I suppose I've forgotten that in earlier days I would get "nerves" before an important sitting, but certainly this time I felt quite anxious. The difficulties are great. Our points of view, our tastes are so different. The result is a compromise between two people and the fates play a large part. One does not know if things will conspire against me, or if the sun should shine.

There have been so many pictures of the Queen in tiara, orders and crinoline that I felt I must try something different. I asked Martin if a deer-stalker cloak would be suitable. No, he didn't think so, but what about an admiral's cloak? Navy-blue serge. That sounded great and when I saw the cape in his office, felt this would be an enormous asset. We have seen too many two-piece suits with brooch and wristwatch. This would be a great solution. "Do you think it would be possible?" "I can only ask," Martin answered. "You know the way it is." I do.

Martin telephoned to say the Queen had agreed to wear the cloak, was rather giggly about the whole thing, and said it didn't matter what she wore underneath it as it wouldn't show if she had nothing on. "Oh, the saucy thing!" Eileen said when I relayed this piece of information to her.

Martin took me to every corner of the Palace and we found no nook or cranny that hadn't been used by me at some time before. Must rely on a plain white or blue background, and determine to be stark and clean and bold. Just to safeguard, we would also take some typical ones with pillars, chandeliers, savonerie, carpets, etc.

[1] Bertrand, third Earl Russell, OM (1872–1970), philosopher, mathematician, writer and political activist.

[2] Verushka (b. 1939), model.

[3] Patrick, seventh Lord Plunket (1923–75), equerry and Deputy Master of the Household. His parents were killed in an aeroplane accident in 1938 and he was more or less brought up at Court.

[4] Lt.-Col. the Hon. Sir Martin Charteris (1913–99), then Assistant Private Secretary to the Queen.

The last weeks have been a new sort of nervous strain, collecting old negatives, having them printed to specific sizes, planning layouts, waiting for printers, mounters, developers and the like. To co-ordinate has been frustrating and exasperating, we have all been on edge. I feel thoroughly worn and know that I've been running on my last resources for too long. I must have one quiet morning before the Queen's sitting. Can't face more rush from a tornado of Dicky, [losing] Eileen, Mrs. Bell, Mrs. Cartwright, Ray etc., to take these pictures. I was called at the late hour of 8:30 and at 10 even had the luxury of a visit from the Indian masseur saviour. The morning did, however, develop into quite late usual dramatic development of surprises and developments, and there was only ten minutes in which to stretch out on bed after a quick lunch before going off, not feeling particularly well, to the Palace.

Martin asked, "How are you feeling? Would you like a Milltown?" No, I could cope. The electricians were installed with enough equipment to light an entire film unit. I gave instructions for alternative "sets" in case the initial

Lord Plunket at Buckingham Palace the day Cecil photographed the Queen

Sir Martin Charteris, Assistant Private Secretary to the Queen, on the day Cecil photographed the Queen

scene did not materialise, and Geoff[1] suggested the balcony might be good. I found a splendid Acropolis-like corner with three columns.

There was only time to make enough plans before Patrick appeared, in uniform, and soon the Queen, mercifully wearing the dark-blue cloak. As a garment it was certainly not very dramatic, a bit scrimpy, but at any rate it was of a clear line and simple.

As the Queen approached, with Martin, from the distance of the Banquet Hall, she noticed the cleaners on the balcony and smiled at them. Later when we moved to this spot the Queen said, "Oh, I wondered what the men were doing there."

The Queen was in a good mood, or still had the remnants of a good mood on her for she gave off, to the crew, unaccustomed hoots of laughter followed by a giggle. She has also developed a manner of making quite a lot of faces, grinning and showing vitality.

She thought the whole procedure pretty strange and all rather odd and inexplicable. The ladders holding the blue background, the mess, the lights, but still she supposed it was all right. She'd do as requested. At first the

[1] Geoff Sawyer, Cecil's assistant.

effects of the lights were a disaster. Nothing went right. I took pictures to cover up my frustration. Each way she turned was worse than the last. The lights dead. We tried, in quick succession, the footlight on the floor, off, the full right light off, nothing came to light. Then *suddenly* she turned to the left and the head tilted, and this was the clue to the whole sitting—the tilt. I kept up a running conversation, trying to be funny, trying to keep the mirth light. She is averse to a big grin, does not like to be told to smile, but is easily amused and I think feels that I am quite a cove, and is ready to laugh *at* me.

By now I felt I had started to get something and was busy duplicating this one pose that I felt had provided the afternoon's solution. (It later transpired that if I had only asked for the stepladder and photographed it from higher the results would have been much more successful.)

Flashing through my mind was the thought of how extraordinary it is what time does to a face in bringing out parental similarities, developing other unexpected characteristics and going off on surprising tangents of thinness, drawn-haggardness or fat. Princess Margaret, of a more hysterical disposition, looks so pleased, the cat after the cream or the canary. Her more passive sister shows signs of suffering, of past anxieties. The Queen has bloodshot eyes, [the] blue glass eyes of her father, and all the while Queen Mary is just round the corner.

The Queen showed her first signs of amusement when I told her that I always try to take photographs without enough light, that Geoff was always up against my instructions to turn out that light. "Everyone looks better when there's less light," I said rather tactlessly and followed this by telling Geoff to kill a vast standard.

I asked the Queen to let me take some pictures in the mauve dress she wore underneath the cloak. This she was willing to do and I felt the streak of sun coming through the blue drawing-room window on to the blue sofa would make a very happy colour combination.

After a few of these were taken came the interval for changing regalia and setting. Preconceived plans were out. The sun was now shining for the rest of the afternoon and I bade the many assistants bring in our background from the dark cavern and rely on God's glorious daylight. Everywhere were sparkling possibilities.

The Queen reappeared in a vivid turquoise-blue dress, the Garter mantle and Queen Mary's pearl and diamond looped tiara. She looked splendid and I felt elated at the possibilities, and not till later did I realise the dress was hideous, the hair still bad and the angles of the head limited. However, we banged away with great gusto, gaiety and real happiness. I don't think the Queen was for one moment bored and she seemed to respond to my flattery and praises. Perhaps I would be disappointed with the results but I felt that I was really getting good results. Photographed in the blue room, in the yellow drawing room and continued to find quite different effects from those former occasions. However, I felt the poor man's Annigoni[1] would be the best, for the pose of the head Annigoni discovered is that which is the most becoming of any today. I said that I liked so much the wistful expression in the picture. She said it was got by trying to watch the traffic. She was placed opposite a blank wall but by craning she could see the traffic and this had been a great solace during the sixteen long sittings as Annigoni had painted like a miniaturist and had spoken only execrable French.

By the time I had been like an acrobat with my two agile assistants preparing for one hour solid plus half [an hour] for change (I thought it nice of the Queen to apologise for being so long in putting on all these things!), I really felt the sitting had come to a natural halt. I was pleased. I was really fulfilled and really didn't want any more. The curtain came down at the right moment.

I walked with the Queen down the picture gallery (she liked the Rembrandt, had I seen the new [John Russell][2] book on Buckingham Palace?), she retired and I relaxed into Martin's office with a great whoosh of relief. "How did it go? You were pleased? Isn't she extraordinary? There's everything 'wrong' with her face, and yet it works. She's a marvellous woman really. I love her," he said. We ate the best chocolate coffee roll I've ever had in the aide-de-camps' room (hearty badinage) and I went home to relay the news to Eileen and the household. Later Tom Blau[3] telephoned to say he thought the Bo Whites[4] were masterpieces—the new Beaton view and some good vintage Beatons as well.

[1] Pietro Annigoni (1910–88), Italian painter, who portrayed the Queen in Garter robes for a famous 1954 portrait now hanging in Fishmongers' Hall.

[2] John Russell, the American art critic.

[3] Tom Blau (1913–84), Hungarian, who founded and ran Camera Press, the photographic agency which distributed Cecil's Royal photographs.

[4] Bo White, rugged film actor, who later played in *Blue Summer* (1973) and *A Very Natural Thing*, and *Bible* in 1974.

I went out to dinner (with the Mark Wyndhams)[1] and when Blau by arrangement came afterwards to show me the pictures, as we sat on M.'s bed, I was very disappointed. Even the ones on the balcony were disappointing as the sunshine had caused the Queen's eyes to be rather closed up.

Maybe I was tired, but no question of masterpiece. How could the camera be so cruel? There was no imperfection it glossed over! I was appalled, really dunched. Blau comforted me, said he thought it a remarkable collection, the Queen shown in honesty as she is today, a woman of 42, no longer a child, not a film star, not made up for photographs, not particularly interested in her appearance. This was an interesting set.

The following day I was fresher. The rapturous cries of others helped me. The slight retouching helped too. Some of the colour pictures were better. Perhaps after all it was a good batch. When the bad ones were wheedled out the effect was better. Martin seemed enthusiastic, liked the cloak, and I left for America (I write on the plane against time) without knowing if the cape will be approved or not. In fact, it is still in the hands of fate what results will come out of this latest milestone in my career. Or is it a nail in the coffin?

THE DIARY

SEPTEMBER 1968

I am still not able to make up my mind to publish the diary Vol. III which Greta would no doubt resent so bitterly. Yet in my mind she does not appeal to me any more. All the nicest things about her are lost in a haze of her selfishness, ruthlessness and incapacity to love. She has nothing against me, yet is as elusive as ever. The fact that I am not really interested any more makes it difficult to bother to see her. Let her stew in her own loneliness. I know she enjoys life, even the life that she leads, alone and full of petty regrets. But to me it is appallingly vapid. I feel angry that she never made a gesture of forgiveness towards Mercedes, and I know she would not give any generous help to me if I were in need of it. Perhaps I am just manufacturing a situation wherein I would feel it possible to go ahead and be damned. But the years are slipping by and the situation will remain essentially the same until either of us is dead.

[1] Hon. Mark Wyndham (b. 1921) and his wife, Anne Winn.

REDDISH 28 OCTOBER 1968

Raining Monday morning, but at last I'm recovering a bit of vitality after near exhaustion, a state that I've seldom reached before. The last weeks or months in London organising from our small house the vast exodus of photographs for the exhibition has been niggling, exasperating work, what with the delays and incompetence of those working on the show.

Then, in a state of near prostration, I had to fly to New York for five days of organising the "club."[1] With three days to go before the opening, I arrived on a Friday afternoon to find chaos. The place looked as if a bomb had exploded, nothing ready, and worse, the electricians had not supplied more than a fraction of the light brackets and no globe bulbs. Worse, the framer, who had been fed with pictures by us over the past three months, had not delivered one finished article. In fact, he had 200 unframed pictures with him and could not release them to others to frame. A few others that had not even been dispatched to him were found by me. I found another framer. "We are in a jam. Would you be so kind as to help out?" "All right, if you come round at 9 in the morning we'll meet and I'll do the best." I wait. At 11 o'clock I telephone. He would do the job. This lack of consideration for others is what gets me down.

I go on a last-minute frantic shopping expedition for lamps. The Negro assistant is determined not to let me buy. In defiance of him I order four lamps which we do not need. At another lamp place the shop is barricaded by a lot of panic-stricken women. Outside the window is a hotbed of young Negroes. "He's been in here twice already. We've called the emergency police, but they never show. Who knows if that man hasn't a knife in his bag?" The Helen Hokinson ladies[2] amuse me a lot. But my short visit is not particularly amusing.

It is a very difficult time, airless below stairs, lightless and non-stop work. I see very little of New York, no new plays, and people become "part of club life." Guests on a list or members. However, the club looks well. I am pleased and it is only I who notice the defects, the things still to be done.

[1] Cecil was designing *Raffles.*

[2] Helen Hokinson (1893–1949), American caricaturist who specialized in oversized women.

The last day was agony. After my own dinner party for 60 (three didn't show, leaving gaps at tables) I have a slight headache, having drunk champagne, which makes my activities that much harder. I tear myself away with work unfinished to go to the skin doctor. This is the last onslaught on my nerves. The place is crowded, a hysterical New York rabbi is desperately trying to find dollars to pay his bill and screams, "He said he wouldn't charge me for the injection!" I am left waiting. Will I get my aeroplane? I return to find no VIP taxi service, no Carey Cadillacs available. However, I get to the air station and the plane is delayed. But I do land early morning in England, very exhausted, depleted, on edge.

A half-hour's sleep before rushing to Westminster Abbey for Princess Marina's memorial service.[1] I am late. The traffic is at a standstill. I get out and run three-quarters of a mile, arriving out of breath, dishevelled, to find myself importantly placed in the nave. Tremendously impressive proceedings, glitter, gold, Charles II copes in mint condition of silver embroidery on grape velvet, and today the addition of the Greek clergy, the Bishop in jewelled crown[2] and one old priest shuffling like the Fairy Carabosse with long heavy tread, a stick and protruding bottom. The weight of the important people so heavy, the aristocracy, the military, government, artists, the Royal Family (the Queen very pretty today, her complexion glowing). A shock to see some near contemporaries for the first time in so long. Noël Coward a great shock. He has become a fat old turtle, split slits for eyes, rather red, no upper teeth, the lower lip bulging outwards, hunched, bald, the lot. Oh dear, how sad, and he was the very spirit of youth.

By now I was feeling ill. But I must go on to the National Portrait Gallery to see what was prepared. Here a tremendous thrill. A real *cri de coeur* [sic] of joy went up when I saw Dicky had almost finished the exhibition and it was marvellous! The first glimpse of the studio made me exclaim with joy. Dicky had done a marvel. The photographs had been transported, the rack of stars a triumph, real excitement. Dicky was pleased. Then no need to go on about health but after three days I'm beginning to regain vitality after almost complete collapse.

[1] The memorial service took place on 25 October.

[2] Gregori Athenogorous, Greek Archimandrite in Britain.

Dicky Buckle, who designed Beaton's National Portrait Gallery exhibition in October 1968, photographed in situ at the National Portrait Gallery

4 NOVEMBER 1968

The apotheosis is over. It went well, really very few disappointments and much to be thankful for. It is only sad my physical state of health prevented me from enjoying it to the full. I returned from the rush trip to New York in a perilous condition. Three treatments from Gottfried helped, but the pills I'd taken in New York had driven out a head cold but upset my whole system. My bladder seized up and I was afraid of the old bogey, the prostate operation. My head ached, my voice was hoarse and I looked like Gorgonzola. Moreover, I felt so tired. However, by going to bed very early each night and rushing to lie down between visits to the NPG, I was able to survive. The workmen and the mess seemed to take for ever to get rid of and the first party was already in progress before the finishing touches had been made. There were still outstanding the photograph of Dicky, Prince Charles, the Queen in colour. Up till the last I had gone on taking pictures.

The sitting with the Prince of Wales[1] was dull in comparison to the recent one with his mother. I blame the lousy London climate more than the Prince who, incidentally, is a simple, nice, cheerful adolescent of 19 years. He has a gentle regard, a disarming smile and the tip of his nose is delicately modelled and like a Gainsborough. He is handsome, inexpressive and his body heavy. He has obviously no great flair, is badly dressed, but at any rate his hair is long and this is a triumph of independence over the influence of his father and others at Court. As I drove to the Palace, people were going off to work in the dark, gloomy rain-sodden early morning. (I was being given an hour between 9:30 and the Prince's attending his mother's Opening of Parliament.)

In the rush of the last days I had told various persons connected with the sitting that the pictures would be taken in the (Bow) Music Room. Hence confusion on my arrival. The attendants at the Privy Purse entrance drove me mad with their delays. Squadron Leader Checketts[2] could nowhere be found and the time for the appointment was nigh. I had just time to see that Geoff was installed in front of the huge gloomy grey windows and to go to pee, when on coming out of an Edwardian lavatory, I faced the Prince.

We talked of Cambridge, ADC and Marlowe Society, and it amused me that he was next week appearing in an Orton play.[3] Very advanced. He seemed jolly, yet sensitive and rather a dreamer. He seemed to look around the rooms we were in as if seeing them for the first time. Sometimes I did not feel like interrupting his reveries. When I left the Palace and returned home, I felt I had done a run-of-the-mill job. I realised that events, particularly the lighting, were against me and I had not the necessary energy to combat them. I was really an invalid.

. . .

[1] This sitting took place at Buckingham Palace on 30 October 1968.

[2] Squadron-Leader (Sir) David Checketts (b. 1930), assigned to look after the Prince in 1967. He served as his Private Secretary 1970–9.

[3] Prince Charles played the padre in *Erpingham Camp*.

The Dicky [Buckle] sitting was also less interesting than I should have wished. But Dicky was on top form. This was something he had thought up well in advance. He was dressed in black and white with a huge heavy muslin shirt on which he hung a garland of elephant tusks. His hair had been beautifully coiffed in early Elizabethan style and his eyes were bright with gleaming joy. It really did one good to see such relish.

The Fortnum & Mason trestle tables arrived, the white lilies, the smilax. The *Vogue* hosts appeared soon and a great crowd of people. They not only seemed pleased to see each other but they paid attention to the photographs. It was a rewarding sight to see the enthusiasm of June, Diana C., Noël C., Gladys C.,[1] looking at catalogues and the exhibits on high. All our little jokes seemed appreciated and the effects were working. The studio a very lively spot with the revolving postcard stand of M. Monroe,[2] the fading lights, the huge plaster bust and stove, a lively scene enjoyed by all.

Django Reinhardt and Bream playing Dowland,[3] the incense burning, the lights flicking, the flashlight held by me going off every second. (Only the toy theatre was on the blink.) My sisters were surprisingly lively and appreciative, and a great number of old friends turned up to cheer. Some, like Lucian Freud, surprisingly enthusiastic. Lisa and John Hope said they were deeply moved. Diana said, "What a harvest! A triumph, and now to be crowned by the Queen Mother!" In a state of near collapse (Dicky's decorations have fouled the air-conditioning) I went to dinner with Nancy and Hugh [Smiley] and ate too much rich food at La Gavroche. I wondered if I were going to vomit, but I had to sit it out listening to their holiday saga (the Dordogne in the rain, with bad food, £50) until at last I was able to hope for oblivion, which aided by pills was later vouchsafed.

But no lying in. Back to NPG for the press view, this most depressing for the Museum has no knowledge of the press, sends invites out to art critics and had not prepared for the fact that the papers would be tremendously impressed by such a different picture of the Queen. At lunchtime I telephoned Blau to ask if he had been "requested." Yes, the amateur photographer of the

[1] June Osborn, Lady Diana Cooper, Noël Coward and Gladys Cooper.

[2] Cecil had photographed Marilyn Monroe (1926–62) at the Ambassador Hotel in New York in February 1956.

[3] John Dowland (1563–1626), composer, singer and lyricist.

Royal Photographic Society's journal had "enquired." I told him to ring the main papers, and by the evening all hell broke loose.

But back to the NPG to show poor bereaved Princess Olga[1] around on a very private back-door visit. Nice as she is, she can be very difficult. She was at her worst, her manner so brusque that Roy felt he was de trop and retired like a stricken deer. "*Ach,* those are hippies. Great heavens! So they've taken their clothes off!" She nevertheless telephoned the Queen Mother and said she had been touched, the show was very nostalgic.

Then a grandmother's steps return home to lie down for a moment while last-minute telephoning kept Blau on the hop, and the Queen's pictures were now in Fleet Street. Then to the Gallery for the private view party preceded by the Queen Mother's visit. As we stood by the awning, awaiting the Royal car's arrival, Roy said, "Oh, the excitement. I think this is the most thrilling thing that has ever happened to me!" The rain came down in torrents. Rush-hour traffic was at a standstill. But the maroon limousine appeared and the Queen Mother, in puce and magenta, being received by Lord Kenyon[2] to the accompaniment of forbidden flashes from the press reporters.

A very leisurely and sympathetic tour. "Oh yes, Freda, I remember that well, and Paula. She died, didn't she?" (It was no good contradicting.)[3] "Oh I remember that sitting [her own]. It was really the end of an epoch. And Gertrude Lawrence, she was unlike anyone else, wasn't she? Unique. I'm glad you've given her a whole group to herself. Dear Rex,[4] what a talent he had, so spontaneous. What a loss. Oh, and the frieze. Yes, I remember that Hesse diadem.[5] That's one of the best of Marina. She was beautiful up to the last, and look at Marie-Louise, what a character!"[6] Laugh. A careful look at the Wind-

[1] HRH Princess Olga of Greece (1903–99), wife of HRH Prince Paul of Yugoslavia. She was in England to attend the memorial service of her sister, Princess Marina.

[2] Fifth Lord Kenyon (1917–93), chairman of the National Portrait Gallery 1966–93.

[3] Freda Dudley-Ward (1894–1983) and Paula Gellibrand (1898–1986). They were both married to Bobby, Marques de Casa Maury at various times.

[4] Rex Whistler (1905–44), artist and designer, killed in the Second World War.

[5] Cecil had photographed Princess Cécile of Greece (1911–37), Grand Duchess of Hesse, when she attended the coronation of George VI. She was a sister of Prince Philip and was soon afterwards killed in a plane crash with most of her family.

[6] HH Princess Marie-Louise (1872–1956), granddaughter of Queen Victoria. Cecil took an inspired portrait of her in 1953 with her arm upraised. The sitting was aided by a large whisky and soda, enjoyed by the Princess.

sors. "They're happy and really a great deal of good came out of it. We have much to be thankful for." I did not over-egg the pudding by saying "We have to thank them for you" but merely responded, "We have *much* to thank them for."

Then the war rooms. Dicky took over to explain how I had not known an RAF badge worn by Princess Elizabeth from a Grenadier's badge[1] so we had had an erratum in the catalogue. I came back in the Act II studio. Much appreciation for the Broadchalke characters. "What a good face the gardener has! What a character!" Interest in the new picture of the Queen. "Yes, she told me I'd be surprised by it. 'It's very different,' she warned me." "Do you like it?" I asked. "Yes, I do. Yes, it has great character!" The Prince of Wales "was delightful, such a nice boy. I'm so glad you liked him!" Jolly, girlish, sympathetic, darling QM.

Then after a tour to the boardroom, a line-up, Nancy and H. (H. blowing raspberries at me), Nancy very disguised as a young dowager in red velvet and chinchilla. When I introduced her as a guinea pig sister, Nancy's upper lip became very straight and she talked with pursed lips. But she adored the evening, and meeting the Queen [Mother] would give her a topic for weeks on end. After an hour and a half the Queen [Mother] had to leave. "But you can't, Ma'am, the traffic is at a halt and your car can't get near." We managed to get out by the back door. "Oh yes, all the milk bottles," said the Queen [Mother]. A prowling photographer surprised us by being by and taking a flash of the leave-taking, as all the cars in Orange Street hooted and klaxoned [at] the Queen's holding up proceedings.

Ah well, sighs of relief. Now the main party. Already the rooms were full. A different crowd from the *Vogue*-ites, Museum friends and the general public with only a sprinkling of friends. The same interest in the pictures, the "effects" and the decor. The great surprise was a visit from Broadchalke of Mrs. Betts and Mrs. Prest, when the latter was seized by the arm by Eileen, her eyes filled with tears.

Lots of Ambassadresses, Rosemary Olivier,[2] John Betts, Trees, Wormald,[3] whom I'd not seen since I'd photographed him in *The Duchess of*

[1] Cecil had photographed the Queen when she was Princess Elizabeth, soon after she became Colonel of Grenadier Guards in 1943.

[2] Rosemary Olivier (1903–2002), niece of Edith Olivier.

[3] Captain William Wormald, MC, son of Percival Wormald, of Fulford Hall, York.

Malfi in my Cambridge studio above the electrician's shop, David H. [Herbert] from Tangiers, a great cross-section. Refugees from the storm continuing to arrive till past 8 o'clock when I had to participate (without having had time to pee) in the most boring dinner (in Roy's nice room) given by the Chairman, Lord Kenyon. I sat next his genteel wife,[1] and however hard I tried I could not get her to come off it, to relax. The evening seemed interminable. Dicky kept saying he must leave to put peace to his mother but then he'd start again on some new conversational gambit.

I knew I was lucky to be thus "honoured," but still the boredom was appalling, and it was for ever before I had occasion to pee. I returned home past midnight to be rung by hypocritical *Daily Express* asking details of the Queen's pictures and had I been influenced by Annigoni, and did I know Ramon Novarro, whom I'd photographed in the early thirties, [who] had been found with his throat cut?[2]

Next morning all the papers (except mother *Times*) carried huge pictures of the Queen in the boatman's cloak. They created a big stir and were incidentally good publicity for my exhibition to which Roy Strong, always an optimist, said 1000 people had come on the first public morning.

Dicky telephoned in high glee and embarrassed me by talking of the "Beaton magic." He said the show was being a great success, interest mounting, 1000 people had been through on Saturday and 1500 today, Monday. All day long there was a queue. He said that it was fascinating to watch the rapt faces of the people, that he couldn't keep away, and the young looked at the pictures of the thirties as if they belonged to some long-forgotten world of Fragonard and Watteau. A lot of the young looked at the pictures of the dressed-up beauties with an incredulous smile on their faces. One young man in a white mackintosh had remained standing in the same spot for ages. Dicky wondered if he was perhaps just listening to Django Reinhardt. Dicky went off to his bank to

[1] Leila Peel, who married (1946) Lord Kenyon.

[2] Ramon Novarro (1899–1968), Mexican-born film star and later a character actor. Two hustlers beat him to death at his Hollywood home in quest of the petty cash ($5,000 or so) that he was said to keep under his bed. He was found dead on 31 October.

cash a cheque and when he came back the young man was still in the same position.

Dicky reported that the old Museum had never known such liveliness and that everyone there was going about wreathed in smiles. Roy, particularly happy, felt that they'd get their expenses back in the first week. Of course, I take a lot of this as exaggeration but it is very rewarding to know that there is a general public for my work. I am most surprised.

Pleasant short week in London now health is recovered, only a pity I am not able to fully enjoy the furore of the apotheosis. Miraculously the crowds keep up a constant stream, 1000 people a day. Roy is now keeping the Gallery open late one night a week. The young are euphoric. A stranger rang Eileen to say he'd spent three hours in the show and thought it delightfully "camp," in the most laudatory terms, he explained. The critics for the most part have ignored the show but Mario Amaya[1] has written that I was one of the world's most interesting personalities! "Now really!" as my friend, Marjorie Oelrichs,[2] used to say.

A football reporter and a sports photographer come to do a thing on me for *Nova*, anything more unsuitable. I know how awful the pictures will be. A woman from the *Daily Mail* came to interview Eileen. We both told her things that we wouldn't say to each other's faces. Eileen said that during the 15 years she has worked for me she had learnt to look at people's faces in a different way. She also said—greatest relief!—that she never wished to leave me. I told her how delightful was her habit of being fresh and unspoilt enough to make such graphic descriptions of everything she had done *en passant.* This well brought out here (Reddish) this afternoon when she returned from a second-hand book shop in Shaftesbury and told how kind and good the Danish woman proprietor was, particularly to a 12-year-old boy who came in for a Dickens and hadn't the 3s. 6d. to pay for it, but must go and ask his mother's

[1] Mario Amaya (1933–84), American art critic, who died of AIDS. He helped found *Art & Artists,* and was an arts exhibition organizer. He was deemed "one of the more colourful and inventive figures in the art scene on both sides of the Atlantic."

[2] Marjorie Oelrichs (1908–37), American society girl, who conspired with Adele Astaire to give Cecil a brisk introduction (one go each, in the same week) to heterosexual sex. She later married the bandleader Eddy Duchin (1909–51) and died in childbirth.

permission. She gave verbatim report of the boy leaving his name and all that transpired.

A quiet weekend, prior to the visit to California, with huge teas, cream on scones etc., in front of fire, and sorting letters into files. If we don't do this properly now, Eileen said, "There'll be such trouble later when they're asking me all sorts of difficult questions: 'Where did he go after the war?' etc."

Concert of eighteenth-century music given by Bream on the guitar in chapel at Wardour. About 300 people turned up on this cold winter's evening, paying £1 or 30s. for this rather rare treat, instead of going to an American movie. The audience constituted the very spirit of the English country folk. They were all individual, however surly and ridiculous. The men, in the biggest, thickest tweeds, broad-backed, wide-shouldered, mustachioed, crisp-haired. (Some of the young had such marvellous shiny, oil-downed silk for hair.) Such clean, clear complexions, but some looked pretty much as if they hadn't had a bath after attending the sheep dog trials or the sheep dip. The women really awful, their hair so badly cut, permed in cart ruts in the mud, awful tweeds, a wisp of chiffon scarf at the neck, gauche in manner if stout in heart. All awfully jolly, and hail fellow, talking no doubt about the batting order, but kind, decent, good.

Julian gave the guitar the sounds of piano and violin. He knew the instrument more intimately than a pilot the dashboard of a DC2. For someone a bit rough in manner his sensibility is amazing. Face contorted in nervous twitches while playing. His services donated to the Rebuilding Fund of the Chapel, a marvel of reconstruction, arrived at by the Arundells[1] selling some alabasters. This whole experience the very essence of Wilts and Dorset at its best and worst. Typical. Dicky talking about his regiment, in military mien, had supper with the Arundells (the Breams and mostly old gentlemen from the Brigade of Guards), then on to Breams where he woke up on a sofa at 4 in the morning, while the others continued to carouse.

Dicky, lively as all, got out at 9 next morning, telephoning about the latest happenings at the NPG.

[1] John Arundell (b. 1931) and his first wife, Laura Tennant (1935–89). They lived at Hook Manor, Donhead St. Andrew, near Shaftesbury. He succeeded as 10th Lord Talbot of Malahide 1987.

TANGIERS DECEMBER 1968

Arrived for a weekend to buy gauzes and spangled tissues from the souks, for the Brighton Pavilion sequence in *Clear Day.* David was so warm-hearted in his greeting and welcome. His house a haven against the cold, wet, blustering weather. He said, "I'm in fine fettle, thrilled to be back here. We made over £1,000 at the auction last night for the prevention of cruelty to animals. But I came back from England really depressed. Two nights before I left, I saw Charlie Linlithgow[1] at the Savoy and he must have been rather drunk for he shouted out at me, 'Sidney will never get well again because he's got cancer!' "

So the ghastly truth has come out in this crude, beastly way. It seems my premonitions were right. When they opened him up, they found he had cancer of the lung, of the spine, and then in the leg. The poor thing has to suffer till the long drawn-out end, for the doctors will never tell the truth, or else the victim just crumbles up. But why survive for all this suffering? It is a cruel stroke that Sidney should have survived for only eight years, at the thing he was brought up to do. That his son [Henry Herbert] should succeed at such a ridiculously young age, without the opportunity he longed for of making his way in a world of his own (films). The change that is to take place will be a great shock to us all.

VISIT TO HOLLYWOOD

Still feeling quite ill, for there was not enough time after the "Exhibition" to relax and recoup from my colitis and sinusitis, before I had again to fly off over the Atlantic, this time over the Pole, a 12-hour journey to Los Angeles. For the first two days I was in a daze, buoyed up with pills, but feeling that I was only operating on a few valves. Nevertheless, during my five-day visit, I got through a fantastic amount of work, though never able to enjoy myself in the evening, for all my strength was necessary for the next day's work. Much to discuss with

[1] Charles, third Marquess of Linlithgow (1912–87), brother of Lady Pembroke.

Koch, Minnelli[1] and the wardrobe people about *Clear Day*, and the meeting with Streisand[2] was an event. Her publicity is so bad that I feared she might be the tyrant, the virago, the bitch that she is said to be. Instead she was particularly ingratiating and amenable. From the moment she appeared, late, at the rehearsal, it was evident she has star quality, is a natural. She is above all else intelligent. Her brain works so clearly, so healthily. She could be a lawyer. She is never hurried. She does not appear to be the type to get overexcited, nor to make the wrong decisions on the spur of the moment. She knows every detail must come under close consideration.

She has flair, natural taste, and knows what is best for her, certainly in appearance, and I'm told she is equally bright about the script. She has no knowledge (she asked if in 1815 the women wore black chiffon nightgowns), but a keen eye for colour and a direct way of saying what she dislikes. ("I despise turquoise," she said.)

One day in her dressing room during the lunch interval she ate a lamb cutlet in her long-nailed fingers and was the most basic and healthily Jewish person you could meet, but great, her Jewishness an asset, interesting and helpful. She told me of how she did a photograph advertisement in return for a fur coat, but the deal had cost her thousands of dollars. The telephone rang and she talked for 15 minutes to a shop that had sent her a bill for $17 when the percentage should have been taken off and she should only be charged $14. She gives priority to everything of principle, no matter how unimportant in detail.

As for her looks, they are fascinating, her complexion is poreless, immaculate, shiny. Her eyes, a grey-blue, are beautiful but for the one fatal fault of a slight squint, teeth pearly and large, beautiful laugh, interestingly curved nose, flowing from eyebrow line of forehead, pretty hands and pretty ways of using them, a good neck.

"Oh, give me some of your French fries." "You shouldn't have them, Miss Streisand," says her coloured maid. Barbra says she is not going to sing in her next two films. She only sang because she had no success on the stage. "But

[1] Howard W. Koch (b. 1916), American film executive and vice-president of Paramount, and Vincente Minnelli (1903–86), noted director, particularly of musicals.

[2] Barbra Streisand (b. 1942), actress and singer, whom Cecil had first seen singing in a nightclub in 1963. He took two reels of film of her, capturing "this strange Cleopatra-like profile with bold flow from nose to forehead."

I want to act. I must do Juliet and all the classics, Ibsen and Chekhov." Meanwhile she will get $1 million for the album of *Clear Day.* Perhaps she is the clown wanting to be Hamlet, but she is a brilliant clown and, as the taxi driver said, "Those sort of people only appear out here once every twenty-five years." She is surely set for a fantastic spell of success. There is nothing to stop her. She has everything, or so it now seems to me.

Here's hoping that we continue to get along together as well as so far, for we have argued, we have disagreed, we have said our pieces, but we give and take as professionals with a job on hand. I treat her as an equal, and only now and again do I realise that I am sparring on equal terms with someone who is 50 years younger than I am!

It was a shock to find oneself, so comparatively soon after leaving one's interests in London, absorbed in the new project of a Paramount film production.

Soon after my arrival I was as immersed as I had been during the long months of work on the *My Fair Lady* lot. I felt like the old fire horse at the ring of the bell. During the four days an enormous amount of progress was made, so many decisions made and so much work piling up for the future.

One morning there was a press call for the stars of Paramount to be photographed, the strangest line-up, people I had not heard of, but who are now the biggest names, Lee Marvin, Vince Edwards, as well as Rock Hudson and John Wayne[1] surviving from the past. It reminded me vividly of my earliest visit as a fan to Hollywood when everything seemed so wonderful, and unlike it seems today.

Cecil then visited Kin in San Francisco, and found him living in a state of some chaos—"the mess is indescribable." But Kin was still quoting Socrates and others, his mind dwelling more on intellectual matters than on domesticity. Cecil was forced to confess that he relied on "certain comforts of life" and was therefore "quite pleased to be leaving for New York and my own clean lavatory and bathroom, and knowing that cleanliness does go hand in hand with godliness."

[1] Lee Marvin (1924–87), film actor, who played villains or unsympathetic heroes. He gave a throaty rendition of "Wand'rin Star"; Vince Edwards (1928–86); Rock Hudson; and John Wayne (1907–79), stocky and breeches-clad star of many a Hollywood Western.

NOËL COWARDISMS

Watching Elizabeth Bibesco[1] at her favourite sport of picking her nose, Noël adjured her to "wave when you get to the bridge."

Looking very old at my exhibition and scrutinising a neon nude picture of Nureyev, he turned to K. Tynan and said, "Cecil must have caught me on one of my off days."

VISIT TO TANGIERS

I swear over and over again that I will never again visit David in his Moroccan house. Once more I returned (this time to buy gauzes in the souks for the *Clear Day* costumes). As before I leave with few regrets. David's house needs the sun. I arrived in the rainy season. The house has no central heating and soon becomes damp, and everything in it. The house does not bear close inspection. Like Kin's, it is not clean enough. The bathrooms are really too small and improvised. Barton Gas is a most uncertain and unattractive form of heating, often resulting in sickness or fatal accidents. This time I found myself bitten by fleas. The dogs were carefully tended and they wander everywhere. But David is blissful. He loves everything he owns. He has no regrets for England, or Wilton. He would not change his house and garden for any other. Such contentment is rare, and certainly he has a point when he criticised me for being overworked, anxious, colitis-ridden, strained, too involved in the rat race. Yet I could never give up and come to terms with his life. A weekend is more than enough for me. I am writing in the sodden airport and my stomach turning over lest there should be delays in the aeroplane taking off.

REDDISH—HEALTH REPORT — 20 DECEMBER 1968

Have come down here with relief, for now I have ten days in which to be quiet, and to regain health and strength before returning to Hollywood.

[1] Lady Elizabeth Asquith (1897–1945), daughter of H. H. Asquith, married (1919) Prince Antoine Bibesco (1878–1951), a friend of Marcel Proust.

The past weeks have been a strain. I have not been able to enjoy myself to the full for my health has been pretty dicky. The colitis has continued for six weeks, gradually getting more and more of a hold on me until the last three weeks have been an awful strain. I have devoured so much kaolin powder that I've become like a cement mixer and all to no avail. Every appointment after a meal has been a strain lest at some sudden moment I have to rush off to explode in a complete magma of bowel evacuation. Gottfried, on his dignity and fighting for his life, says that all is well (the analyst's report is OK), that it takes time. Meanwhile, each night is a preparation only to regaining enough health in order to cope with the morrow. No indulgence in food, drink, cigars, late hours or sex. I haven't really been able to enjoy to the full the great success of my exhibition, for I have had almost a continuous slight headache.

Last weekend, [when] Derek Hill[1] was staying, was almost the climax. In spite of keeping quietly to my bed most of the time, the bowel upheavals were being more disconcerting and frequent than before. My entrails felt as if they were the bubbling waters of a Danté's *Inferno,* and I'd endure the rise and fall of the bubbling tides until no longer was it possible to hold oneself in curb. Derek was worried and said I must go to a specialist. This I did. Even the idea of two days in London exhausted me. So much to pack in (with fittings and sittings) and the dread of the specialist appointment.

This, however, went well. The man himself was unsympathetic and I to him (we had no rapport) and the probing of backside was painful, but his report did me a world of good, and whether it was my physiological result, or the result of the pills that he gave me, but suddenly I felt assured, stronger and on the road to recovery. After the weeks of buttered toast, strong Indian tea and eggs, I could now eat anything. My colon was neurotic. My trouble was that often I got run-down and tired, through overstrain, overwork, and the effect was that my bowels were the first to give out, not chest or heart, or throat, but an upset stomach was a direct result of overstrain.

If I wished to eat anything I knew would upset me, I must take the consequences but they would not be "serious." There was no disease, no microbe, no damage to the gut. Nothing untoward that his cold, unpleasant instruments could see while excavating my back passage.

[1] Derek Hill (1916–2000), painter, who later became a painting friend of the Prince of Wales.

I was still very tired, my voice hoarse, my face gone to pot, but my confidence, beginning to get a bit undermined, was restored. After two hectic days (helped by hired cars) I came to a Thursday 5 o'clock train and sank into a warm corner seat with oh, such relief. I felt that at last there was a breathing space, no terrible rush against time, that I could relax and enjoy a quiet spell in the country.

DEREK HILL

Derek Hill made me feel very amateur as a painter. He quite rightly considers that painting is a life's work, that there is so much to read and learn about the art apart from the practice of it. My lack of technique in all things practical was shown up too by Derek's knowledge of what paint does on canvas, on board, on wood, how it has to breathe (this is why my too quick varnishing has resulted in baubles of sweat appearing on the canvas). Derek knows the use of different brushes. Such is my vagueness that I will use one brush for almost all purposes. It is a fundamental and simple thing to learn but I have just realised that each different sort of stroke calls for a different brush, that his different brushes are just what the clubs are to a golf player.

HEALTH REPORT CONTINUED

21 DECEMBER 1968

It is with the greatest relief that I can say that my bowels are on the mend. The specialist's minute pills seem to have done the job of getting my guts into an orderly regime, or maybe it is just the psychological effect of a "second opinion" and a good notice, in fact a "rave" about my innards. I am now in the process of discarding all the medicine which I have shovelled down my gorge in such vast quantities. I look back on the last two months or more as a nightmare of kaolin powder and precipitate visits to the loo where a Niagara of dirty, chalky water gushes from my backside, befouling the bowl in such an untidy manner that I have to spend considerable time swabbing with paper, water and even sponges. How loathsome a business it is. And how strong is one's inclination not to discuss any of these things. Even with the specialist [I] was somewhat shocked when he quoted Chaucer, "And the mule, he shat with fright."

The reports of the faeces being bandied about from one person to another also humiliates me. But thank God that the report is good, for although I don't think I want to live to an old age, I don't feel like having a terminal disease just at this moment. Why? What do I want to do? Well, come to think of it, it wouldn't matter so much if I didn't make that £7,000 that is being paid (towards paying for my taxes) with the latest film. I am not particularly optimistic about the way my painting is going. I don't feel I am likely to burst into a literary masterpiece. But habit is strong, and with little more than a sigh, if not with youthful élan, I start another day's work.

CHRISTMAS 1968

Nancy and Hugh came to stay for the festivities as for the first time in many years their son was going to be with his in-laws. Nancy has developed along such unlikely lines, or rather such very conventional lines. Everything is "done" or not done. Hours are spent talking about family trees, even if the roots do not go deep. She and Hugh have enormous interest in knowing who people are rather than what they are. It is a subject that absorbs them and each time they go out, even to a small cocktail party, they can add to their information. "Oh yes, we met one day at the Dowdings!" This, at once, produces a bond.

Christmas coming on a Wednesday has created a week of Sundays. It has suited me well as I have been recovering at last from my colitis attack, and have purposely rested a great deal. But during these strange limbless days our imagination has been afire with the progress of the three American astronauts who have visited (within 60 miles) the moon. We have listened on the radio to all the bulletins, and watched, staggered, on TV, the remarkable and so ordinary men go off into the capsule to spend six days travelling further than anyone else has ever done.[1]

[1] Spacecraft *Apollo 8* was launched from Cape Kennedy on 21 December and made ten orbits round the moon, before splashing down in the Pacific on 27 December.

Being of so little a scientist or engineer, their exploit has been particularly baffling to me, but suffering as I believe I do, from claustrophobia, I am haunted by the horror of what could have been the fate of these three. To see Borman, Anders and Lovell[1] having their "last" breakfast was extremely poignant. In silence they ate steak and eggs, and drank a cup of milk. They looked extremely grave, as indeed they might with the responsibilities they were burdened with for the next week. We then watched this grave and courageous trio trussed up like divers in their cumbersome suits and head protectors, getting into the terrifyingly small confines and after an interminable wait—was it three hours?—and no doubt remembering the three astronauts who were burnt alive, being shot up with the power of millions of gallons of petrol aflame behind them. Almost immediately they were rocketing into infinity. We heard their voices in contact with ground control at Houston, Texas as they started to cope with the thousands of intimate gadgets which might be the means of preserving their lives in this perilous adventure. The first crucial stage was over when we saw they had successfully spurted off enough steam and energy to jettison their projectile, and the small capsule soared on its way to higher space.

Then we heard, of all things, that two of the astronauts were suffering from the prevailing flu. They were being sick and had headaches. Doctors, thousands of miles away, prescribed remedies. Perhaps the rocketing and the thin air of oxygen makes them feel light-headed, queasy-stomached. However, they continued to keep in touch with the fast-diminishing earth. Then they took time off their more serious occupation to photograph themselves to show to the awe-inspired below what it was like to be living in such a condition with their cellophane-wrapped turkey legs, forks, camera floating in space.

Then another crucial point was reached when they were to come within range of the moon's magnetic pull. Would they go cracking on to the moon? But everything, thus far, was going to plan. Then their goal was achieved. We saw pictures of the moon at close hand and heard descriptions of the craters, the land being brown or blue. But most silly and almost disastrous was the fact that all but three of their windows were clouded over. Then they

[1] Frank Borman (b. 1928), commander of the mission, William A. (Bill) Anders (b. 1933) and James Lovell (b. 1928), the three astronauts who made man's maiden voyage round the moon and were the first humans to leave earth's gravitational influence.

started orbiting the moon, and when on the far, dark side, they would be out of contact with the earth. Tremendous anxiety, silence. Would they be orbiting until their oxygen gave out at 10:30 p.m. on 28 February? (It is terrifying how all the possible eventualities are known so intimately.)

Then with a joke they continued communication with earth. Round and round the moon they went, until their instructions bade them return to the distant earth. Everything had gone to plan so far, but they were not out of danger until two seconds before their splashdown for then they were to return to the earth's atmosphere and unless they came in at just the right angle they would be immediately burnt to a cinder.

Meanwhile the jealous Russians had added to our anxiety by saying that they would not undertake such an exercise until many of the known risks had been more carefully overcome. Worse, the Chinese let off an atom bomb, which might have been disastrous to these travellers.

Meanwhile these astronauts, recovered from their sickness, recited most movingly in their flat American voices from the book of Genesis, and they remembered how petty were men's conflicts on that little world below. Their flight into space gave them a perspective and they felt men's troubles below were futile. Why must they fight each other and make of earth a hell?

One quaked for the safety of these men as they returned at incredible speed from being 200,000 miles away. The anxiety of their wives must have been appalling: for us it would have been bad enough to realise these men had disappeared without trace or explanation, but for their immediate family the strain must have been unimaginable, also for those who for years have been working on these projects.

Ray came into my bedroom. "They're safe. They're down. Absolutely on time, and within a few thousand yards of where they were meant to be in the Pacific."

The return, as seen on television, was deeply moving. The three appeared thinner and wobbly on their feet. They were elated, such smiles of happiness (and relief?). The captain spoke a few words into the microphone to thank the thousands who had worked on this project. "I guess we are just part of it!"

The whole enterprise had gone like clockwork, but the most impressive part has been the human element. Three not so young men were picked.

They were known to have all the necessary qualities: wisdom, discipline, vision, imagination.

It was a triumph of the intelligence. It was little to do with fun. It was just hard work that they knew they were capable of doing. They had to keep clear heads during a series of non-stop manoeuvres which have been enough to send others into a state of panic.

It was a triumph of nerves, of heroism, but above all, of man's intellectual mastery over mystery.

SECOND TRIP TO HOLLYWOOD

DECEMBER 1968

It is a very poor arrangement that I have to fly over the Pole to fit Barbra Streisand's clothes here and then fly back in order to fit her in London, and this is my second visit half across the world within the last month. But that is the way things work out in films. But there is no minimising the fact that the twelve-hour trip (with one hour's delay) is a very great strain on the system. Luckily I arrived at an hour when I could go very early to bed and sleep for fourteen hours. This helped me recuperate from the ills that I have been suffering from for two months. But my arrival here was in no way a pleasant series of surprises. The old "glamour" that the place used to have for me has entirely dissipated itself into a business routine.

It did not seem particularly strange that having come from the coldest spell of an English winter there was sun here for I saw it only through the slats of ugly windows. The Beverly Hills Hotel, which had seemed such an idyllic haven when I was in love with Greta, now seemed banal and ordinary.

Just as soon as I'm through, I'll get the hell out. But arrangements are bad and I don't know where immediately to go. Kin is away with his parents and has not let me know of his return, and any alternatives sound dreary. Where to go? In my mind I think of the possibilities, and all the while I say to myself "the glamour has gone." This is really a sign of age, of having had it. Or is it merely that in the rush we have not been able to keep the situation under control? Maybe, having had three working days here, I will go back home again. Certainly there are worse things . . .

Not that she gives a damn.

Barbra Streisand is not loved by the grips, electricians and wardrobe. She is far too exigent.

She is always late, and when she appears is never sorry or apologetic, or stressed. She remains calm and intent on her goal, of doing her job to the very best of her ability. Shirlee tells me that she and Scaasi[1] fight like cat and dog, that their fittings on Saturday night started at 8 o'clock and lasted till 2:30 a.m. Shirlee was amazed that we did four or five fittings in two hours. She tells me that Barbra is a tamed human being. But she is ruthless. I don't think she liked our boos or laughter when having given Arda, the head cutter of the wardrobe, a faded little ruin of what must have been a ravishingly doll-like creature, a terrible run-around, working late at night, early in morning, she then sent her on a dozen journeys to the stock room to get veils or tassels or frills. "Let me try some half-made white ribbon."

Arda goes forth on her thick piano legs, her feet in silver ballet slippers. She returns. No, the ribbon is turned down by the onlookers. Barbra thins down till cross-eyed the ribbon, and touching her, says, "Say, this is ⅝″ ribbon not ½″." She twitches at our remonstrances, but goes on with measuring tape, "Yes, it has an edging that gives it the look of the extra width."

The studio powers that be know they have a star of great and rare magnitude and so give way on all sides. At 26 Barbra knows the power that goes with stardom. Apart from her gigantic salary she is going to acquire a great deal from this picture. For instance shoes, and expensive ones, from an Italian shop in New York. She does not make up her mind if she will wear shoes without heels, or low heels or high heels (she likes to look tall), so three pairs of each are ordered in every colour. For the whole production she has over 100 pairs of shoes.

For the Publicity Ball her hairdresser (Fred) was to have gone as a jester in Danny Kaye's[2] old outfit. Seeing him looking rather sad at the ball, wearing an ordinary suit, I ask, "Why no jester?" "Oh, we were too late. She wasn't ready till she came here at 10."

[1] Arnold Scaasi, fashion designer who began designing in the fifties. He also dressed Elizabeth Taylor, Barbara Bush, and Laura Bush.

[2] Danny Kaye (1913–87), comedian and film actor.

She is 26 years old, a tenacity and eye for detail that is quite staggering. But I admire her. She cannot be made to say she likes something unless she is 100 per cent sold. The black and white costume did not please her until we've improved it after two and a half hours' work. She was right.

PHOENIX, ARIZONA

I really suffocate in Hollywood. It is ugly beyond belief and there are very few people with whom I can "speak the same language," I'm afraid this goes for most of America and for really all the Americans I come across. Kin happens to be American, yet I love him. Jimmy Davison[1] is the most American American. My friends in New York are cosmopolitan and even they soon begin to pall. It is only when I'm at home and the telephone rings from across the Atlantic and these strange voices give me a jolt that I realise the effort it takes me to compete with such strangers.

After four days (I could tell by the number of red roses in individual vases that come in with the breakfast tray) I hopped on to a plane to Phoenix, and to arrive at Nicky's[2] and Jimmy's ranch was as if I was breathing freely again.

PHOENIX

More than three days in this sparkle of sun and air has helped me to relax and feel quite remote from the person who has been under such strain for the last two months. I have even started to read, have devoured half a dozen books until my eyes have ached. I have enjoyed the crisp nights with the logs burning in my bedroom grate. Nicky has, without a specific job, a filled life. His interests never flag, he knows a remarkable amount, and Jimmy is a quiet, subtle, ennobling companion. It is quite an event for me to have got on to a

[1] Jimmy Davison, friend of Nicky Haslam at that time.

[2] Nicky Haslam (b. 1939), working for *Vogue,* later an interior decorator. He was then on the ranch.

horse and enjoyed in the last rays of the sunshine a canter along the dried river bed.

KIN

Somewhat disturbed that not only have Christmas and New Year gone by without a word from Kin (that not so remarkable because he doesn't stick to the formalities) but that when on arrival in Hollywood and at Phoenix I ring to find no reply at his home. I knew he was going to be in Maine with his family, but did not realise how long a holiday he would be taking. Now I remember when looking back to last year that the Christmas holidays last almost a month, and that quite probably he had already left before my letter arrived announcing my dates of arrival and suggestions for a short holiday together. He is quite obviously away for the length of my visit here so I am without the chance of seeing him for some considerable time. However, now I have realised what the circumstances are likely to be, I am less tortured than when I thought I might have to go through some awful cross-examination, and ask is this the end of a glorious friendship.

SCOTTY

Scotty is a phenomenon. I heard several years ago that the police had caught up with him, that he had quit his racket and [was] out of the running. This is a blow to me, as I am very fond of him, and I would have liked to have sympathised. I only had a telephone number, now surely in disrepair. But no. Although I woke him early, his voice was as cheerful as ever. It is five years since I've seen him and five years can create havoc in a man's appearance, but no, Scotty appeared among the bushes of the Beverly Hills Bungalow gardens, just as smiling and trim of form as ever. And his enthusiasm is as great.

He is really what is known as a flirt. I asked him how much I owed him and he suggested a sum much smaller than I knew was customary. There is nothing he will not do for me. He is helpful and kind and gentle. He seemed quite worried when I stumbled against a chest of drawers.

He still continues his nefarious activities.

There's always something cooking. There is a man who owns acres of ranch and he arrives with a 16-year-old boy. "Now he doesn't want to be the first to seduce him. He doesn't want any recriminations. So he asks me and I get in a bird and together we perform, and the bird says to the 16-year-old, 'Why don't you ask the old man to join us?' "

1969

Cecil was still with Nicky Haslam and Jimmy Davison at their ranch in Phoenix, Arizona. Here he had time to read, or at least to "skim." He turned to the works of his contemporary at St. Cyprian's School, Eric Blair, better known as the writer George Orwell (1903–50).

GEORGE ORWELL JANUARY 1969

The reviews of the four volumes of Orwell's essays, letters and memorabilia recently published,[1] have been unanimously great, Orwell treated as one of the great thinkers of his age.

I knew I'd never have the time or inclination to wade through these vast tomes, but fortunately the opportunity comes to me here at the ranch, of having time at least to skim through the vast accumulation of his tireless output.

Of course there could hardly be two people further apart than Orwell and myself, yet I am in full flood of admiration for his clear thinking, his avid interest, his non-acceptances. He writes in such a straightforward manner that he carries one along in often difficult and foreign territory, and makes me understand, as if for the first time. One has the feeling that his judgement was always at variance with popular opinion, that he alone was right. His foresight is extraordinary. He is a craftsman, works out his theories in the most effective ways, so that the effect is as he wishes. But every now and again my admiration turns to hatred.

[1] Sonia Orwell edited *The Collected Essays, Journalism and Letters of George Orwell* (1968).

Naturally I dislike his bigoted campaign against the ruthless, cruel, unpatriotic upper classes. I have been inspired to pencil in the margins against his most violent assertions that the British aristocracy in the war had only thoughts for their own survival. I hate his cruelty, of cutting a wasp in half, of announcing with glee that an enemy is now "cold meat." He talks of Stephen Spender[1] as a pansy leftist. I applaud H. G. Wells[2] for calling him a "shit." No doubt he was. He was self-sufficient, 100 per cent masculine, relentless. He didn't give a damn about appearing unpopular. He was certainly unlovable. But what a talent! What a discriminating way of looking through the façades.

His piece on St. Cyprian's is a marvel. It is uncanny how a boy of that age could have seen through all the layers of snobbery and pretence of the Vaughan Wilkeses.[3] It is hilariously funny, but it is exaggerated. God knows I *loathed* the Wilkeses, loathed every minute of the school regime, and was just as appalled as he by the stink and squalor of the loos, the swimming pool, just as appalled by the cold and the filthiness of the food. Even so, I never saw a turd floating in the bath. I don't remember the rind of old porridge under the rim of the pewter bowl, and I have the feeling that Orwell made a fetish of the sordid and enjoyed playing up the horror of life among the miners, of the down-and-outs in any city of the world.

He is looking everywhere for class hatred, and I did not find the boys at St. Cyprian's were themselves snobbish, and heard no word until I went to Harrow of their parents' grandeur, the grouse moors and butlers and chauffeurs. But his description of "Flip" and "Sambo" bring back with an extraordinary vividness these two major characters in the earliest scenes of one's life.

Sambo had a gangling, loping walk with head leaning forward that was somewhat graceful and amusing. His body had a certain elegance. His eyes were ferrety and secretive, even if occasionally amused, and his complexion wonderfully poreless, apricot-bloomed and immaculate. His mouth was a bit simian. And as I write this, I realise that I could also be describing the physical appearance of his wife, "Flip."

She too had a simian mouth, the upper lip the most pronounced fea-

[1] Sir Stephen Spender (1909–95), poet.

[2] H. G. Wells (1866–1946), writer.

[3] Mr. and Mrs. Vaughan Wilkes were the headmaster and headmistress of St. Cyprian's while Cecil was there.

ture in her face, it protruded in Egyptian style over the square teeth. (Were they false? They seem, in retrospect, unnaturally square and regular.) She too had a clean, clear, blank complexion. I was fascinated to study a woman bereft of powder or any form of make-up. I wondered if she used a scrubbing brush dipped in cold water on her face in the morning. She too had the smallest, brightest tadpole eyes. They were lidless, or at any rate the skin above them covered, hawk-like, the lid. She was a non-stop study. I was fascinated by her, terrified, had absolutely no affection for her; in fact, hated her almost as much as Orwell did.

Orwell also brings to mind after an interval of nearly 50 years the presence at the school of the strange, terrifying blind boy, whom one persecuted a little and yet was so terrified of, for he had an uncanny way of using his long, supple fingers like pincers and really torturing one in the most relentless way. He discovered, unseen to others but recognised by him, the presence in a pocket of my corduroy trousers of an old-fashioned nail polish buffer. This was ammunition in his power. I remember also an excessively pretty boy whose mother appeared almost as young as a sister should be, and just as pretty. There was something too pretty, even stagy, about the lady, who had the sad blue eyes of widowhood, and somehow one knew that the Wilkeses only had the boy here on sufferance as his background was too stagy. By the time I arrived at St. Cyprian's, Charlie Cavendish[1] had left, and the only Lord that the Wilkeses could boast of was the ugly, pudgy, toothy Reggie Malden,[2] a thoroughly unattractive specimen in looks and character. Orwell also brings back the Wilkeses' penchant for the Scottish, and two of their favourites, who wore the kilt, were the Kirkpatrick brothers.

The escape from "Flip" when, at last, one left St. Cyprian's was one of the great milestones in early existence (nonetheless I am sorry that later I added my name to a ridiculous letter of abuse that Charlie Cavendish, that most docile and sweet of men, wrote to her in one of his periodic bouts of drunkenness). She was more difficult to deal with (her husband a mere pawn)[3]

[1] Lord Charles Cavendish (1905–44), younger son of ninth Duke of Devonshire. He was a wild friend of Cecil's at Cambridge and, in 1932, he married Adele Astaire, dancing sister of Fred.

[2] Reginald, Viscount Malden (1906–81), later ninth Earl of Essex.

[3] To this Cecil added a footnote: "How when Mrs. W. had gone to London for the day I was bold enough to chuck playing football (in fact, running round the football field in shorts, for the ground was too hard frozen for play) but being spied looking through a window by Sambo, retreated to hide under the stage of the theatre being built, the gym, where eventually I was caught."

than any of the monster figures that loomed later in life, so that having come through the Vaughan Wilkes experience, one felt that the rest of life was a comparative picnic.

Another St. Cyprian's regret is that I remember so very little about Orwell himself. I was intrigued and fascinated by Cyril Connolly with his truffle-hunting nose for talent and quality, and I have a vague feeling that he may have suggested that I should cultivate the friendship of Blair. This I tried, for a short time, to do. I believe we worked together on our private allotments, we each had a small garden, and I seem to remember sitting side by side with a white, veal-skinned Blair, who was growing mustard and cress. His hair and woollen sweater were tough and coarse, and reminded me in colour and texture of a mule, or a seaside donkey, and there was something defiantly poor about him that makes the analogy seem apt. But even at an age when politics had so little bearing on either of us, there was no rapport. I certainly felt no urge to become more intimate and he very soon sloughed me off as a stranger, and very soon he left. I regret that I cannot remember his face, only a vague sense that the cheek by the jaw and ear was long and white, and made of a thick consistency.

I learnt very little in the way of traditional education at St. Cyprian's, but I learnt a little of what one should learn. I wrote out lists of the books I knew were right for me to have read, without ever reading them. But my education was mostly negative. I learnt how to suck up, to curry favour, to be a sycophant, in order to survive, to get "into favour," to get a coconut cake. But many of the things I learnt were those I could have well remained ignorant of for some time to come. Altogether it was a bad school, but not as black as painted by Orwell with his beady eye for the sinister and the unfair.

Cecil enjoyed his stay at the ranch and took his first ride on horseback in 20 years. This he undertook feeling that it was the point of being at a ranch and, though he would have welcomed any excuse for escape, he duly set forth. "At first I was a bit alarmed," he wrote, "but soon I enjoyed the sensation of speed and the applause of my companions was good for morale."

This was the high spot of a stay which proved one of "complete relaxation."

Cecil flew home to London via Los Angeles, exhausted but to find good news awaiting him.

The one nice welcoming news was that my exhibition continues to draw crowds and that it has again been extended until the month of February. Also a telegram arrives to say I have been nominated as one of the best-dressed men of the world! What a farce. If only people knew! I spend comparatively little on clothes, an occasional good suit but most of my suits are made in Hong Kong or Gillingham, Dorset or bought on quaysides during my travels abroad. I do not own a clean pair of gloves and my shirts are mostly frayed. I suppose I should realise the list is entirely phoney when Prince Philip one of the worst, most "square," ugly dressers, is top of the list.

Too bad that a dry through and foggy crackly voice should develop into one of the worst head colds that I've had since adolescence. Too bad, too, that the dreaded fitting with Streisand (in fact, quite a smooth operation and minimum of difficulties) and the attendance next night at the première of *Funny Girl*[1] prevented my taking the precaution of staying in one atmosphere. The result was a real funereal cold, a pourer, a streamer. It was a relief to know it was not serious, that I was not really ill and, in comparison with the recent colitis, amounted to very little, but it put a damper on my activity, my vitality. I did last-minute designs for *Clear Day* at quarter speed, but my head ached, my jaw and teeth throbbed, my eyes were bunged up and red, my nose inflated. I felt a thousand years old. In fact, it was unbelievably my 65th birthday on Tuesday.

In January Cecil retreated to Reddish with a bad cold. All was not well in Wiltshire. The health of the Earl of Pembroke, Cecil's neighbour at the "Big House"—Wilton—was giving cause for further concern.

Sidney Pembroke is dying of cancer. Mary and the children were told that his case is hopeless (for the disease has spread all over his body) but they maintain complete secrecy. It is difficult for friends who have an inkling of the situation who meet with a rigid or even airy dismissal of the seriousness of the situation.

[1] *Funny Girl,* film musical originally a Broadway show, released in the United States in 1968, which also starred Omar Sharif. Barbra Streisand repeated her stage role as Fanny Brice.

Each weekend I go over to give a few bits of information about life in London. Each week I find Sidney less well. Mary, with superb reserve, says in a high-pitched voice, "Sid's not having his meals downstairs for the time being. They bring a tray to his sofa. So it's no use asking you to dinner. Come at tea or drinks time."

Sid is losing his colour, his eyes no longer that turquoise blue. He is losing weight and he lies lower in the sofa, the bottles of pills multiply on the table behind him and every now and then he is convulsed with pain. He has developed, through pain, a habit of clenching his teeth, of bringing the lower teeth forward. We held our talk of his condition, but the others in the room were deadly silent when last evening Sidney asked me if my Dr. G. [Gottfried] knew of an anodyne against sciatica. I talked airily about how he gave me nothing to help when I suffered from shingles and said, "One just has to wait."

"But it takes such a bloody long time. I've been six months already."

I long to break Mary down and, when she sees me out of the hall, tell her that my heart bleeds for her. But I'm afraid she would resent it. It would be too awful if she went on pretending, so each visit is a play acted out somewhat painfully. Today, perhaps I succeeded in raising the tempo, bringing more laughter into the room. We talked of David [Herbert]'s starting to write his life story and the ten tapes so far completed. We talked of the scrapes he used to get into, the early days in "Berlin" and the blackmailing gangsters in New York. For so proud a woman as Bea Paget [their mother], she has had the most appalling humiliations to face in life!

With Sidney's illness and doom hanging over the place, I feel I will never know Wilton again as it should be. The young people have not got the knowledge, know-how or flair to keep it alive, and a sad aspect of the case is that they do not have any wish to be there. They'd prefer to stay where they are able to participate in the world of film making and creative activities on the outer reaches of Chelsea.

Mary tells me Sid has had a very bad week with pains down his back. It isn't a slipped disc, it must just be the result of lying on his side, and his back has given out. Miss Archer, the masseuse, says she can feel the nodules swimming about.

It is extraordinary that Mary can go about kidding in this way. She knows Sid has cancer of the spine. Why elaborate the lies of the defence?

Anyhow, today (Saturday) it is mild and sunny, and helped up with extra pills, Sidney has gone out shooting, a triumph of determination over insuperable odds.

SIR FRANCIS ROSE

Francis Rose has taken up a good deal of Eileen's working time this week. I have been reduced by my cold to a pitch of weakness that has made another encounter with Francis just a bit more than I could muster up the courage to face. I shouted at him over the banisters as he arrived. Five hours later with 15 pages of letters for Eileen to type out for lawyers etc. For me he had written out a poem about Gertrude [Stein] and Alice [B. Toklas]. If not quite a poem, it had a certain charm and conjured up this odd couple in a way that I had forgotten. It had a point and the essence of Francis. If only he would not make life so miserable for himself and his few remaining friends.

No matter how squalid and down-and-out he looks, he still has a quality of grandeur. He has found a woman in reduced circumstances who lets him a room for £7 a week. He calls her his "hostess." But what prevents him from putting his head in a gas oven? *How* can he survive? He has no prospects.

Cecil loved to visit a fellow photographer or a star from his youth. He then recorded their memories in his diary. Some of these visits later bore fruit in the book he published with Gail Buckland,[1] The Magic Image *(1975). One such was the Austrian photographer Emil Otto Hoppé (1878–1972).*

E. O. HOPPÉ — 28 JANUARY 1969

Dicky [Buckle] and I made a pilgrimage to the 90-year-old photographer who lives in a bungalow near Andover.

Here the greatest contrast to Francis, an old man in impeccable condition, clean, soigné, well tweeded up, living in complete contentment

[1] Gail Buckland (b. 1948), American author and exhibition organizer, formerly curator of the Royal Photographic Society Collection.

E. O. Hoppé, photographer, Andover, 1969

although a heart condition ("nothing serious") prevents him going out. "I'm house-bound," he says, but he has a "sort of a" darkroom and he continues to experiment with photography by taking the ordinary things that people overlook, the design of skaters' shadows on ice, iron chairs in rows, a plantain in flower, an onion. He has no regrets, takes everything, including the death of his wife, as an inevitability of life that must be made the best of. His daughter lives in the neighbouring bungalow, so although they live separately he feels that companionship is nearby, a protection. He is a happy man and I find it impossible to write "happy old man." For this he does not seem to be.

He retired from business nearly 40 years ago and, having given up his studio, went on long voyages. His one regret is that he sold all his negatives to Hutchinson's, the publishers, and the man who owned this treasure trove committed suicide, and now no one knows the whereabouts of all these thousands of pictures.

For Dicky and me this was particularly distressing and all that remained for E. O. (Emil Otto—Viennese) to show us were a few isolated prints of little interest. One beauty of Hazel Lavery,[1] exuding the feminine

[1] Hazel Martyn (1880–1935), born in Chicago. Married first Dr. Edward Trudeau of New York. Widowed. She married second (1910), Sir John Lavery (1856–1941), painter.

allure of a great lady of the period, with her silk collars, velvets and pearls, and in his particular picture in the background her little Moroccan slave boy. Another photograph of Epstein[1] with the carving of the figure of Oscar Wilde's tomb in his studio, and a unique Henry James. But little else and his books give a very poor impression of his work, so badly reproduced and whimsical, corny, a great many things his work is not.

Due to circumstances (Dicky having friends arriving to stay etc.), we had a rushed visit for after an hour we had to leave to meet a train with the feeling that we had accomplished little. Dicky pleased that E. O. had told us that Nijinsky, very difficult for he could not speak one word of English, had been the one member of the Ballet who refused to go to the studio, so had to be photographed in his dressing room, where a curtain and an electric light were rigged up, and the proceedings were helped by the presence of his sister (even so the results were not good).

It was, however, next morning when I telephoned Hoppé that this most articulate man was able to give me a "résumé" of his life and photographic career. His father had been the managing director of a bank in Munich and had expected his son to follow in his footsteps. In fact, he was sent to Shanghai to learn the ropes. En route, the young Hoppé stopped off in London, met a young girl whom he married and remained in London for two years, carrying on a deceit with his father, sending letters home that were posted by a friend in China. After two years the wife went as ambassador for the son to Munich, won the heart of the parents.

Meanwhile the son was working in a bank—and disliking it—in Throgmorton Street, much more interested in his work as an amateur photographer. It was when he won a £100 for the first prize in an amateur photographer exhibition organised by *Daily Chronicle* (or *Mail*?) that young Hoppé decided to leave Throgmorton Street and moved to South Kensington, where he took a 50-year lease on Millais's house. Here, from 1905, for 25 years he carried on his photographic career.

Hoppé was influenced by Craig Annan,[2] a photographer from Edinburgh, and Furley Lewis[3] who were purists, tried to get deeper than make a

[1] Sir Jacob Epstein designed Oscar Wilde's tomb in Père Lachaise cemetery in Paris.
[2] James Craig Annan (1864–1946), foremost British exponent of photogravure.
[3] Furley Lewis (d. 1939), photographer.

mere likeness. They used a little psychology to a certain extent. Hoppé tried to dig deeper than putting his sitter in a decorative painted setting. He always tried to talk to his sitters before he made a date for the sitting, and during the photographic process considered it more essential to catch a mood or expression than have complete sharpness of definition. Thus he kept up a continual flow of talk while photographing.

At first Hoppé was considered a black sheep and was attacked for his impatience in disgressing from the stereotyped in photography.

It was Bruce Ingram[1] of the *Illustrated London News* who first encouraged Hoppé to publish a portfolio of four pages of unconventional portraits by a new young man. The Hoppés lived in Chelsea, surrounded by artists, sculptors, writers, who had "publicity" value. Their activities acted one upon the other, and they launched him as an artistic photographer who was responsible for making something which was considered a trade rather than a profession.

Hoppé met the editor, Huskinson[2] of the *Tatler*, Ingram of the *Sketch*, at the Savage Club, and here business was done in a very casual, uncompetitive way. "Taken any photographs lately?" No agent used, a full page was paid for at the rate of three guineas. Hoppé never solicited a sitting, thinking it unfair since he possessed the copyright, but charged a fee of five guineas, after which the sitter could order pictures, as few as he liked at two guineas a copy. These were mounted on card with Indian ink matting lines done by Hoppé himself (never a manufactured mount).

In this way he made such a considerable sum of money that after 25 years in 1929 he retired. He was tired of people. Artists were his friends, society people came within his orbit and he admired Hazel Lavery and, with Catherine d'Erlanger and Epstein, they formed a theatre drama club at the Lyric for performing plays that had not been given before (Maeterlinck[3] was an innovation!).

He admired Gladys Cooper, Spessiva[4] and Queen Marie of Romania[5]

[1] Captain (Sir) Bruce Ingram (1877–1963), newspaper editor and director.

[2] Edward Huskinson (1877–1941), editor of the *Tatler* from 1908.

[3] Maurice Maeterlinck (1862–1949), author.

[4] Olga Spessiva or Spessivtseva (1895–1991), Russian-American dancer in Diaghilev's Ballets Russes. She later suffered a severe nervous breakdown.

[5] HM Queen Marie of Romania (1875–1938), granddaughter of Queen Victoria, married to King Ferdinand I of Romania.

but he was always a lone wolf. He went to Romania, where he lived with the gypsies and wrote down hitherto unrecorded stories and fairy tales. He became a friend of the Queen of Romania and she gave him facilities and encouragement with a book published with an embarrassing title.

After retiring, he travelled—Burma, India, Bali, Australia, North and South America—and took photographs wherever he went, though not portraits. He settled with his wife in a sixteenth-century house in Kent, until three years ago when his wife died. He has a son working for Wrigley. A daughter in the bungalow next door looks after him.

More recently his photographs have been of abstract designs: duckweeds, factory buildings, commercial structures, and experiments with hot water on the gelatine negatives etc. When asked if given the chance to choose again his life work, would it be photography? "Most certainly." It would probably not be of portraits but he would like to develop along "purist" lines, though never descending to mere trickery and stunts, which he abhors. He was proud to think that his efforts had helped to elevate photography from the status of trade to "profession."

Dicky left with stars in his eyes. He considered Hoppé a sort of magician. He thought he had created quite a little magic in that dreary, utilitarian bungalow.

Dicky takes his "research" musician to Stratford for a new ballet. He has had many late nights. He sleeps during ballet, then he wakes. He shouts to his assistant, "You fucking shit, why didn't you wake me up? How *dare* you let me sleep!" He writes an article about George Best, the footballer,[1] instead. The *Sunday Times* rings him: "You can't *not* write about the new ballet. We've got a photograph of it across the page."

"I can't write about it. I was asleep. If you nag me like this I think you've got the wrong ballet critic."

[1] George Best (b. 1946), popular footballer with an extensive love life, whose later health problems preoccupied the tabloids.

GLADYS COOPER

Gladys Cooper acts for the money, now tells her agent that she won't read a script until she's signed to do it.

Says Ellen Terry[1] taught her never to be sorry for herself or say, "Don't feel you're being pathetic, or the audience won't have sympathy. Be courageous and you'll have their hearts." She carries this advice into her own life.

Aged 80, the former great beauty has become a bright, funny, interested, intelligent old woman. There are no pretences, no stage affectations about her, and she expects a certain intelligence in others. At the charity (*Evening Standard*) Drama Awards lunch she took me as her guest. I was quite impressed, against my prejudices and better judgement, by the speech of Jennie Lee.[2] Loathsome as this iron lassie is, I felt she showed understanding and heart. When the final applause came, I whispered to G. that I thought the speech quite good. "A lot of bunk," she replied.

The newspapers have been full of such horrible personalities, events and calamities of late (Wilson worst of all, Callaghan etc., strikes of telephonists, *dégringolade* of England new *Queen Elizabeth* being unacceptable) demonstrations by students at LSE etc., that I skim through the pages, picking out a few items of interest, and I'm sorry to have to admit that such is now my venerable age that the obituaries have an uncanny fascination for me. Almost every week there is a start of shock as I see some contemporary or younger friend has joined the other ranks.

This week in the country I have been feeling very depressed by my continued health (bad cold has turned to bronchitis and my bones ache, and the mucus from my chest into my stomach and makes me feel sick). The papers have seemed worse than before, so one morning with my breakfast tea I turned immediately to find in large letters "Irene Castle—pre-war 1914 favourite."[3]

[1] Dame Ellen Terry (1847–1928), actress who played leading roles opposite Sir Henry Irving.

[2] Jennie Lee (1904–88), Labour minister, later Baroness Lee of Ashridge. Then Minister for Education and Science.

[3] Irene Castle (1893–1969), fashionable dancing star with her husband Vernon Castle (who was killed in an aeroplane crash in 1918).

Another nail gone into my coffin, and another milestone passed, or at any rate an early favourite gone for ever. Not that she hadn't "gone" for the past 40 years. But it was nice to know that the woman who had created such a personal magic was still in the land of the living, and that she was enjoying life and able to talk of the future as well as the past. Irene Castle was someone I never saw perform, but from her pictures I could tell exactly how she must have looked and moved and stunned her audience with her blade-like flash.

Well, I've written a lot about her marmoset cherub face and her star blue eyes with the lids that cut low down at the outer corners, and I'm glad that I went to see her a few weeks ago on her last visit to London when I got her to sign the photographs for Raffles, and she clutched my arm saying, "Isn't old age awful!" But although she had no voice and was in the company of her doctor, whom she admired for keeping her alive, she still had the panache of a star, and among the dreary anonymous diners in the hotel the waiters recognised a great personality.

She had nothing to be sorry for. She had a wonderful life. She has lived to the age of 76, but it is I, one of her few remaining admirers from the millions, who am at a loss. And I find it sad that there are already so few people with whom I am able to discuss our loss. Too much time has gone by. Even the picture papers were not interested in someone who had had her day such a very long time ago.

Cecil then went to the Buhlerhöhe Clinic, near Baden-Baden in Germany, for a long rest cure, hating the imposed solitude, but enjoying walking amidst the fir trees in the forest. He read Thackeray and Gibbon, he was interested to find Herr Willy Brandt,[1] *the German Chancellor, among those in the dining room one evening, and he was saddened to discover, during an attempt to peruse the German newspapers, that Fritzy Massary*[2] *had died.*

It was the most extraordinary coincidence, if such it was, that of the very few German people that I know I should read the name of Fritzi Massary and learn that yesterday at the age of 86 she had died in Hollywood. "*Fritzi Massary gestorben.*"

[1] Willy Brandt (1913–92), Chancellor of the Federal Republic of Germany from 1969.

[2] Fritzi Massary (1882–1969), Austrian singer.

A pang of pain went through me for although I had never known her in her prime I had heard so much about her that I realised that in the field of operetta she must have been unique. She was the "Merry Widow" of Germany and very different she must have been from our lovely Lily Elsie. She had a tremendous vivacity and chic. Her clothes were said to be more works of art than theatrical dresses, the petticoats alone worthy of a museum, and in this there must have been something of the American Ethel Levey.[1]

I first met her in the courtyard of the Schloss Kammer in the Eleonora, Alice, Kommer[2] days. She was a wizened little pixie in Bavarian clothes who sang with great play of fingers the popular "Joseph" from *Madame Pompadour.*[3] One could tell even under these difficult conditions what artistry she had, but those who had seen her were speechless in their admiration. Then, being a Jewess, she had to flee from Hitler's diabolical regime. In London she appeared in a Noël Coward musical but her part was so poor that one could not gauge her real flavour.

She next surfaced in Hollywood when George Cukor had the idea that she should appear for a brief moment as the Queen of Transylvania in *My Fair Lady.* I was given the job of showing her around the lot, taking her to be measured by the wardrobe. But she was not willing to break her retirement for peanuts. Her agent asked the most preposterous amount of dollars for at most a four-day shift.

I was deputed to telephone her and reason with her. "But it'll be fun!" I said very stupidly. "Fun? No. It'll be hard work. It'll upset me a great deal. It'll mean panic here for weeks on end, my peace of mind upset. I've retired. Why should I come and do a day's work if it upsets me?" It would have been good to see her make an entrance, for the way she placed her feet was in itself a creation.

Well, I cannot pretend that at 87 she had not enjoyed a good life, for

[1] Ethel Levey (1881–1955), American jazz artiste with an aquiline nose, married to George M. Cohan (1878–1942), American song-and-dance man.

[2] Eleonora von Mendelssohn (1899–1951), actress, who appeared in many Max Reinhardt productions in Germany before the war and committed suicide in New York; Alice (Astor) von Hofmannsthal (1902–56), wife of Raimund von Hofmannsthal; and Dr. Rudolph "Kaetchen" Kommer (d. 1943), Reinhardt's right-hand man. They were part of a stimulating intellectual circle.

[3] *Madame Pompadour* (1923), operetta by Leo Fall (1873–1925). The song "Joseph, ach Joseph was bist du so keusch?" was a world hit.

although she had had, beyond middle age, to leave her country and all behind, she managed to make a new life of ease and comfort with her daughter Lisl in California. But it is sad when these theatrical stars go out of orbit, for their fame is so transitory, so difficult to explain to later generations: the freshness and originality and vitality that she invented. Yes, that is the important thing, for without these inventors the stars of today would not perform in the mould that they have created from the influences that have come down to them. Maybe a number of older people will be sorry that Fritzi has gone. I blow a kiss to her memory.

FOOTNOTE TO THE ABOVE

With eyes aching through over-reading, I went after the Sunday evening meal to watch television in the lounge. The announcer told us that during the evening there would be a programme in memory of Fritzi Massary! What a gift for me. This I would enjoy. I had to sit through a performance with Grete Moscheim in *The Glass Menagerie.*[1] Although I understood little, I know the play well and was able to realise that the old actress (was she Molnár's widow?) with her face lifted beyond human recognition, used her strange voice with a great variety of inflections. This was bearable entertainment.

Then we must submit at 10 o'clock to the cross-questioning on some vastly intricate technical subject of one of the members of the Cabinet. This seemed endless. Could I possibly sit it out? At 10:30 the programme continued. At 10:40 it ended. Just as I was looking forward to the next programme, the other guests of the sanatorium rose to their feet and put off the TV. In English I shouted, "I want to see the Fritzi Massary."

"No, no, it is forbidden. The rules are very strong here. No television after 10 o'clock!"

I rushed up the stairs to my bedroom, too angry to share the lift with my fellow guests. My heart was pounding in the altitude.

I lay down and was too incensed to sleep.

[1] Grete Moscheim (1905–1986), German actress, member of Max Reinhardt's Deutsches Theater, Berlin 1922–31. She was never married to Ferenc Molnár (1878–1952) as Cecil speculates. Her husbands were Oskar Homolka and Howard Guild. She was in the film *Die Glasmenagerie* (1969).

Cecil returned to England after his cure.

The object of my return from the sanatorium was Aunt Cada's 90th birthday.[1] There were several occasions when the family did not think she would achieve the great celebration. But although Cada was the delicate one of the family and early in life half her inside was taken out, she arrived (minicab trouble delayed her) to be greeted by 30 or 40 close friends whom she had invited to lunch at Pelham.

The proceedings were an enormous success for the blind old girl has shown such courage and such spirit and interest, and has accumulated so much friendship and affection around her, that all were plumping for her, and the atmosphere was unusually friendly and festive.

I had to propose a toast and, as usual, made a fool of myself by not being able to overcome my emotion, but she replied with tremendous aplomb. Faces from the dim past survived to drink a toast. Blanche Mitchell, Dudley Scholte,[2] Bertie Watson, who has made £3 million from inventing a material for aeroplane runways, Dame Eva Turner,[3] and a whole lot of relatives ate Ray's chilli con carne, mutton, Boeuf Stroganoff and three different sorts of pudding. The atmosphere was jubilant and Aunt Cada has something to think about for the rest of her days.

Princess Marina had died in August 1968. Sir Philip Hay[4] *had been her private secretary for many years, and he now had the solitary task of sorting her papers and closing down her apartment at Kensington Palace.*

VISIT OF THE COURTIER—PHILIP HAY

Philip has been perhaps more affected than anyone by the death of Princess Marina. Not only was it a terrible shock to him to lose someone whom he

[1] Cecil's aunt, Cada Sisson (1879–1970) was his mother's youngest sister. She was the widow of Richard Chattock (1865–1936).

[2] Dudley Scholte (1905–90), Heath Mount School contemporary and son of the well-known tailor.

[3] Dame Eva Turner (1892–1990), opera singer with a formidable presence.

[4] Sir Philip Hay (1918–86), private secretary to Princess Marina 1948–68.

loved and worked for through many vicissitudes, but it has been [his task] to work on surrounded by the debris of the Princess's life, trying to put her papers and belongings in order. It has been a bad time for him, arriving daily in an empty Palace going through the past. He asked me if he could come and lunch with me, and a date had to be fixed very far in advance, not because he had much to do, but I had. He arrived early and stayed till half the afternoon was gone.

He enjoyed the gossip because it was one of those rare occasions on which he could let go, feeling perhaps that I was much more of a friend of Prince George and also of the Duchess than I really had been. He was quite at ease, and communicative, yet even so he has been involved with the Royal Family sufficiently long to have become entirely the typical courtier. He has a built-in resistance to people who ask for more than they should, who are inquisitive or indiscreet. This attitude has seared through every pore, so that even in moments of great amusement, and I dare say anger, there is a lever which comes down to prevent the truth from showing.

He told me of the last six weeks, and after the doctors had told them the worst, that Princess Marina was doomed, of the horror of pretence, and the consultation about who should or not be told, Princess Olga [Princess Marina's elder sister] outraged that she hadn't been informed until after her sister lost consciousness, but the reasons were valid (re P. E.[1] at Pratolino possibly letting cat out of bag). The merciful accident of the Duchess falling in the bathroom and hitting her head had hastened the death by cancer, otherwise by degrees she would have become paralysed, losing speech etc.

Philip, when first employed as Secretary, worked in two servants' rooms in Marlborough House (the Kents having no London home). He was at first terrified when Queen Mary summoned him. He would find her lying on a chaise longue and he would stand to attention listening to her for one and a half hours on end. Or she would be sitting in an upright chair and he would sit in front of her, their knees almost touching. Queen Mary seemed to know everything there was to know in the way of gossip and she disapproved very much of much that she read in the newspapers. "You must tell Marina she

[1] HRH Princess Elizabeth of Yugoslavia (b. 1936). Pratolino was Prince Paul's and Princess Olga's house north of Florence.

must not go out with Noël Coward, a most unsuitable companion. Now be sure to tell her." But the old Queen would be sure to double check herself and Philip would always discover that the Queen had written to Princess Marina to tell her of the same directives that Philip had been instructed to impart.

Philip is a pleasant, no longer beautiful, man who is capable of looking after himself and indeed, now is being made a director of Sotheby's, but his manner, turn of phrase and mind are completely moulded in the past. He has no idea of the way things have changed and if he did, would resist the changes with all the wiry strength that he possesses.

ISADORA DUNCAN

The *Isadora* film[1] in a cut version and without the tiresome intermission was at last shown in London to a very critical reception. Seeing it for the second time, its faults were much more apparent and the visual beauty struck one less. However, there is no backtracking; it is a film that I will always remember for its great moments. That Isadora does not come out as either a great woman or a genius of the dance is the main trouble. It would be interesting to see Ken Russell's TV with Vivian Pickles[2] again as I believe this is the truer picture. Certainly, on second viewing the dance sequences are done with great lack of imagination and the sequence during her lovemaking with Gordon Craig[3] is the clue to the way the dancing could have been interpreted to give the feelings of strangeness and originality that Isadora wove over her audiences. To me Vanessa Redgrave[4] is very touchingly beautiful, though I now see her marriage scenes when she appears as a conventional and ladylike Edwardian hostess are quite wrong.

However, others have thought her wildly inadequate. Henry Herbert recoiled at her ugliness. Freddie Ashton thought her a well brought-up horse.

[1] Karel Reisz directed *Isadora,* a film on the life of Isadora Duncan, which was released in 1968. It starred Vanessa Redgrave, Jason Robards and James Fox.

[2] Ken Russell (b. 1927), film director with a will to shock, and Vivian Pickles (b. 1933), British character actress.

[3] Edward Gordon Craig (1872–1966), influential stage designer, actor and director.

[4] Vanessa Redgrave (b. 1937), British leading actress, known for strong political views.

He observed, "I don't like to know the background of an actress. Gertrude Lawrence came from no definable stratum of humanity. Vanessa is a girl who has been to an excellent school." Fred then corroborated Bébé Bérard who said that Isadora, in spite of her late-in-life drunkenness, flatulence, fatness, tiresomeness, could as soon as she got up and derobed and started to dance, hypnotise her audience into making them see something for the first time, that she had the divine spark. Fred elaborated, "Her assurance was so astounding. She was not afraid to stand motionless in the middle of the stage for some considerable time, then very slowly use one hand, then the arm; as a figure of death she stood enveloped in a purple cloak, and only after several bars of music did she slowly move her arms to reveal a hidden sheaf of real lilies. When she came towards the audience, she did so with great slowness, as if in slow motion, and the effect was breathtaking."

I'm afraid in spite of many felicities, Karel Reisz[1] is not a good director, or at any rate not bold enough to simplify, and illustrate his theme in a nutshell. The film will certainly not be a public success either.

Dicky Buckle's much vaunted party afterwards was a dire failure. Instead of having the Banqueting Hall it was given in the dark, dreary passages of the Coliseum. The food was abominable, a cold old chicken leg with three pickled onions, a quarter of a tomato, and Whitaker potato in a basket. A bottle of red wine was spilled over Laura Arundell, who had taken such trouble and had come up specially from the country to put on a Greek dress with freesias in her hair, and Vanessa Redgrave fainted dead away. She measured her very considerable length on the floor, and was taken out feet first. Luckily, there was her "waiting chauffeur-driven" automobile. As soon as she was away from the party she recovered, told the driver to stop at the coffee stall at Covent Garden. Here they both quickly ate fried eggs and bacon, and drank coffee, and she asked to take away the cup and saucer as a souvenir of the most successful part of the evening.

For many years Cecil had endured having Maud Nelson as his secretary. She was the girlfriend of Olga Lynn and was part of Cecil's social set. She came to help

[1] Karel Reisz (1926–2002), Czech-born film director who made his reputation in Britain (*Saturday Night, Sunday Morning*).

him, but was hopelessly inefficient and relations deteriorated so badly between them that Cecil would walk around South Kensington until the hour when Maud went home, rather than have to face her.

Finally he could stand it no more and plucked up courage to dismiss her. She was replaced, in 1953, by Eileen Hose, who was highly efficient, in every way the opposite of Maud, and stayed with him in his difficult last years and until his death.

Cecil remained in touch with Maud and when, in 1957, she was arrested for hitting a High Sheriff's daughter over the head with a broken bottle, he offered to go to court as a character witness on her behalf. This well-meant but possibly misplaced gesture did not prevent Maud from undergoing a spell in prison.

Some years later Maud went to Tangiers, where David Herbert observed "a bald-headed old man with a few grey hairs sprouting unwillingly on his pate." It was Maud.

Needless to say, she went from bad to worse and she finally died on 28 February, 1969.

MAUD NELSON

It is awful that I am not more upset at the news of Maud's death. My first reaction was one of relief. She had an appalling accident two years ago, but in her own words, "She would not give up." And for what? Diana [Cooper] said, "Much better if she hadn't recovered for what?"

Poor Maud was a hopeless case. Useless and a luxury woman without means. I fear the last years were not very pleasant or happy for her in her rudderless state. In fact, the death of Oggie[1] on Maud's return from prison was the end of her life too. At best Maud inspired friendship. She had a way, a little coterie of lesbians were wonderfully loyal, but times have changed and Maud had no place in them. She was totally unable to keep down any job that would bring her in enough money to pay for concert tickets, and pâté and wine. She was a faithful friend and devoted servant to me for more years than I remember but I suffered from her incompetence so much that it is an effort to remember all the especially good things she did for me.

[1] Olga Lynn (1882–1961), small, rotund singer, who was Maud's girlfriend.

Loyal even beyond death, however reluctantly, Cecil attended Maud Nelson's funeral at St. Mary's, Cadogan Street.

Maud's funeral was pathetic. St. Mary's, Cadogan Street cold, dark and almost empty. Maud's coffin under a black velvet pall that had been used at so many hundreds of funerals that it had become shabby, poor and covered with stains. The flowers, too, were very meagre. Her sister had come over from Portugal and Francis Rose, wearing my old clothes, was introduced to her by Beryl Ashcroft. "Ah," said the sister. "These are names I've heard so much about."

The whole occasion was cheerless but tearless. No one was really very sad at Maud's passing. All said, it was a merciful relief, and I'm pleased that Maud was not able to realise her shortcomings, and that she never really suffered from depression and loneliness. Even her best friend Beryl said that since Maud's mind was beginning to go, her having failed to wake up was to all and to herself a blessing.

Francis Rose saga has taken a turn for the best. Amid the lies there are particles of truth. It seems that the Isadora Duncan drawings do in fact exist, and he produced them and they are very amusing documents signed 1927. And they are worth a considerable amount. Better still, Francis has sold three paintings for £1,500 and is now allowed to spend it all in a week as the court order has been quashed.

His high-handed grandeur has suddenly asserted itself again and he has been giving her peremptory orders.

FRIDAY, 14 MARCH 1969

A tiring week of frustration, inactivity and spurts of busyness. Monday a rush by early morning train to Maud's funeral, then on to the Ideal Home Exhibition where my rooms are in a state of unsatisfactory incompletion due to the electricians' strike. The rooms depended on spotlighting. It is as if a theatre curtain went up on a set without lighting. It is the sort of thing that causes people to criticise unfairly. The unions do untold harm, to me, to the Ideal Home, to the country. Fitting for *Clear Day* at Berman's, a most tiresome experience, evening with Patrick Procktor and Gervase at the last Orton play (which makes me realise how much I hate Feydeau and farce). Long session with José about the New York version of my exhibition. A social occasion with Ava [Waverley] to lunch and Loelia [Duchess of Westminster] and Diana gate-crashing and "making" the occasion, Diana telling how her car was stolen, but the messages she sticks to the window, "Dear Traffic Warden—Please have pity on a cripple" or "Please don't be unkind to an old lady taking a child to hospital," must have touched the thief who three days later returned the car.

Diana told of how shocked she was by Evelyn Waugh when asked by a pedestrian in an unknown town the way to the station would make up false instructions and sent the man off to miss his train. "But you can't do that, Evelyn."

"I always do," he replied.

Cecil invited John Gielgud to dinner finally to rest the long resentment he felt about having his sets dropped in the English version of Enid Bagnold's play, The Chalk Garden.

One evening highlight was the reconciliation supper after 15 years with John Gielgud. We were both a bit shy and self-conscious some of the time. Talk never on the main topic but on new plays and actors, and the new influences in film. John keen to do film of *Death in Venice,* but can't get a director. Very realistic about his relationships with [Patrick] Garland and Alan Bennett.[1]

John said Noël Coward or Enid Bagnold[2] (I forget which) was, like all of us, afraid of death. Did not have the opportunity to take this up. But I'm not afraid of death, I don't want a lingering suffering agony but the fact of dying does not disturb me. John got on v. badly with Albee,[3] almost brought a suit against him and thinks him the most mannerless person he has known, would never help with explanation of his play. When asked what a later scene would mean, Albee would say, "I've forgotten." Like Noël he is totally incapable of "rewriting" (Alan Bennett too).

[1] Patrick Garland (b. 1935), theatrical director, and Alan Bennett (b. 1934), dramatist and actor. They were then working with Gielgud on *Forty Years On* at the Apollo Theatre.

[2] Enid Bagnold (1889–1981), author and playwright, whose works should be better remembered. Widow of Sir Roderick Jones.

[3] Edward Albee (b. 1928), American playwright.

No private life confidences. John left very abruptly, apologising for having kept me up so late. 1 a.m.

Next day hard work at Ideal Home. Last-minute galvanising to life but still no bloody electricians. Buying £200 worth of false flowers from Spry, and wonderful gourds and false fruit.

Evening with Freddie for three of his ballets, [*The*] *Dream, Monotones,* Elgar [*Enigma Variations*]. We drank champagne in the intervals. Fred very brusque with everyone, took a curtain call at end, which was as rapturous and roaring of applause as my Gala.

Then with Dicky [Buckle] and Vanessa Redgrave beyond Richmond to Sheen where Rudolf Nureyev has a house with huge garden and enormous furniture. Joan Thring[1] said he bought the furniture so big and bulky so thieves could never take it from house, very Russian, original, of no great fashion, enormous sideboards, gargantuan Elizabethan or Dutch four-poster bed, gargantuan throne chairs of ebony, vast goblets of wine, 20 for dinner at midnight, Mexicans serving.

Rudy, a vague host, without manners or responsibility, leaves everything to Joan Thring who must suffer a lot. Rudy less difficult looked quite funny and bright, stepped on my toe when I said Margot would *never* stop dancing, did a marvellous imitation of Pavlova with her fluttery lips. He is a Tartan and is happy when drunk, when he has sex and 20 hours' sleep, miserable when he goes to bed early and alone. Complains Covent Garden pays him less than anyone else and gives so few performances, but he likes being with them as they are a *marvellous* company.

Vanessa Redgrave, very beautiful and young one moment, quite hideous the next. Her lips the best feature, pale, young, sometimes wore glasses with a pad to protect her nose, hair a mess, dressing gown a mess, on strange terms of intimacy with the fat moustachioed driver of her car. They kiss goodnight in a huge embrace. He says he'll be back later. What can it mean? A lot of "Dears" and "Darlings" and also "deared" the commissionaire of the cinema

[1] Joan Thring, former model and publicist in Australia, married for a time to the homosexual Australian actor Frank Thring, who was taken up by the Oliviers. She became Nureyev's tour manager and later served as secretary and manager until they fell out. Her brief acquaintance with Vivien Leigh in the 1950s provoked somewhat offensive "revelations" from her in a 2002 TV documentary about Vivien.

when he earlier passed to find out how *Isadora* was doing at the box office (well). The Communist racket is brought to strange lengths. She can be charming and also maddening. After her horrid TV appearance on Sunday when she must have antagonised a lot of her fans by her lack of humour, her brashness, her incivility to the interrogator, I am against her, but tonight found her agreeable and although sometimes self-conscious, nevertheless only spoilt in a few flashes, as, for example, when having referred to our first meeting (when she came to be "auditioned" as a photograph model and she was turned down) she now said, "I hope I'll pass next time."

SUNDAY, 16 MARCH 1969

Henry Herbert has become a father again, but the disappointment that the second child was another daughter[1] has added to the sadness of the last days. Perhaps Sidney was even too far gone to be able to take in the fact that there was still no heir to the great estate, but the cancer which has taken charge of his whole body has galloped voraciously down his legs, into his lungs and back so that for the last few days he has been in an agony of pain. Morphia did not placate him, then cocaine was found to help, even so he spent a night of torture watched over by Mary and his sister Patricia [Hambleden]. Henry rang to say his father was dying. Then this morning I was woken by Henry to say it was all over.[2]

It is a great misfortune that Sidney's father spent so long in dying[3] and that Sid has had only eight short years of the Wilton that he loved so much. It is a particular irony that his son would so much like not to live at the big house, but would have liked to devote these early years of his married life to leading a bohemian life and making films.

For Mary, who has been a monolith of strength, the raison d'être of her life has now gone, while the Dowager still survives[4] at Henley-on-Thames

[1] (Lady) Sophia Herbert was born on 12 March.

[2] Lord Pembroke died on 16 March, aged 63.

[3] The fifteenth Earl died in 1960, aged 79.

[4] The Dowager Countess (formerly Lady Beatrice Paget) was then 83.

to remember with remorse how badly she behaved to her eldest son, so that he never forgave her.

Meanwhile, the grandiose funeral arrangements are being made and all the neighbours conjecturing as to where Mary will live and will the young couple move into the big house or will it become a public monument to past greatness.[1]

At Reddish Cecil bemoaned the much-prolonged winter, and wished he had the chance of sun on his "bones." He noted that there was so much flu about that it was quite hard to find a free undertaker. When Eileen came to stay with Alan Tagg and Charles Colville, he enjoyed hearing the latest from the London theatre world.

MARCH 1969

Delightful and quite rare theatrical talk. Alan's stories are in depth. Not just gossip about Sir John [Gielgud] or Olivier and whosoever it may be.

We were all anti-Olivier, the quiet-spoken and discreet manager of the Old Vic suddenly admitting he thought Sir L. must have horns and hooves. When a critic wrote that Maggie Smith acted Olivier's *Othello* off the stage, Olivier burst into her dressing room and shouted, "You didn't act me off the stage. You *bored* me off the stage." A woman pontificating when the publicity woman was suddenly fired was praised by Olivier for "saving" the Canadian tour by her magnificent work, then was immediately sacked.

I remembered when working on *Anna Karenina* at the time when L. O. and Ralph Richardson[2] were such great friends. A picture I'd taken on the set of R. R. appeared full size on the first page of the *Sketch*, a publicity still of L. O. appearing smaller inside the magazine. L. O. kicked up such a row with the *Sketch* that the following week they gave him a double spread.

[1] Mary Pembroke moved into the Old Rectory, Wilton, and the young couple moved into the big house from Bulbridge, Juliet Duff's house in Wilton.

[2] Richardson played Karenin in the 1947 Korda film of *Anna Karenina* for which Cecil designed the costumes.

It seems Miss Plowright[1] and L. O. have both become like the hated Wolfit[2] in that they brook no competition on stage (L. O. refused to have Martita Hunt[3] in *Sleeping Prince* as she'd been too good in the stage version) and surround themselves only with lesser actors. Thus Irene Worth has been sacked from the Old Vic, Maggie S. etc. The result is that business is suddenly doing badly and whereas before tickets were difficult to come by they are now publicised as available for all performances.

Don't let it be said that artists, designers, photographers or whatever are effete and afraid of manual labour. Digging was the easiest of the jobs in the garden. Have run backwards and forwards with heavily piled barrows of earth for an hour on Sunday, yesterday, my brick-carting day. Of course, by doing an hour only one is able to work harder, quicker than one could if at the job all day long, but the forays among the debris of the old cottage garden made me realise how little there was to be feared in doing a navvy's work.

Two Bobs, LaVine and Prairie, came conveniently to stay for a night and were given the job of carting at least 30 barrow loads of manure. They performed manfully. It is interesting how most people really enjoy being made to do things that are good for them and yet would not do on their own accord.

COLOUR TELEVISION

Dot Head, my most marvellous neighbour, was eulogising the glories of colour television. "We've had Tolstoy, Dostoevsky, and now Kenneth Clark on *Civilisation.* It takes you around the entire world. No need to go to London to a theatre ever. You just sit by your own hearth and look at the most marvellous scenes of sun and beauty."

For Dot it is particularly wonderful as she is deaf and can rev up the volume to hear all. I dined with her in order to see K. and was staggered by the

[1] Joan Plowright, third wife of Laurence Olivier.

[2] Sir Donald Wolfit (1902–68), actor-manager. There were many reasons to hate him. Cecil blamed him for killing his play, *The Gainsborough Girls.*

[3] Martita Hunt (1900–69), actress. She played the Grand Duchess in Rattigan's play *The Sleeping Prince,* which opened at the Phoenix Theatre in November 1953.

colour frescos and faded paintings so much clearer than one could see as a traveller, a revelation. I must have a set; the boy from Radio Rentals spent an hour proving that I could not have any result. Dot remonstrates. "Nonsense. It's nothing to do with your hill, the power comes from Harnham and the hill is not in the direct line. You must have it. You've no idea of the interest, you see the most wonderful people arguing late at night, Krishnamurti, Angus Wilson."[1]

The second crew sent out found they could get perfect results. I was angry to think of all the frustration I'd suffered *not* being able to have BBC2 intellectual programmes but soon forgot it in the glory of the colour of skies, water, green fields. The colours have an added luminosity, being seen through glass, and even the most ordinary-looking news announcer has interest with the very clear representation of his skin pigmentation.

But as for K. Clark's *Civilisation* series it is a marvel. One could watch each programme a dozen times and then be aware of extra felicities. He has written an accomplished commentary, so beautifully phrased that one should write down almost every other sentence in a "Commonplace Book." It is so learned and measured, and in the most unpretentious way shows his infinite knowledge and erudition.

He has the face of a tortoise and a cranium so enormous that one realises there is more room for brain than most people possess. Even so his knowledge is astounding.

But perhaps the most wonderful revelation is the way in which he shows us the paintings and the frescos, the painted decorations. We have seen details from the National Gallery, chosen by him in remarkable books, but here the significant details flow into the bones of the composition in a quite staggering way. Botticelli used to be my favourite painter. I now saw the *Primavera* as if for the first time, with the Three Graces as one harmonious composition in ivory colour and the flowers flowing from the Zephir's mouth is a remarkable arabesque, and in the *Birth of Venus* the linked arms of the winds forming such a ravishing linear composition that travelled under K.'s guidance to other linked undulations of drapery. The details of roses and sea and arms and breasts forming a magical transformation scene.

[1] Jiddu Krishnamurti (1895–1986), Indian mystic, and (Sir) Angus Wilson (1913–92), novelist.

This programme has become a twice weekly event. Nothing would prevent me from seeing the latest Sunday instalment, and if one is lucky one has the great satisfaction of seeing the recap on the Friday evening. One sits in the dark surrounded by the coldest, gloomiest, ugliest, delayed springtime on record and one is wafted to Italy and the most lyrical pictures of the hills, with poplars and olive trees in a haze of heat, to be taken by the slowly revealing camera to the hilltop town of soft pink stone to be shown the revelations of the Palace of Urbino. This makes one realise how much of the most fantastic beauty there is that one has not yet seen. It is worth living to see.

Lady Diana Cooper appeared on Desert Island Discs. *She was Castaway 961 and the programme was broadcast in March 1969.*

Ray came in to tell me that Diana Cooper was on the radio doing *Desert Island Discs.* The voice was unrecognisable as that of a querulous, quavery, rather affected old lady, nothing of which is Diana. But soon one translated this feeble voice into that of the strident vital corncrake that we love and the content of the talk was absolutely her own and nobody else's. It created such an impact that for days I remembered every honest-to-goodness word that she said. No pretence. No shirking. She chose her records to remind her of her life, her early musical beginnings, *Clair de Lune,* Wagner, and she told of her affiliation with the Trees[1] and how she was as a child allowed to walk on in the crowds and would answer in the hubbub, "Yes Caesar[2] [sic], we *will* lend you our ears."

The interrogator[3] then said, "Oh yes, you murmured 'rhubarb, rhubarb.' "

"No, not rhubarb," answered Diana, "but, 'Oh poor Caesar, look at your wounds!' "

She told of how she had met with opposition by her family to her marriage to Duff, how he had "proved" himself and what wonderful times they had had in Algiers and in Paris, how Duff at Munich had resigned "to his undying honour." She talked of old age and space, hated the haphazard sprout-

[1] Sir Herbert Beerbohm Tree (1853–1917), actor-manager, and his family.

[2] It should have been Mark Antony.

[3] Roy Plomley (1914–85), who created *Desert Island Discs* and interviewed all the "castaways."

ing of skyscrapers, thought the hippies "all right," said her love of Doggie was absolute. All those who heard her said she was "a great character," so honest, true. I found her surprisingly "well bred," well brought-up. She pronounced foreign words impeccably. "Yes, Mother made us learn our *motifs.*" Doggie = Duggie. The Barbara Freyberg[1] element came out strong, also Iris Tree. It is good to have this on tape.

Suddenly Diana has become older. One realises she cannot be with us for ever.

WILLIAM DOUGLAS-HOME[2] PLAY

William has had nothing but flops for many years. Suddenly even the critics gave *The Secretary Bird* great praise for being a witty, well-constructed play. I felt it so remote from anything I would enjoy that only the arrival in London of the lonely bereaved Princess Olga[3] has precipitated my going to the Savoy Theatre. I arrived to see the audience bitten. Not very glad, but certainly expensive, rags appear, all so self-assured, sophisticated, rich, all in spite of Wilson and taxation and all that has changed. The curtain went up on the most hideous country drawing room, chintz, dead, artificial as if for a mortuary. The old couple next to me moaned, "Beautiful scenery!"

To my surprise I found the evening very much more agreeable than I had imagined possible. In fact, I was vastly more entertained than at Orton's farce or the Old Vic productions or most of the plays I've seen of late.

Cecil had been invited to dress Barbra Streisand for the Brighton scenes in On a Clear Day You Can See Forever, *produced by Howard Koch for Paramount, directed by Vincente Minnelli, with lyrics by Alan Jay Lerner. The film also starred Yves Montand.*[4]

[1] Barbara Jekyll (1887–1973), married first Lord Freyberg VC (1889–1963).

[2] Hon. William Douglas-Home (1912–92), playwright and brother of Sir Alec Douglas-Home. *The Secretary Bird* ran at the Savoy Theatre from October 1968 until July 1972, with Kenneth More initially. It was then replaced by another William Douglas-Home play, *Lloyd George Knew My Father.*

[3] Princess Olga was still saddened by the death of her sister, Princess Marina.

[4] Yves Montand (1921–91), French film actor, remembered for songs such as "Les Feuilles Mortes." He was married to the actress Simone Signoret.

After three hours we were still trying on the balloon dress and headdress. Suddenly she wanted to make it into an Indian prince's suit. She gave us inspiration. We were impressed by her quick eye and gradually the whole costume by trial and error was completely changed. There's no doubt she has an uncanny eye, won't be satisfied with second best. (How did she pass some of her *Funny Girl* costumes?)

But one has to be firm. She is by no means always right. I discovered that she had altered some details of the costumes we'd fitted in Hollywood and I was far from pleased; in fact, had taken away a great deal of the simplicity and style, to say nothing of introducing a different period feeling.

It had been a tiring, emotional afternoon and I came limp to catch the *Brighton Belle,* here to discover the modern new world at my disposal in the form of Tom Parr's brilliant Lewes Crescent flat, here to stay for ten days in his absence while working on the film. The flat is all that is modern in comfort and chic. It has little soul and Ray soon discovered its first impression quickly wore off and he felt it became tacky. Our first problem was to make the walls warm. The cold seared into the marrow and I was terrified of being stricken by another cold as I sneezed to the accompaniment of the latest in TV and radio equipment, and sank into bed.

Having made up his Chalk Garden *differences with John Gielgud, Cecil now decided to let the past settle with the play's author, Enid Bagnold. When he was in Australia, he had sent her a line wishing her well with her latest play,* Call Me Jacky.

During the war and later, he had spent a lot of time at North End House, Rottingdean, where Enid Bagnold lived with her husband, Sir Roderick Jones, the Chairman of Reuters. By the time of this visit the house (or rather three houses joined together) had fallen into considerable decrepitude and Enid was a widow.

ENID JONES

It was quite a strain going to the Rottingdean home of Enid for the first time since what she calls our row over ten years ago. She and friends had sent so many calls for olive branches that on the spur of a moment I wrote her a conciliatory letter. We had exchanged correspondence but this was the first time I had seen her in the background that had once been so familiar to me.

Cuthbert Worsley[1] escorted me and when we came into the hall I saw that nothing had changed by an iota, except that dust had gathered. Enid is now sofa-ridden having an arthritic hip, which will be operated by a surgeon and a team of three helpers for three and a half hours. Meanwhile she says she likes her new life as she lies under a coverlet in a red peignoir, her hair frizzed orange, her face gone to podge. Diana, a wonderful friend, is one of the remaining few who put up with Enid's selfishness, her ego and, in fact, is entertained by her company.

Enid struck me again as being very remarkable, certainly a great individual and her brain delves deep beneath the surface into every topic. Her grasp is as remarkable as her imagination, telling the story of *Clear Day*, she was fired, she had almost the plot of a novel there and then, and so with every subject. She talked with great authority, even in front of Diana, who in her turn can turn others into pygmies.

Occasionally she said something that made me realise she is, in spite of her many kind actions, by no means a kind or even a nice person. She was going to give stick to Edith Evans[2] in her autobiography.[3] Enid entertains plenty of bitterness. She was intolerant of Binkie [Beaumont] who never discovers a playwright but latches on to their third play, often without success. My visit, though fascinating, was not altogether a charitable or Christian experience. I found I did not like Enid any more than I had imagined. She is too interested in herself to bother about anyone else. She attacked Cuthbert for being unobservant. She criticised him for not admiring her table of small flowers, the green globes of the euphorbia. But if one is observant one would notice that the narcissi by her sofa were dead in their vases, that half of the flowers in the room should have long since been thrown out.

[1] T. C. Worsley (1907–77), drama critic of the *Financial Times*, who lived in Enid's cottage for four years, with his friend, Johnny Luscombe. Enid wrote that he had added greatly to her life and that she had shared his "woes and triumphs . . . as he has mine." Later, however, his melancholia depressed her. Author of *Flannelled Fool* (1967), a detailed account of his homosexuality, which was a first among his class and generation. He suffered from emphysema and when breathing became too difficult, he took a fatal overdose.

[2] Dame Edith Evans (1888–1976), actress.

[3] Enid had not forgiven Edith Evans for ruining her play, *The Chinese Prime Minister* (1965). Of Edith's interpretation, she wrote, "I wasn't ready to see my cool theme wrapped in butter." Enid's autobiography was published in October 1969.

But Enid will not change, in fact, is more herself now than ever. She cannot keep a servant, so she is servantless. She is economical to the point that only Diana can put up with such meanness. She is marvellously patient. She is likewise genuinely thrilled that Cuthbert's latest book has been acclaimed as "un-put-downable" by his publisher.[1]

But I came away with the feeling that although built on heroic proportions this character is not really all she should be, that her faults are mean and petty, that she has just missed being the figure that she should have been. I came away with the feeling, too, that here was someone very much with her life behind her and that although she was now on the track of knowledge and devoured books at a great velocity, the real days were over and that she was now rather bravely laughing at the thought of death.

CLEAR DAY

I sauntered off to the Pavilion under the impression that the first day's shooting has to be done in the basement cellar where Barbra appears as an orphan run away from school. Shock to find all my Promenade clothes being inspected. They looked very different from what I had imagined, not as good, but they were planned for out-of-doors sunlight, not the grey cold light of the present arctic weather. The day was full of incident. Felix Harbord[2] at my suggestion brought down from nowhere to give authenticity to the banquet, appalled by the ignorance of the Hollywood team, which I take for granted. They ask where are the fish knives. They start the banquet with salmon and then bring on the fowls! He was appalled, but amused. Petch[3] nearly fainted when told H. wanted £100 a day and said in Hollywood someone would plan a whole battle for $50! Felix got £50. Barbra's hairstyles make no concession to period and she refuses to cut her fingernails.

Her taupe dress, hair, face, coat and dress all the same colour is quite beautiful. She was slightly overwhelmed by the grandeur and prissy elegance

[1] Alan Ross was about to publish *Television: The Ephemeral Art,* a full-length survey of a wide variety of television programmes, in 1970.

[2] Felix Harbord (d. 1981), interior designer, who would have had a good sense of style for such a production.

[3] Petchnikov, one of the production team.

of Mrs. Fitzherbert's tea party scene, and in true Fanny Brice tradition debunked the whole thing by saying "Aw shit." She walks like and feels a comic and this has to emerge every other moment. The improvisation that I'm good at took on masterly terms today when that marvellous comic Irene Handl had no costume for one scene that had been restaged from an "exterior" shot. The muslin cap was too dainty and clean, and she had only one costume to wear later in the kitchen. So in search of a cap I found a Caley's bag for gloves, and put her head in this bag, pinned it at the back and sprayed it dirty.

Likewise a piece of sacking of canvas made in two and a half seconds an apron. What dare we do for a shawl? Irene Handl said she had two chihuahua dogs in a basket and would lend us their crochet rug. This made a splendid shawl. Thus in a charade manner was the mother of the star turned out in less than five minutes as if for a charade.

By the end of the day, admiring, supervising, photographing and hanging about, I felt more overtired than for years. I realised that I had not the strength and stamina that I had six years ago in *My Fair Lady.* I was now too tired to read and, lest I was too tired to sleep, I took a pill which calmed me down. I feel in a no man's land here in this strange modern flat that is rootless, cut off from the world. I have lost both my homes and feel I'm in limbo. It's a horrid feeling and plays tricks with time, too. I feel I've been here a week instead of two and a half days.

It's always rather tiresome after one's days of great effort to telephone home and find things have not moved since one's departure (which seems so much further ago than it is) and that the difficulties that have arisen are on such a picayune scale. We are short-staffed, there is no one to run errands, to do a hundred different jobs, except Eileen. She cannot be expected or even allowed to do so much. Telephoning this evening the saga was of Geoff [Sawyer] not delivering pictures, of no one answering Felix's bell, the bell's out of order. Oh dear, and when I compare the way in which the Paramount photographer operates.

APRIL 1969

For months the whole country has been whipped by icy winds, we have shivered under grey skies and the spring so longed for refuses to show even the slightest indication of its eventual approach. Oh to be in England! Well, the first of April was a bugger. It mattered to us, that little egocentric cluster, working on the *Clear Day* film, as all the Promenade costumes were to be seen in a blazing sun outside the Pavilion. Well, there was no sun, instead rain. Yet the weather report said there would be sunny intervals, and so all those wretched women in muslin dresses have to remain freezing outside on the muddied turf. How cruel of the elements and how cruel that these people (including the aged) should suffer so. And yet the patience of the producer was remembered, for at the cost of many a double pneumonia case they did get the necessary "shot" by the end of the day. My costumes, which were a travesty of the sketches, looked alive and justified themselves once the sun appeared. The white with the bright splashes of colour should be very effective, in spite of the bad taste of the art department. One shot of the carriage arriving at the Pavilion should be extremely effective.

The day had personal dramas. Suddenly, in among this make-believe, a drunken workman appeared lurching in our midst and tried to borrow a light from Minnelli. The drunk had a dried, bloody nose, was harmless but scarifying and was marched off quickly by a friendly bobby. Petchnikov attacked me that Felix had gone off to London to hire a hulk of Georgian silver for the banquet without his permission as to the expense involved and I had my usual trouble with the hairdressers. John Richardson's[1] peroxided locks still far from the desired result and when I made the woman responsible for their care fetch a bottle of oil, she was furious. When I suggested "opening up" his forehead she brought an irate little turkey cock of a man who came up and abused me. "I am the designer and it is my job to see that ideas are carried out." "I don't care who the shit you are." This in front of a crowd of extras. When I said "Well, we'll bring in the producer and director on this" the little jerk said, "Oh, you're going to tell tales, are you?"

He was called to the bigwigs and it seems he apologised, but not to me. Koch told him with typical Hollywood hypocrisy, "We're all together in this just trying to make a good picture and that's all that counts!" One of the more elderly well brought-up extras came up to me and said he thought I had

[1] John Richardson (b. 1936), British leading man, who invariably played in fancy dress.

comported myself so well that he was proud of England. This was indeed a shock.

The day's shooting ended unsatisfactorily and in typical fashion. Having waited so painfully for the sun to come out, we were given a half-hour burst in the late afternoon. The cameraman now said he did not want sun and waited for the clouds to come up. When they did, the rain started, Barbra's dress and umbrella got spattered and we all had to run for cover.

2 APRIL 1969

The plans are changed every ten minutes. It was essential, they said, to shoot the banquet set today. They had spent so much money on the food, enormous pieces, *montées* of lobster, salmon, chicken, suckling pigs etc. But on arrival at the Pavilion I discovered Barbra in her blue and white Promenade dress doing a close-up that could have been done in Hollywood. Then she was to shoot the Récamier dress dancing in the twilight.

Fed up with the waiting, I had my first whiff of the Brighton front as Felix and I went into the town for some gas globes for the dining-room scene. The charm of Brighton and The Lanes has entirely gone. Very sad.

Messengers were out looking for me. "At last," shouted Hopkins.[1] "Well, I've been kept waiting times enough by Barbra," I said rather pettishly. She was dressed in the "new" version of the ball dress and now turbanned headdress, which thank God she likes. She looked very exotic and quite strangely beautiful, and the relief that this dress was a success took a great load off my shoulders. For the moment this is the last dress of the project.

Afternoon's activities divided taking photographs of the extras in their golden banquet dresses, helping Felix with the silver for the table, adding coloured flowers, doing a drawing of Barbra, keeping an eye on the hair. Felix, very friendly with the actors of the Pavilion, shocked by the ignorance of the director and his crew, kept repeating himself. Vincente kept reading out of the *New Yorker* a bit about the elaborate meals of Prinny. Naiveté to the point of infantilism. But I take it for granted. I expect it. I only wished I were being paid

[1] Hopkins, another of the production team.

for my time, like all the others under weekly and daily contracts, but I suppose it is part of my job to be around when the "box office attention" changes her mind about a costume.

Tom Parr's flat is a haven and I thank my stars I have not had to go back to some dreary hotel bedroom. I spend my evenings quietly here trying to recoup forces but my brain is stilted in this igloo of unreality. I do not feel I am able to concentrate on any intellectual exercise. I can write a little, though not read. I therefore enjoyed the treat of having Cyril and Deirdre Connolly come here for dinner.

Cyril is extremely well informed about government and politics. This I did not know. His great brain encompasses everything. He discussed Walter Monckton and I vilified Lord Chandos[1] (mainly for his repulsive appearance). Cyril is all the while looking for slights. (He is guilty at not having seen his neighbour Cuthbert Worsley whom he considers so distinguished.) He is inquisitive to the extent that he cannot help looking at one's telephone number jottings by the bedside. He is greedy but now eats very little and drinks not at all. He was funny about school ties and said I should wear my Leander tie and he would wear his Neanderthal.

A civilised evening in great contrast to the milieu in which at the moment I earn my living.

THURSDAY, 3 APRIL 1969

The unreal days pass without the usual knowledge that one is in the world at a certain place at a certain time. I'm in limbo and when Felix said he had been four days here and would be quitting with £200 in his pocket I could not believe how quickly the week has passed while we move from one "problem" to another delay. Today was an almost complete waste; Barbra in her new banquet dress was very pleased with her appearance and the diamond she had

[1] Walter Monckton (1891–1965), first Viscount Monckton of Brenchley, and Oliver, first Viscount Chandos (1893–1972), both Conservative politicians.

elected to wear in her nose. But camera crew, props, electricians, to say nothing of producer and director, were all baffled and dismayed. The diamond, sadly, had to go.

I admire B. S. for being audacious in these little ways. She likes anything eccentric and making her more of a character. On her arrival at the banquet she then started to challenge the lighting. She knew it was not right for her (Stradling[1] has been at the game 50 years!) and marched up to the camera and across the room, judged its effect while Vincent had to sit as her "stand in." No one knows more about the technique of looking the way she wishes than she does. The left side of nose is bigger than the right, both eyes must show in three-quarter view etc. etc. The company had been sitting for the shot for two hours and were amused by the way she concentrated only on herself. It was interesting to see how, once resigned to the lighting, she then got into the mood for her close-up in which she is determined to seduce the beautiful and rich young John Richardson. By the time she had been looking lovingly, lustingly at him her eyes, which had been those of a basilisk while regarding her reflection in her triple mirrors, now had become swimming pools of love and romance.

Her brain is as clear as crystal, her intelligence such that she is not afraid to trust her own judgement entirely, but somehow I feel she will overstep the mark and become so rigid in the way she is presented that the public will become quickly tired of her, the photographer Larry[2] told quite hair-raising stories of how she gave him hell, destroying such a large quantity of good pictures and limiting him in his approach. In revenge he says she will age very quickly, that once these Jewish types have two children they become thick and shapeless. Already, looking at my first photographic proofs, I see that her basic forms and poses are those of a typically Jewish momma.

The banquet scene was at first amusing to watch. In spite of Felix's advice, Vincente continued to perpetuate some "howlers." The Prince Regent had to battle his way past footmen to get to his chair. The first course, instead

[1] Harry Stradling (1907–70), British-born cinematographer, who worked in America and who had worked on *My Fair Lady* among many other films.

[2] Larry Schiller, West Coast photographer who worked for *Life* magazine.

of soup, was a piled plate of lobster, with everything prearranged on it. No question of having salads, sauces in tureens. The display of food was enough to make the juices run of those sitting at the table so that when Vincente shouted "Eat up. Devour everything in sight. Shove it all in. You're gourmets," the extras were delighted to comply. When the take was over the head prop man in the brown cap rushed forward and shouted, "Don't eat any more!" The lobster plate was then taken away for another "take."

After a bit I got tired of the scene and walked with Felix in The Lanes but the Brighton Lanes are now filled with boutiques instead of ye old curiosity shops. The charm has gone. Lunch with Cuthbert Worsley and his friend Johnnie (Luscombe) was a delightful diversion, C. saying how LSD taken under the supervision of a doctor had unlocked a barrier that prevented his writing, that if only the Frenchaus?? had used drugs he would not have been frustrated and guilty of so many unnecessary things (including the drowning of his brother[1] and homosexuality). C. is one of the kindest men. I feel so very critical and ungenerous about people, and found that I dislike so many people whom he loves and admires. He only dislikes Dadie Rylands[2] who, it seems, has always been beastly to C. without his knowing the reason!

During the afternoon, with no possibilities of photographing B. S., I found time hanging very heavily and I wondered if I could remain "hanging about" much longer. I became very depressed and weary when I heard that the schedule had been changed and that my proposed escape after the shot taken here in Lewes Crescent had been postponed till another week. Have been here five days and it seems already a life sentence. Since I am not contracted to be here I may take the law into my own hands and scram back to my own life only one hour's train journey away.

Too tired to go out at night and in an attempt to escape the film world I rewrote early Tangiers diaries for Vol. IV. But I felt I had been struck with a *coup de vieux* and it was as a man of my years that I conversed with Ray, moved about the room and eventually took myself to my solitary bed.

[1] Worsley's brother, Bengy, floundered in the water with him. He pushed him away and swam to safety, while Bengy drowned. Many nightmares followed.

[2] George Rylands (1902–99), fellow of King's College, Cambridge.

Full of energy but nowhere to spend it, B. S. was being photographed in close-up all morning long. The banquet table around her somewhat depleted, as the guests of yesterday had either eaten too much lobster, or it had gone off, or, as some said, had been covered with preservatives. The result in theatrical lodging houses a night of meal vomiting.

The photographic climax came with B. after lunch but she seemed a bit tired, though delighted when she saw the results of former work. She liked the amateur hit-and-miss element, though I was distressed that my assistant had given me so many wrong exposures. Koch and Minnelli to lunch at the flat. They seem utterly soulless, Vincente the more human. He tried to make an effort while conversation very sticky with H. K. But Vincente will never come clean. He is so discreet he will never commit himself about former "stars" he's worked with, or ever say anything about his life or stories.

Koch looked embarrassed when I said I blamed the entourage for building B. S. into such a monster, that I was at first scared stiff and even now, after an interval, approached her room for a long wait outside her door with alarm. Yet I found her extremely nice and easy once one realised the meticulousness of her approach and detail. "Oh, we love her," they said. "She's easy to work with, a bit late admittedly, not on the button. She's very unsure of herself. But can you imagine her rise in the world? She used to be a waitress in a Chinese restaurant and then an usherette in the cinema. Now she has her own companies and she's just started. She's going to be responsible for her own pictures in future. She's got real talent. She's extraordinary and she knows it. She is so quick to learn. During this picture she's picked up a lot of French from Yves Montand, and her ear is so acute she can hear every separate instrument in an orchestra, so it upsets her if she hears a flute is playing out of tune."

Her hearing is so remarkable that they took her off to an ear specialist who said her hearing was inhuman, that she could hear things that only a dog could hear.

EASTER SUNDAY, 6 APRIL 1969

Brilliant Brighton sunshine brightened the spirit of all holidaymakers sick of a long grey English winter. At the Pavilion, to which I went late, they were doing a small scene, B. dancing with Y. M., so there was no need for me to hang around. Ticked off a silly girl for being photographed in full black eye make-up with false lashes (against rules). Then played hookey for the rest of the day, going to North Street markets, buying odd junk and relishing the cold, windy, but springlike sun. After quiet lunch sunned myself, like thousands of others all along the front, on my balcony. Then read of Brighton in Thackeray, slept in sun, then on my bed, worked on play, and went to Hassocks for perfect evening with the Alan Rosses,[1] most friendly, highly civilised evening of quiet talk, discussing the quality of charm and why it is not enjoyed by the younger generation, though it seems the 17-year-olds now feel a want to return to manners.

Adrian Daintrey,[2] extremely witty and pithy, and Alan, tense and rather hard on nice clever Jennifer, his wife, extremely intelligent summing up of various personalities, from the neighbours, Worsley, Connolly, etc. to Dr. Gottfried, whom he considers a terrifying menace, never diagnosing people's illnesses but boosting them up with rays and injections. It seems Harold Acton[3] has written a libellous short story about his treatment of them. Alan drove me from their well-sheltered dip in the Downs on to the high winding Ditchling beacon where the wind was blowing a tornado, the lights of Brighton in distance real magic instead of the much vaster panorama of commercial Los Angeles. The scale right here, and that goes for the Rosses' life, family, pretty house and garden. One could not wish for more.

Dr. Gottfried illustrating professionals' absorbed attitude to their job, told of the gynaecologist who was revisited after a long interval by one of his clients. "Don't you remember me, Doctor?" the lady asked. The doctor had to confess that he did not recognise her face. "However, let's see what the situation is. Will you please lie down and open your legs." Bringing his glasses to

[1] Alan Ross (1922–2001), editor of the *London Magazine* and his then wife, Jennifer Fry (formerly married to Robert Heber-Percy).

[2] Adrian Daintrey (1902–88), painter.

[3] Sir Harold Acton (1904–94), Florence-based aesthete and writer.

play on her ovaries, he exclaimed, "Oh yes, of course, it's Mrs. Wildbaum. Pleased to see you again."

The Easter crowds should have afforded me an opportunity to take a number of Cartier-Bresson pictures. But it is not as easy as it seems to take a Bresson picture. I took a number of people asleep in the sun, the ridiculous, courageous Salvation Army, but nothing extraordinary will result. But the break from the Pavilion was salutary and the sun quite marvellous. Unfortunately the east wind was cutting.

The film was delayed by Barbra being, as her publicity man explained, "diarrh-attic." She was rolling on her bed with stomach pains, having been to a kosher restaurant with Koch, and then in secret going on a "date" with the new James Bond (Lazenby,[1] formerly a milkman) clad in leather jacket and gold cap on the back of his bicycle. When, at last, she dragged herself to the studio she had to perform in the kitchen, which was decorated for the occasion with great sides of beef, geese, chicken, pies, fish, sugar cakes and every sort of giant banquet food, not the most congenial atmosphere for someone with a weak stomach. The smell of the food, now becoming a little "high," had to be sweetened by atomic sprays.

Larry Schiller, the photographer, came to lunch (in B.'s absence) and gave me a mouthful of information, how he made half a million dollars selling nude pictures of Marilyn Monroe, how he gets paid by Paramount a vast sum to be with this picture, by knowing that he will place pictures in magazines not open to them. He made me feel such an amateur and such a poor relation. He is a real operator. Ray, serving, said he was a nervous wreck or a compulsive eater. He is enormous for a young man of 22. He told me Peter Lawford was responsible for the death of Marilyn Monroe who had spent her last night with Jack Kennedy.[2] He told me he had taken 18,000 "passed" pictures of B. S. on this picture and so many "killed." He has a quick eye and knows exactly how much of this picture is going to be cut, but shot just to please Minnelli or Streisand.

An untidy afternoon at the Pavilion photographing extra girls, then

[1] George Lazenby (b. 1939), formerly seen in TV commercials, the most wooden of the various James Bonds. He only appeared in *On Her Majesty's Secret Service* (1969).

[2] Marilyn Monroe died of an overdose on 5 August 1962, aged 36. Peter Lawford (1923–84) and President John F. Kennedy (1917–63) have been implicated in many a conspiracy theory.

coming home deadbeat to relax, too tired to write or read, so slumped into an armchair and listened to a gramophone record. Kenneth Clark on Rome on a neighbour's colour TV, then a gossip dinner here with Tom's friends, and much information about the Beatles' Epstein's[1] suicide, his dangerous life and his never telling the Beatles of his queer life, the Beatles pathetic and wan, to be pitied in spite of their fortune and Rolls-Royce motor cars.

EASTER MONDAY, 7 APRIL 1969

Another day of waste. At the Pavilion they were doing the ball sequence. B. S. meeting the Prince Regent, B. S. meeting her rich lover. It was all in "mime" but for a few execrable words of dizzy dialogue. Whenever I could suggest a more elegant substitute the answer would be put that the American public would not understand it. The sequence continued all day and I felt little solace in the fact that B. S. changed her clothes for me to put on her purple street dress, for I discovered that this, the best costume of all, is not to be seen full length in the film, only through a coach window. It was the dress that gave the least trouble and turned out the best. It is really very smashing.

The "outside" world in the form of the Alan Rosses came to peek and peer. They enjoyed the glimpse though soon tired and were off for a walk on the front, the holiday crowds given the blessing of yet another day in the sun. There were incidents, a black leather–coated motorcyclist lying on a greensward, surrounded by police and gapers, ambulances rushing noisily "into picture," a policeman poking his finger in the mouth to see the damage. A road accident or a punch-up? On the beach a man had knifed a woman and daughter. But in general the crowds were controlled, and a word of thanks to the Brightonians who, after London, have such good manners. They are really willing to help and so make any enquiry at desk or telephone an exchange of politesse rather than of angry words.

Probably am able to quit tomorrow. The second ballroom will have seen me out as far as new costumes go, and it is really not worthwhile my hanging around in case B. S. has another ten minutes to spare for photographs.

[1] Brian Epstein (1934–67), the Beatles' manager. He committed suicide on 27 August 1967.

Incidentally, the photographer, Schiller, every now and then writes out a questionnaire for her to answer. His latest included "What do you think of C. B.?" In answer she wrote, "A beautiful man, a beautiful talent."

Have enjoyed many free evenings and seeing delightful people a thousand miles away from the Pavilion, and if I haven't enjoyed the technique of film making any more than usual, it has been a job of work done to pay something towards the taxman.

Evening with Cuthbert Worsley and Johnnie Luscombe. C. reminded me of Aldous H. [Huxley] and has the same way of making difficult thoughts sound simple. He is also very appreciative and laughed when I said Peter B. [Brook] was an international monkey, able to speak eight languages and flying from one capital to pick up the latest Prague theatre tricks, or to Romania for a production to copy. In fact, it was a help that he had been born in four different countries.

He also liked, "the Alan Rosses create such a sympathetic atmosphere in their house that they even made 'Auntie Nose' [Violet] Wyndham seem attractive."[1] An exchange of opinions on plays, films, and exhibitions which Cuthbert sees for the doomed BBC *Critics.*[2]

It worries me a lot that it is now four months since Kin wrote to me.

SYBIL CHOLMONDELEY[3]

I arranged to take the recently widowed Sybil Cholmondeley to the première of *Oh What a Lovely War.*[4] "We'll just have a sandwich at my house before curtain up," she said. There are few people who still manage to have the aura of pre-1914 luxury about them. Sybil, during winter, is likely to wear a tuberose

[1] Violet Leverson (d. 1979), author, widow of Hon. Guy Wyndham.

[2] *The Critics,* a weekly programme on the Home Service (Radio 4).

[3] Sybil Sassoon (1894–1989), married fifth Marquess of Cholmondeley (1883–1968), Lord Great Chamberlain. She brought her exotic Baghdad inheritance and considerable wealth to the Cholmondeley family.

[4] *Oh What a Lovely War* (1969), First World War musical satire originally created by Joan Littlewood at the Theatre Royal, Stratford East, with an all-star cast, directed by Richard Attenborough.

pinned by a pearl and diamond brooch to her dress. Tonight she provided a marvellous half-bottle of champagne and smoked salmon sandwiches, and fresh from Norfolk, her keepers had sent three plover's eggs. "Now, you must do what my brother Philip[1] taught me to do with them. You must redistribute the yolk. Now, my hand is quite down. You open the palm flat, place the egg with its flat base in the centre. Now be very brave! Bring the other hand down on it very suddenly and hard. Slap. Like that!" The egg suddenly became a poached egg, flat with the yolk seen through a film of the white jelly, white-bordered. One then ate the egg as a sort of a plover's egg sandwich.

I felt I had had a glimpse of another world, the world I had yearned for as a child. Of the evening, only the film was a disappointment.

Bond's play, *Saved,*[2] caused a furore when it was first shown only a short time ago. Already it has become a classic. I must say its outspokenness, frankness and brutality shocked me. But the shock was legitimate and not for shocking's sake. I find the play a real development in the art of playwriting, subtle and brash at the same time. A young man living with a girl in her parents' house is superseded by another man whom he hears fucking his ex-girl downstairs. He shouts, "Are you trying for the Cup?" The mother sympathises with the rejected young man. "But how do you manage?" she asks. The most terrific shock came at the end of one scene after the mother had inadvertently sexually excited the boy, then scorned him in disgust, and the young man gets out a dirty old handkerchief and starts to unbutton his flies.

Later a scene between the resigned but still vindictive husband and this boy was wonderfully subtle, sad, poignant and strange. Very impressive ending to a thoroughly stimulating evening.

POOR SIDNEY'S MEMORIAL SERVICE

Although the main service was at Salisbury Cathedral, the St. James's Piccadilly church was full for a later memorial. Music beautifully chosen and sung

[1] Rt. Hon. Sir Philip Sassoon (1888–1939), politician and collector.

[2] *Saved* by Edward Bond, a controversial, pornographic and pretentious play, was first staged at the Royal Court in November 1965.

by soaring choirs belting out the anthem, and Kenneth Clark reading the lesson, but the same coldness that permeates S.'s and Mary's taste and way of life, was to be felt here.

Strange that this coldness stems so strongly from the Dowager, Auntie Beeswax (sitting indestructible in the front pew), and is sensed in the food (no matter what the chef), the arrangements of the flowers, the chintzes and cretonnes. Even after death it was present here today, taking predominance over sorrow.

I dare say I was slightly put off before the service started by seeing so many would-be smart people using Fortnum and Mason's as a rendezvous for the sad occasion.

(After a lot of deliberation as to what to give Tom Parr for the loan of his Brighton flat, I thought a croute of pâté would be the thing. I discovered that croutes are only ordered at Christmas and that the last had just gone to Badminton for the Royal weekend—snobs please note!)

Among the pickled fruits, Pat Laycock[1] and Sachie Sitwell were gossiping about personalities. Oh no! We really can't have name-dropping here. When Sachie started worrying about Georgia being late, I hurried off to the church where a great number of young men relatives were helping the congregation to their seats. Harry Hambleden[2] placed me too high among the relations, while he himself sat in a seat alongside, in the empty pews at the far right.

Suddenly, as the service started, an old beggar came in with hearing aid, tousled white hair and a buttonhole of forsythia, and carrying a violin in a case. He is an eccentric who comes to church whenever there is a funeral or a memorial, perhaps even a wedding. Among the carefully arranged and extremely self-sufficient congregation he introduced a note of madness that gave great artificiality to the proceedings. Harry H. and the other stewards looked very embarrassed but had the grace to smile and welcome him. The old man fidgeting with *The Times,* and the violin, was a great source of interest to the stiff-upper-lipped relations and I was thankful to the old man for creating

[1] Patricia Richards, married (1932) ninth Earl of Jersey. Divorced 1937. She later married Robert Wilson, and then Peter Laycock.

[2] Fourth Viscount Hambleden (b. 1930), nephew of Lord Pembroke.

a note of drama into something which should have been a tragic occasion, but in fact lacked all deep emotion.

BETTY SOMERSET

Betty Somerset, such a character. "I'm giving you a hunting, a sportsman's lunch" (steak & kidney). She hides Betjeman's "bad taste" poem about serviettes and fish knives from her nice, genteel housekeeper. "I couldn't *bear* for her to read it and be worried, and why shouldn't she say 'Pardon' and 'lounge'? I always talk about mantelpiece, and why shouldn't I? It's so vulgar of these people to tell us what is now 'U.' "

She talks about the full moon ripening the corn, and "the seed should only be sown at certain times of the moon."

The pleasant evening was a quiet dinner at home with Eliz. Cavendish,[1] Frank Tait and Patrick Garland. We all got along well and the talk was of a most entertaining quality. Patrick, a new friend, extremely funny as a raconteur and brilliant as a mimic. But the mimicry is not overdone and he does not do set pieces, but tells his tales in the person concerned's voice.

He was full of good stories about *40 Years On*,[2] and how John Gielgud had been so absent-minded that he is often late for cues, missed a whole scene and doing an ad lib, said to the audience what was most in his mind, "Oh I'm dreadfully worried about having to pay all those back taxes."

Another Gielgud story out of context: When they were rehearsing *Oedipus*[3] and the gold phallus was first produced, there was much criticism. Irene Worth said, "It should be on a plinth."

John asked, "Prince Charles or Prince Philip?"

Patrick also talked of the very shielded Carola Oman, the designer. Her worst ejaculations are "Oh Christmas" or "Golly." During the fighting

[1] Lady Elizabeth Cavendish (b. 1925), daughter of tenth Duke of Devonshire. Close friend of John Betjeman.

[2] *40 Years On* by Alan Bennett, starring John Gielgud, Paul Eddington, Alan Bennett and Dorothy Reynolds, opened at the Apollo Theatre on 31 October 1968. It was a school satire.

[3] John Gielgud played Oedipus in *Oedipus* at the National Theatre in 1968.

stages of preparations for *40 Years On*, she heard so much swearing that she asked why everyone said to her, "Oh go and fuck up!"

The conversation was by no means all bawdy. Patrick has a very wide knowledge of poetry, literature and the stage, and his honesty is remarkable for one going through the first stages of success. Talk was also of the remarkable "village" and its "inhabitants," bought by Tony Richardson and the goings on, in which Eliz. stayed as a spectator this weekend, a great deal about juvenile delinquency (Eliz., a magistrate, had today sent a child to a reform school for stealing £2,000), about the Budget. We are all having to pay higher taxes for merely breathing, and in spite of the general gloom, the long dark cold winter taking its toll, ill health, Biafra, Czechoslovakia, and all the horrors of the world today, we sat animatedly rising above everything till one o'clock, which is now a late hour for me.

Cecil's cat, Timothy, fell into a tub of paraffin and weedkiller, and was nursed back to health by the Smallpeices. An unknown octogenarian sent Cecil a request for £5 and Cecil sent this because he imparted the information that his childhood heroine, Lily Elsie, had got her name from being known as "Little Elsie." But Cecil wondered if he still cared about these early figures: "But of late I really had felt that at last the scales had fallen from my eyes and that the old operators would in today's times appear utterly fatuous. For a spell I have turned my mind from the nostalgia that has played such a part in my later years. There was so much to pay attention to that was of tomorrow."

FRANCIS ROSE

Francis Rose, apparently quite sane again, brought his other benefactor, George Melhuish, to lunch. Francis has now sold four pictures for £1,500. So his financial situation, according to Sam Blott who doled out the fivers when F. was under restraint, is apparently saved. Francis's sudden change of attitude is remarkable. He is dictatorial and patronising. He opened a letter from a friend who enclosed £5, and Francis sniggered. He would have been only too glad of this two weeks ago, when he was down to his last 7s.6d.

Melhuish, a cold fish, and likely to share a flat with Francis only if it suits himself, looked slightly embarrassed when Francis indulged in his schizophrenic grandeur talks of having, as a result of some Russian art theft, met de Gaulle, Malraux, etc. in Paris recently, but otherwise seems to enjoy Francis's company.

When F. went out of the room M. confided he was very worried, for Francis had told him if he didn't get help, he'd take his cat, Pussy Balou and jump into the river.

I became only a little exasperated by him for one cannot get what my father used to call a straight answer from him—where his early pictures are stored, who bought the four, why he was searched by the gendarme in Paris. All will continue in mystery.

Just before departing for New York at the beginning of May, Cecil spent a weekend at Reddish, working on Vol. IV of his diaries, the one that would follow the sensitive Garbo volume. Timothy, the cat, who might have died from his encounter with the paraffin, was now well enough to catch a rabbit and make what Cecil called "a banquet" of it.

Cecil caught the train for London and, on arrival, he found the theatre critic Jock Dent[1] *waiting nervously for him, "in case I would object to what he had written about my opinions on Vivien Leigh. He is at the last gasp, having been run over, and now having to give up his reviews."*

Then Cecil flew across the Atlantic, where his National Portrait Gallery exhibition was opening in New York.

NEW YORK 4 MAY 1969

The exhibition is not the anticlimax I feared. The "May Day" opening was very brilliant, and the installation just that much cleaner and sharper than in London. But it shows the difference in atmosphere between the two continents. The emotion one felt looking at a life's work, in London, is missing here. Only a few people sense the nostalgia. The exhibition is geared to a less serious crowd than in London, and so far the press response has been entirely social. But I am not disappointed, because I am not surprised. Things have turned out just a bit better than I expected they would, so I am not worrying, only

[1] Alan "Jock" Dent (1905–78) was about to publish *Vivien Leigh: A Bouquet.*

longing to get back to do the things I feel I must do for my greater inner satisfaction, the *Gainsborough* play foremost on the agenda.[1]

NEW YORK VISIT IN RETROSPECT

The inconvenience of travel in the past was a somewhat long drawn-out affair that could easily be borne. There were not the appalling moments of panic, despair and physical discomfort that we put up with today. These thoughts inspired by the sight of John Richardson,[2] whom I gave a lift to in my taxi from the airport in New York (where, of course, taxis are rare). He could not be dropped near his apartment as naturally the road was up. He had broken his wrist and so had difficulty in getting out of the cab with his luggage. In the pouring rain he stood surrounded by luggage helpless, aidless. He staggered across greasy planks and coats falling off his arms, trying to get over the potholes, to ring the bell of his naturally servantless apartment. Meanwhile would someone make off with his luggage standing in the street? This all at the end of a long, harrowing flight of delays, frustration; in fact, the usual inconvenience endured during the Atlantic flight.

But in any case New York life is "tough." You can expect no redress. Robbery, beatings-up, fines, interest, insurance, landlords cutting off gas, defying the mayor, the police, the electricians, by not turning up at the appointed time. People behaving so bloodily to one another and taking it for granted.

But this is not the theme of my visit, which happily is a highly pleasant one, of contentment. During my last visits to the US I have been battling ill health and making a terrific effort to get through the work on hand in the allotted space of time. This time I felt extremely well (perhaps the sanatorium visit helped) and I had never before been in NY at this pretty time of year. In the past I had left just before the dogwood and the soft-shell crabs. Here was the park, a mass of blossom and fresh budding trees, magnolias by the hundreds with wonderful strong silver branches and trunks, all so healthy in comparison to our frosted varieties at home. The climate, after our cold, was

[1] Whenever things were going well, Cecil returned to the long drawn-out drama of his play.

[2] John Richardson, the art critic and writer, rather than the film star mentioned earlier.

summer hot. Almost too exhausting to enjoy walking but the park life was terrific with horsemanship rampant and the happy people in groups playing a guitar or a flute (60,000 people listened to an open-air *Hair*).

I arrived for my exhibition, so the first thing to do was to find out from José of things going well at the museum. He complained of the director but thought things would please me. When I went round next morning they did, everything very spruce and immaculate. Now I must get busy taking more pictures to give a "Stop Press" feeling of New York now. I enjoyed this as the responsibility was entirely my own, no question of pleasing *Vogue* or the sitter, and the sitters were delightful, young Charles Ryskamp, who is to be the new Director of the Morgan Library; McNeil Lowry,[1] who quietly doles out untold millions to the arts from the Ford Foundation. He looks like a Cranach and is to be found in this wonderful Kevin Roche building. Lincoln Kirstein, whom I photographed with his sister, Mina,[2] had made a list of suggested people and they were all interesting in their various ways; Peter Mennin[3] of the Juilliard School, whom Charles Biasiny, my assistant, said looked like an extra in a Hollywood film. David Hockney and his painting of Geldzahler;[4] Anthony Dowell discreetly become even more of a star to rival Nureyev in the Covent Garden Ballet and, most curious and indescribable, the haunted world presided over by the zombie, more dead than alive since he was shot, of Andy Warhol. At first the mercurial groups of strange people, sitting around in silence and moving pointlessly around his huge factory, were difficult to capture. But eventually I felt I had a valuable addition to the exhibition. In fact, I had and I was pleased with the last-minute additions.

Then the exhibition chores, interviews, TV etc. took time and when the tiring "openings" were over I was busy with plans for making money in the future, seeing "Heritage" furniture people from Carolina, a loathsome Freedman about Raffles, merchandise and DuPonts. Perhaps none of these projects will materialise but I suddenly realise it would be wiser for me, instead of

[1] Charles Ryskamp (b. 1928) and W. McNeil Lowry (1913–93), first Director of the Ford Foundation's programme in the arts and humanities from 1957 to 1975.

[2] Mina Curtiss (1896–1985), author of a study of the world of Proust and latter-day survivors, *Other People's Letters* (1978).

[3] Peter Mennin (1923–83), composer, president of the Juilliard School, 1962–83.

[4] Henry Geldzahler (1935–94), creator of the Department of Twentieth Century Art at the Metropolitan Museum. He died of AIDS.

working piecemeal, to try to tap the vast millions in the US. Each day was more crammed than one could believe it possible with dates and strangely enough they seemed to work out well, even managing to keep my "cool" with Alan and the long drawn-out explosion about *Coco.*

Katharine Hepburn brought an element of freshness and honesty to the proceedings, and I was incapable of comparing Barbra Streisand so unfortunately with this woman who doesn't give a damn what she looks like and, poor thing, her face was bandaged and blotched with the recent operation for skin cancers. Here was a New England spinster using rough language and looking like something out of a 1910 schoolgirl story asserting herself with utter and complete honesty and integrity. Everything she said was the pure truth, she could not but be on the level, forthright, down to earth, evading all complications. In comparison, Barbra is devious, cunning, defective, Katharine so distinguished, such a lady.

Barbra behaved in her usual way, only worse, when I arranged to photograph her in the two Old Bailey costumes sent from Hollywood. She asked that I resubmit to her the pictures she had already OK'ed. She wondered if after all it was a good idea to let *Vogue* publish all her costumes. She kept Bibi, a *Vogue* editor, waiting two and a half hours in the lobby. I went to a Jewish party given in her birthday honour and Barbra spent her time going through my prints to OK. A more shrewd critic there has never been, a banquet scene showed the huge Pavilion chandeliers and a wonderful decor. "No, I look awful." She killed the picture although only appearing the size of a postage stamp.

No, Kate is great. I just wish *Coco* were too. I feel the whole thing is doomed and I don't want to spend more time on it.

Meanwhile Sam Green at his nicest, better than I have ever known him. He was at my side during the last day's rush and panic. He got me in exchange for photographs, a Warhol silk screen of M. Monroe. He gave me advice when in desperation I could get no reply to my attempts to call Kin and wondered if I should precipitate a crisis by sending him a wire.

The last hour of my visit was extremely sad. I came back to telephone to San Francisco after almost six months of non-writing. Every ten minutes I tried again. I was very, very sad—I went to the airport intending as per Sam's suggestion to send him a tape recorder, but for several reasons I decided against this. I drank a cup of coffee with brandy in it and then went once more to the telephone to try the San Francisco number.

Miraculously, Kin answered. He seemed cheerful but I was very serious. I told him in no uncertain terms how unhappy his inability to write had made me. I had never nagged or complained in our relationship but how could I write and tell him of suicides and births and everyday unhappiness if I got no comeback. He sighed deeply. He knew it had been a long time. He sighed again and said he supposed he would have to write. He made a friendly remark about my having called him. He did not seem to have changed in his attitude and I was deeply relieved. Deeply satisfied that I had been vouchsafed this last minute of parting to talk. "How long have you been in New York?" he asked and when I told him two weeks, he seemed a little shattered for he knew that if he had not created a situation, I would have called him on arrival.

As it was I was deeply relieved to find that my visit had not ended in a vacuum and by now the flight number had been called and I had to hurry to join the others on the horrible night flight back to London. I was so emotionally exhausted and so fatigued in limb that I could not take in for some time the fact that I had talked to Kin. I only knew the "blank" had been partially filled. It was not entirely satisfactory but I was going back now in the hope that I would receive a letter and that something that was really of the utmost importance in my life was not at an end.

NOT TO BE FORGOTTEN

Cyril Connolly—the classic joke is of his greed (in later years he eats very little). Also Cyril's habit of taking away books from houses he has visited. One angry friend wrote demanding the return of a certain first edition Cyril had borrowed. Cyril returned it. Inside was found, as a book-marker, an old ham sandwich.

Betty Salisbury wrote to her old friend Nancy Lancaster[1] marking the letter "St. Andrew's Day." Nancy replied marking her letter "First Day of the Motor Show."

[1] Elizabeth, Marchioness of Salisbury (1897–1982) and Nancy Lancaster (1897–1994).

K. CLARK

Tonight the last episode of *Civilisation* on TV. This series has prevented my going out on Friday or Sunday evenings. It has been the best programme ever given on TV and the greatest pleasure possible. The most exciting of all was last Sunday's "Fallacies of Hope," with miraculous use of music, but each in its own colour, information or phrasing has been a gem.

It is not to be wondered at that K. has aroused enormous jealousy. He knows too much and he knows he knows more than others. He's offhand, arrogant, unloving and therefore unlovable. He is a cold snake and yet one cannot but be abject in admiration of him. When he is on tricky ground, e.g. a rich man welcoming the revolutions of the underprivileged, one is alert to criticise, but the guarded phrases in which he cloaks his opinions are so exact and clever that one cannot worst him. The text when spoken and printed created very different impressions but the whole work is a remarkable achievement, and one feels how lucky a man he is to have had this opportunity to show to a vast public the fruits of his life work.

MARGOT FONTEYN

Fonteyn is 50. She is admirable, everything that one admires and yet she makes the hackles rise. Her personality is so armour plated. She is so invulnerable and so metallic that one longs to stop that silly giggle. All this makes one feel a cad, for her lot is really a tragic one and cannot but end in tears with her crippled husband eating away all her earnings so that she can never retire, and some of the present criticisms must be wounding.

Americans have no colour sense, or at any rate no understanding of subtleties. The colours you associate with America are the primary ones, red, blue and white. The hideous covers of *Time* (which should be hidden in any room of repute) cleverly strike the discordant, harsh note of conventionalism brought to its zenith.

At Whitsun, David Hockney came to stay, and on another weekend, Diana Cooper stayed.

QUEEN MOTHER OUTING

The lady-in-waiting, Ruth Fermoy,[1] is very musical. She managed to rouse the Queen Mother to take a party to a concert, not in aid of anything, at the Festival Hall to hear four harpsichords being played, accompanied by the strings of the St. Martin-in-the-Fields Orchestra. It was a delight to hear such exquisite and unusual sounds, sometimes the *ping* of the wires managing to make organ sounds that filled the vast hall. The exhilaration of the music, Mozart, Bach, Vivaldi, infecting the players who were obviously enjoying the evening as much as the serious music-loving public.

The Queen [Mother] was received by all the officials of the hall in ceremonial manner and it was agreeable to be part of such a smoothly run procedure, with the cars always available and avoiding any problems of delay or anxiety of traffic blocks. But the evening was nonetheless extremely informal.

The Queen Mother seems remarkably happy in her later years. Tonight she was in fine fettle, making good out of every remark. I arrived the last. "I hope you won't mind this harpsichord concert."

"No, it will be very refreshing" was greeted with gales of laughter, and so throughout. The fellow guests were a young Foreign Office couple, Jenkins,[2] Freddie Ashton a cushion, and Celia Keppel and her now successful, pleased with himself husband, McKenna.[3] Altogether a rather dull gang, which meant the Queen [Mother] had to work hard, and though she had spent the day at some stunt at Hatford, she did work like a trouper. Never a second's pause was allowed. She managed to make these diverse people enjoy an entity.

At supper that entity seemed to be the wife of Mr. Denison, the direc-

[1] Ruth Gill (1908–94), married fourth Lord Fermoy. Woman of the Bedchamber to the Queen Mother from 1960. A keen musician and grandmother of Diana, Princess of Wales.

[2] Sir Michael Jenkins (b. 1936), and his wife Maxine. Later Ambassador to the Netherlands. He accompanied the Queen Mother on her controversial visit to the Loire in 1963.

[3] David McKenna (1911–2003), then chairman of British Transport Advertising and a member of the British Railways Board, married (1934) Lady Cecilia Keppel (1910–2003), daughter of ninth Earl of Albemarle.

tor of the hall,[1] a maypole of a woman who bearded us in the interval and browbeat the Queen Mother into looking at the hall's dreary museum when we were longing for our supper. (The chef must have longed for our return too for the chicken was overcooked.)

The supper was enjoyed, lobster mousse, fried chicken, lots of veg, avocado and salad, and Scotch woodcock (which I couldn't eat). Masses of drink of all sorts and the Queen Mother's bosom acquired what Freddie described as a Dry Martini flush.

After the supper the variety of paintings were admired, the Sutherland portrait[2] quite revoltingly bad in its clever, ruthless, bourgeois debunking way, the Sickerts good and bad, the bad so bad that they ruin the room. We looked at the too copious Windsor Castles by Piper[3] (when he saw the inky skies, the King is supposed to have said, "How unfortunate you were with the weather!").

The evening was over. The highlights had been driving in the Rolls with the Queen Mother and seeing tough American gangsters do a double take as they recognised the Queen Mother as the car careered off at a tangent, the arrival at the box and the backstage jokes (with Eileen Joyce, Princess Alice etc.)[4] but the reality of the evening came when I went back to Freddie's little doll's house and discussed the Queen Mother.

With the Queen Mother we were all very much "on tolerance," but must never come too close. For myself I was surprised how well she talked politics with the bore McKenna, and most surprisingly said she was for the Trades Unions and thought them jolly clever fellows. I think Freddie and I really came alive when I, drinking a glass of milk, and he, smoking endlessly, discussed Alice Delysia, the old revue star of our youth whom Freddie had recently seen as a widow and *bonne petite bourgeoise* at a C. B. Cochran[5] get-together reunion.

[1] John Denison (b. 1911), general manager, Royal Festival Hall 1965–76, and his third wife Audrey Burnaby (d. 1970).

[2] The Queen Mother was painted by Graham Sutherland between 1960 and 1967.

[3] John Piper (1903–92), artist.

[4] Eileen Joyce (1912–91), Australian pianist, famous for changing her frocks between concertos, and HRH Princess Alice, Countess of Athlone (1883–1981).

[5] Sir Charles Cochran (1872–1951), theatrical impresario.

Cecil retreated to Reddish and took Jayne Wrightsman to visit Stourhead just as the rhododendrons and azaleas began to fade.

Although the wonderful honey scent of the azaleas (which sends me back to my first heart-throbs at Harrow school) were as powerful as ever, the mountains of bright cerise rhododendrons had faded, and in the perfect haze of an early morning's ideal summer day, the calm waters and the ever changing, ever beautiful compositions of trees, it was at its most idyllic. Today is the sort of day we wait all winter (and spring) to enjoy. The birds seemed to share our ecstasy. On the water the moorhens took off in dipping euphoria, leaving lines of bubbles in the water as they took to the other element. The swans were appraising their wings.

Charles was at his best, a bit piano as a result of the news that his ex–son-in-law had murdered his second wife before shooting himself and leaving Charles the legacy of two unwanted children, and he was attacked by hay fever.

So altogether the long drawn-out visit was more agreeable than one could have expected, though, as Ray said, after a succession of very rich meals, he felt he couldn't face any more food for many days to come.

A horrible summons to New York shatters the peace of the countryside. I have to make a certain amount of money to go on living in the way I do (two houses, great burden) and alas not enough comes from photography or writing. (I only wish I could live by the latter.) So I have to jump at an opportunity to do a big New York production but as bad luck has it this always happens in the summer so that the garden I've longed for all winter and spring has to be abandoned and my peace of mind upset with all the nonsense of loud theatre talk.

The film Royal Family, *directed by Richard Cawston, was shown on television in July.*

Together with 29 million others Mr. and Mrs. Smallpeice and I watched the *Royal Family* on TV last night. As entertainment it was a breakthrough of a historical kind. The first time the public have seen into the busy and interesting lives of this perfectly delightful family. For the first time we were shown inside each palace, the people who work for the Crown and a lot of interesting shots of the family relaxing at a picnic, trying bull's-eyes and at dinner telling one another amusing anecdotes and how difficult it was not to give way.

The Queen excelled in a story of how one of the courtiers rumoured that the next person she was to receive was in fact a gorilla. When she buzzed the buzzer and the doors opened it was, in fact, a gorilla. Prince Charles said, "If it had happened to me, I'd have *dissolved*!"

The Queen came through as a great character, quite severe, very self-assured, a bit bossy, serious, frowning a bit (and very lined). Her sentences are halting. She hesitates mid-way, you think she has dried up, you prompt her, but she goes on doggedly. She came out on top as the nice person she is. Prince Charles also a tremendous asset and often very touchingly beautiful. The Queen Mother, very badly photographed, came out as a leftover, very sad as she is responsible for so many of the excellent qualities with which her grandchildren are endowed. Princess Margaret mature and vulgar, Snowdon common beyond belief. For me, knowing the backstage a little, it was particularly fascinating, but for the public it was a revelation and one that will do enormous good to the Monarchy.[1] The point being so well taken that the Queen with this tremendous job was herself without power, but was a bulwark against dictators or others usurping power and doing it badly.

Cecil went to Paris to see Chanel and to attend a ball at the British Embassy given by the Soameses.[2] *He returned exhausted. Presently he was back in front of his television set to watch Apollo 11 land on the moon and to see Neil A. Armstrong*[3] *become the first man in history to walk on the surface of the moon.*

REDDISH 21 JULY 1969

Unbelievable thrill of watching, like 600 million others, the television, of man's invasion of the moon. One could not believe that one was actually

[1] This film certainly gave the Monarchy a boost at the time and allowed people to see what the Royal Family were like as people. Some observers cite its making as a mistake, opening the way to a flood of press curiosity and prurience. It is hard to see how they could not have addressed the issue of television at this time.

[2] Christopher Soames (1920–87) was Ambassador to Paris 1968–72. He was married to Mary Churchill (b. 1922), daughter of Sir Winston.

[3] Neil A. Armstrong (b. 1930), astronaut.

watching two men up on that bright crescent that one could see at the end of the garden on this marvellous summer's night. Irene Worth, Eliz. Cavendish and James P.-Hennessy were staying and we sat glued, with pulses throbbing and wondering if there would not be some last-minute unforeseen disaster. The terror continued. How *could* such courage (or were these men bereft of all imagination and anxiety?) . . . The whole thing has been a great American triumph, marvellous beyond dreaming from the scientific point of view, but for once these heroes have used poetic and imaginative phrases; instead of the "Gee, Brother, you should see these colours," Armstrong said, "That's one small step for man, but one giant leap for mankind."

They performed faultlessly their prescribed tasks and even answered becomingly the congratulations of the whole world from President Nixon.[1] Then they left the moon, leaving behind the legacy of an olive branch and medals to the other astronauts who had died in the attempt to reach this fantastic goal.

The household was up at six to watch the touchdown, all but James, suffering terribly from DTs (what a tragedy!) and so vivid was the way that this expedition had eaten into the subconscious that none of us had been able to sleep soundly.

An event that we will never forget but never be able to understand.

All the astronauts look like Kin.

The incredible stretch of rainless heat has gone by while I churn out, like a Japanese on a conveyor belt, the designs for *Coco.* I don't think they are very exciting but then Chanel's work is not theatrical. It is in perfect taste and always has been. I have not enjoyed the job as much as I should, as the background to the whole project is so hysterical and changing. As soon as one has made one gesture of good faith one is rewarded by a slap in the eye of disappointment. At the moment Hepburn is being difficult and wants to look like Hepburn and not Chanel. It is important I make the money.

Two old women heard in Queen Mary's Rose Garden about one another: "What a stupid thing to do! Smelling flowers! She'll still get insects all up her nose. It's her own fault. We'll leave her to it."

[1] Richard M. Nixon (1913–94), President of the United States 1968–74.

BROADCHALKE

Dodo John[1] is dead, a marvellous woman, so responsible for Augustus's taste. He painted anything or everything in front of him. She put the magnolia in the vase, she wore the dirndl skirt and assumed the wonderful natural poses that he painted. She was timid (fey) coquettish, but with innate dignity. Never a pretence or a thought to the reaction of herself on others. Subtle, able to cope with almost any difficulty, she was worn out by the task of looking after Augustus and tending him during his years of deafness.

When he died she managed to enjoy the few years of leisure that were left to her. The anxiety had gone and she retired into herself. She was frustrated at being too old to do the household chores and look after the garden, but she was not lonely for family or friends. Last week she was looking at the astronauts discovering the moon on television. She then went to the dining room where she fell. Her son picked her up. No, she was not shocked or hurt, she insisted on taking herself alone up to bed. Here she slept soundly. The doctor did not wish to wake her and when he called again in the morning he could not have done so for she was dead.[2]

Cecil was disappointed when Patrick Garland rejected the latest rewrite of his play. Cecil knew that he would soon be drawn into the work for the musical, Coco, *which he was designing for Alan Jay Lerner. He wondered where he could go for a quick summer break. He visited the Beaton family graves at Hampstead, which affected him greatly. When he saw his mother's grave, he noted, "This was the resting place of the person most loved by me. An absolute typhoon of tenderness overwhelmed me. I had to gasp for breath, blinded by the gush of tears."*

Soon afterwards he spent a night with Stas and Lee Radziwill at their luxurious home in Henley-on-Thames.

Then Katharine Hepburn arrived in London for her first costume fittings for Coco.

[1] Dorelia "Dodo" McNeill (1881–1969), wife of the artist Augustus John (1878–1961).

[2] According to Michael Holroyd, her son Romilly found her lying on the dining-room floor on the evening of 23 July 1969. She died later in her sleep.

The fittings for Katharine Hepburn's clothes for *Coco* have not been amusing. They have been grim struggles against irritation, the wrong decisions of others and interferences. At each session she is accompanied by her sycophantic entourage who stand around listening to her non-stop yak or make occasional suggestions. These come as the last straw on the camel's poor receding humps. Hepburn has never "worn" women's clothes. For 35 years she has appeared in Dutchman's cap, polo-neck sweater and wide slacks. Hollywood has tucked her out for films in its typical styles, none of which is applicable to the present situation. But on being given anything different in the spirit of Chanel she says, "No, I've never worn anything like this," and once more she stretches for her old Dutch cap, which she wears at an angle far back on her head like a crooked halo. Every time I suggest a waistband or a certain colour she has an alternative suggestion.

We have to try to keep calm but the sessions become a war of nerves, a battle of attrition. Fortunately, she starts to get tired before I am completely "downed." Yesterday's session was a brute. The evening dress which was to be the pièce de résistance turned out a bugger. She looked matronly, misshapen, her huge body capped by a shrunken head. She has huge upper arms, and bosoms and wide hips and when she looked at herself for the 900,000th time, she said, "I dunno why but I must have gotten fat or somethin . . ." A silence was broken by the faithful Phyllis[1] making a breathy noise as if air was expiring from a punctured motor tyre: "No you haven't!" Well, she bloody well has.

At these sessions I have had to evolve a technique to prevent interruptions and harmful suggestions from those who do not know. It becomes very hard to say no a hundred times. If any piece of stuff is lying around, someone is apt to pick it up and ask if this wouldn't be rather useful. "No," therefore the place is void. Don't leave Mr. Locke's embroidery around. If the wrong ones spied it we have a new argument to cope with. Hepburn puts her black polo jumper on her head. It reminds me of Chanel's black satin headdresses. I suggest we might make one just in case but she amends the suggestion. "In grey, like the dress though." This time I do not answer. I lower my eyelids. This is becoming a new trick with me. Perhaps we are both playing tricks with each other.

[1] Phyllis Wilbourn, a few years older than Katharine Hepburn, who had previously worked for Constance Collier. Katharine Hepburn described her as a "totally selfless person," working for a "totally selfish person." She was still doing so when she died in 1995.

I had to do some quick thinking in order to save the situation and my research came in useful. While I was sketching an alternative design, Michael Benthall came out from the fitting room and asked, "What about that printed material we saw?" "No," I shouted without turning round. Luckily he did not continue or fight back.

It is interesting how our relationship has never developed. In New York I was at first impressed by her directness, her honesty and frankness. After Streisand I found her so distinguished, such a lady in the deep sense. I still feel these things but she holds back on me so much (she told James Bailey[1] that she did not feel at ease with me) and since Spencer Tracy[2] has been her man for so many years it is perhaps not surprising that she finds me somewhat different.

I therefore no longer extend the arm of intimacy. I have asked her to the country, but there is no response and we become more and more businesslike and remote, so that I perhaps only see what she shows and this is a very different woman from the one I had expected to find. I see—and this is not surprising—a complete egomaniac. I see a schoolmarm, a Victorian sportswoman or suffragette. I see a woman without a vestige of humour with very little grace.

She arrives at the sittings without a smile for anybody. She dives into the procedures without any opening gambits. No human relationship is indicated even to her "jagger" Benthall[3] who stands twitching nervously in the cramped cabin. I see an extraordinary physical human being, a red-mottled, shiny face bereft of make-up, with wonderful bones and a marvellous, clear, childlike regard in the eyes. I see a raddled face but an extraordinary silky mass of auburn hair, raddled hands like an "old salt" and a strong suburban housewife's body with the agility of a girl. I see someone who is completely uninterested in the events going on around her (she has never even mentioned the moon men) who seems to read nothing, see nothing, someone who is, in fact, a goddamned bore.

[1] James Bailey (1922–81), designer, whose family lived at Lake House, in the Wylie Valley.

[2] Spencer Tracy (1900–67), American film actor whose integrity shone through his work. He and Katharine Hepburn were inseparable for many years.

[3] Michael Benthall (1919–74), stage director on both sides of the Atlantic.

The above, written in exasperation, is slightly too prejudiced. We have now had our last session on the clothes and she is less worried, has come to accept what we have done for her. About her first costume (leopard-trimmed) she said, "This is great, and I thought it was going to be horrid." In fact, I have got everything I wanted. Each dress is the colour I originally chose, but at what a cost! With what arguments! Just before the last fitting she said, "I wonder if this funny little old woman shouldn't just wear one black suit throughout." I had to give her the reasons why this was not a good idea, the part does not develop, has little emotional interest. Every theatrical device will help. The changes of costume will help. She nodded. "I see. You're saying she'd become a damn bore." All those around who had been sweating their guts out for a month were greatly relieved.

I was greatly relieved to see the clothes suddenly come to life. They had movement and when she wore the wig and hat she did become Chanel and at last the dowdy Victorian governess evaporated. At last she started putting on more and more jewels and acquiring a little bravado. "Why are you smiling?" she asked me. I didn't tell her it was with relief. "Well, we haven't quarrelled yet!" she said. "Touch wood," I lamely replied instead of speaking the truth, which would have been, "No, but what an effort it has been to keep my cool." Or, "No, but we haven't become friends. You haven't given me any of your confidences."

I said I'd had a bad time deciding where to go for a week's holiday and when I said it wasn't a particularly good time to go to Ireland she asked, "Why?" Phyllis prompted her, "Because of the riots." When leaving Berman's for the last time, Kate smiled to the various assistants and shook hands, and in the car she asked me for the names of all concerned so she could send them "thank you notes." She then talked about the hurricane that swept her family's house in New England when she was a girl and she was inspired and brilliant, and brought all the characters to life. One could smell the tang of reality and I thought how odd that this person should have become an actress of all things. Yet having become one she is such a real "pro" that she works hard at the important aspects of the job. The car dropped her at Chappell's where she was to have her music (singing) lesson and as I saw her go in the door her face showed complete absorption. Phyllis and I and the fittings are already miles away, and I knew that the experience of the last months had made no impression on her whatsoever. Her attitude towards her awful old clothes just the same, and she knows nothing more about me than she did after I'd taken those photographs of her 40 years ago.

COLITIS

At periods of overstress I am stricken with an additional burden, that I am likely to suffer from nervous colitis. This is a very great handicap, for not only is it exhausting and further reduces one's powers of resilience, but it is a mortifying, horrifying experience to have to keep rushing to the loo. And a question of rushing it sometimes is. Many things bring on this sad state of affairs, overanxiousness, too much pressure against time and more ordinary reasons. One may forget that those raspberries looking so succulent and rare may bring on an attack, or the salad, or the fresh beans and tomatoes. And a cigar seems to ignite a great firework display.

If I am in my own house, it is not so much a disaster if suddenly I have to leave a friend to rush out of the room, but sometimes coming back from a dinner or a dance I am taken short, and this is quite a nightmarish situation. At odd times I have not been able to contain myself until I got home and have had to "let fly" by the garden railings, or once in Paris at the end of a "public" park seat. Coming back from the British Embassy ball in Paris, I walked, in the company of June's son, Christopher Osborn,[1] all the while hanging on to my behind. I cannot think why he did not notice. All this, so far, is more mortifying than serious, but if this complaint should not get better then I will indeed be sorry for myself. In fact, I will have to take the situation seriously in hand and arrange that circumstances will be such that I do not expose myself to these hazards.

Cecil snatched a few days at Glenveagh Castle with Henry McIllhenny, and moved on to "the great contrast" of staying with Derek Hill, sometimes known as "the poor man at Henry's gate." When he left, he saw for himself the first impact of the Irish fighting that had begun that year.

[1] Christopher Osborn, son of Cecil's friend June Hutchinson.

At Bogside the barricades and burnt-out homes, trash of all sorts and barbed wire, seemed merely fatuous and childish, but I suppose during the recent fighting they were of importance. Now the whole mess merely demonstrates the stupidity of the Irish fighting one another with the result that all are poorer even than they were before and life in Ireland today is abysmally meagre. But the Irish love to fight each other. It is their means of getting rid of adrenalin and the present issues are so complicated that they are not likely to be cleared up now, or for a very long time to come. Meanwhile life is always uneasy when the IRA are around and lately their activities have been felt in many sinister ways. Let us hope they will not be vicious enough to resort to their red trucks or destroying beautiful old houses and setting fire to stables without letting out the horses.

We crossed Londonderry Bridge guarded by such very young-looking soldiers with their guns at the ready. It gave me a pang to see them. It reminded one too much of the last war. The day was grey and cold, and the long visit and the cold air front made me very impatient to leave and return to less hilly wide open scenery, back to an easier way of life.

Just before leaving for New York, Cecil enjoyed four and a half days alone at Reddish.

He dreaded "the maelstrom of Broadway."

COCO

Andy Warhol, looking through some art magazines says, "Isn't the art scene today revolting! Oh I wish I could think of a way of making it worse!"

The musical, Coco, *was the inspiration of the producer Frederick Brisson, who persuaded Chanel to surrender him the rights to her life story in June 1954, the year of her comeback as a couturière. Brisson wanted to celebrate the most revolutionary of fashion designers, a woman, or as he put it, the woman who "Chanelised" fashion.*

In his quest, he brought together the top professionals in the theatrical entertainment world. In 1960 he persuaded Alan Jay Lerner to write the libretto

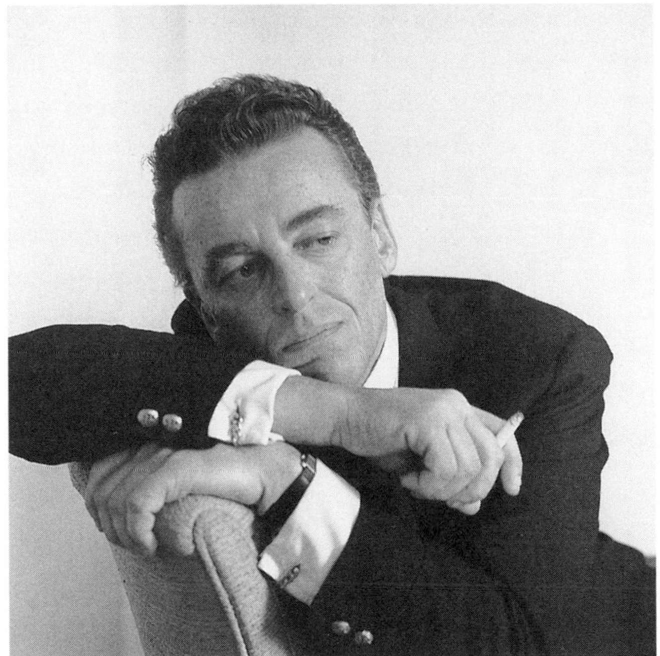

Alan Jay Lerner, brilliant lyricist, who wrote *Coco*

and lyrics. Lerner's many triumphs included My Fair Lady, Camelot *and* Gigi. *A man who can still be widely quoted today, since his songs are so well known, he brought his customary mixture of wry humour and light cynicism to the script. Only a man married six times could have given true feeling to a song such as "Why can't a woman be more like a man?"*

For the music, Brisson engaged André Previn,[1] *to work with Lerner on the score. Since March 1968 Previn had been Principal Conductor and Musical Director of the London Symphony Orchestra. He had collaborated with Lerner on* My Fair Lady, Gigi *and, for the additional songs in the film,* Paint Your Wagon, *which was on the point of being released.*

Cecil had been asked to undertake the sets and costumes from the start. He had already gone through a series of meetings with Chanel and, of course, he too had worked with Alan Jay Lerner in the past.

The Director, Michael Benthall, had previously directed Katharine Hepburn in Broadway productions of The Millionairess *and* As You Like It. *Before*

[1] André Previn (b. 1929), German-born musician working mostly in the United States. In 1970 he married Mia Farrow, but they later divorced.

that he had been artistic director at the Old Vic for nine years. He had also directed Laurence Olivier and Vivien Leigh in their alternating plays, Antony and Cleopatra *and* Caesar and Cleopatra, *in New York in 1952. Unfortunately, he was not entirely at ease in the world of musicals.*

Michael Bennett[1] *was responsible for the musical numbers and the fashion sequences. He had earned three Tony nominations for previous Broadway musicals. He was to prove highly strung and quite confrontational.*

The action of Coco *took place in Paris in the autumn of 1953. Coco herself had been retired for fifteen years and was remembered, if at all, for the scent, Chanel No. 5. She contemplates a reopening, takes on an assistant and hires some models. There is a young girl, Noelle, who represents the curious present and future. Coco muses, "A woman needs independence from men, not equality. In most cases equality is a step down," and later, "The wages of sin don't compare to what you can make in the dress business," all classic Alan Jay Lerner lines.*

The meeting of the old world and the new comes to fruition with the preparation for the opening of the salon, and more cynical asides from the pen of Lerner: "One doesn't get married to escape boredom, one gets divorced." And as the great moment arrives, Coco announces, "Everything is on sale but me."

In Act II, the opening has been a disaster and the news of Coco's crash spreads about Paris. But then four mass merchandisers arrive on the scene and make Coco a fabulous offer. The champagne flows. There is a minor sub-plot involving the love life of Noelle, but the musical ends with Coco solo, triumphant, "Always Mademoiselle."

The cast included only one major star, Katharine Hepburn, who played Coco Chanel. Though best known as a film star in a host of films, from A Bill of Divorcement *to* The Philadelphia Story; The African Queen; Summertime; Suddenly, Last Summer; Long Day's Journey into Night *and, more recently,* Guess Who's Coming to Dinner; The Lion in Winter *and* The Madwoman of Chaillot *(generally deemed a disaster). She had also appeared on Broadway in a number of Shakespeare plays, as well as* The Warrior's Husband, The Lake, Jane Eyre, The Philadelphia Story, Without Love *and, in Australia,* The Millionairess.

 [1] Michael Bennett (d. 1987), choreographer.

Katharine Hepburn (1907–2003) lived to be ninety-six. Her last years were spent in unseen retirement. Her legend was immense. She was one of a very few survivors from the great days of early cinema. She had many admirers and gave many performances that will be known even to the present generation. She retained an air of mystery, not as intense as that of the mercurial Garbo, or the latter-day reclusive Marlene Dietrich. She always had a more wholesome quality. She was a fresh, athletic type of girl, with a winning smile, excellent bone structure. Yet no one really knew the precise nuances of her long friendship with Spencer Tracy, or her friendship with the sharply intelligent producer Irene Selznick.[1]

Cecil had annoyed her with his description of her in his Scrapbook, *as:*

> *Hepburn, with the rocking-horse nostrils and corncrake, cockney voice had become the new heroine in succession to the spangled glamour girl. The type emanated from the sporting-parsonage, freckled, with semaphore gestures and a nasal twang at which all masters of elocution threw up their hands. It was the type to put on an old oilskin and hare off down the drive, in a very battered car, waving and shouting that she would be back in time for the tennis tournament or to feed the chickens. She was tough and boyish, but her main appeal lay in the fact that in spite of the metallic façade, she could easily be reduced to tears.*

Stephen Tennant had mused with Cecil over her "strident voice," opining that to him, "She is that yell, that shriek that is simultaneous with the bell ringing at school, the bell that signifies books clapped together, pencils thrown down, and the rush into the playground for break."

Cecil continued, "She is joyously healthy and undoubtedly eats an apple a day," and he also noted, "Miss Hepburn in a bad mood is dangerous."[2]

Cecil embarked on the adventure of Coco *with optimism, though with certain reservations and misgivings. The opportunity to make money appealed to*

[1] Irene Selznick (1907–90), daughter of Louis B. Mayer, head of MGM, and one-time wife of film producer David O. Selznick. She was a theatrical producer in her own right, notably of Tennessee Williams's play *A Streetcar Named Desire,* and *The Chalk Garden.*

[2] Cecil Beaton, *Cecil Beaton's Scrapbook* (Batsford, 1937), pp. 31–3.

him, but the thought of being stuck in New York for some weeks annoyed him just as when George Cukor had kept him in Hollywood for the making of My Fair Lady.

With Cecil and a big production, there were bound to be problems. His priorities never changed. It was always "Sets and costumes by Cecil Beaton, the play written by the author, starring the actors," in that order. Thus, when his set was criticised, there was bound to be trouble. This would come from Alan Jay Lerner, who thought that Cecil had promised him a cocoa-brown set, whereas he got a beige one. And Cecil also had to cope with the inherent wish of Hepburn to look like Hepburn rather than like Chanel.

Cecil arrived in New York on 5 September, with a headache. He stayed at the St. Regis Hotel. From this day on he kept a daily diary. Though it would have been interesting to reproduce this in full, some passages have been excised for reasons of space. These relate to his mornings in the hotel, telephone calls to Margaret Case, Sunday lunches with Diana Vreeland, other endeavours such as work with Raffles and designing fabrics, which he undertook on the side. There were also daily meetings with Ray Diffen about clothes.

However, certain social engagements have been retained to give a flavour of his existence outside the theatre.

NEW YORK FRIDAY, 5 SEPTEMBER 1969

Arrived in sand-coloured rain, sordid and glimpse of New York as we dropped a Scot in Porto Rican 179 Street district and drove through wet garbage till the St. Regis. Gradual unfolding of *Coco.* Bennett seems to be the "star," baffling me with ideas and making the biggest contribution so far, Benthall still with us, plodding away calmly and having acquired a little more authority.

Fred Hebert,[1] while Fred Brisson is putting his wife[2] on the screen, says the production will cost an arm and a leg. Who cares? But then says, "You've no idea of the interest already; we could 'sell out.' " But we've got to have a show and the work as bad as ever with Alan, very nervous, surrounded

[1] Fred Hebert, associate producer of *Coco,* later a producer and director.

[2] Rosalind Russell (1908–76), film actress.

by good-looking girl sec and ditto chauffeur is only interested in his latest lyric bound in gold and leather case. Not one word re dresses and set. But I am not surprised or disappointed. I only trust I can remain remote from the show.

My assistant Lawrence Reehling[1] turned out to be a most charming blond Apollo in a velvet suit, businesslike, tough, go-ahead, with a deep voice that growls along without much pause. But he seems very nice and I enjoyed his company in spite of splitting ghastly headache. Could it have been caused by antibiotics and aspirin on trip? Anyhow, result was appalling and I had to come back to lie down for two hours. Even then could hardly drag myself back to the theatre but the girls had to be chosen for Berman's[2] to get on with the costumes. It was interesting to see the girls audition, so very much in the US fashion of today with little, brittle legs and no style at all.

By the evening my torture had lifted enough for me to go out with Pat O'Higgins but my patience was strained. Friday night on Manhattan and a gala without means of locomotion, taxi whistles, old blonde beehives waiting outside every awning, every restaurant full. I walked in the muggy tropical heat, arrived to find Patrick bloated, all his looks gone, and he was either drunk or drugged. His dying father in a nearby room made the atmosphere more depressing. I wished I had not let myself in for such an ordeal. But fortunately P. had cleverly managed tickets to the unbelievably successful *Midnight Cowboy* movie and in spite of queues stretching down the St. Germain-des-Prés of New York we got in (though too close) and enjoyed the most entertaining film I've seen in years. It left a great imprint. It is honest and true, terrifically outrageous and shocking. But gosh how good. The fact that the cowboy reminded me a lot of Kin made the evening even more extraordinary for me and I dreamt about it during my fitful night. Hoffman, a superbly talented actor, made a most fantastic accomplice to the beautiful young innocent.[3] One sequence where the cowboy goes to bed with a ghastly made-over old woman on Park Avenue was so entertaining that I would love to go again just to see again the full horror of this sequence in which the woman, instead of paying

[1] Larry Reehling, appointed as Cecil's assistant on *Coco.*

[2] The costumes were made by Ray Diffen and M. Berman Ltd.

[3] *Midnight Cowboy,* directed by John Schlesinger (1969), starred Dustin Hoffman (b. 1937) and Jon Voight (b. 1938).

$20 takes $100 out of the cowboy's wallet. A film that made me feel all my photography efforts were quite beside the point and completely out of date.

SATURDAY, 6 SEPTEMBER 1969

All morning spent with Michael Bennett at his fantastic eerie psychedelic cave of an apartment. Magenta, scarlet, almond green blue spotlights, a favourable and unexpected atmosphere in which to work. If anyone is going to save this show it is M. B. He has worked hard and brilliantly with utterly real and lively conceptions, which have succeeded in getting Lerner out of his morass to make some effective scenes. Plot told in choreographic terms. I did not mind when he asked me to abandon a whole set of costumes because he was right, and they were wrong. The work piles up and so does the expense. But the project at last seems to be an exciting one, such a change from slogging on as I have for years *pretending.* So much time wasted, so much energy gone down the drain and sheaves of notes completely outdated.

NEW YORK

This is the winter season of pornography. *Oh! Calcutta* has given birth to dozens of other rude and louche shows. The movie pages are advertising every sort of sex. Nudity is everywhere. Nothing is left unsaid. It is amazing and wherever does it go from here?

SUNDAY, 7 SEPTEMBER 1969

A peaceful stream of work in my hotel bedroom. Enjoying doing the new designs to replace those that Bennett knew were wrong. By degrees the pressure under which I have been for so long in England (and the nervous colitis too) is subsiding and I begin to feel very much more leisurely in my attitude.

The very late lunch at Diane's (who would love to be a Dame but alas, being an American never can be honoured) gave me an opportunity for a five-hour stretch of uninterrupted work, which is more than I could hope for in my studio at Reddish. The lunch was agreeable, food that tasted of something, Jonathan Lieberson,[1] a bit young in that his enthusiasm carries him too far, so he, with an extraordinary knowledge, is rather apt to say "Aldous Huxley, British, died 1960," "Sandro Botticelli, Florentine painter of the Renaissance." Yet he is delightful, a new find and enthusiasm of Dame Diana and DeeDee Ryan who told me of her marriage coming unstuck, very bad news this.

The first session with Ray Diffen who, contracts permitting, is to make this leg of the clothes. He is sympathetic and professional, and Larry Reehling tactful and efficient. I feel I am lucky in this association. The first "production" meeting on stage concerned me little. Matters of a technical nature (rehearsals, moving in, lighting, etc.) were discussed so that I was able to return to base to carry on my own life and rebound back for the "Bids" session when all the men who build scenery came to look over the latest proposition. They are a tough but necessarily efficient lot, and it amazed me to see them all together being so friendly and amused as they are in cut-throat competition with one another. Mercifully no serious objections were raised and the model, so familiar from the hours spent on it in London with José [Pradera], looked very clean and fresh.

Evening of lukewarm water with Niki Gunzburg.[2] We went at long last to see *The Lion in Winter.* Twice K. H. has asked if I'd seen it and seemed amazed that I had not shown enough interest. Perhaps better if she asks me again I should evade the question, for I loathed the pretentious middle-class

[1] Jonathan Lieberson (1949–89), son of Goddard Lieberson (1911–77), President of Columbia Records, who helped Columbia to make a fortune out of the score of *My Fair Lady* by being sole investor and who signed artists such as Simon and Garfunkel and Bob Dylan. Jonathan's mother was Vera Zorina (1917–2003), the ballerina, who had formerly been married to the choreographer George Balanchine. Jonathan was a precocious young man, lately out of Columbia University who gained a Ph.D. in Philosophy, and went on to be an author, teacher of philosophy and contributing editor to the *New York Review of Books,* for which he wrote numerous articles.

[2] Niki Gunzburg, Baron Nicolas de Gunzburg (1904–81), scion of a wealthy Russian family which made a fortune in the first railroads in Russia, he was well-known in pre-war Paris and spent the remnants of his fortune giving *Le Bal des Valses.* Later he was fur and fashion editor of *Vogue.* A pencil-slim man with morbid interests. He starred in Carl Theodor Dreyer's film, *Vampyr,* in which he also unwisely invested. Invariably clad in funereal black, his imposing demeanour belied an irreverent sense of humour. Calvin Klein claimed him as his greatest mentor.

culture lesson. It is phoney through and through with all the clichés of language in a guise of verbiage. Cliché production of canvas castles, studio lighting, barking hound dogs, flares, heavenly voices and K. H. throughout with Victorian schoolmistress hairdo and false lashes. It is everything I hate and hope the evening will have made me realise that it is only my own stupid fault if ever I go again to see this sort of pretentious rubbish.

TUESDAY, 9 SEPTEMBER 1969

Chorus girls call to decide which should wear what dress. It is fantastic how when a snap decision is made the girl and the dress become an entity, identifiable and unchangeable. The girls very pretty, belegged, some effective beauties but none with distinction. Our decisions crammed into a concentrated two hours with the threat of overtime and union a Damoclean sword. The day a mess—nothing constructive achieved.

To the strange movie *Easy Rider*[1] of infinite appeal to the young. An *original* beautifully acted film, which left me very much bewildered, having missed a great deal, but very impressed that here were a whole new bunch of people with a lot of new things to express.

WEDNESDAY, 10 SEPTEMBER 1969

Lunch with Weissberger[2] who brought the *Coco* contracts to sign (I will wait for the new moon tomorrow) and find him completely lacking in any conventional stimulus. He now no longer likes the theatre. So what else have we in common?

Spent afternoon doing extra designs.

Dinner at the Lafayette with Truman [Capote] the treat of the day. Happily, I find him in good trim, having cleared his head of a lot of social nonsense and having devoted his summer to his book, his arrivals (there is a new

[1] *Easy Rider* (1969), interminable, though undeniably popular, film about two drop-outs crossing America on motorbikes, with Peter Fonda, Dennis Hopper and Jack Nicholson.

[2] Arnold Weissberger, Cecil's American agent.

gold and silver bull pup named Maggie) and to Jack [Dunphy]. He was very alert and on the QT, his brain only becoming less alert as the effect of some very strong drinks began to show. He said he had had to eliminate people from his life in order to devote himself to his work and the 15 people he was fond of. He talked of the new films pandering dishonestly to the shock values of the moment, drugs, homo etc. He seemed to have forgotten the Hollywood influences and [to] have become much more as he used to be, a writer interested in all aspects of life that influence his work.

THURSDAY, 11 SEPTEMBER 1969

This must be the lull before the storm. The telephone remains silent. The others are choosing the cast, flying to California on other business, or merely going to the country for a long weekend. I have scraps, odds and ends of designs to do, but am resting while I may and going to movies. These seem to me to be the only Broadway entertainment that is valid today, all the "shows" so abysmally old-fashioned, witless and vulgar. The *Easy Rider* and *Alice's Restaurant*[1] films have a freshness that appeals to the young, and these are only two of almost a dozen that are worthy to be seen. I found the Andy Warhol *Lonesome Cowboys*[2] extremely fascinating. The spontaneous dialogue and the visual beauty enough to prevent one's being bored.

He has the audacity to show at enormous length a young cowboy washing himself in a bucket of cold water. The long scene with the boy soaking his hands, the back of his neck and underarms, has no significance but its visual impact, and the ripple of the muscles is very beautiful to watch. It was likewise rather beautiful to watch these boys letting off steam by wrestling. It is all very simple but it hasn't been done before with this artist's eye.

He really has made a contribution to films and this seemed to me the most digestible to date. Two films in one day and this would be unimaginable in my busy routine at home.

[1] *Alice's Restaurant* (1969), anti-Vietnam film concerning a folk singer about to be drafted who drops out. Apparently there were a few jokes. It starred Arlo Guthrie.

[2] *Lonesome Cowboys* (1969), a pornographic Western in which Viva plays a rich rancher running into trouble with a local gang of cowboys. It included a gang rape scene. Awarded Film of the Year at the San Francisco Film Festival, it was seized by the police in Atlanta.

During the unrushed day, I put in a visit to the Modern Museum where they were showing photographs of K. Hepburn, where before they showed Garbo. The difference is extraordinary, K. H. never reaching the heights or able to transcend her film material, whereas Garbo's spirit illuminated all the dross. There's no doubt that K. H. has been a great screen personage but, at best, it is all very homespun, small-town stuff, and in certain films it is just plain Hollywood artificiality. Admittedly, it is unfair to judge from a collection of "stills." They are over-retouched, artificially lit and somehow manage to exclude all reality.

FRIDAY, 12 SEPTEMBER 1969

A necessary but time-consuming meeting to discuss the number of clothes needed for the principals in *Coco,* this in an effort to cut down expenses although Fred Hebert said the set and costume department was less than expected, and within bounds, whereas in every other department it was not. But I will not listen any more to these matters which do not concern me.

SATURDAY, 13 SEPTEMBER 1969

I am now down to the last details in creating horrible minor characters. But what a waste of time it is. How much better employed I would be if I were able to get to my studio, to return to where, more than ever, I feel I belong.

It is tiresome that dates can't be arranged that I go home now, but maybe next week we can be very busy, for there is a great deal to be done once the go-ahead signal is given.

SUNDAY, 14 SEPTEMBER 1969

Life continues in my bedroom, working on Vol. IV diary with minor interruptions. The director, Michael Benthall, of *Coco* calling just to feel he is *au courant,* and the co-producer Hebert wanting reassurance that in the absence of Lerner and Brisson he was doing the right thing.

Jonathan Lieberson, met with Diana Vreeland, came to lunch.

J. is a new friend and a great delight. He is 20, incredibly intelligent and wise, and completely unspoilt. He lives in his parents' home and although there are servants, they do nothing for him in the absence of the parents, so he lives off breakfast foods (the equivalent of my childhood's "Force"). He likes it this way for he is of the generation that thinks it demeaning for a human being to look after another, that they should allow themselves to be slaves. For three months he has shut himself away from the world to write papers on Chateaubriand and V. Woolf. These are not for publication, but for his own satisfaction.

Psychology is his main subject, but there is little he is not interested in, particularly literature in all its forms, likewise music, medicine, science, history. He reads, he is desperately interested, but when coming out of his parents' house to discover more about the disease from which V. W. suffered, he made contact with the world again, and he complained of its dangers, the destruction brought about by the poisoners who waste your time for the simple reason they have nothing to do. He is an extremely moral young man, disciplined to the point where he marks down in a book each cigarette he smokes. He drinks little, does not smoke pot and said how sad he thought it was that so many friends wasted Sunday morning by sleeping the entire time.

He is very serious about the mission to express oneself in life. It is the only thing that makes him interested and he likes to work in an un-air-conditioned room so that literally he can feel the sweat of his labours. Without working all day (or reading or listening to music) he feels that he does not deserve the evening. There is a rare purity and freshness about someone born of such sophisticated parents who give him too much choice of richness, knowing too many people of all kinds, but of whom Stravinsky remains the greatest.

I don't understand the cult for celebrities because so often the celebrity has put his "all" in his work and in company can only talk the price of candles. Stravinsky was like this. He could now only interest himself in his work. The fact is that he is dying by degrees, his children hovering like carrions, and he being moved by a clumsy nurse from room to room. "No, don't put me down to sit on my testicles," he cries. I sat upright at a room service table by the window in the sitting room for three hours or more while J. held forth with a marvellous disregard for self-consciousness.

His eyes are like an animal's, they are so unspoilt, so true, he has the perfect means of co-ordinating thought and speech. He looked very beautiful in garish hippy clothes of black satin, flower embroidery waistcoat, organdy striped shirt, orange tie and white duck trousers. His hair is long and biblical, somewhat wiry, fuzzy and formless. He cultivates a four-day growth of beard, which I found merely dirty-looking. He is not nervous or living on his nerves but he has incredible energy.

He talked of his love for Penelope Tree and her situation vis-à-vis Bailey.[1] "Things are so difficult for them that it ties them together like adhesive tape, like spat-out chewing gum on your heel." She is contaminated by the "luxury" world, the demoralising world of modelling, but will now never settle down to educate herself, or make up for her missed years at school.

Without being cynical he is completely apt in his appraisal of a situation and said of Bailey that he was now in the bucket and getting puffier. He talked of the Gores, Stella Astor[2] and others who were supposed to be rebelling against their parents, but in fact were being just like their parents in a different guise. Their revolutionary ambitions only stretching as far as comfort allowed. It was fine to be a gypsy at Glastonbury but they, none of them, did any work. They were all dilettantes, and as such, vicious influences. J. L. has had to give up going to Europe for the summer as he goes like a magnet to the most vicious of the time wasters and he is determined to be dedicated, would possibly like to [spend] a month pressing grapes, while not reading or contemplating.

When he returns from Max's restaurant, he feels like reading Thomas à Kempis, *The Imitation of Christ*.[3] He talked about the films he has reviewed and to each subject he brings a freshness and intelligence that is most rewarding. He's the sort of person I have missed during all my years in New York and

[1] Penelope Tree (b. 1949), the model and daughter of Ronald Tree, was then living with the "hip" photographer David Bailey.

[2] The Ormsby-Gores, daughters of Lord Harlech, and Stella, daughter of Hon. "Jakie" Astor.

[3] Thomas à Kempis (ca. 1379–1471), Augustinian monk and writer. Next to the Bible, *The Imitation of Christ* is the book best known to Christians. Cecil was impressed and borrowed it from the London Library on a brief return visit to England.

only trust that a little of his quality will seep through all the dross into me. He left to read a poem by Verlaine, to listen to Poulenc, to read a book about the physical condition caused by depression or nervous upset.

NEW YORK MONDAY, 15 SEPTEMBER 1969

I did a certain amount of barrel-scraping and feel now that the designing job on *Coco* is nearly at an end, and I should really put my strength to the execution of the job. But there is an awful stalemate and everything in abeyance. The scenery is to be built by Feller's,[1] the best, and the costumes by Diffen,[2] but neither seem in a hurry to start, therefore I have had a big dose of my hotel bedroom, oblivious of life outside, which happens to be sunny and hot, and makes me sad at missing so much. Matters were made rather sinister by non-appearance of my assistant [Larry Reehling]. So much depends on him, and since I've been so lenient letting him off early to the country on Fridays, felt he might have shared Sharon Tate's fate.[3] But he called in the evening to say he'd had a flat tyre, surely an insufficient reason for losing a whole day's work.

I lunched with Natasha Wilson,[4] who has survived God knows how many dis-intoxications and must be as strong as all Tsarist Russians to survive all the beatings she has given herself. She has great character and although she leads a life that would drive me to a quick suicide (hardly ever leaving her hideous flat in New York) she has learnt to live by herself, to read a lot and not be restless. Her only regret is that she has not made friends with the younger generation. She talked about Chanel's affair with her brother and said that it ended because Dmitri,[5] "like all Romanoffs, was no good in bed."

[1] Feller Studios, run by K. Feller.

[2] Ray Diffen Studio Clothes.

[3] Sharon Tate (1943–69), film actress in *Valley of the Dolls.* She had been sensationally murdered on 9 August by Charles Manson (b. 1934), who was spared the death penalty due to a Supreme Court ruling against capital punishment.

[4] Princess Natasha Paley (1905–81), granddaughter of Tsar Alexander II of Russia, she was later married to Lucien Lelong (1889–1958), the couturier, and later to Jack Wilson (1899–1961), the theatrical agent.

[5] Grand Duke Dmitri was her half brother.

TUESDAY, 16 SEPTEMBER 1969

Lull continuing, though the morning was spent in conference about the filming of the *Coco* covers, to be transposed to the scene later. It was interesting to hear men from sound, electronic music, lighting, staging, economy and other departments all giving their versions of what should be done. I feel it is all very tricky and can be agony, and a *great* waste of time for which I was not paid enough. If I had a large *per diem* salary then my face might sag a little less.

Niki [Gunzburg] rang to ask (re *Coco*) if I remembered that in the early twenties Frenchmen wore one ear inside their hats.

Morning spent (likewise most of the afternoon) choosing patterns for the Ray Diffen clothes. The choice of "fabrics" is greater here than in London and all sorts of imitation "Chanels" were brought forth with the easiest sleight of hand. The atmosphere of the establishment is delightful and I am thankful not to be subjected to the factory technique of Eaves or Brooks where money is of the first importance so that no mistakes are permitted.

Made the hideous mistake of saying I would go on David Frost's[1] TV programme thinking it would be an interview like we did in London and discovering I was on a panel with that little monster of bad taste, Zsa Zsa Gabor.[2] I lay in a dressing room relaxing and listening to her incessant gabble, and almost decided to quit. The situation was saved by Lillian Gish[3] being one of us, for she talked so intelligently and with such taste and wisdom that the audience appreciated her worth, and when asked her philosophy of life quoted the euphoria of the Florentines who said, "Isn't life wonderful . . . And how beautiful all these ugly people are." When Zsa Zsa was asked, she squirmed and said her shoes were too tight. Complete waste of two hours.

After the indolent afternoon of rest and massage, a pleasant evening. First to receive an envelope of cash for the sketches I did for Bonwit [Teller], and to get a glimpse of the luxurious calm cool way the top executives operate. Then to

[1] (Sir) David Frost (b. 1939), television interviewer, then crossing the Atlantic with alarming regularity to fulfil media commitments in Britain and the USA.

[2] Zsa Zsa Gabor (b. 1919), one of three actress sisters born in Hungary.

[3] Lillian Gish (1893–1993), American star of silent films such as *Birth of a Nation* (1914). She continued into talkies. She died aged 99.

Henry Geldzahler to sit around a 1930 glass table with good-looking boys discussing all. The apartment is unlike anything I've seen, with Lalique, thirties horrors and all the bad taste of objects made in formica looking like china. But I liked the host, found him sympathetic and kind, and not the pushing sort that he has the reputation for being.

Jonathan [Lieberson] lives in a large house belonging to his parents who are away in New Mexico most of the time. During their absence the servants, who are paid full time, do the minimum work for Jonathan so that when I arrived and could hear him playing the piano on the first floor they screamed "Jonathan! Jonathan!" rather than opening the door themselves. At last one German bun-faced woman in dressing gown with her hair in curlers condescended to open the front door and even to show me as a favour to the upstairs, book-lined study where Jon, looking like Liszt, with his hair cut from shoulder- to chin-length, welcomed me in odd clothes including huge leather boots which he had himself painted gold. He was just playing the *Damoiselle élue* by Debussy. Would I like to wait? It was very "luxurious" but if you considered it in the context of the time in which it was written, it was pretty remarkable. Jonathan kept up a running commentary as he played, quite well, and for the first time in many days I felt the atmosphere to be entirely sympathetic, relaxing, beautiful, and in the reflected light from the music Jonathan looked marvellously romantic with his full lips open, showing the right proportion of teeth, receding chin, receding forehead of his mother, a wonderful summation of health and youthful intelligence.

He is a wonderful creature and it is so interesting to think that his mother [Vera] Zorina, the beautiful, but I always felt rather gauche, Russian dancer and the "suspect" Goddard [Lieberson] should have produced something so absolutely first-class as this. He said he had had a busy day. He'd been to Columbia to ask a professor a certain question to do with a paper he had written, had been to see a very bad poetess, had been playing the piano, as he did each day for several hours. He went to the telephone. At first he'd found himself on to a wrong number. "This is Doctor Hymen's office."

"That must be a gynaecologist," he murmured. He said that lately he had opened an account at Max's, the only way he could possibly entertain his friends, as he had absolutely no money, that he had conned the proprietor into giving him an account, since he found out who his father was. "Like Proust,

I've had to get to know head waiters." With American ease [he] ordered a table at Max's for 9:30. "It will take us 20 minutes to get there therefore we have ten minutes to spare. Shall I play some more?" He has the ease and self-confidence of certain well brought-up children. I was enchanted not only to hear him play Poulenc, Chopin and Beethoven, but also to hear his commentary. He is 20. He alluded to himself as someone who was not too old in years, but he had been playing the piano for seven years, he was not so young. "Now this piece is full of popular chords, but this is so pretty just like a little river," and he played very delicately and expertly but without any emphasis on his own performance. He was merely demonstrating a point. He screwed up his face and said, "That's wrong, but it's the right chord. Now this phrase always opens my tear ducts. I've been very moved by this, and by this," and again he would play certain phrases that he found throughout a piece of music that with repetition moved him more and more. "It is known that certain chords go straight through you and get into the blood stream. Am I boring you? You've no idea how many people I've bored in this chair! Now this phrase upsets me very much," and he started again to play, suddenly stopping to get a score from the shelf above his head with such ease that he knew from practice exactly where everything was placed and in the music itself he knew just where to find what he was looking for.

In fact, altogether he seems to have an extraordinary ease of life, to be able to fall into circumstances or situations just as he wishes. He throws away information. "I found myself at the Engelhards'.[1] The daughter's wonderful, a great friend of mine but the mother's just like a man and she's trained her parrot to speak just like herself, and when I arrived I was terrified because this voice screamed, 'Get out! Get out!' "

He is not as vague as he seems. He takes out a long cigarette from the pack and marks it down in his diary. "A psychiatrist told me about this method. I wrote a paper for a professor of sociology on a theory I had for disciplining oneself but it didn't hold up; this stops me smoking 60 a day and I'm down to 16 instead or 12."

We left the book-lined room, caught a cab with ease and went villageward.

[1] Charles Engelhard and his wife Jane.

We were joined by the George Plimptons[1] and it was Jonathan who, wild-eyed, talked the most frankly. Asked if he knew a certain person, "Of course I do. Do you think I'm ignorant?" He has the raciest flow of words I know, very impressive, and he is businesslike too, castigating me for not remembering what he had written in a letter to me about a possible TV show. It is pretty wonderful to see somebody who makes such wonderful use of his young life as Jonathan.

FRIDAY, 19 SEPTEMBER 1969

A session with Ray who seems to have everything under control. It is tough for an Englishman to compete in New York today, but Ray, of quite a gentle nature, seems to manage it. But I got a glimpse of what he is up against. While we were choosing stuffs a man came to say that he had bought the building and wanted Ray's premises. "But I've a lease for another two years." That doesn't seem to matter if someone can think of a way of making more money and, since rents are going up all the time, no one is safe.

Went on to meet Alan, Kate, etc. who were auditioning the male lovers. I watched Kate do a scene with Papa, and cold shivers suddenly ran down my body and I had to hold back the tears, she was so moving and so intense, every fibre in her body reacting. It was a revelation, and the young man as Papa was so good, has such an excellent voice and sang the pretty songs so well, that I felt the whole thing suddenly had emotion.

Kate after her two weeks' "rest" looked incredibly fresh and well, her eyes like little stars. She, for the first time, seemed pleased to see me and we kissed on the lips, a sensational gesture watched by all the management. We stood in the corridor of the Steinway Building and talked while the elevator with a number of people in it called for "Papa," then went down and returned, spewing forth an Italian Jewess who had the effrontery to come up and tell Kate how much she'd admired her in *Lion in Winter.* Kate was horrified but shook the woman by the hand, listened to her praises, then said how busy she was and must leave.

[1] George Plimpton (1927–2003), editor of the *Paris Review,* originator of participatory journalism.

I'm glad to have had a change of heart about Kate, for she is, in her own way, remarkable and today was most appealing with such vitality, such youthfulness and intensity of feeling that suddenly I feel she may make something of the dialogue.

SATURDAY, 20 SEPTEMBER 1969

The air-conditioned climate of my room made it difficult for me to sleep, but after an hour in the dark felt strong enough to have an evening in the village with Gervase [Griffiths], who was to take me to a strange theatre club where they perform plays in connection with the Tarot cards. Gervase said he thought this the most interesting phenomenon in the theatre today, but after three-quarters of an hour, I begged him to let us leave for the amateur quality of the performances was exasperating and costumes were not good enough. Naked people, all very unattractive and the screams and shouts got on my nerves, though the 40 other people in the audience seemed entranced.

However, one transvestite did a dance à la Isadora, doing *Swan Lake,* which was the most mad, fantastic and really hilariously funny "turn" I have ever seen. A large, well-proportioned young man was clad in the most inexplicable clothes, tights, a scarlet Roman slip, a bandana headdress was worn with chiffon Greek over-draperies. The face half-veiled, with yashmak with a hole cut to reveal the huge rouged mouth, was encircled with seven spangles, and the pale-blue ferret eyes were seen above this, very white and mad!

The dance to Tchaikovsky records was inexplicable, dotty, wildly surprising. He danced as if on points with bare feet, leapt in the air as one only does in dreams and jumped as if on a pogo stick. When he rushed off stage with a wild leap, you thought the dance was over, but a second later he was rushing back with renewed celerity.

Of course, as everything else, the turn went on much too long, but some of the effects with a Pop Art coloured wreath of flowers, and trembling hands, were rather beautiful. I was reminded of Stephen Tennant and some of the most outrageous "mad" turns I've ever seen.

As I left (down the secret staircase), this terrifying eyeless creature appeared and whispered, "What is your name?" I was glad to get out to the comparative sanity of Max's, where we were joined by Henry Geldzahler and gang.

I found Gervase a difficult companion for his stutter has become worse, his voice quieter and he was extremely vague about finding his way to any of the places he suggested taking me. I bought the Sunday papers and felt guilty about the first "ad" appearing of *Coco,* with a sketch of mine for the logo, and I walked many blocks rather than pay the liftman at the hotel the ridiculous excess sum he charges for the morning papers.

Came back to find Hepburn had postponed the photography on Monday. This may mean that I have to delay my departure home. It gave me the horrid feeling that I suffered from so much when notes were put under the door changing the appointment with B. Streisand.

SUNDAY, 21 SEPTEMBER 1969

Dinner by self in oak room, thence to Andy Warhol's *Flesh,*[1] impressive and often beautiful, and made me feel how easy to make a movie and what fun too. Then home to return telephone call of Freddie Brisson in Hollywood. He inveighed against K. H., said she had been very difficult and he was afraid she was a dishonest, disappointing character. He had heard that she had kissed me on the lips in front of the company and this was the act of Judas, that she had been saying awful things about me, that I had been very difficult and that she was not at all pleased with the clothes we had done for her in London.

Coming after the kiss and a somewhat kinder feeling towards her as an individual, this information gave me a great shock. I was quite upset and certainly terribly surprised. I had always thought of K. H. as a straight-from-the-shoulder good fellow. Brisson now said he thought her rather disturbed, quite inconsequential, often contradicting herself and talking in circles. The long telephone call roused me so that I was unable to sleep, so after a while got up and took a pill, and this had a great calming effect on me which hung over till the next day, a good way of making troubles disappear.

[1] *Flesh,* another film in the wake of *Midnight Cowboy,* filmed by Paul Morrissey over two days in July 1968, and starring Joe Dallesandro. It ran for seven months at the Garrick Theater on Bleecker Street.

MONDAY, 22 SEPTEMBER 1969

Session at Ray's talking to the workroom staff and bidding them Godspeed on the journey. Then to a rehearsal of the projectors at the theatre, K. H. loving every moment of it and Benthall having a bad time, and I too when it came to telling the movie people how to light the singers. Alan and Karen dinner and we talked of the idiosyncrasies of K. H. and how she talks for talking's sake, and talks a lot of bilge. How "they" are all maniacs and she no worse than the others, but for me a good excuse to air my grievances and tell how difficult it had been to go through so many objections at the countless sittings. Alan less positive than Freddie that she was against me, but had said that Alan and I were both talented but with bad characters. Lots of imitations and jokes, and I enjoyed the dinner at Lafayette and the good food and cigar, but had to rush back to the loo as I was taken short, and very distressed and sad that I should respond in this way to my first cigar in weeks.

TUESDAY, 23 SEPTEMBER 1969

Early call gave me a restless night. By the time I got to the studios where the recordings and music shots were being made, K. H. was already in her stride relishing every exciting moment of it, never for an instant giving her voice a rest and delighted to hobnob with all and sundry so long as they would keep loneliness at bay. She is in many ways like Chanel. The usual manic studio delays, chaos, so many men taking so long to do childish jobs. Eventually we got up a background effect that was exactly like I've ever photographed since I first started imitating Victorian photographs and the cameras rolled on the actor singing the part of Papa which Coco yearned towards him with such intensity that the air became electric with sparks around her. The emotion that K. H. puts into each scene is absolutely shattering. Her eyes fill with tears, her lips and hands tremble, her body quivers and the whole entourage quake. And she kept up this intensity all day long. I was most interested to watch her, but I could never enjoy being a director, for as George Kaufman[1] said, "Anyone can be a film director if he can keep awake."

[1] George S. Kaufman (1889–1961), American comedy playwright, who frequently collaborated with Moss Hart. He wrote *The Man Who Came to Dinner.*

Lunch in a Broadway steakhouse with Lawrence R. [Reehling], who has been through a very tough time but I hope soon will be able to devote himself more to me as I am impatient to get more important props done. But I doubt if this will be accomplished on this voyage, the end of which is in sight, though due to *another* postponement of K. H.'s picture, will be the usual rush of last-minute panic. The rush continued as a lull all afternoon when I found myself able to rest and do the necessary telephone calls and even to have Joseph to massage me for the last time.

To Jonathan [Lieberson] for an evening of rising above disasters. Everything had gone wrong for him and continued to do so. As he got out of the taxi, looking like Christ with a beard, his belt fell into a puddle. Abstractedly, he said, "Isn't it awful to have your belt fall in a lot of dogs' mess?" Then he couldn't find the Fellini movie he wanted to see and, when he did, he wished we hadn't. In spite of the terrible noise at Elaine's, we talked for many hours. Jon's eyes pretty wild as his brain raced at speed to remember everything from former conversations and everything he has read. He had read for nine hours each day of late after a one-hour lecture at Columbia. He talked of the various Indian religions appealing to the various physical types. He talked of Lord Russell, unknown-to-me professors [and] Hemingway whom he hates as much as I do.

To me a fascinating evening with an original, unconventional young man of acute intelligence and subtlety, able to laugh at himself as much as at others. It intrigues me to think he finds my company as interesting as I find his. He loves New York City as much as I hate it, but he may spend his time in New Mexico or even in a retreat.

The filming continued a bit more calmly after yesterday's long breaking-in. The Archduke with beard was today announcing himself at Chanel's and Kate was as usual doing the responses as if her very life depended on them. She loves the life of the studios and is willing to muck in like a sandpiper. It was a sunny day and so in between takes she went out on to the sidewalk, lay back in a swivel deckchair and with feet on a dustbin, started to read Graham Greene's new novel. I remarked that she looked very Samuel Beckett, but I don't think she reacted clearly. I also remarked on the influence of Greene as a writer. I felt her whole background and parentage came to the surface when she said with clipped woodpecker intensity, "Oh, he's a very good writer, excellent writer, excellent." The morning was almost sublimely frustrating in that there was almost a whole morning in which work could be done at the costumer's, but Ray and his staff were at the Met Museum looking at original Chanels.

I went therefore to inspect miles and miles of theatrical furniture and of course in an hour found nothing that even resembled what Chanel has spent a lifetime collecting. However, I was impressed by the wealth and variety of the stock, which has recently been recovered from half a dozen junk attics and all sorts of valuable things have come to light.

THURSDAY, 25 SEPTEMBER 1969

Still I get a bit of strange angst each time I have a biggish sitting. Today lowering skies after the sun spell gave me a foreboding feeling as I got up much too early for the thrice-postponed Hepburn sitting. However, all was well on arrival, Eddie and Japanese assistant *in situ,* and Kate in curlers already made up and looking twenty years younger. I thought the house[1] so much more civilised than when last I saw it, with simple taste, good pieces of dark-brown furniture, monochrome Aubusson carpets, books, Americana and all very polished, and cared for by a Chinese woman who obviously enjoyed her job. Rather touching little bunches of mixed flowers obviously from the country and not from a florist.

The sitting went well with a variety of yearning ship's prow heads to early golfing beauties 1914, sea-spray sports girl, mad moonstruck maidens, jolly good sorts. When I got her to wear a hat pulled down on her face instead of a halo, she really looked marvellous, clear-cut, stylish, such a change. She has a remarkable conglomeration of features; the bad things that have happened, with the cruel years, only accentuate the telegram of her face (the mouth more bitter in repose, the eyes haunted) but she is blessed with a structure that is made for camera and this is at least three-quarters the reason why she has $20 million in the bank.

[1] At that time, Katharine Hepburn lived at 244 East 49th Street.

The adoring Phyllis sat by, beaming and saying how well her mistress looked, and I agreed that she gave a very good performance, smiling and laughing with great naturalness when needed and instinctively using her ugly hands with grace. The session seemed to me to break the ice of our withholding relationship. Perhaps it was only temporary but we discussed our earliest meeting 34 years ago and when she remembered that I had written she was like a member of a hockey team.[1] I told her I had heard she was still distressed by the things I'd written about her, saying that in early age one had less temerity, more bite. "Oh, I say the things I feel. I don't think people resent it." We ate lunch together provided by Phyllis and I think a good morning's work was done with an enormous amount of stuff in the can and of many varieties.

She off to sing, I to Ray Diffen where things are starting to roll very slowly but surely. The detail work takes for ever and I was tired, and returning to the hotel there were messages to attend to but before I had time to pee, the two Bobs had arrived to take me to dinner before seeing *Oh! Calcutta.*

Calcutta surprised me by being far more stylish than I'd imagined from the reviews, and the dancing and lighting and movie backgrounds created quite a beautiful impression and reminded one of the early photographs of Muggeridge, or of Sandow's exercises. The whole thing is certainly a breakthrough and fills a place in the theatre left void by Minsky's burlesques. It is a place for out-of-town business conventions to go to and certainly this was what tonight's audience consisted of. The laughter was hearty. I found the sketches extremely unattractive and it revolted me to see a row of people on cocktail stools masturbating themselves, worse to hear young actresses describing their sexual experiences in the most basic and banal ways.

Altogether, though, I was pleasantly surprised, although occasionally disgusted, even angry, at the idea of Tynan becoming rich by such means. The evening was more enjoyable than most spent in the present season's theatre.

[1] Cecil had described her as "very like any exceedingly animated and delightful hockey mistress at a Physical Training College" (*Cecil Beaton's Scrapbook*, p. 33).

Katharine Hepburn in two photo spreads by Beaton, September 1969

Sep. 25. 1969
1
2
3
4
5
6
7
8
9
10
11
12

FRIDAY, 26 SEPTEMBER 1969

Last day of New York visit. Tension from waking on.

Larry R. to ask about the list of props. The most difficult to find is a 1953 vacuum cleaner. At an early lunch at the flower-bedecked Grenouille, Freddie B. gave me the full low-down on K. H.'s behaviour against my poster, how she had shown it to three friends and they had all thought it insulting to her. She had thought my name too prominent in the list of credits and behaved in a way that to me is quite inexplicable.

I cannot see that so straight-faced a woman can also be so devious and treacherous. I cannot even see her being totally influenced by Cukor, or for that matter his being so vindictive. However, Freddie continued to say how amazed he was at her Judas Iscariot kisses and how I must get her signature on the back of each picture she passes otherwise she will later complain that the "bitch" has published the very picture she did not want.

When a few minutes later K. H. arrived at my rooms for lunch and to see the pictures, she was so pleased with them that she refused to sign. "It'll take too much time." She never likes to hand me a compliment but she thought "that they were as good as she had expected them to be." I again asked her to sign, saying Freddie had asked me to do so. She then said that she only was particular about this sort of thing with *Life* and *Time* who had wasted so much of her time and been so difficult, and once had come to see her to OK an article which started off "Mrs. H. has always been interested in sex" (K.'s mother being a social worker, educator of children etc.). We kissed goodbye and seemed to be quite "on the level" with each other though I still find her very brash and brusque and strident.

Phyllis could be a catalyst but is too sycophantic to her mistress. Incidentally, K. H. is blessed with the most photogenic bone structure and although almost everything is wrong with her face (false teeth, crooked mouth, appalling skin, hooded eyelids) yet the essentials are there to register on film.

Cecil walked to Ray Diffen's, arriving "bathed in sweat for conference with Michael Bennett who seemed pleased with the designs I'd done at his behest. He had had a good morning's work with K. H., who he said was very bright and quick to learn, and was altogether enthusiastic about the prospects of the show."

Cecil went back to the hotel to cope with Hepburn's proofs and to finish packing before the club car arrived at seven to take him to the airport.

He then spent some days back in England. Sam Green came to stay at Reddish to work on their project about the Baeklands (see The Unexpurgated Beaton, *pp. 32–3). On 14 October, Cecil arrived back in New York.*

On his way to London airport he had been thrilled to catch a glimpse of the motorcade bringing the Apollo 11 astronauts into London, a stay which involved a visit to the Queen.

Meanwhile he crossed over the Atlantic as if he were going off once more to a fitting at Berman's, rather than what could be, and nearly was, a three-month stay.

The arrival was easy. Alan Lerner has a sort of mafia of his own and his men were out to see that I got through the Customs easily with a dreadful gold-painted wagon that his wife was giving him for a first-night film present. I took the Porchesters[1] in the awaiting station wagon with me and arrived without incident back in the rooms I had vacated such a short time ago.

Jayne [Wrightsman] sent me a Gauguin bouquet, a sheaf of not interesting messages awaited me, and soon I was infected and unnerved in the trials of a big production, Brisson telling me K. H. had been difficult all along the line, but then he went ahead and did just what he wanted and although she now said she did not trust any of us, was forging ahead with a tireless energy that had not been dampened by her recent bad notices for *Madwoman of Chaillot.* The hours between London and New York confused me. I took a sleeping draught but woke for long stretches of an endless night to start life on a sunny beautiful autumnal day.

WEDNESDAY, 15 OCTOBER 1969

My morning was spent making and receiving important business telephone calls, not all connected with *Coco.* I was busy in every direction, then went to the Bronx to see the enormous construction of the scenery for which I was

[1] Henry, Lord Porchester (1924–2001), later seventh Earl of Carnarvon, and his wife, Jean Wallop.

responsible, and yet when seeing the blue panels, felt I had so little to do with, and neither could I enter into the technical discussions that went on so long between high-powered brilliant engineers and draughtsmen. If there are no worse snags than those that cropped up today, I will be a free man to get on with other chores connected with this vast project. And considering the temperaments involved this is not likely to be free of resentments, surprise shocks of an unpleasant nature, and the bad ethics that one expects in the theatre but nonetheless come as a shock.

My assistant, Larry Reehling, seems to have the equable temperament that makes him seem to rise above all troubles and he does not listen to the ridiculous nagging worries about mounting expenses and possible economies. He goes ahead and orders what is necessary and argues that if we are working on a budget made three years ago, then we are under-budgeted.

The evening was a bit of a nightmare as I had to go to the opening of an Alan Lerner film, *Paint Your Wagon.*[1] It was a gala première with crowds in the heart of Broadway and all sorts of unknown stars creating stampedes of enthusiasm. The film about womenless men in the Gold Rush days was everything that I loathed. Even to watch the life of boozing, biffing and being muddied all over made me acutely embarrassed. I had had a glimpse of the populace and the star guests, and was lucky to sneak out in the interval and come home to try to reconcile myself to the change in time between London and New York.

THURSDAY, 16 OCTOBER 1969

Tremendous concentration of about a dozen fittings at Ray's. Gradually the musical is coming to life and the dreary personages that have bored me in so many new typescripts suddenly appear in person.

The change of time and the lack of air produce near exhaustion and we had a most welcome though late lunch at a nearby French restaurant. Then to rush off to Brisson to tell about publicity photographs boosting the already inflated ego of Hepburn. Then a rush back to go through charts with Larry

[1] *Paint Your Wagon* (1969), Lerner and Loewe film (originally on stage) about two prospectors in the California Gold Rush who set up a Mormon ménage with the same woman. It starred Lee Marvin, Clint Eastwood, Jean Seberg and others.

Reehling who never turned up. My frustration and exasperation prevented me from resting, as by the hour I waited for him without one word. Half a day wasted, when so much detail work could have been done. The casual young man rang at seven o'clock to explain the muddle.

FRIDAY, 17 OCTOBER 1969

Ragged morning. Chorus girls waiting to be fitted at Ray's while Brisson had arranged journalist interviews with me at hotel. To make me feel more frenzied and put upon, Eugenia Sheppard arrived an hour late.

At usual lunch hour a long interview with *Women's Wear Daily,* a paper that everyone reads, and which is ruthless and can make things tough for me if they wish. They can make or break. Reehling then moaned on in monotonous smart voice about the chores to do, and I can't criticise him for being slow with props, shoes, wigs etc., as he has a full-time job with scenery and had started off to the workshop at 7:30 this morning.

The Greek blond Adonis looked a little frayed. And Ray looked frayed too and yawned when I returned for a quiet session at the end of the week's work. The workrooms are at capacity and it is quite a big responsibility for him but he has a calm disposition and this helps me as well.

Pleasant evening dining at poor man's Côte Basque with Sam [Green] who talked of the significance of the Met modern show last night, of the intrigue involved and of how [Tom] Hoving, the director, clamped his hands to his forehead in shock when he saw a group of dancers strip and, stark naked, start a humping dance. He has had enough of a bad press interest without this. It seems a group lying on the floor started humping and when a *New York Times* reporter asked one of the girls what she was doing, got the reply, "I hate cock, otherwise I'd be fucking."

SATURDAY, 18 OCTOBER 1969

The first run-through of Act I. This came fresh to me as I have been unable to read the latest scripts, having been surfeited with former versions. But although there are still the offensive, unsuitable, damaging remarks that Benthall years ago said he would persuade Kate to omit, the script acts extremely well and I was quite surprised to find how it comes to life, how the characters are delineated and how amusing and informative a lot of it is.

The minor parts are extremely well cast, the comic who plays Sebastian Baye[1] is a marvellous new discovery, delightful, mad, funny, and I am delighted to find that he plays it straight with no faggoty emphasis. It is quite wonderful to see how much he makes of so little.

As for K. H., she is never off stage and she is a marvel of vitality. She does not give any suggestion of Chanel herself, is in fact K. H. as ever, but it is a remarkable tour de force, full of vitality and emotion. K. H.'s voice is very strident and seems higher, more feminine than in life, but her singing is bad. She has no voice at all. She speaks the songs and occasionally tries for a note but it is not there. This is the one aspect of her performance that will not be praised. Otherwise she will be crowned with laurels and the only danger is that her voice may give out as I believe it did in the run of *The Millionairess* in London.[2]

A lot of the dialogue is very moving. This surprises and delights me as I felt the whole show would be lacking in sentiment. It is not. Alan said it was the best first act he had ever seen, better than *My Fair Lady.* It is not. But I feel suddenly that it will succeed and that it has not been a mistake to get involved. I also feel humbled at having misjudged the script and not seen that Alan really is a tried professional and knows the effect that this dialogue will make. The movement given to the story by Bennett is an enormous asset and I was thrilled to think of the opportunities he had given me to show off my costumes. They should really be quite dramatic and this pleased me tremendously. The music is adequate and two numbers from this one act will be standards. Altogether I found myself very elated and even moved, and I think audiences will respond in just the way they are expected to.

Following the run-through there was a conference about the lighting for the "Put Up the Lights" number. This proved to be an agony for me as I had

[1] Sebastian Baye was played by René Auberjonois (b. 1940), who had lately starred as Dago Red in the film *M*A*S*H.* He was a founding member of the faculty in the Drama Department of Juilliard.

[2] *The Millionairess* by George Bernard Shaw had been revived in London with Hepburn in 1952. It was now the basis of a Peter Sellers–Sophia Loren film, directed by Anthony Asquith (1969), which inspired a Sellers–Loren hit record "Goodness, Gracious Me."

planned to be at the hotel at one o'clock to meet Sam to take the plane to Vermont. A dozen of the management sat in a circle in the downstairs lobby and started to get really involved. The minutes ticked by very quickly and I knew that the discussions would last for hours. Sandwiches were ordered. A lot of personality irritation at play. Benthall trying to be positive and authoritative, but no one respects him, and Bennett is the obvious director of the show. Suddenly Benthall suggested that K. H. should be dismissed to rest and study for the rest of the weekend. Alan went to tell her so. He returned saying K. H. wished to have more direction so she could study the new scenes over the weekend. Then, not to be out of any of the activity, she appeared as a Lady Macbeth on the stairs to join the discussions.

It was now time for me to go. My departure was a bombshell. "Where are you going?" asked K. H. rather impertinently. Then she excused herself for her impertinence. When I informed her I was going to Vermont she asked me to bring her back some maple syrup. Benthall had the gall to ask if I was going back to England. I am disappointed that I didn't ask, "No, are you?" But perhaps it is as well to have turned the other cheek. At any rate my departure was considered a disaster, and although most people are free to go off at lunchtime on Saturday, it is not necessarily so in the theatre. But if only I had stayed another three-quarters of an hour my departure would not have been felt so acutely and as things turned out this three-quarters of an hour were not only wasted, but put to the most exhausting and unnerving purpose of waiting for Sam's late arrival.

Sam and Cecil then spent an enjoyable weekend away, working on their project. They returned early on the Monday morning, having bought Katharine Hepburn her maple syrup, cookies and apples.

MONDAY, 20 OCTOBER 1969

Now for urban excitements. *Coco* kept usurping my mind and what panic would be found on my arrival. The panic turned out to be greater than expected as my assistant, without telling anyone, had gone off to Florida and my scene sketch urgently needed by workshop painters nowhere to be found. At the theatre great tenseness. But my tin of maple syrup won K. H.'s heart. She kissed me. Frustration at non-appearance of Larry, but was busy with telephone and chores, and lunch of a hamburger brought to my room in a brown paper bag.

Total exhaustion by bedtime, having had a nice visit from an Italian[1] and a long session with bright and clever Bennett about the wigs at his apartment. It is not fair that we have to work so hard. Back at one o'clock and tomorrow a ten o'clock call at Ray's with a line-up of girls.

TUESDAY, 21 OCTOBER 1969

Tired and tense, I found everyone else tired and tense at Ray's and mentally I soon got a headache. The progress on clothes is good and I was pleased to find so much wit had crept in. Reehling, rather tired and abashed, appeared but told me he will be "off" all next week. I suddenly hated him; however, we continued to work along going to Newall's Art Gallery to get in half an hour what Chanel has taken a lifetime to acquire. Miraculously, luck was on our side and we got two marvellous gilt tables, just what is needed. I also ordered the artificial flowers, which is a chore which I always enjoy in spite of revolting mercenary conditions and loud speaker interruptions.

Was really so tired that the idea of a free evening delighted me, but on arrival at hotel, found lots of last-minute SOSs and spent the evening doing drawings and colourings for *Time,* also being interviewed by a tired woman who had been to the theatre and seen most of the participants but most impressed by M. Bennett. Too tired to talk to Kin, or to make any effort, and put out the light by 9:30.

WEDNESDAY, 22 OCTOBER 1969

Closeted in a small upstairs room at the theatre, working out the boring question of the wigs and the minutiae that are all part of a huge production, watched the brilliantly dressed "Preparation" number, this really a show stop-

[1] There were one or two similarly cryptic notes in this part of the diary.

per, and I was relieved to see Kate in Chanel shoes. By degrees she is doing all the things she fought against at first.

THURSDAY, 23 OCTOBER 1969

After the long summer weather, temperature dropped to arctic, and here I am without warm clothes. Visited Feller's Studios in the Bronx, and a bit worried as to how the painting of Act I will turn out. But they are marvellous technicians and I feel my brain badly trained to take in so much information. The "props" are wonderfully well made and the chandeliers should be great. Thence to choose chairs, screens and props at Newell's and back to cope with the more urgent calls and publicity messengers.

At four a run-through of Act I. The emotion soon goes. And one sees bad spots, but K. H. is good in the "Coco" song and choreography wonderful of the little black dress. Everyone out front very tired, tense or giggly. Luckily I was on a laughing gag, Alan telling me terrible stories of what goes on behind the scenes. Michael Bennett thinks Benthall must be drinking. He certainly looks terrible and may be taken out on a stretcher or, if his eyes close more shut, be given a blind dog.

K. H. brought me home in her car and we tried to warm up into a friendship, but there is a barrier between that embarrasses me.

No time for much of a pause before walking in arctic air to Diana [Vreeland] who had a lovely dinner party where the atmosphere was congenial so that it seemed unnecessary to leave for the rough-house of a [Mrs. H. J.] Heinz party given in honour of Antonia Fraser[1] and her *Mary, Queen of Scots.* Told "Suzy"[2] that she looked like a Gustave Moreau and then Ruth Ford came up in velvet and coral, and she too looked like a Moreau. Talk, but very interrupted by celebrity-hunting bores who are news conscious, and *Coco* is the news.

[1] Lady Antonia Fraser (b. 1932), author.

[2] "Suzy" Knickerbocker, the alias of Aileen Mehle.

FRIDAY, 24 OCTOBER 1969

Arrived at Ray's before anyone in charge had appeared so wandered around the tables getting to know the various helpers. One old woman of over 80 without any teeth gets up at six each morning to arrive in order to talk as she works. She was once a trapeze artist and hung from her mouth but one day the iron clamp broke.

Then to Brook's Costume where the depressing job of pulling clothes from the racks produced in me the inevitable depression. How quickly all these wonderful clothes ideas become junk. Mood lightened at Barney's, a huge men's department store, where all the with-it clothes are to be found at fantastically low prices. A quarter to four before I finished my solitary lunch and, tired out, was able to operate for the rest of the day from my bed. All the magazines are hot on the track for *Coco* photographs and I am lucky to have "early Chanels," but the tension of transatlantic telephone calls makes me on edge and my voice has become hoarse.

SATURDAY, 25 OCTOBER 1969

I hated having to dress and entertain Beatrix Miller[1] to tea, but she is kind and nice, and talk was glib and entertaining. My voice better after the rest but bad by the end of the evening, although it was effortless and delightfully spent with Sam, dining in the King Cole room talking about modern painting, and then to *Last Summer,*[2] a film about the cruelty of young people to one another. It was so successful in its intention that I would willingly have murdered the harsh brash bitch of a 16-year-old girl that seems so typical of Americans of a certain class, a tough beast with sex appeal, brutal to birds and lesser-appealing girls. It was extremely impressing and depressing.

[1] Beatrix Miller, editor of *Vogue* in London.

[2] *Last Summer* (1969), a film about well-to-do teenagers and their summer holiday sexual adventures.

SUNDAY, 26 OCTOBER 1969

Hopefully a day of recuperation. But I was worried in case my *extinction de voix* would develop into the awful cold that I fear so much. Not speaking was the only solution.

Outside a freak spring day but by the time I dressed and went for a foray it was dark. Sam was playing the piano and his apartment, very empty, had charm and guts. We went to the Dakota Building where Charles-Henri Ford was having a poetry reading by that mad creature who appears in all Andy Warhol's films, a wild way-out group, and suddenly Jonathan appeared, looking very messy with his beard, and saying he did not at all like these people, thought them decadent, but he himself disloyal for saying so. My voice so weak, I did not wish to try it. Made me realise I'm not at my best at a party. I feel I have no small talk and merely make enemies. However, there were many nice new faces including that of a beautiful boy whom we are to see in a new Fellini film.

Then down the building, so strangely unlike New York of today, so solid and well-finished, so full of iron, heavy woods and leather, to Ruth Ford's flat lined with Tchelitchew portraits and drawings. She has the finest collection in existence and I'm glad to see that she is not nearly as badly off as one had heard. She's a stout girl, and a good friend. I only trust she will find a man to look after her in old age.

Mart Crowley was there, discussing with the director of the film of *Boys in the Band*[1] and the crowd was all of young people doing things in the world of the arts. Sadly, my voice prevented me participating and I came back to write and read, and just when about to pack it in, Diana V. rang and, although she did most of the talking, it was quite an effort to keep abreast for almost an hour. She talked of Ruth Gordon[2] being so full of vitality that you felt she was whirling loaded revolvers in every direction.

[1] Mart Crowley (b. 1935), playwright who wrote the play *The Boys in the Band*, which was turned into a film about a heterosexual invited to a homosexual party, directed by William Friedkin in 1970.

[2] Ruth Gordon (1896–1985), actress remembered for her parts in *Rosemary's Baby* and *Harold and Maude*. She was married to the somewhat younger Garson Kanin.

MONDAY, 27 OCTOBER 1969

A great stroke of fortune. No reason to leave my room, my voice still on the blink, but I began to feel my energy returning, so perhaps no cold or flu is in store and that my trouble was caused through fatigue.

Bob LaVine sent me round a packet of surprise presents including pornographic literature and luckily I was able to go early to sleep in the hope and belief that life will begin again tomorrow.

TUESDAY, 28 OCTOBER 1969

A return to the grind and my voice stood the test. A taxing morning at Ray's where momentum has gathered and they are conscious that time is running short. Luckily the chorus girls all seem delighted with their clothes and this gives a fillip. Ray is a bit exasperated and on edge but is the kindest, fairest, most sympathetic person one could work with.

The evening a delight for the Wrightsmans have arranged that two of the Kenneth Clark lectures are given for the NYC university students and we were privileged to dine in auspicious company (including Jackie Onassis who now looks a mess with contorted twitching face and dirty hair) before going on to hear the first two of this miraculous series. Here in New York the calm and peace and erudition struck one as particularly civilised. The onslaught of beauty was deeply touching to the emotions. I felt proud that England could produce something so great, and hope that lily-livered slob [Bill] Paley had a little regret that he turned down the series as being too boring.

WEDNESDAY, 29 OCTOBER 1969

Confident that my stars were in good orbit, I went off to Ray's for fittings. The messages keep coming in for more "extras" dresses, and when it was suggested that a "wrap-over" was needed for Hepburn, I thought I'd better go round to the theatre to see what is happening and show an interest after an interval of several days.

I find K. H. in her Chanel hat feeling that the stars had stopped in their courses because she had cut her hair. It is a dark brown, not dark enough, and she refused to dye it. But I complimented her and said how wonderful (meaning young) she looked, and greatly relieved to say goodbye to her hideous Victorian landlady topknot. She did not know anything about a "wrap-around" so I went downstairs to M. Benthall to enquire. This is where I made my mistake. The fat lobster said, "Kate has changed her interpretation of Chanel. Since she saw this pathetic little old lady asleep on the sofa, she wants to play her as Mary Poppins. Some of the costumes will have to be changed, as she wants to look 'mousey.' "

I was too angry to be coherent and got up and left. I am not strong enough for this sort of job any more. I suffer too much. The adrenalin ran over and I felt faint and sick.

I came back to telephone for support from Alan and Brisson's aide. I could hardly eat my lamb chop. Suddenly a car was downstairs to take me to K. Feller's studio and take my mind off the possibility that K. H. will do what she has intended all along, to wear her one Chanel suit, which she bought to "cover" the misdeeds of this vile monster whom she does not trust for one moment. The scenery is progressing. I make decisions, often wondering if they are the right ones and how the effect will be. A ton of abuse will fall on me if the effect is not as expected of me. A thousand details occupied me, fabrics for chairs, for men's trousers, for flowers.

I lay on the bed and telephoned Truman who is recovering from a near-miss motor accident in which he was precipitated through his windshield. I made him laugh so much about Merle Oberon's face being so tightened that she had to be fed at the Grenouille intravenously. Truman said he now knew the meaning of the term "in stitches."

Instead of going to sleep, I lay thinking over the possible disasters that might occur tomorrow when K. H., in the lunch break, does a dress parade of all her costumes. I have asked for the support of all concerned, but feel that this is the moment when K. H. may strike, and if she shows herself the enemy that the management tell me she is, how am I to react? I took some aspirin and still the torment went on. I got up and took more aspirin, then five o'clock registered on the IBM tower outside. When the breakfast tray arrived I felt as if my whole body was made of tin!

THURSDAY, 30 OCTOBER 1969

Felt very tremulous and nervous after my sleepless night and the prospect of K. H. saying she would wear none of my specially designed clothes. The morning of fittings seemed irksome, particularly in view of the fact that dozens of enormous packing cases arrived from London with all the clothes we'd made there. It was thrilling to see them and I feel they may look sensational on the stage. Ray was very generous and sweet about them, and no rancour or jealousy whatsoever. A rushed lunch and then the fatal meeting at the theatre.

K. H. appeared one by one in the clothes before six of us in the stalls in a theatre otherwise cleared of personnel. K. H. with frown and bad-tempered was fighting whole situation. She loathes wearing "clothes" and she did not hesitate to say when she did not like anything. A red suit turned out to be a big disappointment and made her look square.

But Benthall was silent and the great scene which I had feared, when she was to say "Why don't I go through the whole play in one little black dress?" was avoided. Although racked with anxiety, I was so relieved when the session was over that I went off to the Bronx workshop to see samples of scenery in a state of euphoria. But exhaustion had set in too.

FRIDAY, 31 OCTOBER 1969

There will be no *Time* cover of my *Coco* drawing and altogether there has been a great deal of wasted time. The morning in my rooms working in telephone calls left me breathless and with that horrible old feeling that I most dislike of fighting the clock. My scrap lunch was eaten so quickly that I felt I had an ulcer by the time I got to Diffen's to meet Bennett about the "materials" for the number where "bolts of tweed fly through the air"—most dangerous! Bennett tremendously enthusiastic about the London clothes but, half an hour before she was due, K. H. arrived (I think she had intended to get at Ray to do alterations to her clothes before I arrived).

However, the session went much better than any we've had in London. Ray is wonderfully caring with her, recognises that she is just a bundle of nerves, unsure of herself, and has a calming influence. This encounter seemed much more honest than most we've had. We argued, discussed, contradicted one another. She said she knew she had been "impossible" because she loathes all clothes. She said it was remarkable that we had got along since she was as difficult as I was. In some ways she was disarming, but again the act of why are we all in this? Instead of answering to the last, I said, "Oh, but we do have some fun out of it!"

We went through all the London clothes, made great alterations, improvements I admit, we discarded ruthlessly and finally she brought out the Chanel clothes she's bought. They are impeccably made. Real works of art and they will help us with our changes.

Karen Lerner appeared at one moment and K. H. made some extremely rude remark about her having come to have a snide look (she hadn't), then paradoxically she walked through the showrooms to exhibit herself to all the various people in the clothes. This was very nice of her. Altogether there was slight badinage and jokes (I still think she is short on humour). She left with the benighted, bullied Phyllis carrying boxes of Chanel junk, jewellery, hats, costumes, and Ray and I, exhausted, talked over the situation.

There is a lot to be done and time is getting short. But I felt that the worst hurdle, touch wood, had been crossed, that Kate's nervousness was somewhat allayed. Now it is the scenery that holds the greatest difficulties. Ray said how relieved he was that he hadn't had to make all K. H.'s clothes, and I told him that today's session had been a "romp" in comparison with the grim, grinding scenes in London.

With nothing to do for the evening, I was delighted to do nothing. Perhaps mistakenly, I was relaxing because I had the feeling that the worst of this big job was now over. Perhaps there will be some appalling crisis that strikes unexpectedly, but the bulk of the clothes are made and K. H.'s wardrobe complete except for a few numbers over which we can fight during the weeks to come. But it would make everything easier and clearer if she would come out on the level and not tell others behind my back just what she thinks of me.

SATURDAY, 1 NOVEMBER 1969

There was much activity at the costumier's, semi-principals in every room, and chorus dancers not only fitting their new dresses but also those arrived from England. Ray said of one *belle époque* that he knew of no other designer who could do something so bold and simple and experienced. This surprised and of course delighted me.

By mid-afternoon I was pretty whacked but looked in at the theatre to see what was happening. Kate, raring to go, loving to rehearse, to repeat the lines ad infinitum.

She tackled me about her operatic number (Noelle's[1]) wig. "I cannot act with a young girl wearing a wig and she must not have her hair cut in a bang like mine. That would be too lesbian and we can't introduce that element into the play. As it is there have been rumours about me, because I have some very good friends like Laura Harding[2] and we wear trousers. Oh, it's been said millions of times, and Chanel too, she's had that reputation."

I told K. that I did not for a minute believe that C. had those tendencies (lots of women fell for her romantically, passionately, doggedly) but Chanel was far too unrelenting against homosexuality in men to have those feelings about women. She spent her later years inveighing against pederasts, saying that they had ruined fashion by purposefully making women look foolish. "Is that so?" said Kate. "Now come on, let's do 'The Money Rings Out Like Freedom' " (my *least* favourite number) and the rattle voice was at it again. Meanwhile the coverall carpet has been laid on the stage.

SUNDAY, 2 NOVEMBER 1969

Morning spent writing peacefully, no telephone. My thoughts far from *Coco* until lunchtime when Fred Brisson returned from California and, with two executives, took me to lunch. He brought a good deal of hard sense to the gen-

[1] Noelle was eventually played by Gale Dixon, who was a regular in the TV series *Another World,* had played in *Hair* and had played Millie opposite Dustin Hoffman in *Jimmy Shine* on Broadway in 1968.

[2] Laura Harding, American Express heiress, who helped with the costumes for *The Chalk Garden.*

eral situation, said that the last act was going to give us the trouble, that the show would take one and a half years to pay off. He obviously dislikes Hepburn and said Yul Brynner and those who had played with her in *Chaillot*[1] had found her an intolerable bitch. I must say that I was terribly prejudiced against her the whole afternoon as I sat watching her in the run-through. She is extremely good in the part, gives it enormous intensity. She is a dynamic Yankie, never even remotely reminding me of Chanel. And her singing voice is nil. But she will help pull the show through with another great contribution coming from Bennett. His choreography makes one cry. I was deeply touched by the parade of fashions in the finale. But much of the show is banal Broadway fare, the music without distinction, and much of Alan's dialogue is anathema to me, though I realise that it will go down well with the audiences who prefer the accepted copy rather than the original wit.

I went to Kate's room to congratulate her and felt that this time I was being the Judas. I find her energy so overwhelming that unless she has lines to read all the time she becomes a menace. Returning late, knowing the show will disappoint a great number whose hopes have been raised too high.

Came to bed with my head full of *Coco*, and realising tomorrow will be the busiest day with all the London clothes being tried on and my first glimpse of the set on stage.

MONDAY, 3 NOVEMBER 1969

The scenery was coming by very slow degrees into the theatre, so no rehearsals and the chorus were being sent in droves for fittings on the clothes recently arrived from London. Mercifully, only minor alterations were necessary and many of the costumes delighted me, and sent the workroom and their wearers into ecstasy. But ominously, Phyllis W. arrived with a whole lot of old clothes from K. H. and we were all scared stiff in case she would want them to replace those we have made for her. It is difficult to steel oneself

[1] *The Madwoman of Chaillot* (1969), directed by Bryan Forbes, also starred Danny Kaye, Edith Evans, Charles Boyer, Claude Dauphin, John Gavin, Paul Henreid, Nanette Newman, Oskar Homolka, Margaret Leighton, Giulietta Masina, Richard Chamberlain, Donald Pleasence and Fernand Gravet.

against possible shocks and unpleasantnesses, and the next ten days are going to be crucial.

With the concentration needed to scrutinise, criticise and make decisions in an airless emporium, I found myself too tired to stay over the lunch interval with Ray and took myself back to lie for ten minutes on the bed at the hotel, before eating the expensive, uninteresting room service meal that nevertheless preserved my recurring sore throat. The afternoon was a continuation of the morning, the enthusiasm of the girls maintained and Ray seemingly tireless in spite of what must be for him the great strain of organising all those costumes, with always more costumes added, to be ready in a few days' time.

Very little to see at the theatre, but later in the evening Alan rang to say that he and everyone concerned were very worried about the colour of the carpet. It was too light. I tried to pacify him, but needed a little pacifying myself.

Dinner was a delight, with Ruth and Gar[1] at the re-flowered Grenouille. I was afraid they would pump me about their great friend Kate, but mercifully they only asked "between the family" what I thought of the show, which Garson had once turned down as director. We talked about dope-taking, methods of work and, interspersed with the usual name-dropping, Ruth was extremely funny and powerful on a variety of subjects. It amazes me that Garson, who is so bright, no longer seems to write or produce in films anything of the slightest merit. The two seem to live in the greatest luxury and Ruth had what she called a huge "limo" to take her a few blocks home. They are two of my old friends that never play the same record too often and I laugh a great deal in their company. They terrified me with an account of how at the end of a picture, *Suddenly, Last Summer,* K. H. asked Mankiewicz if all shooting, dubbing, play bashing etc. etc. was over, and when told yes she spat in his face. She then repeated the performance to Sam Spiegel.[2]

The Kanins sympathised with me for going through the hoops of putting a big musical on stage, then told the story of how someone had been deliberating whether or not Hitler was still alive and remarked, "Well if he is, let's hope he's on the road, putting on a new musical." Gar said he thought I

[1] Ruth Gordon and Garson Kanin (1912–99).

[2] *Suddenly, Last Summer* (1959) was produced by Sam Spiegel and directed by Joseph L. Mankiewicz. It also starred Elizabeth Taylor and Montgomery Clift.

looked calm and healthy, which surprised me. I came home wishing that the next week would go by in a dope haze of unconsciousness.

TUESDAY, 4 NOVEMBER 1969

Ruth and Gar had appeared so smart and well turned-out last night. They came to the hotel early, having voted for Lindsay,[1] to drop a note of thanks (for birthday flowers) on me. They were transformed into sleazy old theatrical bums. Gar unshaven in awful clothes, Ruth in leather fringe, a Broadway hoofer. But their gay and affectionate spirit remained intact. As I watched them from the back of a taxi, it was good to see a couple getting along so well together and after so many vicissitudes.

Nothing much to see at the theatre except the beige velour which Alan thinks so light, but Feller, the man who knows, says it can always be brought "down" but never "up."

Mercifully the telephone did not shock me, and I felt refreshed by the time I had to go to a "social" lunch at the Grenouille with Lee [Radziwill], recently arrived. She said she was changing her friends in London as the stupidity of the "smart" set was beyond a joke. As we came out of the restaurant, she shouted "Oh shit!" as she saw *Women's Wear Daily* had sent a photographer.

I walked with a heavy heart to the fitting at Ray's with Kate, as if going to my doom. She fills us all with such anxiety and tension, and today's session was made difficult not only with her demands, getting too sweaty or hot in this or that fabric, hating this shape, that colour, but the exigencies of the changes made one costume quite impossible. We added two of her own Chanel costumes to be altered, and by including the red dress that she has always said she hates, she felt that we had the requisite quota of clothes to his. But the fact that she threw out certain things that Ray had made for her, and others had to be made, threw back seriously his workroom schedule. He looked very gaunt, pale and worried.

By the time we were through the Kate session ("No I'm not tired," she said) we were all bushed. But the relief that she was more frank and demon-

[1] John V. Lindsay (1921–2000), Mayor of New York 1966–73.

strative—"You're stubborn, I'm stubborn, but there's no moving Alan Jay Lerner"—made us all rather hysterical and for the first time the fitting room resounded with a certain amount of genuine laughter. In her car on the way home she looked really like a very frightened child when she asked, "Do you think I'll get away with it?"

WEDNESDAY, 5 NOVEMBER 1969

Heavy rain made the city impossible to move in all day and night. Abortive visit to Ray where fittings failed to materialise so I arrived too early for an emergency to the theatre where the portal planned would restrict the vision of several seats up the sides of the stalls. Better to give in over this and fight for later more important issues. So far the beige and background look good, and I am pleased, but from one minute to the other new snags occur. It is interesting to note that Fred B., Hebert and others seem to treat me with a respect that I have never had before: unlike the leading lady, they thank me for being called in at an emergency. My sense of guilt is at full blast now whenever I take time off to do things unconnected with the play, or even to have an evening out.

Bought a hamburger on my way home and slept till the telephone woke me with the good news that *Vogue* has bought Francis Rose's article on Gertrude Stein. My afternoon ruined by having to trudge in the rain to Truman's film *Trilogy.*[1] This much-publicised private showing was delayed while a few spurned latecomers from the press arrived. The grand ladies were not present. We sat in a room of such coldness, under an air-conditioning vent, that I feared for my health. But worse, the soundtrack went wrong. One could hear nothing, but what one could seemed perfectly untheatrical. Even the story of the woman who haunts graveyards in the hope of finding a widower to wed went without any humour whatsoever. A terrible flop.

THURSDAY, 6 NOVEMBER 1969

Still the city disorganised by rain. The girl who wears "my mother's dress" had already had her fitting and left by the time I got to the costumier's. This is a

[1] *Trilogy* (1968) by Truman Capote. Three of his stories were adapted for television.

bleak patch at Ray's, the workrooms full but the progress seems nil, and K. H. has thrown a spanner in the works by chucking out things she'd already agreed upon and ordering new things to be made in order to compete with quick changes. I went to the theatre where things are slow, and my assistants are never present. So I returned to another solitary room service meal, coping with envelopes and telephone calls and feeling quite stale. I would like this all to end so that I can think of other things. K. H. looms as a sort of witch in the background, and I want to be free of her. It is good to have such an ally in Fred B. who, it seems, told Margaret Case that he was not only in *pleine admiration* of my work, but of my character. Alan is edgy and has not yet said he likes the set.

With telephone turned off, I slept deeply most of the afternoon, then walked in the drizzle to the theatre where, most terrifying of moments, the projection was being shown. We all feared that these would give us enormous trouble and after all our work might have to be scrapped, but lo and behold, they were a success. They really looked mysterious and the father in the mirror frame like a Sargent portrait. A success. Now where is the crunch coming? Benthall, never admiring the set, said, "We have a problem. I don't know if you've heard about it." It proved a mere detail. I asked him not to present problems as I found them upsetting to one's creative activities. I told him that Alan's call about the expensive overall carpet being too white had upset me and proved not to be a problem. Benthall, disloyally, said, "But Alan says everything is a problem."

Relieved that this session had passed off as well, I came back in Fred Brisson's car and felt very free for the evening with Sam to go and meet some weirdie friends, hopheads, and thence to the Viva film.

FRIDAY, 7 NOVEMBER 1969

Not a good day, neither of my assistants saw fit to "clock in" by telephone and only by chance did I discover that there was taking place the most important "technical" involving the lights and set. It would have been disaster if I had missed it. As it was, I was late.

However, the lassitude soon left me and I braced myself for a horrible experience at the theatre. It turned out to be more horrible than expected.

The activity at Ray's seemed to be easing down and the clothes now being made are rather depressing, and Ray was sad at just having had a message to say his much older sister had died of cancer. Much activity, though, at the theatre where the set came under long and close scrutiny and was considered very unsatisfactory by M. Bennett, and the whispers that it was too light in tone continued.

Mercifully, K. H. kept out of the arguments for once, but she was in fighting fettle, as healthy and young as a schoolgirl, giving her opinions on all and sundry. She liked her set. "Great set," she said. "Fine colour. I love those tobacco colours." Somehow I don't feel her praises ring true. She picked up a prop mirror and said, "That's no good! That's very vulgar." The roses were too large and it was interesting that she said that her mother never considered that any woman should come downstairs in a dressing gown.

She is one of the greatest show-offs I have ever known and she gave a good demonstration of this as during the tedious hours that are spent fixing the lights on her, she had to lie on the floor near the microphone. Suddenly she had the notion of singing very deeply into this instrument one inch from her mouth. She sang, very badly, "Miss Otis Regrets," which she truthfully said she learnt in order to get this job. Then she wisecracked to her nauseatingly sycophantic ingénue Noelle (Udana[1]), made compliments: "The 'cusstumes' are goin' to be lovely." Such energy as she has is absolutely astonishing. Today she was really galvanised, and what an exciting time for her, singing for the first time with an orchestra.

There is still a lot of improvement to be made to the set and it was tough that it had to be scrutinised in an unfinished condition. The lighting was appalling for most of the time, and Michael Benthall took it into his head to become boss, and spend a great deal of time altering clothes and backings and exasperating us all. However, in all fairness to the great big puffball, it is his job and it is always one of the most painful experiences to have to see the set in rough, without proper lighting and no costumes. Tom Skelton[2] remained calm, with half a dozen different people shouting different instructions, and finally a "conference" was convened. "Mystery" everyone agreed was what was

[1] The actress called Udana was replaced by Gale Dixon.

[2] Thomas R. Skelton (1928–94), lighting director on *Coco*. A pioneer in lighting dance.

needed, but how to acquire this was not known and everybody seemed to have different points of view. Alan was extremely fair and, although there are aspects of my set he does not like, was willing to "go along with my suggestions." Nonetheless I was quite a bit perturbed.

The great big "preparation" scene in which clothes are torn apart while the stage revolves seven times could not be rehearsed as the revolve would not work (shades of the Met's *Traviata*). So we continued quite late at night with the lighting. Suddenly Bud Widney,[1] Alan's right-hand man, said that we should all go home and leave the lighting to Bennett and Skelton. Alan Jay himself did not much relish being turned out of the theatre.

I packed up immediately, feeling both relieved and shocked, but I was much more shocked when I was walking home and passed Bennett and his assistant, and Bennett practically cut me. Only Bob said goodnight. Bennett is a bright boy but I will not allow him to trespass on my preserves and an ugly situation has been created.

SATURDAY, 8 NOVEMBER 1969

The "situation" at the theatre had blown over, so Bud Widney told me on the telephone, and Bennett and Skelton had both now realised what palette I needed for my costumes. I had telephoned to know if I was welcome at the theatre! K. H. was singing in her particularly ugly voice, as full-on strong as a child, and hating to be left out of any conference. She behaved most cruelly to the ingénue, who at last looked good in a wig, but Kate said it was false, too like her hair and gave a lesbian interpretation to the play. In fact, she knows the full head of hair makes her own look skimpy. Maybe she does not realise herself the reason why she is so determined not to let the girl look her best, at best an also-ran. The Ray clothes had all arrived at the theatre and Kate was putting on the new bedroom jacket, which is necessary for a quick change and which I consider quite ugly. She ran through her quick changes and complained about collars and cuffs, and contradicted her former announcement.

Jerry [Adler], the stage manager, told me not to go into her dressing

[1] Stone Widney, production supervisor on *Coco,* later a playwright, producer and director.

room. "She hates clothes!" The fact that she had slept badly was perhaps an explanation for much tough talk. The "Hoedown" was rehearsed, and I think it one of the most horrible numbers in a show that has many duds. Then the finale was rehearsed with lights, a very thrilling moment for me, and my nerves were on edge and raw whenever anyone made a suggestion that would lead to difficulties. Often Alan comes up with some impossible idea, which is suddenly changed to become a great improvement. I felt the effect of the moving staircase à la Busby Berkeley so great that I could not believe it when Bennett and Alan suggested scrapping it. The turntable machinery and the engineering were at fault, causing interminable delays, but I was buoyed up by the conviction that the whole finale will be as exciting as I had imagined.

SUNDAY, 9 NOVEMBER 1969

On arrival at the theatre panting and out of breath, Larry and John, my assistants, broke the news that everyone was ganging up on me to change the set and make it much darker; they thought the fault lay with Skelton's lighting and wanted me to be firm. I immediately tackled Fred Hebert and Fred Brisson to have them on my side.

I thought the atmosphere pretty tense but was delighted by the nice note of friendship from Kate thanking me for my birthday offering of yesterday. The [dress] rehearsal took for ever to start and the "Preparation" scene seemed to go for far less than I imagined, so much effort not noticed. When the performance proper started there were stops for the inevitable snags, the lighting was *impossible.* The little black dresses seen against a crimson background, and all the hot oranges and ambers suffusing the set at most times.

It is agonising to see one's work anew day after day without the changes that one knew had to be made, while prolonged scrutiny only brings more complaints. I was extremely anxious to get the painters to work on alterations but during the very long day as more and more suggestions came in, finally out of bad suggestions good ones came; for instance, since the mirrors on one side of the stage are not used to any effect I am pleased to change them for coromandel screens which, being dark, will please everybody—I hope.

K. H.'s performance does not grow with acquaintance and I feel quite on edge whenever she tries to sing, the sound so very unmusical. She was, of course, very fraught and swore a great deal in front of the entire populace. Things like having no backstage facilities for changing got her mad and I must say she is wringing wet after each strenuous scene. Her clothes in the interval were damp rags. She delivered a great scene to the authors about pornography and why the ingénue should not look like her, but mercifully I was spared today. However, by the end of a long, tiring, unnerving rehearsal, although many irritating criticisms of my work were levelled at me which proved I had not read or at least taken the script seriously, the atmosphere was not hostile for talk of intrigue. Everyone meant to be helpful.

André Previn, while admiring the finale, said he did not think it proved the point of the song that Chanel had freed women by making clothes simple, but had made them in part very elaborate. I felt the whole performance depressing, with little magic even at the best moments and such a deal of banal Broadway trash. Let us only hope Broadway will take to it, the critics won't, of that I am sure. I came back at 9:30, very tired in limb, and mercifully was able to sleep right away as suddenly life seemed very empty.

MONDAY, 10 NOVEMBER 1969

A horrid day of anxiety. The anxiety gave me a headache, which I had to bear, but which got worse when at the end of a long spell in the theatre I came home to recuperate with aspirin. The rainy morning spent choosing last-minute unnecessary pieces of furniture and minutiae like vases and flowers in far-flung parts of this most squalid city. Then to the theatre, where last-minute delays before a dress rehearsal combined with intrigues galore to prolong the start of proceedings. Even the orchestra, appearing for the first time, did not give the necessary lift to the show.

With each performance K. H. becomes less impressive. Her voice is excruciatingly ugly when she tries to sing and she is less effective even than at rehearsals. The music pales with an orchestra and the horrid numbers ("Hoe-down," "The Money Rings Out") are worse each time. All sorts of suggestions made for altering sets and costumes. Bob, the stage architect, said, "Why don't they fix the book?" I felt deeply pessimistic. The thing really would be a flop.

Alan makes me nervous with all his suggestions, some of which are bang on the mark, but he has an inability to cut down his own deathly prose. Benthall is a tactless fool, and when the principals left after their late rehearsal, they were heard to say, "The costumes are to be changed."

I returned late to the theatre to watch the painters making a very few alterations, but by midnight they quit and tomorrow is a holiday, so God knows when we will get anything altered. Meanwhile the scenery comes in for criticism and I fear will continue to do so for the next horrible month. Why did I not quit this show two years ago? Came back for more aspirin but headaches kept me awake quite a depressingly long time. I put on the light to try to telephone Kin in San Francisco but he did not reply.

TUESDAY, 11 NOVEMBER 1969

Black despair. My stomach was queasy. I dreaded the intrigue of the theatre, could hardly brace myself to go over to the squalor of Broadway with its pornographic joke shops, smells of frying foods and appalling ugliness. The morning spent attending to my businesses in my room including lots of telephone calls to deal with emergencies at the theatre. The little Noelle looks so revolting that she is in danger of getting sacked. Ray had to go shopping for last-minute emergencies at high prices and managed to do well. Meanwhile, lunchless, I went to the one o'clock rehearsal—dress—for musical numbers only. K. also on stage, half of the mechanism has broken down, a row about why painters had not come to do the necessary as requested.

I felt too sick to brazen out K. H. I am quite scared of her. It is a terrible effort to make inroads on her and I have nothing to say. I avoided her like the plague. At one point I felt I could hardly bear to remain in the theatre, the goings-on on stage so irritating and unattractive. There are several big numbers that get me on the raw. I told Karen Lerner how depressed and pessimistic I was, and how I couldn't imagine how Alan remained so comparatively calm, but she said he went back home to nightmares and, two nights ago, dreaming that he was being chased, fell out of bed. The day turned out less dramatically than I imagined, for the doom of the first chorus girls' costumes was delayed. I wish I could throw off all the gossip and rumours with a shrug. Instead I suffer.

Luckily my mood changed. I came back feeling there was chaos at the theatre but in other departments than my own. Certainly, it would be appalling if the mechanism breaks down in front of an audience and the show could not go on, but I felt that the last details of my job were going to be attended to, and I came back to sleep and to forget.

The first preview loomed.

WEDNESDAY, 12 NOVEMBER 1969

Had early call for the theatre to show costumes to Eugenia Shepherd by 9 o'clock! Was very pleased that she was so enthusiastic. It is important, but outraged to find that the prop man on his own initiative had arranged the flowers in the vases according to his own taste, had gradated [sic] the roses as if in a funeral parlour tribute. Didn't know I could get so angry so early. Came back to bed, for I needed all my strength and felt terribly fatigued.

Then the usual rush to the usual blundering, appalling, unhappy mess at the theatre. I do not believe in the show and do not enjoy watching anything but my two big costume numbers. The fact that we are opening tonight is terrifying beyond belief. The stage-works in hand present the most diabolical difficulties and if some mechanism breaks down we're for it.

Fred Brisson has behaved to me impeccably and he is my ally. Alan is as untrustworthy as anyone can be and the rest are a lot of sly, conniving sycophants. Hepburn scares the daylights out of me and the less I see of her the better. Fred asked me to dine before the show[1] and we had an interesting talk at Sardi's. I was amazed at his "cool." He has had this idea for eleven years and at last it was bearing fruit, and he was completely sanguine, completely aware of the shortcomings and difficulties, but taking everything in his stride. We went over to the theatre early in order to go round with good wishes for everybody. I was astonished by the size of the crowd, had forgotten that the Mark Hellinger can hold so many people. K. H. was behind her locked dressing-room door, but Phyllis opened it enough to give us a glimpse of a made-up face that grimaced a smile and a rejection at the same time. "That was pain-

[1] This was the night of the first preview.

less," said Freddie. Then on to the stage to congratulate Jerry Adler and his crew.

No sooner had I paid my compliments than to my astonishment I saw the first scene set up with the new corners exposing the coromandel screens, this completely destroying the basic effect of my design. In fact, these additions were only added so that they could be used after the audience had seen the oriental apartment. Jerry explained the corners could not be altered.

I roared with fury, shouted at Alan who promised that this was not a plot, that things would be put to rights tomorrow. My stomach turned over, my throat went white hot, my eyes burnt. The evening was utterly ruined for me. I saw the proceedings on stage in a haze of bile. And how I hated them.

K. H. received the most tremendous reception when she appeared on stage, but her first scene and song went for nothing and the first laugh of the show came about 20 minutes after curtain up. The audience was rich, elderly, stupid. They reacted very quietly to the whole evening, there was real enthusiasm for the "Music Rings Out," ending in wild catcalls after the little black dress number. It is exciting and my clothes looked well. But even after a whisky and soda in the interval, my mood was still vile and I loathed the whole evening and felt the more intelligent people present did too. A man at the back of the stalls, even in Act I, responded to the "Let's Go Home" song by saying, "Yes, let's."

The length of the entertainment was so interminable that dozens of people walked out and never knew there was to be an all "scarlet" finale. As for the "book" the K. H.–Noelle scenes were interminable, the sentiment quite unplaced. K. H. started to become a New England Joan of Arc hearing voices and her little star eyes a-twinkle with celestial thoughts. Withal, her pace flagged to an astonishing extent and her legs seemed heavier, ensconced in clay.

Fred, next to me, began to be amused rather than desperate. "Look, there's another batch of people walking out!" I did respect him for remaining so calm. My basilisk eyes lit upon poor sweet Karen Lerner and I gave her no quarter. I felt she should know how badly the evening was going even if idiotic people like Jane Panza and Sister Parrish[1] drawled that they were enjoying

[1] Sister Parrish (Mrs. Henry Parrish II) (1910–94), doyenne of American decorating, she refurbished the state rooms in the White House for Jackie Kennedy.

themselves. I knew I was making a mistake by doing so, but I was so angry that I would not mingle with the others backstage, walked home, pleased with the fresh night air, by myself.

I knew I was too upset to sleep, so took two pills and somehow managed to get through a miserable night with as little consciousness as I could muster. It was a sad experience, though nothing in comparison with Fred Brisson, to feel that so much of my time and energy, and at the expense of no summer holiday, all this should have gone for so little.

THURSDAY, 13 NOVEMBER 1969

I had told Larry R. to tell the staff that I would not be coming to the theatre again until the corners were fixed and I switched off my telephone. Today would be a complete rest from the theatre and its activities. It was a lovely sunny day, and I would go out and walk in parts of the town that I'd not glimpsed since Broadway had confined my steps.

I was visited by a nice Italian who was friendly and sympathetic, then went across the road for a luxurious dinner with my old chum, Margaret Case.

From Margaret I gathered that there is already quite a good deal of criticism of the *Coco* evening and even the way that Hepburn had influenced me to wear her own Chanel clothes, but worse, trousers, a thing Chanel would never have done. One cannot win.

FRIDAY, 14 NOVEMBER 1969

I spoke to Ray, telling him I was too upset by the first night [preview] proceedings to thank him and all his marvellous staff for the way they'd managed, and he said for them it had been the happiest experience of his career and only sorry if the play was not the greatest "smash."

It seems the Noelle of our play is going to be changed, so a lot of new clothes have to be made. It seems *Women's Wear* has published a bad first report. It seems Alan has been hysterical. So it went on.

Between calls I rested. I could have gone out to meet people but feel too uninterested, and luckily I was able to preserve energy for an evening that I thought was to be quiet and was not. It had been my intention to enjoy the highly civilised company of Jonathan [Lieberson] for dinner after looking in at the theatre, but the first act lasted longer than expected and I was "caught" leaving the theatre. I should not have returned as promised. No one would have bothered.

As it was, my dinner at Elaine's with Jonathan was confined to a half-hour's rush. Jonathan was discovered reading a book on "criticism" as he stood in a huge crowd waiting for me half an hour late. "It's very difficult to read this book here," he said. His eyes flashed as he told me of the *dégringolade* of Penelope Tree. She said of a hairdresser (!) that he was the wisest, most intelligent man she had ever met. Bailey has reduced her to his level.

Jonathan has suffered a terrible shock from the attempted rape/murder? of a maid by an intruder into the family house, and one feels that one great surprise could send him "round the bend."

He is so highly strung, so brilliant,[1] but he has recovered, and returned early to read some more, while I, on edge and furious at Alan telling me he had a "string of notes" to give me, merely inveighed against the leading man's velveteen jacket fading into the background. He told me the clothes for the chorus for "Personal History" were now almost right while I thought the song too long. I'm impatient at hearing of all the new songs and brilliant innovations that are going to be achieved, while nightly having to submit to the torture of hearing the repetition of completely inane, worthless and damaging stretches of bad dialogue, and dreadful production.

Benthall was again smelling of whisky to such an extent that he was a fire hazard, though I'm told not as drunk as last night. Bennett too has employed the technique too long of sloughing me off and saying, "It's going to be done."

Blinking like a mechanical owl, he clasped his fat hands together and

[1] Jonathan Lieberson's later fate was less happy. He developed AIDS, booked himself into a suite at the Lowell Hotel in order to receive his friends and bid farewell to them. He then left for his mother Zorina's house in Kent, Connecticut, and died there about two weeks later, on 16 June 1989. He was only 40. When his book, *Varieties,* was published in 1987, Elizabeth Hardwick wrote, "The depth of his learning and excellence of his style make him the most brilliant young intellectual of his generation," while Bruce Chatwin described him as "one of the most intelligent and articulate men in America."

said, "We've all got to be kind to Kate. We've got to get her through two performances tomorrow. We've got to tell her how good she is."

Later Fred B. said Kate was in tears, feeling that she'd let us all down, but I hardened my heart. K. H. can expect sympathy from no one, certainly not me. She'll get $1 million for being herself on her own terms, and if she's overwrought and wondering if she's as good as she's pretending she is, then it's all grist to her mill. It's her way of filling an empty life.

I came away from the theatre feeling ten years older and on edge, and wondering if instead of having had the quiet evening I'd expected, after such a nervous strain I'd be able to sleep. So just in case, I took a sleeping pill.

SATURDAY, 15 NOVEMBER 1969

A quiet afternoon. Joseph [a favoured masseur] came to give me a massage and at the moment when all was over and relaxation desirable, the telephone took on a terrible life, with all the noises of the theatre backstage as calls were put to me to meet the emergency of putting in a new Noelle, perhaps adding a number about the Chanel suit etc. etc. Alan wishes to see me, so a meeting is called for tomorrow at 4. It seems I am to be on tap at any time until we open. My stomach turns.

Sam Green then arrived with a huge "bladder pearful" of pâté before he and Cecil went to the theatre to see Kopit's Indians, *a play about Buffalo Bill, a response to the Vietnam War.*

Sam quite rightly said it would be good for me, while in theatre land, to call on K. H. whenever possible and give her kind words of encouragement. I arrived at the theatre to find the interval over. Her door open, she was making a quick change. I stood in a senile way in a dark corner near where she would pass to go on stage. I would make some pleasant remark. But the face of intense concentration with closed mouth and eyebrows down was something that scared me so much that I knew I had made a terrible mistake.

My stomach dissolved. I imagined her later creating the most appalling scene about my amateur behaviour and lack of respect. Sam said he could not imagine how I was so in awe of her, that my contribution to the show was as good as hers, that I should "come off it" and alter my attitude. It is true that I am completely terrified of this rather mad and certainly quite unaccountable, untamed dog.

It took me a long while to recover my equilibrium. Came to bed, feeling happier, but the waking was not good. The K. H. episode and the lurking danger of the theatre haunting me, and I'm not so sure that I'm not starting another cold.

Lunch with Diana Vreeland.

SUNDAY, 16 NOVEMBER 1969

Her reaction to having seen *Coco* was baffling to me. I could not believe it. She has never been a K. H. fan, is tired of this woman telling us she's the only well brought-up lady in America and all the snobbery "doesn't count any more." "No, I've never liked her, wouldn't be dragged to *Lion in Winter*, but in this she is so extraordinary I cannot believe it! She is so moving, so exactly like Chanel!"

She had no praise for the book, or for my "nostalgia" dresses, only for what I'd done for Hepburn. I was tongue-tied. To me it is the greatest shock.

Cecil would have liked to stay longer, but he had a date with Alan Jay Lerner and Fred Brisson at his hotel.

It was as well that it was done here in quiet as we were able to confer without interruptions. Some of the intrigue surrounding the "replacement" was divulged before Alan's arrival, how K. H. accuses them all of lying and hiding things from her. Alan's suggestions for improvements sound good, but I was aghast at the idea that they're altering the finale. It is sensational, and even to alter a detail could take away the impact. As it is, they intend to subtract about ten costumes. I could not resist telling Alan of many of my suggestions for improvements to the play, some of which he said he would consider.

The meeting went well and cleared the air for me. I felt much happier about the whole thing, though appalled at the amount of time I was likely to have to spend in New York hanging around the theatre when I intended to go to sunnier plots to regain lost health.

MONDAY, 17 NOVEMBER 1969

High-powered meeting with the re-implaced ingénue at costumier's. Having before been a terrified mouse, she is now back on her own terms, dictating and saying what *she* wants in the way of costumes (and no doubt salary too). Quite a transformation.

Bennett appeared and we tackled him about not changing the finale, or cutting out numbers of girls. He *seemed* to be convinced. Having decided to give in to the ingénue and allow her to wear strong green, Freddie rang to say the president of Chanel No. 5 had seen the show, liked a lot of it and had told Coco so, but raised certain objections, one of which was Chanel detested and never used green. My sore throat was beginning to get me down and the hectic condition in which we were trying to work was most exhausting.

My shell lurched off to lunch with Weissberger, but I had little to relate, or vice versa, and was impatient to leave, to get back to arrangements and sleep. Went to doctor who gave me penicillin and B12. I returned to bed for the rest of the day and night. Such a relief!

Telephoned news of outside happenings. K. H. had taken it upon herself to tell "Udana" she was sacked, lest she hear by other less fortunate sources. I begged leave to go to Jamaica to get rid of cold.

TUESDAY, 18 NOVEMBER 1969

Not at all recovered, Mary the maid advised me not to go out, to cancel all plans for the day. The relief of this was great. People who must would come to see me. My voice sorely tried by the telephone.

Truman telephoned to report on his visit to *Coco.* He did not spare me, thought my work the only good thing in a show with lousy book, lyrics and music. He was not impressed with "old Hepburn" and complained of the *longueurs.* Betsy Bloomingdale[1] then called in such a state of euphoria that I thought she must be mad, her euphoria followed by flowers.

It was soon lunchtime and I got out of bed for a room service Oeufs

[1] Mrs. Alfred Bloomingdale, friend of Nancy Reagan.

Benedict with Bob LaV., who drooled on about how much money I should make and don't. In his own way he has done extremely well out of Broadway this year in spite of working exclusively on flops. Joe Biaggi of the firm ludicrously named "Swank" brought his manufacturer to see me about the designs I have made for jewellery. This visit followed by Ray and Jack with patterns for the new Chanel suits and the new ingénue, who in spite of her preference must not wear Chanel's hated green. I found myself once more churning out designs, when suddenly Ben Rosenberg,[1] the accountant, appeared and, with all the time in the world, sat down and told me how he started out life as a banker, and of his experiences going a long way back in the theatre.

WEDNESDAY, 19 NOVEMBER 1969

At Ray's the atmosphere was very anticlimactic. K. H.'s understudy being rigged out and, although ten new dresses are being made and others designed for Noelle, the aftermath was a let-down. Ray looks tired and sad, his sister died.

THURSDAY, 20 NOVEMBER 1969

Early call to be at the theatre to stand over the painters to do their art deco decoration to the main doorway. Slow work but I went round the corner to Ray's where the new ingénue was being rigged out in quite new designs. Also slow work, but Ray enthusiastic, said, "I like what you're doing to her." Back to the theatre. Progress encouraging but I had to return again before the painters' day was over at three. And this meant a rush from taxiless area of New York where I was brunching most feebly with Anita Loos, Natasha and Whitney Warren.[2] I'd thought it was Anita's brunch and there'd be roars of laughter. Not a word

[1] Ben Rosenberg, general manager of the *Coco* company, later a theatre producer.

[2] Anita Loos, author of *Gentlemen Prefer Blondes*; Natasha Wilson and Whitney Warren, from San Francisco.

of any interest. Whit completely fatuous and no opportunity to talk uninterruptedly to anyone.

Came back to a sheaf of telephone messages, a chore that I'd cope with after sleep. Today I feel better for the first time, though I fear the inevitable cold presaged by sore throat will prevail. Sam very late in arriving to go up to K. Clark *Civilisation* and honour-conferring at the Met, which was the reason for my standing out in cold, windy street, and likely to add to the prospects of illness.

The speeches were unbelievably tedious and K. made a marvellous Freudian slip when he said "I'm very conscious of this horror" instead of "honour." Too near the knuckle for general laughter. The reception afterwards gave a great opportunity to see the splendid new hanging of marvellous pictures.

Sam sat while I had a pre-theatre steak sandwich in an opposite hotel, and I had to clock in at *Coco* to see if K. H.'s hats covered her face, or if they should be altered. Any more tedious reason for sitting at an unexpurgated, too long, too unfunny performance I cannot imagine. I was hardly able to remain in the theatre but Alan bullied me to remain afterwards, though he had no notes that made any sense. There is always some reason to be upset if I go to the theatre and that is why I like to keep away. I was unnerved to find that Bennett had told one of the dancers to take off her hat for the finale. We can't have this sort of thing or everything will go to pot. Walked home feeling the whole evening had been a complete waste of time.

FRIDAY, 21 NOVEMBER 1969

A depressing, wasted day. Nothing seemed to be accomplished. The effort to get out of the room between telephone calls caused an ulcer feeling in stomach and any appointment with the skin doctor is never exhilarating. Today he added more scabs. These in themselves are lowering to the morale. Truman in the country seemed to be on the crest of the wave, having an easy, effortless, but successful life. I felt envy of him. Margaret Case gave her résumé of last night's visit to *Coco* with Rattigan and Glenville.[1] They realised what a job of

[1] Sir Terence Rattigan (1911–77), playwright, and Peter Glenville.

ingenious designing my set was (few do!), they realised the importance of the style I had injected into the production, they realised the importance of my costumes. They realised the importance of K. H., though saying she could not project the lyrics and was often at a loss for direction. They realised how poor the book and music. They thought it would be a hit.

SATURDAY, 22 NOVEMBER 1969

Would clearly have liked to have the morning off like most people but here was an occasion to get away from the theatre chores and concentrate on trying to make money in another direction, that of selling ties and scarves.

The shadow of the late afternoon's meeting hung over me with anxiety and dread. I feared that there'd be a horrid row, that I'd lose my temper, that I might walk out over the criticisms of my work from the people who are least likely to know what is good or bad.

I got to the show in time for my most loathed "Hoedown" and had to squander half an hour's valuable energy before the "after the curtain" meeting on stage when electricians and all the chorus girls had to be assembled while a panel "judged" my clothes. Would this pass? What was the test to be? No one knew.

Freddie had heard Chanel had become furious at the idea of plastic being used, so he was against plastic. Someone else was against the Christmas tree balls, but who? No one would say what they thought when these dresses were exhibited. I made a few concessions. I'd alter some of the dresses criticised, and if they could make up their mind to censor the Christmas balls then I'd do other designs. But Ray brought a little sense by whispering, "Imagine, here are 12 grown-up men giving all their expensive time in this fatuous way."

Benthall went on about sequin shoulder straps and it was hard for me not to say that he had missed his vocation in life. What does Bennett think about mauve? At one point I almost turned to two old women in the stalls clearing away that matinée debris of programmes, Dixie cups and used French letters to ask them what they thought.

I used some pretty strong sarcasm and Alan L. said, "Oh come now, we've not asked you to change many things!" At any rate the scenery was no longer criticised and after a fatuous waste of half an hour a few decisions were arrived at, and Alan then herded us all into an office to hear about the improvements and cuts he was making to the show.

But when can they go in? Monday? No, not till Friday—if then. Meanwhile the show goes on in its overlong dreary way, though the audiences like it and the applause at the end delights Hepburn so much that I can't think she will be willing to leave this for a solitary life as long as her health holds out (again at this matinée she had another nosebleed). I'm told the show is bringing in more money (at $15 tickets) than any other Broadway show ever has. Even I, with my minute percentage, have earned a pittance with the last week's vast takings.

I came away from the theatre so relieved that there had been no real unpleasantness that I felt as if I was in a holiday mood. There were still extra clothes to design and others to supervise, but I felt the end was in sight and that I could have a nice quiet weekend in which to look after my frail health.

SUNDAY, 23 NOVEMBER 1969

I think now that she is ensconced, K. H. has feelings of remorse that she was so difficult about her clothes. "I hated them, but now I like them," she admits and she chastises herself for having been so difficult, so impossible, now that her friends think she looks great in her clothes and now that the audiences give her a standing "reception." It is heady wine and she is quite high with delight, but the fact that she has nosebleeds is worrying, a symptom of high blood pressure and nervous exhaustion. Alan says, "Give her work to do. The busier she is and the more she has to think about, the healthier it is for everyone."

MONDAY, 24 NOVEMBER 1969

To the theatre where Kate was rehearsing with the new Noelle. I find myself trapped in the stalls watching as the hours speed by and Alan talks of how great the show is going to be. "Truman and Lee will be proved wrong. Wait till you see the new material!" Kate was extremely ungracious, shouting to Alan, asking René if he were on marijuana, and she has recently hit two stage managers. We had a talk about a hat of hers being altered and again she said I was very stubborn. She is the least determined-to-be-loved of many women I know. I came away fairly calm, thinking everything was under control for the new girl but with one's back turned anything can happen.

I dined with Fred near the theatre (Pyrenees) and sat through first act in close seats. It was a very smooth performance and the audience liked it in spite of the non-cuts.

TUESDAY, 25 NOVEMBER 1969

Woke to find an awful attack on my *Coco* work in *The Times.* They really had it in for me and some of the criticisms are valid. All will stick. It means a great deal more work. The telephone howled with indignation from Fred B. and Alan L., the latter having already sent off an hysterical telegram complaining of the lack of ethics of *The Times* in reviewing a show before it was officially opened. Diana V. very upset on my behalf and at the theatre Jerry [Adler] showed his loyalty by saying it was outrageous.

K. H. had not seen the article (very unflattering about her too) but Jerry whispered what had appeared and she rushed down the corridor to me shouting, "Cecil, I hear you've been roasted! Well, take no notice of them. Other people love all you've done, and it was just the same for me when I did *Jane Eyre.*[1] They came out to Chicago and roasted me. The only thing to do is to ignore them." This was the only moment when I felt a bit sorry for myself. By the time the day had passed I had no longer any memory of the attack.

The usual delays at theatre and at Ray's where fittings continue without the excitement of working to a "first night," so that there was only just time for me to bring a hamburger and Dixie cup of coffee up to my room before the afternoon's photography began. I had rather looked forward to taking some pictures after such a long interval but the strain of fitting them in with so little a margin took the edge off the enjoyment.

 [1] *Jane Eyre* (1937), play written by Helen Jerome, which closed out of town.

Andy Warhol at the Factory, New York, 1969, with his team, including Candy Darling and Brigid Berlin

I felt I hadn't done rightly by Viva[1] who is such an extraordinary character as well as Luini-esque beauty. She kept up the incessant running commentary that is so effective in Andy's films, and much of it is entertaining and strange. She looked quite beautiful in the camera which does not show that the whites of her eyes are greenish grey like the outside of a hard-boiled egg yolk, and her teeth a dead colour; her nose is an anteater's. Yet she is a photographic marvel. Ed and his Japanese assistant then accompanied me to the Plaza Hotel

[1] Viva (b. 1942), actress who appeared in several Warhol films, including *The Nude Restaurant* (1968) and *Lonesome Cowboys* (1968).

where, after hours of arrangements, telegrams galore and appointments set, the ghastly gang that moves around with pop groups or stars were ignorant of my intentions to photograph Mick Jagger at 4 o'clock.

One young man said, "I was never told, but I'll go and wake him up. He's been travelling all night and sleeping all day." Later he returned, saying, "Mick is waking up by slow degrees, he'll have some breakfast, then bathe and he'll be with you as quickly as possible." I felt this was frying pan into fire stuff. What *was* I doing hanging about while all these high-powered kids were on telephones to all parts of the world offering $50,000 to some firm to make a film of the performance at Madison Square Garden on Thursday. (During the past week the Stones have grossed one and a quarter million.)

Eventually someone came in and said, "Mick'll be here in five minutes," and sure enough, smelling very strongly of Floris lime bath essence, he was. Very pale and soberly coiffed, in tight white silk trousers with bulging jacket and a pale-green design on a sweater, he did not present a very dazzling picture. But he is nice, on the level and unbelievably photogenic, and I hope his magic will come through to save the situation for me. He later wore an extraordinary old-fashioned conjurer's cloak made by Ossie Clark, of black silk and tassels and black velvet bands, reminiscent of a doctor's degree cloak and a judge or Mephistopheles.

By this time I had no respite since waking and my head was aching and my bladder in need of being emptied, so I was in no mood to accept Mick's invitation to go with him right away to watch them do their show in Philadelphia. "We're motoring from here at 7:30. We do our show at 10."

If I were not to have been getting up early to catch a plane for Jamaica tomorrow morning, I might have been tempted to "cut" the theatre, but hell would break loose if I were not there to discuss the new Noelle's new clothes and an idea (rotten) that Alan now has of adding a scene showing Coco's private dining room. All these abortive and beside-the-point attempts to improve the show take up so much time. For years, now, one could count the wasted hours discussing things that one has to give the benefit of the doubt to.

Anyhow, when Mick asked me to have a drink with him in his room I was pleased to do so, headache still raging but I could go to his bathroom and enjoyed seeing Mick, so self-assured and yet so completely simple and natural, in the same suite in which B. Streisand had once played the superstar role.

Mick, walking about barefoot, talked of his recent visit en route from Australia to Bali, and how impressed he had been by the dancers and the beauty of their gestures. He did an imitation of the young boy who did the lion dance and every fibre of his body was alive with movements that were "new" to him. He is all the time experimenting in his "art" and has now the intention of making his "show" much more of a theatrical visual experience with coloured backdrops and lighting in which he would like my help.

He *hated* the complacency of Australia, enjoyed the Ned Kelly experience and although he feels Tony Richardson is an egomaniac, is impressed by his knowledge of the pictorial side of film making. I left Mick after a quiet sympathetic half-hour, feeling he was really a very sensitive and exceptional person with a quiet way of doing things that go from good to greater.

Late dinner with Larry Reehling whom I feel I'll never get to know better. He has a way of shelving anything difficult and tiresome, and of talking when he senses one is going to ask him to do other things. He has a real theatre sense and could possibly be an excellent producer. His views on this show have always been excellent.

The backstage scene, with Alan like a frenetic cat on heat, was more ridiculous and hectic then ever before. Everyone at cross purposes. Benthall being the last straw of stupidity, ignored by all. V. difficult to get anything arranged. But I escaped with incredible feelings of relief that from tomorrow morning my brain would not be filled with all these tiresome distractions and with luck these horrid songs and orchestrations would not be making my waking hours an unpleasant continuation of all these unpleasant memories with the terrifying ogress, K. H., at the base of so much trouble.

On the following day, Wednesday, 26 November, Cecil and Sam Green left for Jamaica to stay in the Spanish-style 1920s house of Lady Sarah Roubanis.[1] *Here they remained until the end of the month. Cecil recalled a "loveless, lovelorn honeymoon" here with Peter Watson, and later visits to Ian Fleming and Noël Coward. He found Sam "a delightful companion" and one evening he told Sam about his past.*

[1] Lady Sarah Spencer-Churchill (1921–2000), daughter of tenth Duke of Marlborough. She had two husbands before marrying (1967) a Greek, Theo Roubanis. In the 1970s she was raped by natives at her Jamaican home.

The half-hour of daiquiri drinking before our excellent lobster dinner was given up to my relaying the most serious of my love affairs. I found myself remembering all sorts of long-forgotten details about Kyrle Leng,[1] Doris Castlerosse[2] etc., some of which were wonderfully salacious. Sam particularly liked Doris's effort to delay my orgasm by ordering me to "think of your sister's wedding."

Sam and he worked on their project, Sam even writing out Cecil's notes in long-hand for the typist.

Although we get along extremely well, every now and again the generation gap does assert itself. A native in the duty free shop asked if I was Sam's father. Then, when told I was not, asked, "Then you are travelling together?"

SUNDAY, 30 NOVEMBER 1969

Tomorrow our holiday is over. I feel I have made a really delightful new friend.

MONDAY, 1 DECEMBER 1969

Suddenly the telephone called me and Fred Hebert was wanting to know where I was as Alan had a lot of memos. This raised the tempo of my blood, my holiday was over.

There was a terrible rush in the heat to the airport, and muddles over the flight and departure. But they got on the plane and arrived in New York in a blizzard. Cecil found his hotel room double locked. He was in a panic to get to the theatre.

[1] Kyrle Leng (d. 1958), early friend of Cecil's, with whom he fell in love, but Leng went to Oxford and formed a life-long partnership with Robert Gathorne-Hardy, while Cecil went to Cambridge.

[2] Doris Delavigne (1901–42), wife of the corpulent gossip-columnist, Viscount Castlerosse. Her spirited attitude to sex was that there is no such thing as an impotent man, only an incompetent woman. Cecil had an affair with her in order to annoy Peter Watson. During the war, Doris became depressed and committed suicide.

So in unsuitable clothes rushed to arrive just as curtain was going up at theatre. Fred to greet me, worried in case I'd missed out, but the list of Alan's "memos" very slight, a lot of fuss about nothing. But a meeting called for tomorrow and all costume suggestions then to be made. Meanwhile the show was an improvement undoubtedly, though still many "cuts" should be made.

Kate very elated at end of performance and, never one to pour oil, said they were all furious at your going away. *Tant pis.* K. H. brought me back and in my room found a sheaf of messages, proofs, letters from home. It was late and I was very tired when I finally accepted that my holiday was over and tomorrow would be another busy day.

TUESDAY, 2 DECEMBER 1969

Early start, but then early for theatre isn't early for the rest of the world, so I was able to contact the other world and, just as I was leaving, the unexpected extra call made me late. However, Ray was later than I at his office. I had to make many snap decisions before going on to the "conference" at the theatre. This seemed to go well with nerves calmer, and a lot of "home truths" were accepted. Bennett says he is going to do this and that but so little is done. I nagged Alan about cuts.

Back at Ray's it was difficult to concentrate on all there was to do with conflicting personalities arriving and leaving, but we are getting towards the end of another phase. The new "Chanel suits" about to be finished. I now have the fun of designing a lot more vulgar Fath-ish[1] "Sebastian Bayes." Diana [Vreeland]'s Diana did secretarial work for me at our sandwich lunch half-hour and soon the telephone was ringing from all sorts of unexpected directions (including Kate photography) necessitating more arrangements.

WEDNESDAY, 3 DECEMBER 1969

The inevitable battle against time. This gives one the ulcer feeling if not the ulcer. Even at Ray's it was difficult to keep calm in spite of the comparative lull.

[1] A reference to Jacques Fath (1912–54), Paris couturier who was known as "the couturier's couturier."

There were so many decisions to make and so little time. The new clothes are funny, but so many considerations to other people's tastes have to be made. It is now time when so much effort has to be made to please the obvious. Alan ruined my peace of mind by telephoning during the matinée where the audience was particularly sluggish to say Hepburn's hats must be changed because of apocryphal complaints from the gallery. I lost my cool, but also my preserves of energy.

The midday treat of seeing Lincoln [Kirstein] was a rare exception to these days. He is so alive and brilliant, so modest, so helpful. I broached the subject of whether I should publish Vol. III[1] and he was perturbed. If I had spare energy to face the onslaught of criticism, but "Gentlemen don't do those sort of things," and there'd be awful criticism about a "love affair" between a faggot and a lesbian.

Afternoon of trivialities including a visit to talk to 300 women fashion editors corralled by Eleanor Lambert.[2] Walking with Fred B. down Park Avenue we tried to unravel some of the present difficulties, but I should not get involved in a hopeless situation. K. H. will not hear of a new director being brought in to replace the completely incompetent Benthall. But as soon as I get a new job of work outside *Coco* there is sure to be an interruption. I am telling other people as well as myself that this is my last stage job.[3]

THURSDAY, 4 DECEMBER 1969

How to throw myself back so far as yesterday? It seems an aeon ago. So much emotion and feeling have been spent. On arrival in calm spirit at Diffen's, I was suddenly faced with the knowledge that Alan's assistant, Bud, had either been in or had sent word to say that the costumes of the following mannequins needed alteration. This return to the criticism by Alan of the colours and non-colours in Act I struck me as being so exasperating that I went to the telephone and lost my temper with Bud to such an extent that I could hardly talk. My voice came out as a full-steam foghorn. My body was a highway of flowing

[1] This was the controversial Garbo volume of diaries, published in 1972 as *The Happy Years.*

[2] Eleanor Lambert (1903–2003), fahion guru.

[3] And so it proved to be.

nerves. I felt shivers of cold throughout. I don't think I ever remember being so angry as I let off my fury at all the pinpricks of the last weeks.

When I had finished I had to sit down. The skin on my face felt so taut I wondered what I would look like. What colour? The Diffen personalities were amazed and shocked, didn't know I could do it. Eventually, after I'd recovered, I felt refreshed and pleased that I had been able to give myself such a catharsis. Of course, a rude letter from Alan was forthcoming, and although I acted hurt at the theatre and he avoided a confrontation alone, I minded less about this than the unjust intrusions into my professional domain.

The row really coloured the whole day. Luckily there were diversions. Fulco [Verdura] painted a very funny picture of Coco Chanel at lunch. He repeated many of her most characteristic and appalling bons mots. He gave me her *real* flavour (unlike the rubbish we are portraying at the theatre). The afternoon was one of interviews (first time furniture reporter) telephone and a short abortive visit to the theatre where the eight new suits arrived but [were] not shown on the stage.

An hour later I met for dinner with Freddie at 21 and we talked of the glorious gossip connected with the show, all hair-curling and easily forgotten. The evening performance showed alterations and some improvements, the audience only wanting to be amused, laughed at the serious *longueurs.*

FRIDAY, 5 DECEMBER 1969

Since Alan, having sent me one of his spontaneous letters, had obviously been avoiding a confrontation with me last night, and I would probably not get a word in edgeways when next we would meet, I decided to send him a letter in reply. This I read for approval, readily given, to Freddie B. But by the time this was coped with a valuable slice of the early morning and a lot of energy had been wasted.

Felt guilty as I played hookey from *Coco* and went downtown to discuss making money by choosing colours for reprinting classical fabric designs.

The afternoon passed with a visit from Joseph, more telephone calls, then a strangely long silence when for hours on end the bell never rang. It created an uncanny feeling. Of course, when it was time for me to leave there were two extra calls (Natasha [Wilson]'s 64th birthday had to be celebrated), which made me late.

I waited at elevator door while the elevators rushed up and down without stopping. Exasperated, I shouted to myself "fuck" but discovered it was not to myself, for a married couple had appeared, all dressed up for their Friday night out, to whom I most embarrassingly apologised. But in the icy streets the taxis were all "off duty." I walked for miles on the way to the Bobs[1] for a pre-theatre meal. We were to see *Salvation*, a sort of amateur *Hair* done by even younger people. It was enchanting, of such gusto and spirit, the whole form refreshing and new. Back projections of abstract patterns, old photographs etc. gave the impression of immense scene changes. The combo of five people was brilliant.

Altogether a great evening, only too short. It made one realise how ridiculous it is that we are doing such an old-fashioned, outdated show at the Mark Hellinger, 33 in the orchestra! And no music! And no lyrics in comparison. I felt suddenly allied to a world that has long gone. No wonder that we'll get such a roasting from Clive Barnes.[2] Back to the Bobs for some healthy pornography in which a young negress showed innate dignity while performing the most shameful acts.

SATURDAY, 6 DECEMBER 1969

I have a feeling that, since I don't believe *Coco* will be a long-time success, this visit is not really the moneymaker that it was intended to be. So I must make money on the side. Today I did simultaneously two coloured sketches of K. H. as C. C., which I hope to sell. The drawings, which were done in bed, even when on the other end of the telephone was Diana V. [Vreeland], took me to a late lunch.

Eggs and bacon fortified me till teatime when Fred started nagging about whether I was going to see the matinee or evening performance of *Coco* and if I'd call him back on various subjects. He wants Lerner to call me as a

[1] Bob La Vine and Bob Prairie.

[2] Clive Barnes (b. 1927), English critic (reviewed dance for *The Times* 1961–5), became drama critic for *New York Times*, 1967. His influence was considerable.

Princess Lee Radziwill (sister of Jackie Onassis) photographed at Pelham Place, 1967

result of what Alan terms as my "nice" letter, but I was just as happy not to be bothered and feel that the more days that pass without my having to make further concessions the better. Out of town reports read to me by Fred's secretary Linda are appalling and I fear Clive Barnes will give us a complete roasting. By the end of the day my two sketches were complete and I felt tired but satisfied, and considered I had deserved one or two telephone calls.

The evening at Lee [Radziwill]'s was relaxed and enjoyable. The G. Liebersons rejudged by me came out with high marks. There is no doubt he is bright, and after one gets over her [Zorina's] gauchery and lack of feminine grace, she is extremely observant and alert. Her imitations of other Russians who have never mastered any other language was incredibly funny—Valentina,[1] e.g. "She looks what Garbo want but don't." The description of Nemtchinova[2] going to have the expression on her face photographed, when she had been told by Auntie that Mummy had died, was incredibly funny.

[1] Valentina Schlee (1894–1989), widow of Georges Schlee and still living at 450 East 52nd Street, in the same block as Garbo, though the two ladies tried never to meet.

[2] Vera Nicolayevna Nemtchinova (1899–1984), Russian dancer and teacher.

Lee quite a mysterious character with a lot of unexpected things going on in the background of her life. We gossiped, perhaps too freely, about *Coco*, and other stage, film, music, ballet subjects, and of course the youngest generation, until very late. The Liebersons have made good, Zorina in a sable coat dropped me home in their chauffeur-driven limousine. The lights were on up in Jonathan's room where he has been studying so concentratedly for the past months that unfortunately I have not been able to see anything of this pure and remarkable human being.

SUNDAY, 7 DECEMBER 1969

There were the usual necessary telephone arrangements and I had to get out of my bath to hear that the date of the photo call had to be changed, Hepburn saying that if the new material was to go in on Monday it could only be as a result of a rehearsal and to hell with the *Life* cover. I admire very much her always putting first things first and her respect of her audience is of paramount importance. But she has no thought for advancing the prospect of the show itself.

An impromptu dinner with Lee. This time her sister [Jackie Onassis] and David Frost made up the evening. It was not as interesting as the night before, and D. F. is first and last a slick journalist, and the TV world does not look well in private life. Nevertheless he has qualities even if perhaps without a heart.

Jackie looked quite hideous, square-faced, fat-cheeked, double-chinned, with old hands, her hair worn in straggles and her body disguised in a sort of Barbarella cowboy suit. She seems interested in every newspaper item, but without the aura of the White House becomes suddenly an ordinary creature far less pretty than her unphotogenic sister. Jackie, a nature nut, wasted, having spent all morning in the hunting field, insisted on walking home through the sleet and snow. A pleasant evening with quite good opportunities for talk and it was not necessary for once to feel that one was spending too many evenings among the alien corn.

MONDAY, 8 DECEMBER 1969

Fred B. seems to enjoy talking to me and calls every hour upon the hour, but to put the talk on a business basis he generally ends by giving me some extra chore that will necessitate other calls, then calling him back to report on unnecessary developments. He still asks if Alan has called me in answer to my letter, which I am glad to say he hasn't since I'm afraid this would necessitate being closer to him and therefore at the mercy of many new sources of irritation.

There has been much praise of the revival of Noël's *Private Lives,* and since so many people have told me how great Tammy Grimes[1] is, I decided to take Margaret Case (our five hundredth visit to the theatre?) to see the phenomenon. Such it turned out to be. Tammy is a freak. In this she is without doubt a man dressed up as a woman. As such, a claque roared with laughter every time she moved or said anything. I was appalled at this terrible transvestite ugliness, the boxer's neck and jaw, the huge forehead, shapeless arms, body and legs, the croaking and squeaking of this freak's voice. I was staggered at the ugliness of her appearance, her unpressed clothes, her feet. But she does act with a great variety of talents. She sang her small hit brilliantly and the audience accepted her as the most alluring woman that she is supposed to be. But my mind went back to Gertrude Lawrence, and I realised again her impeccable style, grace, distinction, sexual allure and evocation of beauty. I felt very sad.

But the play stands up amazingly well to the changes of fashion. It has heart and seems so much less brittle than it is said to be. Meanwhile poor Noël is extremely ill and weak, though perhaps his latest success will buoy him up and add to the enjoyment of his 70th birthday celebrations.[2]

TUESDAY, 9 DECEMBER 1969

By the time I've gulped coffee and a club sandwich, and got to the theatre, she is already there half an hour early and complaining that others are not ready for her. She is the most bossy of schoolteachers. It takes a great effort to pull

[1] Tammy Grimes (b. 1934), stage and film actress who had briefly had her own TV show (1966).

[2] Noël Coward was too ill to appear at the main celebration of his 70th birthday in London and got Princess Grace to stand in for him.

oneself up to face her bark but one mustn't let her see that one is frightened. The half-dozen photographers were working on stage while I rigged up a studio in the lobby.

Once on the job Kate became human for the camera, being touching, winsome, gay, appealing in turn. But not one word of give and take or friendliness in between shots. The egomaniac in her was given full sway and she even acted her part out to add to her enjoyment. She manages to have the company on her side, was photographed with the crew and did all the things she should have except be a human being. I felt the photographs I took were of quite a good average and some even interesting. I said, "My God, you are lucky to be so photogenic." The chorus girls were very pretty and the bright ones knew how to pose.

Alan seemed calm as Fred watched our reconciliation. The whole atmosphere seems to have calmed down and the final alterations are going into the show. Kate is now "frozen."

It is awful that I am still nervous before a routine job of this sort, and when Sabinson,[1] the publicity man, said "Things are going well," I begged him not to prognosticate.

Ten days more to go.

It seems the morale of the company is very low. K. H. pays no attention to anyone but herself and the incessant rehearsals have got the chorus down. Alan Lerner had to send telegrams to the company bidding their gracious presence at a Sunday rehearsal and saying they would receive a $60 bonus.

WEDNESDAY, 10 DECEMBER 1969

The evening was very festive with Ray Diffen and his friend Harry. I took them to Mr. & Mrs. Forster's, the extraordinary restaurant run by the Virginia lady cook who supplies individual meals for people with special tastes. We gossiped

[1] Harvey B. Sabinson, one of two publicity directors for *Coco*, later Executive Director of the League of American Theatres and Producers Inc. (1982–96).

all evening about *Coco* and its personalities, who was a snake in the grass, who against, who loyal etc. Of course, the "boys" hear everything, see everything and are very intuitive. Ray is kind, funny and appreciative, and I am glad I made the gesture though it was an expensive one and it's time I stopped getting into New Yorker habits.

The colour *Coco* photographs have come in, of great splendour. K. H. photographs like a 16-year-old, fresh, clean, untrammelled. As I told her, she is damned lucky to be so photogenic. Very late by the time I'd gone through the countless slides.

THURSDAY, 11 DECEMBER 1969

Hoped to oversee the new costumes going into *Coco* tonight (Sebastian Baye and Noelle) in a short while. But Gale, the Noelle, with a snivelling cold in the head, was so difficult and tiresome that one of her dresses took us an hour to conceive. Her demands based on the fact that she has bad legs and no posture but she made other excuses. Am now at the end of my tether and easily roused to anger. At lunch with Weissberger conversation hung heavily after I'd talked to him about our business. His funny stories appal me, but he's a loyal friend.

[Sam Green] made an excellent suggestion about showing the little girl in red Communion dress to introduce and explain the red finale dream sequence. Sorting of photographs and with eyes aching and very little time to spare, met the Freds for quick dinner before show. Audience very alert and performance greatly improved. Still the end is too long but the big numbers now pull together and the new clothes a success. But Hepburn had not been told of the new arrivals and on finding herself vis-à-vis a new Noelle outfit "blew her top."

Anything seems to throw her. The fact that the turntable brought her on stage on her sofa from the P. side instead of OP upset her mightily and she created a great scene. Poor Jerry.

She blamed me and dressmakers, she blamed Alan, but it was for the stage management to tell her. In any case we can't get near her closed door. I argued hotly, lost my temper, and I think she responds to rough talk, and she disappeared. However, the scene upset me so much that with all the extra amount on my mind I was not able to sleep. I got up and had a pill but even so the night was made unpleasant and unrelaxing for me.

FRIDAY, 12 DECEMBER 1969

Wakened by a London call, in answer to mine, by Blau[1] to try to get *Coco* pictures out to press. It is all so unnerving and upsetting. I'd like to pack it in, but I must make this final effort. Then I can relax in the country in England.

Alan, who had been the first to bear the brunt of Kate's displeasure about the new clothes, had recovered his sense of humour enough to give word that lest she be put off her performance someone must go and tell her that the man in the box office was today wearing a pink tie.

Later in the day I discovered that one of the little dancers in the show who had been busy photographing at the "call" had sent his negatives to be immediately developed. He then took one print to K. H. that night and in spite of a clause in her contract that she would give me first preference for the publication of herself as *Coco,* gave the dancer a go-ahead, and thus the picture will appear first of all in *Life.* I then remembered how this little dancer had come Judas fashion to me in the lobby where I was working, offering me a cup of tea; he knew he was betraying me.

Meanwhile [the man at] Pix had later received a call from Blau and he came hotfoot to pick up the negatives and the "passed" pictures from K. H., who graciously conceded that I had done a good job.

Later in the day Fred Brisson telephoned to say that he really believed Hitler was alive on 51st Street. He had never in his career had such unpleasantness with any actress. He and Alan had got together in mutual hatred and both had said that such troubles as these were not worthwhile. K. H. was still refusing to do the record album, was ranting against the "logo" and bawling out everyone who was nice enough to come and beard her in her lair.

I was not in good shape for the evening's entertainment, a great dinner, followed by a little dance, given in her white over-decorated house by

[1] Tom Blau, of Camera Press, the photographic agency.

Mary Lasker. It was a Democratic Party gala graced by President and Mrs. Johnson. I suppose snobbery and propaganda make one alter one's opinions, but having been revolted by Johnson during the time that his ugly face appeared every morning on the breakfast tray, I now thought him quite passable with even a certain charm and gentleness of manner.

At the end of dinner he got up to make a speech in honour of Mary. It was done with grace. Naturally, he has had a great deal of experience, but it was wonderful to see someone's brain at work, while in a flash he shut his eyes and decided what he was going to say. He rounded off long and complicated sentences with style.

The dinner was divided into two rooms and it was only later that I heard how Brooke Astor, who is always springing to her feet to make a complete fool of herself, had again risen and had delivered an oration that left everyone gasping. She pointed to the ex–First Lady and said, "You are Lady Bird. What a fitting name for a bird like you. You are a lovely bird who reminds me of a bird that flies everywhere dropping seed from which flowers grow." Dead silence. "Everywhere you go, over islands in the Pacific, everywhere you drop your seed and the flowers flourish."

The evening should have been interesting for there were certainly interesting people present. Doctors, including the greatest heart operation surgeon in the country, bankers, politicians, journalists, but also there was complete dross, people who, as Margaret Case said shockedly, "should not have been there."

Unfortunately, I was not able to extricate myself from bores and since the noise was so appalling, I soon found myself drained of remaining energy, and beat early retreat.

On Saturday, 13 December, Sam drove Cecil to Long Island so that he could stay with an old society friend, Alexandra Emery Moore (Mrs. Robert McKay) at her Oyster Bay home. He enjoyed being in an old-fashioned, luxurious house, "a hangover of the great days of wealth now gone."

On the Sunday Cecil had to leave in order to fly to Greensboro, North Carolina, on a moneymaking expedition to meet Mr. and Mrs. Nathan Slack, of Heritage furniture, for whom he was undertaking some fabric designs. Stricken with a bad cold, he was relieved to get back to New York.

MONDAY, 15 DECEMBER 1969

Seldom have I felt more joyful than when told they had got me on a 6:40 plane this evening. Another night in that motel room avoided and a present of a free day in New York at this time was indeed a godsend.

On the way from Newark in the taxi we passed the Mark Hellinger Theatre so I took the opportunity of getting out and clocking in at the performance. I let myself be seen backstage and again at the back of the stalls, saw the results of the "touch-up" job to the books, chandeliers etc., then left to the womb of my room.

TUESDAY, 16 DECEMBER 1969

Noël C.'s 70th birthday. He is not well enough to attend all the celebrations in his honour. It is a shock to think this young blade has suddenly become elderly. It is a nail in one's own coffin.

It is a strain wondering if one will recover in time for the last-minute rush and for the Atlantic flight. Later in the day with a bit of packing done, and the wall piled with envelopes ready to be sent out, it became apparent that I would not be well enough to go out to Sam's dinner party, also that Diana V. was a flu victim and would not be able to come with me to the [First Night] opening of *Coco*. She called me late at night and was in a wild state with a high temperature and exaggerated emotions.

Very much the feeling that the end of this visit is near. I took a very hot bath and lay sweating between blankets, then having started to sleep, remembered the Vick's rub and, tingling like a boiling lobster, welcomed sleep.

WEDNESDAY, 17 DECEMBER 1969

Much recovered.

My lunch date was the head of the Morgan Library, young Charles Ryskamp. He has a freshness and purity that is very rewarding and rare.

As luck would have it the hired car[1] passed by the hideous Mark Hellinger Theatre where I clocked in for the end of a matinée performance, showed myself. For the first time I saw the incredible speed with which the chorus girls rush off stage to various vantage points to be met by hairdressers, or dressers who rip their clothes off with brutal force. In a matter of seconds the changes are made. It was quite a revelation and so much more interesting than anything going on on stage.

I had intended to call on Hepburn but she rushed to her dressing room without a gesture or a smile, so I left forthwith, thinking how miraculous it was that at long last the date of opening was finally upon us. One more day and then freedom.

The day of the First Night of Coco *finally dawned.*

D-DAY THURSDAY, 18 DECEMBER 1969

This date has loomed large the past six months. At last it was terrifyingly upon us. The whole day really spent in preparation for what the night might bring. Although we knew a musical was of little interest, this one took on great importance, for it would be the result of many years' talks and of many months' whole-time job.

The telephone morning was quiet, a young fan with her Jewish mother came to show me her portfolio. I hurried to the theatre to leave packages at the door, then to lunch with Tammy Grimes at a hamburger joint near her. Back to prepare for the evening, making a *place à table* for my 22 supper guests, having Joseph knock me into shape (my cold is miraculously better), then the incredible last-minute panic and rush.

I waited at the corner of 55th Street in awful draughts for the Wrightsman car in which Lee [Radziwill] was my special escort (in the absence of Diana V. ill with flu). Lee looked very beautiful with Japanese landlady hairdo. At the theatre the usual mêlée of excited onlookers, a vast crowd of not very impressive first-nighters, expectation, cool excitement backstage, packages, flowers, K. H.'s door tight shut.

[1] Cecil had undertaken a photographic assignment, hence the car.

Katharine Hepburn as Coco Chanel, on set at the Mark Hellinger Theater, New York, made to look like the famous Chanel salon at rue Cambon

Our seats were in the second row, nearer than I've ever been even at rehearsal and they gave one no feeling of the bulk of the ship at back of one. It was like being in the prow, and perilously near K. H.'s mottled face and legs. I enjoyed the evening, for the show has improved enormously and goes with a zing. There are lots of things that could and should be changed, but Alan is above everything stubborn.

I enjoyed enormously the choreographic numbers, was thrilled to have the cheers for the little black dresses, and there seemed to be applause for many of the sets and costumes. But in the interval people said there was no show but for me. That did not forebode well. However, I was buoyed and excited. The audience enthusiastic about everything they could enjoy, but quite silent when not amused.

For me K. H. was without any magic, her timing as erratic as ever, her overemphasis quite horrible. She was in no way resembling Coco, in no way doing an impersonation of anyone but herself. Lee cooed that the improvement in the show was immense and I was buoyed by the general enthusiasm and really enjoyed myself. Then the finale cheers, the red dresses having created their usual effect, and a standing ovation for K. H., who suddenly shed 30 years and looked far too young for the part.

The usual first night detritus backstage and in quick time to the Boîte of the St. Regis. Here my 22 guests turned up in driblets, a few extra places had to be added. Quite a nice mixture of young and old, staid and "way out," pretty and beautiful and freakish. Excellent supper of pancakes, salad and soufflé, all very well done by the hotel. Sam [Green], Jonathan [Lieberson], Penelope [Tree], [David] Bailey etc., very pleased with life and Jayne [Wrightsman] quietly enthusiastic about everything and Charles in a good mood.

Then on to the party for the Brissons. Fred put his arm round me and praised my work and behaviour. Then he told me that the notices were bad, that Clive Barnes did not like anything—not the book, music or my work—except K. H. This put a damper on the proceedings but I kept telling myself that I knew C. B. would hate the show, that it was not his at all and that I should not be surprised.

Later, with snow on the ground, Penelope Tree, putting two sets of fingers in her mouth, made a marvellous shrieking clarion call for a taxi, no doorman with his whistle was so effective. We tumbled out into a taxi for home and I felt pleased to think that, at last, I would be escaping from my hotel room and all its recent professional associations.

FRIDAY, 19 DECEMBER 1969

I woke at the accustomed hour, rang for all the papers, and quietly read them. Clive Barnes was far worse than I thought.[1] I knew he would not have time for

[1] Barnes wrote "Mr. Beaton has never struck me as a particularly accomplished designer—although his dresses were often pretty—and nothing in *Coco* causes me to revise that opinion" [*New York Times,* 19 December 1969].

this sort of show and he has a prejudice against me, but I did not expect him to be so vile in his attack on my work. The real sting came with his comparing the set he liked the most as being like "early Oliver Smith." This made me mad.

It was awful to hear such unmitigated praise for K. H.'s performance. All the papers were unfavourable for the play but euphoric in praise of K. H. "Without her there'd be no show." This is just what Fred B. had hoped not to read, as it means the bookings will fall off disastrously when she leaves the company. Quite probably they may not try to replace her and certainly they will not attempt a road company, or take the show to London. I was strangely undisturbed by the sudden cold douche (not unexpected) and continued with my packing and making plans for the afternoon departure.

I noticed that the telephone for once was completely silent. It seems that bad notices are the only way to keep peace at home. At 12 Diana telephoned, full of heart and reality and good advice. "New York critics don't mean a thing. They're something for the birds," so unlike her to use this vulgar phrase. After hearing my reactions she said, "But you're talking as if the show was dead! Why, everyone had a great time and you're leaving with the town at your feet. What you have done is masterly. You couldn't have done better!"

The morning went by with a visit from a bright journalist with a tape recorder, and then Sam came to cheer me up and together we went out for a late lunch. He behaved like a real friend, helping to put all the last-minute rubbish into my bags and coping with the awful French secretary girl that Margaret had kindly sent me to help with the agonising emergencies that one has to face before leaving. My three-month bill seemed astronomical, but Sam pointed out that with the $40 per diem from *Coco* I would have been more than covered.

Fred Brisson telephoned to tell of his great disappointment at the notices and how he had not told me of the full horror last night as he did not want me to be worried, particularly about the disgraceful way Barnes had alluded to my work. He is a gent. He said they had thought of having Barbara Stanwyck[1] as a replacement for K. H. and how Alan and his entourage had been completely and utterly amazed at the press reaction.

 [1] Barbara Stanwyck (1907–90), enduring American film star, known for playing sultry ladies.

A quiet half-hour on my bed to say goodbyes and to be comforted by Sam, a new and nice companion who has really been a great prop and mainstay. I love his trickery so and he is resourceful. We will miss one another.

Thence by expensive car to the airport. But the Friday night Christmas traffic was so appalling that the 40-minute drive took an hour and a half and I was terrified of arriving too late to check in. But Pan Am are better than BOAC for welcoming last-minute arrivals and also for winking at their excess baggage. I made the grade and managed to overcome the journey quite painlessly, sitting next to an extremely boring "advertising" salesman, whose lot in life was obviously a lonely one.

ARRIVAL SATURDAY, 20 DECEMBER 1969

The dark rainy early morning of London. At the house the news that Ray [Gurton] was ill with double pneumonia and could not come down to the country but miraculously Eileen had hired a temporary cook. The house was falling apart and builders having to repoint, but otherwise no bad news and I went off to the doctor. My blood pressure high, instead of the usual low. Of course, the New York doctor, according to Gottfried, had prescribed the wrong medicine, so no wonder I had had a return of the chest troubles. Now I must fill up with vitamins and rest.

I could hardly keep awake and longed to get into the train for Salisbury and as bad luck would have it, Seymour Berry,[1] a reformed drunk, got in the compartment and bored the pants off me. I told him I wanted to catch up with a sleepless night, but he droned on. At last I slept and never heard him leave the compartment at Basingstoke.

A nice welcome from Smallpeice in new corduroys and soon I was back where I belonged, welcomed by pots of Roman hyacinths and lilies of the valley. For two days I was unable to keep awake. I am now wondering if I am suffering from sleeping sickness.

For two days—make it four.

[1] Seymour Berry (1909–95), second Viscount Camrose. He lived at Hackwood Park, near Basingstoke.

CHRISTMAS DAY, THURSDAY, 25 DECEMBER 1969

This is the first morning I have woken up feeling that I have any strength in my body. I have slept morning, noon and night ever since I came down here. My body is made of cotton wool.

POSTSCRIPT

For Cecil's résumé of Coco *("I knew the show would be no good with such a rotten book") and for what he thought of Katharine Hepburn in retrospect ("She is a rotten, ingrained viper"), see* The Unexpurgated Diaries *(2003). The play ran better than expected. But on 1 August 1970 Katharine Hepburn performed her last show and was replaced by Danielle Darrieux*[1] *who, though good, did not pull in the crowds. The show closed on 3 October 1970 after 329 performances.*

Cecil's prediction that Coco *would not come to London was fulfilled.*

And so he entered his last decade, exhausted, better off financially and, above all, relieved to be home.

[1] Danielle Darrieux (b. 1917), vivacious French actress.

INDEX

This index identifies figures in the text and occasionally those in footnotes, who are not otherwise mentioned in the text. Since most people are identified in footnotes on their first appearance, the distinction "& n" is by and large omitted, unless the footnote happens to appear on a later page. Normally I insert dates in the index but as these appear wherever possible in the footnotes in the text, they have not been repeated in this index.

Nor have I indexed names mentioned in footnotes that are only there to identify characters in the text. These have been omitted since they are secondary characters, and anyone looking them up would therefore be disappointed.

Cecil's work on the musical, Coco *appears on every page from page 418 to page 506. It therefore seemed pointless to list individual page numbers for the major participants, Katharine Hepburn, Alan Jay Lerner etc., as anyone interested would wish to read those pages in full, and they appear in most of them. However, for a detailed breakdown of* Coco *activities, the entry for Cecil himself should be consulted. H.V.*

A NOTE ABOUT THE AUTHOR

Hugo Vickers is the author of Gladys, Duchess of Marlborough; Cecil Beaton; Vivien Leigh; Loving Garbo; *and* Alice, Princess Andrew of Greece, *among other books. He lives in London and Hampshire with his wife and his three children.*

A NOTE ON THE TYPE

This book was set in Minion, a typeface produced by the Adobe Corporation specifically for the Macintosh personal computer, and released in 1990. *Designed by Robert Slimbach, Minion combines the classic characteristics of old style faces with the full complement of weights required for modern typesetting.*

COMPOSED BY

North Market Street Graphics, Lancaster, Pennsylvania

PRINTED AND BOUND BY

Berryville Graphics, Berryville, Virginia

DESIGNED BY

Iris Weinstein